SACKVILLE STREET

Oliver St John Gogarty was born in 1878 and was educated in England at Stonyhurst and Oxford, and in Ireland at Trinity College, Dublin, where he was a contemporary of James Joyce, whom he never forgave for portraying him in *Ulysses* as Buck Mulligan.

Gogarty was a Fellow of the Royal College of Surgeons of Ireland and, like W. B. Yeats, he became one of the first Senators of the Irish Free State. He died in 1957.

Three classic volumes of autobiography, now at last available in a single omnibus edition.

SACKVILLE STREET

As I Was Going Down Sackville Street
Rolling Down the Lea
It Isn't This Time Of Year At All!

Oliver St John Gogarty

AN ABACUS BOOK

As I Was Going Down Sackville Street first published in Great Britain
by Rich and Cowan 1936
Published by Sphere Books Ltd 1968
Rolling Down the Lea first published in Great Britain by Constable and Company 1950
Published by Sphere Books Ltd 1982
It Isn't This Time Of Year At All! first published in Great Britain
by MacGibbon & Kee Ltd 1954
Published by Sphere Books Ltd 1983
This omnibus edition first published by Sphere Books Ltd 1988
Reprinted 1989

Printed and bound in Great Britain by
Richard Clay Ltd, Bungay, Suffolk

ISBN 0 349 10142 6

Sphere Books Ltd
A Division of
Macdonald & Co. (Publishers) Ltd
66/73 Shoe Lane, London EC4P 4AB
A member of Maxwell Pergamon Publishing Corporation plc

As I Was Going Down
Sackville Street

A PHANTASY IN FACT

"Ω μοι ἐγώ, τέων αὖτε βροτῶν ἐς γαῖαν ἱκάνω;
HOMER: *Odyssey,* xiii. 200

CHAPTER ONE

Quaintly he came raiking out of Molesworth Street into Kildare Street, an odd figure moidered by memories, and driven mad by dreams which had overflowed into life, making him turn himself into a merry mockery of all he had once held dear. He wore a tail-coat over white cricket trousers which were caught in at the ankles by a pair of cuffs. A cuff-like collar sloped upwards to keep erect a little sandy head, crowned by a black bowler some sizes too small. An aquiline nose high in the arch gave a note of distinction to a face all the more pathetic for its plight. Under his left arm he carried two sabres in shining scabbards of patent leather. His right hand grasped a hunting crop such as whippers-in use for hounds. His small, sharp blue eyes took in the ash-dark façade, topped by a green-white-and-orange flag, of that which had been the Duke of Leinster's town house; but it held the Senate now. He saw a sentry dressed in green, staring at the green pillar-box which stood a few yards in front of him, near the angle of the footpath where two tall T.D.'s, heavily moustached and carelessly tailored and coiffeured, were bidding good-bye to each other, hiding in the fervour of their handshake all the contempt they mutually reserved.

'*Slaun lath*, now. And there I leave you.'

'*Bannacht lath*, Shaun. I'll be seeing you soon again.'

The sentry stared on at the letter-box, his eyes not raised to the martial cricketer, for Dublin had accepted him as the present representative and chief of those eccentric and genial characters whom it never fails to produce in every generation. Only when he muttered close to the ornamental iron gates which the sentry guarded, did he disturb his brown study.

What were the memories he 'represented' by his accoutrements and his dress? What turned him into his present lunatic condition? To answer these questions we must go back to the days when the great Lord Lieutenant, the Earl Cadogan, held state in the Phoenix Park. That Viceroy, hearing of an act of gallantry which had cost the man his reason, sought him out, and finding that he was but slightly 'touched', gave him the run of the vice-regal grounds, with their pageants of state and their cricket matches. He was but slightly 'touched', for he had wit enough to realize his trouble. So, when his doctor told him that his mental disability was likely to become progressive, but that he would never be violently unbalanced, he remarked: 'Endymion, whom the moon loved: a lunatic ...'

So 'Endymion' he became. There was method in his madness, and more than method. But let that more reveal itself to those with eyes to see. This, however, will not be contested; the sabres are his cavalry escort, for he must have been impressed by the cavalcade of sixty well-mounted troopers who attended the vice-regal carriages; and the cricket flannels — his memories of summer evenings on the smooth pitch; the whip, his runs in winter with the staghounds of the Ward. All gone now; alive only in memory and regret those peaceful, prosperous days when life was fair and easy and man's thoughts were the thoughts of sportsmen. If he be held treasonable now for regretting those days, all the more reason for this investiture in motley. Dublin saw him only a man gone 'natural', and Dublin has outstanding examples in every generation.

Endymion was preceded by Professor Maginniss, who turned himself into an Italian professor of deportment by eliding the two terminal letters of his name. But what if Endymion were a Dean Swift *aneu malakias*; a gentle Dean gone genial and given more to mockery than to fierce indignation? There is evidence that this theory in no way exaggerates his worth. But let us not delay him by considering his pose or its significance.

With a word to the sentry, he passed into the National Library.

Up the street a tall figure, blond as a sun of Italy, could be seen approaching – the figure of a young man who walked thoughtfully, as if dictating to himself. He was walking past the National Museum, for there is a museum at each end of Kildare Street. Coming along, he must have seen the merry droll.

I will ask him a question which I wish to have solved, for he is the brainiest fellow in Dublin, an honest man, and what is more, an honest solicitor.

'Austin,' I said, 'tell me, am I right if I see in the cuffs on Endymion's ankles the proclamation to all who run and can

6

read such signs, that he is standing on his head and walking on his hands, as it were – upside-down?'

A smile flickered, but he answered as if considering the matter profoundly.

'You are right. And what it more, if Endymion's world is upside-down, then he becomes the only one who can be said to be related to it correctly. What is the use of our walking upright if the world is upside-down? If we stood on our heads in a topsy-turvy world, there would be no disharmony. Endymion becomes the only sane creature in the world as he sees it.'

'I guessed it. By God! A good fellow and a fantastic fellow to boot. He shouted "Noom" to the sentry as he passed. "Noom to me, and moon to you." '

Austin pondered a little while. 'You see, he may be symbolizing his ideas or theories more thoroughly than either of us imagines. He may be going backwards in Time as well as reversing in Space. Just let us see if it be a crescent or a waning moon.'

'I have thought of that,' I said; 'waning it should be. Just let us look down the street and see.' The ghostly crescent appeared. 'Of course, that is a last quarter ... He is more thorough than we think. I wonder if he is mad at all?'

'Well, he is allied to great wit. It must be wonderful to believe yourself to be the only sane man in the world. More wonderful still to have your past before you again, and becoming your future. Having been completely reversed, he is going back with the moon to the fullness and the foison. We are declining to darkening days.'

'To think of my having laughed at him! He has outsoared the shadow of our night. Envy and calumny and hate and *gain* can touch him not. And I laughed at him!'

'He would like you to do so. He does not want to lessen, he wants to increase the amount of mirth in the town. There certainly is room for more mirth in Dublin. His pose has the advantage of silence for the most part. He cannot be held up for being captious. He cannot be held up for anything, in fact; for who can prove that he is a symbolistical critic of our time? At most we can only say that he is amusing himself and us too, and this is a kinder form of amusement than the more common, which is at the expense of someone else.'

I thought for a while, envying Endymion, who had achieved

7

an attitude towards things that had made him not only a laughing philosopher, but an amusing one. That transient envy, itself a form of flattery, which never fails to touch me when I see great work, now assailed me momentarily. Why had I not thought of that? To be Endymion, to speak – if not my mind – to act my part protected from the hates, jealousies, and trickeries of the days about us now; to scorn them symbolically . . . to turn myself right about, not only right about face, but upside-down, and journey ever onward to the Golden Age.

'Praetulerim delirus inersque videri.'

As Horace, Rome's less sententious Kipling, has it. What a wonderful thing it would be if we could choose and control our madness! Not that awful insanity which King Lear prayed Heaven to withhold: that uprooting of the Reason from storms within as destructive as the ruin of the elements outside: breaking the age-stiffened oak: a brain set adrift by the ingratitude of its own flesh and blood. Not that, sweet Heaven! But to be able to adjust the Reason to the phantasmagoria of Life. And, while maintaining the steadfast lapis lazuli within, to have it played upon by every delicate shading of the weather, deepening its azure now and lighting it again in tone with the luminous and magical haze which is tremulous with life. To be magical as Life itself, and as irresponsible: to be lunatic enough to take the hard edge from knowledge, to be irrational enough to temper Justice with Mercy, and to be able to adjust oneself to the changes in intensity which the waxings and wanings of Reality assume in the shimmerings of its cloud – this would be an ideal adjustment and a poetic opposition to outrageous Fortune.

'But surely he could not have been symbolizing when he jumped into the empty vat in the brewery, when his companion fell in? They say that he thought that it was full of some fluid, and that his friend was in danger of drowning. But it was only full of carbon dioxide gas.'

'Are you so very sure that he may not have meant something by his plunge into the gas? Anyway, retrospectively I am sure he means it now. For all we know, he may intend in the course of this cavalcade backwards of Dublin life, when he reaches again the point in time when he fell in, to fall out – in fact, to

8

regain his sanity. But we should not insist too much on the appositeness of symbols. Their value lies in the breadth of interpretation they allow.'

'A cavalcade of Dublin life backwards for thirty years! When was it he fell into the vat of gas? Thirty years ago. Shall I ask him?'

'No, no. Leave him to his studies, whatever they may be,' said Austin, smiling.

'Yes, indeed, whatever they may be.' I knew that if I could arouse a curiosity in those 'studies', that I might get Austin to look into the Library – that home of the Dublin Muses and its Sybil ... that porticoed place which has made so many philosophers but so few of them Stoics. I wondered, would Endymion ask for books such as those which walled the library of Pantagruel? What books would he ask for? ... it was a matter for investigation. My imagination could not supply the authors who would be likely to interest so strange a fellow.

'If we go in there, there is no knowing whom we may meet ...'

'But they cannot talk to us, and we can slip out again, I will merely glance at the form he has filled to get a book, and the name of the book on it.'

'It's not improbable that he brought some book or even a newspaper to read in the library – yesterday's *Evening Mail*.'

I remembered the fissure on the left of the wayside at Delphi, as you ascend the Sacred Way, whence the gaseous vapour still issues that at the time when the Oracle was at its best used to intoxicate the fasting priestess and induce the prophetic frenzy. It is by the roadside, only moved by an earthquake a little distant from the ancient cella of the god. After all, I mused, if a whole nation, if the wisest nation of the world once, set its course by noxious fumes, why not Endymion?

I described the finding of the fissure in the ditch beside the Sacred Way. I told how I bent down and leaned my head to inhale the very breath of those hysterical hexameters which steered old states and kings. It smelt as a hothouse smells – of deep earth and warmth. It did me little good, probably because I am a prophet in my own country (which accounts for my being a nobody), and, anyway, the last Oracle announced its own extinction.

9

Speaking my thought aloud, I said, 'Is it not strange how reputable the Oracle was?'

'Almost any form of words may prove oracular, provided the soul is sufficiently agitated. On the morning of any momentous day, do we not begin by looking out for signs of good luck or bad, the left shoe to the foot first, the white horse, the red-haired woman? ... These cannot help as much as, if we are anxious enough to notice and attach value to them, their presence or absence may mar. It was the direction of the mind inward to the business in hand that made the reputation of the Oracle. If an Oracle to-day said, "Please keep off the grass," we might take it as a warning against investing in Land Bonds, or a hint that a sea voyage would prevent a nervous breakdown.'

'The priestess had to be a woman of the canonical age, as we call it in Ireland. Apparently no pretty flapper would do ... Greece, like Ireland, was, therefore, immoderately influenced by hags.'

Austin raised his hat.

'Who was that who passed?'

'Miss Bellowson. Surely you know her?'

'Let us cross the street. I am somewhat superstitious, I have a strange idea that certain spots of earth are fey or haunted; certain houses are unlucky. This street corner is evocative ... Yeats holds that to speak of ghosts is to conjure them up. Let us move along on the other side.'

'Stop! Look! There's Endymion. He did not stay long in the National Library.'

We watched him emerge, cross into the middle of the street and halt. From his pocket he produced a large compass. He scrutinized it carefully through his monocle. He turned it, looking up now and then as he did so. He set his course for home. 'He goes home by compass! He cannot trust the ebbing town.' He raised his whip-hand to the north, and entered Molesworth Street again.

'Going home by compass! Was there ever such a fellow? I wonder where he is off to now?'

'He lives in Pleasants Street. I hardly like to mention it. Things are getting so appropriate to him that I feel slightly moonstruck myself. What an idea to live in Pleasants Street! I should have thought of that.'

'Where is Pleasants Street?'

'Off Camden Street. It is a charming street full of old-world two-storeyed cottages; steps ascend to hall doors on the first floor, they are all the same pattern save one, which has a pagoda-roof-like shade of green above its window. It is a sunny street, and the yellow bricks seem to catch the sun, for it is more sunny than any street in Dublin. Round the corner you can see, as the light grows fine or thickens, green and blue, the Dublin Mountains with their hanging fields. Endymion's house has a white horse in the fanlight. But, for Heaven's sake, let us not inquire into what that may mean, or what he may mean by that. It is our chance to see what he has been reading.'

The Reading Room is a large building roofed by a cylinder arch. George says that the National Library has two domes, the second being the bald head of its librarian, Lyster. One of the attendants, who sits at the inquiry desk, provides a third dome. His head sends heliographs of warning when the light beats down to those who disturb the silence of the place.

The great Reading Room was almost empty. Two lady medicos, with their fair heads together, were studying Gray's *Anatomy*, and shaking with suppressed mirth. Opposite to them, surrounded by little blocks on which 'Silence' was printed in large letters, sat a clergyman with a 'fire-red, cherubini face'. From time to time, in regular intervals which synchronized with the maximum pressure and suffusion wrath produced on his countenance, he hissed out 'Whist!' like escaping steam. Another clergyman wandered, lonely, round the shelves which held the dictionaries. He looked like a parchment-pale Oliver Goldsmith. He moved his lips silently, as if quoting to himself. In truth, he was gently masticating a small piece of carrot, which is full of vitamins.

'The saints are equal to the doctors – two of each.'

'Whist!' said Father McQuisten.

We turned to the desk. In the Signature Book, spreading fully in purple pencil across a page, was the signature of Endymion. It read, to our amazement:

JAMES BOYLE TISDELL BURKE STEWART FITZSIMMONS FARRELL

'Damn his symbolism,' said I; 'he's got my name and the names of my friends and acquaintances included in his title.

11

There's George's, Joe's, and the Shamuses'. You've escaped. What's the idea?'

'Whist!' said Father McQuisten.

'He cannot have been christened in all the surnames he has included in that line – that almost reads like one of Phoebus Apollos' gaseous hexameters!'

'No one can say for certain why he has made a conglomeration of the present-day well-known citizens, and taken their names to himself, unless . . . well, what's the use? You cannot prove a surmise. He may mean that he represents in his person an amalgam of the ingredient races that go to make up the nation.'

'He means that he is Ireland? Poor devil!'

'Its countless Jameses, the Norman, Elizabethan, Cromwellian conquerors, merchants and mediocrities – all the incomers, in short, that make the Irish mosaic.'

'That he is a walking amalgam?'

'Or that the Irish Farrell has to bear on his back all the rest of them – Normans, Elizabethans, etc. Or that he is leading them in triumph – settlers, planters, merchants and mediocrities, as well as the Shamuses of the people. So he is a nation in himself.'

'Whist!' said Father McQuisten.

A red-nosed little rat of a man with sooty eyes, who wore a long, faded overcoat for shirt, waistcoat, and jacket, and had just seated himself, looked up, and answered 'Whist!' antiphonally.

Perhaps it was hearing this profane voice subconsciously that brought the Librarian to the desk. His bright scalp, added to the light from the attendant's dome, sent double rays of warning towards the little man, who sank into his greatcoat, and remained motionless as a hibernating rodent.

Lyster is a lovable man, and I felt grateful when he beckoned us to his Librarian's office. His brown beard moved a little as he smiled, with cheeks fresh as a child's, while his whispering, diffident, feminine voice invited us.

I saw him better when we had passed the barrier; a large, broad, short, soft, suave man in a greyish-blue suit. He indicated two arm-chairs and fussed about, though it was evident that they could not be moved. With a sigh, he prayed us to be seated.

12

'It is trying work, conducting a National Library,' he said. 'You can have no idea of the difficulties which confront me. I am worn to a shadow, as one might say, endeavouring to keep the peace. I am at the disposal, at the mercy of a public, some of whom are not trained for a room, not to speak of a library. And then, even the students who come here from the Universities are wholly undirected in their reading. Without direction among so many books from the different ages and countries, it is as if (nay, worse, since a library is undying) the young students were suddenly to be exposed in an arena to any danger. That is, if left undirected. Any country can be an arena, without culture. And who is to lead the mind in the direction of educational reading but I, the Librarian? I believe that, next to the irremediable harm of a general education by which they are left open to any influence, any sinister author, the second grievous thing is undirected reading. Do I bore you? No. Then let me give you a few instances and examples of my difficulties. They are equal to and almost – I will be bold to say it – quite on a par with the responsibilities an Ambassador has to bear, and charged with as great import for his nation. Think of the harm Nietzsche could do to the half-informed minds of some of our undergraduates. And yet, because doubtless of some "review", I find his name put down not once but twice, for those authors which are to be acquired by us. Some little undeveloped fellow wants to glory vicariously in Battle!

'A medical student called the other day and demanded the lastest book on Surgery. We required that he fill in the name of the author or, in these cases, editor. He said he did not know it, but that we at least should know what were the latest books. Do I bore you? No. Happily, I heard the argument with the attendant at the desk. Infinite tact, as you will see, is so necessary when dealing with a surly person. The last thing is to be resentful, and our much-tried attendants are apt so to be. "If you don't know the name of the book you want," said one, "how can you expect us to get it for you? This is not a thought-reading salon you are in." Gentlemen, we were on the verge of a scene ... a scene in a library! Unthinkable!

' "But it is a thought-reading salon – what is a library? May I help you, sir?" I said. He seemed rather taken aback. I merely meant that the thoughts of all the greatest minds are here to be read. But either that appealed to him or did not, or he had deeper forebodings than I could fathom. Much to our relief, he left. If this is boring, pray interrupt me ...

'An engineering student fills in a form for Stott on Strains and Stresses. What strange and invariably monosyllabic names these writers have! I interpose: "May I just offer for your consideration – and I know it is cultivated – this most appropriate poem of Kipling? After reading it, I am quite convinced that you will have no time, nor, indeed, inclination, for mere stresses." The sons of Martha! How beautifully and fully, without trigonometry, he indicates their function! Not for a moment, mark you – and this is important – hinting or indicating that they are dissatisfied with their lot in life. Do I bore you? No. "It is their care that the gear engages, it is their care that the switches lock." What book on engineering could be so satisfying? Turn to his picture of the sons of Mary, the first-class passengers through life. Let us look at them lolling in a Pullman to Bath or Penzance. We see the lighted windows of the restaurant coach. We see the sons of Mary sipping in careless ease the good things of this world. Outside, the sons of Martha in the reasty tunnel! Is it not a masterpiece? If I bore you, stop me. So many schoolmasters are unable to realize the help I have given, the fillip I have endeavoured, in this my responsible post, to impart to higher education. Think of asking for a book on mathematics!

'Worst of all, perhaps, are the little uniformed fellows who are studying to be bank clerks. I commend them to Browning. Other brands saved from the burning.'

'But not saved from the Browning,' Austin whispered.

'To-day, Mr Farrell had the grace to call in. He is interested in medieval astronomy. He presented himself before the attendant, muttering "Lytel Lewis, Lytel Lewis." Did I allow my subordinates to put him to the question? No. The moment he quoted the title of Chaucer's dedication to his son, the "Lytel Lewis" of his essay on the Astrolabe, I was there to have it sent for. This is one of the few consolations of the librarian – to direct reading, not merely to serve it. Do I? No? Well, then, never forgetting that without my efforts this great library might easily degenerate into a mere annex of the Alexandra School or Wesley College, you will realize my difficulties. I am not ... ? Put my problems another way. A medical student has pawned his books. I have actually known it occur. He comes

14

here. But what is my position? If I am to offer sanctuary from the Dublin pawnshops, I must wean him from the mere unimaginative side of his medical work, and take him into the higher realms and romantic fields of that great and noble profession. Rose and Carless on Surgery, or Osler on Medicine! One or other of these books are all he can envisage as being representative of the great tradition of medicine, wide as the ages! What are our educators doing? What an account shall they not have to render, deprecating imagination and degrading medicine to a rule of thumb! Separating man from the Universe, from his starry bourne. I say to medical students, "Before perusing Osler, who is quite a modern author and divorced from European tradition, might I not" – Do I bore you? – "suggest that you dip for a little into Paracelsus, that Doctor of both Faculties, neither of which he deigns to define? Surely your mind is not impervious to the charm of those inadequately appreciated Middle Ages?" He signs a docket, gentlemen, for Theophrastus von Hohenheim, that "Para" which, as you know from your Greek, is derived in the sense of "beyond" Celsus, who held the medicine of the Mittel Zeit in fee. These students rarely revert, once having tasted Castalia, otherwise this great library would be the ante-room of the dissecting-room, a morgue, or, but for my vigilance, a pathological department. We are under the protection of the Muses and the Minister for Education.'

Of whom does he remind me, I wondered, as I watched the Librarian? Not of the skipper on a Thames lighter, nor the captain of a trawler in the North Sea. His burly body and that pleasant beard, the brow of a philosopher above the broad shoulders of an athlete, and then that diffident, whispering, virginal voice. I have it! Plato, of course. He is Plato, the Broad. And his subtile, inquiring, reasonable, if fantastic, mind! Will he reveal a tendency towards myths? Out of his time; but yet associated in character with a Library, an Academy for the whole town. I should have thought of it long ago! Plato!

'You are very silent, gentlemen. If I am boring you, do not hesitate for one moment to call me to account. But to continue: If I am in difficulties with the lay and those untrained in thinking, imagine how multiplied those difficulties must be when I am dealing with the theologian and minds which are both subtile and sensitive. But if I were to retreat or to shirk my duties, I might as well abdicate. Instead of coming here for books, the danger would be that books would be brought in to be perused here. Then why a library? Exactly! And books of the same kind as those in the library of the late Boss Croker, who ordered a thousand volumes of Algebra to decorate his walls. Breviaries, not Algebras. That was the possibility until, with the most delicate tact, I met a situation which indeed wanted it. A clergyman – a friend of mine since the incident – called one day and, without filling in any form, took up his place by the radiator and proceeded to immerse himself in his Breviary. Had I not known of the spiritual problem which beset poor Father McQuisten, of his struggles with the Fiend, his wrestlings with visions of lingerie, or rather with the thoughts which a lady's underclothing gave rise to, I could not have been in a position to extend to him my help. A very delicate position indeed! I could not have had the advantage of his understanding of my difficulty had he not been a man of wide reading and common sense. He was no Mr Pepys and she was no Lady Castlemaine. Merely the bride of the neighbouring rector.

' "You read your Breviary by the radiator," I said. "Well, what about it?" said he, challengingly. "Nothing, that is nothing of import," said I, "but I mean . . ." – You know how easily one becomes confused in affairs of eschatology? – "I do not mean to imply that reading of your Breviary means nothing to me; but I was about to ask if your learning extends to a catholic appreciation of our treasures." Now here, gentlemen, you observe my tact – "We have a very early edition of the controversy regarding the Priscilliantists and other Docetic heresiarchs with whose work you are doubtless well acquainted." "Docetic" – let us keep our Greek constantly in repair as Dr Johnson advises us to keep our friendship – comes, as you gentlemen know, from " δόκεν ", to appear. These heretics held that our Divine Lord was a mere apparition, a wraith. A dreadful heresy! To some extent encouraged, of course, by the importance of his appearances after death. But yet, a dreadful heresy! Our library rather prides itself on its heresies, of which we have most erudite commentaries. The Ages of Faith – do I bore you? – when hearts believed and built, one should couple with religious reading, works on architecture: Byzantine, Transitional, Gothic, and Baroque.

' "But, Father, if you would care to have a table set apart for your deeper studies I shall arrange it if you please, where you would not be disturbed by the more frivolous and female students of Medicine. I find it so hard to make them read anything but mere note-books, one might call them enchiridion of Medicine: but your table, I will see to it myself, will be kept well supplied with the more authentic records of the heresies; and of what befell Pelagius, who opposed the view that God's grace was destined for all men, but that man must make himself worthy of it. St Augustine, who, as you are doubtless aware, 'endears himself to us by his mistress and his illegitimate child.' I quote not myself – far be it from me – but George Moore, a frequenter of this library and a friend of our wistful stylist John Eglinton, who rebutted him. Moore had the Dark Ages in his mind so far as a sense of historical perspective went. Yes, there is a translation of the Confessions. What Latin! Only to be compared with Lyly's Eupheus ... *'Nondum amaren sed amare amaban . . .'* quite an obsession . . ." Do I bore you? Ah yes, the book will be with you in a moment.

'Father McQuisten is a charming man, charming and scholarly. If you already know his story, forgive me – or, rather, the story of his tragedy. I am demanding too much of your attention? No? How shall I explain it? Let me put it like this. He was as much the victim of propinquity as of delinquency.

'The Vicarage and Parochial House, as is natural in Ireland, were separated as far as could be considering the size of the village; but their gardens abutted on each other at the end of their sheltered walks. Their gardens abutted! The Vicarage garden ended in a clothes-line, the Parish priest's garden ended in a privet hedge over which the clothes-line was clearly to be seen. Clothes hung out to dry! So long as they were bachelor's garments they could by no means be regarded as sails of escape from the daily round of unromantic fancies. Oh, do I bore you? The vicar married, the Vicar married! When his young bride was brought home and her undies waved in the winnowing airs at the end of the Vicarage garden, how futile must it have seemed to Father McQuisten to read, *"ne nos inducas in tentationem"* when the herbaceous border led directly down thereto! There was a disembodied ballet dancing in mid-air, where the sparrows of Venus fly (you remember the first of

Sappho?) "like an embodied joy," as that exquisite fellow Shelley has it, "whose race has just begun." Do I bore you? Can you forgive the over-zeal of the devotee who, after three days' distraction, loaded his twelve-bore with double cracks and let fly, not at the para-virginal cami-knickers, but at four of the Vicar's shirts which in the interval good taste and modesty perhaps had interposed for his lady's lingerie. The shirts hung upside-down!

'The outrage could be forgiven, the mistake never. Imagine taking a shirt for panties!'

'Appearances were against him,' I ventured to suggest.

'Ah, of course – I relied on you to see it! A form of Docetism, nothing else! A form of Docetism!'

'That recasts the creed of the Phantasiasts.'

'All we want is to be understood.' And he smiled suavely with a twinkle of mischief, as I thought.

At length we escaped.

'What an extraordinary fellow!' I said to Austin. 'One is never allowed to get a word in.'

'No, nor the books one wants.'

'Why should one be? I thought the fellow most amusing: saving engineers by Kipling; budding bankers by bad verse; suspended priests by heresies. He calls it snatching brands from the burning. I heard you whisper that it would be better to snatch the bank clerks from Browning.'

'I did not quite say that. Why are you so hard on Browning?'

'Because he didn't keep on banking. He introduced jazz into English verse, on account of his mixed blood no doubt. There is black blood in him somewhere, that is why he was called Browning – it comes out in the tom-tom of his verse.

> "Beautiful Evelyn Hope is dead,
>   Rumpity, rum pity; don't look dour!
> This was her table, that was her bed;
>   And here her last leaf of geranium flower."'

'I rather like it. The economy with which he makes a scene is amazing.'

'But, then, the cross-word puzzles of his poems. He anticipated cross-words. He kept so many people guessing that he got a reputation for depth and for poetry out of all proportion to the beauty he evoked in words. Instead of "fundamental

18

brainwork", there is only something foundered beneath the surface. What porridge!

'The nearest he got to poetry was "A chorus-ending of Euripedes", and Mrs Browning. He depends for half his effect on our associations of ideas with the Greek; for the rest on his wife. His inspiration is rarely original. It is literature begotten on literature, Caliban upon Mrs Browning. Where is his equivalent to what is created out of nothing:

"Come unto these yellow sands"?

'His muse is as much invalid as his wife was invalide. I much prefer Longfellow, who does not turn your mind into a war dance, but he leaves it cool and smooth.

"As he leaned upon the railing,
And his ships came sailing, sailing,
Northward into Drontheim fjord."

And smoothness is one of the three indispensables of poetry. Yes. Browning is only suited for reading in banks. There is a Browning Society in England whose members assure each other that they understand him. When I read his translation of Aeschylus, I find it very useful to have the Greek beside me so that I may find out what the English means. He does not write poetry, but his prose pulsates.

'Then those medical students for whom he has prescribed a course of medieval quackery! And his priest studying heresy! What an amusing fellow!'

'I never listened to more suave and childlike irreverence in my life.'

'I saw nothing irreverent in it.'

'You would not be likely to, being irreverent yourself.'

'So you have succumbed to the Pelagian heresy, which would deny me God's grace. A heresy whose chief was an Irishman from, as Dr Macalister suggests, Tibroney, where a lot of "Fly Boys" from Roman persecutions had collected. An archetype of Bray. The people who think that priests must be regarded as dehumanized sicken me. You would respect the butler more than the nutriment, the barometer more than the weather, and would be afraid to tap at it . . . I am, as I have often sadly realized, the only true Catholic in this town, who lives his religion and does not excommunicate the clergy, who are a large part of our life, from a share in that life, as if they were already relics. If we are to have living Catholicism, you must not treat the clergy as outside life. You may have the Faith but, like a score of Irishmen, you have lost the tradition and the great amplitude of the Church. You are as bad as ex-President Cosgrave, whose piety greatly embarrassed His Holiness the Pope.'

'Is that why the ex-President took you to Rome?'

'Precisely. He knew that I had been there before and that I had lived in Austria when that great Catholic country was a living Empire. The Holy Roman Empire, in effect. There one could see the clergy sharing the lives of the people.'

'That does not explain why it was necessary to take you to Rome.'

'He wanted somebody who would not be considered to be bringing coals to Newcastle. Had there been the least doubt about my orthodoxy, do you think I would have been given a large gold medal by the Pope?'

'You got it by mistake. He probably intended it for the President.'

'Nonsense. Have you lost your faith in Infallibility? The Holy Father is infallible as I have reason to believe. It is you who are heterodox, and not I.'

'You are irreverent.'

'It makes me sad to hear people, who never went to Rome, talking of irreverence in Ireland. They are all suffering from a feeling of inferiority to Protestantism yet. They deny themselves joy in religion, and they conduct themselves as if their clergy were a lot of old maids or parsons' wives. They forget that the Devil is the Spirit who Denies.'

At that moment a strange desk-deformed figure appeared, leaning to one side with head cast down sideways over a despatch case: the despatch case, the invariable sign of revolutions which end successfully for the petty intriguers and bureaux rats. He was low sized, in a blue double-breasted overcoat and the usual black trilby hat. His face was thin, with loose, lemon-coloured flesh hanging down on each side from his mouth, which looked as if someone had suspended a bat upside down from his nose. His eyes were like zinc.

'Who is that?'

'That's Cascara the Economist, the greatest catabolite of the

20

new system. I don't care whether you think me superstitious or not, but I'm off now! This place is uncanny.'

'That's the way you went on when Miss Bellowson appeared . . . Don't let me think that you really are, after all, only a figure in the mind of a lunatic.'

'Forgive me, old man, but I really must be going. What are any of us but figures in the National mind?'

I had to remove myself. I should have had too much hatred to sustain, and contempt, had I remained in the precincts of the Government building, with that nasty little Cassius hard by. All that is scheming, mean, humourless and vile resides in that sinister figure: all that makes for the eternal ineffectuality of the native. The little bagman, the Firbolg, with his sinister little lack-lustre eye on the look-out for recognition he had never earned. That's the first phase of Communism in this country. His teeth are black from mouthing 'The Republic'. Soon it will be the Union of Soviets. Ireland a Society of gullible slaves dominated by an over-salaried hypocritical bureaucrat. There is, I am glad to say, but one other scoundrel in Dublin equal to that fellow. He is the under-sized, big-skulled, streamy-eyed solicitor, who is making up by an old age of viciousness for a middle age gone grey in regularity and religious duties, which he found an unwelcome but indispensable preliminary to stalking rich widows in Gardiner Street. Even now, I suppose he is sneaking to Mount Street on his way to take out in kind what he can no longer extract in cash from some poor woman whom his tentacles surround. This is known as 'being kind to his clients'!

My mind cannot entertain hatred long. It upsets the physico-chemical equilibrium of my blood . . . Mount Street: Pleasants Street, Mount Pleasant Avenue! What a wonderful town! There was one thing that made Our Lord lose his patience, and that was hypocrisy. Then who can blame me for my Christian attitude to these humbugging sneaks? That coffin-worm of a solicitor devouring widows and orphans, and the little yellow leprechaun who stole power through a confidence trick on the ignorance and illusions of an electorate equally narrow, and who now persecute the Irish people in the name of The Irish People, and seek for a continuance of power by bringing about catastrophic collapse of all the old honest forms of profit-making.

21

Get this into your head, Austin: it behoves us more than
ever to support the Church at this moment, seeing that it was
never before so gravely threatened, and by self-seeking deceptive curs such as that. I would be the last to weaken it, seeing
that the alternative to it in this country is a reign of plague-
bearing rats.

> O Signor mio, quando saro in lieto
> a veder la vendetta, che, nascosa,
> fa dolce l'ira tua nel tuo segreto?

The heresy politicians suffer from is belief in themselves.

*

The three best streets in Dublin are those that run from south
to north parallel from St Stephen's Green to Trinity College –
Grafton Street, Dawson Street, and Kildare Street. Grafton
Street is connected to Dawson Street transversely by Duke
Street, and likewise Dawson Street to Kildare Street by Molesworth Street. These streets are a little over one hundred yards
in length. The three first-named streets are closed by three different views of Trinity College, which redeems their present-
day drabness by the grey, substantial dignity of the eighteenth
century. It is hard to say which street has the loveliest vista.
Grafton Street shows the great window, wreathed in roses of
sculptured stone, of Professor Tyrrell's spacious rooms. The
campanile beyond, with it beautiful cupola of newer stone,
leaves dark the shoulder and the mighty roof of the library in
the full majesty of its age. But Kildare Street has to pay for its
two museums, its Government Houses, and its Royal College
of Physicians, by giving up any vista but that of the railings of
the College Park and the roofs of rickety houses beyond. Dublin, on the north, is bounded by the eighteenth century, as
Seumas O'Sullivan says.

Pointing to Trinity, 'That is where all the trouble originated,'
I said to O'Duffy, one of the few men left who can understand
a reference, and debate a theory without flying into a rage or
seething with hushed hate. 'That is where it all began in the
early seventeenth century, when the Virgin Queen founded
Trinity College – the College of the Holy and Undivided
Trinity. The very term "Undivided" is almost a prophetic cynicism.'

'The Virgin Queen,' he repeated. 'I saw somewhere how a little girl in a history paper said, "Queen Elizabeth was the Virgin Queen. As a queen she was a great success."

'She succeeded in throwing a pretty apple of discord into Ireland when she founded a college and promulgated the idea of "Freedom" to break up the native chieftains. There was no word in the Irish language for Freedom as she wished it to be understood, or as she wanted it for purposes of disruption. And it was not very hard to win the native from his "allegiance" to his chief, or to send that chief on the run before his "tenants". She made him about as popular as a latter-day landlord by suggesting the new idea – and any new idea, no matter whence it comes or how rotten it may be, will stampede the Irish into enthusiasm. We have Moscow's anti-God and anti-mother love and anti-family. Our little Dermot McMurroughs invite not the Normans now, but Friends of the World to Ireland. So she told them first of "fixity of tenure". Instead of merely having grazing lands annually allotted to them, on which it was not worth while and probably forbidden to build, she said, "Pay me a shilling and your chiefs cannot shift you," or words to that effect. Why, it was as disastrous as a Methodist Mission to the naked and non-venereal natives of the South Seas. The mere Irish became infected with Freedom, but they quite characteristically cornered it for themselves, as they do to the present day. Every tribe became a monopolist of "True Freedom". Whether they fought with each other mattered little to the Chieftain, who was not included when the new-found panacea was being dispensed. But they all fell into Elizabeth's hands and the hands of England: "enslaved", as they call it now; but it was "freed" while it suited them.'

'Poor devils!' I said, 'at the mercy of an unexamined catchcry! – as they are down to the present day.'

'I have not the least pity for them. They may be poor devils, but they can still make those connected with them devilishly poor. Look at them now, they are trying to "free" themselves from civilization: "to be self-contained" like a wild cat with an imperforate anus. We are told that it is an impertinence to call us British. It is we who are to be made *remotos ab orbe*, by ourselves.

'Politics is the chloroform of the Irish people or, rather, the hashish.'

23

'They are the stock-in-trade of that little skunk, what's-his-name. He will soon be discredited.'

'He is discredited already in my mind in the term of your description. He is not a skunk. That animal, as you know –'

'I know.'

'But it is the other end with him.'

'I saw him the other day with a despatch box. The usual symbol of sovereignty of these little commissars. He secretly was on the look out for a salute from a policeman. There is nothing more sinister than the humility of the mean. The earliest natives were "bagmen" too. The low-grade Firbolgs, the Plain Men!'

'His bag is probably full of notes on a Catholic Socialist Republic and other deceptive contradictions. He would prohibit the sale of contraceptives, and yet in mercy to his wife not wear a gas-mask. We are ready to impose on others the shortcomings of ourselves.'

'You remember how those citizens in *Julius Caesar* "threw up their sweaty night-caps, and..." '

'Oh, my dear fellow, don't go on with it. How Shakespeare hated the plain men! He knew too much about them. He had to live too closely to them when he was side-stepping the Puritans, to whom he was a public enemy. Professor Hotson, who discovered more about him from Harvard than all England from London, showed that he was what we would call a gunman of sorts with steel on hip, an associate of Falstaff's "harlotry players" and touts. How he got time and peace to write amazes me. "Sometimes he excused himself as one in pain." He would not go the way Jack Green went. He had to be sober sometimes, and yet he had time to indulge in whatever gave him that stroke which is apparent in his last signatures: hemiplegia. Otherwise, why retire and die at fifty-two? Eighty would be more like it nowadays: Tennyson, Bridges, Watson . . . Only the other day Yeats pointed out to me the curious fact that Shakespeare never praised Elizabeth.'

'What about "Who is Sylvia?"?'

'Yes, who and what (the hell) is she, that swains commend her? How he escaped from being drawn into politics is a mystery. He must have had a close squeak when Essex was discredited. He must have been a kind of George Russell, one recognized as a literary man and one of whom politics is no more to be expected than meanness from a parish priest.'

'Perhaps you have met a mean politician?'

By this, we are come to College Green. Grattan in bronze hailed with uplifted right hand the statues of Burke and Goldsmith, the gentle Irish Virgil, but who, of course, now cannot be acknowledged as Irish by the little unreckonable rats who have done nothing for Ireland save use the word as a fool-trap for votes and office from the uninformed and unemployed. 'Ireland' has come to be as deadly and as degenerating an incantation as 'Freedom' was in the days of the Virgin Queen. Virgins have done a deal of harm in this island. And marriage does nothing to soften their dissatisfaction with life. It cannot be all the fault of the men. It must be the hardness of our women that is driving men to politics. A little slogan formed itself in my mind, a cry to the women of Ireland: 'More petting, less politics.' I was able to tell it to O'Duffy. I find it so hard to withhold what seems to me to be a witticism, especially when it is just born. But O'Duffy is bad enough on the Present State of Ireland, without drawing him out further on the subject of all the old trots who go about wreaking their insatiable illusions and desire for exhibitionism on the youth of the land. No, I said to myself, I will wait until I meet Hackett. He's the lad that will laugh. Or O'Connor, when he comes up again. His nose will cream and wrinkle when he expiates on Our Hard Women ...

While I absented myself momentarily in thought from my friend, he was looking down Dame Street.

'What are they doing over there?' he asked, pointing to a platform of timber which was being put up.

'There is to be an address by the True Republicans this evening, I believe. I saw it in a copy of their paper, which has since been suppressed.'

'Suppressed?'

'By the less true, because more prosperous, Republicans. Once Republicans get into office, it becomes the turn of the disgruntled to delve deeper for the pay-dirt of the "Republic" through adits so narrow that they can be counted on to defy anyone drawing a salary as a Minister. They become *truer* Republicans ... so inaccessibly true that the only way one can co-operate with them is by giving them a vote towards office

25

and a thousand pounds a year less Income Tax and free motoring. Then they hand on the baton, or rather, the baton is taken up by a still lower stratum, who in turn become inaccessible, or rather, in what is to be the next turn, unapproachable . . .'

'Which Truists are holding the meeting this evening, did you hear?'

'Naturally the ones with an axe to grind . . . Let us come to it.'

'My dear sir, not for worlds would I listen to those scoundrels. I would put them into a labour battalion with no labour leader, but a British infantry sergeant instead. And when one of them had done even one honest day's work – voluntarily, mind you – then that one could go out. He would have been handled and made. The only good Irishman is an ex-Service man.'

Now, why did I not think of that? I asked myself, envious again because without the friction of my mind, where would O'Duffy's flint have been? However, I will remember it: I shall say it, as Whistler prophesied of Oscar Wilde in like circumstances. But what good is an epigram if it lacks a receptive hearer? To whom shall I repeat "The only good Irishman is an ex-Serviceman"? I don't care from what army. Will I be brave enough to father it or to put it back on O'Duffy? That's a good idea! If it be not too well received, I shall take the authorship on my own shoulders; whereas if it score a success, I will give credit where credit is due. There is this truth in it, anyway: Discipline is our greatest need. Otherwise we are only yeast to raise other people, among whom we are transplanted, to prominence, if not success . . .

*

So I shall have to go alone to the show. I will not stay long. The crowd is always more interesting to me than the speakers. I cannot help regarding politicians as that genius, poor Tom Kettle, saw them, 'partly mountebanks'. But the crowd. There is nowhere a wittier, or cheerfuller, or more good-natured crowd than in Dublin. Profane, obscene, they come out of the seventeenth century with a power of expression that rivals, or rather, is that of the English of Elizabeth, a language in which it was possible to say more with a few words than we can say now with all the abused words in our swollen vocabulary. I will try the effect of this on O'Duffy. I waved my finger as if marking time for a quotation. I caught his attention. 'Listen:

"The natives leave the right arms of their infant males unchristened, as they call it, to the end that they may give a more ungracious and ungodly blow when they strike, which things not only show how they are carried away by traditious obscurities, but do also intimate how full their hearts are of inveterate revenge." '

He picked it out at once with a little mocking laugh.

' "Traditious obscurities" – the very words to describe what it would take a page to demonstrate: the mutterings, ill-feelings, that "hushed hate" which, as Shane Leslie declares, is the root of Irish melancholy, the withheld minds, emotions instead of reasons – all that goes to the make-up of the soul of a race that never beat anybody but itself and hates itself for others' excellence, is summed in "obscurities". And as for "traditious", I suppose it means treasons of sorts, or perhaps traditional and race inability to fling words straight and true . . .'

We were stopped by a sudden figure, a stout, middle-aged man, with an immense W-shaped black moustache like the horns of an aurochs, under a green Tyrolean hat.

'Ha, ha!' he said. 'And to what problem of the time are my eminent friends devoting themselves? I am waiting for the White Terror. I have not shot anybody for ages. I must begin again!'

'The White Terror, Marshal, I never heard of that?'

'Never heard of the White Terror? Ah, my good friend, it is well for you that you did not. But I have heard of it and experienced it. It comes after the Red Terror. Have you never heard of Bela Kuhn?'

He closed one eye and moved his right arm in a martial gesture which made me see him, a sole survivor, surrounded by innumerable dead in some quite unaccountable battlefield. I tried to feel impressed, but I could not spur myself into an ardour for a terror, which had a terror interposed. I gazed at the Ionic pillars on the curved bulk of the edifice, which Shelley regretted had degenerated from the Temple of Liberty to the Halls of Mammon. The light caught the bayonet of the sentry and shone on his 'Nugget'-polished gaiters. The leather leggings of the Free State soldiers are the brightest things in the town.

27

I found myself ignored and my companion, possibly for his greater credulity and access to enthusiasm, not to mention admiration, preferred.

After some time the Marshal observed my inattention and noticed that my eye was on a soldier of the guard. He bade farewell to O'Duffy, but to me he said on parting:

'Ha! the bayonets will be flashing. Wait until you see.'

He marched away, leaving me feeling that soon, through some obscure fault of mine, I was to witness and even be involved in some hosting of bayonets which boded me no good.

What am I to do? I asked myself. Am I to believe in all his nonsense, or make an enemy of him for life? He always alarms me with his ancestral voices 'prophesying war'. I saw the bemused look O'Duffy wore.

'Does that man really exist?' he asked. 'Do you think we are in for another revolution?'

'My whole field of vision is unreal,' I said. 'It is peopled by extraordinary beings. The moment I begin to think martially, this absurd impersonation of militarism appears, but his presence here somehow reassures me. You see, I met him some years ago when he was just about to march in triumph through Hyde Park. But do you mind if we turn into Trinity? We can emerge by the Lincoln Place Gate.'

'Have you met the O'Donovan of the Glens?'

'Yes.'

'And you know the Glen of the Downs in wooded Wicklow?'

'Who does not?'

'Well, the Marshal and the O'Donovan announced themselves full-titled to a nervous parlour-maid in Kingstown, who opened her mistress's door in a hurry and called : "The Glen of the Downs, ma'am." '

'*Intonsi montes!*'

The red brick behind the campanile fulfilled the note of warmth amid the grey stone of the College quads which the pink hawthorns lend it in spring.

The way through the Front Gate divides the great quad of Trinity College, which opens on a large cobbled space on the third side, into two equal squares. In the lawn of each stands a great oak. Old grey houses with windows framed in lighter stone shelter the immense trees. In front, the graceful campanile stands between the library and the Graduates' Memorial, backed by two lawns and the Queen Anne wing. Nearer, the Chapel faces the Examination Hall. Equal lawns intervene. It took me a long time to accept the intrusion of red brick among the grey walls, but now it lends a warm background to the campanile and tones with the hawthorns in the grassy spaces.

Is there any College in the world that for its size has sent within the few centuries since it was founded more famous men near and far? I asked. Sterne, Burke, Goldsmith, Hamilton of Quaternion fame, Fitzgerald who anticipated Marconi and was the first who had the courage to put his convictions of flight to the test in a glider from the parapet of the Engineering School. Her degrees are honoured farther afield than many colleges go.

Untidy undergraduates were grouped about the chains. Lady undergraduates unwilling to relinquish cap and gown floated across the path.

Left and right the dark portals of the house gloomed sullenly. That one over there, the last next to the Examination Hall, leads to the Provost's house, but no figure emerges. I remember the time when in full light on the cobbles stood the greatest Provost of them all – Sir John Pentland Mahaffy. Over six foot and over seventy, unbowed, with head slightly inclined, I see him talking to some attentive Fellow, and I await the dismissal with a wave of the hand and the supercilious smile. 'If they must learn Irish, teach them that beautiful pre-Gaelic speech of which only three words remain. Anyone with a little aptitude can learn them in a week . . .' and he would walk away slowly with the right toe turned in somewhat, as if he stood at a wicket. But nothing appears in the doorway, and I try to realize my feelings. Yes, I know to what to compare my disappointment at the loss of animation at the doorway. It is as when I went to the Zoo as a child and, wandering round in the overheated house, I came to a cage with a little box with a black opening. The tenant hid within. Where is the Marmoset? 'Ah, you should come here, sonny, at feeding-time.' Why are there no Mahaffys now and none to take their place? Because great figures belong to great periods, and great periods are those in which the eternal truths are assured. There is no slithering of the very cardinal points of life, nor is religion regarded as a mere historical phenomenon subject to waxing and waning. There is no one left now to point out with a sneer, with that thing the Greeks called eutrephelia, well-bred arrogance, the fallacy of all this modernism and Bolshevic 'philosophy', no one to draw the student's attention to the answer to sidelong truths such as these modernist professors of history teach. We ourselves wax and wane, but that alters not our nature or the value of our beliefs.

A space between the buildings revealed Botany Bay.

'Just look at that slum, built after the Union. It is enough to justify any Revolution. The misery began in Trinity College the moment the Irish Parliament left College Green. And not a word of protest. They haven't the daring to say a word for themselves even now, or to raise a voice against the travesty of Freedom which has come to be more disastrous to Trinity College than the Union of 1800. If the Botany Bay quad was justifiably called after the Penal settlements more than one hundred years ago, what should they call it now?'

'It ought to be the first object for clearance by the College Society for demolition of the slums. What culture can penetrate such hideousness? It is almost as great an eyesore as the Rotunda Gardens. What is the Provost doing?'

'He is engaged in the study of old Irish.'

'I cannot quite see the connexion.'

'No, but you can see the slob land of Botany Bay.'

We pass under the Library, one of the five great Libraries which can lay claim to a free copy of every book printed in Great Britain or Ireland. We passed the results of Ruskin's *Stones of Venice*, the Engineering School. They were open to intimations in those days. A beautiful building – perhaps the most beautiful modern building in Dublin. The sweet smell of new-mown grass flowed from the spacious Park.

'What a beautiful space in the grimy city! A kind of sunken plain between the raised rampart of Nassau Street, which was made when the Thing-mote was demolished. This Park must be very wide.'

'It extends, roughly, from the wall over there to the place where the first Norse founders of the city landed and erected their stone. It stood where the Crampton Monument now stands.'

'Oh, the Crampton Monument. I know it – in Brunswick Street. Strange, that a monument should be erected to Crampton. You know the story of his rather unfortunate marriage? His wife and he suffered more from incompatibility of stature than of temperament. So she left him *a mensa et thoro*, to stand, as it were, "on the floor", like my grandfather's clock. I always think of my grandfather's clock when I think of Crampton and his monument.'

'Surely you do not mean "it was taller by half"?'

'No. It is much taller. It dwarfs his bust as the Parnell obelisk dwarfs Parnell.'

'And there was Coffee, with a reputation like Crampton's, who took part in private theatricals, but classic drama would have made him. He was cast for a lead in the Lysistrata playing opposite to the widow of a late Lord Mayor. His funeral was magnificent. It is a pity that these warriors who have fought in love *non sine gloria* should not have a funeral with military observances instead of a plain lid to their coffins.'

'With music.'

'And to be buried at St Satyr, like Michel, as Villon has it!'

'I see that they are rolling the pitch. We shall have cricket soon. I like to drop in of a summer evening to watch the cricket here. What town has so central a playing-field? I was amused one day – I forget the match – to see Endymion solemnly stalking round the field. He said, "I must walk round four times sun-wise so that the other side may win."'

Endymion again! I thought; will I never get away from him? How can I, if I believe the uncomfortable innuendo of Austin that I am but a figment of his mind?

Recovering my good spirits, I said: 'I bet one thing, and that is that Endymion never revealed for which side he was circling the field.'

'Now that I come to think of it, I really believe he did not. Isn't that odd?'

'Quite, quite,' I said. 'Oh yes, quite odd, and maybe more so . . .'

O'Duffy looked disturbed: 'Have I? Is there anything wrong? I meant nothing more than what is on the surface, Endymion . . .'

'Oh, let us drop cricket . . . prepare for the Black Death. We are passing the Pathological Laboratory. They had a goose there once with enough diseases, tropical and otherwise, to kill half Dublin. The yard of the Laboratory abuts on the back of

31

Fanning's snug (as it used to be then) in Lincoln Place. About Christmas we snared the goose with the blind-cord and hauled it up, *pâté de foie gras* and all; and, having quietly dispatched it, presented it to Fanning.'

'But surely he must have heard the row?'

'It made very little row. You are not allowing for its reservoir of sleeping sickness. Our gift was gratefully received and lavishly reciprocated.'

'It laid the Golden Egg; but what happened to Fanning?'

'It did more. If you saw Fanning you would realize that nothing ever happens to him. Even Time has not happened to him. He has not lost a hair of his head, the best head of hair in Dublin, a sable silvered, and he is as straight as a cricket stump; lively too, though seventy. Not to be caught napping. I attribute it all to our antidotal Christmas present. That goose laid the Golden Age in Lincoln Place. Perhaps you would like to drop in and have a word with Senator Fanning. We can put his vintage to the proof. You will then be able to verify my miracle.' But the dapper little man drew away. He was afraid of entering a public-house. So few of us are really emancipated. And yet we have more freedom than we can dare use. It is our bogies that enslave us, not England. 'Cannot I have mine ease in mine inn?' The most pathetic cry in all literature. And now in the 1105th year from the founding of this City of the Taverns by the great Wassailers from the North a Dublin citizen fights shy of an inn. You might think that this city was Belfast.

As we entered Lincoln Place my eye caught on the opposite side of Leinster Street a spare figure of a man about sixty. His back was turned. His arms were outstretched at full length sideways from his shoulders and his hands, upturned at right angles to his wrists, followed each other in parallel movements like those of a figure on the wall in a tomb in Egypt.

'What is that fellow doing?'

'Too well I know (I'll say good-bye to you here): he is explaining to a friend a patent device for motor signals.'

'Good heavens!'

'Good-bye.'

I dived into Fanning's.

The Senator looked up from his evening paper.

'Good-evening, Boss. A moment now?'

A bolt slid back, and a door of a snug opened immediately

on my left. 'Come into the fire,' and he waved his hand to the sun which lit the cosy.

'And how has the world been using you?'

'The world's all right, if it were not for this Government.'

He was started. He refrains from speaking in the Senate, for he is choleric and eloquent. But – 'Gyroscope yourself up into a region of calm now for a moment!'

Surprised, I subsided, I who imagined myself to be tranquil.

'Lookit here, now. Those flounders have the country bloody well ruined. Do you know the latest? They have issued permits to send cattle across to England, and there's a regular trade in these permits most of which have got into the hands of Jewmen and blackguards who never had anything on more than two feet in their houses except a cockroach!'

'Is it as bad as that?'

'Worse!'

'But why should there be permits at all?'

'Now you're talking! The country's fallen into the hands of a bunch of gutties whose knowledge of land is confined to the clay round the geranium in the tenements in which they were born. Then they talk of factories! Then they talk of factories, and they have taken the backbone out of the best factory in the world, the land of Ireland, and lodged it up in Mountjoy prison – that's where the real farmers are!'

'I blame it on the Long Fellow listening to that little yellow bittern,' I said. 'Look at us now! We have lost in fourteen years what it took forty to achieve: fixity of tenure for farmers and our fiscal freedom. Freedom is hard to come by, but harder still to hold. If De Valera was in the pay of England's secret service he couldn't do Ireland half the harm that he is doing it now.'

The dark eyes blazed with indignation. Words failed him. He shook his head. Suddenly the fresh face relaxed: 'What are you having?'

'Some of your excellent sherry.'

He called to an attendant. 'That's all right. This is on the house.'

'I wouldn't hear of it. You must let me . . .'

'Well, the next one, then. Pay of England. He's worse! England never leaves a country so crippled that she cannot do business with it, but this –'

He was called away, but I knew that between calls he would look in at the first lull. He reappeared bodily.

'So that's what "Freedom" did for us: made us poorer under a native Government than when we were being "robbed and held in bondage" by Great Britain?'

'Aye. And they haven't got enough of it yet. It's a Republic they want for the thirty-two counties, when they are afraid of taking it for the twenty-six. "Bring in the North" me neck! Think of the chance they have of bringing in Ulster when Ulster sees those it threw out as failures and mischief-makers running this country to worse mischief and greater failure still! "Bring in the North" indeed!'

A lull. I sipped my sherry. He returned.

'There was a fellow telling me the other day that the real reason Guinness is leaving Dublin is that they are afraid of the Communism that this Government is letting grow up from its blundering and incapacity. Lord Iveagh's responsibility is so great that he cannot risk stoppage of supplies even for a week. And with the recovery of England that we are supposed to be bankrupting, he must go where he has an increasing market. There has been a transport strike going on now for two months. Who is it that would be bankrupt?'

'It's what they are accustomed to that they extend to others, bankruptcy and failure.'

'And what are strikes but the preliminaries of Bolshevism?'

'They certainly have succeeded in making politics incompatible with prosperity,' I ventured.

'There'll be plenty of prosperity for Mesopotamian rats and mongrels that are sneaking into this country to benefit by the countless tariffs and Orders-in-(bloody)-Council. God, it's awful to see a fine rich country turned into a poorhouse for manufactured paupers and unemployed.'

'I cannot see a grain of hope anywhere,' I said sadly.

'Hope, is it? You might as well be looking for an earwig in the Phoenix Park.'

'With the Silk of the Kine slaughtered, the slums increasing, and the cream of our youth transported by thousands, De Valera is about as good a nation-builder as an advocate of birth-control.'

'Abso-bloody-lutely!' said Mr Fanning.

34

CHAPTER TWO

As I left the hospitable house which was 'too clean' for James Joyce I thought I saw a movement in an incredible place. High up in the blank wall of a house, the first letter in Oxo opened to disclose a window, and revealed a head with the lined, vexatious, aquiline face of a clean-shaven, middle-aged man. It looked like the head of a cavalry officer. 'Dammit!' it said; and the window was closed. It was Thwackhurst, a collector of graffiti. As I went, I thought I heard the mewing of a cat.

Debating what this apparition might mean – was he looking for his cat, only to find it in the precipitous yard from which it could not escape; or was he merely giving vent to emotions necessarily pent up during a conversation with his landlady? I passed the Kildare Street Club, the landlords' Club, the Club that 'dear Edward' used to call the cod bank, from the silver heads shoaled high in its great windows. It is a museum of such as are left now; where the old ornaments from the past century compare with the gold ornaments of more archaic days. 'With silver and gold . . .' So that is where Yeats found at last the Land of Heart's Desire. I wondered what possessed that wise man to become a member of such an establishment. His wish must have come from that protective and self-inspiring dream of his which exalted the Anglo-Irish in his mind to become the 'greatest breed in Europe'. We have to sing our own Magnificats, or go mad. I thought of the poet of Sicily 'pasturing his visionary flocks', and it explained the poet of Sligo's wish to patronize his visionary tenants. A safe proceeding, provided it occurs only retrospectively in imagination. The old landlords betrayed their country, so the popular rumour has it. But nobody can betray Ireland: it does not give him the chance; it betrays him first. The landowners merely fell between two stools and two railway stations – Kingstown and Euston. Since Lord Dunraven died and Horace Plunkett, they have not left a notable name in their Club, save that of their last comer, Yeats, and he will be about as sib to them as Daniel O'Connell's memory is to the Masonic Lodge round the corner in Molesworth Street, where his regalia are still preserved. Between these thoughts and considerations whether I should attend the meeting fixed for the late evening in College Green, I lost my alertness.

A voice challenged: 'You were trying to cut me,' and, looking up, I saw the Bud smiling. His arms were by his side and his attitude was full of quiet hopefulness. 'You have a chance to come in on it now. There never was such a time as the present for initiative and enterprise. There are hundreds of thousands of tons of it; and a deep-sea harbour at Port na Cloy. The world's market is about a hundred thousand tons short every year. Mullin is interested, and has gone over to study the problem in Cornwall, where they are finding ever-increasing difficulties as they go down. I can let you in on it if you can put up the money at once. I have to be off to Paris to make arrangements . . . I may have to be away for a fortnight. It's practically now or never. We have an option on Mrs McNulty's holding.'

'But,' I asked, confused and yet trying to retain my reason, 'what is it?'

He stood back and regarded me sternly for a moment before letting the righteous contempt, which his regard expressed, melt into commiseration.

'You don't mean to say you don't know? You don't know that there are about three hundred million tons of it, of the finest quality in the world, lying untouched in Mayo and the deep-sea slip at Port na Cloy! One hundred pounds a ton f.o.b., and there you go.'

I knew that if I asked again, again the pantomime. I hoped he would think I guessed. I replied as if considering a revelation.

'But why must you go to Paris if the stuff is in Mayo? Can't you ring them up?'

'My dear sir, my very dear sir, who could do business with Paris satisfactorily by long-distance telephone? Most unsatisfactory, not to add impossible. But business – no, sir, nothing doing on the line.'

If I had stayed where I was happy at Fanning's this would not have happened, I thought. I will certainly tell George about it. This is a matter for that stern daughter of the voice of George – his Muse.

'I have no money,' I faltered. 'Who has, these times?'

36

'Then you or they will never have it, and never deserve to have it, if chances like this are let slip.'

A bright thought: 'What is it for?'

'What is it for? Why, for all high-temperature cement, for "gilling" paper – for making anything, in fact, that is to be made out of kaolin.'

(So it's kaolin.) Nevertheless I'll tell George.

'Was it you I saw demonstrating the robot signalling apparatus half-an-hour ago?'

'Now don't get off the subject. There is a world shortage of a hundred thousand tons, and the Cornish mines are petering out. They may be ballsed up already for all I know. We just want to get a few of us together and to form a syndicate: not a Company, mind you – that will come later, but we must all be in first on the ground floor.'

'Why don't you apply to the Government under the Trades' Accommodation Development Grant?'

'The Government! Is there one of them what knows what China clay is?'

'Kaolin,' said I, glibly.

'But you're an educated man, quick on the uptake; and you understand things. (A twinge of hypocrisy made me more tolerant: maybe I will not tell George after all.) And you realize the importance of keeping it to ourselves.'

'Well, I wish you luck. But as things are at present there is no hope for anything that requires foresight and enterprise developing, while there is so much uncertainty as to the future.' I was going to sketch the difficulties of getting a market, but I wanted to be off.

'I will walk as far as your corner,' he said.

We turned the corner. I made a minatory sign as I pointed to the bank. It suggested that I could not pay the expenses of his specific visit to Paris.

'I'll be hopping off.' And he was gone. A good-hearted fellow caught in the dream that there was anything left that had not been skinned long ago from the country.

After all, curiosity brought me to the Republicans' meeting – that is, the meeting of the true Republicans. As I guessed, all signs of the platform had gone. The speeches were to be delivered from a lorry which would drive up without advertising itself to the Guards.

There was little trace of a crowd, but that one would form as quickly when the lorry did arrive as it forms when you are swearing at a collided motor, I was aware.

Down Trinity Street it came. It halted where once the statue to King William stood, destroyed by those as regardless of historical landmarks as the Vandals who seized the Four Courts and burned their country's records – records which had been spared even by the Danes.

There were six men, and, of course, the inevitable pair of hard women, seated on a bench which was secured midway in the lorry. One stood up. He had a long, dark coat which was buttoned close about his neck. This made him, by hiding linen he may have had, a Plain Man, a Man of the People. This is what he said. He said it three times, addressing the swiftly arriving newcomers as they collected:

'Fellow citizens of the Republic of Eireann, we have come to address you in the cause of Freedom and Democracy, in spite of the interference of the paid assassins of Liberty . . .'

Behind me two women were describing a scene, gaining much in the telling by the slowly charging atmosphere of indignation. I knew the overtures of Liberty speeches by heart, so I lost nothing by turning to more interesting eavesdropping.

'I said to her, that is when they got him snugly into the accident ward and she was sending for her sons to break up Mrs Durkin's husband . . . "You know . . ." I soothed her. "Hands off me!" sez she, "till I quench the bastard." "Now, now, Mrs D.," sez I, "take my advice," I sez, "and lave him to Gentle Jayshus; and he'll play bloody hell with him . . ."' Vengeance is mine, I thought. The brawler above me on the platform continued:

'The present Free State Government, in attempting to coerce us into recognizing Free State institutions, is no more entitled to describe itself as Republican than Michael Collins was . . .'

(Cheers: 'Up Collins! God bless the Big Fellah and may the Lord have mercy on him.')

'There can be no compromise between Freedom and bondage.'

(A voice: 'Take it out of bond, and we'll all share it! Won't we, be Jayshus!')

> The plainer Dubliners amaze us
> By their so frequent use of 'Jayshus!'
> Which makes me entertain the notion
> It is not always from devotion.

Behind me the women asked each other: 'Who's the fellow in the long coat? One of them new Politicals?'
A feeling that the police had finished supper and were apt to emerge from the barracks hard by, damped the curiosity of the listeners. In the expectant lull his voice grew louder. I was able to draw nearer to the platform. I gazed in horror at the faces of the two women who sat grimly behind the orator. Is the harem life so reprehensible, after all?

'Your duty is clear. There can be no wavering in this crisis, no turning back. It must be onward to the United Front . . .'

His voice rose to a scream. The two grim women clapped their hands, but what they shrieked was inaudible. The speaker was working himself up, and as he gesticulated his coat opened and, after a little, fell down to his elbows, showing his shirt-sleeves . . . The applause was more deafening now. I realized then that the more inaudible he became the greater the effect he was producing. I thought of Wesley, who, when his voice failed in the pulpit, kept on moving his lips and hands and affecting his audience, who thought that they heard him more by his inaudibility than by his eloquence.

'Rally,' (he cried it) 'O men, O citizens, don't let what cost us so much, down. Close the ranks of the United Front! Rally round the flag. Rally, ral . . . raw . . . the flag!'

He raised his arm, and sat down suddenly. The silence that held the mesmerized mob was ludicrously broken by a little girl of eight or so, who emerged from under the wagon with a rusty tin of Jacob's biscuits suspended from her neck. One side bore the faded legend: 'Digestive'. On the top of it she beat a brisk tattoo breaking the silence, singing in a shrill innocent treble:

39

'Rally, men, rally,
Irishmen rally!
Rattle a fart in a band-box!'

As the women stretched to seize her, she disappeared.

While the next speaker was disappointing the crowd by her immobility, I stood pondering in my mind the more serious problem presented by the little girl's adjuration. Mixed with this in my mind was Yeats' advice to his daughter never to take up politics, never to become 'opinionated'.

Have I not seen the loveliest woman born
Out of the mouth of Plenty's horn,
Because of her opinionated mind
Become an old bellows full of angry wind?

But the wind in a band-box! There were frozen words which fell on the deck of a certain ship which was voyaging among enchanted islands before Dean Swift wrote *Gulliver*. One of these frosted things when thawed emitted a loud noise and was gone. Now that in a band-box, provided always that there was residual air in sufficient quantity, might possibly enable Irishmen to perform that rattling feat. What an orator, then, and appropriate leader would not he be whom St Augustine mentions in his *De Civitate Dei* (XIV. 24), who could make such sounds at will? Like a pied piper he would haloed by halitosis, lead the 'Irish People' by adjusted detonations to – a bombinating Republic.

The applause was disappointing. Women speakers are not popular with the men in Dublin. Maybe they are too mindful of oratory at home.

While there were consultations going on between the speakers on the lorry, I listened carefully to the effect on the crowd.

'A cook should be able to rule Russia. That's what Lenin said. He meant that government should be so simple that any member of the country should be able to take over if needed.'

'But who would do the cooking?'

'Ah, Jayshus! What's the use of explaining things to the likes of you?'

Evidently there was a convert already, and one whose intellect only required clearing, or in lieu of brains some wild enthusiasm.

40

'Look on both sides of you' (said the speaker, a short man with the accent of the "Glasgow Irish", a muffler on throat), 'look on both sides and what do you see? Banks extravagantly built. The palaces and strongholds of the Capitalists, built with our sweat to be debtors' prisons. We must take over these workers' Bastilles. (Applause.) Or lie rotting in their grip. They will be turned into Clubs' (more clubs!) 'and Recreation Rooms for those whose sweat of blood allowed them to be reared. Where did the money come from that went into their stone and mortar? From usury, from the interest on money. What it cost to build them would build decent houses for you, US ALL. The day is not far distant . . .'

The best statue of an orator drawing fire from the central flame of the land that bore him is in the National Bank, I remembered. I hope they will appreciate that, when the Communists take the banks, at least as much as the ignoramuses ignorant as those in England who set up a committee to assess the Elgin marbles, who have put it aside in a corner instead of making it the central ornament of their hall. Their one justification cast aside! Thereby the bank fell off the gold standard in the immortal standards of great art – O'Connell's statue by O'Connor. Of course, the sculptor has to live and work in Paris. If he lived here he would be in debt to the Bank. I thought of the £4,000,000 spent on Gaelic culture which consisted in bemusing children with Esperantisized Irish and making them fall more readily victims to the Communist and Demagogue. And I thought of the fate of Harry Clarke, that supreme colourist in glass, who lived in Frederick Street, to see the window he did for the Irish Hall at Geneva (of course it had to be Geneva, for the eyes of a fool of a Nation are on the ends of the earth) turned down by the Government who commissioned it because a figure or two celebrating Irish exiled authors were in the nude. The money spent in attempting to turn this nation into a race of bi-lingualists ignorant and gullible in two languages, would have given Dublin spacious streets and boulevards and restored it to the place it held as the Seventh City of Christendom before Napoleonic Paris was built. It could provide, if not 'houses for you, us, all,' at least homes for O'Connor and Harry Clarke.

As I looked up at the brawling demagogue, I thought of the régime he would usher in: a state of horror in comparison with which the muddlers from whom we suffer would appear ideal; a state of things that would involve a ruin of loveliness and beauty widespread enough to make the horrors in the lorry ideals of femininity!

Again a speaker:

'Money is not wealth, no more than your hat-check is your hat when you go to a meeting in the Mansion House. But by juggling with the tickets and tallies of wealth – always a point or two of interest higher here than across the water – you get the paradox of wealth and want. Why? Why? Why? Because they can hold up your hat which is your food and clothing, and they can hold up production and transport of goods and decent housing while they are taking a rake off on the tickets of your wealth which is not money.'

And from the walls of the street of the Banks came back the echo – Money!

It will take more than a band-box to hold that, I said, for now he is telling the truth.

And that is the way it goes. With Good and Bad, Truth and Falsehood in unequal fermentation, there will always be a rumble in the bowels of Life.

CHAPTER THREE

Dublin has one advantage: it is easy to get out of it. Unlike London, which is bottled on three sides and uninteresting on the fourth, Dublin has the country and the streamy hills very near, and nearer still the sea.

It is but three minutes' drive to Ballsbridge, which was widened recently by 'Contractors', which is about as much of a 'Bull' as the statement that the Sussex heights are downs. And Ballsbridge is by Serpentine Avenue, in which you can get a horse for an hour's canter on the wide sands of Merrion. One must choose the time when the tide is out, or at least not fully in. And as the tides – uncharacteristically – of Dublin are predictable and punctual, there is very rarely an hour of a morning when the sands are covered. The morning sky is a sight worth more than a morning's sleep. Before the reek ascends from the old houses in which now nearly every room holds a fire – so different from the days when one family held a whole house – there is always a glint of sunlight to be found at the edge of the distant tide. The little waves that cannot rise to any height on the level sands may be the better part of a mile away, and you can canter for five minutes before you meet them and watch them bearing rainbows and spreading on the tawny sands their exquisite treasures brought, as it were, overseas from the inexhaustible and sunny East.

On the right is the smooth outline of the Dublin mountains, rising like cones and rippling into nipples like the paps of Jura, where Wicklow shows Bray Head. The Golden Spears are softened and magnified in the golden morning haze and the greater nearer mass of the Two and Three Rock mountains is half translucent and unreal. Far away, twin steeples catch the light at Kingstown; and the great house at Monkstown, built where the Dun or stronghold of Leary stood, begins to blink its windows at the sun. The outline of the little granite town between the hills and sea is the colour of the sand, and recalls some such sight as must have gladdened pilgrims' eyes when dawn showed them Florence or Fiesole. But the irregular formation of the Wicklow Hills preserves the mind from forming a pattern or formula for their formation. They are subject to no one design as the herringbone ridges of the Apennines; and they will never by repetition offend or limit imagination. And yet in the morning light they rival the hills of Italy in the beauty of their form; at other times their beauty must depend, like all Irish mountain scenes, on the play of shade and light. The uncontaminated breezes flow in with the gentle tide. Howth is amethystine yet, and the long, high horizon is unbroken by a sail. I can see the parallel valleys shared out from a central ridge running along half Italy, steeped in monotonous and assured sun. Here, before I turn, all may be changed. The luminous mass may be angry brown and fuming at its edges with luminous vapour. The whole canvas may be erased.

The morning sky along the coast may be seen as late as 9 a.m. on a morning of February or March. Dublin is, during the months from October to March, a winter resort. The summer gives us delights in their proper season. It is only the winter months that would lie heavy were it not for the advantages the town has of egress to the wilds. We inhale the Atlantic vapours and they turn us into mystics, poets, politicians, and unemployables with school-girl complexions; thus these vapours have lost their enervating and transforming powers before they reach England. And yet her only thanks is to send us for April her eastern winds, whose influence is influenza. No one makes allowance enough for us who live in this vat of fumes from the lost Atlantis.

You must not think that Merrion is like this every morning at the beginning of the year; certainly not, but I have seen it thus on occasions when beauty reigned in the air and made it receptive. All we have to do is to dwell on such moments of beauty. The other moments matter little, and should be dismissed as interlopers and of evil origin. It is the same with life: few moments are allotted to us free from concerns or boredom. These can be counted on the fingers, but as they shall have to stand for us for whatever is desirable and tolerable in life, engrave them in golden letters on the marble of memory and let the rest be forgotten, or remembered, by the happy moment's foil.

It costs one hour's sleep and half-a-crown to ride out to meet the winnowing tide at Merrion. You could not do it for that in Rotten Row, nor there, for all the money in the Treasury, could you make sure of being alone. There may be a corpulent and cheery bookmaker striding the foundation of his profession along by the sea wall, but he will not come near you. He

44

will think that you are melancholy mad or that your horse is restive: that you are better left alone. One thing is sure: you will not waken Dublin, which insists on nursing its misery while shutting its eyes to its delights. Your horse will be hard to hold once he is turned. He sees the squat tower of Irishtown Church. He knows the slip that leads to the roadway. He wants to get back to his stables. No matter how far you may take him beyond them, he will gallop back.

It will not take me long to get through my hospital work this morning, I thought, as I was breakfasting. I shall have time to read the morning papers, particularly the *Daily Express*, for things have come to such a pass now that we have to look into an English paper for uncoloured news and for news suppressed at home. Either through pity for the Government, or an endeavour to leave it unembarrassed, the two untied papers 'go easy with the news'. A leader or two criticizing finance, or such impersonal theme, is the farthest the criticism goes. The Government here has freedom from the Press. This is compensated for by the fact that it owns a Press which has no freedom from the Government, and so the whole round earth is every way . . .

If I am late I shall have to talk to Sir Chalmers, the historical surgeon at the hospital. He is an asset to us, for without him the tradition of surgery which comes down from Nelson's hard-battling fleets would be broken. He is a type of the old and lost school of the days when a doctor had first of all to be a gentleman. After that he could be qualified. How few could be qualified were such a condition to be made primary! A genial man, a great host. 'That's sloke and piping hot . . . with the mutton . . . with the mutton . . . What was this I was about to say? Oh, yes! I believe in top-dressing women, and in helping them, if occasion arises afterwards. And why not, poor creatures? The under sex.'

Sir Frederick will be there, he whose memory goes back so far that he has forgotten his survival in the present. And the 'workers' of the Staff will, mercifully, be engaged. Thank goodness, my line of work seldom involves calamities. In the scramble for beds no one has yet suggested 'slabs' for me. I will be discreet and ask no questions about the winner of the overnight's Sweep. Well, I know, but unofficially – which covers a multitude of inquiries – that there is a Sweep nightly in most of the wards, and he who draws the 'stiff' – the first to die in the morning – wins. Thus it is differentiated from horse-racing, which is gambling; but Death is certain! 'When we beat the Incurables, I was in the Hospice for the Dying. We beat them by nearly ten degrees.' The degrees were degrees of temperature. Rival nurses took the temperatures of a selected team from the ward in each hospital, added them up and reported. 'We beat them by ten degrees, and if Mr Purvis Puris is operating to-day, we'll knock hell out of the Fever Hospital next week.' Such are the advantages of Surgery over Medicine!

There are nineteen hospitals in Dublin, and all of them unmergeable into one. That is due to the fact that many grants and endowments were denominational. There is a greater vested interest in disease than in Guinness's Brewery. This explains why it would give rise to far more trouble than it is worth to run the nineteen into one. Besides the unemployment it would create and the disease it would end! Disease is not always a heartbreaking and melancholy affair, as might be supposed. Where there are so many hospitals for so small a city the diseases thin out, as it were, in proportion to their deadliness; they tend to become chronic and tolerable. The cheeriest people I have come across are cripples or invalids of some sort. A robust or 'hearty' person is looked on somewhat as askancely as he would be in Magdalen or 'The House'. The same applies to an independent spirit . . . I sometimes feel that even I am wanting in popularity.

'So St Vincent's beat us. I am sorry to hear that, Sister. Who had we running against them?'

'The Grattan Ward.'

'And they?'

'Their Gynaecological.'

'They must have had a few puerperals, for they won by 6.80° over our side: we were playing eleven. I hope none of them rubbed their thermometers on their sleeves or put them on the hot-water bottles . . . I have known that kind of thing to happen, and it's not fair. When patients take such an interest in these inter-hospital sports competitions, which help them to bear their trouble and add interest to the weary hours, they should at least play the game.'

'There was no cheating. I took the temperatures with my own thermometer.'

'Sister, that is an excellent report.'

'But, sir, I am afraid there is to be a Board inquiry.'

I was puzzled. I felt that I had been putting my foot into it if the inquiry involved the sister.

'A Board inquiry? What about?'

'About these inter-hospital matches. Matron says they are disgraceful, undignified, and full of unbecoming levity.'

'I will make a point to attend that meeting.'

'We'll all be grateful if you will, sir. I need not say how grateful I will be, for it was I who took the temperatures.'

But I had no time to compose a defence because one of the physicians came in, with 'Look here, I'd be glad of a word with you.'

'Yes. Out with it.'

'The hospitals are going to blazes. It seems that for months most unseemly competitions in temperatures have been going on: whole wards vying with each other, not only in their own hospitals, but against wards in other hospitals. It will bring us into disrepute and lead to a collision with the other staffs. We are holding a meeting in the Board Room this afternoon at four o'clock . . .' (Just as I might have guessed, when I cannot be there, I said to myself.) 'A Board meeting to find out what is to be done.'

'It's quite clear: reduce your temperatures on the medical side, and we will look after our surgical side, so that our hospital will be scouted out of the Senior League or whatever it is; and let the others set their own houses in order.'

'That's all very well; but Matron says we must show our authority and maintain discipline by administering a stern rebuke.'

'I'm perfectly sick of authorities and administrations of stern rebukes. If I go to that meeting, I warn you I will blow it sky high. What sort of Sadists are you, that you must stuff your authority into patients, when probably all they want is a clyster? Anyway, this department, which was built for me by the Irish Hospitals' Sweep, is hardly the place to deprecate sweeps in hospitals. If it ever occurred to you to ask yourself whence comes the amazing courage of the half-fed sick poor that makes ailing and terrorized patients face operations – all the more appalling because of ignorance exaggerating terror — and makes them "frivolous", as you call it, in the face of

47

death, you will find it is due to this camaraderie and good-human-natured joking among the patients themselves. The alternative is disciplined efficiency run to such lengths as would turn the establishments for the relief of pain and the cure of disease into vivisection societies. Let them have all the fun they can, and good luck to them. They are better men than I would be if faced with half of their disabilities – of which not the least is the arbitrary discipline planned to exalt "Authority". Every little pettifogging (no, no, that is not the word, for they don't leap as to the tabor's sound and they have no joy in the jumping), every trumpery little commissar is trying to bolster up his lack of personality and character by becoming a disciplinarian and an authority. And now they want to put a stop to the only game in which it may be truly said that the side which is beaten is not disgraced. Some women have no gumption; they would offer to nurse St Anthony through his struggles with the flesh.'

'Well, you are busy now, but we can go into the matter thoroughly at four o'clock.'

My own character must be weak somewhere, I thought, after Crowningshield had taken himself off. The moment I gain a point I feel like a bully and I want to apologize. Now, Crowningshield is a nice fellow if not driven by 'Authority'. I do not want to hurt his feelings. The more I dwelt on that the more I saw he was right in a way: most of us are – because there is something to be said for discipline in hospitals, something to be said for measures against frivolity in the ante-room of death.

I remembered what happened to a beautiful young woman whose father took up Spiritism, or whatever they call it, late in life. The growing girl was taught that Death is not, and that the supersession of breath was no more than 'passing over'. After two attempts to poison herself, she jumped from a high bridge into a shallow stream and drove her splintered thigh-bones into her beautiful body. Once we relax the fear of Death something happens to Life. It would appear, then, that Death is an astringent to Life. It is verily. This is borne out by the fact that those who are near to Death fear it not so much as those who are in the fulness of health and the enjoyment of life. These are conscious of what they have to lose, and so the contemplation of the opposite condition becomes frightful. Death holds life together. We are borne onwards by the black and white horses.

Long ago I was greatly shocked when I saw patients for operations being trundled on a tumbril of sorts into the anaesthetic room *en route* to the theatre, where they would be operated on by a man whose job it was, and who neither knew their names nor circumstances. But the reverse of the picture converted me. Were the surgeons to know that perhaps he had under his knife the breadwinner of a family of eight, would it help or hinder him? It would be in degree like operating on a relative. And where was the sympathy to end? Surely you could not permit dirty friends to accompany the sick man up to the moment he was put to sleep. There is plenty of discipline where it is wanted. Try to relax it where it is not. The whole problem of the treatment of the sick appeared at one time to me to be full of wastes, overlappings, and abuses. Suppose, for example, forty little hunchbacks are gathered together under the new disease description of 'Surgical tuberculosis' in a mansion sold for the sake of the rates. Any syndicate who owned the premises could call it the only hospital for the exclusive treatment of bone tuberculosis, a staff of sixty could congregate – proprietors, doctors, nurses, laundry-maids, porters, wardmaids, etc. That is one and a half supers carried on each little hump! Why is this not scandalous? Because the expense falls on no one in particular, and one and a half persons to serve each hump is not as good as two, or even three would be. The more, the sooner the hump may disappear . . . No one in particular is paying for the upkeep of this imaginary example of a hospital. But many get their living out of it, and each child gets an extra chance of life. So long as we consider life precious, this must continue. Humaneness is our claim to existence in a civilized mode. The higher the type the more humane. Humanity is all that matters to human beings. There is so much of it among the British people that it overflows into the animal world, as is witnessed by the Societies for the Prevention of Cruelty to Animals and the pampering of dogs. The corollary: disregard of animal suffering is a disregard for human life; as soon as animals are maltreated it will not be far until children, women, and men will suffer. It is a good thing to have an overplus of humane feelings. The multiplication of small hospitals might be objected to if they

49

were a drain on the community. The Empire of Austria had but one for the whole of its wide and mixed territory. The conditions there were the next thing to inhuman. There were no nurses, as we know them, for there were no middle-classes whose daughters would enlist. Old street-walkers took their places, and, what is worse, took the places and performed the duties of qualified men. And if a student wished to get into personal relationship with a teacher, without which it is hard to learn, he had to go round the corner to a little half-private hospital run by the nuns of some Order. Any personal sympathy with the patients was out of the question because of the system and because of the multiplicity of languages. The different departments were marked by coloured stakes: red for surgery, blue for midwifery, yellow for eyes, etc. And the flag that announced no deaths was never flown . . . We have discovered a way to deal with diseases and to subordinate them to man. We keep disease in its proper place. If Death walks the world, why not make it walk the streets and suffer us to be its souteneurs like George Moore's *Alfred aux belles dents?* Yes! We must meet it with a serious aspect. Let us make disease 'keep' us all.

Thus we make disease pay for its own upkeep, but keep those concerned with its cure or treatment. Those who fell victims to suffering – the dead – have endowed most of our hospitals. The rest of the upkeep of hospitals falls now on sportsmen, no longer on the banks. The banks have thus lost the last link that bound them to humanity, and sportsmen gained the first links which give them possibly something in common with religion – Hope and charity. The Archbishop of Canterbury points to an eternal reward after death, and bids his followers live in Hope. The Hospitals' Sweep sells us Hope of an earthly reward three times a year. Thus the Archbishop and the bookmakers have a common interest: both hawk Hope; but the hoping sportsmen, seeing that they are not required to die tri-annually before chancing into their reward, endow the dying so that they may take their eternal chance. The Archbishop requires that men should spend their lives righteously and in corporal works of mercy. The horsey people propose that you should live your own life and spend ten shillings, and the Sweep will look after the mercy by endowing charities. It is Cantuar *v.* Centaur.

Three great inventions came from Ireland – the invention of soda water whereby whisky outdoes champagne, the invention of the pneumatic tyre whereby was made possible the evolution of an engine to scale the blue, and the invention of the system whereby disease is made to support patient, nurse, and doctor, and horses to carry hospitals!

There are proportionally to population not half so many hospitals in London, and this in spite of the many vocations which lead to disease. This is only apparent. The truth is that every Englishman's house is his hospital, particularly the bathroom. Patent medicine is the English patent. Liverpool to London, judging by advertisements for food, sauces, soups, purgatives, and hygienic porcelain, is an intestinal tract. Millions have been made out of patents for purgatives, not to include the patent medicines which are intended to deal with the various results of eating too much. And most of these patent medicines, very nearly all of them, are taken in the bathroom. The most amazing results are advertised. You can lose pounds of flesh by taking a patent form of Glauber's Salts, or put on pounds (only if you are a lady) by the same taking. Agonizing aches in people unseen and unheard of by the patentees disappear, regardless of idiosyncrasy, or a positive Wassermann. And the Englishman believes all this. He believes that a purgative can fatten or make him thin; he believes that either there is only one kind of ache or that one medicine can cure various kinds. His empty churches would be filled twice over by the faith he wastes on the permutations and importance of his lower bowel. And yet, in spite of his faith in one medicine for many unseen and unknown diseases, he cannot accept miracles; he burks at the infallibility of the Pope, but unquestioningly accepts the infallibility of the pill. 'Just as much as will fit on a threepenny-piece' instead of as many angels as will stand on the point of a needle. So faith has fallen in England to the level of the lavatory. And yet it cannot be said that it gives rise to less appreciation of love of righteousness, for it makes *Mens conscia recti*. But it saddens me to think of the pent-up faith misdirected that liberated could rise to Heaven in minsters with flying buttress, curious pinnacle, and soaring belfry. Perhaps, fearing lest he be made to hop on the Day of Judgement, the Englishman is keeping something in reserve.

51

CHAPTER FOUR

It is time I moved onwards by horse-power of a different and non-metaphorical kind.

If I go by canal, I will be at the aerodrome in twenty minutes. If I go by the road that borders the canal, I shall be slow but the associations of the bordering elms should make up for it. They are lovely even now, in spite of their neglected elms and the garish hoardings which are allowed to deface the only boulevards we possess. Old elms, open and half hollow, which were planted to be conduits for water in days before cast-iron or earthenware could be made, gauntly stand in their decay, more sinned against than sinning, and shelter by night the fugitive loves of a city, as the Bard said when he compared a lady whose reputation was disputed to the trees on the canal. The path is lovely because it runs beside the long water over-arched by bridges of cut stone which complete their ellipse by reflexion in the calm water. From Dublin to the Shannon, one hundred miles away, these two great examples of eighteenth-century engineering extend. They cross valleys and enter marshes, such as those which alone could hold up the onsweep of the Roman roads. Lonely through the rich brown bogs they run, to little towns whose white cottages brighten the pale green water, and on through short borders of sheltering trees. Reliable, unleaking, linking Dublin to the largest river of the three kingdoms, to the 'lordly Shannon spreading like a sea . . .'

When my mind longs for that peace which is Death's over-ture, I think of myself as a lock master at one of the country locks beyond the edge of Dublin, where the sound of living water never ceaseth. I would appoint myself to the Ninth Lock, which is not far from Clondalkin. There is a great stretch of water on one side and a well-appointed public-house where one might rest and spend some of the three pounds a week between boats. With a well-chosen form of peculiarity or moroseness one might preserve the privacy of the inner man . . . until you opened the great gates for the last time, and the skipper of one later boat would say: 'Lift the coffin over here and I'll cover it with turf. He was all right in his way, and it will save something to float him down to Harolds Cross, and that's handy for Mt Jerome' . . . 'And on the mere the wailing died away.'

'Contact.' That is the thing I wish to be rid of – contact with earth, for a while, but contact it is. The brown shallows pooled far beneath are in the circuitous River Liffey; where it steps down in white water are the weirs. Leixlip Castle on its mound is there, with the dark, paneless windows of its ancient heronry. Save for that at Rathfarnham Castle, there are few of these remaining. How winding the river is! If it ran straight it could reach the sea in ten miles, and it takes seventy-three. None of us wants to reach his end straight away. That great white-fronted house is Castletown, said to have a window for every day in the year. And those ruined walls the walls of a great mill. The mill-race runs through Celbridge Abbey, owned and decorated worthily now by Lady Gregory's daughter-in-law, famous for her good taste. Hidden in the laurels is the maze, and beside the river running under the private bridge is Grattan's Walk. In the days when *ex tempore* speeches were considered bad form, Grattan thought out his speeches by the softly-singing river. And in those stables Dublin's edition of the Gloomy Dean, Dean Swift, tethered his horse before his brutal interview with Vanessa. Under the Abbey's embattled roof her heart broke and she died. What was the matter with the Dean? I wish Yeats had given his mind to that, even though he forgot George Moore. I had a chance to ask that question of an expert on such subjects and the inventor of explanations on everything germane to sex 'problems' when William Bullitt, the late President Wilson's unofficial ambassador, was going to Vienna to see his friend Sigmund Freud. 'Take the *Journal to Stella* with you,' I implored, 'and ask him to give you his opinion on the enigma of Dean Swift's amours.' But I heard no more of the enterprise. Maybe it appeared to that citizen of the United States to be no more than an attempt on my part to substitute old loves for new. To bring love problems to Vienna may have seemed to be the latest and most delicate cynicism. So the Dean's libido remains undiagnosed. It is gone now; the Abbey and Lyons come into view below its hillside lake and woods. There Lord Cloncurry's daughter, Emily Lawless, wrote her *Bog Myrtle and Peat*.

The great mansion is yet held by her sister one of the few lovely places left in the family which planned and cherished and preserved them. I wish I had asked the pilot to come along. I may spin if I let my mind wander from the machine. It may be as well to seek safety in height. It needs about three thousand feet to separate oneself from the coil of earth and petty concerns. Up here, were it not for the noise, there is heavenly peace. Swinging to the east, the bright buff-coloured Hill of Howth and the sands of the two Bulls can be seen. The Danes 'took a great prey of women from Howth' somewhere in the tenth century. Such raids are discontinued now that each woman has become a host in herself: such is the development of individuality. A great prey of women . . . The finely-drawn hills are on the right, lighted on their southern side. And at the end of the range, where it falls to make the plain of Dublin, can be seen Dundrum and Rathfranham, where Yeats lives. I will look him up this evening. There is nowhere to land if the engine conked except on Leopardstown or the Phoenix Park when one flies over the city. It is worth noticing the roof-like, flat, floating island of smoke which, seen sidelong, looks as opaque as plank or as a piece of plate-glass. We can see through it from beneath, but it diminishes the brightness of the stars and refracts the violet rays. However, there is the great brewery that has done more for Dublin than any of its institutions. It cleared the foetid liberties long before philanthropists took to improving the houses of the poor. It provided one of the loveliest *volks garten* in Europe, and it set the model to employers long before Henry Ford expounded his theory of high wages. It went beyond that, for what happens in the U.S.A. to employees after the wage-earning age? – too old at forty: in Guinness's you are in your prime. If I were beginning life again – (oh! a pretty bad bump from the smoke of the chimneys to remind me that I must hold on to the life I have, such as it is) – if I were beginning life again I would seek a job in the brewery. I have often longed not only to take, but to make drink. And by making Guinness you make so many other things as well – garden villages, dependable workers and the brew that savours of content. Like dark sleep, it knits up the ravelled sleeve of care, and, what is an achievement, it wastes the time that might, if we were not drinking, be devoted to scheming, posing, hypocrisy and money-making.

'The silted Nile mouths and the Moeritic Lake': Clouds.

What a wonderful communion Guinness provides! You can drink yourself into helping the poor by better housing; you can drink yourself into St Stephen's Green, or at least into appreciation of those who gave it to the city; and you can, if you like, drink yourself into poverty and become an object, if not a dispenser of charity. Old martyrs fought with beasts in the arena and those tore out their victim's viscera in a minute; now you can dedicate your liver, fair and softly as they did whose custom provided the sums that went to the restoration of Christ Church, to the erection or maintenance of holy fanes. When you see a face that would act as a bed-warmer, as Will Shakespeare has it, scorn it not. Salute the *bon nez* to which went so much drink in the making. And think of the Rose window of some great cathedral, gules and purple, wing on wing. Drink to the Lord Ardilaun who gave us the Green. Drink until you see the ducks swimming in your tankard. Drink your liver into martyrdom . . . take your time: there are no Neros here. Where is my funnel?

Where am I? At three thousand feet, and instead of over the great brewery, I am near the Hill of Howth. It is time to turn. 'Rudder and bank together,' as that best of instructors, Elliot, used to sing out. But all his skill could not save him from a fellow who ran into him at a thousand feet. Back over the Fifteen Acres, the most wonderful aerodrome any city could ask for, only seven minutes from Dublin's centre. But it is not open spaces that make aerodromes, but open minds and enterprise. There are twin chimneys of Clondalkin that beckoned me home – in gratitude to them I confess it, no matter how it reflects on my 'navigation' – many and many a time. What I want is a balloon.

And now for the landing. There is a chance of a three-pointer, since there is no acknowledgeable and critical head in the front cockpit, to make me self-conscious. Just let her in at sixty-three. Crab a bit of height off and . . . Back, back! Yes, poor Elliot! Your old pupil's remembering. Stick *right* back! Just my luck! When I do land well, there is nobody about to see it.

And now for lunch.

What would Dublin do without the Shelbourne Hotel? The host of fashion and of whatever interesting visitors arrive from overseas. Well-dressed women with vivacious voices; tall men with shining hair and rubicund faces, who order things. The Boers call them *rooi-necks*, but they are the Boers' master in spite of – no, on account of – their colour scheme. For it is the beef-eaters and the beer-and-whisky-drinkers that inherit the earth. It does me good to see them, tall and carefree, walking about as if they owned the hotel with the rest of the Empire. Careless and carefree people, for whom the best is about good enough. They hate no one, for they consider the world their household. They have built an Empire and ruled it, and they have attained that air of carelessness by having so many subject nations to master by disregard. This quality of the British drew the attention and criticism of a German philosopher, who reflected that the English rule as the best lovers of women succeed, by a certain amount of casualness. But it is not with one of them I am lunching.

My host is an American 'columnist', and he represents a large publishing firm in the U.S.A. I do not know him by sight, but George, the hall porter, who knows everyone, will point him out. It was George who first noticed our decline and fall when he saw the new Minister in a morning suit with turned-up trousers and *yellow* boots. He was quite right, it was the beginning of the end: but what puzzles me is, why should such solecisms make such a difference? It may be because there is something of subjection and flattery in imitating the fashions of another people, or is it not that the nation that sets the fashion rules the world? That must be the reason. But there is something deeper yet. I remember being given a great compliment – an hour's talk with Doctor Lowell, the founder of modern Harvard. He wore a frock coat and *brown* shoes. No matter what he said of interest or wisdom, it was lost on me. I only remember those brown shoes . . . Now, why should the wrong colour in shoes discredit his words and take away any good from whatever message he was conveying? No one but myself would have been light-witted enough to care. That is not quite the reason. The reason is that observance instead of observation, manners – that is, *'mores'* from which *'morals'* is derived – instead of knowledge are the marks of the older Universities. Founded, like Greece's foundations, on the crystalline sea of Thought, they are aware that there is nothing new, unprecedented nor likely to be, so that having drunk deep of Castalia, the next thing is to observe the *convenances*. The blue serge on Sunday, the bowler and the cherry cane . . . I did not exactly weep tears of pity on the Principal's polished shoes, but I came away in a confused state of mind, annoyed at myself for being unable to remember what my hour with Lowell should have given to me, and angry that I was the victim of feelings which I could not analyse. I have it now! His shoes were *immoral!*

A columnist is a person who writes like this in American papers and earns, or draws, five thousand pounds a year or more:

New York:
The age of magnificent contrasts:
An ex-Bank President hailing a Street car.
Dave Apollon's King of Heart's hair cut.
Wonder how John D. Jnr. would look in a beret.
Look alikes: Bud Kelland and his son.
What became of Zelma O'Neal?

He shall have my sympathy for it. It must be harder to write like that than to do brainwork. It is a hard thing to make the trivial significant, or to make mediocrities interesting. And yet the Press, by thrusting publicity on people, gives them a significance in publicity. No! It gives publicity a significance. The Press becomes a Temple of Fame. And those whose names are written on its columns achieve a momentary immortality, an ephemeral fame. And, strange to say, even those who are quizzed are pleased: notoriety at any cost, as was the early way with Ford's motors.

But it was easy to find Kurt Kelner, for he was with my friend, Captain McLoren – clipped moustache, trim figure, grey eyes and straight. He is always the gallant captain to me since I was made aware of his sad story. It might be called 'The Vengeance of Shiva'. He was stationed in India, and one day he had the chance of saving the life of a priest of a sequestered temple. Curiosity born of the apparent contradiction to Western minds by which it seemed incomprehensible that courtesans should be associated with a holy shrine, made him ask as a favour if he could visit one of those ladies who had dedicated themselves to religion in so strange a way. The priest was evidently in a difficulty. He was caught between his gratitude and

57

his fidelity to his trust. He explained that the women were really girls of high rank who devoted their bodies to the service of the Temple and that, as it would be clear to them that he could not possibly share their belief or approach them except from the most obvious motives, he would leave the matter to his better judgement. But judgement in a man of twenty-three can be obscured by concupiscence, especially in the absence of officers' ladies who had dedicated themselves to arms. He had his wish, and will.

'She saw through me at once,' McLoren said. ' "You only come here out of lust and curiosity. You have no prayer to the god." ' He acknowledged that he had not. ' "This is a form of prayer. We have dedicated our bodies to the service of those who have neither the leisure, the philosophy, nor the power to remove from their minds the veils of the flesh. We drain their concupiscence from them. They are then in a better frame of mind in which to reach communion with the deity." '

'That was pretty hard on me. I thought at first that the priest had put her up to it, but no. She insisted on me going through with it; said it was her vow. And I never experienced anything like it in my life, before or since. That's why European women are utterly without interest for me. A bit of a tragedy, you know.'

How much of a tragedy I learned later, when from two sources I heard of the despair of my friend obsessed by maddening memories. He forgot that he was overlooking the fact that his youth, at the time of this meeting with the priestess, added to the transports; and he failed to take it into account when brooding on his lost delights.

'If it had been love at first sight, I could understand it,' one of my informants confided.

'But it was, and far more,' said I.

'Yes, but what I mean is, that I have heard of men never marrying because the woman they loved died or married someone else; but to be dreaming still as McLoren is carrying on, twenty years after, of some coloured woman . . . It's incomprehensible.'

'I have learned that she was not coloured, but had an ivory sort of skin . . .'

'Oh, he told you that, did he? But what about the snowy skins that he turns down? He groans when a really good-looking girl meets him. The prettier, the worse it takes him. Sometimes he's damned rude.'

'Perhaps it is that women in Ireland are not a form of prayer?' Let it not be thought that I was heartless or that I did not do my best for McLoren. At the risk of being misunderstood, I wrote to India to a Diotima whom I knew, to a lady who 'had intelligence in love', asking what might be done. This is her reply:

'Should your friend indeed have had ingress to a priestess learned in the art and practice of the African Aphrodite and Diana of the Ephesians and Venus of the Triple Gate, whose mysteries are alive in India alone to-day, then truly would he go sighing for evermore after that memory of unendurable pleasure indefinitely prolonged. And certainly would he find the women of the West amorously inept.'

What more could I do? But I was all the more interested in watching McLoren.

'I want you to meet Mrs Kelner, Miss Babette Vyse, Kelner. And now we will go in and have lunch at last . . . Hold on: I was told to ask you if you'd care for a cocktail.'

The mixed drink of a mixed race and yet more characteristic than the drink of any other nation save, perhaps, absinthe or the vodka of the Russians and the butter tea of Tibet . . . And yet how preferable to any of these! . . .

'Yes, a cocktail.'

'What kind?'

'Oh, the yellow one with lemon juice in it . . . it has a faintly green look. I used to get it in New York.'

'You have been in New York?'

'Yes. And what surprises me is that I am able to answer that embracing question which someone is sure to ask: What do you think of New York?'

Irony, however slight, is either not understood or misunderstood and the subject of suspicion to an American.

'I was going to ask that very question,' said Mrs Kelner. 'Well, what do you think of it?'

'Seen from the air, or from over the Hudson in the evening purple, it is by far the loveliest city I have beheld. It rises like fabulous Troy . . . there is no city in the world to compare with

59

it . . . It is greater than Troy not only in its buildings, but also in the beauty of its Helens. The most characteristic thing in America, mechanical America, is that it can make poetry out of material things. America's poetry is not in literature, but in architecture. But one must have seen the sun from the East River on the dark silvery pinnacle of the Crysler Building, to believe it. I lived with a friend for weeks in Number Two Beekman Place, and I saw, through the clear winter morning, that marvellous sight. Like newly-cut lead the pointed roof shone . . . The sight was as new to me as my first sight of the slender pillar of a mosque . . .'

'Where did you see a mosque?'

'When I went to Crete . . . the pillar stood out against a calm, apple-green sky. It was unusual, and full of alien romance to me.'

'Yes. It is refreshing to get away from our traditions for a while . . . They are apt to be overwhelming if they are not interrupted occasionally. Getting away from them accounts for the popularity of touring, and that itself is a new development of the last twenty years.'

'Do you think that explains why Germany went off Christianity this year?'

'I don't get you.'

'To assist her tourist traffic. I can imagine hundreds of clergymen rushing there in mufti.'

The way a waiter sticks up conversation with a dish is most annoying. That is one reason why I hate food. It interrupts good talk, and just as I was making an impression (whether favourable or not does not matter), or just as I thought I was doing well with my 'reactions' to architecture, the waiter hisses, 'Sauce tartare?' I must have shown my temper on my face . . . Is it any wonder I prefer drink to food? It promotes, or at least does not hinder, conversation. And it limits the waiter's chances of asking questions. A man can give an order. The initiative is with him. He is not at the mercy of a man who has to fill him up with comestibles within a limited time.

When he had smeared my plate and departed, I said: 'Sorry I was interrupted, but in the pause it occurred to me that I was probably talking too much and taking advantage of other people's weakness for food.'

'We were talking about the wine list.'

Splendid!

'It would be an awful thing if the ancient drinks were forgotten during the tyranny of the chocolate-makers, Quakers, or whoever they were who dried a great nation. Gin is the enemy of good drink. I suppose no American can remember what good claret tasted like. To whom would he go to recover the lost information? If there was one good drinker left in London, and if he were endowed by the American Senate to come over and to preach on the merits of Château Latour, that would not help: you cannot tell people about taste, any more than you can explain light to the blind. Now, before you forget its flavour, drink thoroughly of some red or amber wine.'

McLoren said, 'I prefer a whisky-and-soda.'

That is one of Dublin's famous inventions – soda. It was invented in Sackville Street. The well is under Nelson's Pillar. It is a temperance drink, but it is fated to be associated with whisky until the end of time. A perfect proof that not only is there a Providence, but that Providence disapproves of teetotallers.

'Large or small?' interrupted the waiter.

I had a dear old friend who detested that disastrous question. He often rebuked the fool who asked it, with, 'There is no such thing as a *large* whisky.' He could always imagine and drink a larger one; but a small whisky did exist, to the detriment of all good drinkers . . .

'What are you drinking?'

'Oh, something from the Valley of the Moselle. It is one of the loveliest valleys of the world. I always think of that quotation from Claudian when I drink Moselle:

"Immemorial vines embower the white houses,

The earth yields to the labour of the slaves

The incense rises from the temples where the distant
    Emperor is honoured:

Fortune is seldom invoked, for men desire no change."

That shows that there was at least one period in the world's history when people knew they were well off.

' "Fortune is seldom invoked, for men desire no change." Our peak point as a nation was reached about the time of Queen Victoria's Jubilee. Even in the public-houses there was no talk of politics then.'

61

'Oh, nonsense!' McLoren exclaimed. 'What about Parnell and Healy, and all the bad blood?'

"What I mean is that we had no politics thrust upon us. We were not responsible for our condition. We had always England to blame. Now we have only ourselves. Politics and prosperity go in inverse ratio to one another. This town will soon be another modern Athens, dirty and full of lawyers. A gong should have announced forty years ago: "The golden pomp is come." '

Mrs Kelner whispered: 'Kurt wants to get you for a book for his firm. He represents a big syndicate in the States.'

'Sure. We must have your book.'

'What kind of a book and on what subject?'

'Why, the whole show.' He looked out of the window. 'All your memoirs.'

'Alas, a medical man has no memoirs. It isn't done.'

'Now, come. Was not Axel Munthe a medical doctor? And he wrote *San Michele* to get money for a Bird Sanctuary.'

'I am a Bird Sanctuary. Any of my little sisters, the birds, will find my sanctuary inviolable and their confidences respected. If I write, it will be to win a sanctuary for myself.'

The ladies did not quite 'get' this. Our slang differs from the American, which aims more at statement than innuendo. I feared to explain, knowing how poorly my effort about the Germans going off Christianity to improve their tourist traffic had been received, and so forbore to point the reference to St Francis and his sisters, the birds.

'But, sure, Doc, you could do a book that would not give away any medical secrets. You have been right through the whole movement and you knew all the figures of your own time. You could include an historical perspective from the inside that would be a valuable contribution when the history of the time comes to be written.'

'Don't expect me to write a perspective. The only way to treat this town is the way the Chinese treat their pictures: eschew perspective. Perspective is too facile. Read Desmond MacCarthy's wonderful description of a Chinese landscape in his "Experiences" to realize my idea. Taking a point of view, any point of view, is certain to fill one with sorrow. But if you make Dublin the hero of a book and let it portray itself as it is every day, you may get an effect such as the wisest of Masters, the Chinese artists, achieved.'

'Well, I hardly know. I guess you know best. But it seems to me that you would be throwing a lot away if you were not to give the history of the men you met as they appeared to you and the effect of their new-found liberty on the Irish people.'

'The effect of their new-found liberty on me is easy to perceive. I did not grow fantastic deliberately: I thought I was going towards Freedom and breaking down a Bastille; it was only opening a lunatic asylum. So I have, in order to protect the ego, or whatever you call that which likes peace of mind, accepted my *rôle*: I am a mere figment in the National mind, and that mind is not quite sane. And, by the way, what is Freedom?'

They thought that this was a joke, and a good one. That is my fate: to be misunderstood jocularly. But what of it? So much depends on those who misunderstand. Would it be worth while to set them right?

'What do you think of the present situation?'

'Remember I faced your question, what did I think of the U.S.A., but this is altogether beyond me. I can tell you some facts. We have less than three million inhabitants in the Free State, and more than three hundred thousand whom you will not permit any longer to enter the United States and to enjoy its fuller life and its higher standard of existence. These un-emigrated hate Ireland because it is not the U.S.A. They look upon it as a prison, and the position of any government which depends on so many adult votes is somewhat similar to that of warders when the convicts have taken over the prison. But the most ephemeral things are politics. They are the passwords to oblivion . . .

'Ireland at present is parallel to what Greece was in the age of myths. We never had, as England had, the Roman school-master to teach us logic. Therefore, fairy-tales are our politics. I am not anxious to compose fairy-tales: I can always send out for a daily paper.'

Kelner smiled and said, 'Yet I am not sure. I still think that there is a mighty lot that has not yet been told about your country. You are not all dreamers.'

'Maybe not, but woe betide the reputation of anyone who wakens us up from our dreams. It is worse for you in the

United States. There you have got the permanent dreams of half-a-dozen nations who are the hyphens, to deal with. In order to avoid loss of national or homeland identity in the great merger of humanity, the newcomers rally round and cling to the totem-poles of their country of origin. The Lutheran becomes more Lutheran, and the Irish Nationalist never moves from the politics of a hundred years ago. The reaction of this on Ireland, whose politics are supported by the American-Irish, can be imagined. It leads to a perpetuation of the politics of the Famine. It keeps alive resentment and encourages the demagogues here to hawk hate. And hate is anything but a policy of progress. It keeps us back, and the more backward we become the more we hate those who present us with the object-lessons of success and prosperity. We save our faces by hating England. It would be far better to shave them and to emulate.'

'We'll talk about this another time.'

'Those men think only of themselves and their plans, and it's always at some meal that they do business.' Mrs Kelner was feeling left out.

'It is altogether my fault,' I said. 'I am as bad as a friend of mine, a barrister, who went to condole with the widow of one of our presidents. He spoke for an hour without a break and without giving her a chance even of a sigh; and then, coming out, remarked: "A nice chatty little woman." Now be as chatty as you can.'

'Thanks, but I am a complete owner of myself, and you could never succeed in snowing me under. I only refrained from talking because I had nothing but questions to ask. And it's rude to ask questions?'

'No. It would be worse if you took so little interest in us that you asked none.'

Babette began to laugh. 'She has them all arranged originally. They are original kind of questions. We drew them up between us this morning.'

'Oh, don't betray me. But if you don't mind' – turning to me – 'do tell me what are the things you would regret most if you left this town?'

'Now, isn't that a swell way of finding out what we ought to see!' Babette exclaimed.

'I would probably regret the informality of life here. I hate

64

dressing up vocationally. In London the medical men are as distinctly got up as the chimney-sweeps.'

'But here you cannot tell the difference?' – from McLoren.

'Now, that is a nasty one. A bull's eye! But even at the risk of being taken for a sweep, I prefer not to be judged by the cover exclusively, even if it is an old college or regimental tie.'

'Humph!' said Mac.

'Next to the formality, the easy egress to the country. We have wild geese two hundred yards from Merrion in the mornings, and the dells of the Dublin mountains are not ten miles away. Hills, rivers and sea, and an almost winter resort temperature. And perhaps it would be my greatest regret leaving the best water and water supply in the world: the Vartry water.'

'Millie's questionnaire has not taken us very far. What she wants to know is what we ought to see.'

'Just round the corner from this hotel the Gold ornaments are to be seen at the Museum. What they have to do with the Muses, or why a building for housing antiques and not poets should be called a Museum, beats me,' said McLoren. 'But don't let me deter you from inspecting the most interesting native ornaments evolved by a nation which lived apart from Europe for centuries, almost as far off as the Government is trying to put it to-day. They are made of pure gold, which may have been plentiful until worked out on the surface of the Wicklow Hills. But they cannot compare as objects of Art with the Cretan and Greek cups, daggers and ornaments, earlier by one thousand five hundred years.'

'Listen to me,' I said; 'you are under the curse of tradition. You expect that you will add to your statures and gain a feeling of superiority by borrowing from the poor unhistorical dead. If you find in the country into which you are born certain examples of a "culture", no matter whence it comes, you immediately take unto yourselves all the little tradition it may be presumed to bring you, at the same time withholding yourselves from any primitiveness with which it might identify you. Let us be truthful for about ten minutes. There is nothing to be gained from this dream of our superiority in some Golden Age, except an excuse to shirk life in this age in which we find ourselves.'

'You don't say!' said Kelner.

'But I do. I would tell you all about the foreshortening fallacy of history. Mrs Stopford Green was our best example. Her history of Ireland left you under the impression that Ireland was as colourful and as humane as *The Pilgrim's Progess* but for – but for – but for . . . anything except hard fact . . . The Gold ornaments mean nothing more than a date in decadence from what was reached in Greece fifteen hundred years earlier and more marvellously.'

'But, say, what are we to see after these barbaric ornaments in the Museum?'

'Ask Dr Mahr, whose appointment was a miracle because it meant modern science in archaeology, what his opinion is of the "Gael" in contributing to modern civilization. But don't embarrass him by asking him to describe that sole specimen of pre-Christian "Art", or of even collateral Christian Art, the quaint wooden figure he discovered in Mayo. "Up, Mayo!"'

'Don't mind him when he scents some racial contradiction between the ancient observances and those of our day. He is so mischievous that he loves to expose any proof of contradiction he can find,' said McLoren.

'Well, I know this much about Irish archaeology: there has been only one example of pre-Christian sculpture found in the country except the Phallic deity of northern Mayo. I grant you that it argues badly for a people who had to "say it with" a wooden image instead of with the orchids of Fifth Avenue. Don't mind McLoren. Let us admit that the age of the Irish Gold Ornaments was a bad time for Blondes. There is one exhibit not from the Golden Age. It is the present President's boots.'

'Boots?'

'Yes. Upstairs in a glass case to prevent anyone else stepping into them. They are long, thin boots with fallen arches. De Valera's boots.'

'Fallen arches?'

'Possibly symbolical: to commemorate the fallen arches of the Mallow Viaduct destroyed in his civil war.'

'I don't quite get that.'

'Certain Rakes of Mallow blew it a quarter of a million pounds' worth to make Cork a Republic by isolation. If they were triumphal arches, it would suggest Empire and Imperialism. But these boots are calculated to appeal to the flat-footed man in the street.'

'That is if the man in the street has boots.'

'The Museum is not open to the barefooted. Besides, these boots have already a semi-sacred character, exhibited as they are in the Nation's Invalides. They may yet be regarded as relics and touched to cure corns.'

'But not "cold feet"!' said McLoren.

> 'Who dares the pair of boots displace
> Must meet Bombastes face to face.'

'We must see these boots!'

'A cult of the Boots may down the arches of the years arise; the Order of the Boot, its insignia. The boots in which the President went to America only to hear them called "shoes". This will provide the characteristic schism. The boots may be taken out at the annual, triennial, or even bi-annual election of the President and used as a test of his fitness for the post, somewhat in the way the Tanist was elected of old. Then the Lia Fail or stone of Destiny sang approval, now the Fitting of the Boots.'

'Shoes' would be anathema even though it might bring in the United States, to which in immemorial times the President took his departure. It would be too suggestive of that old woman (Eire) who lived in a shoe.

She had so many children *he* did not know what to do. It would distract the devout by statistics of unemployment.

I noted that the boots were placed parallel to each other. A somewhat more divergent attitude would have given them character.

'I will not take coffee, thank you. And really, Kelner, you ought to know why. I tried in vain for three days on an American train to get white coffee, because the tea was a sort of half-hearted poison and the black coffee too racking on the nerves. I hate all coffee since. And I would hate your trains, only you make up for your earth-bound, slow and overheated furnaces by your futurist air services.'

'But Doc, what are we to see after the Museum?'

It is strange how much it takes to make me drunk in boring company; I can get drunk without a glass with my good companions. But to be unable to shelter the mind from questioning friends gave me to think . . . seriously.

'Well, when we have done the Gold Ornaments in the Museum?'

Yes, yes, I thought, the Museum . . . the Museum . . . Museum . . . House of the Muses. 'Oh, you must go straight ahead down the street in front of the Museum until you come to the Royal Hibernian Hotel . . . a bonny hostelry in its way. I could tell you of a night with a few Scotsmen there, but . . . You won't lose it. I'll die dictating . . . Take a bayonet turn to the right; half-way down Duke Street is the Bailey. Its windows are nearly flush with its walls. That spells the seventeenth century. Scylla and Charybdis prove its desirability. They are the horrid flower-sellers which haunt its portals . . . Of them anon, no later. But the Bailey is the true museum of Dublin because it is the House of the Muses. If you are lucky and if you can work yourself into the confidence of James or Lewis, you may be given a glimpse of the Symposium. You remember how Plato placed all the best of Athens at, what we in our degenerate and envious days would call a "Drunk". He called it a banquet. He does not, if you notice, interrupt good talk by food. They called for larger cups.

'The Bailey entertained Parnell; and, because of that tradition, Arthur Griffith, "the greatest Irishman of all time," according to Deputy Belton. I always thought it detracted somewhat from Griffith's sense that he should judge a hostelry by its old patrons rather than by its mellow beverages. The Bailey has the best whisky and the best food in Dublin. I took a young friend of mine, a wealthy fellow, and between the unreality of riches and his chef, he declared in the Bailey, and at the bar, mind you: "You have the best eating-houses and drinking-houses in the world." He knew what food could be. We know what food is. Good cooking is an excuse for bad food. But our prime beef defies camouflage and our Jameson . . . Well, you can see it in the hall of the Bailey, with its silver label on its barrel before it is consumed. Later, those for whom whisky is the chief event of their day come in. "Its Protestants to be." The smoke-room upstairs, where Griffith took his ease after his day in the slum of Crow Street, is now a dining-room, but there is a room behind it with a corner fireplace. There you may meet a bard or two, but they are on the wing.'

68

A light touch on the arm. A tall figure bent and whispered: 'Is that George?' She went away, looking back with a laugh over her shoulder like a figure in Botticelli.

'Who was that woman with the clear skin and eyes like grey ice?' Miss Vyse asked.

'If ladies praise her she must be beautiful,' I said.

'Why, sure. And she seems to know you pretty well. Surely you must see that she is lovely? We are wondering what she whispered in your ear.'

'I'll tell you without the least hesitation, but it will take some explaining.'

'She asked if you were George.'

'If I was George?'

'I heard her,' said Miss Vyse.

'I don't want to puzzle you, but the meaning is this: I have a great friend who is a stout poet and a good writer. He does not publish or advertise. When I quote him, people pretend to think that I am trying to pass some of my own lucubrations under the name of a character I have invented. I cannot get the wife of one of our Consuls to believe that George exists. So, mockingly she asked, "Is that George?" It's very annoying to be given credit for a character you have not invented and to meet with no recognition for the characters you endeavour to create.'

'Why not bring him in to call?'

'I did! But he is shy, and, as I failed to draw him out, she still insists that he is a "false creation".'

'Say, I'd rather meet George than see the Gold Ornaments.'

'But you cannot meet him to-day, so –'

'Well, before we leave for "The Chieftain Harrington".'

'I have never heard of the Chieftain Harrington. Who is he?' Now what had I said? Their faces fell.

'Oh, but we met him on the boat. He is the hereditary Chieftain down somewhere – you have the address? – in Cork. He invited us to see his stronghold. How extraordinary!'

'Oh, I just thought that "Harrington" was not an Irish name. But so many Irishmen have odd names now, one cannot be sure.'

'But an hereditary Chieftain?'

'I will inquire and let you know.'

'Now who the hell is Harrington?'

'And one thing more – where can we buy antiques?'

'Nassau Street, Sackville Street, Liffey Street, where Naylor's is and all along the quays. Have you not heard?'

> 'Two Jews grew in Sackville Street
> And not in Piccadilly.
> One was gaitered on the feet,
> The other one was Willie,
>
> 'And if you took your pick of them,
> Whichever one you chose,
> You'd like the other more than him,
> So wistful were these Jews.'

It is hard to break away from those who have infinite leisure, but I closed the entertainment as soon as I could. Going forth, I met Butterly, a spruce little barrister with a large red face who always seemed to be leaving in a hurry, though no one knew where he went or where he slept. He was now leaving the scene of one of his famous jokes, the lounge where he gave his well-known advice to the two young officers who were complaining about conditions on the Gold Coast ...

'It is all darn fine, but think of having to wake up with a Negress's head each side of you on the pillow.'

'Think imperially,' said Butterly.

He was mysterious now. He beckoned me and took my arm as we walked out.

'I saw you pointing at the bank when you were talking to the Bud,' he remarked. 'It's in there you should be ... or I should be.'

I looked at him closely. I saw that the redness of his cheeks was composed of countless tiny purple veins which looked like little star-fish under the skin. There are places, I thought, from which he does not hurry away in time.

'I in a bank?' I asked, surprised.

'Of course you will: in your next incarnation anyway,' he said. 'Your friend Æ must have told you long ago that we all became our own opposites after a cycle or an era or one of those things.'

'It will take more than the Great Platonic Year to get me into a bank.'

'Platonic? Ho, ho! I don't know so much about that, but what I do know is that that is the greatest bank in Dublin.

70

Don't mind its reserves, but just look at the view there is of all the finest women in Dublin. They pass along by the wall there twice a day. Twenty-three steps on an average to the sixteen yards.' The little eyes gleamed with mirth. He dug me in the ribs. 'I'll run you down to the green room in the Abbey and fix you up, as a typical bank manager. A little more silver in the hair, a little more tightness about the mouth until it suggests a savings box, a little hint of parchment about your skin, "this indenture witnesseth" and a fund of meaningless small talk. We would call you Chitchat the bank manager.'

I toyed with the idea, I might for a moment and count up. Five, six, seven, eight, nine ... 'Her little heel fits in a shoe!' No! I could never do it! I could never keep myself from distractions: were they numerals or steps I was counting? ... ten, eleven pounds and tuppence ... a damn fine figure of a woman ... and one halfpenny! She is stopping ... It was not at me she was looking, but at that fellow crossing the street ... Who is that fat little man? Then aloud: 'It's only nonsense, after all.'

'It's far from being nonsense,' he said. 'Just as the Orange pogroms in the North are a direct result of the hypocrisy of Belfast, which has its middle classes suppressed with so much respectability that they are afraid of being seen in public with a woman or a whisky for 364 days in the year ... they have to break out and take it out by beating drums and their fellow citizens on the feast day of that homosexual King who was financed by a Pope. It's far worse among the bankers of Dublin. They have no one to whom to look up. Lives of great men do not remind them that their mistresses were fine.

'Nelson, Wellington, O'Connell, Parnell: saviours of civilization, empire-makers, liberators, statesmen, lechers. Sailor, soldier, liberator, statesman ... but where, oh, where are the bawdy bankers? Can it be that because none of them is truly bawdy, none is truly great? Can it be that the further men remove themselves or are removed from the opposite sex the further they are removed from the service of humanity? And they have not even got a "Twalfth". That's what makes them so sadistic. They have to take to helping fair clients with "The Authorities", who, of course, never see the letter ... I doubt if they exist – but it's great sport having the pretty girls writing letters to yourself. If you cannot work that you can write:

71

"Madam, I trust that you will be in a position by the 1st prox."
God! Man, you've missed your vocation! There's a new
movement in English prose there. You could be counting the
girls' steps if you were in that bank.'

And put it in the ledger, I thought, at the close of the day. A
little grey elfin creature with a peaked hat took up her position
squatting on the kerb in front of the bank window. She never
raised her head from her banjo, but, playing to herself, glanced
sideways along the strings as if to follow the little notes in their
flight from an indifferent town.

Butterly looked at his watch, evinced surprise, and was gone.

My hostess dispensed cocktails. The room was full of laughter, which is not the least of the contributions that alcohol
makes to conviviality. A great, blue-clad figure dominated the
scene as he moved lavishing the good cheer, an engine of
mighty force to dispel the gloom of endless icy forests and immeasurable wastes, but over-strong for the little islands. Breast
to breast the ladies whispered. A laugh rang out. 'Let's all hear
it. That's not fair!'

Too far away to hear the explanation, I realized what it must
be; as laughter is some form of short triumph, and what would
make a woman laugh more than a short or long triumph over
the male sex? She can rarely see fun in mens' jokes, unless she
is degraded, because, before they can amuse her, she has to
accept some measure of degradation for her sex. Was it, I
asked myself, what I took for maternal instinct, aggressive
though I felt it to be, an outcome of the concern Mrs Gallagher felt constrained to show for our failing? Had her husband's weakness strengthened her? Had she from the transitory
(and the trumpery), been transformed into the Eternal Feminine – that is, into a representative of the feminine element in
nature? And her deep wisdom that suggested no more than her
knowledge of the inherent weakness of men. Was she not endeavouring to dry Nature's tears at my expense? Nature has
tears, that's the way to translate 'rerum': 'Galen calls it
"natura".'

'By introducing contra-conception to the Vistula? Here are
half a million unborn sturgeons. No lemon with caviare.'

'Silence!' roared Mr Shillington. 'I see an obvious pun which
I want to anticipate, while there is still time. It might easily

have been "Caviare to the General Public". Thank me for saving the assembly from the lower form of wit, which is the pun.'

'The Doctor is now about to recite. I crave silence for the doctor.'

'Do you indeed?' said I. 'When the "Grand Duke" has danced his Bear Dance, I will consider dispensing with what little reason remains to me ...'

'Clear the floor! And carry on!'

With arms folded in front of his face, the Grand Duke danced his bear dance, revolving heavily and grunting as he lifted himself up and down. Now and then he moved forward as if threatening; again he retreated into himself, symbolizing the hibernation of winter sleep. He growled ominously in his awakened mood. Over his thick nose his honest blue eyes affected surliness, which was contradicted by his cheerful intellectual face; his bulky and apparently unwieldy body plopped up and down with the nimbleness none could have expected of a bear. Mrs Gallagher, whose husband manufactured soap, retreated from his proffered embrace. The men of the party had by this become enlisted on his side; it was as if he were restoring them to self-respect; the very indifference of his growls awakened a wonder in her and an uncertainty, a wonder changing to a wild desire; were men justified in their aggressiveness? Her experience was the experience of a maternity nurse. Hush-a-bye, baby! but the Grand Duke growled. The married women took his dance and all it suggested for matter of fact as it were. Why was she the only woman in the room to whom it was left, by implication of fault, to maintain a kind of obscure objection to all that the bear dance implied? The Grand Duke was hugging imaginary mates. Ladies who had intelligence in love were withholding themselves and, thereby, egging the dancer on to the suggestion of inaccessible ecstasies. Mrs Shillington clapped her hands. Mrs Gallagher, still sipping Schnapps and chewing caviare, saw the room suddenly filled with sturgeons. They were swimming by her, and as each passed, each regarded her with a reproachful eye. 'College of Sturgeons!'

'Francis wishes to speak on the newly-discovered Fifth Gospel.'

'But we got it all in Dawson Street before it was discovered in Oxyrhynchus. Æ gave it to those who believed in him.'

'Yes. But Æ probably believed in a Fifth Gospel. Francis's claim to a hearing is his capacity to disbelieve twice as much as any orthodox Hermetic. If a man is to get credit for belief in something that does not exist, all the more is he worthy of approbation who does not believe in the non-existent. And this in spite of the fact that it is much easier to believe in the non-existence of Nothing than to pin your faith to the nothingness of existence.'

When a Viennese girl of twenty sits on your knee and you are finding reasons why you should be considered an exception, even though you are fifty, from the category of the middle-aged, it is time that you considered your sanity and, if she is not your daughter, hers.

'Dementia Praecox,' I said, releasing her.

'Amazing person,' said she, letting her pupils dilate.

> 'Der stolze Dom –
> Das ist mein Wien
> Die Stadt für Lieder,'

I remarked, trusting to its inconsequence to save me. Vain hope! Entranced, she continued:

> 'Am schönen blauen Donaustrom.'

Two sharp words in the German of Vienna's dialect recalled her to herself. I saw her glide away, and I could not help recalling a somewhat similar incident, when a charming girl in a great house in Hesse was sent to the servants' quarters before midnight after having dined as an equal with the family. Morganatic, they called it. But Morgan, the Pirate, was surely less punctilious.

I was asked for a recitation or a song. I said, 'I have none of my own, but if you like I'll give you one of George's poems. You know him? He is the Juvenal of Dublin. Better, indeed; for his work is more learned, smoother and more restrained.'

Mrs Shillington laughed. 'George!' she cried, 'George?' Of course you all know there is no such person. He is one of the Doctor's inventions. When he does not wish to speak in his own name he calls up "George".'

I raised my hand in a gesture of futility.

'If I could only write his verse, I would gladly accept the soft impeachment, and your flattering belief.'

74

'We had a great deal of "George" from the Doctor at the wonderful dinner the new Irish Academy of Letters gave.'

'Oh, do let's have him again!' some young woman gushed.

'Yes, yes, yes, yes! We want George!'

'Provided you give him at least the credit for his own existence. I cannot imagine anything more exasperating than to turn up in the flesh and blood and find no one to take you seriously; that is, your existence seriously. I know to what use I would put such a position. I know that if you all insisted on disbelieving that I was in the room now, it would suit me very comfortably. But, alas! we are all held responsible both for our existence and, what is worse, our actions. If you are not apologetic I will produce George before the end of this orgy.'

'This what?' asked Mrs Shillington.

'Orgy,' I repeated. 'When there is any pleasant and private feast from which a few who think that they should have been invited are excluded, they invariably call it an orgy. I have always regretted that I was never at an orgy; I am trying to repair that shortcoming now. As I say, I will produce George . . .'

'Well, until you do, just recite his latest.'

'Very well,' said I. 'You must know that George is not only the *arbiter elegantiae* of Dublin, but a critic of the grosser forms of licence.

Sidelong I could see, across the angle of the hawthorn-bordered square, George's car, outside his house. As no one believed in him, no one believed that he lived not far away from where we were junketing. I made up my mind to slip away for ten minutes and return with George. Judging by the noise that human beings make when a little alcohol loosens a lot of languages, the party would go on for an hour or two yet and few would notice my movements.

'I suppose that I may bring a friend in?'

'You are not going out?'

'As a matter of fact I promised to introduce George to you, and if he is not too shy, I can bring him in in ten minutes.'

'Still insisting on George?'

'That settles it, then. I will leave your hall-door ajar and be back again in a moment.'

As I went out I hoped that George would not be too shy for

his *rôle* of gate-crasher. Ha, there he is, leaving his house. His evening stroll. How to circumvent it?

'Hello,' said I.

'Where did you spring from?' he inquired.

'Oh, I was in that house across the way, having a cocktail or so at a party. It is full of jolly people.'

'Do I know any of them?'

'You do. There is one odd thing about it, I warn you. There is a Viennese of twenty or younger who sits on the knees of those she imagines are poets. And she kisses them. Fame always wins women irrespective of men's looks. Let us give thanks for women's lack of aesthetic sense! The older I grow, the more the truth is borne in upon me . . . I am beyond the age of self-deception.'

'Where is all this?'

'Oh, just in that house there. Drop in with me and have a drink. They asked me to bring as many friends as I could and I feel that I have failed them. Besides, I have been stealing your thunder. The little lady thought that I was you.'

George snorted. I knew that he was saying to himself, 'I must see about this.' He pulled the handles of his car to make sure that it was locked.

'Promise to get me out of it in half-an-hour?'

Dear, dependable George! That great, well-formed head of his, complemented by a full face, reminds me both of Mahaffy and Walter Pater. The grizzled moustache was more a reminder of Pater, for it was more juvenile, than of the full Saxon, arched head of the great Provost. George has great planes and 'values' in his countenance. He is *sehr solide*. Under middle height, as were Julius and Napoleon, he moves like a bear in action.

'How have you been stealing my thunder?' he asked uneasily.

'Just this, George. When I recite a poem of yours, Mrs Shillington and Mrs Skafting insist on its being mine. I am too honest . . . well, hang it all . . . you know I don't want to rob any man. "Who steals my purse . . ." But his verse! That is a far more serious matter . . .'

'How did my name come into this?' George asked.

'Oh!' – I felt embarrassed. 'Well, Mrs Shillington and Mrs Skafting – they both persist in believing that I am trying to pull

76

their legs by pretending that the best satirical verse of modern times is by you and not by me.'

'By you and not by me?'

'They think that you do not exist.'

'And who writes my verse?'

'That's just it. They insist on believing that I am the author of all your verse; and that I use your name to save my own from the fame which it deserves but which in Dublin is merely my reputation for more "intimations of immorality".'

'I must see about this.'

The hubbub had not diminished a jot when we got back to the great front drawing-room. We were unnoticed. Mrs Liddle, whose husband printed most of the primary school books, nearly made George self-conscious.

'The "Side-cars" are nearly finished. Try "Une rêve d'amour".'

'Mrs Shillington, this is George. And Mrs Skafting, this is George. And Miss Hoult, this is George. And Madame Meyler, this is George. If I hear anyone laughing at me when the poet is quoted, here he will be for the next ten minutes to establish his own existence.'

'Whom has he got now?' asked Mrs Shillington.

I was in a nice position. If I let George realize the extent to which I was dependent on him for any notoriety I possessed, all the more would I have to explain to him how far I had been drawing on him, and also the absurd incredulity which attributed not only his fame but his existence to myself.

McViking said, 'Glad to receive you, Mr Boyle. Don't mind my friend. I am the guest master, and a large vodka with a small sandwich is what I condemn you to. Boy, attend here! Mr Boyle is here as guest the first –'

'I am not, I fear –'

'He says he isn't here,' Mrs Shillington whispered.

'I am not a gate-crasher, but my friend drags me about.'

Six-foot-three, bald, youthful, bellied, our host bore down on us. 'Only what you call a tumblerful.'

'When in Rome,' I said.

George gulped half of the white liquor.

Mrs Shillington and a barrister gathered around, awaiting epigrams. I felt that anything I said in the circumstances of expectancy would be taken for witticisms, just as the banalities of the obsolescent jarvies are accepted by holidaymakers as *merum sal*. So I left it to George.

He held his glass steadily, unmoved, while he said, 'Thanks, thanks,' and sought a quiet corner.

'You think that you will get away with it?' Mrs Shillington asked. Mrs Skafting said, 'The Minister for the Interior.'

'Whose?' asked I, getting rattled.

'In Vienna we have men *sehr solide*, just as your friend is, but we do not attribute to them our verses.'

George drifted away to a low arm-chair by the hearth. He was farthest from the prawns and the many kinds of liqueurs. What I have achieved, I thought, is simply this. I have lost the ear of the company by going when I set out for George. Now the company has doubled, and it is more out of accord with a personal and topical note. Almost as tall as the Consul, the finer figure of the Flemish Minister, rapier against battle-axe, rose. His Excellency from the U.S.A. was announced. And all the better, for there was now no danger of being asked to address the company. It is aggressive to monopolize the attention of a free conversazione. As bad as the intrusion of comic songs on good talks, when it can be heard, at an official dinner. Miss Purser asked why there was no protection for stained glass. Why is there no tax on French saints made of plaster of Paris?

'I think there is,' someone said. 'That accounts for the increase in robustness. Not robots, but robustness.'

'What do you mean?' asked Miss Purser, who financed a stained-glass factory, kept many girls and pretended that it was not one of the many disguised charities of the great family of Purser.

Monty fumbled. Someone said:

'It's high time that we were allowed to design our own saints, and not take them in plaster of Paris from a lot of French sculptors. I believe the increase of tuberculosis amongst our peasantry is traceable to chapels which depend on Parisians for their pious, emaciated images. You cannot dwell long on or with anything without becoming like it, or to like it.'

This shocked Miss Purser.

I caught Cunegunde. 'Do you see that grave man near the window? Go over to him. Wrap yourself round his neck. Kiss him, and say, "But are you really you?"'

'Why should I do that?' the child inquired.

'Just for fun. For a joke; for a charade. But don't leave him too long alone, or he will go home.'

I tried to avoid the Marshal's Pilsudski-looking eye.

'Hah, a little touch of grey attracts them. I saw her rapt attention as she gazed.' With his fingers he indicated the hair above his ear.

'Don't be jealous,' I implored. 'It leads to duels, and I am a bad correspondent.'

His eyes converged as he made a mental note of continuous hate, but he said blandly, 'We cannot spare our able-bodied men.'

I did not like to jibe too openly with, 'Ah, soon the bayonets will be flashing,' 'I have seen the red field of Carrhae,' was all I said, 'and "the Balbian funeral torches".'

'Every telephone pole has a white wire decoration to prevent him running into them on his way home.'

Now, to whom is that referrring? But, returning, Cunegunde said, 'I nibbled his ear.'

'Good girl! What did he say?'

'He said that I had eyes like ice.'

To my hostess, as I was departing, I said, 'Thanks for the quiet orgy. I told you I'd bring him.'

'I'm still unconvinced.'

'Then you are as good (or as bad) a Berkeleian as Yeats, who holds that all existence depends on the percipient, or rather he held it until Æ pointed out an objection with, "Very well, Willie, then I am responsible for both your existence and your poems".'

Outside, the first thing I noticed was a certain pensiveness in George. Lilacs before the hawthorn, pink and white, the laburnum gilding both. The men of old knew how to enfold their squares and city gardens. The sward of velvet green glowed through the breaks in the railings. I respected the pensiveness of George. Heavily, my most dependable friend walked on. I sense brooding in another perhaps as quickly as a woman. Was he labouring a resentment to grow against me?

'That girl is no nymphomaniac,' George at last said, with deep conviction.

How relieved I felt! Had he said, 'Why don't you recite

yourself and not me?' that would have been a difficulty. But all that was on his mind was Cunegunde.

'Sorry,' I said. 'But she is in good company. I left her with Captain McLoren looking after her, and he knows European women's weaknesses and their shortcomings. I only meant to express the bewilderment I felt when she sat on the knee of a fellow as old as I.'

'You are always parading your age.'

'But a kid like that!'

'She is old enough to choose her friends.'

'Yes! Yes!' Distractingly: 'Did you notice how they appreciate prawns?'

'So would we if we were two thousand miles away. So would everyone if what they were offered were exotic.'

'So would I,' said I.

Step by step along the deep brown granite footpath we walked, aware of the rose-red city in its evening glow; George deep in thought on some moral problem, or deep in composition of a satire of other men's lapses from the curbing line.

Had I offended him by taking him to a drawing-room that was, after all, but a vaudeville of the Dublin of old? . . . 'They told me, Heraclitus!' . . . but if we remember it, what does it matter who forgets it?

West against the sunset the roofs of Mercer's shone: Union Street, Aberdeen is its counterpart. Again, on our left the glory of the Spring, as the men of Dublin of old knew it: purple with lilac and gold with laburnum; and the hawthorn about to whiten. Old enough now to be acceptable as natural and not artificial, these old squares must have represented the height of landscape gardening in the days when they were laid out. Powder and peruke and sedan chairs: as gracious as Versailles. The façade of the College of Surgeons gleamed like a Greek temple beyond the lake and waterfall of Stephen's Green. What a magnifying lens was that country that made Parthenons for those who had eyes to see in every city! The pillars on the Acropolis are honey-coloured in the bright air, but these are white and grey, through moving veils of green. How soft is the yellow-green of Spring! I thought. Dante has no Spring in his *Inferno*.

'Shall we go down Grafton Street?'

'Not unless you want to hear how kaolin in Mayo can be developed by a fortnight in the Boul' Mich.'

'So you have heard our latest scheme for developing the country's resources?'

'Many times,' said George.

As we emerged by the Dawson Street gate, I saw across the road a trim figure in a blue reefer jacket who looked like a seafaring man. It was Monty, and he was smiling as one who had seen us first. Monty is the wittiest man and the kindliest wit in the town. But it is I who have to bear the laurel for him. He censors films and compensates for this by making jokes for me. I like it, for they are better and kinder, perhaps, than any I repeat.

But look at the position in which I find myself! Between George, whose excellent verse and solid presence are attributed to me, and Monty, who wants to make me into a kind of George for himself. I am the author of their poetry?

'We are going to the Bailey,' I said.

'I can't,' said Monty. 'She is waiting for me at Mitchell's. She is not in too good a humour. When we were walking past the Bailey it reminded her that we were twenty-three years married to-day! "What do you propose?" she asked. "Three minutes' silence," said I.'

'I hope you did not tell her it was my suggestion. I hope it's you she's angry with and not me.'

Monty went off through King Street. The best Dubliner of us all, James Montgomery: Welsh-Norman or Norman-Welsh in descent, with no dismal heritage of resentment: witty without pathos. His wit is light and no cover for self-evasion. I wish I were called 'Montgomery', for then I could sing to myself with more relish that catch from Burns:

> Ye banks and braes and streams aroun'
> The Castle o' Montgomerie.

What a lovely scene it calls up! The grey walls and the fresh braes below.

'We will go down Dawson Street.'

In the space before the Mansion House, with its potted shrubs and suburban rock-garden, we met Thwackhurst, the collector of graffiti.

'Did ye see that?' he said without preliminaries. 'That bloody budget report? That's where we are landed by the Dago. Taxes and taxes, and no tax on their own incomes! What an abscess Griffith opened when he took up the sword for Irish freedom! Freedom, me neck! Freedom to be bled white by a gang that keeps in power by coddling poor country louts with: "John Bull, the enemy!"' '

'I do not think you are correct in calling the President a Dago. He is no more a Dago than Deputy Nugget. A Dago is a citizen of San Diego, and one who would certainly think it an impertinence if you called him an Irishman or held him responsible for the present mess. He is more Irish perhaps than any of us, seeing that he looks like something uncoiled from the Book of Kells. Besides,' I asked, 'which of the gang possesses the grand manner of a San Diegoite or is capable of a chivalrous gesture?'

'It is true what a man from Waterford said yesterday – "the English refused freedom to gentlemen like Parnell and Redmond, and gave it to a bunch of louts, knowing bloody well they could do nothing with it that would be any good".'

'You are as bad as the old charwoman who blamed the English, first for living in the country and then for leaving it, and herself without a job.'

'I'm sick of politics,' said George.

'God blast you and them, anyway,' said Thwackhurst cheerily. 'You have ruined all the graffiti. You can't find anything in a piss-house now but political remarks. It's always a sign of decline in the fortunes of a country. Even at their moments of ease the people are obsessed with thoughts of politics. Instead of thinking of the matter in hand. And just when the spread of popular education was bringing the graffiti lower on the walls.'

'Lower on the walls?'

'Sure. Don't you see the little children were beginning to add their quota, when all this damn politics comes along.'

'What would you consider as a graffito of the golden Age?'

Thwackhurst fumbled for a note-book, but before he found it he started reciting:

'Here lies the grave of Keelin,
And on it his wife is kneeling;
If he were alive, she would be lying,
And he would be kneeling.'

He waved his unopened note-book, saying: 'It is fundamental. It expresses the difference between Life and Death, Love and Loss. It is touched with the *lacrimae rerum* above the Weeping Wall. Terse as a Greek epitaph,' he murmured, fondling the words in his mind.

He must be thinking of the Wailing Wall. But I said:

'There is one about Shanks's patent in Trinity College.'

'Is there?' he asked eagerly. 'In the Muses?'

'Yes,' I said.

'I must get the Provost's permission to go in and photograph it.'

'There is no need for that. Anyone can go in.'

'The Provost likes formality,' Thwackhurst said, with a twinkle in his wrinkling eye.

'The Baths of Caracalla,' I remarked.

'For God's sake, come on,' said George.

'They must have had their walls covered with wonderful graffiti scribbled by the young men as they lay cooling. It was the Silver Age of Rome. But tell me, where did you find Keelin's epitaph?'

'In the lavatory behind Nelson's pillar. There is a version in a pub in Dalkey, but it is corrupt.'

'God blast you and your politics,' Thwackhurst repeated. 'They are as bad as glazed tiles! which have ruined the finest town for graffiti in Europe, and ended its Elizabethan Age.' He was gone.

'The writing on the wall,' said George, restored to humour. He had forgiven me for suggesting that his admirer, our admirer, little Cunegunde, was mad.

The furies which we ward off from Griffith's memory, the flower-sellers whom he encouraged by his largesse, beside his inn, attacked us. We paid toll. Joe was awaiting us. Joe with the forehead of a Spanish grandee.

'You took your time.'

'This fellow brought me to a party and kept me there when I wanted to be here,' said George.

'So, that was it,' said Joe.

'Don't blame me.'

'Listen,' I said. 'Do you know what I found out to-day? Endymion has all our names in his list of his Christian names. If you doubt it, go to the National Library and look in the

83

signature book. "James, Boyle, Tisdell, Burke, Stewart, Fitz-simons, Farrell." We are all included . . . in his lunatic make-up.'

'Figments in the mind of a lunatic! I like that,' Joe commented.

'Where do I come in?' George asked.

'I have not instigated him,' said I.

'I never did him any harm,' said Joe.

'It is his way of aggrandizing himself and of paying us a compliment. He includes the life of Dublin at the moment in himself. He regards us as all that is worth anything in the town.'

'I wonder. What a "final famous victory" — we end not as ideas burning on the hand of the Creator, but as loonies in the mind of a lunatic!'

'You are somewhat pessimistic,' I replied.

'Even in the Irish Free State there is room for pessimism.'

'Gentlemen?' large-nosed, red-haired Lewis inquired.

'Two tankards and a small one.'

The Bailey is the only tavern where there still are tankards of pure silver. A few now, but one time one hundred and sixty. Trophy collecting and other forms of theft have reduced their number to seven or eight.

The fire in the corner fireplace was smouldering. The north light fell on the mirror which closed what had once been the folding-door to the smoke-room where Arthur Griffith held his sway, and before him, Charles Stewart Parnell. Joe sat side-ways across the little room, George in the corner at his left, and I faced the fireplace and the mirror. Doors to the left and right of us.

'It's very quiet here,' said Joe.

'If we're not interrupted by the famous bores, we'll be right enough,' George remarked.

'We can ascend,' said Joe.

In Arthur Griffith's day Mr Hogan gave us the use of a reserved room one storey higher. In it, some of Griffith's messages to the Irish people were composed. Solemnly, when invaded by the town's tiresome ones, we were wont to bid ourselves good-evening publicly and to go up privately and unobtrusively to the privileged room. There we could sit *lauda-*

tores temporis acti: living in the imagined successes of our past.

Now no Whelan holds the gate against intruders on Arthur. Griffith was dead and we, his disciples, meet but rarely in the upper chamber. We can let our talk range freely in the smoking-room until we are driven out by some insufferable but respectful bore, who calls us "Sir".

'We met Thwackhurst on our way here. That delayed us.'

'He is one of those who cannot be accused of being *cupidus rerum novarum*,' Joe said quietly.

'Nor quite satisfied with their results.'

'He prefers poverty and freedom to observance and respectability. I like him well. Seumas brought me to his digs high up in a gable, where he lives with his cat. It was the morning of Christ's nativity. He got out of bed, put on a short reefer jacket over his naked form, stepped into his boots and, nether naked, squatted before his fireless grate with: "It was the winter wild . . . God blast my old huer of a landlady. Which of yez has a match?"'

'Has she forgotten the mistletoe?'

'She has forgotten the bloody fire.'

'I saw him looking out of his window in Oxo after his cat this morning,' said I.

'Another character, Maturnin, the best authority the *Encyclopaedia Britannica* could enlist, used to do his work at the bar downstairs.'

'It's a great tavern right enough.'

'What amazes me,' said George, 'is that the Germans are sending over professors of English to trace out the imaginary itinerary of Joyce's imaginary Mr Bloom through the different pubs he is supposed to have visited. They all miss the one that Joyce liked.'

'The Bloom that never was on sea or land! He is quite unconvincing. A mere chorus to Joyce.'

'Was he Elwood?'

'Lord, no!' said I. 'He was a dentist in Clare Street.'

'I should hate to have my pubs stalked by German professors who took pub-crawling seriously. The moment our pubs become the subject of literature, that is the moment they are undone. Even we who patronize them would become self-conscious. The last thing drink should do is to make one self-conscious. We would become actors, as it were, in a play, and not simply patrons of our pub.'

'Even in our ashes live their Reuter's wires.'

'Talking of ashes, we saw that wonderful doctor Ashe who thinks that he is the cigar. He passed us in Dawson Street in a hurry, in his Ford.'

'Probably he was going to lay another wreath on the grave of the "Unknown Soldier".'

'To whom he was related.'

'In that he was more or less unknown.'

'Just the same again, Lewis,' said I.

'Right you are, sir. Fawcus rode another winner to-day, sir.'

The unnecessary boy who makes a noise with the grate lingered to overhear, but left the fire slacked.

'How's Yeats to-day?'

'I heard he is better. Hackett is preparing a festival celebration of his seventieth birthday. I hope he'll be all right for it.'

'When he's gone, the next in line is O'Sullivan,' George affirmed.

'What about Stephens?'

'No. The Bard is the next best. Listen to this:

'Have thou no fear, though round this heart
    The winds of passion are.
The image of your love is set
    Within, serene and far;
As in some lonely mountain lake
    The reflex of a star.'

'My idea of lyrical poetry is different. I like it earth-free like a lark and devoid of sadness. James Stephens' is a good example.

'Lovely and airy the view from the hill
    That looks down Ballylee;
But no good sight is good until,
    By great good luck I see
    The blossom of the branches
Coming towards me
    Airily.'

'It is light bright and echoes with "lovely" and "good". Or take that light and witty stave born out of merriment – if the Bard would adopt that style, he would be as witty as Willie Shakespeare. You know the stanza about the intermittent wife of a learned ornithologist who spent her week-ends with a tramp.

> 'That two-backed beast of which you speak
> He has no horns upon his beak
> And the reason is not far to seek –
> She needs strong back where a back is weak
> And there's wisdom yet in the ancient rann:
> "She's away with the gaberlunzie man!"'

> Then guard your forehead whatever befall
> For the tallest forehead amongst you all
> And the wisest scholar that ever was born –
> He yet may wear the cuckold's horn.'

'How gay it is and in the great tradition! – "a word of fear". Why should wit be inadmissible to great verse? But you would have a little sermon concealed somewhere in a song. You stand for Wordsworth . . . I'm "light as leaf on linde", and I stand for Burns. There is always a hint of hypocrisy in Wordsworth:

> 'Will no one tell me what she sings?'

He doesn't want to know. If he did, he would run off from his love-making as he did once before from the girl in France. He is the one person who does not "Endear himself to us by his mistress and his illegitimate child." He certainly does not. Yet he had both. He never wrote a love song . . . He never put up a fight.'

'Burns' fight against hypocrisy does not necessarily make him greater than Wordsworth.'

'Not his fight essentially, but his attitude towards life. The ease and clarity of his song. Honestly now, George, would you prefer a thousand Wordsworths in this pub to a thousand Burnses?'

'You have drawn a red herring of religion and the rest of it in.'

'No. But I'm trying to show that your judgement of poetry is basically religious. You want the pulpit in the poem. You have not got over your public school and Matthew Arnold's influence yet. Your poet must be a preacher as well as a teacher. However, Shakespeare diddles you all. What does he preach? Is it not significant that Wordsworth took after Milton, and that Milton took after that arch-hypocrite, Cromwell? Give me the pre-Cromwellian poets, no "stern daughters", but "Doxies over the dale". The English people are afraid of Willie Shakespeare, and yet Wanton Willie and Rantin', Rovin' Robin are the best poets in the English language. James Stephens is no black-leg in the domain of the parsons; he's a great spirit, one that outsoared the shadow of his youth and outlived it unsoured. . . . After your pals are dead and buried, "he will hoist his flag and go", as his reincarnated Rafferty went with the Spring always at his back.

'Now with the coming in of Spring, the days will stretch a
    bit:
And after the Feast of Bridget, I will hoist my flag and go:
For since the thought got into my head, I can neither stand
    nor sit,
Till I find myself in the middle of the county of Mayo.'

Joe, who cared little for either of us, said, 'I believe in George.'

I was left confronting a silent George with an arsenal of unexpostulated energy. He kept so silent that somehow I felt wrong and was beginning to feel concerned when he smacked his lips. I thought he was about to speak. But George is a great friend. The minute that he found that the discussion was turning into an argument of conviction and that the position was about to drift from that most delightful of all communions when friends are found 'affirming each his own philosophy', he suddenly changed the whole front by producing a little manuscript from his pocket-book. Silently he handed the page to me. I read:

'Yes, you are right. There is no doubt. No balance sheet
Will be made out; A call, maybe, On you and me.
We shall not see A Company At God knows where In Far
    Mayo.
But should the Bud to Paris go, Oh, there will be
The Company Of hearts' desire, That stings like fire,
Of sweet young things In silken hose, And other with-
Out any clothes; When shapely limbs Are twirled in air,

88

He will not know, He will not care; They will not run
Before him there – When he goes down. A fervid man,
To plump Louise Or swift Susanne, He will not know
Or care a pin, If China clay Or Kaolin Be white as snow
Or black as sin!'

'Splendid!' I shouted. I looked over it to find what caught
my eye as I read . . . the verse mastery:

> 'Of sweet young things
> In silken hose,
> And other with-
> Out any clothes.'

The jerk between the 'with' and 'out' is like the pull off of the
last stocking.

'Great writing, George! It would keep Cook occupied touring this town to Paris if he used your verse as publicity for
"The White town far away", as George Moore calls it.'

'I like "twirled in air".'

'More of the French actresses,' said Joe.

'Where did George get "Susanne"?' I asked.

'That reminds me,' said Joe. 'They are all Susannes.'

'Are they?'

'At Boulogne, at Rouen and Amiens, I never met anyone
who was not Susanne.'

'Why?'

'*Nom de guerre*, I presume.'

Gently the influence of Bacchus, that divinity who convinced the world of old that he was indeed a god and one
whose influence could be proved; on whom unbelief needed
no help, who suffered not from atheists, but only from fanatics,
overcame us with his gift of peace. Past grew as considerable
as present: more important, too, magnified by the mists of
time. I gazed at my reflexion in the mirror; and I haloed it
with clouds of smoke.

'Talking of ashes and Unknown Soldiers, Monty got a good
one in to-day. When the Bailey reminded his wife, whose eloquence is well-sustained, that they were twenty-three years
married, she asked, "How do you propose to celebrate the
anniversary?" – "By three minutes' silence".'

'Oh, you told us that before!'

'We may repeat our drinks, but not ourselves.'

'Repeat!' said Batt, as he entered suddenly.

'Repeat? What we want in this country is a vomitorium so that we can vomit out all the bloody fools who are ruining it. England has a puke-point, but we have not. That is why we cannot get rid of the sickening fools who try to boss us. The worse we get the more we revel in despair. Look at us now. Thirteen years or more of home rule. Who gets the rule but the poor bloody fools who have to stay at home? The fattest and most easy country in the world wrecked by selfish government in half a decade, and turned into a Spartan Helot's warning to the Commonwealth.'

'But if we were totally free?'

'When were we? If there was a when, when we were? The first gang from overseas could walk through us. Was there ever a conquest we resisted? Was there ever a conquest by which we benefited? Whom did we kick out? Only the men who could have made men of us as they were themselves. Arthur Griffith's Ireland costing twice its revenue for one year's government. And the Government afraid to send criminals before juries unless they want to get them off. We're half-beggared and twice taxed.

'When it comes to governing under democratic conditions you have either to reduce the people to your own level of mediocrity or reduce yourself to theirs. As a rule it is a compromise which brings both to a lower level than either held.'

'We were just discussing verse,' I murmured in expostulation. I was not heard.

'I know, I know,' said Joe. 'I would prefer to hand the whole place over to Bohane, who manages the Spring Show and the Horse Show. He would make an excellent Dictator. He knows the country and we know him.'

'We know that he comes from Yorkshire.'

'Where does De Valera come from?'

'The Devil only knows! That's his strong point, that he's unreckonable. We won't be ruled even by one of ourselves. A native would be too wise to try, or too harassed by jealousies to succeed. We simply are not a ruling race. Politically we are fodder for any foreigner to exploit: culture beds for any political microbe.'

'Bohane could run the country rationally first, but he would need to have been cast ashore from the unknown, like Arthur Pendragon.'

George said, 'No country is run rationally. Even rationalist Russia has to stage pageants of force and to use the sex symbols of the Hammer and the Sickle.'

'I see McGinty has been talking about the Sickle in his latest speech.'

'So I saw,' said Joe. 'What's the idea?'

'He has probably been dallying with it of late in its relation to the "social transition" he mentioned. We are drifting straight for Celtic Communism.'

'Griffith said, "I believe in the Irish people." Well, I disbelieve in them.'

'Why then, you will be asked, do you go on living here?'

'To go on disbelieving. I should hate this country to be ruled by reason, and the certainty that it never shall be tempts me to remain. If this place were to be run in the interests of reason, do you think that we should ever get a drink?'

Suddenly the golden light of the door-panes was shadowed A heavy figure, with a mop of hair hanging over one shoulder, literally blew into the room. He lurched down the three-inch step, straightened himself, and shouted:

'Bring me a cup of sack, boy, I would be merry.'

We raised a little welcoming cheer, and at once began to babble. Blue-eyed, vigorous, generous and reckless, Shamus de Burge takes the drabness from life. He has an open face and a winning smile that shows his fine teeth.

Turning to us, he inquired in a loud voice:

'How are all you huers?' (It seems that in Dublin that word is bi-sexual. Or is it a relic of the Elizabethan days when 'whoreson knave' was quite common?) 'I'm writing a book on Richard Cœur de Lion; he was a great huer. He was the real artist. He bloody well laid them all out. He knew his stuff. He knew how to fight. Fancy being called "Lion Heart" in days when every man was brave! A great huer, and a relative of mine. He was the hell of a lad. He bloody well forked them all up on his thirty-foot spear. He was the real Norman. The de Burgoes came over with him.'

'With Cœur de Leeon?' Joe inquired.

'De Leeon or de Lion, it's all the same . . . What other Richard is there?'

'There is Richard Lynam, who was King of the Kips,' said Joe.

'Blast you, anyway. You are nearly as bad a cod as my old friend here.'

'Thanks,' said I.

'But he was always a cod; you're only coming into it. As I was saying, Richard Cœur de Lion forked them all up, and so did Eustace, the Monk. He sent the boys over with de Burgoes to Ireland, and we had our thirty-foot spears and we bloody well forked the natives up.'

'I was waiting for that,' said Joe.

' "He fought with Love even to the end," ' I quoted. 'Like the great Achilles.'

The blue eyes flashed and smiled.

'Well, you are right. But no one else waited for the spear of the de Burgoes. We went through the country: "Men who rode upon horses!" Yeats has us right enough. We came in and conquered the whole place in half-an-hour. And we forked all the natives to hell.'

'Tell me, Shamus,' I asked, 'has the spear any phallic significance in your family?'

Shamus laughed. He could laugh at himself, which is perhaps a proof of his non-Celtic origin. But his fine frenzy was not finished.

'On the distaff side I'm a descendant of Kubla Khan.'

'In Xanadu?'

'No, you idiot, in the thirteenth century . . . Where's that bloody waiter?'

'He has gone off, thinking that this is de Burgoes' day.'

'If that waiter thinks that he is getting the day off on account of the victories of my family, he is bloody well mistaken. What's yours?'

'Shamus,' I said, 'I am so overcome thinking of the "pleasure domes" of your ancestors-in-law that I do not think I can sustain another drink. But don't mind me; I can become as intoxicated on good company as on drinks. I am thinking of the "twice ten miles of fertile ground which the Sacred River girded round".'

'You bloody well ran into the River Liffey. What's wrong with that? And you scrambled out at Liffey Bank because you couldn't pass Guinness's.'

'Surely you could not be expecting him to be looking for another wet?' said Joe.

'Another wet? Where's that waiter gone?'

'To caverns measureless to man.'

' "What's wrong with that?" reminds me,' George said, 'I met Endymion the other day, and he told me that he had invented a cure for constipation.'

'What is it?'

'Take salt, take salt.'

'But that will give you a thirst.'

'Well, what's wrong with that?'

'What's wrong with Lewis? Hah! mine ancient, here thou art! Get us something to keep the intellect afloat over these shoaling tides.'

'Right, sir. Right sir. Fawcus won again to-day.'

'We were never a very militant nation,' said Joe – 'that is, compared with the Scots. As late as 1746 they fought Culloden, where one thousand of the Clansmen went down in one battle for the House of Stuart. Where is Scotland now? Dominating, directing and leading the British Empire. And where is King George? Down at Balmoral every summer, dressing himself up in a kilt and wearing a – what d'ye call it – a sporran. And his son married to a Scotswoman. The Scots were wise enough to get a share of what they built. They are as honoured as the English now.'

'Winning battles in the spirit in which they were lost?' I asked, thinking of Æ.

'Do you suggest,' said Batt, 'that if Ireland lost more men and had a better beating than the Scots at Drumossie Muir, that the King would come over here every year and dress in a caubeen and knee-breeches and twirl a Shillelagh and stay with Buckley near the gas-works in Monkstown?'

'I don't know what you are talking about, but I do know that a wise nation can fit into the team which is the British nation without losing its identity or self-respect.'

'He'd look better as a National Forester,' George thought.

'What's the good of singing "Soldiers are we" when we hate the very sight of the results of soldiering and all that it implies conquest and Empire? It's time we gave ourselves a chance to do something else than wail and hate. We are the only nation

93

in Europe who were never in a European war, hence we have to assure ourselves that we are soldiers.'

'If we were totally free –' I began.

'By heavens,' said Shamus, 'if we get any more freedom we may as well all become teetotallers, for we will then be free to develop our spiritual side, which is to allow no one to do as they please. If we get any more freedom we'll all be chained together. I didn't notice any slave-driving British names among the Executive Council. They are all Irish but two . . . There's only one thing to do, and that is to go on the dole and eat out of these fellows' hands and degrade yourself so far that even they will be superior to you and feel what mighty monarchs they are.'

'What about becoming one of them?'

'Not so good. You would have to associate with them and see Irishmen dominated by a foreigner in their own rooms. Besides, who wants to be guilty of having fooled and betrayed so many of the kindly Irish? If our countrymen can stand such slave-driving from a home Government, the wonder is that they lost any men at all against the outsider.'

'Perhaps we like the privilege of enslaving ourselves,' Joe remarked.

'Our idea of Freedom,' said Batt, 'is unrestricted opportunity for victimization.'

'Well,' I said repeating an old thought, 'politics is the rumble in the bowels of a nation. I will now leave this intestinal tract. Let me solace myself with song.'

> 'There's nothing left but ruin now
> Where once the crazy cabfuls roared,
> Where new-come sailors turned the prow
> And love-logged cattle-dealers snored:
> The room where old Luke Irwin whored
> The stairs on which John Elwood fell –
> Some things are better un-encored:
> There's only left –'

I quoted.

'Jayshus! What kind of a kip have I come into at all?' Shamus inquired, smiling. The very question Odysseus asked of his homeland.

94

'There's only one kind of a kip or brothel and that is mentioned by Goldsmith. Farewell all.'

'Hold on a minute!' Shamus shouted.

'He doesn't believe in the Irish people,' Joe remarked. 'That's why he's going.'

'I want to be out of the way when the Irish people start believing in themselves.'

'Where's that guy of a waiter?'

'Guy Fawcus?' Joe remarked.

We were just getting into the mood when laughter was beginning to come as readily as the drinks. I was sorry to leave. Suddenly the golden glass was darkened for a moment. A bright-eyed, intelligent face appeared and disappeared.

'Come in, Cahal!' I said.

'Well, aren't you a cook's blind bastard!' Shamus shouted, angry at being deprived of female society. 'That wasn't Cahal O'Shannon. That was Norah Hoult!'

'I never saw more intelligent eyes in a human face.'

'The Bagmen are up. Don't let the little Firbolgs get you on your way home. The Bagmen broke out before in this country, but we always put them back in their places, and we'll have to do it again. Do it again with the spear of de Burgoes!' and Shamus lunged at the incoming waiter with an imaginary spear. ' "Those *natives* will never rule," as Paddy Hogan said.'

I quoted

> 'But I, the last, go forth companionless.
> And the days darken round me, and the years,
> Among new men, strange faces, other minds.'

The problem confronted me. Why does every educated Irishman regret that he is Irish? Is it the education, the country, or himself that is wrong? Or is it wrong to be educated? Or is it wrong to regret? Perhaps regretting is a sign of grace. Shamus is right in his instinctive wish to be differentiated from the herd among which he finds himself. Why is it that most Irishmen seek that differentiation? The cleavage is not wholly between Norman and native nor between gentleman and farmer. There is no difference here between the gentlemen, such as are allowed to live in their land, and the men who live on the land. I remembered what McLoren once said to me: 'Most of the peasants are gentlemen and have an immemorial courtesy that can only have come from a ruling race.' What has happened to our race? Who are the race? For the most part they resemble Shamus, big, blond, and blue-eyed. These are the remnants of conquerors and a conquest of time out of mind. They are descendants of that Milesian stock which conquered a country inhabited as parts of isolated Africa are inhabited, by little pigmy fellows, the Firbolgs, or Bagmen. We resent identification with the defeated. The Bagmen with their little despatch cases are for the moment in insurrection, and it is against Milesians they are revolting. And they are in the ascendancy just now. This explains a great deal. It explains the desire not to be thought 'Irish' in the narrow and narrowing sense which that word has come at present to have. They do not wish to be identified with all that is small, narrow, vindictive, cowardly, and vile. Irishmen, be they de Burgoes or Milesians, are not happy with this 'freedom' which has only thrown them to the mercy of the tinkers in the land. I wondered how many of the government were of the Attacotti type of mind. Was there one of them worth Shamus de Burgoes' little finger? It was his like who were in ascendancy when Ireland was getting its name for spontaneous courage, generosity and the open hand. His history may be at fault, but his instinct is not. I longed for that magical spear, no matter who wielded it, that could 'fork them all to blazes'.

Up Shamus! You are of the true and sterling stuff. The Bagmen must be put back in their place, which is the Republic of the ditches. And the magnanimous Milesian must come into his own once more. An end to this Tinkers' Dream! The problem is solved, if there ever was one. The problem why an Irishman is reluctant to be considered as an Irishman. Why? Because he is loth to be identified with the defeated, and with dirt and defeat and multitude. Before history recorded battles he was a conqueror. Now that there is a record, he is an underdog to his immemorial inferiors. What is this I smell? Class conflict? What does it mean when only one class, and that the lowest, is alone to be paramount? – Communism! Of course! I should have known this long before, and not have been confusing myself by obstinate questionings about the meaning of an Irishman's reluctance to be thought an Irishman. He does not resent being considered Irish. What he does resent, and what I more than most resent, is identification with Communism. I am in two minds whether to go back and ask the liberating Lyaeus, Seumas, if he still is in the mood for a pint of sack. *Par le splendeur Dex!*

One of the harpies selling matches approached.

'Buy a box, Sir.'

'I'll do nothing until Ireland's free!'

She looked puzzled. Then she broke out –

'Ireland me neck! A Dago President, an English King, an Eyetalian Pope! Ireland me neck! Up the United Front!'

'That two-backed beast.'

The queues were forming up outside the cinema house in Grafton Street: Dubliners willing to buy a dream that will let them escape for an hour from their surroundings. I passed the prosperous betting house of Jack Martin.

'Fortune was seldom invoked, for they desired no change,' I remembered grimly.

I turned in to the Green, and left Grafton Street behind me, with its temple of Fortune and its cinema crowds seeking solace in their shadowy 'stars'.

CHAPTER FIVE

To gain admission to the Vice-regal Lodge it was necessary to stop your car at the guarded gate and remain stationary until a policeman had examined it and questioned you. He would then inquire at the sentry's box if anyone of your name was expected at the Lodge. This was before De Valera invested himself with the functions of the Governor-General.

I was met by His Excellency's Major-domo, the tall and impressive Mr Doyle, late of the Gresham Hotel. His fidelity to Collins and his help in the movement as well as his undoubted ability placed him where he was.

'He is upstairs,' said Doyle.

'Vidi presso di me un veglio solo.'

The first Governor-General of the Irish Free State, Tim Healy, walked across to the window of one of the upper rooms, and pointing to the view, said sepulchrally: 'Louis le Grand Monarque had nothing better than that.'

Immediately underneath red geraniums blazed in their formal beds; the beautiful greensward was bordered by a paling of graceful stone pillars. On either side, trees threw up their fountains of young green. From the plateau of the Phoenix Park the shallow vale of the Liffey appeared deeper than it is. Afar through silver mists the Dublin mountains rolled smooth as a dim wave. The smoke belt which roofs the city was transparent and roofs and spires looked like a mirage.

> 'The people of Pa do not care for flowers;
>   All the Spring no one has come to look.
> But their Governor-General, alone with his cup of wine
> Sits till evening and will not move from the place.'

I quoted, having gazed my fill.

'What audacity!' Tim exclaimed, and smiled. 'They have not come so far,' said he, thinking of his well-guarded gates. 'Where did you get that?'

'That is a translation of the Chinese of Po-Chu-i when he was Governor-General of Chung-Chou.'

'Chung-Chou,' mumbled Tim into his beard. 'I don't think I

98

will invite them to look at my geraniums. Not even for the Jubilee Nurses' Fund.'

I said, 'Well, the Vice-Regents who lived here knew how to live. They chose the highest and nearest open space to the city.'

'They took it over,' said Tim.

I thought of the spacious days of Lord Wimborne's Lieutenancy; of the stir when he, himself a Grand Monarch, and his escort 'came sounding through the town'; of the bustle when her Ladyship went a-shopping in Grafton Street, and of the many cars walling the polo-ground of a summer's evening; the diners gay with uniforms every night.

I looked at the ivory face, the black-and-white beard and the high brow above the bright eyes of liquid brown, such as some Chief Rabbi might possess. I thought of his marvellous and astute career. *He* 'took it over', I thought, and he sits with his collection of Waterford glass in the corner of the morning-room where he entertains his old cronies and new friends to lunch.

'Most cities extend in a westward direction. Dublin is an exception to this rule. Why? Because of this Park, Guinness's Brewery and the Kingsbridge Railway Station. There is also the valley of the Camac and the gloomy bulk of Kilmainham to prevent the speculating builder.'

'What a blessing!' I exclaimed.

'I suppose it is. They would be overwhelming my house at Glenaulyn but for these safeguards.'

'No city neglects its river as Dublin does. There is not a pleasure-boat on the Liffey from Butt Bridge to Lucan. If the river and town were in England there would be water-gardens and boat-houses and people delighting themselves in the lovely amenities of the water.'

'And drowning themselves,' said Tim, in a comic sepulchral voice. 'You can see, but the trees are grown, the edge of the road where Joe Brady killed Lord Cavendish and Mr Burke.'

Was he thinking of his far insecurer position than that of the Vice-Royalists of 1882?

'That was a terrible affair,' I said.

I remembered hearing, as a child, the story of the deed, and of how it was done with an 'amputation knife'. I remembered the fascination which made me take out my father's surgical case when his back was turned, and examine the longest of the four or five long, narrow knives, so narrow and with such thick backs that their blades were almost triangular ...

'With a terrible weapon,' said Tim.

'And a terrible end for Joe Brady. Marwood, the executioner, had to go down into the pit and hold on to his legs to kill him: he was so strong, and they miscalculated the drop.'

I let my mind dwell on the other side of the question. What strong sense of overwhelming wrong had constrained a man of such good character as Brady to put his head into the halter? But Tim's politics were in abeyance in the Lodge.

No man who ever practised at the Irish Bar had a more deadly simplicity of phrase than Tim Healy. He knew the popular way of thinking, as if every juryman took him into his confidence and confessed his point of view. The story of his defence of the Insurance Company that resisted payment because of the suspicious way in which a timber-yard they insured was burned, is an example. The two night watchmen, Tim told the jury, 'neither saw a spark nor heard a crackle or even smelt smoke, and yet during the hours of their guardianship the whole timber-yard of acres and acres is destroyed. Gentlemen of the jury, the Babes in the Wood.'

We left the room and descended by the lift to the great drawing-room where he had put in two antique Georgian mantelpieces at his own expense. He showed them to me and began a history of the Lodge. Then, without finishing it: 'For fear I forget it, if you are doing nothing better to-night, come here for a lantern show of an attempt to ascend Mount Everest. And we will have a little dinner first. Another invitation – will you bring your friend Yeats, the Salley gardener, to my box at the Spring Show? I have asked the Army Band, so I must entertain some of the officers and their ladies, who may want to dance afterwards. Some of them are Generals.'

'They have attained suddenly very high rank?'

'Now, don't be too sure of that. Their mothers may have been "generals" before them.'

He smiled rather grimly as he was wont to do when he let his memories criticize the present state of things; not dwelling for the time on the fact that but for the fighting of these 'generals' he would never have sat in the House of the Satraps. I wondered why his intimate knowledge of the Irish mind should allow this contempt. Was it because he could not

100

emerge from the generation which he knew? Was it because he could not forgive Griffith for his policy of ignoring Westminster and all that it meant to Tim? Honoured, trusted, consulted at Westminster, Tim Healy sought for and accepted the position of Governor-General of the Irish Free State and all it connoted merely as a compensation of sorts for all that he had lost? Was he the first to foresee the futility of the future and the earliest to cash in on his losses by making the better of them? He had a profound knowledge of the popular mind, of its temperament, its character, its limitations and shortcomings. Therefore, immediately after his appointment there were rumours of his resignation. Knowing as I did the energy and the influence he brought to bear in London to obtain his appointment and his gratitude to Lord Beaverbrook for his decisive aid, I asked him what he meant by threatening to resign. 'Nothing, Oliver, but the minute these fellows here think I am enjoying myself, that is the moment they will begin to undermine me.'

He believed that his was a life appointment. He set about furnishing the Lodge as a home, making it a liaison office and a bridge between irreconcilable and uncouth elements and those who had already, with Scotland and Wales, nations with national features more marked than ours, been content to join in the Celtic hegemony which built that Empire which is Rome's successor. '*Ab orbe terrarum remoti*' once: but now making the orb of the world revolve round them. I do not say that he condemned or had little faith in what the undefining politicians call 'Gaelic Culture', but he knew the difference between culture and civilization. He knew that folklore, native dances, cottage life and the Gaelic language could never fulfil the proper destiny of the different classes of the Irishmen or bring Ireland to take its place once again as a contributor to the civilization of a Europe far beyond it in progress.

To offer our island as a funk-hole or a retreat from the wars and ambitions of Europe might be quite in character with the tendency of the representatives of that part of the Irish race which seeks sheltered occupations and longs for ease when it grows tired of belligerency, or, rather, irresponsibility after disturbance. It may never have appeared to him in terms as succinct as these, but his instinct for 'sizing up' a jury made him size up his own countrymen and act according to his percep-

101

tions. He did his best to heal the 'split': 'As an expert of splits, take it from me that there are some fellows who are depending for a livelihood on disunion. And one of them is De Valera.' He could only bring those together who were already in one camp. To wean men away from the hopes of gain to be derived from opposition was beyond him. He called himself the 'Invisible Mender', but what he might regard as a rent or a hole in his seat was a *modus vivendi* to De Valera and the Irish who took up arms against the majority of their countrymen. Mending an Ireland split in two from the Vice-regal Lodge was about as hopeful a proposition as that of a tailor would be, who offered to sew from the Escurial the rents of the garments of the beggars who lived by exposing their sores. He had few delusions. I think that he was gratified by being able to rise from the dead of the Redmond *régime* which Griffith ended, and to take the plum from Griffith in the end. He would have an added satisfaction had he heard Griffith's 'I don't want Healy; he betrayed Parnell.' This was said to me by Griffith as we walked along Nassau Street some months before Tim Healy's appointment to the richest office in the New State. In certain ways, by his non-aggressive astuteness, by his leaning on forces greater than himself, and, like a glider pilot, getting a lift from any cloudy formation, he resembled De Valera. The Rabbi-like eyes and skin they had in common, but for deep-hearted and sympathetic understanding, for the ready hand that had not to be sought but was proffered, for loyalty to Ireland as far as he was akin to it, and for a faith that envied only those whose faith was simpler, Tim Healy had no equal. He was too wise to let it be seen that he enjoyed the Vice-regality while he had it, though he must have known that it was a transient and, to the new Ireland, an unkindred thing. How could an Irish Viceroy improve on the genuine article? Worse, he took the shilling of the Sassenach, without spending in the city the Sassenach's pound.

Henry Curt Mantel was shocked by the familiarity of chief and serf in the Dublin of the twelfth century. He sent over his professors of decorum, his royal tutors, to show the chiefs the unwisdom of their ways and their want of a dais and a withdrawing room. Uncle Tim's Cabin, as Lady Lavery called it, had no withdrawing room. You met all the founders of the new *régime*; and they could meet you on level terms. If any signs

102

of inferiority were manifested they were due to artificial and arbitrary rules of conduct, British in origin, which sought to lay down laws even for eating asparagus. The asparagus, to give it its due, revolted and refused to be hung up by the green end. Lady Lavery, who was usually at the banquets, could be counted on to come to the rescue by demonstrating by dainty gesticulation the nice conduct of the flail-like food. But woe betide you if you thought that your ways with asparagus were enough to constitute 'a national record'. Table manners could be confused with the habits of, or with attempts at apeing the ascendancy. There were days when Tim would not have hesitated by his contempt for such pomps.

As I drove away I went over in memory the few visits I had paid the Vice-regal Lodge of old. When the Aberdeens first held office I was taken, a very small boy, to some 'drive' of theirs for Irish goods, dressed as an 'Irishman' – knee breeches, top hat and the legendary shillelagh; the real article I have never seen in the hands of any Irishman since that day. Then, the Wimbornes' *régime* full of imperial hospitality to a little clan. I pass over the second coming of the Campbells. I prefer the liberality of Conservatives. The Dudleys and the Wimbornes spent £50,000 a year or more above the salary attached to the office of Lord Lieutenant.

I recalled the last time I was at the Vice-regal Lodge before the change of government. I drove there in one of Lord Fitzalan's cars; I returned on foot. As far as guards and precautions against assassination went, they were somewhat the same then as now. Can it be that all governments have to be protected from the governed? Is the multitude never at ease? In Sweden, I believe, the King can walk about unguarded and also unmobbed.

As I drove along the Liffey towards O'Connell Bridge I thought of two journeys I had made in that way before. One through the firing with Hugh Law; the other when, rescued at midnight and escorted by many gun-turreted tanks, I sat in an armoured car listening to desultory rifle-firing, and was driven to the government buildings. To how few is it given to have the sensation of driving headlong through a supine city!

> What a thing it were
> To ride in triumph through Persepolis!

103

True, it was easier for me to visit now the Lodge than in the days before the change. Did this mean that the Lodge had come down, or that I had gone up in the world? That is one of those questions which are best answered by having a Yes on, 'each way'. One thing was certain: it could never be a bridge between the warring factions in the biggest faction fight Ireland has had for centuries, particularly since almost half the country was 'out on its keeping'. The Lodge had to go in the course of De Valera's march to Cloud Cuckoo Town, towards that City of Contradictions, his Irish Catholic Socialist Republic. But was Collins's dream any more realizable? It had not the elements and the makings of Communism, but it was just as inadequate and . . . but he was capable of seeing facts and of adjusting his position in the course of events. So, he would have enlarged on his ideal Ireland. Had he not written:

> We must be true to facts if we would achieve anything in this life. . . . The true devotion lies not in melodramatic defiance or self-sacrifice for something falsely said to exist, or for mere words or formulas which are empty, and which might be but the house swept and garnished to which seven worse devils entered in.

And one a foreign devil!
Who could blame a man who had dared and done so much for an ideal to be still somewhat led by his dream?

> One may see processions of young women riding down on the island ponies to collect sand from the sea-shore, or gathering in the turf, dressed in their shawls and in their brilliantly coloured skirts made of material spun, woven, and dyed by themselves, as it had been spun, woven, and dyed for over a thousand years. Their cottages also are little changed. They remain simple and picturesque. It is only in such places one gets a glimpse of what Ireland may become again . . .

He forgot the brothers of the young women! He was assassinated by his fellow-countrymen not far from his birthplace; and he died in Emmet Dalton's arms:

'The much-loved and trusted "Big Fellow" – statesman and soldier too – now leaned against me in the darkness, rigid and dead, with the piteous stain on him, Ireland's stain, darkening my tunic as we jolted over the road . . .'

There were no Englishmen about when that occurred, but Mr De Valera was not far away, he who has done more damage in a decade to our country than England did in seven hundred years. England never sapped Ireland's morale. De Valera and degeneration are synonymous.

The south light was on the beautiful dome of the Custom House behind its hideous grid of loop-line railway. O'Connell and his four lady guardian angels looked after me as I turned to cross his bridge; how they would fly away were his monument to come to life! I looked along the curving river of the seven bridges to the city's steeples on its southern bank. At evening this is one of the loveliest views. The steeples gain in height; and, if the tide be full, the seagulls brighten the river as they float with their breasts held high against the current to the sun.

A crowd collected at the Ballast Office clock; that clock, by which all watches are set, caught my eye. I saw that the crowd was looking at Endymion the cricketer, as he saluted the clock with drawn sword. The ceremony over, he took from the tail of his coat a large alarm clock, set it carefully and replaced it in his pocket, from which it began to ring loudly as he walked, greatly to the crowd's delight. The people cheered good-humouredly. It was high noon!

I passed the bulging bank of Ireland, that squats on the city like a usurer with his money-bags, and so home.

A bulky figure was being assisted outside my house on to a side-car, that almost lost conveyance; a bulky figure with a dark trilby hat above a mane of unkept hair. I saw the sackcloth on his chest and belly. What a narrow escape! The reigning bore of the moment was leaving my house, doubtless having been told that I was not at home. A narrow escape! If I retain any of my youth in age, it is chiefly due to my avoidance of bores. My bore-point is very low. I flash off and I am gone. But this was the most tiring and, to women and young girls, the most offensive bore in Dublin. He owed his impunity to the religious attitude he adopted to bully women about their clothes. It made the police tolerant when they saw him with his apron of sacking and his girdle cord. He would sit in a tram and accost the passengers roughly about their low necks, bare

105

arms or legs; was a self-appointed censor. He was one of those cases that suffer from frustration of sex . . . and to whom all sex is anathema. Also, it should be persecuted. This is not an uncommon attitude of mind in elderly adults who have nothing left to think about when the flesh is ignored. Subjugating their sex becomes an object in itself, as if gelding were godliness. This explains their hatred of women and the desire to make them suffer, as was apparent in the attempt of the Boston Methodists to persecute the beneficent inventor of ether the moment he applied it to the relief of birth throes. But Philip Francis Little was calling on me, not to call me to the sackcloth, but to leave me a book of his poems.

Philip Francis modelled himself, so far as his way of speaking went, on old Dr Sigerson, and Dr Sigerson, conscious always of his Danish or Scandinavian origin, used to speak as if he were translating a rune.

The amazing thing was that the poems were quite competent. This is the foreword:

> The aim that all we poets have in writing is of pleasing
> Ourselves, which is the object each one has when he is
> sneezing.

After all, he is more interesting that Gerald Manley Hopkins, who fooled Robert Bridges with his tricks with language. Philip Francis Little's

> No throstle cock, no blackbird
> Chrysostome upon a tree,
> Could sing a song of saxpence
> So merrily as he.

Chrysostome, golden-mouthed! Of course he got it from his religious studies, but it must have been almost profane to him to employ it for the 'Ousel cock so black of hue, With orange tawny bill.' What a pity he didn't stick to rhyming and leave preaching alone! He is taking his immortal soul too seriously; already he is eccentric; soon he will go mad. And now he was heaving off on a side-car, leaning over to talk to the jarvey who kept humouring him. Often as I have heard of that humour, I always took it with a grain of salt, with the suspicion that it was assessed by tourists who came prepared to see fun in anything Irish. But the remark from the quayside hazard to the men on the Guinness lighters, who comported themselves as shepherds of Ocean though their voyages were limited to a few miles of the river. 'Eh! Bring us back a monkey or a parrot!' justifies them. And the jarvey who asked the famous surgeon who defended a divorce action for alleged misconduct in a cab, leading his bride in *secondes noces* out on his arm from Church *en route* for a honeymoon, 'Cab, sir?' had a terse turn of phrase.

CHAPTER SIX

Sir Horace was dissatisfied with his death, of which the Press notices were quite unworthy. He had just died in New York, so that his loss would be all the greater in Ireland, which could not compansate itself by a public funeral. But so inadequate were the obituaries that, without waiting for the Irish Mail, he wrote on the fourth day to the newspapers pointing out certain omissions and misunderstandings, and assuring 'those who worked with him' that the announcement of his death was premature, but that they and his country would have whatever years were left to him, devoted selflessly to their service. He then collected enough money in America to found in Dublin a paper of his own.

The reason of the paucity of cables of regret from Dublin was simply that 'those who worked with him' were incredulous. They knew that there was so much of his usefulness still undemonstrated that his death was, at the worst, merely a means of getting a public assessment of his life-work and a criticism of their help – a method as it were of reporting progress. So, unimaginatively, they resented more than mourned him.

Therefore, I was all the better able to sustain the shock when I discovered that the Session of the Senate was about to open with a letter from Sir Horace sending in his resignation. He succeeded in hitching the Senate to his retirement, a thing that many could not do in the course of their full activities.

The Chairman read:

'MY DEAR GLENAVY,

After too protracted and earnest thought, I have come to the definite conclusion that I am no longer justified in remaining upon the Senate. I therefore place my resignation in your hands and ask you to take the proper steps to have the vacancy filled. I wish to tender to you, to the Vice-Chairman and the members my grateful thanks for your kindness to me at my two attendances and your indulgence in regard to my many absences. To you all, as well as to myself, it is due that I should state the reasons for the course I have taken.

They are two and can be briefly summarized:

1. The Senate may, if its members give sufficient thought to the problem submitted to them for discussion and disinterested advice to the Government and the people, build up and exercise great influence for good. It is a small body, and cannot afford to have members who are unable to attend at least a majority of its sittings. I could not do this for reasons of health in the near future, and do not believe that such attendance will ever be the best way of rendering that service to my country which will continue to be the chief aim and object of my life for the days I may be spared to see.

2. My work lies in spheres of voluntary effort – especially organized voluntary effort – and not in that of legislation or public administration. It is true that when much younger I represented an Irish constituency for eight years in the British Parliament. I presided over the Irish Convention, worked for the Dominion Settlement (without the Partition that had to be) and accepted the honour of a nomination to the Senate. But in the first case I was seeking State assistance for agriculture and industry. This came with the creation and endowment of the Department of Agriculture and Technical Instruction of which I was the working head for its first seven years. The other political activities were dictated by the recognition that, failing an Irish settlement, all the work I wished to do had come to nought.

I joined the Senate from a wish to take some small part in supporting the Free State Government, well knowing the personal inconvenience my doing so would cause. I would not leave it now if I could be reasonably suspected to be thereby safeguarding my person or my property. But, as things are, I do not wish to make a bad precedent in our public life by occupying a position the duties of which I cannot adequately discharge.

I need only add my earnest wish that the fellow-countrymen with whom I shall no longer be officially associated will realize the high ideal of public service they have set before them.

Yours sincerely,
HORACE PLUNKETT.'

'To that letter,' said Lord Glenavy, 'I replied:

'MY DEAR SIR HORACE,

I read your letter with very great regret, in which, I am certain, every member of the Senate will share. I should have asked you to reconsider your determination were it not for your statement that your conclusion was definite. I shall, of course, communicate the contents of your letter to the Senate, and have only to add that I welcome your assurance that the resignation of your seat will not involve any interruption of your constant devotion and unselfish services in the interests of your country . . .'

Mr Bennet said:

'I think we might consider whether it might not be reasonable to ask Sir Horace Plunkett to reconsider his determination to resign . . .'

That is better, thought I. That short letter of Glenavy accepting, almost with alacrity, Sir Horace's resignation, will never be forgotten as long as Sir Horace lives; and Sir Horace is likely to outlive Glenavy, for, not content with founding his own paper, he is bringing to Dublin his sanatorium from Battle Creek.

The Earl of Mayo said:

'I should like to say a few words with regard to the resignation of my old friend Sir Horace Plunkett. We were boys together. I have known him for many years . . . We in this Senate must remember that Sir Horace Plunkett has been consulted with regard to co-operation by almost every leading man in Europe and America, except, of course, from Denmark, where the system of co-operation has been carried on successfully for many years . . .

'I am glad to tell you his health is very much better. I think it must be better, because I saw an excellent letter from him in *The Times* the other day, dated from his house in London . . .'

The idea of Sir Horace's health having the same curve as his letters to *The Times* was something I had not considered. But the Earl has just assured us that 'it must be better!'

Colonel Moore did not like to let the occasion pass. He had not always been in entire agreement, but –

110

Sir Thomas Grattan Esmonde, waving the lanyard of his eye-glasses, said:

'May I say how deeply I regret that Sir Horace Plunkett's health has compelled him to sever his connexion with the Senate? I think it is a great pity when our country is struggling to her feet that the Senate should lose the services of a man who has given his whole life with absolute disinterestedness to further Irish interests.'

Sir Nugent Everard said:

'As one of Sir Horace Plunkett's old colleagues in his co-operative work, I think it would ill become me if I did not add my voice, as I believe it is the wish of the Senate to ask him to reconsider his resignation ..."

This brought the Chairman, Lord Glenavy, into the discussion again:

'Of course, personally, no one would more sincerely welcome Sir Horace Plunkett back but ... Perhaps I might suggest to Senator Bennet that he would consider that it might be more dignified and complimentary to Sir Horace Plunkett if he would frame a resolution somewhat to the following effect: "That the Senate, while accepting his resignation with regret, desires to place on record its appreciation of the pre-eminent services he has for so many years rendered to his country." I only throw that out as a suggestion. It is entirely in the hands of the Senate.'

Mr Bennet:

'I am quite in your hands and the hands of the Senate.'

Who was it muttered: 'A washing of hands'?

The passage in Sir Horace's letter that referred to the wild state of things when Senators' houses were sent up in flames, not by any Englishman remaining in the country, but by the natives themselves; when losses of irrecoverable treasures were being inflicted daily, when the Record Office that contained irreplaceable records of our country went up in smoke burned by men of the class that never makes history, was the most remarkable because of its modesty. 'I would not leave it now if

111

I could be reasonably suspected to be thereby safeguarding my person or my property.'

No man could reasonably suspect Sir Horace Plunkett of lack of courage. His drive right up to the kneeling British soldiers who were holding Dublin put any such thoughts out of my mind. Sir Horace was intrepid. He may have had a high disdain for danger, but it seemed that it never occurred to him to notice it. His passenger had cause to regret Sir Horace's intrepidity. He was beside Sir Horace in his two-seater when the British opened fire. There were traffic regulations which Sir Horace had disregarded – after all, he was on his way to the Plunkett House – so they opened fire without warning. Sir Horace drove on. His passenger was shot through the kidney. The mascot on the car was drilled. A few bullets pierced Sir Horace's clothing, but Sir Horace drove on, hastening slowly. *'Festina lente'* is the motto of his family.

'My dear fellow, I will see about this.' He asked the kneeling rifleman: 'Where is your officer? This is scandalous. I will have him here at once!'

Men of the race of Plunkett cannot be reasonably expected to stampede.

CHAPTER SEVEN

To-day I will be a millionaire. I will do just as I please. Have I come into millions? Yes. The heavens have endowed me: it is a fine day in Dublin, and my tastes are more than money can buy. I have never confused money with wealth, that is why I am a millionaire: I am as wealthy as any, though not as monied as the least. What are my wants? Already I have the first of them gratified – it is a fine day in Dublin; and the second, which needs a high barometric pressure to fulfil, has got it. Freedom from the tyranny of meals, appointments, and even friends, any man can have by embracing Sister Poverty; but there is one thing that she must give me in return for my attentions, and that she cannot give – the power of unimpeded movement. Her vehicles are the ambulance or the Black Maria. I would desert her for a Baby Ford.

A child has an extra appetite; one in addition at least to those a grown person has – it is the necessity for movement. To keep a child motionless would as assuredly kill it as it would kill an old man to confine him to bed. Young and old must move; and the desire for movement is overflowing into the hunger for speed. The eternal feminine, the female force in Nature, led the men of old upward; speed is taking her place in this generation. What is at the back of this hunger for and need of speed?

Just as there are tribes who are unacquainted with the facts of parenthood, with children who do not know their fathers, so we are unaware of our heavenly descent, our cosmic relationship. And yet the thrill of the electric atoms which make up the substance of our bodies is slowly being felt and interpreted in terms of speed. Our bodies are desirous of swift movement now: speed for speed's sake. Soon our minds will realize the electric nature of our being and deliberately direct our bodies' movements towards the All-mover, the *Primum Mobile* whose glory thrills and penetrates the universe.

Call them profanely protons and electrons, these are but names for matter in the immeasurable Mystery of Being which vibrates through the whole of space, or rather of creation. The

113

body is vibrating in harmony with the universe. The more we grow conscious of this, the more we will to move. Movement is the ritual and recognition of the divine nature of our substance. It is a recoil from that which is dead, an act of life. To satisfy the desire and to make an action of recognition, the power to move must be provided. Else we remain still as death.

My motor, therefore, takes me far to-day from the Eternal Feminine of the Vice-regal Lodge with her *gentil babil*, into the hills or even into the air. I will arise and go into the granite mountains, and sit on a stone in the middle of a little yard-wide rill, and watch the water move over the clean golden sands, or by a heathery stream watch the sub-aqueous grasses wave, while far above go the high cumulus clouds that look down upon it all.

I remember Talbot Clifton once asking me, 'What the devil were you doing on that hill? You had no gun.'

There was not the least use in trying to answer him. The answer would, for peace and for understanding's sake, have to be 'nothing'. And that would seem an offensive and unsatisfactory reply. He did not know that I was a millionaire and can let others shoot my imaginary birds and catch all my fish but the Salmon of Knowledge.

With these blanketing clouds there will be a warm dell above Ticknock, where I can do nothing until it is time to fall down on Dundrum and give Yeats the Governor-General's invitation. Will he accept it? Of course not, at first; but a little strategy, a little strategy. I have already in my mind a little scheme to endow him with the necessary distinction. He must be made to see that he has an opportunity to take up the position which he likes beyond all others: the position from which he can both dominate and endow.

His mind provides me with a realm of beauty beyond the beauty of woman. It will be a relief to be independent in thought for an hour or two while I sail in the shadowy waters or sit with Cuchulainn grown old. Seven lean years he endured of love, only to win at the end emancipation from – what was it the aged Sophocles called Love? – 'a relentless master'.

Now he leaves to Love the perfervid sunlight. He has refracted his rays, as it were, through the pearl of Paradise, and they fall with so gentle a softness that they are only visible under the moon. How different this from George Moore,

114

caught in the ugly snare and wry-twisted with curiosity; how different even from Keats, whom he makes to appear somewhat treacly and relaxed. Keats, Gates, Yeats: etymologically these three names are one and the same. They are names found in Cornwall. So Keats and Yeats are neither English nor Irish originally, but Cornish. And Yeats' mother being a Pollexfen makes Yeats closer to Cornwall than Keats, and closer to Parnassus as it rises to our modern eyes. I must remember that: Cornish! He will be delighted to hear it. He is growing somewhat tired of being irretrievably Irish, which has come lately to mean Celtic, which means nothing. He wants a change. But with Yeats a Cornishman! He shall have sailed with Tristram, sung hopelessly of Iseult for seven long years and reproved the facetious Dinadan. And he shall disapprove of present times. Already I hear the sailors singing the oldest of sea shanties as they near Tintagel, where Yeats is waiting beside King Mark.

> They rowèd hard, and snug thereto
> With Heveloe, and Rumbaloo!

It's enough to give him, with this new outlook, a new lease of life. And that is the function of anyone who is a well-wisher of the Muses' son. And he can find an excuse to escape from boredom, which is the only thing that ages, an excuse to get out of the Kildare Street Club.

I will gather myself up and hurry down. I can see the old grey mole of De Lacy's Castle from here, and past it the Yellow House; a mile this side is Yeats. Yes. Yes. How pleased he will be! But, of course, he has to discover this lineage for himself.

Why did I not think of this before? There could not be a Gaelic Yeats. It won't take 'O' or 'Mac' as a prefix. Now that he is recovering from a cold, is the very time to complete the cure and put him up for the Round Table. He will elect himself. Merlin will not be in it with me as a magician! He had better be Sir Lancelot than Sir Tristram, for 'Lancelot was better breathed.'

Yeats lives in Rathfarnham in an old house in lovely grounds, a house built before cement took the place of stone and thin-walled clangour for the stately repose and long silence of continuous dwelling. His gate is on a bridge which spans a stream fresh from the golden granite of the hills. The walk rises through a well-gardened wilderness of flowering shrubs, and the old grey house is screened by a blossoming orchard. His croquet lawn is beside it, and the hills form an ever-changing picture as deep and as glowing in colour as a picture by his brother, Jack Yeats, in his latest style. The door faces you. 'Yeats' on a heart-shaped brass knocker. As it used to be simply 'Yeats' on his London house in Woburn Place before the place was demolished.

'I am glad you have come,' he said, 'you are the very man I want to see. I have just been reading George Moore's *Memoirs of my Dead Life*. And a question keeps rising in my mind which you can answer. Take that seat there. This is the question: Do you think George Moore was impotent?'

The great Cornishman was sitting up among his pillows, his magnificent head, with its crown of white hair and satin-like brown skin, toning well with the fawn dressing-gown he wore. His nose, like an eagle's, was broadest between the eyes. At the foot of the bed a gas-fire burned; outside the open window birds were seeking food in a coco-nut shell which he had fastened to the sill. He was recovering from a cold and 'enjoying his illness' for the peace it provided and for the immunity it gave him from his friends.

Good Lord! but aloud: 'I don't know. It is rare for a man to be impotent. He may be unable to propagate, but organic impotence must be very rare.'

'Was he a man?'

'He had the pelvis of a woman, as artists are said to have. There is little to be deduced from that. The only arguments that come to my mind are based on deduction more than on facts physical or otherwise.'

'Well, go on.'

'Take the evidence of women. Susan Mitchell sensed something lacking. Women are like that. She wrote "Some men kiss and do not tell, some kiss and tell; but George Moore tells and does not kiss." Kiss may mean . . . Well, she was hardly likely to say more.'

'Go on.'

'You remember Goethe says' – how well Yeats remembered, I knew, for I remembered long ago mentioning Goethe to

116

Moore, and Moore pointing to Eckermann's *Life of Goethe* and saying with a snigger: 'That's where Yeats gets all his information. That's his text-book' 'that the "passing of a genius is measured by the woman it leaves behind." Now, where are Moore's surviving lady friends?'

'There's one.'

'Oh, we all know! But did Moore hold her exclusive affection? He did not. She was faithful to him only in her infidelities, *splendide mendax*. "I could not love thee, Moore, so much, loved I not others more." That's argument number one. Then, one evening I sat with him in his bedroom in Ebury Street. He was recounting with a reminiscence so devoid of melancholy that I suspected it was but a work of the creative imagination. Suddenly he looked at the rug in front of the fire and addressed it and me: "O rug, thou could'st tell many a pleasant tale of love!" What's wrong with the bed? thought I.'

'Exactly,' Yeats exclaimed, with the excitement of a triumphant detective, jerking himself up in the bed. 'Exactly! His accounts of his adventures are all one-sided. There never is – he never gives one, a distinct feeling for the woman in the case. I have just been reading these Memoirs, and I am wondering more than ever what form his impotence took. I remembered this: He was passing along Merrion Square one night with Best and he saw couples standing upright, immobile, speechless with heads on one another's shoulders. "But they are not saying a word!" he exclaimed. "I wish I could do that! Best, could you do that?" Best said that it was about the only thing anyone could do. But psychologically it reveals that Moore never felt the silence of love. His scenes leave you with no account of the woman. It is only of his own sensations he talks. Now we all know a woman has far fiercer sensations than a man. She cannot conceal them. She cries out. Moore never tells what the woman did. Why?' – pointing and shaking his finger at me – 'Because she was not there!

'A woman in Paris told me that the earlier emotions are apt to become obliterated by the later. Moore only recounts his earlier emotions!'

I said: 'I consulted a woman novelist about the Moore problem and I put the objection regarding the one-sidedness of his love scenes. *"The Lovers of Orelay"* for instance, where there is more writing about the locale than the love.'

'What did she say?'

'That Moore was an artist and was both sided, woman and man, as artists should be.'

'She was a woman novelist, you say? That accounts for her defending him. His works are admired particularly by women.'

'Wait! I begin to see a further argument for your thesis in that. Women admire him because they feel instinctively that he can never give them away.'

'Admirable!'

'Love must have ever been to Moore "All a wonder and a wild desire". His curiosity was undiminished, and yet, it could be argued that that was chiefly a proof that his interest in women was undiminished. An argument in his favour.'

'Would you mind closing that window? The birds will not come back until it's down. I interrupted you?'

'Not at all. I remember since we spoke of the absence of the woman from Moore's description of his love scenes, his telling me of something a lover – no, he preferred to call her a mistress – of his was supposed to remark . . . it is so much on the lines of the ignorance he revealed to Best that I forbear telling it; but you may take it that now I come to think of it, it bears out the conclusion we come to from what he said to Best.'

'What was that?'

'Oh, never mind. But don't you remember the way in which he tried to make me to personate him in Vienna shortly after I had returned from that most delightful of cities?'

'When the lady that admired his work threatened to come to Dublin so that she might bear a child of his?'

'Precisely. She was, according to Moore, a beautiful Viennese . . .'

'And you had just come back from Vienna. That's what gave him the idea. The idea of the Viennese admirer. You had been extolling Vienna?'

'Very likely.'

'Go on.'

' "How am I to know her? And do you imagine for a moment that she will not find me out?" "My dear fellow, I will show you her photograph. And as for finding you out, she only admires my work, she does not know me, and that is why she insists on bearing a child to me".'

'Yes! Yes! Go on.'

118

'Having, so to speak, screwed my courage to the sticking-place, I asked to see the photograph.'

'And did you see it?'

'I cannot remember.'

'Try to think.'

'I did see a photograph, but he might have forgotten that he had shown it to me before I left for Vienna the year before. It may have been the photograph he used for Pearl Craigie ...'

'Now, listen to me. I saw that photograph, yellow with age. It had become, when I saw it, the photograph of a beautiful Virginian who was threatening to come to him from America desirous of his services. He wrote a play about it. That was all.'

Yeats lit the lamp beside his bed. The birds were twittering in his apple-trees, settling for the night. I might open the window now.

'After all, he was a great artist and greatly loved art,' I said. 'He was a devotee to that and creative in that sphere at all events. He was a great person and he never forgot it. His air of perpetual cantankerousness was to defend himself from rational little critics "while the work was in progress"; to defend himself from Reality and common-sense. Had he not said, "We must keep up the illusion"? And while he attended to his garden, the garden of his prose, he resented what anyone can have if they bear fools gladly – comments.'

But while Moore wrote much about Yeats, Yeats remained silent about his contemporary. Why was this? I think that Moore's inordinate jealousy, a jealousy which flew at the fame of Hardy like a pettish child, realized a greater genius in Yeats than he possessed, and so he tried to subject by ridicule what he could never have outshone. Yeats disliked Moore, first of all for his 'position', – a landlord – and then because he was attacked by Moore before his friends for taking a Civil List pension. Also, Yeats feels that his words may easily confer fame, since he has never allowed his literary judgement to be persuaded. Making your rival ridiculous is the chief aim of Irish opponents since the duel was abolished. And in his trilogy *Ave, Salve, Vale,* Moore mocked at Yeats. *Ave atque Vale*, I have recorded it was at first, until he pilloried Professor Tyrrell, who, aware of Moore's ignorance, remarked on hearing of his portrait drawn by Moore, 'Moore is one of those fellows who think that "Atque" is a Roman centurion.'

The problems that confront the mind of man are innumerable, some of them incalculable. My problem was not one of those which may be described somewhat hyperbolically as vital; nevertheless it was, considered from the point of view of Art, a cardinal one on which much hinged. And I was nearly forgetting it! I had to persuade a real poet to accept a invitation to a pseudo court. Yeats is the greatest poet of this and of most of the last generation. Tennyson, his predecessor, built a world of song on ready-made foundations. Yeats had to create it all from 'airy nothing'; and to protect it from marauding hands. I had to persuade him to accept a word-of-mouth invitation to the opening ceremony of the Spring Show. The Show might have opened itself, but its success was contributed to by the presence of His Majesty's representative. Dublin is loyal at Ballsbridge. Horses connote knights, 'Men who ride upon horses' (I will quote Yeats to himself), and therefore courtliness. This may help me to persuade the poet to join the 'Distinguished Visitors' in the 'Royal' box.

'By the way, Yeats, the Governor-General has asked me to invite you to the opening of the Spring Show. He will be in his private box, and we can go up to it or take tea under it in his private apartments.'

'I will not go. I am suffering from a cold.'

'You are not, but you are making your friends suffer from your cold.'

'I will not abet this trumpery mockery of a throne. I will not meet Tim Healy or Lady Lavery in the Royal box. Really I am surprised that you take this mummery of kingship seriously.'

'No. I do not; but I think that in the Decline and Fall of the British Empire in Ireland, and Ireland with it, you and I should stand like your Triton in the stream, and resist the lapse from grandeur with dignity. I am going in a tall hat, as it were crowned by remembering happier things. I am sure that mine will be the only tall hat at the Spring Show. Half the Kildare Street Club will be there, but they will hesitate to honour the King lest they offend Democracy by meeting his Viceroy suitably attired. I, as you know, have not the least concern for popular opinion.'

'Neither have I!'

'I am going in what I hope will be the only silk hat to be seen at the first official function of the Free State. We must not conform to the unceremonious.'

This roused him. 'Look here, I think you are right. Unless we are to let the country drift without a protest into the loutish ways of the bog, we must stand for the observances of good manners. We must wear tall hats.' The grandeur innate in the man was coming out. Quietly now! Leave him the tiller.

'You are quite right. If we do not give our countrymen the lead, who is there left courageous to sport a tall hat?'

I hope, I said to myself, that the proposition will not appear to his mind as 'Silk hats save Ireland!'

He was agreeing, but it did not mean that he was coming to the Show.

'Quite so. But it is neither here nor there this mock court held by a barrister, in what is no more important than an agricultural show in one of the shires. I will not go. I am not well enough. It is a travesty: a revolution in a palace.'

My last card: 'Yeats, we need not ascend the grandstand at all. As poet of the Lake Isle, you ought to see the country girls producing the island's fare. It is a goodly sight. I saw some of the dairy-maids at work in the last Spring Show, and they were very comely. The butter-girls are so clean and wholesome you would think that they were personally selected by Dr Russell of the Department of Public Health. Wonderful sight, the churning! Lassies of seventeen, with white elbows.'

'Why white elbows?'

'You must know that the skin of the elbow retains to the last any trace of pigment that there may be in the racial species. If there is the least Eurasian, Arabian or Semitic blood, for instance, it shows in the browning of the skin of the elbow: some skin diseases are diagnosed by a spot or two at the elbows. Now the dairy-maids I saw churning have snow-white and ruddy arms like strawberries and cream. Their work at the churning had made them rosy, and still they kept on with the old-fashioned churns, plunging up and down the long handle. It is a very graceful attitude. I wonder why your brother Jack has not caught them at their work. In a year or two there will be no more churns with long upright handles, nothing but revolving barrels with glass windows. The old and homely things are ebbing away, ebbing away.'

121

'You do not expect me to rise from my bed to see Tim Healy; and a few country girls churning?'

'Whoever suggested it? I merely threw out a hint that you and I could attend the Spring Show, wear silk hats where no one else dared, and slip away from the Royal box in time for the butter-making competition. I will drive you home.'

'Perfectly preposterous!'

'Very well – you are missing a lot.'

'What am I missing?'

'Oh, nothing, perhaps. But I am deep in the folk-lore of the churn. Most of the treasure trove from Irish bogs is butter, and we get that unique and beautiful form of vessel the mether from the bogs. The three- or four-handed goblet. The descendants of those who made the mether and put butter into firkins are churning at the present moment, unconscious of the long tradition of the churn; and the awful tragedy of it is that no one realizes what is being lost. The sea chanties were nearly all gone until a few late-comers collected half-a-dozen Bowdlerized stanzas or so. But the churn! Only one song of butter-making remains.'

'Have you got it?'

'Father Claude overheard it in Tipperary, when a buxom maid was churning as she thought all alone. She had buttocks like a pair of beautiful melons. Her sleeves were rolled up. She had churned from early morning. Her neck was pink with exercise. Her bosom laboured, but she could not desist, for the milk was at the turn. Up and down, desperately she drove the long handle: up and down, up and down and up and up for a greater drive. The resistance grew against the plunger. Her hips and bosom seemed to increase in size while her waist grew thin. In front of her ears the sweat broke into drops of dew. She prayed in the crisis to old forgotten gods of the homestead! Twenty strokes for ten! Gasping, she sang:

"Come, butter!
Come, butter!
Come, butter,
Come!
Every lump
As big as
My bum!"

122

You are missing not one, but many milk-maids' songs. And when we are dead, they too shall be; and the folk-lore lost forever of the dairy and the byre.'

'How does it go?' – He beat time to recall the rhythm. ' "Every lump As big as My bum!" '

'Yes. You are correct. But my proposal is that we get these chants at first-hand and be not depending on Father Claude for such songs.'

'When does Tim expect us?'

'Any time from four to six.'

' "Come, butter, come, butter," ' he murmured. 'I think I will join you. Let me know when you can send a car. And there's my hat to be brushed.'

'Sir John and Lady Simon are the guests of honour.'

'There was not a word about them when I was out at the Lodge this morning.'

'They arrived by the evening boat. Can you call for me to take me out to dinner?'

'With pleasure.'

'At eight o'clock.'

Lady Fingall put down the telephone. Now what is up? I wondered. What brings Sir John Simon over here?

The telephone rang again. Lady Fingall, it seemed, had been cut off.

'You know that Hazel is staying there and acting Lady Vice-Reine in the Lodge? Lord Lovat is there and some American friends of Hazel's. It is a very private dinner; quite informal, but not informal enough for you to tell my stories. I am quite able to tell them myself. But you may remind me if I forget.'

'Telling other people's stories? I suppose I do, when they are not other people's stories about other people. We shall see.'

'We will see how it goes. We may have a pleasant evening. No decorations!' she laughed. 'Eight o'clock.'

I am presumed to know all Lady Fingall's stories by heart. Perhaps I heard them independently from other sources. I will tell no stories. I detest the set story which is brought to dinner, as obvious as a stud on one's shirt. I prefer personalities, for what are stories without characters whom we neither know nor are made alive for us?

123

I thought of the last time I heard Tim speaking in public. It was at the dinner of the Tailltean Games. The Committee were undecided until the last moment whether they would invite the Governor-General or not ... When they had made up their minds as to the exact amount of vice-royalty athletes could sustain, it was almost too late to invite him with any propriety. In fact, it took a great deal of diplomacy on my part to persuade him to accept the half-hearted invitation.

There were almost a thousand guests in the Metropole. On the right of the Governor-General sat Prince Ranjitsinhji, the famous cricketer, magnificent in his jewelled turban. When Tim arose to speak, I marvelled at his rhetorical or rather histrionic device for commanding attention. It is hard to hold an audience, particularly from the outset. They do not prick up their ears until the first quip or telling phrase. But Tim arose and putting his hands behind his back, leaning his head forwards and swaying it from side to side as if about to utter an incantation, he waited, then made his voice assume a dismal and sepulchral sound like the echoes in church. The effect was to make his audience as attentive as a congregation. Thus he held us from the first word.

'Your Highness, Ladies and Gentlemen, I don't know why I have been invited here to a banquet of the Tailltean Games. The only game I ever played was a game of marbles. But we have here on our right a splendid and world-famous sportsman, and deservedly so – His Highness, Prince Ranjitsinhji of Nawanagar. He is, as you know, a great sportsman, a wielder not alone of the cricket-bat, but of the salmon rod . . . His presence here is a sign of the affection he bears our country. Gentlemen, he might have fished in the Ganges; but he prefers the river at Ballinahinch!'

The laughter and applause were deafening. The company saw the absurd vision of the Prince casting a fly and raising a crocodile. Only the praise and applause reached the Prince.

Another great Irishman who adopted this subterfuge in public speaking was our dear Tom Kettle. He had as great a force of genius and as great a gift for concentrating his force in a phrase. He is the only orator whose loss is a national deprivation. His fine gift for friendship sounded in his voice, which was the sonorous proclamation of the presence of a great soul.

'I went "Home" to one of the ruined drawing-rooms of eighteenth-century Dublin with a girl whom circumstances, all remediable, have turned into what is called a prostitute. There was a family living in every corner but one of that dilapidated *salon*. As we approached the prostitute's corner, we approached civilization. There was a screen round her bed.'

He said this to shock the apathetic and venal mismanaging Housing Committees of the day into dealing with the awful tenements which still fill up as soon as a family is housed elsewhere and sap the lives of the incoming countrymen.

It was useless to seek to divert him by pretending to be shocked by his meeting a prostitute. Kettle was too big to be affected by the calumnies of hypocrisy or of those who had not only the prostitute on their conscience, but also the lives of the three Christian families. He condemned the Committee with, 'It's your housing makes whores.'

Lady Lavery was acting as Vice-Reine. So far so good. She was one of those Londonized Americans who are adept hostesses. She could make a funeral feast entertaining. Wherein lay her accomplishment? In thoughtfulness for others and a genius for tact. How often have I left her hospitable house feeling as elated with myself as that guest described by my friend Pearsall Smith, but without the reaction which the cool evening caused. Women such as these know the knack, not necessarily of flattering men, but of standing aside and acting as prompters with the certain knowledge that men will do their own flattery in their own way. That makes them great entertainers.

In her own drawing-room she would have jumped up and half crossed the floor to meet us, arms outstretched. Things were stiffer at Tim's uncertain court. The ladies were casting about for some indication of Tim's attitude. Would he expect them to curtsey? Would it embarrass him if they did not do it before Sir John? Would he be cynical if they did? Lady Lavery's tact saved the entrance problem. She got in the way and led us to His Excellency. Soon he led us, with Lady Simon on his arm, to the small dining- or breakfast-room. As usual when he was in private, the table was decorated with his Waterford glass.

The American London hostess friend of Lady Lavery sat on my right. I never catch names, so, for all I knew or remembered, she might have been 'Prudence'. To heap coals of fire upon my head, she remembered me. Had we not met in London? Yes, of course. (My Lord, but where?) ' . . . And what an amusing evening it turned out to be in the end!'

'But was the issue ever in doubt?'

'Well, I was not too confident of my powers to entertain.'

This is where I flounder, I thought, if I say one word. But I was saved – or was I? – by Lady Fingall, who asked me in a loud voice with everyone's attention already captured: 'Tell us about the party you were at in London where Sargent was, and what he said to you when the Negro minstrels sang.'

In a flash I remembered the identity of the lady on my right who 'was not too confident of her powers to entertain'. It was to the big party she gave us in Chelsea she referred. I was a guest, but so unobtrusive was my hostess that I might just as well have been a gate-crasher. And I was by no means saved. Lady Fingall is hardly a lifeboat from a social predicament. I found myself now in danger of being represented as ungrateful enough to mock in Dublin the hospitality accepted and enjoyed in London. After all, it was Sargent's remarks I repeated to Lady Fingall. Had these become one of her stories? My face is not very expressive but I tried to make it register – Fire! No use! 'I heard it from the Duchess of Rutland, who .was there,' said Lady Fingall; 'I'll tell it if you don't.'

'Is there any mystery?' asked Tim.

I said, 'I met Sargent, or rather, I was in a room with him. I noticed how tall and portly he was, and I remember the iron-grey on the back of his head and the light coming through his rather large and rosy ears.'

'What was it the nigger sang?'

'Oh, something from Shakespeare,' said I, and dropped my voice and wriggled as one loth to continue.

'I remember it now,' cried Lady Fingall. 'He sang "Take, O take those lips away". And Sargent said, "Yes, do. They are nine inches long."'

'You must forgive me for Sargent's jokes,' I said, turning to my neighbour.

'I am glad you enjoyed your evening,' was her reply.

Ah me!

'Sargent made another joke about the other black man's song,' persisted Lady Fingall.

'What was the other black man's song?' Tim asked, cavernously.

'He sang about journeys ending in lovers' meeting; and Sargent said: "Lynchings end such lovers' meetings in our Southern States."'

'I did not think that Sargent had such an outlook. I thought that he had become as British as Henry James,' said I, hoping to reinstate myself. But to my rescue nobody came. It was hardly a tempting speculation. No one cared what Sargent thought. They knew him as a painter ...

'I want to hear the story of Baldy Doody's Pig,' said Tim.

'That is not my story.'

'Has he never a story of his own?' Lady Lavery asked. 'But you cannot escape from telling it. It is his Excellency's command.'

'Well, I don't want to steal Joseph Conlon's story, but here it is.'

'That ruffian?' asked Tim. 'Go on.'

'He said he was told to investigate on the spot a complaint from a village near Cloughjordan about an outrage of the Black-and-Tans. In order to get accurate details he approached the parish priest, who was a fine specimen of a man about nineteen stone weight.

'"That'll do you, Mr Conlon," he said, "it's so distressing that I could not talk of it till after dinner. And you're just in time. It's three o'clock!"

'I was ushered into the dining-room, where there were five curates about a table: three on one side and two on the side near me. Before each of them was a turkey on a plate. "Boy, another bird for Mr Conlon," his Reverence shouted.'

'As if it were a snipe,' gloomed Tim, greatly amused.

'Well, it showed fine instincts and considerate hospitality on the part of his host,' said I.

'Go on with your story,' said Tim.

'My friend goes on to say that when he had cut sufficiently through the turkey to see his companion on the opposite side of the table, the bird was removed by the boy. Apparently it was only a hors d'œuvre, or his delayed deglutition was taken for lack of relish. Then dinner began in earnest.

'"Towards nine o'clock," said 'Conlon', "with my back

teeth floating, I said: 'Father, you promised to tell me of the outrages of the Black-and-Tans.'

' "His Reverence sighed, and took a sip of green Chartreuse, and said: 'Mr Conlon, I'm sorry you broached that subject, I was just getting over the shock. There are outrages in all parts of the country, but there are none of them as bad as those scoundrels perpetrated here last Saturday week back. I've hardly got over it yet.' "

'He paused and looked round the table, but the chorus was too reminiscent for words. Finding an atmosphere charged with sympathy, he went on: "Two lorries full of them came down the principal street, sitting back to back, covered over with wire, as if they were a lot of hens, to protect them from bombs which were never heard of in our village. When they got opposite the parochial house they thought fit to fire a salvo, and they bombarded the place and black-and-tanned it up, down, right, left, and centre. Fortunately they hit nobody, but they killed Baldy Doody's pig. She had a litter of thirteen, and he was a family man himself. It was a terrible and irreparable loss."

'A vision of the curtailment of the Harrogate cure crossed Conlon's mind, he confessed to me, when he heard of the outrage on the village livestock of the "family man himself". "The times are bad," said he, lamely enough. "They couldn't be worse," his Reverence replied, "I don't know where they are leading, but you're forgetting to help yourself, Mr Conlon . . ." '

'You're an awful ruffian,' said Tim to me.

'I told your Excellency it was not my story,' said I. 'I know too much about the Church, especially the Orders, to leave an unqualified impression that all clerics have easeful lives; even the old men in some Orders are treated as if they never passed twenty-one. They are up early and they have every hour of the day taken up with duties. There is not a comfortable chair in any of the rooms I have seen. For too much secular ease, there are, as Lady Lavery told me, "Retreats".'

So I had some slight revenge for her 'command'.

Lest Sir John would carry away a wrong impression, Tim described some of the exercises of abstinence and the rigours of religious life.

'The jokes about the Church are reminiscent of Rabelais?' Lord Lovat asked.

'Yes. Jokes show the healthy affection in which it is held.'

'Very likely,' said Tim, who had never heard of Rabelais. And, to use the amazing provisions of legal phraseology, would not have read him had he heard, or, having read him, would not have approved of him. To confirm his statements he welcomed the reference to a 'Retreat'.

'Tell us the story of the Retreat for Parish Priests . . .'

'Lord Lovat will be disedified,' said Lady Lavery. 'He is probably a Presbyterian, and so out of sympathy with the austerer forms of celibate life.'

Tim smiled: 'If it happened in Milltown, there cannot be much harm in it. Go on.'

'Father Tim Fagan was giving a retreat for parish priests, and he warned them that the loneliness of their lives might lead to indolence if they were not perpetually on their guard. This is the kind of thing, I mean:

"Mary, get me my slippers.

"Mary, put the shawl on my back.

"Mary, is the pillow behind my head?

"Mary, poke the fire.

"Mary, bring in the hot water, I'll attend to the rest myself."

"Till in the end," said Father Fagan, "you wouldn't know which of them was Mary." '

'Your Ladyship is worse thán the Senator,' said the Governor-General, who was not at all pleased. He had been caught out by Milltown. Turning abruptly to his neighbour he changed the subject: 'You were in the House the other night?'

'Yes. I heard Austen speaking. After the debate Asquith passed him a note saying that he heard him read the last Will and Testament of the Liberal Party; but that for his part he intended to die intestate. Austen's reply was quite as witty but I did not see it.'

'Ireland always got more from the Conservatives than the Liberals, though she expected more from the Liberals. Did that ever occur to you, Sir John?'

'Possibly, if it be a fact, it may be accounted for by the longer terms in service of the Conservatives.'

'It's not the Way, but the Will,' said Tim.

I gazed at the high intellectual brow and the pointed chin of the man who sat opposite. An Heloiseless Abelard, and like Aberlard, tall and comely: a dialectician of the first degree, an intellect like a ray in its penetrability, capable, for unbound, of taking either side: Nominalist or Realist it mattered little, for his pleasure lay in the triumph of the acuteness of his thought.

We were talking of the Pipe Cemetery at Salruck where the strange custom survives of putting pipes on the graves of those who lived on land but oars on the graves of those who won their living from the sea. A custom old as Time. I tried to recall the name of the helmsman in Virgil who had an oar erected on his tomb.

'Could it have been Palinurus?' Sir John prompted politely.

He has at his instant disposal everything he has read or experienced. A *lux perpetua* of a mind. And I remembered the impression the last act of *Hamlet* gave me of that other intellect not inappropriately associated with Sir John's, pervading like the light of lights and rapidly destroying its creation by a clear irradiation of inexorable reason, terrible as electricity, inevitable as Fate.

It saddened me to think that he could never be popular. To be popular one must be somewhat pitiable: the British crowd is won by weaknesses; but who could purchase or persuade that inflexible intelligence as clear and as amiable as a glass bulb?

He quoted from three poets and a line or two of his own.

The Governor-General said: 'Here's a poem of Irish manufacture,' and he quoted *Down by the Salley Gardens*.

Then Sir John gave an example of the shortest witticism he had heard. Two Cricklewood bus drivers, in the days of horse-drawn buses, were in the habit, in the negative English Blighty way, of hailing each other in a friendly manner by imprecations as they met. One morning a driver missed his friend, only, after weeks of sorrow and loneliness, to find him perched aloft driving a four-in-hand – a hearse. At the moment they were recovering from surprise a little child ran under the leaders' hoofs. The hearse driver reined in desperately just in time.

'Greedy!' said the busman.

Sir John knew Dublin. He had been over for the Compensation Claims Committee. The Royal Hibernian Academy had been burned, and the artists who had lost pictures at its exhibition were claiming for them. He did not know how the artist Gray, a painter of Highland cattle, arrived at the estimate of his loss. Or, rather, he did discover it. Gray was a painter of

Highland cattle and he claimed for the loss of a characteristic work. He could not make up his mind. It was a great picture. If it had not been burned in the Royal Hibernian Academy, it might have been in the Tate Gallery. He got great delight out of painting it.

'How much is it worth?'

'Worth? You can't talk like that to an artist!'

'Well, at how much do you assess your loss?'

'That u'd be hard to tell. It depends on the demand and on my patrons.'

'Yes? Yes?'

But it was time to adjourn for lunch.

'I'll have to get expert advice.'

'By all means.'

During the lunch-hour the artist sat with a crony of his in the nearest pub. They exchanged drinks and resolved to get a reward in some proportion to the needs of the occasion, seeing that art is inestimable. On the Commission's sitting being resumed, Gray explained:

'There are twenty cattle on the hillside.'

'Twenty?'

'And at fifteen pounds per head that would work out at three hundred pounds, besides those hidden in the mist. My friend here is an expert on values. He is the best known butcher in the town.'

How can Reason, however pure and serene, prevail against an artist? Yet he made no claims for the mist!

'That is not absurd at all, but the finest thing I have yet heard about Dublin,' Lady Lavery rebuked me. 'It only means that an artist is found taking his creations for real, and Shelley calls artists' creations "more real than living man". It is splendid to realize that there is a man left in Dublin who values the creations of an artist's mind as solidly as his own cattle. Where is that splendid butcher? Or is he only a figment of your mind?'

'On your own showing, even if he were only a figment of my mind, he should be as substantial as if he were not . . . what I mean is, as if he were real . . . Where am I getting? Your Ladyship is quite right. I remember now that somewhere in the Purgatorio, Dante provides local habitations for Antigone and

131

Ismene *"si triste come fue"*, and the daughter of Tiresias and Thetis, the mother of Achilles, and yet these are but the creations of poets, placed in a poet's purgatory: dreams within a dream. Had Sir John sent Gray to prison and impounded his cattle we would have comparable situations.'

'I'd like to buy some of his Highland cattle,' said Lord Lovat.

'Could you tell us,' said Tim, 'if they're liable to foot-and-mouth disease?'

'Beyond me, sir,' said I.

Tim entered into a history of the Waterford Glass factories at Waterford and the factory for glass at Cork. I had heard it all before as well as the history of each piece. Celery filled four large Irish glass celery-bowls. I waved a stalk gently to attract the attention of Lady Fingall, since I was to jog her memory; and her story about Tim's celery was more amusing than the history of Tim's celery-bowls. But she was not to be drawn, so the tale must be left untold like that of old grouse in the gun-room which, however, I can guess: there were flint-locks in those days! But I dare not pirate Lady Fingall's story. That was the only piece of celery I took from her bowl.

'Ramsay MacDonald has a fine head,' Lady Lavery was saying, 'but he is totally devoid of humour, which, after all, is a blessing; for if a Prime Minister does not take himself seriously, who will?'

'How do you know that he has no humour?' Lord Lovat asked, standing up for his countryman.

'I told him how Bernard Shaw went to church the other day and, when they passed him the plate, moved aside murmuring "Press".'

'He probably thought it was irreverent,' said I, who had ground to make up.

'And he would be quite right,' said Tim, who had suffered a good deal.

Lord Lovat, who presided over the Colonization Committee, told how successful he had been when he got a whole village to emigrate from Scotland: 'Parson, doctor, dentist and all . . . No home sickness.'

'And all what?' growled Tim.

'And all the scandals, of course,' Lady Fingall interjected.

132

'It is the absence of scandals that makes the heart grow fonder and long for home.'

'Can the reason why the English are great colonists be that they make their own scandals wherever they go?'

But no one took any notice of that presumption.

Sir John was telling of a rebus in the Sonnets of Shakespeare which I wanted to hear. I often wondered why there should be such a search for lines that more than their meanings tell in the Elizabethan poets. In those days there were only seven Worthies, and anyone who wanted undeserved immortality had to put the come-hither on a poet as the chief journalist of the time, just as the Romans tried to bribe Tacitus for a chapter in his history; yet he gave from his admiration of him more space to Arbiter of the Elegances than to all the 'prominent people'. Nowadays, all are famous, because Fame itself has become ephemeral in order to escape from the makers of ramshackle immortalities. The men who 'feature stars' and judge books by the sales and read 'best-sellers'. The *Rubaiyat* of Fitzgerald never sold at all.

In Shakespeare's days the poet was the photographer, reporter and, if he were the dramatist, the producer of notable men and events. Hollywood was now in Whitefriars and then in Southwark. And the actor in the Puritans' time was Public Enemy No. 1. But now Publicity is Enemy No. 1, because it has undermined fame and substituted itself for Good Report. Virtue and Nobility must yield to notoriety. Thus it happens that the directors of publicity can juggle with values and ideas, hide what is excellent and exalt what is mediocre and worthless. The advertisers become the advisers of public taste and the Arbiters, not of the Elegances, but of vulgarities. To the vulgar you must appeal through vulgarity.

Is it any wonder, then, that the aristocrats or those who wish to remain private and apart should come to have a horror of publicity and to hold all purveyors of 'ideas', as well as ideas themselves, suspect, and to prefer life to literature?

Only in the secret precincts of their own homes and among their intimates can they safely relax into genius. They must in public confront the over-informed and under-educated Public with 'good form', their armour against 'information'. And they succeed in appearing to believe that intelligence is the prerogative of the intellectual classes. And the intellectual classes are persuaded to believe that there are fools in high places. They fooled even that immortal School Inspector, Matthew Arnold, who found them polite and admirable: but they were impotent of ideas and had a 'dangerous tendency to become studiously frivolous'.

When we find ourselves confronted by 'best-sellers', movie 'stars' and fashions which are 'put over', gilt edges, go-getters and magnates clothed with ephemeral fame, is it any wonder that a man of taste should shut himself in from such things, 'closit in his tower'? Not content with manipulating money, the Mesopotamian mongrels must dictate 'ideas', make it virtuous for you to turn the other cheek while they pick your breast pocket. They put that 'across'. Now they seize on every thought of man and take it to their bazaars and sell it shop-soiled, spoilt or copied at second-hand. The Public is deceived instead of being inspired by the thoughts of humanity's finest minds. Is it any wonder that the 'landed gentry' should hold all 'ideas' suspect and fight shy of them and these dealers in the virtues? They are, after all, from the 'eminent' novelist to the share-pusher, but trammels to catch and to exploit the men who have won and inherited the land.

They know that in the past their ancestors got on very well without letters. Unable to read or write, each had his 'latimer'. It should not be necessary to be clever to retain one's property. They know that frequently they have lost their estates through the machinations of clever people from the steward to the pettifogging attorney. In a world of false notions and false 'values' the aristocrat born can trust no man. He has come to place his trust in the horse: the totem of his conquering tribe! Hengist and Horsa! To comfort himself he has invented and built up a wonderful form of symbolism, Fox-hunting. Here, he who rides may read the meaning of the symbolic ritual – the cleverest animal hounded down by men upon horseback. Foxhunting is the ritual of the aristocrat. In vain does the socially ambitious stockbroker strive to rise socially by falling off his hunter. His bandy legs may be more tribal than vocational, but they have not become bandy from horseback. In vain does he seek to emulate the 'best people' by affecting concussion of the brain. He may implore the surgeon at the cottage hospital to add to the report of a broken collarbone, 'suffering from concussion'. The hereditary Masters of Hounds are not to be fooled. They would not accept him were he to have his brain removed. Acquired confusion cannot open the doors of country houses. The better classes are born concussed, as my friend Aubrey Hammond informs me. It is a protective characteristic. (Pardon my stupidity!) According to the librarian, Lyster, 'All we want is to be understood.'

I remember realizing this when I dined with an author among polo-players. It was at Wimborne House. Augustine Birrell, who had been spoiled by being taken for granted, bored me and the majority of the company. He looked like an old headmaster come out of retirement by (ordered) special request of some boys who had no choice in the matter. We had to wait on his words. So had he. This made us word-conscious, self-conscious, with no hope of becoming unconscious. Polo was opposed to pedantry. The horseman won. And then began a light raillery far wittier than any *obiter dicta* could be from the steady collection of a life-time. Give me sportsmen such as the great poet Pindar sought. And let the best-seller men sit silent staring at each other, each game-keeping his gaggle of words.

Suddenly I came to myself. Had I ever been in Scotland? Frequently. There is no country I enjoy so much: from 'Auld Ayr' to the Outer Hebrides. Lord Lovat knew Islay well. What was I endeavouring to remember? Ah, this.

'Did you ever shoot on the Kildalton property?'

'I did.'

'And you swam a small loch after some duck?'

'How did you come to hear that? It's rather interesting.'

'Not so interesting to me. I suffered for you. I was the guest of Talbot Clifton, who owns Kildalton Castle and forest. The first days' sport took the form of a correctional lesson for his head keeper, who had described some birds as having been seen "by Lord Lovat's loch".'

'By my loch?'

'Yes. It seems that you swam in after a wounded bird and so the deed was perpetuated by naming the loch after you. Now, the birds were as numerous as in an incubator, but it was not the birds that concerned my host but the fact that the keeper had forgotten to transfer his name to the loch you swam.

'My friend was six-foot-four in height, and when he jumped

suddenly down a steep bank into a four-foot torrent holding his gun high above his head, I was amazed because I could see a hundred yards upstream a pine tree cut plank-wise for a bridge. He waded across and made secret beckonings to me to come on, putting his fingers to his lips. Thinking that he had found some prehistoric quarry awakening from its pliocene slumber, I took the plunge and drowned the gun and very nearly myself. When I retrieved both he helped me up the bank and said, "Now Ramsay has to come on and he's not as tall as you; and this will teach him to talk about other people's lochs on my property." '

Lord Lovat was amused. He knew Talbot and what a sportsman he was, and, like every hereditary landowner, jealous about property.

'It must be hard to get Highlanders to leave Scotland?' Tim observed.

'It is much harder with Lowland miners. Segregation on a flat Canadian ice-bound prairie has little attraction for them.'

'They could not bring the mines with them, and if they did they would still be on the dole.'

The gathering of the guests for the cinema show grew audible.

'I wonder if we are segregating ourselves too long,' said Tim.

At this the ladies rose and curtsied to the half-risen Governor-General. He grunted, embarrassed somewhat; then turned to me at once when he had sat down.

'You were at the Senate to-day? Was there a debate on my Address?'

'There was a debate as to how to debate, and some confusion as to the procedure ... it seems that there are no standing orders framed to deal with either the hearing of or receiving the Governor-General's Address. Glenavy suggested summoning a meeting of Senators and informing them in the Summons that the Address would be open to consideration.

'The Earl of Wicklow asked "What address? The Governor-General's speech is not an address."

'Colonel Moore protested that an amendment which he handed in was objected to because there was to be no vote of thanks.

'Glenavy sat on him. "Really, it's too bad if the Senator

136

does not pay attention to what takes place in the Senate. I told the Senators that it was entirely a matter for them what their procedure would be. I suggested the best procedure until we had framed Standing Orders; and that recommendation of mine was adopted without the slightest dissent. I must say that I think it very unfortunate that any Senator should wish to go behind it, because it puts the rest of his colleagues in a very unpleasant position before the public and the country." '

'You're lucky in one thing. You have got the best Chairman in Europe to preside over you in the Senate,' said Tim.

I thought that very generous, for I remembered the well-known story how, when they were rival counsel, Mr Campbell, as Lord Glenavy then was, wept at the close of an action for divorce in which he represented the plaintiff. Tim rose, and, to undo the effect on the jury, with awful solemnity began: 'Gentlemen, we have witnessed to-day the greatest miracle since Moses struck the rock: tears from my learned friend.'

He was about to rise when I hastened to inquire, 'Sir, you know everyone in Cork, who is the Chieftain Harrington?'

'Oh, that humbug! Is he about again? I'll tell you all about him. He is one of those Americans who want to make the impression on other people that they failed to make in their own country. He left New York some years ago and . . .' – the pause before the thunder – 'his only recommendation was a kick in the rump. And now he's an Irish Chieftain. He picked up a rich Irish woman on the boat and married her.'

'He must have descended from his wife.'

'You'll see him any day walking, with white spats, beside a woman as fat as himself. Are you coming?'

Before it was darkened for the screen, the lecture-room looked gay enough with the uniforms of the men who had fought to hasten the settlement with Great Britain which is known as the Treaty. Many have claimed since the truce which preceded the treaty credit for a share in the warfare in which they were not endangered or engaged. But most of the men present went out in arms against Great Britain, and by so doing placed a halter round their necks which failure would draw tight. It was possibly born of his hatred of humbug that Tim Healy sought about in his mind for a sly dig at the post-truce heroes. Every one of them had half died for Ireland if you would believe them, or were related to those who had died. To them alone Ireland owed its freedom. Taking my arm, Tim whispered, moaning gravely in his deep voice, while his eyes twinkled as he indicated the assembly of a free country, 'Baldy Doody's pig has not died in vain.'

Canada may be cold enough, I thought, as I watched the Tibetan mountaineers screened sleeping in their cloaks at 19,000 feet, on icy Everest, in an atmosphere so moistureless that one side of your face could be frostbitten while the other was sunburned. The climber told of how at 19,000 feet, birds cease to fly; how the air in the columned glaciers became so disintegrated that it acted like laughing gas on the carriers; and how, for a while, it was thought that these men were drunk. I saw the awful frostbitten fingers, swollen like pears, and the heroic rescue of the sun-blinded doctor of the expedition. But what brought the rigour of the ascent most to mind was the casual remark that dropped and rang, as casual remarks usually do, into my consciousness, which at the moment was as receptive as a gong:

'At this elevation (26,000 feet) the climbers were taking sixty gasping breaths to every step they took upwards.'

As I went to thank the Governor-General for a most enjoyable evening, he said, 'On Tuesday I have to open the Spring Show. I want you to come here to lunch and to take some of the ladies in your car. I am afraid that you have disedified Sir John Simon with your *contes drôlatiques*. Good-night!'

As I drove home I forgot the deep satisfaction and faction in the town, thinking of the possibilities of a lecture on *The Disedification of Sir John Simon*.

CHAPTER EIGHT

Mr Cullinan was growing restless. I had asked him to dine and to meet Sir Horace. Mr Cullinan was the man who had subscribed the second largest sum towards the foundation of a paper for Sir Horace. Mr Doherty had been the greatest sponsor. Mr Cullinan is one of those Americans who are deprived by Nature of revealing their greatness in words. Had I not seen part of his fleet of bronze oil-tankers each as large as the liner to Holyhead, I should never have realized that I was in the presence of a man who could have bought an Irish county. I did realize that if Sir Horace was absent from dining much longer the charm which might well make such an experiment (in co-operation) possible would be broken, and Sir Horace might be judged on strictly business lines and found wanting in punctuality.

The servant called me to the telephone. There had been some firing audible as Mr Cullinan left his hotel. Mr Cullinan tried to glean some inkling of what the telephone message was from the man's countenance – a hopeless task; but I knew from the tension of a voice which I could judge that something serious was toward.

'Ah, my dear fellow, I am afraid that I will be late for dinner, so I just rang you up to ask you and your guests to have a little patience with me . . . No! no! You must not wait. You see, I have been held up on my own drive and my car has been stolen by armed men. It will take me a little time to get another car. But I will come along.'

The car of one of the most chivalrous, influential, and patriotic Irishmen stolen on his own avenue! By 'armed men'! I was sure that Sir Horace had not asked them for their 'officer'. I was not surprised; but how would Cullinan take it? What would he think of the wisdom of endowing a newspaper in the midst of a guerrilla war?

All I said was, 'Sir Horace has just rung up to say that he will be along presently. We are not to wait.'

'I hope nothing has happened to Sir Horace?'

Regarded in one way, that was the trouble. Nothing had

139

happened to Sir Horace during a life that was singularly thronged and ineffectual – about as ineffectual as Shelley's . . . In the swirl of thought ideas followed – Sir Horace has a nephew Shelley-like but hardly ineffectual: Sir Horace, when he should have been a military man, is a reformer; so was Shelley, when he should have been a monogamist.

'Mr Ryan, Mr Cullinan, we are to dine without Sir Horace. He will be here presently.'

No one should endeavour to entertain two American millionaires, at the same time, at the same table. They may be vegetarians, but they are not gregarious.

'That was during your Pittsburg period?'

'No, sir, I was never in Pittsburg for any period.'

'I should have said?'

'I do not know, sir, what you should have said: but you should not have said that my town is Pittsburg.'

'Mr Ryan, surely you know Mr Cullinan is the founder, we might say, of Houston, Texas. These succulent and delicious grape-fruits with their pink flesh are his gift. He travels about supplying his table, no matter where he stays, with the produce of his estates.'

The background of my mind was disturbed by wondering, would Sir Horace, with his usual imperturbability, ignore the cause of his delay in meeting his American admirers and turn it aside with a murmur of polite phrases? A shot, rather close, judging by its noise; but possibly far off, allowing for the echo of Ely Place, rang out. This recalled old times in Texas not, unfortunately not to Mr Cullinan of Texas, but to Mr Ryan of Philadelphia. If he loves his brother man he will put Philadelphia 'on the map'; but I want peace in mine inn until Sir Horace takes over.

'Mr Ryan,' I said, 'you may not know that Sir Horace has devoted his life to his country.' – Insincerely enough, I thought that Mr Ryan deserved this kind of clap-trap – 'There is hardly any act of his which is not in some way bound up with the advancement of his plans. "Advancement of his plans" should be one of those censored phrases.' Then, more daringly, 'We all know what those plans are?'

'Sure,' Mr Ryan replied.

Mr Cullinan, who had contributed in cash to the advancement of some of Sir Horace's plans, felt that he should assume

140

a proprietary air, at this juncture, over Sir Horace, and commenced to enumerate without elucidating the plans. I knew that he was a true disciple of Co-operation. Meanwhile, the mind of Mr Ryan was losing the freshness of its insight and becoming sicklied over by the paleness of Mr Cullinan's explanation.

' "Everything for Ireland",' I intoned pontifically, hoping that the emphasis of the asseveration would enable me to discover how Sir Horace's latest loss came under this category. For it was accepted by his disciples that everything he did, no matter how inexplicable, was bound up with Ireland . . . But we heard his voice in the hall. It sounded full of little hard, crackling consonants, inarticulate and cultivated monosyllabic sounds, not at all unpleasing. These preceded him into the room.

'Ha! ah! Aah! I am so glad to see that. Ah! It might have been worse had I let the soup grow cold . . . However, now that we are all together . . . there is . . . No? . . . Ah, don't mind me, I never eat soup . . . You have been at Battle Creek, Mr Cullinan? An excellent sanatorium. I am urging and making representations in the proper quarter, of course, for the necessity, the very urgent necessity of having a sanatorium in Ireland run on the lines of Battle Creek. Diet has not been considered: that is to say, the importance of diet has been overlooked in the treatment of medical cases – internal medicine, as they call it there.'

'Unless you ignore diet altogether, Sir Horace, do take a little food.'

'Ah, my dear Cullinan, you should know that two kinds of proteins, those represented by the potato and those by the flesh of lamb, are opposed and should not be taken together. In fact, in the potato alone there is almost sufficient to rear a family, as indeed families were reared in Ireland before the famine. Water, if I may.'

'We have progressed a long way since then, Sir Plunkett.'

Sir Horace looked almost coy, as one embarrassed by praise. Surely he cannot hold himself responsible for the improved condition since the famine? He was 'explaining' to Mr Ryan. By the end of the explanation Mr Ryan was confused, but vaguely conscious of Sir Horace in some *rôle* in which he was hardly distinguishable from Providence.

141

'We have only about one-third of our pre-famine population for whom to cater. The Home Brighteners have done exceeding well. They are devoted ladies who have helped enormously in the improvement of domestic conditions. They are associated with my I.A.O.S. They go into the cottages and make suggestions. The standards of living which are not wholly dependent in this country on wealth are considerably improved by their advice. What I mean is, that a farmer may be wealthy . . . I mean to say . . . suppose a poor farmer were to come into a considerable fortune, he would go on living as far as comfort and the raising of the standards were concerned, exactly as he had lived before and as his father had lived. The Home Brighteners . . .'

Crash! went a rifle in the street.

Mr Ryan said, 'I was talking to our friend here, Mr Cullinan of Pittsburg, Sir Horace, before you arrived. He tells me . . .'

Mr Cullinan rose with, 'Sir, I tell you here and now and once and for all . . .'

'Houston Texas, Galena!' I interjected.

'I can hear you, Cullinan, better if you remain seated,' Sir Horace drawled.

There was what would have been elsewhere an awkward interval. But that would have been in company which did not know Sir Horace. He went on as if resuming a conversation held in New York but a moment ago.

'Your two visits to Ireland, Cullinan, have given you an intimate knowledge of the present political situation, which cannot be understood without getting, as you have done, into close touch with the chief actors in this extraordinary drama. This experience will enable you to explain the complex state of our public affairs to other leading American friends of Ireland. (Mr Ryan had to come into this now or be for ever frozen out.) But also to place before them the project of re-starting the *Irish Statesman*.'

A bomb fell at the other side of St Stephen's Green or just behind Ely House. 'Echoes,' I murmured. It might have been a cork popping for all the deflection it caused in Sir Horace's flow of speech.

'In cases where you have to present the proposal by letter, it may be helpful if I here summarize the reasons why you and I, after many conferences . . .'

142

'Count me in on this, Sir,' Mr Ryan exploded.

Sir Horace took not notice. His confidences were Mr Cullinan's exclusive 'option'.

'. . . have come to the conclusion that a very real service may thus be rendered to those who are striving to bring order out of chaos' – another bomb – 'chaos', continued Sir Horace, 'into which Ireland, with her proverbial ill-luck, has once more been plunged.'

'She'll come right out,' Mr Ryan, reduced to the status of an acolyte, responded.

'As you know, Cullinan, the original journal had a brief career. The rapid rise in the cost of production . . .'

I waved the coffee aside.

'. . . exhausted the available funds, after it completed its first year of publication.'

How hard it would be to anticipate an end to one of Sir Horry's sentences! I found myself thinking.

'Competent observers are satisfied that the education it gave in Britain . . .'

Mr Ryan nodded. 'Competent observers.' But he was losing his chance of becoming one of Great Britain's educators. Cullinan was about to be made *for Ireland* a 'Matthew Arnold' under Sir Horace.

'The Dominions, and the United States (Ryan, how fallen!), were factors in enabling – some say compelling – the British Government to make our country the largest political concession in the long history of the Anglo-Irish conflict.'

'And to think that I only backed Mick Collins!' thought Mr Cullinan's rival.

'It had no small influence in persuading Irishmen that they can now enjoy in common . . .'

But the share in Ireland's greatness that Sir Horace was not inclined too readily to share, brought the business men, starved all their lives of imagination, to his feet. His perfect, cool rhythm made their eagerness to enter at the eleventh hour, as it were, the vineyard of Sir Horace seem indecorous.

'Freedom to develop the human and material resources of this country . . .'

Somebody broadcasting for the resources of civilization threw another bomb nearer to the festive board.

'. . . but even when peace is restored, the Government will

143

need for this task a far clearer realization than now prevails in Ireland of the scope and limitations of that representative and responsible Government . . .'

His nephew, Lord Dunsany, is a poet in a far less hackneyed and constricted field than this in which Sir Horace's imagination towers. Who has the greater power of compelling dreams?

Dunsany wrote: *The Kind of Elfland's Daughter* – our best modern example of romantic prose. Sir Horace wrote (helped by Æ) *Ireland at the Cross Roads* – (where it always has been, and shall be). Dunsany banished politics into Elfland: Sir Horace restored Elfland to politics.

'For the first time in seven hundred years,' the crackling voice went on. What a response that 'seven hundred years' is striking! 'with this indication of the general end in view . . .'

Dunsany's imagination appeals to imagination. But his uncle can create imagination even in millionaires. Judged by the fundamental brainwork . . . Oh, but he is marvellous! I must look upon him as a prose poet and a leader of the leaders of men. And he does it all by merely adumbrating, never expressing an idea.

'I will now set down the precise method by which it is to be attained . . .'

'Precise method' is good. 'Mobled' is good! But how wrong I was! His next sentence refuted me.

'There will be registered in Dublin the Irish Statesman Publishing Company, Ltd.'

I, who hate all business talks, plans, constructions, and syndicates, was casting about to escape, when one of his mesmerized millionaires inquired:

'Say, Sir Horace, may I call on you to-morrow?'

'I am afraid I shall be entertaining a British Cabinet Minister. But, let me see . . . I will get Longworth to telephone to you when we ascertain how our day is taken up. But why not come out and lunch with us at Kilteragh? – and meet Mr Fisher?'

'Delighted.'

If I am to prove a good host I must know my cue. Everyone could count on Sir Horace's being too tired to do more than to permit some rich American to distinguish himself by an exceeding-greatly-rewarding subscription to Ireland's illimitable future.

'Sir Horace is tired,' I said. 'If you will go upstairs you will find that some people have called who are anxious to meet you. I will run Sir Horace home.'

Sir Horace groaned accordingly.

'Now that is very good of you indeed. Once cannot do more than give rich men a chance of expressing themselves against the background of the Nation. Meanwhile, what is the least valuable car you have? Naturally, with all this highway robbery there are no taxis, and if I stay here for the night as you so very kindly suggest, Kilteragh may be burned.'

As we passed in my Ford with its left-hand drive the church at Donnybrook, and the long walls were beginning, Sir Horace asked, 'Have you a gun?'

'Two.'

'Let me take them. You cannot do two things at a time, and I have been in Texas. You must not mind if I shoot at sight. The important thing is to carry on.'

'The safety-catch is on.' I heard a click.

With the wind-screen raised as high as it would go, I drove rapidly through the dangerous darkness. With the corner of my eye I could see Sir Horace, wiry and alert, with a parabellum in one hand and a 43-Colt in the other, weaving them warily side to side in a small arc.

'They seized my car on the lower drive. They will hardly expect me to return the same way, therefore let us return by it.'

'They have cleared off long ago, fearing reprisals,' I asserted.

As the small, fearless figure sat beside me, I remembered the suit of armour in Dunsany Castle where Sir Horace was born. I thought that it was only a figure such as his that would fit into it. Back into the Past I rejected him – the beginnings of his family tree, a Norman knight repelling a raid against the bretesche which must have stood on the great mound or motte which guarded with wooden tower the road to Tara before the stone castle which stands beside the great dun was built.

The Norman-French crackled in my ears.

'Steady, men! Keep your horses on firm ground! Stop the pursuit there! Let them hide in the woods!' My mind flew back to the present, hardly to be distinguished from my dream.

'They have cleared off long ago, fearing reprisals,' I repeated.

'I expect they have. By Gad! it's remarkable how history repeats itself. The indigenous Irish could never do more than

145

raid and burn, because they resisted the discipline of their chiefs who might have kept them longer in the field. Once they found themselves confronted with asbestos block houses of stone which they could not burn, castles as they call them now, which protected for the Normans both serf and steer, they had no organization to conduct a siege.'

'They lacked co-operation,' I ventured.

'Ah, spasmodic destruction was the only way in which their militarism could find expression; and you cannot found a civilization on that. Now to-night, they may take our car, your car, as mine has been taken, they may set fire to Kilteragh and I will lose my library: but are they any nearer to a civilized way of living?'

'Don't let their pretensions excuse their performance. They are nothing but a lot of rogues and ruffians calling robbery Republicanism.'

The locked-up houses were ominously still. The long demesne walls which flanked the road, with their belts of trees within them, were ideal for a snipers' ambush. When I am in danger I grow exalted, which is a form of excitement little different from hysteria. Probably my flood of talk was distracting Sir Horace. He interrupted me with a cackled, 'Ha! It has just occurred to me that, unless they want to collect every car on the road, they will not take this, for they cannot possibly know who are in it. We will only be identified by going into Kilteragh. I may relax a little. There is always a certain amount of strain in being on the *qui vive*.'

He crossed the pistols in his lap.

'Every country goes through this kind of thing, raids and destruction, at some time or other. The remarkable thing is that Ireland has gone through it so often. It never appears to learn a lesson.'

I thought of the Border forays and the relish of the balladist as he recounted the harrying:

> Now they have harried the dales of Tyne;
> And burned all Bamboroughshire;
> And Eskadale, they have brent it hale,
> And left it a' on fire.

The glaze through the night! Ireland, too, all on fire!

'The side-lights should be sufficient about here. We turn to the right, then right again up the drive. You can go straight on through the other gate. I hardly think . . . Ah, my dear fellow, this is all right. I will jump out. Do not stop the engine . . . No, on second thoughts, go right round the rockery and back by the way we came. It is too obvious that a driver in a hurry would carry on through the second gate. It is really extremely kind of you. Safe journey! The guns are on the seat.'

I had neither the courage nor the *sang froid* of Sir Horace. The night for me was peopled by surly men nursing an immemorial grievance or inventing one to justify outrage to their peculiar consciences. 'Traditious obscurities.' It was no use to drive off in a hurry. If one could not pull up when the highwaymen stood in the road, it meant a hail of bullets through the wind-screen. I thought of Sir Horace's drive in midday against a storm of British bullets. What a stormy petrel he is: I hope no adverse mascot. I wish I were driving home some stout fellow like Joe Magrath. It is half-past eleven. There are the lights of Kingstown and Blackrock. There is something encouraging in a light. The fighting Greeks hoped, if they had to die, for sunlight. Electric light would be better than this midnight darkness about Kilteragh. At Blackrock I became heroic retrospectively. But soon I became indignant. Here am I, Irish of the Irish, to save my property, running away from Irishmen, and for no other fault than I backed Arthur Griffith, who, as assuredly as Sir Horace Plunkett did, fell among thieves. They can hide in the woods. But Griffith is exposed to the howling storm of ingratitude, an Irish Lear, with Goneril and Regan, aye, and Cordelia too; for Ireland has three characters, like the three ladies whom the hero of the old Dublin ballad 'As I was going down Sackville Street' informs us that he 'chanced to meet.'

CHAPTER NINE

Kylemore House, Connemara, stands on Kylemore Lake, which lives clothed in purple and silver under windows lit by the southern sun. A blue-eyed giant of a man, with a golden goatee, is standing by the door giving orders to his spaniel, Judy, his chauffeur, Timmins, and his Scots terrier, Billy, at the same time. 'In Judy! Keep the door open, can't you? . . . Billy, come along!' His silver Lanchester is simmering in front of the house, against the wall of which a salmon-rod is leaning with the fly stuck into the cork of the handle. He has tried a spell of fishing, but it was too bright. He cannot remain inactive. He is driving seven miles to look up his next-door neighbour. He is coming to see me.

My house, too, stands on a lake, but it stands also on the sea. Water-lilies meet the golden seaweed. It is as if, in the faery land of Connemara at the extreme end of Europe, the incongruous flowed together at last; and the sweet and bitter blended. Behind me, islands and mountainous mainland share in a final reconciliation at this, the world's end. I am sitting on a little terrace overlooking the lake, watching the wider shimmer of the ocean beyond a thin line of green in the middle distance. It is good to let the eyes relax and to lose accommodation on wide prospects.

A butterfly, like a small, detached flame, is making excellent landings on the faintly pink blossoms of the thorn. Two bees disturb him alternately. But there is no harm done, and the morning is flowing on, filled with brightness and peace. No trout ring the lake with sudden ripples. It is too sunny for fishing: trout should pray for '*mehr licht*'. The indolent sound of waves receding from the shelves of gravel on the beach near by, or the singing of some insect projectile, are all the ear can discern.

Behind me a wing of the long sea-grey house stretches for forty yards. In the evening the lake will send the westering sun dancing on the dining-room panels, the oak of which sun and age have reddened until it looks like the mahogany of a later day.

The sun is shining up at me from the lake and down on me from the sky. We have not long to live in the sun; and here even the sunlight is not assured. Therefore let us enjoy it while we may.

'Work while ye have the light.' What an idea! As if one were an Italian navvy. It sounds like something from one of those Hebrew 'Prophets' who prophesied nothing but uncomfortable things, or from that pre-Bolshevic, Leo Tolstoi. While the sun shines is the time to enjoy life.

O quid beatius solutis curis!

As the poet said whom mistresses and mortgages had never left carefree.

Galway is always inclined for peace. They called it a rest-cure for Black-and-Tans in the 'Troubles'. At any rate, it is fairer and more peaceful than Dublin is at the present moment. It is good for me to be here where no one comes to break in on my rich indolence.

Ah, but a warning horn is blown on the crest of the rising ground which flows in a semi-circle round the house. A great car dashes up the drive and grooves the gravel into brown lines as it is pulled up. My friend the Squire of Lytham, now residing at Kylemore House, has come to call. He is one of the mightiest sportsmen in the world. I, the introvert, am caught by the greatest extrovert I have ever known. What have I to say for myself? Convert him to loafing and inviting his soul? A hopeless hope! He has taken it for granted, since I was given no chance to deny it, that I share his passion for sport. And I have not the courage to protest now, and to lose caste, however undeservingly gained. Were I to disavow it now, I would die in his opinion and he would lose a friend.

He hailed me in a jerky, deep-sounding voice.

'Hell-el-lo! If you haven't been fishing, why aren't you out shooting seals?'

I answered somewhat evasively, 'It's too bright for fishing, and even if it were not, the bottom feeding is so good here that the big trout never rise in this lake. I once caught nine, all over two pounds, in ten minutes, during a hot wind from the west; but that was long ago. I haven't had a rise since.'

This seemed to give him food for thought. Evidently, to him it was a matter of concern. I dared not say that I had never fished since that memorable day. It would have been honester than to let him go on puzzling his brains challenged by such an important problem, to give me good advice. After a while he jerked out cheerfully:

'I'll tell you what you must do. Drain the whole lake.'

'The whole lake? But how?'

'Oh, have it pumped out. Then, very, very carefully . . . sod it. Then let the water in again; and stock it with rainbow trout. You see? Rainbow.' To him, with the wealth of Lytham, St Anne's, and the half of Blackpool behind him, it was a simple and necessary proceeding.

'Already I have lost a hundred acres through the agitation of Canon McAlpine, who butted in to make mischief out of his own parish. If an additional hundred acres of good grazing land were to appear at the lake's bottom, I would have other people's black cattle up to the windows of my house.'

'Why did you give the hundred acres up?'

'Oh, I did not want them. So long as the lake is not contaminated, and I am left with a certain amount of privacy, I don't care who grazes. But I did care when I lost my forty-acre wood of ash trees with its green arches carpeted by lawns. An ash wood is the cleanest wood there is. And the poor fools who felled it, felled it to use the wood for fuel while they sold the coal they got in relief during a shortage of turf. Now, like all ignorant peasants who hate trees, they have left themselves with no winter grazing or shelter for their cattle. And there is no milk in this district from November until May . . . Their children are their victims, fed on stewed tea until they are old enough to enter the asylums, where their parents should have been.

'Damn it all,' he said, not so much in commiseration as annoyance at the problem invincible ignorance presents. Then he bent down and played with his dog. Suddenly he rose, to his full height, and with, 'Come along', moved towards his car. As he stood, I marvelled at the figure of the man. He was very tall and straight, but his hips had an un-English appearance. Something of the Arab, I wondered?

'What about a drink?' I asked.

'I never allow myself a drink until after six o'clock.'

He looked out over the sea and made several suggestions.

'What you should do is to keep a motor-launch here. You

150

should open up the outlet from that lake of yours so that the salmon and white trout may get up.'

But there was something on his mind which he had not revealed.

'Also, you must put down some grouse. But have the vermin destroyed first.'

'But where can I get the grouse?'

'Yorkshire. I will get you as many as you want.'

'The Irish grouse is a bigger bird with more comb. I don't wish to mix the breed.'

'That's all very well, but if there are no Irish birds to shoot why not get hybrids that you can shoot?'

'Thanks for the tip.'

After a pause: 'It looks a good day for having a pot at some seals?'

'Last year I shot twelve, and only recovered one. They sink.'

'Then how did you get the one?'

'I went overboard for it and caught it by the flipper. It dived between my knees, and I turned an under-water somersault.'

'Very stupid thing to do. Now let me tell you, when I was with the Esquimaux, the thing was to use a light harpoon. We'll get a harpoon with a very long shaft: then . . . !' He transfixed a visionary seal.

'It's rather murderous shooting them at all. They come out of curiosity quite close to the boat with their intelligent brown eyes, wondering what you are doing so far out at sea.'

This was too much for the great hunter.

'Ho! Don't forget that they are ruining the salmon-fishing in my lakes. They take a piece out of the shoulder of the fish and then leave it to die. They should be shot. The harpoon's the thing.'

'I don't want to land them. Nobody can cure hides properly here. The few skins I have are like Zulu shields.'

The treatment of the skins of the grey Atlantic seal did not interest him. He was considering the ways and means of getting them.

'What kind of boat did you use?'

'The ordinary curragh. It is a most sea-worthy boat, though it is only made of canvas stretched on wicker.'

'Hopeless! We must get a launch . . . By the way, how did you get back again into the curragh?'

'Over the stern. You wait for a wave and heave yourself in. It is impossible to do it at the side.'

'I should think so. Now, lookey here . . .'

'Yes?'

He walked over to his car. As he walked he said, 'Do you see that Lanchester? Now, the gears of that car are never out of mesh. It has a continuous gear. You can slip into reverse at seventy-five and come very slowly, very slowly to a standstill; and then, very slowly back.' He illustrated the gentleness of the reversing movement by his hands, which he held parallel as if about to join them in reverence.

I knew where an implied disparagement was being aimed. I was not going to have my Rolls disparaged. I became brave, for I knew that at one time he had six Rolls-Royces to take his friends about his Scots shoots. 'Who wants to slip into reverse at seventy-five? Has it no brakes? I should simply hate to find myself going backwards.'

'Not the point, not the point. The point is in the gearbox – worm drive!'

'Leave the worm that turns; and come along into the house.' I had a feeling that there was something on his mind which for once was not a problem concerning game.

In the library he produced a large golden fountain pen, which he laid on an inkstand, and, turning away from it abruptly, 'I want you to have that,' he said.

He cut short my expostulations with, 'From me.' Then he flung himself into an arm-chair and, with a change of voice, began: 'Now lookey here! I came over to ask your opinion. I want to go over to see my cousin Lonsdale next week . . .' He paused, as if embarrassed by having to take counsel with anyone but himself. Then solemnly, 'Do you think if I leave Kylemore, my wife and children will be molested?'

'Surely not! Certainly not.'

'You are living in a fool's paradise, my friend.'

I could have answered, 'I prefer to be in a fool's paradise than in the Board-room of a rationalist,' or 'Just at the present in Ireland, if one is to be loyal to the Government it is necessary to be a fool.' But it was the wrong moment for facetiousness when such a man was struggling to confide in me. Instead, I exclaimed:

'Nobody molests women and children in Ireland.'

152

'There is a lot of unrest, far more widespread than you seem to realize. You may be the first to suffer.'

'I? But I have never done the people any harm.'

'That's just it. You see, I have been in many uncivilized places where human life was of little consequence. I have met savages of every description. And the worst position you can place yourself in with them is to do them no harm.'

I thought – 'Anoint a villain, he will prick you: prick a villain, he will anoint you.' Then aloud: 'Do you think you will be attacked?'

'Oh, no! I do not think it. I told them what they may expect if they come sneaking about my place. But it's while the man is away that these kind of fellows gather courage and show it by intimidating the women and children. I thought you knew something about the people among whom you are living.'

'Well, all I can say is, that I will be astounded if Irishmen attack women and children in a defenceless house.'

He drew within himself. Suddenly the awful thought struck me – 'Can he suspect that I am only lulling him into a false security? Does he really believe that I am living in a fool's paradise and am not in collusion with *canaille* who would avenge themselves on women and children?' I felt uncomfortable and embarrassed. I almost wished that I were attacked first, to exonerate me from all suspicion of duplicity to such a fine fellow. Nor was I relieved when he suddenly leaped up with, 'Well, I'll be getting back.'

I thought of his tall, dark, beautiful wife, his little daughters and his two sons, still children. As I pondered I began to have misgivings. How much 'hang over' of hatred, centuries old, remained in the country to instigate 'Revenge, by Jayshus! on the Sassenach'? True, the hatred had become more or less diverted into civil war, Irishmen hating Irishmen. Hatred's the thing! Perhaps the English would be overlooked. Then I remembered the louts who were playing at campaigning by stealing motor-cars: Sir Horace's, one of mine. Talbot Clifton had three cars at least at Kylemore.

'If I thought as you do, I would not go.'

'I have no intention of going just yet. I wanted to talk with you. That's all.' He only waved his hand as he drove off. He did not look back. I was left feeling uncomfortable for the rest of the day.

Damn the vampire dead who have left us nothing but an heritage of hatred which operates equally against the 'Foreigner' and against ourselves. In the Tenth and Eleventh Centuries the natives took sides with the foreigner. Against him now, and, a year later, allied to him, with the facility of the professional footballer for changing sides. Post-mortem hatred met by living suspicion of all our tribe makes a comely life impossible.

There was never a more attractive man than Talbot Clifton in many ways; but now I stood before him mottled by the corruption of a dead hate, whilst he was poisoned by living suspicion. Damn the dead! When will they cease to infect both Irish and English with their mortality? Here am I, who never 'let down' any man, a suspect and an accomplice against my will, and through no fault of mine, in every fatuous act and brainless brutality of the past, of the present, and of days to come. The 'he who is not with us is against us' of the narrow sect! A curse on both their houses of hate. They stand between me and my friend. Is there no place in Ireland for a man of good will? There is in the monasteries, perhaps; but even monasteries provide no unbroken sanctuary in Erin.

There are many burnings besides the burning of the church of Cashel's rock to be remembered, before the English or the Foreigners could be accused of producing any excuse for such outrages. No; even the house of God is not safe when the tribal passions of Ireland are aroused. The object lesson of peace and aloofness from passion which they provide seems to have aroused vindictiveness all the more. And if this be so, what chance is there for me and for Talbot Clifton to be left to the enjoyment of neutrality? None. I should have pointed that out to him. But to make him believe it I should have to be victimized first. And I have not the least desire to be a martyr to 'smallholders' even to show how right I am.

Leisure, and the accoutrements of leisure, lakes preserved, pictures, silver, and motor-cars, these are as red rags to the congenital 'Reds' – the under-dogs of all time. We shall be 'taught a lesson'. In other words, all we possess that is the outcome of the creative imagination of artists who had the leisure to dream and to give their dream a local habitation, all that took time and loving care to accomplish, be it the cover of the Book of Kells or a silver inkstand, by all that appertains to a household

154

of continuance, aye, even the house itself must be destroyed. And not that anything may live but hate.

If this were told to me by anyone else, I would believe in it so much that I would at this moment follow Clifton and warn him to take himself and all he held dear to the safety of a country which has had only one or two civil wars. But in my case performance follows slowly on prevision. I know what will happen, but so great is the margin of the incalculable in Ireland that I wait to see. Should I have told him that fifteen pounds of mine was stolen from a post-bag in the name of the Republic which gathers public property? I only withheld the knowledge out of shame. Were he to hear it now, nothing would convince him but that I, through jealousy or some such motive entertained by 'natives', was planning to have a rival expelled. In England he rivalled successfully the greatest sportsmen, from his cousin Lonsdale down. But he was no rival of mine. To become my rival he must needs loaf for weeks refraining himself from many things. He had the mind of a child in many ways. Some of his visits to me were due to his preference for the site of my house to that of his own. I had both lake and sea. He had only lakes. And the sea was seven miles from him. He had bought a derelict place, restored, equipped it, and now he was running it expensively. He considered me, humble as I was, a rival because Nature was my fairy godmother!

Petey, who was low-sized and broad-shouldered, because he was a hunchback, said: 'there's an Englishman at Leenane helping the Republicans.' He waited ready to interpret my comment later on, to my greatest disadvantage.

'How do you know?'

'The Beach told me.'

'And what did he say?'

'Just that.'

'But how did he know?'

'He heard him drilling them, and giving them orders and telling them tactics.' (Tactics: my fifteen pounds!)

Now, I knew this well. Mrs Clifton took pity on him, and invited him to dinner. He must be so upset by his own tragedy that he must come over to upset this tragical country. But to discuss him with Petey would be, no matter what I said, twisted

155

into an excuse for the conscientious ruffians who were by some cowardly euphemism called 'Irregulars' to annex some more of my belongings. Petey threw the net again.

'They have taken – commandeered' – he corrected to a military word for robbery – 'Mr Clifton's big car.'

For a moment I was shocked but soon that something 'not altogether unpleasing in the misfortunes of our friends' came to me, or rather, anticipation of the misfortunes which would rapidly follow my non-friends who had stolen Clifton's car, consoled me. They were in for it now. The Lanchester was the apple of his eye. His fearless blue eyes would blaze.

On Sunday I came back from church to find my house had been ransacked by armed men, 'looking for Mr Clifton'. On the breakfast-table was a red silk handkerchief, thrown down carelessly. It contained a diamond tiara, a large pendant and many more jewels. The frightened servants said that Mrs Clifton had been in.

'How did she come?'

'In a pony trap.'

So they had stolen all Clifton's motors, and he himself was hunted. What could have happened? He never would have left his wife and family to the mercy of the ruffians who stole his cars. Things must be bad at Kylemore when, in her desperation, she tried to save her jewels by getting them over to me. Mysteriously my one available car had ceased to be available. I could not go over to make inquiries. The journey might cost me my car, and cost her her jewels. I wondered if the servants had seen the handkerchief full of diamonds on the breakfast-table. I knew I was being watched. If I buried them, I would be observed. The best thing to do was to take them to Dublin as soon as the car could be put in order, and then travel by night circuitously. Surely Clifton's three cars would satisfy the rabble for the present.

I began to realize how the country victims of the French Revolution felt, and how it came about that, in spite of their numbers, they never organized themselves generally to resist. They were lulled separately into a false security because each family believed, until it was too late, that their relations with the local tenantry would make their case exceptional. Even if the local tenantry loved them, the new passions in the air abolished loyalties and any affection that might have been

156

hereditary; but what none of them realized was the fact that, willy nilly, the local tenantry were themselves the victims of a grim central gang who could order the outlying units to arrest their own parents if need be. (In some cases this may have been done unwittingly.) Thus it was, so gradually did the civil war affect us, that we took but little notice of it locally and ignored the extent to which it had spread. *Ucalagon ardet!* But, though next door, it did not necessarily mean a conflagration for me.

Presently the news came in, magnified by rumours. Petey said that Mr Clifton had ambushed his own car and had shot one of the men who had stolen it. This had a great effect upon the narrator. He was frightened.

'I take off my hat to him, Petey,' I said. 'You can tell them that when you are making your report about me. He has only given them a taste of what they have been giving to others.'

Petey was frightened. He began at once to agree with me, but tentatively.

'Oh, sir, indeed yes. These are terrible times, anyway.'

One would think that the times had put themselves out of joint. I got rid of Petey and prepared to go to see Mrs Clifton, to hear, if possible, what had happened.

But she had gone to the nearest secure place, Galway, fifty miles away, and had taken the children and some of her belongings with her.

This is what had taken place. The day after his visit to me, Clifton's Lanchester had been seized in his absence by a gang of men and used on journeys between Leenane and Clifden. This brought it past his doors. The thought of his farm-hands taking their girls to fairs and races in his car! It was insufferable. Having seen it pass to Letterfrack and knowing that it would return about midnight, he took his Star two-seater and his Ford, and barricaded the way at a crossroad some few furlongs to the east of his house where the ground rose high enough to cause a car to slow down. He waited alone, with his Purdey in his hand; alone, to hold up, how many armed men? He did not care. After a while the great headlights could be seen searching out the invisible hills, sweeping up and down as the front springs gave to the bumpy road. He could hear the hum of the engine at intervals. Nearer and nearer it came on. At last the full blaze of the headlights met his obstructing cars. He switched on his lamps and stepped out from the darkness.

'Hands up!'

All threw up their hands. One occupant of the stolen car could only obey partially. He was a prisoner. His arms were tied at the elbows, behind his back. In the tension of the silence as the stately figure approached, one man's nerve went. He leaped out of the car and started to run back, onwards to Leenane. Thinking he was about to execute a flanking movement, Clifton let him get almost out of range, then discharged a barrel at him. Mrs Clifton suspecting what was toward now arrived on the scene, imploring for mercy: 'You can get many Lanchesters; but you cannot bring back human life!' She hampered her husband's movements. This gave the gang time to draw their revolvers and to threaten Clifton. Neither side would yield. Mrs Clifton extracted a promise from the car-stealers that if they were allowed to keep the car they would not alarm her children nor molest her house. They promised accordingly. But later, armed men notified Clifton that if he did not leave Ireland that night they 'would not be responsible' for his safety. Single-handed against a whole countryside, without telephone or any means of summoning aid, with the lives of a family which he could neither remove nor protect against a host, the only chance of saving them lay in falling in with their conditions.

In the dawn he drove across the island with his valet and a suitcase, knowing quite well how little Republican promises could be relied on to curb the itch for destruction.

This was the result of the promise not to molest his family:

> *'Oglaigh na H-Eireann,*
> *Headquarters,*
> *4th Western Division,*
> *Castlebar.*
> 14/3/22

To Mrs Clifton,
Kylemore, Connemara.

On the night of March 12th, 1922, your husband, Talbot Clifton, with others who are known to me, lay in ambush at a point on the main road between Kylemore and Leenane, and fired at officers of this Division who were proceeding to Castlebar.

As a result of the shots fired, Captain Eugene Gilan of the Irish Republican Army is now hovering between life and

158

death in Mr McKeown's Hotel, Leenane. I am satisfied from information received, that you also participated in the ambush, and this is to notify you that an armed guard will be placed on your premises, and that you, Mrs Clifton, are to leave Connemara before 12 noon, Monday, 27th. Otherwise other steps will be taken.

If you desire to make any statement, it will be necessary for you to come to Castlebar, and I promise you a safe conduct.

(Signed) MICHAEL KILROY.

G.O.C. 4th Western Division,

I.R.A.

N.B. – The armed guard will remain on your premises pending the return of your husband.'

As the outcome of this intimidation, Mrs Clifton drove away with her jewels to Renvyle. We were out at the time, so she left them on the breakfast-table, and hastened back to Kylemore to prepare for the journey to Galway without delay. Her children were more precious than her gems, and if waylaid for the prize the precious stones offered, she could say that she had left them behind.

There was little time to be lost if we were not to be marooned. Roads were dyked, bridges broken, trains derailed. Yet before I set out for Dublin with her treasures I went to Leenane.

I could not find the teacher of tactics. But it gave me little comfort to reflect that, though they exonerated me from suspicion, this Englishman's tactics led directly to the theft of his host's car. It was not the Irish this time who were wholly responsible for Irish miscreancy, but one of this country's particular curses, the renegade Englishman who invariably inflicts, morally and materially, more damage on Ireland than he would be suffered to inflict at home. In spite of their adoption of Gaelic names there is hardly an 'O' or a genuine 'Mac' prominent in Irish rebellions. Since the days when Englishmen revolted in Boston against their King, they have been renegading in every country but their own.

I wonder, is the popularity of the Gaelic language due to the camouflage it provides for English names?

The only worse thing than this intrusion of the English renegade is the female of the species. We have both.

I went into the bar, where men were hulking and drinking their melancholy from pint measures. I learnt nothing. They stood silently.

The jewels reached Dublin safely. West valued some of them for insurance. There were others he could not value, for they were unmatchable and irreplaceable. These were the brown diamonds her husband had given Mrs Clifton because they matched her eyes. The insurance rates on the first consignment were so prohibitive, for even the post was not safe, that an employee of the Estate Office was sent from Lytham to bring the remainder to their owner.

Perhaps it is just as well to be back in Dublin, I thought. Not that anyone is safe against the Mafia if once it marks him down; but it at least will not be a case of 'Lonely unto the Lone I go', as it would be if I were to be kidnapped in the country. A gallery must make dying easy for the vain or the contemptuous. But to be done in seven to one in a cellar underground would be likely to make too great a demand on a man's courage, even though it equalled his fate with that of the Tsar. There were forces in the country not too widely to be differentiated from the forces and inflaming sentiments that led to the cowardly murder of the women and children of that unhappy king, forces that were bound to grow in the land if its prosperity was diminished, or if justice became venal and relaxed.

As I left West's, I ran into Kevin. I told him of my errand and Clifton's ambush.

'Do you know that Kilteragh, Sir Horace Plunkett's house, is destroyed by fire from the revolving box on the roof, in which he used to sleep, to its cellars?' he said. 'Nothing was salvaged. The mentality that could ruin not only the frequent home but the repository of some of the best work of Irish artists is hard to analyse, and harder still is it to present the results of the analysis in a credible way.'

'Don't think I don't know it,' I answered. 'The chief factor in the obscurities, traditious or spontaneous, of this mentality is Resentment. This resentment is not necessarily political at all, but is born of the under-dog's envy of the man who can build. Dull resentment against the cultivated and apparently idle

160

and leisured figure is an attitude of mind not at all confined to Ireland, but found in almost every country where there is civilization, for civilization itself is the enemy of the under-dog. And its disappearance will not help him. Civilization is a veneer on the unremitting forces that seek to drag down all that is elevated. It is a veneer on a quagmire that underlies all blossoming. The periods of what we call the efflorescence of the arts or the great cultural periods hardly exceeded fifty years in the history of any country. And when we remember in this paradoxical country that its own period of artistry was contemporary with a time of raids and burnings, we can hardly look to the villain to respect the outcome of an ordered life so much as to spare specimens or examples of it. Even if it were possible to separate from the political the biological characteristics of civilization, they are better omitted.

'The best pictures George Russell painted were those he painted for his friends, the men he loved. Thus Kilteragh held the finest examples of his art. It held books, all the first editions of the short-lived movement that placed Ireland amongst the nations whose citizens were awarded the largest international prize in history for eminence in the arts. It held letters from every great contemporary, corner-stones of future history, if this country is to remain an historical country and not to become a fermentation that matures nothing, but merely sours all that brews.'

'Hold on,' he said, 'you have not heard half the destruction nor half the humbug.'

The Earl of Mayo lost his house. Sir Horace's family established themselves in Ireland in the twelfth century. The Earl of Mayo was a Burke, a de Burgo. No, they were not as Irish as the non-historical Irish or the Firbolg failures, or as those who came over thirty years ago from England to teach Ireland how to be Irish. That is the second ingredient in the mentality of destruction, a reserved belief or feeling that the native has a longer history, and therefore has more claim to a land he never honoured, ornamented, or owned. The third arises from that frustration which makes him wish to remove all traces of what mocks his incompetence and points a finger at his failure. When these passions are aroused and justified by a national movement, by a fiery cross, you can imagine the result. But it is not, alas, left to the imagination.

161

It was saddening and maddening. What was there to do but to curse the half-breed who had split our country? But what was the use? Public representatives are the results, not causes, of popular behaviour. It is better to regard them as *les yeux du bouillon*, the grease-spots that floated to the surface in the cauldron in which Beatrice Cenci boiled her father. 'And the eyes of the soup were the eyes of her father', as George Moore loved to quote from his friend Villiers de l'Isle Adam. They are the grease-spots in the Irish stew; and as results they are not to be blamed for causes. But wait a moment! – I said to myself, thinking of the tendency that representative Government has to become static, *i.e.*, not immediately amenable to the national need or popular demand in an emergency; and with its power of resisting a general election for years, maybe, combined with power to abrogate Parliament or to draw some red herring of a 'war' across the trail when it should go honestly to the country; the public man or, as he has become, the party leader, is to be held almost personally responsible for public defalcations and outrages. Never was there such an instance of the responsibility of one man within the country, and he not an Irishman, for the country's wrongs. Our ruin is more one man's doing than ever before in Irish history since Cromwell.

'And freely to speak my thoughts, it argues a strange self-love and great presumption to be so fond of one's own opinions, that a public peace must be overthrown to establish them, and to introduce so many inevitable mischiefs, and so dreadful a corruption of manners, as a civil war and the mutations of state consequent to it always bring in their train, and to introduce them in a thing of so high concern, into the bowels of one's own country.'

Sir Bryan Mahon's house is burned.

Sir Thomas Esmonde's house is burned. He had an ancestor hanged for fighting for Ireland in '98.

If the English proletariat, nine-tenths of whom are wage-earners, choose to elect a Government nine-tenths of whom are landowners or capitalists, they may expect but little relief from the employers and masters of men. But England can trust its aristocracy; and the system which it has spun voluntarily from its own vitals, to maintain and safeguard above all individual liberty. Ireland cannot trust a system which has been taken over and retained and worked for the opportunity it

162

affords of the most unworthy as a rule attaining office and an income they would not have a chance of obtaining in an open market. The Irish people do not trust their Government. They elect it, hoping to lead it when it comes into power. That is why Ireland always outruns its 'leaders'. The leaders are well aware of this and stop short of few subterfuges to retain their leaders' jobs. Thus it comes about that into the hands of one man in Ireland, and he not an Irishman, was placed the power to do Ireland more harm than any external 'tyrant' in the last hundred years ever did: never did, if what she had to lose in the old days be compared with what she has lost in these our times.

And thus the Irish farmer has, by exercise of his vote, only succeeded in placing over him, instead of the old-fashioned landlord, a new inhuman and merciless vote-buying and tax-collecting syndicate.

The calibre of the men who tried to be superior to Arthur Griffith may be judged, if the documents and reports of the dispute regarding the Treaty (a dispute that should never have arisen) be hard to come by, from their behaviour against the majority of our countrymen after the Treaty was signed and partly repudiated by members of this group. I go so far as to say that Irishmen, if left to themselves unfomented and un-instigated by alien foolishness or knavery, would soon settle into a give-and-take existence. Little constructive, much *laissez-faire*. The one man who could have given them an interesting and progressive policy was Sir Horace Plunkett. His house was the first to go. He tried to co-operate with, and not to exploit, serfs that could only sulk and conspire when not exploited.

I said: 'If Government could be so simplified that a cook could govern Russia, then a market gardener should govern Ireland. Instead of this, it is governed by born blunderers and the banks. And this in a country that has less than half the population of London, which is governed by a few aldermen and a Lord Mayor. Three Commissioners reduced Dublin's rates in a year. Three Commissioners could run the whole country, which is not half so complicated as the City of Dublin. But it won't be worse before it is better; it will be worse before it is worst. Ireland is about to become a crannog in the Atlantic Ocean. And the Government will act as eviction agents, not of the Sir Horaces and the Lord Mayors, but of the very men who backed them and nursed them into power. The Irish people, whatever layer that term applies to now, always outrun their leaders. The present hosts and backers of the Government, the men who, believing in their promises, nursed them into power, are about to be betrayed – in fact, are betrayed already in favour of a still lower and more out-at-elbows order. Thus the host is betrayed as Talbot Clifton was betrayed. And they can be removed only by the methods that removed the landlord of old. This is what the brother of the murdered Minister for Justice said not long ago:

' "The Government has given a legal existence to the most unjust and harshest landlord that ever cursed the people of this country. If Balfour with his battering-ram had sucked £21,000,000 a year out of the Irish agricultural industry and had in the same year used armoured cars to get the landlords' rent collected, landlordism would not even have lived so long as it has lived in this country. The farmer of the country could not easily differentiate between a lie and a statement calculated to deceive. The whole campaign of Fianna Fail had been to assure the country that if Fianna Fail got into office the farmers would not have to pay any annuities.'

'Government by deception cannot last long.'

'How will he end?' asked Kevin.

'Howling,' I said. 'He will go out making a virtue of Frustration and probably get away with it, or he may give one of his endless interviews to Ceres' son-in-law.'

'So long as we get him away, what does it matter?"

'Before that gang relinquishes office they will give us what they gave us before.'

'What?'

'*Si monumentum requiris . . .*'

'Ah,' said Kevin, with a grim yet pleasing smile, ' "Even in their ashes . . .!" '

'But come with me, I am going to Switzer's.'

'What for?'

'To buy an egg cup.'

'You can get one at Woolworth's.'

'Switzer's egg cups are far more fashionable.'

CHAPTER TEN

I looked with a fresh eye at the shabby street that had once been fashionable and prosperous. It was timidly walked in now. Double rows of troops, dressed in 'fedgrün', set back to back in great lorries, gave it an appearance of unhealthy robustness as they rolled by. They were looked at indifferently by the passers-by. But some, the shabbiest, glared at them furtively after they had passed.

It takes some courage to put up with this and to sustain the weight of despondency it engenders. Have I to carry the town's and country's melancholy on my back? 'By the Light of God,' I swore, 'I'll not let the bagmen or the bogmen drag me down.' Melancholy, indeed! All because a few thousand men have not the guts to protest and agitate against third-rate tyranny! The town and country seem to be in a state of melancholy unrelieved. Only I refuse to be *atrabilious*. Am I an Irishman at all?

Suddenly the thought struck me. Irishmen like to be melancholy. It is the national pastime to brood full of black bile. I remembered the dark figures in the Connemara pub. Even their drink is black! They chew on melancholy as a cow on the cud. Shane Leslie attributes it to 'hushed hate'. It is more than that. It is independent of external circumstances. They take pleasure in darkening with melancholia God's sweet air. They sin against the light. 'Accidia!' Of course, the obsolete deadly sin. There were once eight deadly sins. They are now only seven. Why? Probably the whole country were sinning, and what everyone does cannot (or can it?) be a sin. Something wrong somewhere with my reasoning, I think. It may have been found that there was no remedy for accidia in Ireland and so they let it slide. But what an escape I had! I might have been living in the eighth deadly sin and taking it for a form of patriotism. What an escape! It's a pity it is not a better known sin so that I would have more merit in exemption from it – Accidia!

How pleasant it would be if all sins were things one did not wish to do! This is one of the few which can never tempt me.

I refuse to be 'sullen in the sweet air', or to be with those who wilfully live in sadness. No! I will not!

I steered for the Bailey.

McLoren was describing, over a whisky-and-soda, the austerities of India. A copy of Pater's *Renaissance* lay on the counter beside him. Instead of seeing Shamus, and telling him how I enjoyed a letter that morning with its paragraphs flowing bravely as banners from a castle wall, I found Chich, whose name rhymes with 'which' and denotes our Dublin etymologist. To his researches I owe the discovery of the meaning of pettifogging. To his more advanced researches I owe the amendment from '*pettus*' and '*facere*' to . . . Well, let him speak: 'My dear fellow . . . Just a moment . . . Waiter! I find that . . . You see, curiosity prompted me to discover the real derivation of pettifogging.'

'But I am quite satisfied with your original discovery. Leave it so. Many things are ruined by being traced to their derivations.'

'It is "petty" and an obsolete word to "fog", to cheat or deliberately to blind to something or other, and, also, there is the old Dutch "focker". It is a pity that my little theory is incorrect.'

'Let it be correct until I have done with it! "After me the Truth!"'

Undiverted, the scholar continued: 'With regard to those old tenures, Langdale in Norfolk was held by one Baldwin *per saltum, sufflatum et pettum*. That is, he was to come every Christmas into Westminster Hall, there to take a leap, cry "Hem"; and . . . precisely!

'When he got old and stiff and could no longer leap, he must have sent his subtle lawyer. So it comes to the same thing in the end. I would like to take one of those old tenures and to send my man of business to hold it and renew, claiming audience of his King. Now, if Sir Thomas Beecham . . .'

He had just come down from Henry the Third to Henry the Eighth with his Laureate, Skelton, when I excused myself and left, only to find Sir Plunkett Barton looking into the window of a fashionable hairdresser. He is a type that will not be long left to us. His gentle, scholarly mind has long ago been ruled out as extra-national. I spoke to him about his book *Shakespeare and Ireland*, thinking of its erudition and pellucid

166

style. He seemed embarrassed at hearing it acclaimed; or was it shyness? Perhaps it was neither, but that he sensed an impertinence on my part in posing as one qualified to pass an opinion. I became infected by his indifference. I felt that in some way or other an apology was needed. I began to explain myself: Fatal! I floundered somewhat. It is hard to explain that you did not mean to praise a thing when you wish to be taken as appreciating it! I looked into the hairdresser's window and saw myself as in a glass darkly. That only made it worse. It seemed now that I had come spying to see what he was looking at! Had I a faint touch of epilepsy this morning?

Turning from the multitudinous bosoms of wax in the window, I gazed at Sir Plunkett with an aggrieved eye, and hurried round the corner.

Instead of the spear of de Burgoes I nearly ran into the sabres of Endymion, who was advancing up the street.

'What are you doing this morning, Endymion?' A relief to meet a better fool than myself.

'Verifying, verifying.'

I noticed that his speech was not so thick as before. He was more coherent. He had replaced his cuffs by leggings.

'Verifying what?'

'I would have you know, if you would know,' he said, 'that the Professor of Gaelic Astronomy in the National University announced in a lecture that the sun rose in the East.'

'Well, so it does. It is universally accepted.'

'Wait a while. I had to verify it.'

'Well?'

'It did rise in the East. And that shows . . . and that shows that a thing may be a universally accepted fact, and yet be true.'

'Of course it's true.'

'Wait, wait! Can't you hold on? Is not New York our West?'

'Yes.'

'And the sun rises for the people living in San Francisco in our West?'

'But it is east of San Francisco.'

'Our West is their East?'

He threw an arm out, fixing me with his little merry eye.

167

Rumbling with laughter, he asked: 'But where does it rise at the North Pole? The eternal verities, the eternal verities!'

He grumbled and laughed in his throat, and went his way.

There surely cannot be a Professor of Gaelic Astronomy? Astronomy is a universal science. More of Endymion's imagination, I hope. Otherwise this 'nationality' rampage will narrow the very heavens if it goes on.

On the left-hand side of Kildare Street I met Father Paddy, possessor of one of the greatest brains and the best memory of any Irishman. His broad face was smiling broadly. 'You'll be glad to hear that Mallow Viaduct is blown up. Cork is cut off and a Republic has been declared.' To my amazement he seemed in earnest.

'We shall soon be all cork when we are cut off from the Commonwealth.'

'The sooner the better!'

'A cork won't be much use without a bottle?'

'The British Empire will go flat.'

I did not wish to be short with a priest even when his politics were preposterous and dangerously charged with disaster to his Church. I said: 'The British Empire has a knack of effervescing when necessary. The only thing that will kill it is suicide. And it has attempted that, without success. *Deo gratias!*'

'They have bled this country white for the last hundred years. They have taken millions out of it. They have blighted every colony they touched.'

'You talk like a babu barrister,' I said. 'An Indian who, seeing British Civil Servants lolling through his country in their Rolls-Royces, forgets that they have brought it to the law and organization which enable it to produce wealth. Let the natives have a try and it would quickly return to the Juggernaut and the Suttee, not to mention child-marriage and inter-tribal atrocities. But who is bleeding it white now? England? Ireland had a trade balance of fifty-two million pounds a year when enslaved. What has it now under its Republicans?'

'Freedom, anyway,' he said.

' "He who is in a state of Rebellion cannot receive Grace," ' I quoted. 'There's no use talking to you.' Then suggested cheerfully, 'Ireland's a free country, shoot whomever you please. We have too much liberty.'

He withdrew his mind from his face.

'The same could have been said in Athens long ago, when Persia threatened Greece. There were faint hearts and merchants who were ready to drop the struggle for freedom.'

'Of course it could be and, as a fact, was said with a variation. But with our case there is a parallel only in the respective sizes of the countries. Otherwise the positions are reversed.'

'How! Reversed?'

'There is more potential tyranny of opinion and tyranny in the name of liberty in this would-be bully of a country, and less culture, than in all ancient Persia. Athens fought for freedom. Ireland has to be anchored to it in the Commonwealth, or we couldn't call our soul our own. Suppose Ireland conquered England! . . .'

'That would be just the same as if Athens conquered Persia? Of course! Can you imagine an Ireland fed on hatred of Imperialism conquering anything? Think of the activities of the English fleet once it had become Hibernicized: "The Rathmines broke off action; on the Brian O'Lynn the firing died away."'

He roared with laughter at 'Brian O'Lynn'. The name recalled something. Soon he quoted:

'Brian O'Lynn had a house, to be shure,
With the stars for a roof and the bog for a flure;
A way to go out and a way to go in:
"Shure, it's mighty convenient," said Brian O'Lynn.'

'Yes,' I said, 'we of the O'Lynn family have the stars above us and the untrammelled air, but we have neither the desire of nor the capacity for building – empires least of all.'

But there is no use talking to a clergyman gone political. It means that he has gone polemical too.

'I saw you talking to the fellow who fell into a vat. I saw you,' he said, with a show-me-your-company innuendo.

'Endymion? Yes. He is our *vates*.'

He laughed uproariously, with a laughter that was annoyingly out of proportion as the laughter by which some people deluge a *lapsus linguae*. But it was a joke or a pun which was forming in his own mind at which he was laughing.

'Don't let him fall into the vat again,' he said.

But he must be getting back. Driven in a Ford, he would

pass through the Sphinx-surmounted gates of Maynooth's old manor house and the porter would salute – the same porter who, when asked what the Sphinxes were, not to appear ignorant though they had no connexion with Maynooth, told him, 'Them is for strength.' And what a symbol of political Ireland is provided by a Sphinx! In front, a beautiful face and bosom to allure, and wild beast's claws behind, to tear and to disembowel those who are mad enough to throw themselves on her breast.

'I have been wondering what's come over you,' he added. 'You must have had a bad conscience. You are walking about as disgruntled as if you were Timon of Athens.'

' "By him who drank the hemlock 'tis not true," but Timon had an Athens behind him.'

'There you go again! What's come over you? You must be suffering from Accidia. You are gloomy in God's day. You used to be merry, hopeful, sprightly.'

'Sprightly?'

Again he laughed uproariously, because of the recollection the adjective brought to his mind. *That sprightly girl who was trodden by a bird,* he quoted from Yeats. Yeats, anyway, is quoted in his own town. He repeated the quotation, *Sprightly girl who was trodden by a bird,* with mock professional emphasis and seriousness, to make it all the more ridiculous. A sly glance at Yeats' pontifical paganism. I caught a glimpse of the mind of the man I loved. A mind full of imagination, with all the charm of all the Muses at its call . . . a mind to which myth and metamorphosis were as present as if he were a denizen of the translunary world.

But the Untouchables had touched him and claimed him politically for their own. He walked away still smiling, glad that he had got over a meeting and the awkwardness of conveying to me that he regarded me as a foe.

I saw his long, slightly curved legs, walking as if they lacked an ash-plant, carrying him away for ever.

'Accidia,' I said to myself. 'Accidia: I suffer from it? Well, dammit, that is very strange! It was what I thought that a great part of the country had. And now I am said to have it myself, by one who is, after all, more or less of an authority on the deadly sins.'

I wonder, can it be that we attribute to others our own diseases? It would account for so many paradoxes if it were true. Gangs in power moulding their countries in their own images, infecting the masses with the sourness of their souls. And I imagining that everyone was queer but myself.

How would it be, were a doctor to dispense diseases instead of healing them? Specialists . . . but the train of thought faded, and I turned towards the Green.

It was disheartening to think that such an intellect could be so purblind when 'patriotism' put its finger in his eye. He was able to hide from himself the fact that a minority was devastating the country and murdering fellow-countrymen. He no doubt compromised with his conscience by condemning the majority as having been 'bought' by England and as traitors. But the logical conclusion, that if this were always the case then it was a natural national condition, never was allowed a moment's hearing.

A lorry, a great heavy lorry with its driver ensconced on high, pulled up beside me on its wrong side. A short, wiry figure, growing stout in the early fifties, descended.

'How are you, Gussie?' I held out my hand. He took it, and stretching it downwards, pressed it hard. I looked at the genial, good-natured snout for the smile that always surrounded it. It was gone. Turning sideways, still holding my hand, he said solemnly:

'They're after you.'

'As my red setter is when I walk out.'

'Watch out, now. And, coddin' apart, don't say I didn't warn ye.'

But I should have been more grateful. He had taken a grave risk in giving me warning. He climbed up to his seat and, as he sat, he produced an imaginary revolver from a hip-pocket, fired from his knee and jerked it away. With a slam of the gears he moved off. A good friend! I have known him for twenty-five years. We raced together, reckless on the track. That was his tip to me to carry a revolver. But I had carried one until my back was sore and I could not sit anywhere in comfort. I carried one until I realized that it must appear that I was suffering from *spina bifida* if anyone noticed the bulge in my back-pocket. I carried one until I realized that the crew I had to deal with would take care to arrange the odds. Their idea of duelling had lost all sense of proportion. Besides, to be a good gunman

171

you have to take your gun to bed, and who can suffer Republicans to appoint his bedfellows? I carried one until the detective who used to take me under his wing whenever I crossed to Holyhead advised me to get a permit for it in England, or to hand it in to Scotland Yard. This I did, because I was curious to see the inside of Scotland Yard innocently. My 'gun' is in a desk high up in a storey, with a view of the river, of the County Council Buildings and of St Thomas's Hospital, where the Inspector's son was a house surgeon when I handed it in. It was better than having it taken from me in the Irish Mail. I carried a gun until I had to put it away for safety's sake. I was glad to be rid of it: 'He who lives by the sword . . .' And one cannot go through life always thinking of death. It is a great bore. It requires too much concentration and tends to make one self-conscious. Besides, death is like a woman, in that it largely depends for existence on the interest taken in it. We have to a great extent invented death.

CHAPTER ELEVEN

'Save my bos anoa.'

It was a wire from Talbot Clifton.

Good heavens! does he expect me to return to that destroyed area for the sake of a stuffed head? The *bos anoa* is an animal said to be a cross between an ox and a stag. It is found only in Celebes. It is so rare that when the special expedition which Talbot led had reached Celebes, the only specimen he could get was brought in wounded by his snapshot by the natives. All the precious things he had left in Kylemore faded in his mind before the importance he attached to this head. If I have to go back . . . but Mrs Clifton had left it in my Dublin house. I could look after it now until a messenger arrived, or safer still, put it in the bank. The idea of lodging a cross-bred calf's head in the house of those who worship the golden calf had the attraction of novelty. I could say that it was more important than ivory and gold. Not being sportsmen, they would not believe me. Then when they found out, they would realize what they had missed: possibly Talbot Clifton's account. There was a time that *pecunia* meant heads of oxen . . . no use expecting them to go back to that standard now, even though in Ireland of old seven oxen would buy a handmaid. I will myself preserve the *bos anoa* with its budding horns, its bee nose and its little black calf's head.

I was expecting to hear his cheery knock at any moment now. Five or six taps, and we knew that it was George Russell the mystic, the poet and the economist (economics being more fanciful still than poetry) who is called Æ. Had not Sir Horace, his chief, wired to a friend – I am quoting Hone – 'We men of affairs keep a poet in our office'? His pen-name came about when he was devoted to Theosophy, and Æ was the short for Aeon. Anyone who heard his knock in my house could have told that it was Friday evening. He never failed us. I felt that he would not fail us now, though it was not safe to be out after nine when the firing began at the fall of night.

In he came, the Angelic Anarchist, his great Johnsonian body clothed in a brown tweed, his flowing tie half seen be-

173

neath the rich brown beard, his kind eyes shining more than the lenses of his glasses shone. He crossed the room amazingly light-footed and took up his accustomed place to the left of the hearth in the corner of a short sofa. As he sank in with a sigh of contentment, he said, 'Ah, well!'

Some small talk was necessary as an overture before he could get going and hold the room in a harmony of sound.

'You were very good to come, Æ. There is a lot of firing in the streets and it gets worse as night falls. My street is particularly unhealthy between nine and eleven.' He waved the implications aside. Luckily Monty appeared. An audience was gathering.

'Oliver, I thought you were ordered into the Government Buildings?'

'So I was, Æ, when it was reported that the corner boys who kidnapped me and let me escape had condemned one another to death if I were not recaptured within a fortnight. But I could not stand life in the Government Buildings. The members of the Government have very little conversation. They are charged with so much statesmanship that silence is the only form of expression, between elections, by which their significance may be conveyed. That is why they play cards.'

'Do they put their cards on the table?' Monty asked.

'If they did, it might put an end to the most persistent heritage of the illiterate Middle Ages, cards. I like the King and Queen and the Knave, but the pips!'

'The pips represent the proletariat.'

'I would rather be taken "for a ride" again than live with people who play cards.'

'He has guards instead of cards now!' Monty, of course.

'I have,' I acknowledged. 'And they are causing me the greatest anxiety. They fall asleep during the night: one night they were all disarmed by their own sergeant – and I have to lie awake to guard them from my enemies. In the day-time they are in danger of shooting my household or themselves. Last week one of them shot the hand of a companion and two legs: his own leg, and the leg of a Chippendale chair. Words could not express my alarm and concern: it was the only leg by Chippendale, the one from which Hicks had reconstructed the whole chair by help of Sir Thornley Stoker's Chinese "museum piece" as one reconstructs some wonderful thing

174

from a limb in the Gobi Desert. The house is not safe with all these guards.'

'They give employment,' Monty observed, 'to the other side, whose activities in turn provide them with the job of guarding you.'

'I cannot see why I should have a guard. It is like shutting the stable door when the steed is stolen. I had no guards when I was kidnapped. Now that no one wants me, I have seven guards who draw the Republicans' fire and the Free State Government's pay. My personality is diluted. Seven spirits have entered in. My guards are more important than I.'

Æ was growing restless. The problem Monty raised was more or less an heterodox form of political economy.

'I hardly like to ask Yeats out this night, though he lives very near,' I remarked.

'Better not,' said Æ. They blended badly, Yeats and Æ.

'Would it not be better if Mr Russell were to pull that settee away from the bay window?' Monty asked.

'Perhaps it would. There is a machine gun which sweeps the street and protects me at intervals of fifteen minutes.'

'That's the worst of bay windows. If you sit in one, you may find yourself in "the Waveless Bay".'

A small piece of moulding became detached and fluttered to the carpet. We pretended not to notice it. Æ was served with a cup of tea and the piece of cake which he never exceeded. An odd shot only now. The peace that just preceded nine o'clock fell on the street.

'They are breaking up the old moulds,' Æ began. 'You see, when empires have been cast into the melting-pot and crowned heads deposed, one naturally expects that the small nations will strive to change their polity and to alter their regime.' He sighed contentedly. His words were finding their ranks now.

De Valera, as Jeffries said, was marching on Dublin at the head of 20,000 words. But Æ was there to defend it with an inexhaustible arsenal. His words were filing past.

'Senator Phelan of San Francisco, sir!'

Two young American ladies, who had letters of introduction, and copies of the *Renaissance* by Walter Pater presented by Captain McLoren, came in at the same time. The great beard awed them a little: Tolstoi? They were placed near Æ. Senator Phelan, who had spent most of the afternoon in

175

Plunkett House, already knew Æ. He must have benefited by his experience, because, 'Don't let me interrupt you, Mr Russell,' came quite naturally the moment Æ sat down. With a little purr in his beard, Æ went on:

'I was just explaining to our friends here that it is quite natural that there should be some disturbance at first at the birth of a new state or polity. "One must have chaos within them to give birth to a dancing star," and the chaos is but the prelude to a newer loyalty, to a newer system that will come sooner or later to be devised.'

Good Lord! Is he excusing the Republicans?

'The signature of the Irish mind is not apparent anywhere in this new machinery for self-government. No one has taken the trouble to ask if the adaptation of the British Parliamentary system will suit our people, or if it is adaptable at all. The obvious failure of representative government taught our politicians nothing, though its shortcomings must have been obvious to them.'

A spatter of bullets splashed the street.

'We obtain our political freedom under the old rules. I do not criticize those who devised the new machinery of self-government; but those who did not devise it and damped down and discouraged the exercise of political imagination in Ireland ...

'Political imagination. Sure!' said Senator Phelan.

The acrid smell of cordite from the rifles of my guards who were 'replying' from upper windows after allowing a decent interval to the fire of their trade unionists on 'the other side', drifted down into the room.

'Imagination ...' Æ continued.

'This is a real thrill,' said one of the girls.

'Say,' said the Senator, 'someone will be shot.'

'The only thing that will be shot is a bullet,' Monty said. 'Yes, Mr Russell?'

I looked unobserved at the letters of introduction. – Bryn Mawr! At once the ladies came to life and were clothed with personality in my mind. They were pupils of an old friend of mine. And no one in Europe who has not been to America is safe in judging an American girl or an American scholar by limiting their excellence to the cover.

'Æ will be impatient in a minute if people prefer to listen to his military hecklers than to him. You were just talking of

176

the discouragement of political imagination. Go on, Æ,' I requested.

'Visitors to our country should know that revolution is De Valera's idea of evolution.'

'His ideas of constitutional representation must be falling short,' the Senator said.

'I hope his leaden ideas will keep falling short' – Monty.

I though I heard a knock, but it was hard to tell at the moment with the noise. Windows of the opposite houses could be heard going up, hopeless hopefulness as to casualties urging their languid occupants to look out.

'There was an artist once,' Æ continued, with his gaze on the ladies, 'whose fantasy it was first to paint his ideal of womanly beauty, and, when this was done, to approximate it, touch by touch.'

'Cell by cell,' I whispered mischievously into a coral ear, recalling to her Walter Pater. She brushed down her skirt.

'General Collins!'

He marched into the room in front of his name. Everyone stood up. The delight on Æ's face glowed. He had been longing to meet him for years. He extended his delicate hand, and instead of withdrawing, tried to lead him to the sofa. But Collins had to be introduced and refreshed.

He was a burly man, whose burliness hid his height. He was a smooth, burly man. You could see it in the unlined face and the beautiful, womanly hands. His skin was like undiscoloured ivory. His body had the unroughened strength that a woman's limbs might have or the body of those wrestlers who are bred to incredible feats in Japan. I have seen such athletic limbs in a Spanish swimmer whose arms, when extended, were hardly dimpled at the elbows.

Low forehead, but what was seen over the clear-cut brow was straight. The hair grew down and his head tilted forward as if his chin sought repose on his chest. Napoleonic! But a bigger and a more comely specimen of manhood than Napoleon. In his newly acquired position, he kept his distance by an aggressive but good-natured abruptness. The finest and most life-like portrait is that of his head in white bronze by Doyle Jones. It gives the countenance in all its swiftness of the quickest intellect and nerve that Ireland bred, of the kinsman by antithesis of the author of the 'Ode to Evening'.

177

I took him to a side table and poured out a full measure as if for myself. 'My nerves are on edge,' I said jokingly.

'If they want all that to soothe them they must be in the hell of a state. If it's for me put half of it back.' Then, as the babble hid our talk, 'You're a bloody fine host,' he whispered. 'You had me nearly killed on your doorstep. I knocked three times and I could not get in.'

I was astonished. Everyone else had got in at once from the darkened and dangerous street. Why was Collins's admission delayed? I could trust the servants.

'I can't imagine why they did not open the door. If I had heard you I would have opened it myself. What happened?'

'I was stalked by three.'

'Gunmen?'

'I think that they were only spotters trying to find out where I sleep. I went for them. Two ran off. The fellow I caught was not armed.'

'You will never be delayed on my doorstep again,' I said. 'Here's the latchkey.'

He took it with, 'Right! . . . How's the President?' he asked. 'Look after him,' and he turned his back to the room.

A few weeks later Emmet Dalton sent that key back from the blood-stained tunic of a murdered man.

Just like Collins to walk about unaccompanied by a guard after nightfall. Just like Collins unhesitating to attack regardless of odds. Just like Collins to send his enemies flying before the terrible exhibition of his courage. One of the constituents of courage is contempt. Collins's contempt for the men who turned on him after his battle against the glorious Greenwood's criminal militia was terrific.

However silent Senator Phelan had been trained to remain in the presence of Æ, silence, now that he was in the presence of the man who had taken on and successfully defied that part of the British Army which was held to be too scoundrelly to associate with soldiers and so was sent over here by a Canadian to prepare us for Dominion status, could no longer be sustained.

Senator Phelan took the fireplace.

'Say, General, to-morrow night I am giving a little party to some very particular friends who have done what in them lay in their different vocations to promote the cause of Irish

Freedom. As its chief promoter – and I feel honoured by the opportunity now presented to me by our good friend here to hail you as its achiever – I hope you will join us at the Shelbourne. Sir Horace Plunkett, Æ there, our host, and half a score of other devoted . . .'

Collins smiled, shook his head and laughed good-naturedly. His laugh conveyed his 'I'm afraid I don't dine out much these nights,' inoffensively as a refusal. A shot outside sounded convincingly.

I saw in my mind's eye what awaited us on the night of the morrow. The festoons of smilax on the rich dining-table; the festoons of oratory before and behind each guest as he was introduced to speak to those who already knew him perhaps far better than his senatorial host; and the festoons with which he would be draped when he concluded. After-dinner speaking is the national pastime of the United States. Only for alcohol it would go on for ever. The people of the well-chosen words are even more numerous in New York than the Chosen People. And there would be no escape. I had to see President Griffith before midnight at latest in the nursing home where he was lying; for the rest, they would have to listen until 'Time' was recorded; and with Senator Phelan living in the hotel, the ordinary licensing hours might be extended.

I did not want to go. Apparently the Senator's call on me had been made with the intention of inviting me personally. He had done so much for Ireland in California and he was a man of such outstanding good-will that I would not have, in ordinary circumstances, thought of refusing him. But as Collins had a bedroom and a bathroom set apart for him in my house, so that he could come and go and put those who believed that he returned nightly to the heavily guarded Government Buildings off their ambush I felt that I should stay at home. The Government Buildings were not four hundred yards down from me on the same side of the street. They made the third block on my side and the last. They were flanked by Leinster House, and the great space of Merrion Square faced them.

Members of the Government who could not endure being as it were confined to barracks during the civil war, took the risk of leaving the Buildings and visiting me after dark, for I also refused to be confined. Thus they could communicate with the outer world and with those who could not be expected to face the grille of steel and sentries' scrutiny.

Collins had heard so much of Æ's wisdom that he was filled with curiosity and glad to meet him undisturbed and at his ease.

'The English mistrust genius in high places,' Æ announced. 'They choose forceful average men as leaders. Intensely individual themselves, they fear the aristocratic character in politics. They desire that general principles should be asserted to encircle and keep safe their own national eccentricity. They have gradually infected us with something of their ways, and as they were not truly our ways, we have never made a success of them.'

'What do you propose doing, Mr Russell?'

'Well, General, we must fall back ...'

Fall back? I silenced myself.

'We must fall back on what is natural with us, on what is innate in character, what was visible amongst us in the earliest times, and what, I still believe, persists amongst us – a respect for the aristocratic intellect, for freedom of thought, ideals, poetry and imagination as the qualities to be looked for in leaders; a bias for democracy in our economic life.'

How well the Plunkett House provides these contradictions! I mused. The General's glass was held somewhat sideways now. He could gesticulate without spilling it. A reflection on his host. I hastened to replenish it.

'We were more truly Irish in the heroic ages. We would not then have taken, as we do to-day, the huckster and the publican and make them our representative men, and allow them to corrupt the national soul, as if Irish Nationality was impossible unless it floated on a sea of liquor. The image of Kathleen Na Houlihan anciently was beauty in the hearts of poets and dreamers. We often thought her unwise, but never did we think her ignoble; never was she without the flame of idealism, until this ignoble crew declared alcohol to be the only possible basis of Irish nationality ...'

Senator Phelan confided to me in an audible aside his reasons for being a life-long abstainer. In vain I quoted Yeats:

> 'And one who found in the redness of wine
> The incorruptible rose.'

180

To encourage the others I pressed a syphon. Our Oracle went on: 'We are losing the Ideal of Being for the satisfaction, or rather the blunting of the senses. We are putting out the eye of light.

'I have never had the high vision of those who have gone into the deeps of being and returned rapture-blinded by the glory and cried out in a divine intoxication to the Light of lights:

'Spread thy rays and gather them. The Light which is thy fairest form . . . I am what he is.

'I do not think that many have brooded long enough on that distinction of soul and spirit which St Paul made when writing to his friends at Corinth. He speaks of many unexplained things: of a third heaven, of a soul and spirit, of psychic bodies and spiritual bodies, of a mysterious power which seems to be the fountain of all powers, which enables one to discern spirits, and gives to another eloquence – poetry in fact – and to another magical and healing power. Some of these powers I tried to wake, but I will not speak here of them, for I am trying to supplicate the flame which gives wisdom rather than that which gives power.

'While I could comprehend a little about the nature of the *psyche,* I could not apprehend at all the spirit which transcends the soul; for, as the seers said of it, it is eternal, invisible and universal. Yet because it is universal we are haunted by it in every motion of the mind. It is at the end of every way. It is present in the sunlight.'

Suddenly Collins sought his pocket, revealing as he did so, a large revolver strapped to his thigh. He produced a stubby pencil and a little book.

'As we pursue it,' the much-encouraged golden voice went on, 'it ever eludes us, but it becomes more and more present until all that we see or are swims in a divine ether:

'It will meet thee everywhere, and be seen of thee plain and easy when thou dost not expect or look for it. It will meet thee waking, sleeping, sailing, travelling, by night, by day, when thou speakest or keepest silence. For there . . .'

Sharply Collins said: 'Your point, Mr Russell?'
Consternation seized me. I had overlooked the fact that

Collins could not have been expected to share with me the little mysticism of which I am capable, by which I hear a voice from out the Golden Age speak, whenever Æ indulges in a monologue which is all music and half poetry. There is no other golden age but that which we bring about ourselves. Æ's voice and ideas shed the light of an endless day about me. No one questions a moral organ in the dim religious light when it unrolls the banners of Heaven. 'Your point,' indeed! The quotation did sound alarming, I admit; but the proper mood for Æ is one in which his waves of sound are allowed to undulate over your mind. Any or all of the three waves of Eire. 'The wave of Toth, the wave of Rury, and the long slow-heaving wave of Cleena.'

Had Collins said, 'Your Tangent,' or even 'Your Cosine', he would have been slightly nearer to the third heaven. As things were now, we are all 'earthed'. The Senator was 'one up on' the General in that he paid the tribute of silence while the spell was being woven. Eager for facts though they all are, the American girls were entranced beyond the exactitudes of everyday existence.

But why had I allowed my attention to be distracted while Æ was getting off the subject? If there were only a fusillade now or even a little bombing to relieve the tension, it would be welcome. 'Your point,' indeed! But no. The only time when such sounds would be welcome they were not to be heard.

Boldly I myself plunged into the gulf.

'Will you kindly tell these ladies, Æ, the promise of God to the Thrice Great Hermes, if he followed the straight way?'

Now, I always admired that title, Trismegistus, Thrice Great. I even forbore to ask myself what constituted his first greatness, or even his second, just as I never would think of asking what were the Faculties of both of which Paracelsus was doctor: 'Doctor of Both Faculties.' The name, not the meaning!

'Perhaps, the General?' Æ asked tentatively.

'Blaze away! Don't mind me!'

I pulled Senator Phelan into the breach. With a whisper to Collins that Phelan was a big noise in San Francisco and should not be ignored, I made a 'contact'. Collins was not trained for a room. He would not move. The Senator had to lean over him. I heard him saying, 'Imagine my position.' While attention was taken up in this way the ladies pleaded to hear the promise of the God. Thus the golden chord that Collins broke was repaired.

An intermediate thought occurred to me, it would: are not all we who look back to the Golden Age traitors to the present?

Æ glowed on, and repeated the interrupted oracle:

'It was not a promise of beauty in a heaven world but an illumination in this world:

'It will meet thee everywhere and be seen of thee plain and easy when thou dost not expect or look for it. It will meet thee waking, sleeping, sailing, travelling, by night, by day, when thou speakest or keepest silence. For there is nothing which is not the image of God.'

The faultless memory that was an illumination in this world ceased to recite.

There was a difficulty ahead of me. Collins could not leave. It might meet him anywhere! He would have to outstay the rest. But would the Senator go before him? I could not let it be known that he was sleeping in the house. To Æ – 'Friend, take Phelan with you when you are leaving. Important. I can't explain now.' He nodded. Well he guessed. For all his unearthliness, he was as practical as Collins himself. But Collins, who had driven up from the Curragh, was tired. He solved the difficulty, and with a sudden 'Good-night now!' he bade us good-bye and left the room. As to where he slept no one was any the wiser.

The ladies woke to life. They learnt more about the General whose tenacity, capacity, and courage had saved the movement for independence when it was about to go the way that every other effort went. I did not allude to the danger his fellow-countrymen had been incited to provide. His heartbroken disappointment could only be exceeded by President Griffith's broken heart.

They were over here to study Oliver Goldsmith, who was to be the subject of a thesis for the Ph.D. They were going down to Athlone to visit the Deserted Village.

'Dublin is a far better example,' I urged. 'It has been deserted by nearly everything that makes a town worth living in. You know that line of Oliver –

> 'Ill fares the land to hastening ills a prey
> Where louts accumulate and lords decay.'

They had never heard of it. Suddenly I remembered how taboo irony in any form is in the United States. They looked incredulous and puzzled. Incredible must have seemed my gratuitous rudeness. It was as if I went out of my way to misdirect strangers on a journey through my country. I hastened to laugh it off. One asked Æ if he knew Mr Yeats. Yes, Æ knew Willie "Yeets" – so he always pronounced the name. The girls said Mr Yeats had lectured twice at Bryn Mawr. The first time it was not so good. But the second time, after he had gotten tortoiseshell glasses, it was a great success. What the subject of the lecture was was not quite clear, but he looked every inch of a poet, and he had a most beautiful voice, like Mr Æ's voice, more so in some ways, but it was not so rich in sounds. They had no poets like him in the United States, no poets at all.

'What about Witter Bynner, the author of *Rain*?' I asked. 'And what about Robertson Jeffers, that lone eagle on his granite tower by the green Pacific, who looks towards the illimitable West? Of our own Ossian he wrote:

> 'This is the proper fame to have, not cornered in a poem:
> Fabulous, a name in the North.

'How I would like to have written that! And what about your Robert Frost, with his Wordsworthian feeling for American landscape? And what about Vachel Lindsay, who galvanized the English language, every word of it, when it was becoming about as empty as urns in a graveyard!'

It fills me with a moon-cold fury when I hear American poetry decried. No, no. I mistook their meaning. They did not mean that they had no poets in the United States, but none who looked so good as Mr Yeats.

Æ, who, once he had risen, used to hurry down to the hall to put on a thin overcoat in winter or to take up his broad hat in summer, turned round to the ladies and said:

'17 Rathgar Avenue. Sunday night.'

They were invited to his Sunday gathering of friends. They had made an impression. Æ had been too often in the United States not to know the mental capacity of American girls that conversation quite often insufficiently reveals. Read their letters and you will find an infinite variety of ways of seeing the facets life can present on its surface. Superficial, of course. But is there any life which, if it is to be tolerable, must not be superficial? Try to probe or dive beneath its glittering surface, and it is as if the sliding beetle ruffled the well and broke the smoothness of the bright, still lymph.

Language is living and growing in the United States. There is a vivid eye and a courage in the use of adjective or metaphor that we do not hold in our 'Outworn hearts in a time outworn'. I have a line or two that one of these girls wrote after she had visited Connemara, that illustrates very well what I am endeavouring to say.

> There is a garden by a lake
> That greener grows for Nature's sake,
> Than any garden ever planned
> By squinted eye or craftsman's hand.

Our wild natural gardens, compared with the formal ones of England or Versailles, where the engineer looked along a line or squinted into his theodolite. Women in the United States are not only amorous but artistic:—

> There is no lust like poetry!

I went with the ladies as far as the hall. Senator Phelan would see them to the Shelbourne. I would walk with them to the turn from which it could be seen.

'But is there not danger?'

'Not at this hour.'

'Wasn't he just marvellous, your Mr Æ?'

'Of course he was.'

'I thought him wonderful. I never heard his equal.'

'No one can hear his equal. He has no equal.'

'If he would only lecture in the States, the halls would be booked out.'

'But on what would you have him lecture?'

She was somewhat hesitant for a moment, then she said:

'On just what he's been talking about upstairs.'

'Now, just what has he been talking about upstairs?'

She was taken aback. She looked at her companion puzzled, then reproachfully at me. It seemed so disloyal to suggest that Æ's talking had no meaning or that no one could tell what he was talking about. It would take some time to explain and to absolve myself from a suspicion of insincerity to my friend. I felt that they would think even worse of me were I to recount, by way of explanation, excellent example though it was, how O'Leary Curtis lost his faith one night through listening to Æ, only to find it again next morning when he tried to explain to Father Paddy exactly what he had heard.

'Aureoles for the outcasts; and all kinds of problems solved.'

'Your problem at the moment,' said Father Paddy, 'is "Who is going to stand?"'

Father Paddy was thinking of Seumas's joke:

I met O'Leary Curtis, and he took me by the hand,
Saying, 'How is poor Old Ireland? And who is going to stand?'

No. It would never do to explain away Æ that way. Instead:

'Girls,' I said, 'you are as bad as General Collins, who you remember made us all to feel so uncomfortable when he took out his little book and pencil with, "Your Point, Mr Russell?" And just at that moment when the wave of Toth was about to break into the room.'

'The wave of what?'

'Oh, forgive me! It is only a way I have of recording the different stages of Æ's influence upon my mind.'

'But there must have been some point?' And they looked at me more puzzled and reproachful than before.

'To explain my meaning, I want you to think of this house of mine as a house for artists, and not for lecturers, readers, preachers, teachers, or people with points. It has been said of Æ that he is one of those rare spirits who bring to us a realization of our own divinity and intensify it. He enlarges the joy that is hidden in the heroic heart. He is a magnifier of the moods of the soul; and he communicates them more naturally by music and murmuring sound than by messages or points. Don't forget what Robert Louis Stevenson said about geniuses like Æ. "Such are the best teachers. A spirit communicated is a perpetual possession. These best teachers climb beyond teaching to the plane of art. It is themselves, and, what is more, the best in themselves, that they communicate." That is the secret of Æ. He is an artist. He teaches nothing. He communicates himself, and the best in himself, which consists of poetry, loving kindness, and a passion for beauty more than for anything

186

else. So you see he is far more like Plato than like the Tolstoi whom I saw that his appearance suggested to you at first sight.'

They blushed, looked at one another betrayed by my penetration.

'It sure did,' was all the bemused girl could say.

'You have forgotten your *Renaissance*. What will the Captain say? A moment, while I run up to bring the books to you.'

When I returned, Senator Phelan would not hear of me leaving, as he knew the way to the hotel.

CHAPTER TWELVE

There was smilax in the Shelbourne as it had been given me to behold in vision. The dinner-table was beautifully decorated, and Senator Phelan received his guests in a well-appointed room; but the sight of an ebony piano in one corner caused me grave misgivings. The speeches would be familiar. I could write a formula for them all. Given so much declared achievement and self-satisfaction on the one side, hospitality and generous self-assertion on the other, the resultant would be National Aspirations and tributes to our host. But the piano brought in another note.

Some men have music forced upon them at public dinners, others pretend to like it. I am in the first category. The piano I like is not a black ebony one by Bechstein with a kind of jib-boom to hold up its lid, but one of those little ones that harmonize symmetrically with the wooden 'art' coal scuttle on the other side of the fireplace which you can plug in as a counterblast to the song of the vacuum-cleaner, while you leave the room on pointed feet, your face Saharaed in a smile.

The dinner, which made a table-cloth a platform for orations, had lasted some hours. It was nearing midnight, and still the Senator's unhastenable drawl groaned on. Æ had just sat down. He had spoken for forty minutes, using only two gesticulations, which consisted of short downright choppings of both hands at once.

'Having introduced Mr George Russell' (to me, and even to closer friends), 'it is now my privilege, before reintroducing Sir Horace Plunkett, whom I may truly and justly describe as his chief, to make a few appreciatory remarks about the oration to which you have just listened. He has, as you are well aware, opened to us a heaven of his own imagination. Sir Horace has laid the foundation stone of many Irish "Movements". Æ edits the *Homestead* and lends his inspiration to the lowliest cotter, cottager – that is to say, farmer.

'Sir Horace will now reply. Sir Horace has very obligingly, earlier this evening inaugurated this little dinner, to which he came at very great personal inconvenience and risk to his health. No more auspicious auspices could hearten any host. Sir Horace has brought Battle Creek Sanatorium to your notice. Sir Horace himself has been an inmate . . . that is to say, a visitor, guest, or, rather, patient at the Sanatorium at Battle Creek; he hopes, if his life be spared, to set up a Battle Creek in your green and pleasant land where cases which are not as yet registered as pathological may be diagnosed and treated accordingly. Only by institutions such as this will lives as useful as Sir Horace's be prolonged and the age of retirement from active public service be indefinitely delayed.

'I call on Sir Horace Plunket . . .

'Sir Horace.'

Sir Horace rose and inclined his head.

It was 11.45. But coyly Sir Horace began:

'I cannot detain you, Gentlemen, as the night grows late, but there are a few remarks of Senator Phelan's which I feel bound to deprecate, flattering though they be. Perhaps a short revision of what my work has meant would not be out of place. My work, as you may know, Gentlemen, lies in the spheres of voluntary effort, especially organized voluntary effort, and not in that of legislation or public administration. It is true that when much younger I represented an Irish Constituency for eight years in the British Parliament. I presided over the Irish Convention – its ivory gavel is one of my treasured possessions – I worked for the Dominion Settlement, without the Partition . . . And now I come to the actual work of the I.A.O.S., and must explain why its services are needed, although, as I have told you, it calls upon us all to do all these things for ourselves. When bodies of farmers in any parish have made up their minds that they have got to join together for any of the purposes I have described, the first question they naturally ask is – How are we to set about it?

'Of course, it is essential that they should learn to trust each other, and take my word for it, before they have gone very far in the practice of co-operation, they will find that mutual confidence pays . . .'

Sir Horace was getting thoroughly warmed to his task of revising his life-work when, most unexpectedly, as I was slipping, unnoticed as I thought, from the room, our host the Senator joined me at the door.

'You are going to see President Griffith?' he said.

189

'I have to see him before twelve o'clock; it is close on that hour now.'

'Bring me with you,' he requested, 'as I am leaving early in the morning . . .' and then hesitated, realizing that he could not leave the room while Sir Horace was speaking.

'Well, it is your only chance of seeing him,' I said, 'because if you are leaving early in the morning I could not bring you in.'

He looked doubtfully at Sir Horace.

'Sir Horace is good for half-an-hour or more,' I assured him, 'and I will tell you all that Sir Horace will be saying while we walk along the Green.'

As we turned the corner into Leeson Street I saw a little barefooted urchin on the steps of No. 97 deliberately fire a pistol in the air. I charged upon him, but he ran down the lane, dropping the pistol as he fled. This was part of the nightly fusillade provided to keep Griffith awake and to add to the torture of his mind, which was seriously disturbed.

He must have heard our voices, because, as I pushed in his door, he sat up in bed challengingly and irascibly: 'Who's that? Who's that?' he said, pointing to the door through which the Senator had not yet appeared.

'An important American Senator – Senator Phelan, from San Francisco.'

'I'll see no Americans,' said Griffith in a voice which could easily be heard by the Senator, whom it was too late to withdraw.

A very short and constrained interview took place which, however, Griffith's natural courtesy did much to relieve. The Senator must have been satisfied with his 'contact', because, on our way back to hear Sir Horace's peroration, he thanked me effusively and was genuinely grateful. We were in good time.

The guests departed after a rather sleepy discussion on general principles.

Senator Phelan left early in the morning. I never saw that good-hearted man again.

By the quay-side we waited: midnight and as yet no ship. All communications with Cork had been destroyed. Only by sea was there a way to Dublin. The corpse of Collins, the vital, the mighty, was being borne by a boat long overdue. I stood for hours at the North Wall. Drizzling rain added to our gloom. I stood by the river-side hour after hour with the officers in their uniforms blackened by rain – officers of an Irish National Army that Griffith created by a stroke of his courageous pen.

At last in the silence of the dark a moving light appeared, coming slowly up an invisible stream. The death-ship carrying the mortal remains of the most rapid and bright soul that alien envy in Ireland ever quenched. Troops formed up. A gun-carriage received the coffin. It was bound for the City Hall.

I reached home in the early hours. I had to make provision for embalming the body.

Never in our life cycle shall we see the like of Mick Collins. He dwelt among us as our equal. Now that he is dead, we find that we were the familiars of a Napoleon who knew no Waterloo.

No matter how it may be diminished, the fact is that Michael Collins beat the English in the guise they chose to adopt at a time of great stress: England's extremity was his opportunity. He kicked it hard. Opportunity brings more than opportunists to the front. Ireland's struggle was old and long sustained tenaciously through the years, opportunities or no opportunities. Hundreds of Irishmen in every age were glad to put their necks in risk of England's halter and quick-lime. Collins alone pulled his generation out.

My guest was coming home to me to be embalmed. Not England, but his fellow-countrymen murdered him.

What an unlucky shake-hands De Valera gives! He shakes hands to speed Collins and Griffith to London. They are dead within a year.

I had to be up betimes if the embalming was to be completed before noon. Hardly had I slept when a loud knocking summoned me. Desmond Fitzgerald, Minister for Defence, to keep me company. It was 4.30 a.m. As he knew little of such processes as embalming, he was anxious that no time should be lost. In my bedroom slippers, I walked him round through the empty streets to awaken the porter of the College of Surgeons. No answer. We went round to the great gate at the back of the dissecting-room. Loudly we knocked, hammering with the flat of our hands to make the greater noise. A bullet embedded itself above our hands. Hastily I kicked the door. Oh, my slippers! I had forgotten. But the invisible sniper guessed

191

what we were about. Another plunge of lead in pine. We must get out of this.

'Leave it to me,' I assured the Minister. 'The job is not a lengthy one. I will come back at six o'clock. Meanwhile, I will try the Anatomy School of Trinity College.'

Arthur Griffith lay on a small mattress in a room off the Ministry for Justice high up in the Government Buildings, as the place intended for a College of Science in the days of the British Administration was now called. He was besieged by a large part of the 'Irish People' in whom he believed. He could not leave the building without risking his life. His guards were troops drawn from as distant places as possible. They spoke like Scotsmen. If you wished to see him as a medical attendant, you had to put your face into a large letter-box-like grille and hold it against the revolver of the sentry on duty, before the door was opened. When you were admitted into the Hall you found yourself in a small chamber, walled by bullet-proof sheets of steel. Search and interrogation preceded your admittance. The lift was not working, neither were the charwomen. Through dirty marble halls and up dirty staircases of a building never designed for dwellings, at last you reached the fourth storey. A long corridor led to the Ministry. Past both, you reached the small closet where Arthur Griffith lay. At a glance you recognized a man who was very ill. He had a solicitor administering to him. The hour was nine o'clock of a morning. My mind was made up at once. Out of this he must be taken. But before removing him permission had to be got from command. I drove without loss of time to Portobello Barracks. There was no nonsense, no red or, what is worse, green tape about these men.

'Griffith is ill and I want him to have adequate nursing and attention, which is impossible in a building designed for offices, not for homes.'

'Certainly. But we must know where you intend to take him so that we can provide the necessary guard.'

Griffith has to be guarded from the Irish people! I suppressed the chain of thought for my patient's sake. No. 96 Lower Leeson Street recommended itself to me because, being as it was the private hospital of the Mercy nuns, I hoped that their sacred character would prove a bulwark against the assassination of the man who believed in his fellow-countrymen.

With military formalities complete and adequate guards, the Father of the Free State was taken secretly from the Government Building and as far as possible from De Valera and his besieging Irregulars. I could never countenance this euphemism 'Irregulars'. They were mostly town riff-raff misled, or country dupes and discontents whom De Valera aroused when he found that his methods had landed him in a minority.

'I see you have Arthur in the front drawing-room of 96,' one of the hard political women said to me with a knowing smirk, an hour later. She had seen Griffith from the top of a tram as he moved restlessly to and fro in front of his windows.

Knowing that there was not a moment to be lost before she would spread the news amongst the gang that aimed at breaking his heart, I ordered that Griffith be removed from the first to the fourth floor.

'There is the fireplace and there is your armchair, Arthur, and don't expect a single visitor until I come again this afternoon.'

Arthur grunted. 'What's wrong with me?'

'You've had a hard life for fifty years and you think ease is a disease. But you have got to resign yourself to rest, and even to comfort, for the first time in your life, and to obey your doctor when you would resist a friend.'

That he did not 'stay put' in his armchair was only too evident. I was returning with shaving tackle and pyjamas for the suddenly removed President, when I found him sitting crosswise from the fire with a chair on each side, on which he placed the daily papers as he read them. He could read print as easily upside down as upright, for he was at one time a compositor.

I moved and turned his chair with him in it to the fire, saying, 'No Irishman ever sits across his hearth. For God's sake, Ireland's sake, and all our sakes, give yourself a little relaxation and behave as if you had escaped from 17 Crow Street for a day or two.'

'What do you mean?'

'I mean . . .'

'I'm all right!'

'I'm not; for I have to look after the worst and most fatal

193

kind of patient – the healthy snob who will not look after himself.'

'There's nothing wrong with me.'

'That's one of your symptoms. But I am carrying your complaint. It's up to me to get myself right with you.'

'Ugh!'

'All the newspapers! No visitors. No telephoning. Me thrice daily. And all the Cabinet stuff can wait. You are going to be decorated for the first time in your life with carpet slippers.'

'I must keep on the telephone.'

'No. Unless it is laid on to this room.'

He took his pince-nez off and polished them resentfully. I knew that so much depended on his complete removal from affairs that I was anxious to remove myself before he could formulate objections to his isolation. You are handicapped as a medical man when it comes to making an invalid believe in his illness. An Englishman likes to be invalided with his back to the wall so that he may summon to his aid his *vis medicatrix*. He fights best in a tight corner. A man like Arthur Griffith looks upon disease or illness as a nuisance and something to be shaken off as we shake off an importunate bore. He cannot react to that which he will not recognize.

'Try to think you are taking a holiday.'

'I never had a holiday in my life, and I don't want an artificial one. I'll go back to the Building. Kindly send for my clothes.'

'Do you really imagine or think that I am keeping you here in order to provide myself with a patient? I want to provide you with regular meals and rest. Consider yourself a "nudist" meanwhile. If in three weeks . . .'

A nurse brought in a large envelope containing reports from the Cabinet. Knowing that these would make him restless and increase the irascibility which was manifest of late, I said that I would permit his secretary to see him or allow him one or two of his colleagues in.

Not for a moment did he refer to the report. He kept his troubles to himself and his responsibilities unshared.

Next morning nurse telephoned: 'You are wanted at once, Mr Griffith is very bad.' He is fighting hard against my orders, I thought. But I went round without hurry, thinking that he had been enraged at my restrictions on the visits of his secretaries

194

and friends. Sir Thomas Myles laid it down that a doctor' should never hurry. No Athenian gentleman did. If the condition be fatal, what can you do? If it be not, the probabilities are that a minute or two will make no difference. But what you can do in the first instance is to avoid arriving at the critical moment. Callous philosophy, were it meant to be taken seriously!

I was at the nursing home within four minutes. This absolved me. At the stairs' head President Griffith, the man who believed in the Irish people, lay on his back. His left arm was outstretched and bloody. A long incision of four inches gaped where his pulse was. It was not bleeding, though the artery had been severed by Mr Meade, who was on the spot, the only attempt that could be made to counteract cerebral haemorrhage. Nurses and porters were fussing about asking each other if it were not terrible. Did they think he was really dead?

'Take up that corpse at once,' I said, letting something of the bitterness of my spirit escape into that harsh word. A moment after, I regretted it. 'Take the President's body into the bedroom.'

'I perish by this people which I made' – KING ARTHUR

Rumours take the place of prodigies in Ireland. Instead of risen corpses in the Forum and chickens with three legs which would have satisfied ancient Rome's superstition, it was given out that poison slew Arthur Griffith. Much as I hate the 'Republicans' and their spurious pretensions, I will affirm that the only poison about them is turned against themselves. They are poisoned by false doctrines. But they do not poison their enemies, only themselves. It would have been a simple thing for me to order an inquest and to have the viscera examined for poison. But the poison that slew Griffith was envy and jealousy and calumny, which can be deadlier than prussic acid, and, what is more mortal to a martyr, ingratitude. He had not the armour with which I, for one, was invested, be it irony or motley. His sincerity was a bow and his belief an arrow which, if deflected, slew his faith. His limitations allowed neither for torrents nor for lakes. Precipitation was as intolerable to him as delay. From the ideal of Louis Kossuth, from the idea of a Dual Monarchy for Ireland, he never advanced or retreated. Therefore it is absurd to write of his parley with English

195

Ministers, Churchill, George, Birkenhead and that ilk, as an 'ordeal'. It has been presented lately to the Irish public as if it were a campaign in which Griffith fought a rearguard action. A battle wherein Griffith was on the retreat. What is the truth? When I think of what Griffith set out to acquire and the character of the man, which was indeflectible, his achievement of the 'Treaty' is a conquest which excelled all that he set himself to accomplish twenty years before. His 'concessions' were conquests. His camp followers may have expected more loot, but the General's plan of campaign cannot be decided by the avarice of the hangers-on or the *vivandières*. A Dual Monarchy was Griffith's ambition. His triumph went beyond it.

CHAPTER THIRTEEN

Renvyle House is burned by the I.R.A. The long, long house in the ultimate land of the undiscovered West. Why should they burn my house? Because I am not an Irishman? Because I do not flatter fools? If the only Irishman who is to be allowed to live in Ireland must be a bog-trotter, then I am not an Irishman. And I object to the bog-trotter being the ideal exemplar of all Irishmen. I refuse to conform to that type.

So Renvyle House, with its irreplacable oaken panelling, is burned down. They say that it took a week to burn. Blue china fused like solder.

How few pictures make up one's memory of a place continuously dwelt in!

I see the long, nervous hands of Augustus John tearing at the ivy which threatened a window of that ancient house – Lu, the Long-Handed, the Gaelic Apollo, god of all the arts! – Also, I remember the giant fuchsia bush spreading like a banyan tree and the garden paths blinded by its growth. The walls six feet thick which left little rooms between their doors, doors which opened and closed of their own accord unnoticed, until Yeats, the poet and mystic, visited us on his honeymoon and saw sights invisible to mine unenchanted eyes.

The Blake family who held the place before me, having taken it over from a member of the Clan O'Flaherty, Princes of Iar Connaught, left a ghost behind them to resent newcomers. It resented Yeats of the second sight even more. At least it could make its displeasure manifest to him by more than the sounds and strange happenings, which by me might have been attributed to the noise and movements of Atlantic gales.

It is true that there were unaccountable happenings noticed before the coming of Yeats. The door of a north room, the only second-storey room with barred windows, could not be opened one evening. Men were sent up by a ladder to remove the bars. They entered the room to find that a chest, heavy with linen, had been moved a few inches so that its edge overlapped the door.

197

Alone in the house one winter's night, lying in a room at the end of the corridor which passed the haunted room, I had heard unprogressing footsteps in the passage. It was about 1 a.m. I was so frightened that I knew I could have no rest that night unless I brought the affair to an issue. I opened the door as the footsteps increased in loudness, strange steps that seemed to approach without ever coming immediately outside. But so suddenly did I open the door that its draught extinguished my candle and I was left in darkness; for the matches could not be found. Silence ensued.

On another night, when the main seas were disturbed, I heard the sound of a siren far off shore: no hope for any ship on that shark-toothed coast. Nearer the sounds came, until I imagined that there was a motor car feeling its way along the back drive to the yard by the beach. And, finally, drowsily I put the noise down to the drumming of some night insect that had entered the room. To me there were no further manifestations, or they were forgotten. Not so to Yeats.

'Willie,' said his wife one evening, 'do not leave me to dress alone. I do not want to see that face again looking out from the glass.'

Doors had been opening quietly and shutting quietly as we sat in the library before dinner. I never paid much attention to them, attributing their opening and shutting to the opening and shutting of doors in the passage side of the very thick walls.

'What face?' I asked.

But I was not answered. Yeats and his wife left the room. I was resigned to being treated as uninitiated, but my friends looked at one another. Evan Morgan, a Cymric Celt, from immemorial Wales, felt the supernatural at once.

'You never told me about this,' he complained, all alert.

Now, you cannot ask a man to meet a ghost, because ghosts are not to be counted on.

'I did not care to talk about it,' I said. 'I thought that Yeats . . .'

I could not say – 'If you met Yeats you met enough of faery, as much as I am ever likely to meet.' I implied that it was far more in Yeats' province than mine, and, that being so, the omission was not mine wholly. But he was not quite satisfied. My hospitality fell short of the necromantic.

After dinner there were very few in the library – in fact only

198

Seymour Leslie and one or two. Evidently something was going on. Seymour could not be left out when anything exciting was taking place. He left the room to investigate. I lolled in front of the fire, hoping that something, no matter what provided it was exciting, might occur. A maid brought me a note.

'Take your friend Leslie away from us. He is a regular vortex of evil spirits.' It was in unmistakable and distinguished calligraphy. Good Lord! What is this? There must be a séance in full blast going on somewhere and Seymour has butted in: 'A regular vortex'! If Seymour is a vortex, I must be a regular maelstrom. I drown evil spirits. Seymour, it seems, circulates them. But, crestfallen, Leslie returned.

'What's up?'

'They are all at it. Lord Conyngham, Yeats, Mrs Yeats and a fourth. They are getting after the ghost.'

'But how?'

'I just looked in to one of the rooms. Lord Conyngham was at the Ouija board. When I appeared, everyone stopped. Yeats said significantly, "We cannot go on until we hear what Mr Leslie wants." That meant that I was politely asked to go. I am to see you.'

'To see me?'

I am determined not to trespass. I want the poet and his party to be left alone. But I must be on my guard if I am not to be used by the very inquisitive and masterful Seymour as a stalking horse. If he goes back it will break up the séance. I know Yeats.

'I for one shall not butt in,' I said. 'I don't hold with séances. I am not sensitive enough.' Winds moaned reprovingly in the chimney. 'I was kicked out of the Hermetic Society on the only evening I went with George Moore to see what it was all about. Let us have a smoke.'

'I don't smoke.' (Oh, don't you?)

'Have a drink and we'll "hit the hay".'

'It's far too early.'

'Séances,' I said, with the authority of one who makes a premise suit his needs, 'usually last many hours. There are people in the next room. Would you care to make a fourth at bridge?'

I knew that Evan Morgan was in the drawing-room with half-a-dozen friends, who saw Shelly plain in him with his long, white open neck, high forehead, chestnut hair, and aqua-marine eyes. I hoped that their company would prevent Seymour from spoiling what, if left to itself, would prove to be one of the most interesting psychological experiments in our country. A ghost which had been felt first hand by me and many others. None of your 'I-heard-for-a-fact-from-a-friend' ghosts, but one I had heard myself, and two of us had *seen*.

As the folding doors closed behind the reluctant Seymour, 'Evan is psychic,' I called after him. A moment later, I was left alone . . .

How this one memory furnished the lost house for me!

I believe in ghosts: that is, I know that there are times, given the place which is capable of suggesting a phantasy, when those who are sufficiently impressionable may perceive a dream projected as if external to the dreamy mind: a waking dream due both to the dreamer and the spot.

The book I read was becoming a crystal because I was merely using its pages as a screen for the subconscious.

Smoke from the fire we light on summer evenings in Ireland for the sake of homeliness, puffed down. A puffing chimney was unusual. But there it was. It proved that I was not asleep, for smoke is hardly a soporific. But I did notice suddenly, as if awakened, that the folding doors were opened and that there was no one in the room beyond.

If it was too early to go to bed some time ago, perhaps it was not now. Where had they gone? What was the restless 'Regular Vortex' doing? Not interrupting Yeats, I hoped. But it would interrupt him were I to search him out in mid séance. This ramshackle house has many chambers. If the guests are not gone to bed they may have gone to the kitchens to listen to the fiddlers at the dancing, or gone somewhere else to play ping-pong.

My lamp is making little noises. The room is gloomy. I will go into the next one, which is brighter and is not filled with smoke.

Ah, well! There is a lot to be said for rooms furnished by a woman's hand. They are devoid of design. They elude and defy calculation. They have so many fancies and knick-knacks. What is that famous paper *Vogue* but the 'Woman's hand' in journalism! Thick crowding fancies, notions! I remember promising to give Sir Thomas Esmonde that cameo of his long-nosed grandfather which is on the mantelpiece. Beside it is a Chinese mandarin with a short nose. Was this the fact that justified their juxtaposition? Below, the Venetian mirror, for all I knew, may have suggested Marco Polo to counterbalance the Chinese porcelain. Vague, *Vogue* and the exotic chintzes!

Suddenly! Was that a scream? There, it shrieks out again! Now what the devil? It must be a very loud scream, or very near, to reach this part of the house. With the thick walls we never hear the fiddles and the dancing in the kitchen. Lights are moving on the stairs of the west wing. Frightened friends in their nighties peer out, but someone is running towards me.

'Quick! Evan is dying!'

'Where is he?'

'In that room there!'

Evan was being supported on a chair by two ladies. His face was deathly pale and his head had fallen forwards. Seymour was hopping in front of him saying, 'Don't take it so seriously, old man!' A table had fallen on its side, presenting a cool shield of green baize.

'What's all this about?' I demanded.

'Evan suddenly became hysterical.'

His pulse was racing. He was but semi-conscious.

'What on earth were you doing?'

'We were holding our own little séance, and just as we were getting results Evan got the jigs or something rather like them.'

Relying on me, the lady supporters released their hold. I was barely in time to catch him as he fell sideways.

'Leave him to me and run to get some brandy.'

I carried him into a dressing-room and laid him on the bed. Presently three returned with brandy, Seymour expostulating 'He shouldn't have taken it so seriously.'

I put them all out of the room. No audience.

His body was smooth as marble: heart firm: no aspirin about. I could not understand the collapse. Presently he broke out in a cold perspiration. Slower pulse, breathing audible.

'What did they do to you, Evan?'

'The ghost!' he gasped, and tore at his open collar.

'The ghost? What ghost?'

'Seymour sent me into the haunted room to raise the ghost, but when it came it transferred into me all the thoughts by which he was obsessed before he went mad.'

'Now really, Morgan, you know very well that there is no ghost; no ghost anyway here who is insane.'

'It was Seymour's séance. Yeats was having one . . .'

'I know. Quite.' A rival séance! Wait until I catch that 'Vortex'. 'Try to sleep, old man. I will sit here until I can get someone to take my place – unless you would care to come down with me.'

'Seymour heard that Yeats spent hours in the haunted room. "Now it's up to you," he said. I went in about 12.30, and after they had locked the door . . .'

'Locked the door?'

'Yes. Locked me in . . . I felt a strange sensation. A sensation that I was all keyed up just like the tension in a nightmare, with the terror added that nightmares have. Presently I saw a boy, stiffly upright, in brown velvet with some sort of shirt showing at his waist. He was about twelve. Behind the chair he stood, all white-faced, hardly touching the floor. It seemed that if he came nearer some awful calamity would happen to me. I was just as tensed up as he was: nightmare terrors; twingling air; but what made it awful was my being quite awake. The figure in brown velvet only looked at me, but the atmosphere in the room vibrated. I don't know what else happened. I saw his large eyes. I saw the ruffles on his wrists. He stood vibrating just as I was vibrating. His luminous brown eyes reproved me. He looked deeply into my eyes. Then, oh then! . . . Oh, my God! . . .'

'Old fellow, you know I am solid enough and all damned spirits steer clear of me. Don't talk about it any more. What about a large one and a spot of soda?'

'I must, I simply can't go on until I tell you.'

'Yes, but don't weep because Seymour sent you into the worst-furnished room in the house.'

'Yes, but let me tell you. The apparition lifted his hands to his neck, and then, all of a sudden, his body was violently seized as if by invisible fiends and twisted into horrible contortions in mid air. He was mad! I sympathized for a moment with his madness and I felt myself at once in the electric tension of Hell. Suicide! Suicide! Oh, my God! He committed suicide in this very house.'

I'll 'commit' Seymour when I go downstairs, I determined.

'But what about your yellow dressing-gown and a few of

your black-and-yellow Chinese sleeve-birds in it? Just to show the girls that you are your own man again?'

He seemed to consider it. But again he wept in pity for the ghost.

'How did you get out?' I asked foolishly; yet thinking to relieve him by the story of his relief.

'Seymour let me out. "It seems to be a poltergeist, Evan," he said, "from all the row you are making" – and I was not making any row. But, oh, that . . . !'

'Your Moroccan slippers are here. Here's your dressing-gown. The birds are in the next room. Don't you think you can do your bit in the drawing-room now? I'll just peep into the haunted room. I don't believe the Yeats party have started for it yet.'

'Oh, you mustn't. Don't leave me. Don't risk that room! I'll go down with you. Promise me that you will never go near that room again.'

'Well, all right. As a matter of nerve-training I used to look into and grope around it for half a minute whenever I was left alone of winter nights in the house. Not a thing! Nothing but my own fears, with which I refused to people the room. I'm afraid I'll never make a gigolo for ghosts; nor allow myself to be terrorized by the cellars of my own imagination.'

Perhaps it was curiosity for the results of the prolonged séance which was still sitting in the opposite side of the house that decided the skiaphobe and obsessed youth to follow me. He put aside his delirium as suddenly as it came. I did the decanter drill once more.

It must be awful, I reflected, to get the horrors before the excesses. Delirium without a drink! The shock before the shell! That would do very well for a definition of madness. I recalled the words of my well-loved friend and mentor Dr Tyrrell of Trinity – 'My dear boy, believe me, there is nothing more disconcerting than illness one has *not* brought on oneself!'

How true! We can cure the results of excess by excelling. But a visitation of uninvited disease! The effect without the cause!

Downstairs Freddy Conyngham was asking for perfume and flowers. Presently Sabaean odours filled the room. There were many contributions. Flowers were taken from bowls here and there. Yeats's ghost had asked for flowers.

At 2 a.m. Yeats appeared.

'She should be down any moment now,' he said casually. 'Yes, she should be here presently if all goes well.'

But where was she, Mrs Yeats?

It transpired that the ghost had communicated with Yeats through automatic writing. He objected to the presence of strangers in the house. But he was in for a course of adjuration he little expected from the Archimandrite Yeats.

1. You must desist from frightening the children in their early sleep.
2. You must cease to moan about the chimneys.
3. You must walk the house no more.
4. You must not move furniture or horrify those who sleep near by.
5. You must name yourself to me.

Now, Yeats could never have guessed that it was the custom of the Blake family to call their sons after the Heptarchy. And yet he found it out and the ghost's particular name. I had never gleaned it from the local people, though I lived for years among them.

The troubled spirit promised to appear in the ghost room to Mrs Yeats, as he was before he went mad sixty years ago.

'She should be here any moment,' Yeats repeated. 'We must wait. We must wait. He has promised to appear to my wife as he was before he went mad.' He waved his beautiful hand up and down, on which a ring as large as a wrist watch gleamed on the side of the armchair.

Far up behind the great flue round whose hearth we were gathered was the gaunt, deserted room, in which Mrs Yeats was keeping solitary vigil. I felt a strange fear, a fear that nothing could combat. What courage she had! But we attribute courage to those whose professions to us are unfamiliar: to the soldier, sailor, aviator, none of whom claims credit for it for himself. So, too, the psychic researchers are unfamiliar with fear in their vocation.

Presently Mrs Yeats appeared, carrying a lighted candle. She extinguished it and nodded curtly to her husband. 'Yes. It is just as you said.'

What was? We all wondered.

After a whispered consultation Yeats announced:

'My wife saw a pale-faced, red-haired boy of about fourteen

years of age standing in the middle of the north room. She was by the fireside when he first took shape. He had the solemn pallor of a tragedy beyond the endurance of a child. He resents the presence of strangers in the home of his ancestors. He is Athelstone Blake. He is to be placated with incense and flowers. Lord Conyngham!'

With grace, and saving presence of mind, Lord Conyngham presented flowers and his collection of scent bottles to Mrs Yeats.

Memories, nothing left now but memories. In that house was lost my mother's self-portrait, painted when she was a girl of sixteen. Her first attempt in oils. And her sampler of the big parrot, made with thousands of beads, outcome of patience and peaceful days half a hundred years ago, under the tuition of the nuns of Taylor's Hill. One of the many Irish convents which, as an Irish-American kinsman truly said, 'train girls to be ladies'. Books, pictures, all consumed: for what? Nothing left but a charred oak beam quenched in the well beneath the house. And ten tall square towers, chimneys, stand bare on Europe's extreme verge.

CHAPTER FOURTEEN

There must be 'something of the sea' all sib to my spirit. I go down to it as if there existed an understanding between us; as if the 'pathetic fallacy' of external nature's indifference were not fallacious but true. I trust myself to the sea with the abandon of a confidence I never feel on land. It may be because I was born with a caul. The fact remains and is always to be relied upon: I can rest on the sea as I can never rest on land. So when I lay in my bed on the British and Irish boat to Liverpool, I felt an inexplicable peace flow up from the depths. The very marrow of my bones softened; and I was filled with honey-heavy peace, a peace that comes but once in a lustrum.

Could it have been that I was under a strain for years without realizing it? Or is this peace due to the lulling movement of our prime mother, the world-enfolding sea? Relaxation is not of the will. It comes from a release from care; and it cannot be turned on as those who begin noonday entertainments in America with an order to 'relax' imagine it can be. America rings to that pitiable appeal 'Relax'. Into what will they re-relax at 1.1 p.m. ....?

I am fondled by the sea in which I trust. Strange it is: never through the many thousand miles I have sailed has there been dangerous weather. And I have sailed in my time far into the blue deep. But what is more unnatural than a voyage without undulations? All noises of the ship's mechanism without motion obtrude. A calm passage is unnatural. I do not ask for a storm to leave me suspended three inches above my falling berth, or to tear my pyjamas as I correct the sidelong roll. Up and down three feet, up and down above a mile depth of element more viscid and visible than the air. Charged with terror is the unplumbed deep. Horror and horror float and dart in the saline vat which, bottled, is our blood. And even in our blood, on the battle goes. Invisible fishes drift and multiply; and we are no more masters of that stream than of the outer sea. I must be a go-between, a liaison officer of sea and circulation. Else, why do I feel more at home and freer from care at sea than on land? Panics on deck move me not. I never shall be drowned. All who sail with me are safe – 'Back! One by one to your boat stations! Women and children first. Call that gynaecologist back! This ship will keep afloat. I am here!' – I should be endowed by steamship companies to sail on special voyages assuring calm and halcyon weather. I have fancied myself in many *rôles*, but never before as that symbol of azure days, the halcyon or kingfisher. 'By jove, a bird!'

And now I am sailing to Liverpool in one of the well-equipped cabins of the 'B and I', the best way to sail to England. If the electric light were only behind and not in front of my eyes, I would recognize a sympathizer and not a cynic in the marine architect. He did not believe that any of those likely to travel by his boats ever concerned themselves with a book. So the light is midway to help the stewards with the drinks. But a bookworm, no! They are not supposed to sail with the 'B and I'. If he read at night he may be blinded by the dazzle that sheds light upon the navel and the eyes. Two feet towards the bed-head . . . but this is asking for intelligence and imagination where maximum illumination is provided.

The sun is getting behind me, but I know all about Dublin in the evening glow. I have not the least desire to look upon it. It is too typical. *Der Untergang!* The Sugar Loaf, called the Golden Spears, will be visible on the south. Howth . . .

Hoved, the Head . . . Well, what about it? Men from Norway named it and took a 'great prey of women from Howth'. For all their sailing these are still in Moore Street, sturdy, snub-nosed, hawser-haired 'Danes'. But no one in Ireland knows Irish history. So we are suffering from a nightmare culture of imaginary Gaels.

I will not have my peace disturbed by thoughts of my town house in the hands of guards, of my visitors subjected to searchings, hatred mistaken for patriotism.

I was astounded at how little I regretted leaving my native land, where patriotism consists in going native, or where usury enjoys an extra two per cent.

> Confound their politics;
> Frustrate their knavish tricks;
> Shut off their 606.
> God Save the King!

I will lie *solutis curis*. The last time that phrase entered my head, my peace was magnificently disturbed by Talbot Clifton, who came bearing a gift of gold. He is endowing me this time with a goldener gift – the gift of peace. What is the cause of this peace? 'My Native Land, Good Night' or the fact that I am on the sea? The sea whereon all can sail and become brotherly by so doing. Why is it that I don't accuse myself of lack of patriotism? Or why – and is not this a further dereliction? – do I look upon patriotism as paranoia and a kind of restricting curse? The sea has neither confines, prejudices nor politics.

Against the light I read his invitation – 'And stay here with all your family as long as you like.'

I have experienced much hospitality in the United States, which seems to be its home. But this man's hospitality is illimitable. The salvation of his *bos anoa* could not account for it.

How wonderful was his Lancashire welcome! The Clifton gold plate was out in our honour. We feasted long and sumptuously. Our host wore a scarlet tail-coat faced with lapels of light blue silk. It was a uniform he had designed for the President of the Lytham Golf Club, over which he presided.

I gazed at him as he sat in scarlet at the head of his table in the great dining-hall hung with old-rose velvet and gold. Golden candelabra expanded all around. He sat magnificent and munificent. And for all its arbitrariness, the uniform in which he was attired was not bizarre. It well became the scene. I watched his long, bony hands, golden from many suns. I thought of that Emperor, a great gift-giver, who had golden fists.

> Voire, ou soit de Constantinobles
> L'emperieres au poing dorez.

I had been sailing to Byzantium: but I am in it now!

But he was taking great trouble to entertain us. After dinner he would deliver a lecture on his adventure in Celebes, and as he hated speaking in public it was a compliment indeed.

He imagined that he had an impediment in his speech, but it was not a stutter, only a little halt now and again which gave it emphasis and the charm of distinction.

Nevertheless he was ill-at-ease when the tenants began to file into the Long Gallery.

He beckoned me aside.

'Lookey here, this kind of public lecturing always upsets me. Not that I am nervous. No, of course not. But there are so many things to be synchronized. The lantern fellow, and the last man in. I hate the noise of boots after the lights have gone out. However!' – cheerfully – 'I have arranged to allow myself a drink for every minute that lantern fellow delays me.'

He held a long billiard cue like a lance over his right shoulder.

'When lecturing, the thing is to seize the attention of your audience. You see! Now, these locals know nothing of Celebes. Nothing! If that damned lantern fellow is late bang goes this whisky – Here's, "happy days". What more can one wish for? Happy days! Damn it. It's nearly 9.56. The lecture is at 9.45. Well, it's not my fault: oxy-acetylene or something of that sort . . . Have another with me. Well, then! Do you think they'll like it? I only lecture now and then as a duty, you see. When I was President of the Orchid Club of Great Britain I chartered a rather large yacht and just succeeded in capturing that rare orchid after which I called one of my daughters. But this is a more serious affair – addressing one's own people. Have I time for another? I never allow myself . . .'

Cheering and 'barracking' drew his attention to his tenants. The oxy-acetylene lantern evidently had projected its beam and proved itself. 'Squire! Squire!'

'By gad!'

He rose magnificently against the screen.

'First picture!'

A map appeared.

'You see here Borneo and Clebes. Borneo is to the East, West . . . and . . . It is upside down! What are you doing? Oh, well! that's better. Borneo and Celebes. You may ignore Borneo. This is Celebes, and the blackened marks are our tracks for five hundred miles by sea, swamp, and forest. Next picture!'

A group of natives and thin-legged native children with enlarged spleens was projected.

'Now! Well! Yes. That's it! Now you see here a group of natives. These little cads are very camera-shy. It is hard to take their photographs. They thought that they were going to be shot. They were quite right. Next picture! . . .

'Here there are no little cads. They have been exterminated since the last picture.'

The tenants moaned in 'Oh!'

'Not at all! They have been exterminated by the Dutch government – quite rightly, because they resisted civilization. Next picture!' The house acquiesced in some finer shade of justice.

A bleak landscape appeared. Natives by a beach with what looked like a dug-out canoe.

'Now this is our boat. We have two hundred and fifty miles yet to paddle. Next picture!'

Sun-stricken desert. Four posts holding up a roof of palm thatch. Desolation.

'Our hotel.'

The oxy-acetylene hissed like a snake. But the lantern, after much blank light, at last projected a Chinaman.

'This is our host. He came from that shack to welcome us at the beach which you see here with "Good-bye! Good-bye!" as he led us towards his house. Next picture.'

Surely the greatness of the Englishman may be deduced from that depth of character wherein even the ludicrous becomes invested with a kind of grandeur and significance.

The long itinerary, as Thomas Cook would call a journey, was displayed and described. Mrs Clifton, festooned with leeches, had followed her lord and master through tropical swamps for miles and miles. Aigrettes it seems were sighted. So were humming-birds – in coveys, packs, broods, ascensions, or what?

The journey charmed me because its purpose was so unapparent. 'It is better to travel hopefully than to arrive.' Besides, he did not arrive. He was exploring. No explorer arrives. If he were to have a goal he would be merely a traveller, and not an explorer, whose chief claim to distinction is that he does not know where he is going. He is finding out.

On the whole the lecture was a success. The lecturer was concerned for his audience, and his audience were concerned for their lecturer.

A reciprocal success! That is as it should be. The lecturer had demonstrated what some governments do to their nationals. But the lecturer's tenants went away with a dim, instinctive feeling that one who had visited so many lands for

210

no apparent reason must be a good landlord and the last man to exploit his own retainers. A most successful lecture! Their Squire had to go for hardships to Celebes because hardships were far from home.

The next lecture – if any – was to be 'On my explorations in the Arctic.' This, if told from the Esquimaux's point of view, would have told of a jam he got them into, into which they would never have got themselves and of how, when the ice was cracking, they turned to him and asked 'What do we do now?' They believed that he had taken over the administration of the North Pole.

One day while speeding along his thirty miles of highroad by the discoloured sea, he said:

'You must have lost considerably by the upset to your work.'

'Of course,' I acknowledged.

'Now, lookey here. You can have one of my Lanchesters, a short wheel-based one, for a mere song. You see, with a short wheel-base you get a little, just a little more speed. And it corners better.'

'I couldn't raise wind enough just at present to inflate one of its tyres.'

'Oh, in that case, just drop in and name some little sum to Elwes, who has it at present in Brick Street, Park Lane. He will let you have it. A man cannot be without a car.'

I heartily agreed. Life would be endurable – that is, one might retire and trust to Life if one had the means of un-restricted movement, wheels and wings. Rest, even peace – immobility of any sort – is a form of death. But for all that I could not take his property, though offered with a tact and consideration which only those who took the trouble to know him and to put up with his sudden passions and impulses, could realize were deep at heart in the man. He had a golden heart as well as golden hands.

But the kind days among magnanimous Lancashire men could not go on for ever. My host was growing restless. One night towards the end of dinner he said suddenly:

'Let's look up Lonsdale.'

'Lord Lonsdale?'

'Yes. He's my cousin.'

My hostess intervened mildly, without astonishment.

'But he's in Scotland just now.'

'Of course he is! Everyone must be there in a day or so – that is,' looking at our group, 'if these good people will come along . . . But I can run up to Lonsdale's this evening in the Lanchester.'

The progress proposed was clogged perhaps by our presence; perhaps by something that diverted his attention.

'A little speeding will take us up there. He'll be surprised to see us.' Is an invitation for life to Lytham as short as a life sentence for some political outrage in an Irish gaol?

That I could believe. But we were bound for Scotland with no escape.

Kildalton Castle is not antique. It is modern, comfortable and desirable. Its 17,000 acres of deer forest, moors and covers constituted my only misgiving, together with the Thorburns which walled the dining-hall with water colours of every kind of game birds.

I am in for it now – 'Sport!' I said to myself.

But off my bedroom was a bathroom. Books were at my bed's head. Mine host had printed 'Private' in his own hand on a card – I have it yet – which he hung on the library door, so that I should not be disturbed. Kindness could go no further, nor his toleration of a literary lout. But still there was 'sport' staring me in the face during the daylight hours.

He broke it gently.

'To-day is a *dies non*. To-morrow, when you are rested, we might look about us for a bird.'

My father had an estate in his time on the banks of the Nore. He looked about him for a bird, but my memory of his sporting activity consisted of a newspaper opened under a bough and shot at from sixty, seventy, and eighty yards when it was too dark to walk the moors any longer. My share in this 'shoot' was to count how many pellets had hit the papers at the different ranges, and to record in my childish calligraphy whether they were No. 6 or Swan shot. What ensued next day at dawn was worse. My father threw saucers, cups, the breakfast set – many sets, up from behind a haystack. Unless I hit them, breakfast was omitted.

My eye improved with inanition.

'What about the teapot?' I inquired after an exceptionally destructive morning.

'Don't be impertinent,' he said.

Though grouse were easier than sidelong saucers, I could not even now dissociate them from alarming repercussions and a bruised collar-bone.

'I am quite content here,' I said. 'I am under no misgivings about being a shot. Long ago I have hit enough to last a lifetime.'

'Nonsense! No one sets a limit beforehand to a bag. Just you see.'

I who had blamed Yeats for forgetting his bathing-suit while being driven seaward, now said:

'I have forgotten my gun.'

He roared with laughter.

'Ho! ho! There are Purdeys in the gun-room for every kind of man. Take your choice. Get one with a balance to suit you!'

Condemned to heavy Trulocks thirty years ago, I am now promoted to Purdeys.

'You very kindly set your library apart for me. I think, if you don't mind, that I'll stay in and look round it.'

'Now, lookey here. We must think about our boys. We cannot set them a bad example. What will my son Harry think if his friends' father does not turn out? If you are not in form, the Chaplain here, who has very bad sight, will save your face. Come along!'

The line advanced, spreading out for about 120 yards. Mine host's son, my son, myself, my son, the Chaplain, and mine host. The setters were perfectly trained.

Bang! from the left. Tawny feathers floated in the air. A dead bulk thumped vertically downwards to the ground. Dermot had scored first shot. He awaited recognition.

'Now, what the devil do you mean? You have murdered a grey hen, the potential mother of eighteen black cock, which are getting rarer in Scotland every season. Fall out of the line, Dermot!' Stricken, the child retired.

Rather unfair, I thought, on a lad who was concentrating on not missing anything that broke cover and who had not been warned about grey hens, much less had he seen one.

'Now let us walk on.'

I watch with admiration the well-trained dogs and the way our host picks birds instantaneously out of the sky by his magic wand of a gun. They are setting again. Careful now.

A brown pack of whirring wings radiates out from the heather. Bang, and then bang!

His heir has stopped one with his left barrel as accurately as his father. Grouse falls from the air. His right only wings and wounds. Unforgivable in a Clifton.

'Out of the line, Harry!' Though Harry was shooting with a 20-bore.

Two sportsmen in disgrace. O Lord, what am I to do? Miss? But then it will put my mentor in an embarrassing position. He can hardly kick his senior guest off the grouse moor. Twenty minutes elapse. My left wing supports me no longer. They are somewhere in the rear. I alone am in command on the left. Hah! Under my feet a pack breaks. Not yet! No, by no means. I am too old a hand to shoot at radiating birds. They are not twenty yards away and flying fast, low and slanting. Forty yards. Yes! That's one. The middle member of the brood swings high to the right almost in front of the Chaplain. I give him the second barrel. He has twenty yards yet through which to fall. Suddenly he blows back towards me again, a mass of scattering feathers. He is bandied like a shuttlecock. My host has given him his left barrel as he falls. His Reverence solemnly fires a salvo over the grave. However, I am still in line. What will my remaining son, who by this time must be rather nervous, do? But his sight is superb and his aim accurate.

The moor falls to a burn. A rowan or mountain ash is the only tree to be seen. It stands branchless save above some distance to our right. A quarter of an hour. The birds do not like reeds. On we go. The dogs stand still again right ahead.

I am sure that I shall fall into one of these bog-holes two feet deep. I cannot watch my step. I cannot even 'see what flowers are at my feet' and keep an eye on the setters. If you fall into a little bog-hole I can hear the command, 'You stay there!'

I thank God I am to the left. It is up to my son now or mine host, or to his Reverence, who intervenes.

More birds! Left! That's one; but another diverges far to the right: eighty yards at least. Will Noll ever get it? Ah! It topples just in front of the mountain ash. But our host is rushing on in front to reach the tree before all the shot-shent leaves have fallen. What does the tree conceal? Why is he in such a hurry? He stands beneath it and points to the leaves which are still coming down over his head.

'You damned well might have shot me! Out of the line, Noll! Harry and Dermot back to stations again.'

'Don't worry, old chap!' I said to my retiring son, who was bruised in his heart by this, his first experience of injustice.

'Harry and Dermot back! No grey hens! Now, Father Chaplain, you must get a chance!'

'Uphill! There was a pink glow towards the east, a reflection surely from a fine sunset behind me, but I dare not turn my head. These setters and the concentrated alertness they demanded!

'Turn back!'

O, thanks be to all the gods of harbours and homesteads! We opened out as we met the gamekeeper with his two thin boards between which the necks of the game were held.

'You see, Father Chaplain, one must be always alert. Perhaps your gun is just a trifle, a very little trifle, too slow in coming up. Now, if a gun is unbalanced you can never hope to shoot, that is, instinctively at sight; and after all what else is . . .' Bang!

'Ah, that was just so that I might illustrate the excellent balance of my Purdey. – Mackenzie?'

'A grey hen, Sir.'

'Damn! Well, all right! Add it to the bag, for who can be expected to see against a level sun? Home all!'

Home we brought the grey hen dead, trying to break our steps lest anything funereal should appear to creep into our march.

(I wish I could hire a wild ass to 'Stamp o'er my head' tonight so that I may be 'fast asleep'.)

In the game-book I traced lightly and almost invisibly in lead pencil after the list of birds 'and 36 black cock'. Because the death of the two grey hens, as we had been informed, added to the potential bag 36 black cock.

I am feeling somewhat Homeric this morning: like a man who strove with gods. But to be the guest of a god entails strife of a sort. Had Clifton, that great hunter, lived in the Stone Age, he would have been feared for miles and miles around in all game reservations. The skulls of his wives would

215

have borne the biggest bumps and presented with pride the bluest wooing bruises.

'No morning tea! Take it away: who the devil invented this degeneration? I will not have my bath turned on either to cool or to overflow. That will do. You may go.'

A quiet shave while soaking in hot water! Like Julia in her bath. I

Lay at length like an immortal soul
At endless rest in blest Elysium.

Certainly Clifton has turned Kildalton Castle into an Elysium were it not for the agonizing recreations he pursues. I must look into his library to-day. He has marked it 'Private' to protect me from interruption when I am reading, but I haven't succceeded in getting within its sanctuary yet.

He never took breakfast. He sat at the breakfast-table like a warder waiting until I had finished masticating. I knew that the moment my jaws stopped chewing he would deliver sentence for the day's diversion – I was quite right. I laid down my cup.

'Deer-stalking! Be ready at ten!'

To this, like Pantagruel, I 'replied nothing'. But inwardly I was self-possessed and I met the challenge bravely. I met it as a matter of fact, half-way. The reason was that I had provided myself with such a good deer-stalking suit by such a good tailor that it reduced the grassing of a deer to the least of things that followed my investiture. It had all the colours of brown heath and shaggy wood, though woods were not necessarily included in a deer forest. It had hints of bracken, gorse, heather and heath so well blent that I said to my tailor:

'What does one want more than the sentiment of the Highlands? Here it is! You have done me very well! This felt on the shoulders lest the rifle should saw through my collar-bone shows admirable consideration. Such forethought! And my cap crowns all the moors as the high place of Edinburgh crowns Scotland, or Branksome's lofty towers its banks and braes. No need to go to Scotland, now that I am invested in it.'

'If Ah wiz you, Sir, A'd think twice before turning down an invite for deer-stalking. Many of our clients pays around £1000 a head when all comes to all. That is considering entertainments and friends.'

I appealed to my host. 'May I have a minute to jump into another suit?'

'A minute, yes. No more!'

I reappeared looking like a moving bog or one of those mountains which could 'skip like rams'. The general effect was greenish, although heather, streams, rocks, tartan, and the counterpane of Mary Queen of Scots' bed had been suggested in the woof.

As he realized what Savile Row thought of Scotland, the imperial on his chin shut up against a smile. He thought – the poor devil has done his best. His heart's in the Highlands!

As we drove to the forest, 'The great thing is not to be seen,' he said, and, 'This is your spy-glass. Put it on!'

I strapped a shoulder.

When the road ended a Ford met us. We went on until it could go no farther.

'Out!'

We walked or stalked for twenty yards.

'The first thing is to learn how to spy.'

'My sight, that is one eye, is pretty keen. I don't need a telescope.'

'It's not a telescope. It's a spy-glass. Who ever used a telescope stalking deer?'

If it goes on, I thought, I will find myself Victor of Trafalgar or the Nile. We are going backwards at such a rate.

'Now!'

He plopped down on a dry tussock and extended himself backwards until he lay flat. He crossed his legs and slowly brought his head upwards. Between his knees his balanced spy-glass rested.

'Now we spy. Fallow!' he jerked out. 'Take no notice! Spy! And – don't stand up. Lie down just where you are!'

'I am in a puddle!'

'We are stalking!'

Poole is in a pool, thought I. I opened the unnecessary telescope, spy-glass, or whatever the yard-long sections of tubing were. Water oozed through my symbolic knickerbockers. I jerked my hips towards higher ground.

'Stay still, can't you? Or you'll never spy a stag!'

There is a 'One-day Valeting Co.' in Dublin. Perhaps they may be able to do something with my ruined breeks, I hoped.

217

'What do you spy?'

The coast of Antrim was distinct. Ireland my home! 'Oh, to be in Antrim now Craigavon's there!' Out of focus! I shot a section or two into my only eye. What is this? A moving barn with black spots? No. A ladybird!

'There's five on the brae side,' the voice of the keeper was heard whispering cautiously in my ear. What a Christian the man was! But what and where was the brae?

'Now you see why we have to begin at the beginning. Spying is of paramount importance. You see nothing?'

'There's five on the brae,' I echoed.

He was far from convinced.

'Oh, are there? Then count the tines.'

I worked the telescope in and out like the pipes of a trombone. At last far off, what is it? Distinctly deer. The leader is a great dark grey stag with eleven tines . . . I shall have lumbago . . .

I hope they are in Scotland and not reindeer, I thought, as I announced:

'Eleven tines.'

'Eleven tines?'

He jerked himself into action on his back from his bed of dry heather. Apparently I had discovered a rare species of a sport. Under the circumstances he could hardly ask his pupil 'where?'

During the long delay I managed to slide landwards from my nine-inch pool. I waited until he had, having handicapped himself as much as possible for the ritual of sport, at last seen what were quite plain to a naked eye, five royal heads with the leader who had eleven tines. The deer ignored us.

'Oh, it's not eleven tines, but the velvet hanging down from a brow antler.'

'They are coming our way,' I ventured.

'Nonsense! Get up! After spying, stalking begins! Now!'

He threw some thistledown into the air and watched it as it floated past.

'Wind's in the right direction. Watch me!'

My tall and forthright friend suddenly became furtive. He stooped down and made little unaccountable forward rushes. Now he lay *ventre à terre* and wriggled on. Then he stopped behind a rock. He looked back to find me standing gazing in admiration.

'Do I do it now?' I asked.

'Dammit, of course you do! Lie down.'

'You told me to watch.'

'Dammit! We're stalking.'

I lay down.

'Now crawl along and take cover.'

I should have covered myself in an older suit.

'Never, never let yourself be seen!'

'They are miles away.'

Luckily he did not hear me. He was advancing crouched along a ditch.

Where is his gun? The keeper, invisible but slightly audible on account of his laboured breathing, followed. He probably bears the gun.

'Does this go on for long?' I whispered.

He put his finger to his lips, then pointed ahead. He trailed a gun in a green canvas bag. I could see a dagger in his belt. Kit Marlowe had one. So had Willie Shakespeare. Tradition! He looks frightened. Maybe we are in for an attack. I distinctly saw the deer moving in our direction. It may be soft with the velvet, I opined, but I am absolutely unarmed. If I had only kept the Browning (not the writer) that I carried in Dublin, I now might have a chance. It is five to three. And of course Clifton will demand the only gun. I remembered hearing somewhere that stags or bulls cannot gore you if you lie down. But I am lying down. I am getting miserably damp – thanks to that puddle – and nervous. I elbow myself into a rounded hollow thick with grass and little ferns. This would be a good place to hide – no, 'to take up my position'. I crawl head on into a large pair of hobnailed shoes. A long finger comes back and waves at me like the barrel of a revolver.

'Have we far to go?'

'Shut up! Who can teach you stalking if you talk?'

I am putting him in a bad temper; but, dammit, he is putting me in a most uncomfortable position, into a series of uncomfortable positions. When will this entertainment stop?

We reach a smooth open space. I can see the Paps of Jura. Above them long drawn strato-cumulus clouds streak across a watery blue sky. It must be lovely and pleasant to be over there on a fine day like this.

Now, how had he got himself half across this tennis-court or putting-green? Of course, it could not be one or the other, but it were just as flat as if it were. He was moving by inches, crawling forward like a tortoise on his elbows and the sides of his shoes.

I go next. I think I will make the passage a trifle slower to register zeal and compensate for my mistakes. He disappeared. But presently I caught his eye glaring at me from behind a rock.

With his free hand he beat a slow time like the conductor of a soundless orchestra. He crooked a finger and beckoned me to advance. I rubbed my face well into the fragrant sward and by a mixture of the movements of a *danse du ventre* and my toes, I moved as if the place were being re-sodded.

'Very good!' without words.

He raised his wrist-watch and pointed to the sun. His meaning was beyond me, but I nodded. I could not be cross-examined just then. The head keeper made the passage. And, in answer to an inquiring look from his master, inclined his head in some sort of understanding.

Now what was going on? This is collusion between them. They must have the stags under observation all the time. Look at me! I am not allowed to raise an eyelid!

We caterpillared up a slope fringed with a natural wall or bank breast high. He stopped here. Now he rolls on his back. The keeper crouches at his feet.

What a relaxation! I could see the sky and a wide prospect. I who had been prospecting and nosing roots of ferns. I hoped my face was dirty. It would show what a sterling stalker his pupil was. We lay for twenty minutes on the restful bank. But he was moving one foot. The keeper slid the rifle up towards him. He is going to shoot something soon, I thought. Soon I hope; this mountain sickness makes me very hungry. It is long past time for lunch. Quietly he undid the cover and disclosed a little rifle with a barrel of dark blue.

'Two forty,' he whispered. 'Flat trajectory, full bead up to two hundred yards.'

'Yes?' I said. 'Quite.'

'Take it, can't you?'

220

Good Lord! So it is I who am to shoot. I had never imagined that.

What was it the fellow said? 'Some gents pays up to £1,000 a head when they takes a deer forest in Scotland, all said and done.' And here was my good friend handing me £1,000 and I not even grateful!

I pulled myself together. I must make whatever slight repayment the gratitude and enthusiasm of a guest may mean to him. I must shoot a stag and revel in the griolloching. I must cast away apathy – Accidia? My God, of course it's Accidia! My besetting sin! If only I were Sir Horace, then even this act would be altruistic. This blood would be shed for Ireland; or to make room for reindeer whose milk is tubercle-free.

'Give me that gun!'

'It is not a gun. It's a rifle.'

'Sorry! Rifle.'

'Hold on now. Just a moment. Let me tell you one thing. No good sportsman wounds a stag. One of your singing friends rented a forest and sent his beast skipping across Scotland tripping in its own entrails. That kind of thing is simply not done.'

'What do I do? Kill it?'

'No!'

Good gracious! Does he mean me to catch it alive single-handed?

'You grass it.'

Well, I suppose if it stays on the grass it will be pretty well dead, I reflected. Suddenly, he remarked:

'They'll be getting up now. They usually get up about four, but the flies may be annoying them. See what you can spy.'

Forgetting the unwieldy spy-glass I peeped through the blades of a grassy tuft. To my amazement I saw the whole opprobrious hillside moving. There were from fifteen to twenty or more stags. I withdrew my head cautiously in awe. Never had I been so near to such large animals in the wild.

I signalled on my fingers – twenty. Instantly he became alert. He verified my observation in a second. Tapping the lock and whispering 'full bead two hundred yards', he passed me the little rifle.

Very cautiously I pushed it through the blades of grass. A great dark grey stag was leading the rest slantwise down the side of the opposite hill. He was about two hundred yards away, judging the little I knew of distance by the space between targets in the Royal Toxophilite ground where they shoot at a hundred yards.

Thank heaven for the 'full bead two hundred yards'. If I had to juggle with the little metal bootjack on the hither end of the barrel, all would be lost. I did not forget the safety-catch. Maybe he thought I would.

I could see the leader better now as he felt his way down the steep slope. I was afraid to look at the others. I waited until the royal beast should reach the level ground. A small spray crossed the sights. But a gust removed it. Three points were in line: The great stag's shoulder and my near and fore sights. I pressed the trigger. Again the leaves! Too late. Thunder in the hills. What a sudden rush of windy hooves! Not one left now! – But, ah, I had seen a lordly beast crumple when my view was cleared from the gusty ferns.

The stag sank down backwards but did not subside. His forelegs, placed apart, balanced his splendid erect antlers. His paralysed hind quarters slanted to the ground. He looked like an heraldic figure. What had I destroyed? Grace and speed and an untameable heart! I felt disconsolate. But for the first time a cheery note sounded from my host.

'Just four inches too high! Too full a bead. You would not believe that the trajectory is flat for two hundred yards. You have not done too badly, though. His spine is blown to bits. Come along!'

The keeper who had lain at his feet now appeared fifty yards in front of us. Respectfully he waited until the Laird inspected the stag.

Antler high, crouched with back sloping from the shoulders, the terror-stricken, immovable beast regarded us with reproachful eyes. Men had never come so close to him before. His instinct was true, no good comes from man's proximity. But he could only rear his antlers. The swift haunches lay sideways inertly on the ground.

'Now!'

The keeper went towards the noble head. He seized the right antler and forced the left to the ground. On this he stood with one foot, and while the great beast was nailed sideways but yet fully conscious, he unsheathed his long blade and plunged it

222

into the root of the neck. He was digging for the aorta. Presently his knife work was rewarded by pints of hissing blood. The stag slumped down. It rolled on its back, dead. The moist knife cut out, first the genitals, then the great white-bluish sack of stomach, full of grass and moss.

I looked on bemused, thinking how like to the inside of an oyster shell is the colour of a stag's full stomach. Mine host was stooping down. He appeared to be dabbing or looking for something amid the bloody guts.

I was no longer concerned about his attitude towards me. Surely I, his pupil, had justified his teaching. A dead shot, first time, at two hundred yards. Suddenly he straightened up. He slapped me smartly across the face. Red dew splashed my eyes. Cheerily he exclaimed:

'You are blooded now!'

No novice can afford to be angry when he is learning a game. I tried to make my face assume a 'We are seven' innocence through its five-fingered streaks of blood.

Signals may have summoned them or the sound of the shot; but it seemed as if the Highland pony and his keeper appeared out of the hillside. The stag was tied dangling across the sturdy back of the little steed. We made for home.

'Were there not at least thirty stags when you spied them first?' he inquired, solicitous for his forest.

'To make an honest confession, I got such a surprise when I saw your hillside, braeside, alive with moving game that I could not count. But they were some lengths apart from each other and they extended sideways about as far as they were from me. How many stags go to two hundred yards?'

'Nonsense! That would mean fifty or sixty.'

'Well, you saw the stampede. They had nothing to do with our five of this morning's spying.'

'Yes; but you may have counted the hinds.'

('Don't show your ignorance,' I warned myself.)

'Anyway, home we go! You were just six inches too high. I said full bead.'

'You gave me a tip which made it possible for me to bring off that amazing fluke.'

'Just a trifle high; but you grassed him in spite of a bad shot.'

I remain modest.

'And for the first shot a record stag is not so bad, considering the way you stalked.'

Now to show my humility.

'But, Laird, I deserve no credit. The deer are more or less tame. My friend, Inderwick, champion bowman of England, could kill them with an arrow. So could I, and my score for a York round rarely tops two hundred.'

(Which of you can kill a buck? And who can kill a doe?)

'That's because you are not musical,' he said, and he laughed in sudden mockery. 'And you did not gut him. Fluke. Ho? If you were a singer you might have only knocked off his horns.'

It was ordained that the guests in Kildalton Castle should sit two-some at little tables in the dining-hall. The principal guest sat with his hostess, while the host sat with the wife of his guest. There was feasting in Kildalton and toasts in my honour. I felt dishonest. I had never shot anything save an arrow more than a hundred yards.

'And no *nouveau riche* shot!' he exclaimed, raising his glass. He is still obsessed by that shot, thought I. What am I to do? Here I find myself, through no merit of my own, in the most delightful place I have ever seen or ever shall see – if I know my destiny. How am I to reply? How am I ever to convince him that I am grateful?

The refrigerating larder held three deer when I looked in. One he had given to my son to grass; one probably was his own; and now a third which was mine. Not his cousin Lonsdale with all his lands and sportsmanship could extend more generosity and largesse (*Au poing dorez!*) to what, as at best, I must have appeared to him – 'a little Dublin doctor'. The immediate tribute I must pay is humility. No boasting! I must not accept congratulations for a fluke!

I lolled and revelled in his library. 'Private'. Now be very fair, I said to myself, and differentiate hospitality from domination. If my father had not died when I was twelve, what would have happened to me? I might have been (no, for I never exceeded high grade mediocrity at anything), for the sake of argument, a second-rate shot and a first-class ignoramus.

The radio on the tower of his Castle is out of order for the moment, but the receptiveness of his wife and his sensitive son to sentiments and ideas is not. Poetry is sacrificed to the poultry we call 'game'.

What a tragedy! His eldest son ordered out of the line for no fault. His wife never allowed any prominence for her excellence. I think of Lady Lavery, who was an admirable painter, but, for her husband's sake, she suppressed her talent. Stags instead of stanzas, and grouse instead of verses. How many birds and deer fall annually, and have been falling for the last hundred years, and of all who shot them,

> How many lie forgot,
>   In vaults beneath,
> And piecemeal rot
>   Without a fame in death?

Well I know the difficulty – forgo sport altogether and become a prey to pretenders and poetasters: is there no middle way between Helicon and the heather? Men like Lord Dunsany prove that there is.

Why do I allow my mind to dwell on the normal or the unexceptional? Here am I who always pretended that I would like to meet the mighty and the unsurpassable. The moment I do, I find myself endeavouring to reduce them to the ordinary and to make them amenable and comprehensible. Why?

Talbot Clifton is, as his wife divined, only to be judged by rules made for himself and changeable to suit circumstances – like cricket at Dunsany. He is to be judged, but not by us – so why judge him at all?

A unique and dominating personality which cannot or will not express itself within the measures of mediocrity is reduced to the survey of us who can never be his equal. Why this straining for the Overman when we can neither recognize nor bear with him when he appears?

Talbot Clifton was metaphorically the last bachelor, though he was of the breed of William Rufus, and the first of that great race whom modern Nietzsche called: the Uebermensch, the Blond Beast, the Uncompanionable, the Fearless and Lonely One.

Of what use were all his expensive and spasmodic excursions? What did he achieve? Nothing. Nothing in the huckster's view or the view of the solicitor's clerk. He was noble, aimless, irascible, bullying, dauntless, extravagant, generous, scorning craftiness or thrift, golden-hearted, golden-fisted, fast

225

to his friend, sadistical and successful – a figure unhorsed into our humdrum days from Roncesvalles or Fontarrabia.

Let us give up the pretence of wishing for the times of Charlemagne again if we cannot admire in our own time Talbot Clifton.

What does he see in me to make me his guest-friend? I know not. But I do know that the first time he does anything that can be construed in our safety-vault box age as 'helpful' or 'practical', I will disbelieve in Homer and Malory and spare 'no lord for his piscence'.

My greatest tribute to him is that he is incredible in these our times.

It is no use cavilling, 'His Life – What was it all about?' I can answer. He is the figure of an ideal predominant in the mind of the yeomen of England. A friend of the people, a Robin Hood. A man they choose to represent. A man they hail, acclaim and depend on. Because he is to be trusted to obtain and maintain for them that indomitable freedom he impersonates and represents.

The piper who had played a merry skirl three times round the dining-room had just retired. The sounds of the pipes faded, sobbing in their bag. He had worn the Royal Tartan of the House of Stewart. The laird sat at his table, also wearing the Royal kilt. He and his wife were descended from the Merry Monarch through the Duke of St Albans. But the Stewart tartan in a Campbell stronghold! Well, I have had enough of politics. In Scotland such things may no longer provoke.

But we spoke in whispers, maybe because we were tired from, or thoughtful of, the afternoon's sport.

Suddenly the Laird's voice rang out:

'Harry! Second picture from the top corner on the left?'

'Canvas-back duck, Father.'

'Right, go on with your dinner ...'

'Dermot! The one in the corner?'

'Sheldrake, Sir!'

'Correct!'

During the ensuing lull my voice audible. I was merely remarking without any suggestion in it of relief that darkness put an end to a day's sport.

But I had been overheard.

226

'Nonsense! Flighting begins at eleven. The duck will just be coming in as you will see, or hear!'

Why had I spoken? Flighting. Now what is that? I was to have a night sport just to refute what he took as an implied slight on his property: that it could not produce sport at any hour.

After much clambering down through tunnels over-arched with shrubs, we reached a little cove. I resolved to explore these paths by day. Beside the sea, in the cliff face, they must be very beautiful. There was hardly enough light in the night to show the cove's water floor. You could feel that the rocks were well covered in seaweed. I was given the best upholstered one. I tried to find something drier. I trod on one of the retrievers. Blunders are concatenated. We shall have no luck, or rather it is I who shall have no luck, to-night. I tried to comfort the dog.

'Hush! not a sound!'

Nor a sight.

'What is the idea? Who can see to shoot in the dark?'

'That's just it. When the eye fails the hunter's ear comes in. We may be able to hear them swimming about!'

In the sultry dark we waited for over an hour. The unfamiliar sounds of the night brought many surprises: a lapping wave that made a noise as if some animal were lifting itself shorewards; the seaweed crackling and sighing, tinkling sounds behind me on on the sand. These were not immediately audible. There was no sound of them from the first ten minutes after we had sat down. Did the ear become accustomed, or were they really made by unseen living things that had grown bold?

An hour passed. The air hung limp in the stillness. Invisible woods were reversing their process of exhaling fresh air. The damp on which I was stationed was unevenly distributed. This means a cold, I thought.

'Would it be any harm if I just took off my things and slipped into the little bay for a swim? If I cannot see the land I will whistle and you can call.'

'Good God! And the duck waiting to come in! Have you any knowledge of wild life at all?' And this to me who had been with him in Ireland.

I gazed crestfallen at the dim brown watery plane. Perhaps he is right, but I never heard of duck flighting, or anything flighting except owls, bats and mosquitoes in the dark. I must wait and see. I had to, whether I liked it or not. The next thing he would have to be angry with would not be me, I resolved. He could take it out of the weather, or the stillness of the night. I will not make another remark for fear I might blurt out the word 'Dawn'. And that might suggest to him an all-night sitting; for he knew that he would not sleep well during the heat wave.

A moth or some insect was trying to land on my ear. I brushed it off. He heard the sound, 'Hist!'

Ah well! I thought, it is better to be here by the quiet, the very quiet sea, than in Dublin with my guards who shoot each other and the furniture. But is it? If he heard my slightest movement, what will happen when he is shooting by ear? And though sideways, I am between him and the sea. It would be ironical if I were to escape from enemies in Dublin to be peacefully shot by a sporting friend. If my guards shoot each other it might be just my luck that my host should shoot his guest in the dark. If I could keep still it might not be so alarming. But I simply cannot sit still, wait for people, or stay still. I attribute this disease to being deprived for hours, when I was but a tiny boy, of freedom of movement, which in children is an additional appetite. Perched high up beside my father in his 'mail phaeton', I was driven round while he visited patients. And forbidden to clamber down, I had to sit still when the coachman took his place to walk the horses.

It must have been nearly two o'clock, when:

'No flighting! They are waiting for a moon. Come along!' There is not the least good in writing to George about this, I thought. My avenger must be Dunsany who will throng the air with feathers if I can get him invited for a shoot.

'In those days, Harry, the world was reclining on its elbow.' I hastened to explain to the puzzled Harry that it was a figure of speech intended to call up the image of a patrician at a banquet or a statue of one of those river gods who lean on an urn from which water pours its beneficent gifts. I was reclining in an armchair in his father's excellent library. 'Civilization had reached the most distant lands to which the Peace of Rome had spread. There are very few periods in history wherein the peoples are aware of their good fortune. Augustan Rome

228

was the Golden Age of the world as it was then. Slaves there were, and hostages, injustice and persecutions, forests were felled and roads were made and simple tribes conscribed; but for the lords of creation prosperity was at its height. Augustus the Emperor, the Divine, the descendant of Venus through Aeneas (that is what the little dolphin means that follows in that statue at his heel, the Sea-born's son), was a mixture of Kitchener and the Archbishop of York, soldierly and sententious. He patronized the Arts. He listened patiently to deputations, addresses and the hexameters of his civil servants until he was rendered immune from insomnia for life. But there was one who made hexameters in a way that no one realized was possible in the Roman tongue. You would need to read Lucretius, who was his elder by years, to see with what easy grace and silver light Virgil had flooded his page when compared to that didactic atheist who preceded him. I cannot tell you whether Virgil was a great poet because it was a great period, or whether it was a great period because Virgil was a great poet. There are questions which do not admit of an answer because the fallacy lies in their being put at all.

'Virgil was a great poet because of his style, his lofty outlook and nobility of soul, and because of the Tiber-like flow and volume of his verse which reflected cultivated hills and stately towers.

'*Fluminaque antiquos subterlabentia muros.*

'He came from the north of Italy where beech trees slope to little stream that had as gentle a course as the Evenlode or the Windrush near Oxford. I think it is better to imagine it as the Windrush, for it was "crowned with vocal reeds". And it must have flowed as gently as sweet Afton flows gently by its silver birches, for the very sound of the poet's name is gentle, not a rod to battle down the proud, but a wand to lean to all the winds and spread its leaves to airs it turned to sound.

'A man from the north meant something very different to Rome than it means to us. From Scotland many poets have come. Very few have come from Ulster to Dublin, because they have sold their souls for common-sense. Facts are not the stuff out of which dreams or poems are made. There must be something far off and strange, "fine translunary things", as Ben Jonson has it, for the fabric of good verse. Something unworldly and even a little foolish. Virgil was a dreamy man. I think he had a little asthma and that he suffered from sinusitis. He suffered from headaches and he preferred to live in the neighbourhood of Naples than in the skyscrapers of crowded Rome. I can see him so distinctly; tall, stooping a little like Shelley, but walking by no means so fast. Shelley had a squeaky voice and his verse at best is somewhat strident. Virgil's voice is always smooth, therefore he never hurried, and his utterance was low and soft.'

'Won't you read me a few lines of the Eclogues?'

'It is not necessary, my dear Harry, we should only bore each other, and a feeling of affectation would result. We should never read poetry, we should make it. I was put off from ever becoming a Latin scholar by having to read Latin. Had someone told me about hexameters and the way their long lines went I would have read for myself. Now I know nothing of Latin, but I can talk of Virgil and so can you, provided you do not read him. Parsers killed his poetry just as medieval logicians killed the Logos, the Divine word or Reason with their mnemonic "limericks", Barbars, Celarunt, Darii! The world forgot the Muses for eight hundred years ...

'Your father, by the way – where is he now?'

'He will be back any minute. He went to look after some eggs.'

'Those paths by the sea, Harry, where do they go?'

'For miles along the coast.'

'Will you show me them? I would like to go at once, if you don't mind. Bring a book along ...

'Can you bring it to your mind's eye? It was the greatest tragedy from which Humanity ever suffered. It was paralleled perhaps by the ruin in Russia; but in the darkness that fell on the world Virgil was not forgotten. He was given the only tribute ignorance and superstition can pay genius. He was regarded as a wizard. He became a kindly fiend. It was as if Shakespeare or Tennyson were forgotten and their pages turned to amulets or charms.

'Think of the greatest and most silenced betrayal in history: Rome's dereliction of British Romans. For four hundred years England had the privilege of being a greater Rome than Romulus's town. Her climate was better. The stature of her men was better. "Sed Angeli" and she had the blending of many Northern races to fortify the South. In a day the legions

230

are recalled. Girls engaged to noble Romans find their betrothals nullified. Hairy and horrible the Greater Scots burst in over Hadrian's Wall. They helped their kinsmen to ravage and to destroy. Never to rebuild or to replace. Mark that! Gardens were weeded over. The hypocausts or central heating systems which went under the floors came into light and were, later, taken to be, to your knees bared, "journeys to Jerusalem". Was there ever such a collapse? I stood with my friend Boni on the Palatine Hill on the floor of Nero's Golden House, and he showed me how in the Middle Ages pilgrimages to Jerusalem could be curtailed at Rome by shuffling bare knees round an ancient central heater. Plumbing had caught the pilgrims.

'When our Heroic period consists of the destruction of the World's greatest civilization, who can blame the attenuated resentment of our tribes?'

If I am not careful, I said to myself, I will end by making Harry regard literature as he must by this regard the stern discipline of sport. Let me leave at least one young person to forage for himself. 'Where Helicon breaks down In cliffs to the sea.'

We reached without interruption the resinous woods. To the right the upshot light of a silver sea. Harry led the way. He did not speak. He had been taught to be so 'observant' that the wide prospect and the revel of light and shade were to him blotted out.

'This is the kind of thing that gave Virgil his pensive, preoccupied and almost melancholy note. The necromancers put it down to a mood of prophecy. Prophecy of what? Rome's ruin, nothing else. You might as well see in Tennyson a prophetic welcome for Lenin as in the fourth Eclogue an advance publicity notice for St Paul.'

Harry said: 'Are you bored by stalking?'

I reassured him. I had set aside Accidia. I had resolved to be full of gratitude.

'I just wanted to know how you will like a much bigger stalk to-morrow.'

'Virgil,' I said, giving myself time to pull myself together, 'got that peculiar pensiveness of his from a realization of the unintermittent war between civilization and culture. Fell the woods, and what becomes of Pan, Sylvan and the Sister Nymphs? Leave the woods and the barbarian threatens Rome.

231

Simplicity against civilization: civilization a safeguard from contagious terror and taboo. *"Sunt lacrimae rerum"* balanced by *"Tantum religio"*.'

If one year's seniority at the University is unbridgeable, what must twenty-five years between pupil and tutor be? And when the tutor is himself a pupil of the youth's father, authority goes for nothing. That is the way it should be. But how am I to get an inkling of the thoughts of youth?

'It's one hundred yards from the last tunnel,' Harry said, and Harry had been taught to be observant.

'If you must be observant, note how a grey cloud shadow becomes purple on the sea. And feel no deprivation because you are not in Sicily when you read about the "Green and purple glow of Syracusan waters". Only the blind, not the observant, count their steps.'

Who tunnelled this solid rock to make a riviera? Who planted the estate with magnificent forest trees? Nobody observes them. I am aware of the many shades of green which make up to me in exquisite delight for the neglect and want of development of music within me. Is it not a sign of some sort of depravity to be moved overmuch by the shades of green? Maybe, but the harmonies of the tones by which Spring astonishes my eyes are more to me, though transient, than all the vocable glories of everlasting noise.

If I sit by a little brook, Harry will not think that I am thinking of its significance in terms of trout.

'Let us sit here for a while and wait and see. There is nothing to see but that four-foot waterfall, and nothing to wait for but the thoughtlessness it brings.'

If I in my youth resented rest, naturally this youth did too. How few are there who take their pleasure in looking for hours into the amber depths of a mountain torrent! But it brings me moods of mysticism – the transparent becoming visible, or serves as a reminder of the harnessed torrent of Pindaric verse.

'Why wouldn't you let me read Virgil?' Harry asked after a pause.

'Because if you read other people's poetry you will write about it instead of making your own. It is not poetical to write about poetry. You become second-hand and easily dated. Europe has not as yet recovered from the Renaissance, nor has English poetry recovered from Alexander Pope.

232

'We might go hunting in the village for living words, words such as those with which the tramp in Kylemore hailed your mother's house. "It's a fine still place you have here, Ma'am, surely." Remember it was near one of these Isles that *Aiken Drum* was written, and that poem contains more live poetry than any pastoral verse I have read. The goblin Aiken Drum promises to "Ba the bairns wi' an unkenned tune." Now, that's what poetry is, "an unkenned tune", not a repeated air. And listen: "Last night I dreamed a dreary dream beyond the Isle of Skye." That is beyond what was Ultima Thule to the Scots poet, beyond the edge of the known world where the Land of Dream begins. We are nearer Ultima Thule here than we ever were before. Magnificence amid mountains islanded and for the pettiness of Life no care. Your father stalks like Achilles on the island of his translation. And I feel just about as much at ease as if I were spending a week-end in his tent.'

Next morning I was reclining on both elbows in the library which was marked 'Private' but not sound-proof, and I heard the loud command,
   'Stalking!'
I read no more in the book that day.
Three hours later, after almost subterranean creeping through the deepest and narrowest dykes, we emerged into sun and dryness on a hill. A little hill fifty feet or so high and separated from its fellow by a valley eighty yards in width. The position lacked humour and was even too heavy for sport. I was under a cloud, and I had to wait until it burst. What had I done? Whatever I did, must have been done before the morning of the present day, for the stalk began under penalizing rules. The deer were evidently wilder and more alert than ever in their career. We lay without talking for half an hour on the hill. Mine host's flask, which he had invented so that its covers, becoming separate, made two drinking-vessels instead of one, was almost empty. The air was full of midges, which were spiteful and had constantly to be repulsed. Under a rock-roofed ledge half-way up on the opposite hill 'royals' were lying down. The head and antlers of the first were plainly visible, which meant that he could see us if we showed. The second and third had only antlers visible. In a corner where the rock sloped so that it was hard to rise if startled, lay a fourth stag

with a very poor head, a 'switch'. He lay back in the dark recess of the rock. His companions were full in daylight but out of the sun.

'Surely,' I asked as I smacked a midge, 'they will get up if the flies keep on pestering them?'

'Put in your cuffs and turn up your collar, or you will frighten the hinds which are over there about a mile away.'

I obeyed.

'If you give me the gun – rifle, I can get a close-up if I slip ten feet down the valley so that the first stag cannot see me. I then can walk straight over the rest of the way.'

'There are no valleys in a deer forest.'

He drained his flask, and ten minutes later added:

'Only corries.' Later, after an equal interval:

'And no "close-ups".'

'Sorry,' I said, 'I am totally ignorant.'

'Only too evident.'

Perhaps this was a part of the training of a hunter, to irritate him so that he should be able to shoot even with his temper frayed. It may be a means of obtaining the equivalent of the fatigue of a long vigil. If I have to slap another fly my cuff will appear. The hinds will be startled, and then good-bye to the stags. It must be worse, I brooded, in the swamps of Africa where they temper the Cyprian extravaganzas of their chieftains by exposure to mosquito bites. But any hunting megalomania that may have threatened me is already anticipated and cured in advance. I am humbled in the presence of the Laird. If I lie on my face and bury it in the grass I can cover my ears with my hands and so avoid the pests.

I could not have fallen asleep; but I evidently had not heard some whispered command. He kicked the rifle towards me: 'Have your close-up.'

Head-first I slid at an imperceptible pace, not daring to look up until I had descended twenty feet. I marked the dark rock and its two tufts of heather. Then, rising, I walked briskly towards the ledge and began to climb. It was at an awkward height, with a shelf about the height of a mantelpiece beneath. As I was wondering how to mount it unheard, a loud voice just behind me said, 'Remember your beast is lying down.' There was not a moment to be lost. With one hand I grasped the rock above the mantelshelf, and with rifle under my arm, made a leap. But the stags were startled, all but the one hampered by the rocky roof. He stuck against it as he scrambled to his knees just as I got a moment's equilibrium in which to pull the trigger of the rifle that touched his charging breast. It must have seemed as if a shot had gone off accidentally in the air, to anyone who saw me rolling down the corrie after the stags, who were already two hundred yards away.

My host was exultant. 'Ho! Ho! Ho! So you thought they were tame, did you? You see where they are now.'

I sat where I was and wiped the grass-stained stock. The cloud was bursting. I had called them *tame!*

'Let me tell you something. You thought it was all beer and skittles, deer-stalking. Now perhaps you realize that it is the sport which requires more skill than many outdoor sports. It is a very difficult science. Everyone misses a stag now and then. King Edward missed his beast and had his stags driven, thereby ruining his forest. My very good friend the Duke of Leeds missed six and he actually wept.'

'Am I supposed to break into tears?'

'Certainly not, but you are supposed to acknowledge that you thought it was too easy. You should have said, "Clifton, I am very sorry, but I got buck fever and consequently missed." '

'Buck fever?'

'Yes, over-excitement in the presence of the quarry which makes a fellow lose his head.'

'But I assure you that I killed the stag. Not any of the "royals", but one you could well spare.'

'Lie number one.'

'I am not in the habit of lying gratuitously, as I will say to fit in with the estimate you seem to have of me. I have nothing to gain or to lose.'

'Lie number two. You have your lack of moral courage to conceal.'

'Dammit! I only did what you told me to do – have a close-up. If I had missed, it would have been worse, for you would have thought that your teaching was wasted on a ham-handed ass.'

'Lie number three. I never told you to shoot from your hip like a German shock trooper.'

I could feel the slow anger rising which floods the brain

until reason is drowned and the irrational instincts are set free. Thus it appeared to me that I had been deliberately taken out to be made to miss, to be shown up – that it had been taken for granted that I was a vain coxcomb, proud and presumptuous at another man's expense.

But it is all very easy and sometimes self-indulgent to yield to anger. How will I appear to my wife and family if I return no longer on speaking terms with my host?

And how am I to stand on my dignity and borrow at the same time the means of transport? There is not a car to be hired on the island, and it is seven miles to the nearest port.

While I was about to cast decency to the winds in spite of the fact that my host was breathing heavily in anger and to let resentment loose at what seemed an abuse of hospitality as a trap, an *ex machina* gillie appeared.

'Me Laird, the stag is dead!'

'How? Where? What?'

'Aboon your head.'

He looked up. The tawny throat lay limply upside down from the shelf of rock.

'Oh!'

A sudden thought.

'Go and see how long it is dead.'

'Ye can see the blood oozing the noo!'

I pitied the spoilt man-child now. He stood flabbergasted.

'Ho,' he said to himself and 'Ho!' again. I could not be separated from the slaughter. Lie number one was no lie. And those arising from the assumption no lies.

I hate being witness to anyone's embarrassment. I tried to walk away. I handed in my 'gun' slowly to the gillie. I walked, as I had told Harry I thought Virgil must have walked, with the natural sorrow that is at the heart of all things on his shoulders. Buck fever, indeed! What had Clifton now? Increased irritation with me for putting him in the wrong.

'At any rate you'll acknowledge that it is the sport of kings,' at length he said.

'No,' I said, 'I will not. King Edward ruined his forest according to you.'

On reaching the Castle he yelled for my wife. She failed to appear. He shouted for his own. She appeared immediately. Mine appeared soon after to inquire what it was all about.

Round the circular plot in front of the hall we went, careful not to overtake each other. I tried to explain. I could see by his back that he was denouncing my duplicity and unworthiness.

'And could you not have humoured him, you who know him so well?'

'Yes. But what would he think of his teaching if his pupil bungled?'

'You say that he wanted you to bungle so that he might demonstrate to you the results of over-confidence.'

'He certainly did.'

'I have no patience with you!'

'I am leaving to-morrow.'

The dressing-bell relieved our restrained stalking.

Again, the munificence in the dining-hall. But we spoke in whispers, overshadowed by the guilt of my success.

'Imperial Tokay since the war is unobtainable,' I ventured to remark.

'Mackenzie! The cellar keys, a tumbler, and a torch.' Me, he summoned with: 'Come along.'

The Castle must have been built on an old foundation. The cellars extended far underground. At last through tunnels we reached an over-arched shelf. Ten or twelve squat flasks – Imperial Tokay!

'My cousin Esterhazy kept some for me. Here's your very good health.'

He looped his finger round the neck of another bottle and swung it as he moved along. It was broached in the dining-room.

'My mother,' he announced, 'never realized that a child was born to her who had the making of a most excellent flautist. She discouraged my music, and my flute-playing never got a chance. And I could have been a rather outstanding . . . Ho! I bet you don't even know the word for one who is proficient on the flute?'

Although he had just said it, I said, 'No. I don't.' (Lie number one!)

'Well, then! Let me tell you, and you boys remember this – it's "Flautist".'

To the butler he said, 'Bring me my golden flute.'

A case, like one of those which contain fish slicers, was

237

presented. It opened and disclosed two golden tubes. These he screwed together and began to play.

'Will you play upon this pipe?'

I determined that I would be the most perfect failure he had ever triumphed over, even if I were to be drawn like Marsyas from my sheath of skin. I put one end to my mouth. Luckily, not a sound. 'My Laird, I cannot.'

'I pray you.'

'Believe me, I cannot. I know no touch of it.'

'It's not a tin whistle. See here! 'Tis as easy as lying. Govern these ventings with your finger and give it breath with your mouth and it will discourse most excellent music. Lookey, here are the stops.' He set it sideways and fluted a few notes. 'Now try.'

I tried, making sure that not a note would escape.

'Why are you sticking your tongue into the stop?'

'To get out some of the Imperial Tokay you blew into it just now.'

He was on his feet instantly, with the flask and an apology as he brimmed my glass. After all, I was his guest.

'My friend, I am very, very sorry.'

Surely I took my 'fill of deep and liquid rest forgetful of all ill'. He expanded imperially and told us how he discovered the Yukon gold before the money-grabbers, and inestimable wealth in iron on an Hebridean property his men of business would not allow him to buy.

I have met some of the world's greatest men. If I dared to interfere with the march of death, I would like to petition that fell sergeant for leave for a hunt again with Talbot Clifton.

With what a problem would we not be presented were it given to us to bring back one or two of the dead! Would we choose from the throng of the world's great shadows or of our relatives and friends? It would depend very much on how recent was our sorrow. Immediately on the death of a relative or friend, or some great personage, we might be tempted to exercise our gift of recall. But given time to recover from grief and to think, we would not be so hasty, having philosophized. It comes to this then, that Time justifies everything, even its own outrages.

What would it avail to recall Julius Caesar from the dead?

238

His work was done and Time's procreant waters rose and made it fruitful. How could he, who hardly knew the direction in which he set its sources, deal with the majestic river's emerging deltas? If those who were to be redeemed from beyond the irremediable river were to be, not only aware of all they caused to grow, but to be held responsible for two thousand years of Time's trend and magnification, would the recall even of Pontius Pilate from the dead to-day be fair or just to Pontius Pilate?

This means that only our contemporaries or friends still unforgotten might be given the benefit of our gift of resurrection. But would an heir recall his father to his own disinheriting, and to the double death of his parent? Would Lloyd George recall Haig, or the British Navy, Nelson?

The only recall I can think of without hesitation as desirable has been imagined 2300 years ago. The recall to her orphaned children of the young mother, Alcestis. It is not quite so safe to recall an infant dedicated to death. A foot-bound child exposed whom a shepherd found, came to but little good from his rescuing. But the younger mother whose breast grows cold to her infant's fingers, appears to present the tragedy of tragedies to me who am loth to tamper with Time or teach the prophetic world its business.

I can only pray that Time will match its step to its funeral march and teach its striplings slowly.

It was no use. I am not born to the purple. Like the girl in Bobbie Burns' lyric who

> Wadna hae a laird,
> Wadna be a leddy
> But she would hae a collier
> The colour of her daddy,

I could not be a laird or stalk beyond my walk in life contentedly.

239

CHAPTER FIFTEEN

I reconciled myself to fall back on myself, so I practised my profession for a while in London.

Often I stood aside and looked at its ordered greatness. A city is the face wherein a nation's character may be read. Disciplined might and millions organized! 'Make no mistake,' Tom Kettle used to say, 'the English have organization!' Here was Freedom visibly being founded, apportioned, and assured. The queues outside each theatre witnessed to this order, as their humour and their patience witnessed to their goodwill.

London is a university with ten million graduates qualified to live and let live. And the use of the English language makes all nations undergraduates to this Freedom. 'At a great price purchased!' ... But I was born free.

There is no poll tax on newcomers to this town, this navel stone of civilization. No charge for protection against molestation or robbery. The *Pax Britannica* safeguards all. How many 'nationals' who had sought to overthrow her order were glad to seek Great Britain's sanctuary in the end?

And here was I, an Irish Nationalist all my life, 'on my keeping' not in the Glens of Wicklow or Connemara but in the neighbourhood of Mayfair.

When working to restore Ireland to nationhood, I should have ascertained first what a restored Ireland's idea of a nation was likely to be. Would it give leave to live to all its nationals? Would its idea of freedom be universal or restricted to a gang? When working to release Kathleen, the daughter of Houlihan, so long imprisoned by the Sassenach, I should have asked myself what sort of soured harridan was likely to emerge. Would her long incarceration not have perverted her and made warders and turnkeys and worse warders the fancy men of her free choice? Had Freedom dazed her?

Too late! Kathleen was out, and she was quickly picked up by those men who knew her for a jail-bird, being themselves so apt for prison service.

Thank God none knew me for a patriot here in London! I could walk without a guard. But walking without a guard did away with a Senator's identity. It was as if a barrister had lost his umbrella. I found this out when I called on Lord Granard at Forbes House. He wanted to hear my news. So I walked round to Halkin Street, but the dark iron gates were closed, and it took a long time for his detectives to believe that I was I. Lord Granard was a Senator too, and it was a Senator's privilege to be escorted! Unescorted, so much the less Senator he!

I had no news, only that *The Field* had an account of what had happened to me and a stag in the Isle of Islay.

'You know my Galway house is burned?'

'They have exploded a bomb in the hall of Castle Forbes. I do not yet know how much damage has been done.'

We were partners in affliction. Our country was afflicting itself into a republic of ruin where all that is outstanding is levelled to the ground.

Next to the Percy and the Douglas families, I would like to be one of the Forbës Clan, for they are mentioned in the Border Ballads. And I cannot even as yet bring myself to believe that anyone can be any good who is not mentioned in Song. The poetic predilection in me is more ineradicable than the poetic licence.

The best families of England and Scotland and even of Ireland are ballad Worthies. 'Colonel Hugh O'Grady is now lying dead and low' – gone with the Wild Geese!

But listen first to the record of the great swordsman of Lord Granard's family, the family of Forbës:

> The first ae stroke MacDonald struk
> He gart the Forbës reel;
> The first ae stroke that Forbës struk
> The great MacDonald fell.

The measure of the man is not felt until his loss! He is great because his fall has great consequences: Leaving Forbës greater still.

Yes, the place mentioned in the ballad is still in the possession of the Forbës family. They could not become families, nor retain their hold, had they not had the physique and prowess of the sword. Greater the Forbës proved themselves than the Lords of the Isles – Halkin Street houses a branch of the family whose chief was victorious because he was the first to recover from a blow.

As for England, I can see the plumes swinging in the press of the verse as the knights swayed in the battle riot.

> Suffolk his axe did ply;
> Beaumont and Willoughby
> Bare them right doughtily
> Ferrers and Fanhope.

'By the way, would you care to see the dining-room? His Majesty is dining here to-night.'

I pulled myself up sharply. There I had been off again with my babble about great verse; and my addiction to monologuing the conversation without ascertaining whether my listeners cared for verse, or rather for my gratuitous recitations and sound-intoxications.

'Yes. Of course! I would very much. Sorry for so much talking.'

We entered the great dining-room. Sixty places; golden plate again, fit for a king!

And then I thought of a lonely kingly man, striding about a far Northern island companionless, who had spread his plate of gold for me. Gladly, if he wished it, would I give a few years of life to revive Talbot Clifton at the expense of my own expectation of life. The measure of a man is not felt until his loss.

CHAPTER SIXTEEN

Joseph Chamberlain may never have stood 'stiff in stour' like a Forbës or a 'campion' in the battle dust; but he dealt in steel, and founded a fortune which gave him respite to found an Empire. I was dining with his son.

Of all the men I have met no one stands more clearly and simply to my mind than Austen Chamberlain. Because his simplicity needs no conjuring from the memory's shadows, there is nothing dim about him. He is the finest and most forthright spirit I have ever had the luck to meet. Upright, blond, with an odd sweeping gesture of his arm, he says his say with assurance. His father's greatness was his prerogative but not his privilege. He is great in his own right and in his own way. And that is the grandest way ever a man had. Right and simple and unswerving. His honesty is contagious. We talked of anything but Irish politics. In the middle of dinner someone who directed *The Times* came in. He was scolded in a way that elsewhere might be turned to party advantage, but no one could betray his host's sheer faith in the common honesty of men. He made what statements he had to make subject to no conditions. In any other country they might have been made the subject of a 'Stop Press' and the fodder for the curious upsetting indiscretions. The grandeur of the man lifted all about him above pettiness. No need for Wellingtonian 'Publish and be damned'. You were damned in your own estimation if you ever entertained the thought of taking an advantage of his expression of opinion.

He told me of his early years, of the time he spent in Germany and in France. I saw his father's ambition for him justified as largely as his own life had justified and fulfilled that lofty patriotism.

The story of Arthur Griffith self-consumed by his indomitable and unswerving purpose, of his abject want and his refusals of wealth and notoriety, astonished him. Later he paid him the tribute which is now historical. 'He was the most courageous man I ever met.' He said it with solemn assurance. He who had met the most outstanding persons of our generation said Arthur Griffith was the most courageous. I have met not a few in my day. But one of the grandest human beings I ever have met is Sir Austen Chamberlain.

In the cool of the night dominated by Westminster Cathedral, I said to myself: Now what have I done? I have dined with a ruler of England, therefore I have become a traitor of course, a spy consequently, and a betrayer of what? – A betrayer of the Bog of Allen. The residence attributed to Brian O'Lynn. I will go down to history as the man who betrayed Brian O'Lynn and the O'Lynn idea of Ireland! But will there be any history for that? Will the pygmies ever forgive me when they hear that I have met a man? I cannot pretend that I am greatly concerned. But is it not sad to think that even if they had their dreams, such as they are, and their ambitions, such as they are, fulfilled an hundred-fold, never could they imagine a man in all their Utopias equal to, or even to be compared with, Austen Chamberlain. What's wrong with us? There's something rotten in Rathangan.

I walked secure through the silent city as if I were in a pleasant park, released from alertness, thinking of the magnanimity of governing souls such as Austen Chamberlain's, whose material expression is strong and established peace.

Never had I kept an engagement book, for the simple reason that I had no engagements which I could not hold in my head. But now many names and unfamiliar addresses needed tablets for my memory.

Once a traitor always a traitor, so I might as well dine with Lady Lavery and take the risk of the fact being distorted in my country. Everyone who dines in London is a traitor in Dublin nowadays. This will go on for a few years until the traitor-setters themselves become entertained and so traitors in their turn and a new set of unfeasted appears. It is like the 'orgy' which I have defined before.

I sat on the left of Lord Birkenhead. He was commiserating gently with himself for the ten years he had been a Don at Oxford. He had worked hard. I said, 'And you walked hard.' He held the record for the walk from Oxford to London. A great athletic figure. One of those natural athletes who require no training – in fact, who seem to thrive in spite of indulgence. He had risen to great prominence against all the rules. Turmoil helped him, but he was there to seize 'glittering prizes' and not to suffer. He was an example of what happens only once in a century, the Rake becoming a success. Caius Julius Caesar and Pitt were his antecedents. When a rake succeeds why is it that most of us are secretly gladdened? It does me good to think of its ingredients. And why? Because we feel that his humanity is not sacrificed to success. It is like the award of the Garter or a prize in the Irish Sweep. That is one reason why Galloper Smith, Lord Birkenhead, High Steward of Oxford University, Lord Chancellor of England, endeared himself to his friends. He was not the first to make Ulster a springboard to the Woolsack. The art of politics is to get some sort of prejudice in your favour; and for prejudice what place was ever more exploitable than Ulster?

I admired the way he kept his figure without exercise. I loved the way he filled and emptied his glass: no half measures about it. He laughed heartily at Dr Tyrrell's remark when the unnecessarily inquisitive waiter who, instead of bringing 'whisky drinks for two' forthwith, stayed, ruining business, to ask and to make a guest self-conscious, 'Large or small?'

'Get this into your head. There is no such thing as a *large* whisky.'

'You have had a pretty strenuous time?'

'In Scotland, yes. In Ireland it lacked humour.'

'Like the lady on your left.'

The 'lady on my left' was the wife of a Continental Ambassador who had been insistently cross-examining his Lordship.

'Don't you think Winchester is the best school in England?'

'I do not.'

He rotated his 'balloon' glass, which held half a pint of brandy, leaving no room for the aroma. He raised it to his lips. His left elbow nudged me as the lady again put him to the question. 'Horrible,' he said.

'After all, you must admit that the best men in England were at school there.'

'Name one.'

'Mr Asquith.'

'Who happens not to have been there.'

'Perhaps it was someone else.'

'I should not be at all surprised.'

'But don't you think I ought to send my son there?'

In judgement: 'If you wish to stereotype mediocrity, I do.'

And there an end.

'There's not much use in drinking sherry at this time of night,' he remarked.

That puzzled me. Could he be under the impression that his brandy was sherry, or had the butler been under orders to replace the lighter for the stronger drink?

Napoleon brandy! There is some at every well-regulated board, so much indeed that it is easy to see why Napoleon had such a victorious career – half Europe must have been making brandy. There is no Napoleonic vodka. As soon as he clashed with countries who were not absorbed in labelling his name for posterity, he met with reverses. Who ever heard of Wellington brandy? Beer was his Waterloo.

His pallor increased as he drank, as if it were an outward sign of the cold clarity of his mind.

He was a sentence-maker, not an epigrammatist or even a *diseur*: Isocrates!

'So you chose Wuggins when you went to Oxford probably because they acted *Comus* in its gardens. It is what I would expect you to do.'

'I only went to Oxford because I was not clever enough for Trinity, Dublin, as Mahaffy said of Oscar Wilde.'

'What's that about Mahaffy?'

'He said, "My dear Oscar, you are not clever enough for us in Dublin. You had better run over to Oxford." '

He smiled as if thinking of some severe remark.

'Mahaffy! Do you tell me so?'

From the way he said 'Mahaffy' it dawned on me that he was at least as familiar with him as with Jowett, whom he did not revere. Mahaffy is better known in Oxford than in College Green. Again his glass was filled! No wine could o'er-crow his reason.

'Why he stayed on in Dublin is a mystery,' he remarked.

'Why? Can you enlighten me?'

I suggested that a Fellowship in T.C.D. brought more immediate emolument and promised more in the end without chopping and changing than any comparable post in Oxford.

'But Mahaffy?' he objected.

'He is Provost. He has been knighted. What Fellow in Oxford can be knighted without being benighted first?'

Again the Foreign Ambassador's wife leant across me and tried to catch his attention. He was not to be diverted.

'There is a lot to be said for Dublin according to Mahaffy, as a step-ladder to social success. He may have been ironical, but he used to say to Oscar Wilde, "Now you have been to Greece, go over to London and tell them all about it." '

'And he did, too literally, perhaps,' mused Lord Birkenhead.

He contemplated his glass, thinking of God knows what. His mind was leaving the room. I remembered his quotation of Lloyd George earlier in the evening.

'There is no slump of Dukes in this house. Their two "Graces" Sutherland and Argyll at the head of the table.'

'The third, of course, being our hostess?'

'Yes. That is what I meant to say.'

But the question about a slump in Dukes brought Lloyd George into the conversation again.

'Have you met him?'

'No.'

'You should meet him, he ...'

'I would rather not,' I said, 'I am over here convalescing from Celts.'

'What are you convalescing from?' asked the central Grace, our hostess.

'Celts of all denominations.'

Their Graces were silent as the Dreadnoughts to which the Welsh solicitor had compared them, who had begun by disparaging England's foundations and then rushing, when self-advertised and successful, to the maintenance of all for which England stood. It would sicken me had I not had experience of the 'codology', as we call it in Dublin, of politicians; and a conviction of the soundness of that Roman system which can enlist with impunity all sorts and conditions to its preservation.

'He did a great deal for the Empire,' said Birkenhead.

'It is for what he didn't do that I don't want to meet him.'

'What was that?'

'Let one of your own countrymen answer.' I quoted from a friend's great verse:

'Chiefly to-day in *this*
Your mastery towers – that you forbear to stir
A finger, while your missions fierce and fell
Shatter doomed Ireland's homes and build in her
A suburb of the great metropolis
Of evil and woe, whose name on earth is Hell.'

247

He listened, greatly impressed. At last cross-examining:

'An Englishman?'

'Yes, one of the greatest left, Sir William Watson.'

'Are there any Englishmen in England?'

'I am one,' said Birkenhead.

'Yes, but let us examine that. Cuchulainn, the Hero of Ulster, its Achilles came from the Mersai tribe who dwelt on the banks of the Mersey about Liverpool. He was called the Hound of the Smith, and the Smiths were honoured in the Ireland of those days, that is 1500 years ago. And you cannot deny that it was in Ulster recently that you made your name.'

Dinner at the Lavery's brought you into the company of persons of incalculable importance. A house which was welcomed as an unofficial meeting-place for rebel and ruler was of inestimable use and service to both sides – Ireland and England. Without it what is the picture? Mr Collins makes his statement to the powers that be, and is answered with all the stiffness which such statements must have for the followers who put each side into power by utterances. Formal, public, inelastic, irrevocable. But at 5 Cromwell Place men could meet as human beings beyond the scent of herded wolves, and exchange views and reveal difficulties. Arthur Griffith was grateful for this accommodation, as once under less important circumstances he was grateful to me. The Lavery's did more to bring about a settlement than all the weary official and overlooked weeks at Hans Place.

No one can call me a spy to-night even though I have dined with two Dukes, an Earl, Knights, and a few Excellencies. No! A useful clearing-house for 'obscurities'. Griffith was grateful and so was Collins. And they were not spies. Well, that's that! But what is this I heard O'Higgins said: 'I laid my guns at Lavery's only to find that the targets were shifted.'

When a guest is not a spy, the hostess must be, to satisfy the inordinate suspicion of a primitive tribe. Lady Lavery as a spy! O'Higgins was as suspicious as that famous member of the police force he helped to create, who when a puny little Frenchman inquired during the war (when every foreigner was a spy) the way to Westland Row, took his pronunciation of English for French; but as nothing should be beyond the purview of a Dublin Metropolitan policeman, he answered him in a set of three wonderful enigmas which concealed ignorance of everything but of the fact that a question was being asked.

'You don't know?

'You could never tell?

'And what would you be after doing if you did?'

And thinking of spies, I thought of how different a spy had been sent in the old days of Dublin Castle's detectives' rule to trap Arthur Griffith. We had been in the Bailey one night, where Griffith met Hubert Murphy with:

'Hello, Hubert! Where have you come from?'

'I was on holidays in a country where there was no income tax.'

'There should be none here!' said Griffith, reaching for his hat. It was eleven o'clock.

Boyd-Barrett, Griffith and I had got as far as the Provost's Wall, when a well-spoken young woman accosted us: 'Good-night, Mr Griffith!' Evidently she did not know him, for it was to Boyd-Barrett she made the remark. Griffith jerked himself forward with 'Come on, boys! Take no notice! Dublin Castle is on me!'

We walked in silence, pondering the infamy of Dublin Castle that could employ foreigners like Pigott and an unknown prostitute indiscriminately. A prostitution in face of the rule of Queen Victoria. Suddenly as we crossed Earl Street at the foot of the great Pillar from the top of which the admiral took the midnight watch, the silence was broken by a woman with a broad Cockney accent.

'Oh, Alliver, that waistcoat of yours saved me and the choild!'

It was somewhat embarrassing. Quickly I pulled myself together and got rid of the encumbrance.

'Take no notice, boys. Scotland Yard is after me!'

'Good-night!' said Griffith gruffly, and left us standing.

'Dammit!' I said to Joe Boyd-Barrett. 'Am I to have no political significance at all?'

'So that's what became of your gold-buttoned waistcoat?'

CHAPTER SEVENTEEN

I said to my heart: don't you remember when you promised to compensate yourself for a self-centred and sensuous talk with Tim Healy's lady guests by an intellectual discussion with Yeats, only to find that he was concentrated still more on the self-same theme, you resolved never to fall from the frying-pan – and so on? And yet you fell. By that disappointment, resolve never more to have to do with Dukes or Earls or grandees, so much the less traitor you shall be. The notice in my appointments book gave promise of respite. 'Call at 5 p.m.' It was near the top of Park Lane.

I called at five o'clock.

Mine hostess said hastily: 'They arrived rather early. They don't usually come until everybody is going away. They are two Crown Princesses. Don't speak until they speak to you: no politics, no local topics, no cosmetic themes and so on. Blonde and buxom. Very attractive.'

'I am. Yes! Quite so. Only three months. Even in spite of autumn fogs. Not so bad! Hospitable. I agree.'

I was getting on famously, even though my best-laid scheme for not meeting any more notable people was going somewhat agley.

'His Royal Highness, the Duke of Connaught!'

'Bow lower than ordinarily and only call him "Sir".'

A tall, spare, active, blue-eyed, soldierly figure entered the room. His presence, instead of embarrassing, put everyone at their ease. He nodded then, and took a seat. 'Who is this?'

I was introduced. I bowed low and named myself.

'You are from Dublin. When I was in command in the Curragh, Nanetti was Lord Mayor.' Faultless memory summoned instantaneously.

'What do you say? Eighteen holes of golf to-day and three hours in the saddle. What do you say?'

'You are threatened with immortality, Sir!' No restraint. Days later at lunch, the genius of the Duke revealed itself. How can such things be translated to those who have lost, or have

250

never known the grammar of greatness? Something better than ourselves!

There must be something if not of the courtier, then at least of the flunkey, in my composition. I like to have people better than myself about me. They radiate on me a security similar to that Julius must have felt when he had men about him of his own liking. Every Irishman loves an aristocrat. In all the sagas of Erin there is not the name of a commoner mentioned. Even the charioteers were noblemen. Let my critics digest that. Anyway, I dearly love a Lord, and I think I can analyse the reason: he stands for an established order of things, for a household of continuance with the obligations its traditions confer. 'The men who dare not be afraid,' for there is no spot on earth that can hide a disgraced member of a noble English family. There is the knowledge that they, like kings, seldom have any selfish or personal interest in mundane affairs. Their axes were ground long ago. They can be trusted not to lower others in order to gain height themselves. Long ago they 'bare them right doughtily'; and, stock-raisers as we are, we Irish, believe in good blood.

Not only do my countrymen believe as I do that there is something innate in noble beings that may not be achieved fortuitously – Pindar had a faith much like it – but it is borne out by the fact that they cannot do themselves justice if far removed from the inspirers of their chivalry. They must not be separated far from their springs of valour, which are in their case the aristocrats, their superior officers. Blame me not at all or as much as you like when I honestly betray what may not be called a weakness in me, but a yearning towards the better than myself, to the 'Beyond Man.'

If Irishmen cannot fight but fail the farther they are removed from their aristocrats, how should I be blamed who appraise and honour this ideal of great men? When you find Irishmen taking up arms for 'Labour', look to some outside instigator. You will not find the warriors who loved to follow the inspiration and example of their breed's best, casting all to the winds for an increase of wages.

The nearer they are to their own superiors the better is their battle. The cause matters not so much as the Captain. And is not this as it should be? When you review the world's long wars, the motive, the reason for them, even the justice of them, succumb before the personality of the leaders. The victorious Captain makes his own political good and evil. Victory engenders Justice.

These thoughts increased my admiration all the more for the soldierly, indomitable figure, which was upheld so upright by the unbreakable spirit of the Uncle of the King.

'Threatened with immortality?' he said a few days later as if nothing and nobody in his crowded hours had, meanwhile, intervened. 'That could be such a threat!' In a few words he left me to consider the philosophical implications of my spontaneous remark.

What a kill-joy is a scientific training! What is called 'observance' becomes a form of observation shortly removed from spying. I was taught to observe. And I cannot lose that lowly second sight. To me the gestures of the Duke as he sat at the table bespoke more than even his terse and considered words. He had what beauty seldom companions, and that is Grace. Even the movement of raising his glass seemed more like a dispensation than a personal movement. Every gesture suggests largesse. I was shocked and stilled by the realization that his intimates about him were as blind to these things as he himself was unaware of them. How far I am removed from intimacy with greatness may well be guessed. Else how could I have sat observing?

But how uplifted I am now that I am near to that which I recognize as better than myself! Far be it from me to suggest that my reason for leaving Dublin was that I could not find anyone better than myself, but who in Dublin could make me feel as exalted as I am now? A Republic will make me feel about as lively as a recital of its Soldier's Song. I must have 'a kingdom for a stage, princes to act'! Here is a soldier, who can make a nation sing, 'God save our gracious King!'

But too much hero-worship is bad for the worshipper. It makes him lean his weight upon the hero at the cost of his own responsibility and power of initiative. Wait a moment, I assured myself, and I shall recover and contradict myself.

If the Irish warriors saw something of themselves in their chieftains, if like seeks like, what have I in common with two princesses whom it is not permissible to address? And they, poor creatures, are losing the best gossip in the town. Out upon it! I will call upon my friend Augustus John. There's a name

252

for you like a fiat of creation. Something accomplished, something pat, something John. 'John' suggests the last stroke of a
hammer dulled on a malleable metal; a foundation stone laid,
the blow of a mace.

Through the 'long slum' of Ebury Street, 'where I live' – so
George Moore described it to annoy Lady Ebury – I walked
and passed Moore's house, 121. I knew that he was in its warm
old rose room, but the hour was too early. The last time I
called about this hour he kept me waiting ten minutes. 'I had
to keep you waiting until the strain of composition had faded
from my face.' I will visit him, I resolved, on my way back –
that is, if I ever come back from calling on Augustus John.

I found the bell of the flat oaken door. 'Yes, Sir, he is in.' I
descended to the great studio. In an alcove he sat brooding,
great-headed, golden-bearded – Leonardo da Vinci!

The aura of the man! The mental amplitude! He raised his
hand in welcome. In silence I sat down. I must wait for him to
speak . . . Now what kind of majesty is that I have 'escaped'
into, I wondered, if, even in Chelsea, I am not allowed to talk?
It is the majesty of genius. I could feel its force and the force
of him in the room. And never since the athletes of Olympia
has there been a man of such beautiful stature. Tisdall, the
Wicklow athlete, is as well built, but John has grace concealing
strength. I thought of that great lyrist, the lover of athletes:

'Yet, withal, we have somewhat in us like unto the Immor-
tals, bodily shape or mighty mind.' Augustus John has both.

'Have a drink!'

So the jury within him had reported favourably on my case
and he had decided. I felt somehow that it would have been
just as appropriate had he said:

'Get out!'

The pleasant business of the glasses – sweet bells jingled into
tune for minds that are not harsh – and the gay gurgling! I
revived. I was about to break, not exactly into song, but into
speech, when he forestalled me with:

'Over here for long?'

'I don't know. I cannot make up my mind. London with its
law and order sometimes chokes me. There are three or four
people too many in it. It takes an hour to drive to the edge
of it, and then I find that the countryside is almost as much
built on.'

253

'Come to Alderney and stay with me.'

'Now, that is an idea. I will drive you down any day,' I said. 'I hate inhaling exhaust fumes and seeing everyone getting yellower and yellower. Besides, I don't like the hard water over here.'

'Neither do I.'

He pushed the bottles in my direction and suddenly his cheeks islanded themselves in an exceedingly genial smile. The smile of Augustus John can only be compared to that of the All-Father on Ida's summit when Love and Sleep conspired.

In mid studio the great portrait of Madame Suggia stood. Her rounded right arm slanted across the canvas to her cello. What an advantage the painter has over the poet! He can make his dreams visible! They are there for all to see. He who has an eye to see will see more. Like a rain-maker he can manifest the power of his soul, the power of his creative imagination, independent of languages and the abuse of words. But the poet needs happy moments, leisure and sophistication amongst his readers. Second sight compared to the Vision Splendid!

And yet I feel that, master without compare though he is of his medium, his medium cannot carry away the torrent of his imagination. He needs another outlet for the swollen streams from the mountain of his thoughts. Poetry? He has written poems. But only one poem in the world is fit to be attributed to the fire within his mighty heart. And no one knows who wrote it – The Red Haired Man's Wife

> But the Day of Doom shall come
> The earth and the harbours be rent ...

Augustus John's inexhaustible force!

It was very pleasant, this bathing in the glory of Augustus. I felt myself growing so witty that I was able to laugh at my own jokes. To think that they spelt Sherry with an 'X' in Spain. 'Xeres.' Absurd! Just as absurd as the people in Dublin who persist in calling Guinness's Double X Guyniss Twenty! I was thinking of the Tommy Atkins I heard in the railway restaurant at Crewe who ordered 'A Guy-niss Twenty, Miss.'

'Why do you call it a "Guy-niss Twenty"?'

'Aw, Oi don't call it. They calls it that, I suppose, because it supports you twenty times longer than any other beer.'

'In Dublin we call it Guinness's Double X.'

'Just loike you Irish!'

How magnificently I was turning the tables on Reality by making it wax and wane to suit my ebb and flow of consciousness! My philosophy was quite a success. Quite!

'Be careful. Two steps!'

Two flights led down from a kind of platform in front of John's hall door. It would make an excellent rostrum from which to address the men hidden in the mighty motor sweeping brushes which whisk behind each other up Mallord Street long after midnight.

'Let us put a stop to the brunettizing of Europe! Keep England fair. Blue-eyed! Sweep out the brown, bring in the blue!'

'Are you?'

'Yes. Yes! Quite all right, thanks! There are all these taxis, you know!'

'Good-night, old man.'

'Good-night, sweet Prince!'

Days and days after, I called on George Moore. He sat in the ground-floor room with his back to its deep red curtains beside the fireplace, over which a Muse leant on the dial of a clock. French Empire. Rather 'Ompire', as a Great Lady corrected a friend of mine. 'Ours is the Empire.'

Two rooms were thrown into one. He liked space. So too at No. 4 Upper Ely Place, Dublin, he opened the folding doors.

He rose, subsided, and said with an expiring sigh, as if exhausted by my presence:

'It is good of you to come!'

He thinks I travelled over specially to call on him since his illness. How shall I gently disavow my merit in his eyes? He gave me no chance.

'Let me see. Ah! Why did you not warn me that the young novelist whom you sent to consult me was quite pretty?'

'Was she?'

He affected an air of the deepest disgust at my attempted hypocrisy.

'Oh, my dear friend! That will do!'

The maid came in with the broken Sèvres tea-pot and set, and quietly withdrew. He swept his hand about to indicate side tables and flower-loaded shelves.

255

'To-day she sent me flowers!'

'In America it is the other way about.'

He resented what seemed to him an implication. He could 'register' impatience either by a shrug or grimace, or a suppressed ejaculation, better than any man I know.

'Surely you didn't come to Ebury Street to wrangle about American customs?'

Moore was the most potentially cantankerous man one could meet. An explosion was always imminent. Petulant should be the word. He had all the petulance of a spoiled child. And he was spoiled. A spoiled soldier, a spoiled painter, a spoiled boon-companion, and a spoiled Parisian Bohemian. Light-footed as a woman on the rough *pavé* of Life, he sheltered himself from its robust jostlings. His epicene genius gave him a double advantage. He could describe all his experiences, and all his acquaintances, from a detached standpoint, and include himself in the pageant. It was impossible to be a friend of his because he was incapable of gratitude; and we all know that friendship lives only on interchange of companionship, confidence, understanding, and affectionate loyalty, one to another. With him you could never count on 'auld acquaintance'. You could never be sure of George Moore. This must be qualified by the outstanding fact that he never betrayed you; but you had to find out that by experience. You could never count on him beforehand. Even though this sense of uncertainty may have been unfounded, he lost a lot of human fellowship and confidence through this withholding of intimacy and his inability to be man to man.

'So she sent you flowers?'

He did not answer. Perhaps he was thinking that I was laughing secretly at the reversal of the order of things. I tried again.

'I know her well. She is writing a novel. I told her that no novel could be written unless it was in a form that might pass muster with you. If it appeared without your being consulted – well, then too late!' I waved my hand as over the abyss of despair that might open if anyone were to write without his sanction.

'How often have I told you that no woman can write a novel? No woman! They can if they will only realize their *métier* is to inspire . . .'

256

I thought an interruption would be fruitful:

'No woman. What about Pearl Craigie?'

'Pearl Craigie?' His eyes were upturned at the thought, and he threw up his arms, delighted to surrender to the delicious impeachment it implied.

'Ah! My very dear Friend!'

We were all supposed to suspect that Pearl Craigie was his Mistress and his Héloise-like pupil.

> Pour qui fut chastré et puis moyne
> Pierre Esbaillart à Saint Denis.

'Too apt a comparison!' I can hear Yeats saying.

But if you were not shocked by the enormity of the suspicion, he would proceed to betray her in the indicative mood for fear that scandal might be missed.

CHAPTER EIGHTEEN

Island England, this Isle – silver sea and so on, has no strands, only watering-places. Water-carts wet the seaside cement while children and adults put pennies in the slots. Brighton – cement, shingle and companionate Semitics. Drive desperately off – Selsey Bill: shallows and tide races. Weston-super-Mare! Even the water in the syphons is salt: and Frinton-by-Sea depends on tennis-rackets. Ilfracombe is an arena for competing restaurant-keepers. Scarborough is in Yorkshire, but Blackpool is Yorkshire's Elysium. It comes to this, all England has only one watering-place from which the sea may be seen and bracing airs inhaled: but Blackpool has to recuperate all England.

Now, if the long sands of Tramore, the great strand, or silver Portmarnock whence Transatlantic planes take off, or the unimaginable West coast of Ireland where 'twice-washed' Renvyle is, were known, what an invasion there would be! But trippers do not expect sea at an English seaside resort. They look for girls in Thetis-thin habiliments, and they are there. I can imagine bathing-dresses being worn years hence as far inland as Winchelsea is now. And no one to dig up old customs! The tradition of land and sea!

But such holiday-makers would hate Ireland with its 3,000 miles of open ocean and nothing to do save swim or sun-bathe, *sans* suits, *sans* slots or listenings-in. Can it be that England owes its greatness to its 'watering-places' because they drove men in desperation to go down to the sea in ships to look for water, and thus they came to rule the waves that knew no shore?

'Nevertheless,' said General Macready, 'Dublin has also produced the greatest poltroon of our time. You have often heard that So-and-So went on his knees to this or that magnate, but it was my embarrassing experience to see one of your townees approach me actually on his knees. When he was ushered in he knelt down and waddled up to me, saying, "Surely it is not the policy of the Great British Empire to have anyone killed as a set off against the murder or death of O'Callaghan, the Mayor of Limerick?"

' "Get up, damn you!" I said.'

'All I asked you, General, was to agree with me when I said that Dublin, in Bernard Shaw, produced the greatest genius of our time. You cross my track with an exemplary coward.'

But the poltroonery of one of our citizens depressed me. I was more or less a refugee. How then could I pose as more courageous than some citizen who was possibly too paralyzed by terror to move?

'I have a great deal of Irish blood in me,' the General said, 'and it made me rather sick to see an Irishman on his knees crawling to me for mercy, as he called it. Had he told me to go to Hell and shoot, I might have asked him to lunch. But what are you to do when confronted by the negation of all manhood?'

'I know. I know,' I said. But I myself had already lost caste through the irrefutable fact that I was a townsman of 'the greatest Poltroon of our time.'

'Forget the crawling seeker for sanctuary, and answer me, General, or deny it – you who are the grandson of a great actor: what country has produced a greater genius than our friend, Bernard Shaw?'

Long fingers swept my hair. The tall American triumphs over the awkwardness of great height. The insufficiency interested in George Moore, Lady Ebury, intervened:

'Leave him alone, General; he never crawled. Would he be here if he did?'

Both of us expostulated. The General rose and held back the tapestried division. The ladies sought the dining-room.

'A magnificent curtain!' said Seymour Leslie.

I cannot bear unmitigated facts for long. And the matter-of-factness of the downright honest Londoners, their surprise at a mind that had to fly if Reality was becoming too rigid – in other words, my inability to stand boredom – together with a warning that was daily growing more insistent, made me long for a change. The warning came from a remembered saying of the greatest poseur Dublin ever produced, Oscar Wilde: a genius, a poseur, but no poltroon. 'You may have one season's success in London, but not two.'

Now, it had never occurred to me that people's hospitable kindness could not go on for ever. I, for my part, could not go on for ever accepting it. I could part with friends whom I

259

would never see again. Mr Asquith, who was equal in years and almost in wit to my friend Dr Tyrrell. With him I should never lunch again, or hear his remark whispered to me, at the young Countess Odescalchi's exuberance, 'Youth would be all very well if it only came on later in life!'

The town where somebody knew me in every street was drawing me from the town where I only knew those who were somebodies. The people whom I could please and shock as they shocked and amused me.

A dinner with Larkey Waldron booming at the head of the table would be more amusing: when the ice-pudding, served half-way through it, transformed your stomach into hemispheres, and the dinner began again for a conquest of a New world: the butler sent in mid repast to the library to verify a quotation which was forgotten with the next mouthful . . . I would like to see St Stephen's Green again with Father Sherwin, young and silver-haired, as Cardinal Newman must have walked to his lych-gate at Littlemore. Father Sherwin, who had the photograph of a ghost, a photograph which would mysteriously disappear. Father Dwyer, keen and scholarly, who takes an interest in politics and knows everyone for miles about the Green. I will listen to the angelic anarchist Æ again, and see Endymion's cricket trousers that are whiter than the whitewash on London taxis' wheels.

What is wrong here, I thought, is the absence of the metaphysical man. It is nearly as bad as the town of Buffalo, where fast-driven human automatons are engaged in 'go-getting' all day long, 'relaxing' for a minute and looking at their watches. Nobody has leisure for speculation. But it is not quite as bad, because here those engaged in speculation of another kind at least compose Limericks, the only poetry that London produces now. We want more village idiots over here. A country without village idiots is not worth living in. Without them there is no way of knowing who are sane. True, they may have all been voted into Westminster, as Al Smith suggested, when he told me that American's village idiots had all gone to Washington.

I want to go back to the town where we are all so poor that we can dabble in ideas without being imposed on or robbed.

Society in London goes in circles and tight compartments: you cannot flit from one to another without letting your hosts down. There are no Fannings here. If there were, it 'would not do.'

They are all watching one another; they are all gossiping about one another. Gossip is the national pastime of the English. What constitutes the Englishman's silent strength? He is loth to say or waste words on an outsider. He wants to keep them all for his club. He won't let a foreigner in on it. Is it any wonder that I was forbidden to talk to the two Crown Princesses! Gossip is the national vice. It is worse in the country villages. England extends freedom to everyone but its own citizens. They are all watching, watching! Commenting and criticizing among themselves. Let me get out before I go back on all my ideas of the freedom of Englishmen. Before I appear ungrateful. The visitor never realizes this. Unlike us, they keep all their drawbacks to themselves.

A taxi rolled by with its tyres newly whitewashed. This has to be done by the driver every morning, I thought. He probably likes doing it, though the tyres will be covered in dirt by the end of the day. It is a labour of love, or rather a duty he has invented and imposed on himself. 'England expects!' every man to invent a 'duty'. The best is just about good enough for the Rulers of the World. But I am not a ruler of the world. I am an ordinary medical man, and if I don't return soon, I will lose whatever little knowledge I may have of medicine. Here the doctors are so kind and professional conduct is so nice that they never contradict each other. To maintain this harmony it is taboo to make a diagnosis. In Dublin, where the conspiracy is unfriendly, it is necessary to keep the wits keen if one has to live on his professional brethren's repairs.

I went to do a little flying with my friend Uwins. My visit to Bristol was all that was needed to make my nostalgia irresistible. I saw the masts of ships at the end of a street! It might as well be the Custom House docks with George's lighters by the river wall, and the sunny gulls on the water!

'You may waken me as early as you like,' I said to the steward. I must drive through the streets before the lame men come out. The clerks are in their offices by 9.30. But between 10 and 11 the streets are full of lame men: whether their lameness keeps them late or no is not the point. What I complain about is that there are so many: men with stirrups under their boots, men with thick boots, men with crutches, and agitated

261

men who spring along as if they were shearing invisible sheep with their knees. At eleven o'clock their places will be taken by housewives with magnificent manners to impress irreverent greengrocers: but the impression goes with the cabbage, and it has to be imposed all over again next day.

Had I thought of it some years ago I should have sent a wire to Dublin Castle 'advising' them that a new Chief Secretary was coming. Nobody would have known what he was like or what to expect. And in return I could have pretended not to know Sir Henry Robinson. He would be at the pier with his well-kept automobile, and before I had time to look about he would whisk me off to his favourite hotel in Recess, Connemara. With a wave of his hand he would point to that lovely desert full of peace, comparatively. This would save the Chief Secretary, who, in any event, could only hold office until his Government went out, from a boring visit to Dublin Castle and possibly many 'deputations' and other vexations, particularly the idea that Ireland was not peaceful and content. But for Ian McPherson to be with Sir Henry in Connemara! What a change after London! And how well the Irish Constabulary in Co. Galway had been trained to salute men in positions of such responsibility or in the company of Sir Henry, which was much the same thing.

I like to think about Dr Bodkin's story of the Chinese mandarin who sat for his portrait looking at a landscape through a window with his back to the artist. His choice of landscape was a better clue than his face to his true self. With my back to England I am looking at Dublin with its central river and its rolling quays light on its spires in the West.

How I love the old town where every man is a potential idler, poet or friend! I love the old town where sock-suspenders are less important than poems! And directions depend on inns. 'Up past the yellow houses, where Robert Emmet hid, to the Lamb Doyles.'

What, I asked myself, has Dublin to offer me in place of the town I have just left? It has neither dignity, majesty, rank nor fashion. Where are its aristocrats? Then I wondered if the autoch-thrones ever invisaged majesty as we know it; if they ever wanted dignity as we know it; or indeed if they would tolerate it if it were presented to them now. What, then, is the native idea of an aristocrat? Obviously he is not a landlord: even 800 years' residence will not commend a landlord to the Gaelic heart. And yet they had their chieftains, their aristocrats. If I could ascertain what the native idea of an aristocrat is, I would know one when I met him. Long descent is so taken for granted that the tribes never thought of recording their antiquity in any Register of Gotham. Long descent is tribal, not personal. The name of the person, if it be a well-known Irish name, secures him his quarterings. But what personal qualities and characteristics must the hero have if he is to be accepted as a hero? First of all he must be physically great, big-bodied, burly, the full of a door. His personal courage must be outstanding and unquestionable, he must be rosy, generous and chivalrous. He must have some noble, endearing fault which is easily forgiven, extravagance for choice. But, outside battle, he must be gentle and courteous and capable of comradery. Such a one was Goll MacMorna, and Finn and Conn the Hundred Fighter. To-day such a one is Sean McKeon. He took on a hundred and fought them to a standstill. In an unchanging people it is evident that there must be repetitions and reincarnations of type. Conn is now McKeon. Who would Dan Breen have been in the old days which are now elevated into an Heroic period? Cuchulainn, I think. Cuchulainn was more his type, which is not as big-bodied as McKeon's. Goll McMorna or Conn for McKeon: Cuchulainn to-day is personified in Dan Breen.

Deep in the heart of the Gael these heroes are enthroned. Long they lie hidden under the hills or in the lakes like that great Earl who waits beneath Lough Gur but at times is seen to ride in armour by moonlight on its surface. We have not reached him yet. We are deriving from a remoter past, but his time shall come.

I gazed up Sackville Street. The grandest thing we have in Dublin, the great Doric column that upheld the Admiral, was darkened by flying mists, intermittent as battle smoke; but aloft in light, silvery as the moonshine of legend, the statue in whiter stone gazed for ever southwards towards Trafalgar and the Nile. That pillar marks the end of a civilization, the culmination of the great period of eighteenth-century Dublin, just as the pillar at Brindisi marks the end of the Roman road. The men who first founded this city set up their pillar where Brunswick Street is now. How long, I thought, would it be before the Gael if left to himself would have set a pillar up? A long time, and a longer before he would have crowned it with Griffith, Collins, or McKeon. It took a hundred years to set Michael Dwyer up in Gorey. More likely a pillar would be set over his heroes as it is set over Parnell.

We are not pillar-builders, nor do we erect trophies, and we shall never erect anything so long as we keep up the pose of setting our faces against Empire and Conquerors and soldiers of trophies. Would this pose ever have permitted a people to be anything else but shirkers? Would it ever have countenanced the British Empire or the Empire of Rome? Yet all we have and most of what we are proceed from these strong sources.

'Excuse me, Senator,' a sailor said, as he wound a cable round a mushroom-like protuberance on the quay, 'there's a few stanzas in my pocket that I would like you to look over if you have time.' A patron of Martin Brennan's, I believe! 'I'll have time enough now that I am home.'

*

Father Paddy met me one morning.

'Home again?' said he.

'I was never away.'

'Oh, weren't you?'

'No. I only thought I was. You know that Ireland is a place or state of repose where souls suffer from the hope that the time will come when they may go abroad. I was only in London.'

He slapped his leg with an invisible ash-plant and passed on.

CHAPTER NINETEEN

It was the 13th of December, 1921, so in a way one of the omens, the unlucky 13, was already set. The Dail was to meet on the morrow to decide whether it would approve the 'Treaty' that Arthur Griffith had signed in London with Lloyd George. If Griffith was of Welsh descent (ap Gruffydd), Lloyd George was a contemporary Welshman, and we had misgivings about anything to which he set his mind. But none of us had misgivings about Griffith; any misgivings we felt were centred on the man who lurked in the background and sent Griffith and Collins – 'Plenipotentiaries' – to bear the brunt of responsibility while his watch-dog, Childers, never lost touch.

Would the Dail accept the Treaty? It was a measure surpassing by far any dreams of Home Rule our country had imagined for many years. But the Irish public always outruns its leaders. Griffith had been a leader of a party for twenty years. There had been an armed rising in 1916. How far had he been outrun? He had founded his whole movement on Kossuth's in Hungary. The foundation here of a Dual Monarchy was the farthest point he had reached or desired to reach. He never altered and never trimmed. Probably, with his deep instinct for realities in politics, he knew just how much 'freedom' the Irish people could sustain, or possibly his character admitted neither change nor evolution. So far as he was concerned, the Treaty supplied all that his life-long devotion to his country had desired, and even more through the *vis a tergo* of the Republican movement. Therefore, those who represent Griffith as making concessions to Lloyd George may have inside knowledge of the proceedings during the many interviews, but they do not know Arthur Griffith, nor do they take account of the scope of his demands. They have probably not taken the trouble to acquaint themselves with his teaching.

To some extent, then, Griffith found himself in a false position when he set out for London as the delegate (plenipotentiary?) of a Republic. Yet he brought back more than he had ever envisaged, only to be repudiated and condemned for not bringing back a Republic for which its chief advocate preferred to make Griffith a scapegoat, than go fearlessly and face Great Britain as Griffith did, who at least secured his demands. This treachery is so characteristic of members of the sub-races and so utterly unfair to honest Arthur that the contemplation of it and of Griffith's betrayer has a physiological effect on me. I cannot proceed.

But we are assembled in 15 Ely Place, on the eve of the Dail decision. We sought to satisfy our anxiety for the future by invoking omens. Happily, men with a knowledge of the classics and the traditions of the classics happened to be present. Father Dwyer, Professor Alton, J. M. N. Jeffries and one or two more. Mrs Bentwick, Talbot Clifton's sister-in-law, was among the ladies and can witness to the experiment. But there is an excellent account of it in *Blackwood's Magazine* for March 1922.

We decided to put the *Sortes Virgilianae* to the proof. Virgil through the Dark Ages was regarded as a necromancer. Some dim memory of his magical mouth flickered in the Central Darkness. And his book was used to foretell the future, for had he not foretold the Golden Age that Christianity was about to bring in his Fourth Eclogue?

There are two ways in which a great poet may foretell the future. One by his aloofness from mundane affairs, which gives that distance which makes stars so fixed that they may be used as guides. Something afar from the question is necessary, why else should not a *sors* with a newspaper or a volume of Ella Wheeler Wilcox suffice? And the farther it be the vàguer and more mysterious is the atmosphere conjured up for prophesying. If a bridegroom as vacillating as was Panurge were to put his key into a volume of Shakespeare and to find that it rested on the first two lines of the first sonnet, need he 'take counsel' any more? And the second way which helps the first is the exultation which the muttering of great verse alone can give, an exultation which in those attuned can produce a magnification of soul which makes everything possible and the future pliable.

But you cannot initiate a ritual suddenly and without seriousness. Professor Alton called for the book and for a key. I produced my folio and a large key. That is what is done. The book is placed on the table and cut by inserting a key between the leaves. The prophecy shall be read down from the line which the tip of the key shall indicate.

'Right!' I said.

'Wait a moment! The key can only be inserted by a chaste person, a child or a priest.'

There were no children present, so I retired in favour of His Reverence.

Yeats, I said to myself, would propose that I should send across the street for George Moore.

Now we must be unanimous as to the question we want answered. What was disturbing my mind at the moment was what would happen to Arthur Griffith, who had seized what he could for Ireland before all chance was lost in a slough of debate. What happens to all who sacrifice themselves for her? Well I knew; she sacrifices them.

This anxiety may have imparted itself or have been already shared by others. I found them setting down the question, and then Father Dwyer advanced to the Book. He inserted the key and carried the key and the book to Alton, who, holding the key in position, opened the book. He paused as if he had difficulty with the translation, gazing over his glasses at the page. We knew that it was not difficulty but shock that made him pause. At last he read, translating as he read:

'... spretae Ciconum quo munere matres
Inter sacra deum nocturnique orgia Bacchi,
Discerptum latos juvenem sparsere per agros.'

'What will become of Arthur Griffith? *Spretae quo munere* – spurned by which gifts – repudiated by the Treaty; *matres Ciconum* – the Maenads – the mad women in the celebration of the gods' ritual amid the orgies of night-wandering will tear the young men to pieces and scatter them over the wide plains.'

It was a passage referring to that 'enchanting son' who spied on his frenzied mother. But who could have seen Griffith lying dead, tracked by one of the Maenads to the holy place of a nursing home owned by nuns with his left arm sliced open?

Solemnly the Professor laid down the book. No one spoke. A mysterious and strong fear enveloped me. I felt all the terror of the fabulous darkness when such prophecies were fulfilled with import for those whose minds were credulous and necromantic.

Instead of being deterred by the gloomy oracle, we were fascinated and drawn, as it were, to test again the Virgilian lottery.

'What will De Valera do? Are we all agreed that is the question we want answered?'

Again Father Dwyer inserted the key. Again the Professor gazed over his glasses at the magical hexameters:

'Quaere age et armari pubem portisque moveri
Laetus in arma jube et Phrygio, qui flumine pulchro
Consedere, duces pictosque exure carinas,
Coelestum vis magna jubet.'

But lest I be thought to have forced the translation let me quote from the account of a disinterested commentator and his rendering of the Latin.

Rouse thee now, and with joyful heart bid thy young men arm themselves and move to the fray and destroy the leaders of the foreign oppressors who have settled on our beautiful river, and burn their painted ships. The might of Heaven orders this to be done.

And even as the Professor continued reading there flashed to my mind a sinister remark made by this same De Valera to one of the Southern Unionists in the days when he was still bandying words over Mr Lloyd George's initial offer of peace. 'If the fighting starts again,' he is reported to have said, 'the Southern Unionists will not be treated as neutrals. And many unpleasant things will happen.'

And now, with De Valera's challenge to the Treaty already thrown down, and the possibility of his overthrowing the Free State, either in Dail Eireann or in spite of it, looming like a dark cloud on the horizon of Irish peace, not I alone but all present were thinking of the unpleasant things that might happen – if the Sortes told sooth. I am, as I have said, no scholar, but as a schoolboy I often laboured long and woundily at the *Aeneid* after my more prehensile fellows had gone forth to play. And now the story of that weak and egotistical young man, Turnus the Rutilian – another De Valera if ever there was one – came back to me: how Juno, ever harassing the

Trojans, even as some malign fate seems to sow perpetual discord among the Irish peoples, sent Alecto disguised as Madame Markiewicz, or rather as Calybe the priestess, to urge Turnus to attack the Trojans. What the others were thinking about I do not know, for the hostess, with unerring instinct, was already urging us to replenish our glasses, and setting the frozen stream of conversation flowing again. And so we continued to talk, mostly about Ireland and what the morrow's meeting would bring forth, until it was time to go home. But nobody suggested that a third attempt should be made to consult the oracle.

Endymion's landlady wished to see me. Her lodger had barricaded his door for two days. He had eaten nothing. If I could persuade him. I went at once to Pleasants Street. After some persuasion I heard his chairs and tables being removed. He let me in. It seemed he had composed some music for his violin. He was afraid that the score would be stolen.

'But can't you copy it out and give me a copy to keep for you?'

'I could if I had a copy.'

'But where is the score?'

'In my head.'

'Thieves never come through doors. They use windows. Let me secure the window, and come out for some lunch.'

But as we went away my work was nearly undone by the landlady allowing her relief to express itself in '*Pax vobiscum* to the pair of ye!'

Indignantly Endymion turned and shouted:

'*Nux vomica!* my good woman, *Nux vomica!* . . .'

'I never allow the common people to outquote me in the classics,' he explained.

*

I must go down to Dunsany and see how the playwright is getting on. Dunsany Castle is about twenty-five miles from Dublin, and the journey takes about three-quarters of an hour in a useful car. The great gates are seldom opened, so you go through a short drive through a gateless Gothic ruin, a 'reproduction' as Sir Thornley Stoker, the connoisseur, would say. Sheer up from the dark gravel rises the grey pile. The square

269

tower beyond the door is half covered with ivy. The hall is filled with armour and trophies of the chase.

'His Lordship is not at home, sir.'

I well knew the difference between not being at home and not being in.

'Are you sure that he is not on the top of the tower composing? If you just say ...'

'He is not in, sir.'

'Then, where is he?'

'He has been arrested, sir, by the Black-and-Tans.'

It was Maunder, the major-domo, speaking. He could be relied on, with such a master, carefully to frame his sentences and to choose his words.

By the Black-and-Tans! Well, of all the countries! But what the devil was Dunsany doing to be arrested by the Black-and-Tans? Was he after all a rebel at heart, following in the footsteps of his ancestor, the Blessed Oliver Plunket, who was condemned on a trumped-up charge and hanged, drawn, and quartered in 1681? If so, it is a surprise to me. I thought I knew a good deal about his points of view in literature, criticism, and politics.

I have it! He has been comforting Ledwidge, the Bard of Slane. That he had been supporting and educating him I knew. And now the master is arrested for the man. And there was in my mind the memory of a poem which Ledwidge broke off, dissatisfied. 'I got weary,' he said, 'as it was no good.'

Let me see how it went. I can never remember prose, but I cannot forget verse if it be smooth:

> What rumours filled the Atlantic sky,
>   And turned the wild geese back again;
> When Plunkett lifted Balor's eye,
>   And broke Andromeda's strong chain?
> Or did they hear that Starkie, James,
>   Among the gallipots was seen,
> And he who called her sweetest names,
>   Was talking to another queen?
>
> Now all the wise in quicklime burn,
>   And all the strong have crossed the sea;
> But down the pale roads of Ashbourne,
>   Are heard the voices of the free.

> And Jemmy Quigley is the boy,
> Could say how queenly was her walk,
> When Sackville Street went down like Troy,
> And peelers fell in far Dundalk.

They probably found a copy of that when raiding Dunsany Castle and so were sure that Lord Dunsany was the Plunkett who lifted something. So they lifted the Plunkett. They had to lift something. But it was the wrong Plunkett. The Plunket who died in 1681 had but one 't' in his name. Norman Plunkett, corruption of 'le blanche jenette,' may not have been his ancestral line. His name has lost a 't'.

But what am I to do? Here I am undoubtedly under surveillance coming from the great stronghold of Dunsany. It was a stronghold in 1181. It is a stronghold still. But a 'rebel' stronghold now. At last the Dunsanys have become Irish! No longer can it be said of them, or of the Irish, that they refuse to blend. Magnificent! With a leader like Dunsany this rebellious movement will be lifted out from the rut of the commonplace. All that Ireland wants is a lead from its gentry. Now Dunsany is striking a blow for the country of his ancestors conquered over 800 years ago! What though his life gives Ireland another martyr? Where he leads, I follow!

'Geordie, give me my lance!'

But Maunder had heard nothing. General Hammond, the nearest neighbour, might supply particular news.

Coming from this rebel, bretesche, peel tower, castle, or stronghold, I will be suspected of connivance with its chief. I begin to grow nervous. What persuaded me to come?

'Maunder, when the Black-and-Tans came, what did they do?'

'Searched the house, sir.'

'Did they arrest his Lordship?'

'His Lordship was not at home.'

'Not at home?'

'Not at home, sir.'

Lady Conyngham told me the whole story. It seemed that Dunsany had been raided by Hamar Greenwood's Black-and Tans. They could not find its lord, simply because he was out in the bogs shooting snipe. But everyone in Ireland was forbidden the use of guns under a penalty of death – more or less –

death in Cork for Nationalists, a reprimand in Ulster for its conditional loyalists.

Snipe sent to 'friendly' members of the Kildare Street Club (where has a poet a friend?) rather got on the nerves of those who had sacrificed their snipe-shooting to the Empire. And here was Dunsany sending them snipe when their loyalty forbade them to shoot. Couple after couple appeared. None of your 'jack' snipe, but Meath snipe from the Red Bog, with breasts on them like wood-pigeons. They were nestled and nourished in the succulent bogs of the perennial and abounding Boyne. Great birds, great herds, great eels and a great river – Royal Meath!

But Dunsany was betrayed by his club mates, not by a poem. Nevertheless his Lordship was captured.

Through his tenants he was driven in a motor tumbril to a Dublin prison, to be tried in Kilmainham! Dunsany, who had been shot for wearing His Majesty's uniform in 1916 by the men the Black-and-Tans identified him with now. Seemingly he had backed Ireland both ways!

But Maunder never lost his poise because, as the lorries drove away, he asked:

'Who shall I say called?'

How England loves to show how impartial her Justice is at the expense of her noblest and most loyal sons! Dukes in prison give a sense of distinction to the house-breaker. But if a Corkman is hanged in whose house an obsolete revolver is found, and a Carsonite in Belfast merely admonished for possession of remnants of the rebellious super-loyal Galloper Smith gun-running of 1914, the obvious impartial path lies midway between Cork and Belfast – Meath.

A peer may claim the privilege of a silk rope. But a silk rope has its drawbacks – that is, it draws you back; and you may be jerked up and down like the game called yo-yo, until you are dead. There was a sack of clay in my garden. This would stiffen the rope if the rope were wetted, and if the sack were left in suspension overnight it would be as abrupt as a hempen collar.

I tried to cheer his Lordship with this idea, but he said, 'There are some subjects which are not jokes, and one of them is my hanging.' This was disconcerting. I had imagined myself a cloud-dispeller. Now look at the gloom I had evoked!

'From a medical point of view a broken neck is more merciful than slow suffocation, and less indecent.'

'My solicitor thinks that on the whole it would be better for you not to bail me out.'

'But who else will come forward?'

'You are identified too much with the Sinn Feiners!'

But, utterly mystified, I exclaimed: 'Is it not you the Black-and-Tans have arrested – not me?'

I did not like to obtrude my goodwill further. But here he was arrested for bagging snipe, when those with whom he was identifying me, who derailed and bagged trains, were at large. Later I learned that all the Sinn Feiners around his Castle were marching on Dublin to bail him out. He was a good landlord.

'Would you say that eight hundred rounds of ammunition will look a lot to the Court Martial?'

'Oh, my God!'

Dunsany used to sing of his Uncle, Sir Horace, in his relation to Æ.

'My Uncle has a poet, and he keeps him on a string,
  And what do you think he keeps him for?
  He keeps him for to sing.'

And he took to himself a poet with the result . . . 'on a string'! It was too horrible!

And now the gloom began to invest me. No more golden evenings in Dunsany in the mellow lamp-light before the great fire, listening to the latest lyric recited or read in that vivid and pleasant accent of his. Exquisite language, excellent verse! Shall I see never again the well-formed knuckles holding the leaves of manuscript, and the long limbs outstretched? The only living man who could write romantic prose, the architect of Pegana, the meadow of Pegasus, peopled with, not heroes, but gods, as Homer peopled his *Iliad*, the playwright of the *Gods of the Mountain*, *The Flight of the Queen* and thirty other works, including the *Sword of Welleran*, arrested for being in possession of a gun!

If I could only send him some of that ale in a Saxon rumkin which 'bids valour burgeon in tall men,' or play him a 'spring' such as McPherson played when

Sae rantingly, sae wantonly,
Sae dauntingly gaed he;
He played a spring and danced it round
Below the gallows tree.

But meanwhile, would it not be a good idea if I hid my revolver under a tree-root, just in case, just in case I am searched on my way home? It is not in falling between two stools that the tragedy consists, but in falling off each stool in turn.

You can see along a straight road for a mile and more on the way between Dunsany and Clonee. I saw a heavy car that looked like a lorry well ahead. But it must be going very slowly. I am catching up on it rapidly. It is going very slowly. It is glinting strangely in the sun. I am nearer now. Gun barrels! rifle barrels! It's a lorry load of Black-and-Tans! I don't want to catch up on that. But I have been sighted. It is going at walking pace. I have no chance of turning. I must go on. They are waving to me to approach. I notice that the lorry is not full. There are two of its number scouting in the fields behind the hedges on either side of the road. They fear an ambush; another ambush, it would seem. They look as if they had been ambushed already. There is blood on one of their bandoliers and one of them seems to have lost a finger. His hand is bound over the stump.

'Get out!'

I put on the brake and, leaving the engine running, stepped out on the road. Two of them advanced white with nerves and pushed their revolvers into my stomach.

The smaller, a pasty-faced little fellow, asked:

'Wot are you doing alone 'ere?'

'Driving home.'

The second, who spoke more correctly and quietly, said: 'Let me see your permit.'

I produced a chit of pink paper which gave me permission to drive 'within a radius of twenty miles from the place of issue.'

'Where have you been?'

'You can see it there,' I said, ignoring the direct question.

They both examined the paper, which was issued, the last

274

time I was held up, from Chapelizod. They knew no local geography.

'Was you at Chapelizod?' the little cad in khaki, who looked like someone who was dismissed for dishonesty with a gas-meter, asked, regardless of grammar.

'No. I was . . .' I said, adding, 'If you don't stop trembling that gun will go off.'

'It can be loaded again.' But the reference to the state of his nerves galled him. He smiled wryly. I thought of that old Irish triad: Three things to fear: the horns of a bull, the heels of a stallion, the smile of an Englishman. He tore off my hat and ripped the lining out. 'Nothing 'ere! Hands up! 'Ere, search him, lads.' He slammed my hat down on my head.

A tall figure of a man in a black uniform, with a black tam-o'-shanter worn rakishly, approached. He rapidly ran his hands over me and searched my pockets. His fingers slipped in before and behind a cigarette case which he neither opened nor even removed for examination. It contained a collection of rather biased cuttings enumerating the atrocities of the Black-and-Tans.

My first surmise was correct; they had lost a comrade in an ambush. I was ordered into my ransacked car to lead the way to Dublin. Two of them sat behind me with rifles. 'Thirty miles an hour all the way!'

If the 'Boys' knew we were coming, I thought, it would be well worth taking a sporting risk and running the whole gang right into them. They have the wind up badly and will scatter like deer.

I take my hat off – well, a better hat than this – to Dan Breen, who, single-handed, shot up a lorry load of ruffians such as these, and then, wounded with his arm hanging useless, came back for more. And to Sean McKeon, who beat eighteen first-class soldiers with eighteen untrained men, and then beat eighty-four Auxiliaries the same evening.

Flames! I said. That was a great fight. It does not matter who was right or wrong. The brave man is always right!

My brand new hat! 'Nothing 'ere in the lining.' Indeed! And I used to think I had something in the lining of my hat. There was this reflection for one: the best thing that happened for Ireland was that the Germans invaded Belgium. Whether Great Britain first broke the guarantee of neutrality by fortify-

275

ing Belgium, as the Germans claim, matters not to the argument; but the self-righteous blather and skite about the rights of small nations which followed had bound more or less the upholders of the rights of small nations to practise what they preached. Great Britain hates to have her preachings cast in her teeth. She is loth to loosen her grip until her hand trembles. Well, her hands were trembling already in the persons of her representatives in Ireland for the rights of small nations, her Black-and-Tans. Her financiers were trembling about the terms of the American loan, and her sailors were trembling at the prospect of having to race the proposed naval expansion of the United States. Therefore it was of paramount importance to placate the feelings of the Greater Ireland which exists overseas in mighty America. And you do not placate popular feelings among nationals by turning loose the offscourings of English ergastula on Irish fathers and mothers and sisters and brothers. Thus Greenwood was manufacturing rebels at the rate of thousands a day. I was the latest and enthusiastic recruit.

Grimly I quoted that great and magnanimous Englishman Sir William Watson, great verse sent by him to me after the outrage:

> To Sir Hamar Greenwood.
> No thin, pale fame, no brief and poor renown,
> Were thy just due of thee shall wise Time say:
> 'Chartered for havoc, 'neath his rule were they
> Whose chastisement of guilt was to burn down
> The house of innocence in fear-crazed town
> And trembling hamlet, while he had his way,
> Converts untold did this man make each day
> To savage hate of Law and King and Crown.
>
> Great propagandist of the rebel creed!
> Proselytizer without living peer!
> If thou stand fast – if thou but persevere –
> 'Twill be thy glory to complete indeed
> Valera's work, that doth even now so need
> Thy mellow art's last touches, large and clear!'

So three fears freed Ireland – Fear of charges of Hypocrisy, Fear of High Interest, Fear of an Invincible U.S.A. Fleet.

We dawdled back to Dublin. In the Phoenix Park they called a halt by the Wellington Monument to send me on my way. Why not have Clonee incised at the base of that obelisk to Wellington? It would be a famous victory where England had fought, for the first time without allies, and defeated me unarmed, by eleven to one. Or it could be cut in letters of gold under the beautifully engraved 'Copenhagen' on Nelson's Pillar, for that was a victory also with overwhelming odds on.

'You ought to go to the Abbey Theatre to-night. There's a play there called "A Serious Thing." It will make you laugh. I wrote it myself,' I said as a parting shot.

I drove along the quays revolving many thoughts. The background of all of them was angry. I recalled another passage in a pamphlet sent to me 'Across the by no means estranging sea' by the poet to whom England in its junker ignorance prefers Kipling, who never rose from the Sergeants' Mess.

Referring to the crass British want of understanding Sir William Watson wrote:

I do not know whether it testified to our curious English unawareness of the typical and very natural, or to a callous determination to insult and outrage that pride to the limit of endurance and to trail it wantonly in the mire. As to the statesmanship that dictated or sanctioned the whole hideous proceeding (the rounding up of unarmed boys), it should be borne in mind that many individual members of that village throng, or rather that human drove, were no more than boys in their teens. All those boys when they grow up to be men will carry within them to their grave a blazing hatred of the very name of England. For my part I should despise them if they did not.

But my spirits improved as I passed along Brunswick Street. A crowd had collected outside the jail. A merry crowd. What had happened? A crowd seldom laughs at the discomfiture of one of its members. Presently, fuming with indignation, Endymion emerged. He was set free. But he was not satisfied. He was indignant still. 'I paid for it this morning and I hold the receipt. I am arrested for illegal possession in the afternoon.' Another pistol? What had he bought?

At ten o'clock, when there were few people about, he had demonstrated with a cutlass before a ham which hung with

277

twenty others on a rail outside one of those shops which are called Italian Warehouses in Dublin. They would be called grocers' shops elsewhere. He chose the last one on the line. He paid for it. 'No, no! Leave it there! I will call for it this evening. Give me my receipt.' Whether or not there was a change of staff when Endymion returned at five in the afternoon to sabre, transfix and run off with his ham, is not known. Probably the police did not wait to inquire. All they saw was a fugitive shouldering a sworded ham. After some chase they overtook and apprehended Endymion. He was now being set free. But this freedom brought him little satisfaction. 'Arrested for claiming his own property.'

But so much depends on the way the claim is made.

CHAPTER TWENTY

Arthur Griffith's dislike for Erskine Childers and his cousin, Robert Barton, made him sense a contempt for them among the Representatives of Great Britain at the Treaty debate.

They had nothing but contempt for Barton because they saw in him a renegade to his own class. But they accepted Collins and myself at our own valuation.

He told me about his manoeuvres to prolong the debate until a Friday, for he knew that the week-end is the English Sabbath, from observance of which no Englishman exempts himself. If he could only get the debate spun out until Friday, he might count on a respite and time for consideration until the following Tuesday. He began an historical explanation which spun out the time. Again and again Birkenhead or Lloyd George would either anticipate or ask whither it was leading. He held on until Friday called the Ministers away.

'Chamberlain was the best of the whole lot. A clean and honest man.' He withheld his admiration from Birkenhead. Like to like: Griffith to Chamberlain; Collins to Birkenhead. He had nothing but distrust for Lloyd George.

He said something in Welsh to his secretary, Jones, when we were discussing the occupation of Haulbowline, and Jones went out to return with a map stippled with red crosses off the south-west coast of Ireland; each cross marked the watery grave of a British victim of a German submarine. The Germans sank two a day. There was nothing to be said.

He might have asked how would the continued possession of Haulbowline and the other ports make the British Navy more efficient. But this might have altered the humour of his opponents.

'There was nothing to be said.'

Had we, who have not a ship to catch a herring a hundred

miles off Kerry, undertaken the naval defences of Ireland, the awful drain for the upkeep of a navy equal to such a purpose would have been almost as ruinous as the loss of half or three-quarters of our trade.

'There was nothing to be said.'

There was one thing to be said to the Five Plenipotentiaries in the room on the fateful evening when they were discussing the terms proposed by the British government. 'I will not break on the question of the Crown.' Gavan Duffy, who was making balls for Barton to throw, sat silent while Edmund Duggan broke down Barton's resistance to the British offer.

> I sat in a cell in Kilmainham during two days while my best friends were taken out and shot. I was inside. They were outside dying for their country. I was in Mountjoy in a cell that overlooked the execution shed. Nine times I saw the English hangman go in and out. There are often times I wish I had been hanged, for they merely followed the course we laid down. And I, who am not hanged for my country, will not spit in the face of those dead men whose sacrifice brought us the terms that we are offered now.

Barton left the room to consult somebody, presumably Childers. Apparently Duggan's eloquence held. He voted for a Treaty crowning the sacrifices of Ireland's innumerable dead, and he prevented, for a while at least, the life-work of Arthur Griffith from being directed by an Englishman. Barton was the first to repudiate his signature.

But those who resent the Englishman Childers' influence on even one of the Plenipotentiaries have refused to consider him in one decisive moment. What sent Barton back to vote? When a weak man leaves a room to consult a dominating character, is it to be supposed that the stronger has no influence? Childers may have sent Barton back to vote for the Treaty. Let me crave for him the benefit of this doubt, for he was as gallant a man as ever died in Ireland.

Since I was defeated by the Black-and-Tans at the battle of Clonee, I have grown rather particular. I don't like soldiers or pseudo-soldiers, especially when they are dressed as soldier chauffeurs. Therefore, on returning rather late one evening, the sight of several of them in a large limousine at my hall-door made me meditative. It would be a good idea before my latch-key identifies me to retreat to some place and to ring up my house. It was all right. Mrs Clifton, who had been dining with Lord French at the Vice-regal Lodge, had dropped in for an after-dinner chat. I wonder! But I hasten home.

They do not send ladies from the Lodge with warrants for arrests. The soldiers are merely escorts for Lord French's car.

Like a young man's dream of Andromache, she stood tall and darkly lovely by the fireplace. She had important news for me. At dinner that night the Provost of Trinity had warned Lord French that I was the most dangerous intellect unapprehended in Ireland. Did not this mean that I was likely to be arrested any minute?

'I have been frequently arrested, but only for a few minutes, and I don't expect that Lord French will listen to a sneak. Intellect indeed! And the Provost is now trying to intellectualize himself into the Kingdom of Heaven, having resigned the Archbishopric of Dublin. It is not done, this resigning an Archbishopric to take up a better job. But Dean Bernard, Dean of St Patrick's, as Dean Swift was, Dean Bernard, whilom Archbishop of Dublin and now Provost of Trinity, has a strange way of dealing with its alumnus which is I. Probably someone told him that when he took up the Provostship, I commented on the translation by remarking that he had exchanged the Thirty-nine Articles for the Thirty Pieces of Silver, which, if anything, brought him closer to his biblical archetype. We must not blame him if the only truth in him is that he is true to form. Probably he blames me for the showers of pennies which the Undergraduates throw at him whenever he appears.'

'He was certainly most vindictive.'

'Lord French is a soldier, and with him a renegade archbishop won't cut ice.'

'What can have made him hate you so?' Mrs Clifton asked anxiously.

'Cardiac cases are often unaccountably irascible.'

'Has he heart disease?'

'Did you not hear that the Lord punished him by substituting angina pectoris for his pectoral cross?'

Gratitude and contempt! Gratitude to the lady who took the trouble to obtain a car from her host to warn me, an acquaintance of a few years' standing, against the Provost, the Head Master of my College. She has repaid now any discomfort I suffered from the suspicious peasants through my association with her husband: to these such as he was a 'spy'! And contempt for the pusillanimous breed the Provost represented, a breed that rightly incurred the hatred and contempt of all Irish Nationalists, old or new. The mimmouthed crew that Bobbie Burns fought against without means or backing. The gang that denies the splendour of God and would turn His grace into a narrow monopoly. The parson caricatured, penurious and opportunist. I cannot imagine Dr Fogarty of Killaloe selling out and doffing his pectoral cross to manage a technical school or to become Chairman of the Electricity Supply Board for the Shannon Scheme. But here is Dr Bernard 'going one better' than archbishopric to take over the well-paid Provostship of Trinity College. There was a time when its soul could bear Molyneux and Berkeley and Burke and Davis ... But it remained for Bernard to cash it in.

'How did French take it?' I asked.

' "He's operating on me to-morrow," was all he said. Are you?'

'I am more concerned for Trinity,' I said, without answering, 'than for Lord French. The fate of a patient of mine is within my control, as Epictetus has it, but the Provost is beyond me; and he will make the College as narrow as himself. You cannot expect to turn a University into a gangster's conspiracy to get a rake-off from the "wise-cracks" of the classical world and at the same time raise its alumni above narrowness and pusillanimity.'

'He never forgives himself for his *faux-pas* with the Provost ...' remarked someone, laughing at me.

'Maybe you are right.'

'When and where was it made?' Mrs Clifton inquired. 'And what was your *faux-pas*?'

'I don't want to elaborate it,' I said, 'but I was staying at Castle Forbes and, because some people like to show their catholicism by entertaining the narrow-minded, Lord Granard included the Archbishop, as he was then, in his house-party. It was dark when we got into the brake from the train. Everyone going to a house-party dislikes and disapproves of the other guests, as is the way of guests before they, all amiable, unavoidably meet at dinner. I could see the silhouette of the Archbishop like one of those old *Freeman's Journal* cartoons of a rival newspaper, where the sheaf is humanized by an angular nose and a pair of thin legs. The Archbishop's nose left his high, flat forehead like a gnomon at an angle of inhuman rectitude and, as he walked, he walked in perspicaciously.

'Things were growing dull at dinner while we waited for some enlivening or even an interesting remark; but the Archbishop remained in his purple clothes as silent as a statue in a Catholic church on Good Friday.

'Just to cheer myself I told the story of Dr Tyrrell's dinner at the Deanery of St Patrick's. It never occurred to me to ask myself who was the Dean at the time of the story.

' "Once," said Dr Tyrrell, mildly cynical with the mellowness of his pleasant seventy years – "once I received an invitation to dine with the Dean of St Patrick's. Well, you know, I could not give it to that old curmudgeon to say that I got drunk in his house." I found myself wondering how and when my friend, Silenus-like in his wisdom, had found grace to refrain. I was not left wondering long. "Oh, no! I took the obvious precaution of coming drunk."

'I laughed at my own story of the delightful old man. A few of the guests simpered, but the Archbishop's nose registered disapprobation and disdain. After an awful pause, he said, shooting a sharp momentary glint in my direction, "That actually happened at my house."

'And I had spoken of him as "that old curmudgeon"!'

'That might explain some of his disapproval of you, but hardly all,' Mrs Clifton said.

'Then there were my bad manners in not waiting for him to speak. But what assurance had I that the Holy Ghost wanted such a mouthpiece? I tried to dissipate the effect of my *fauxpas* by defending the Germans from charges of torturing their enemies – "Woe to Great Britain's foes, they get a bad Press ... After all, the Chinese torture people, and they represent an old civilization."

' "The Chinese tortures are a little more austere," the Archbishop, very much to my surprise, remarked; but with such an emphasis on *austere* that I felt myself somehow rebuked. But

283

then my conscience automatically becomes bad when I meet an Archbishop.'

Be that as it may. He himself is the explanation of my disapproval, but nevertheless, if positions were reversed, I would never felon-set him or act the informer to have him imprisoned or hanged.

CHAPTER TWENTY-ONE

Arthur Griffith had something on his mind. We walked in silence along Duke Street. He had been telling me that he modelled his style on that of Dean Swift. And I had recorded how Dr Tyrrell asked Carlyle whom he considered the greatest writer of English Prose. 'Swaft! for his parfaict lucidity.' Arthur rolled in his gait 'like a dove,' the Kaffirs said when he went to the mines in South Africa. 'Cugaun' they called him. He used it for a *nom-de-plume*.

Suddenly: 'I want you to do something for me.'

'Consider it done.'

'It is this. I have got word that Smuts is on his way from London. He will arrive at Kingstown early in the morning. I want to catch him before he reaches Dublin Castle. Can you have your Rolls-Royce ready at 4.30 in the morning? Meet me at the church in Lower Merrion Street. Not a word to your man. I want you to drive me yourself. Barton and the Lord Mayor will be with us.'

'I will be there punctually.'

'Right!' He gave himself a jerk, straightened his shoulders and marched on. We entered the Bailey. He made no further reference to the arrangement for the morning. It seemed as if he were relieved from a burden – the burden of having to ask anyone to assist him in his plans.

When much depends on a car starting, it is all you can do to prevent yourself lessening its chance of starting by over-attention or tinkering with it. I kept a bottle of ether ready in case. But it never gives me trouble, I reflected, yet at that hour of the morning, without a chauffeur, even the car may be asleep.

But all was well. Griffith and Barton were met, but where was Larry O'Neill, Lord Mayor? We did not like to cruise about too noticeably, but Griffith was getting anxious. The Lord Mayor's presence will make it harder for General Smuts to escape from us and to consult the Castle first. Round the Square, then round by Westland Row. Will we just make one turn before giving him up?

In the stillness of the empty streets a car was heard approaching. Soon we sighted Larry in his black clothes, sitting at the back. He changed into our car. Off. We must be at the pier by five, or our bird may have flown. Along the Merrion Road we hummed. Black smoke far down on the horizon to the east far out where the Kish Lightship rocked.

'Plenty of time!' I said.

We stood on the pier while the boat was being made fast.

Larry was the first up the gangway. 'Tell General Smuts the Lord Mayor of Dublin wishes to greet him.'

Griffith grunted. That was spoiling our plans. We were to surprise the General, and now Larry had damped the effect with his 'Lord Mayor of Dublin'.

The steward said – he had learnt his lesson well – 'General Smuts is not on board.'

'Stand by and let me know if he slips ashore. I want to see the passenger list.'

Griffith examined the list many times, looking for any South African name that Smuts would have been likely to adopt. To all our repeated inquiries the crew persisted in knowing nothing.

'We can only wait until they are all out of their cabins. Everyone has to be ashore by eight.'

A pleasant prospect for me, who detest waiting! But there is one advantage which food has: it helps to pass the time.

All four of us breakfasted. Still no sign of Smuts. We dawdled about after breakfast until 'all ashore!' rang out. We had our journey for nothing.

'Where to now?' I asked.

But Griffith never answered. He appeared not to have heard me. He was deep in thought. On whatever information he had he could implicitly rely, and yet there was no Smuts.

Let Larry rouse him.

'Where do you want to go now, Mr Griffith?'

'Five Merrion Square.'

That is Dr Farnan's house. So Farnan is in the movement. We were not long in reaching 5 Merrion Square.

'I'll be back in ten minutes,' I said. 'I don't want to have this car seen outside the house. It would give the show away. I'll put it out of the way. It might lead to an arrest.'

De Valera was breakfasting with Dr Farnan. I was not present when Griffith arrived. I do not know how he explained

286

missing Smuts. De Valera was supposed to be in hiding. We were supposed to be in the secret, but of course not to divulge it under pain of death.

Presently the telephone bell rang. I think I took the call. It is not important; but what was memorable was the consternation of both Farnan and De Valera when blandly came the voice, 'May I speak to Mr De Valera?'

'Who is it?'

'Alfred Cope, speaking from Dublin Castle!'

And De Valera's hiding-places were such a secret! This knowledge of where he was to be found meant that Dublin Castle could lay hands on him at any moment, if it wished. It rather lessened his importance. Collins could not be found. But De Valera was 'on the phone.'

'Is your car at the door?' he asked me testily, thinking that its presence might be associated with a meeting of the group and so I might be blamed for giving his whereabouts away.

'I am not quite such a fool,' said I.

Cope, it seemed, had telephoned to say that General Smuts had arrived at Dublin Castle and would like to confer with the Irish Leaders. Would eleven o'clock at the Mansion House be suitable?

At the Mansion House I learned afterwards that Smuts advised them not to insist on a Republic.

'I tried a Republic, and it was a failure,' he said.

Afterwards, too, I learned that he had purposely eluded us and avoided meeting Griffith, by hiding on the lifeboat deck, until he should first have reached Dublin Castle.

CHAPTER TWENTY-TWO

As a rule I go to the Abbey Theatre to look at the audience. One can derive much interest from observing them, especially if they are looking at a play by the observer. Lennox Robinson attributes so much importance to the audience that sometimes I begin to ask myself: Is it the audience or the play that is the thing?

But the house had two rows filled with Black-and-Tans. They were much amused by 'A Serious Thing.' A play which showed Judaea occupied by troops in khaki in the days when Pontius Pilate was Procurator. Two were on guard on a wall beside the tomb of Lazarus. Judaea was under curfew, permits to move were necessary; notes, mental and written, were made by Rome's constabulary, of every speech. Great exception was taken to moral apophthegms to disorder. There had been a swine drive of sorts at Gadara.

Lazarus came forth and walked out without a permit, disobeying the sergeant, who ordered hm to halt. When court-martialled subsequently and asked why he had not killed Lazarus, the sergeant answered simply enough, 'Because he was already dead.' Of course Rome could make little headway against a nation of resurrections.

It did me good to see the Black-and-Tans laughing, unaware that their legs were being pulled. Nevertheless, the author did not respond when the call for 'Author!' came.

Edward Martyn asked me to let him read the text. I never saw him at the Abbey. Like every Irishman who can afford to be an individual, he ran an opposition show, a theatre of his own in Hardwicke Street. I went round to his rooms in Nassau Street beside the Kildare Street Club. He was living with monkish austerity – plain oaken chairs and table; church-warden pipes galore because they were so brittle. His austerity appertained to everything except his appetite. He read on in his short-sighted way while I looked at the deep pink cheeks which festooned his collar. His pince-nez made his nose and eyes appear even narrower than they were; and so belied the promise of his broad head and brow.

This is the man whom George Moore calls 'Dear Edward.' This is he who entertained Yeats and Moore in his Castle of Tullyra, hoping to win their approbation of his play.

I wish he could read faster. I hate being kept waiting, particularly in a kind of cell in a low-ceilinged mezzanine between the first and second floors. But soon it will be eight o'clock and he will scent the beef in the Kildare Street Club. He will seize his stick and his man will help his protein-crippled limbs to the carnivorous festival of rheumatism and gout. Strange last survivor of an ancient Galway family, the Martyns. For their liberality and humanity in the bad seventeenth century one of them was exempted from the confiscations which robbed the contemporary chieftains. Jaspar, James and Nimble Dick! Nimble Dick, who challenged the O'Flaherty, Prince of Iar Connaught, to single combat for an insult levelled at his mother, and who carried the combat, unattended by seconds, alone to the Castle of Auchnanure, only to be treacherously stabbed in the back by a retainer: then Humanity Dick, the originator of prevention of cruelty of animals. Yes, the Martyns were a noble clan, I heard myself saying. But suddenly a fat shout from the plain oaken chair.

'The Divine Voice!'

'Yes?'

'You have brought the Divine Voice on to the stage!'

His gills cardinalized into crimson.

'But – well – what harm? There has to be a miracle to get Lazarus to arise.'

'Ugh, ugh! But the Divine Voice!'

'Well, if you can devise a means to get Lazarus up, I will omit it. The play, if we can call it a play, is symbolic. The Resurrection of Lazarus symbolizes the nationhood of Ireland re-arisen from the grave wherein it lay dead – dead from the dilution of its individuality by identification with that of every Tom, Dick, and Harry nation on earth, as a result of the system of "Intermediate Education" and regulated ways. Lazarus has found his soul. He is alive; he is risen. He defies Imperial Rome and its Black-and-Tans. The nation's call has aroused him. Is not *vox populi, vox Dei*? And what is that but the Divine Voice?'

But the thought of horse-radish and succulent rump steak attenuated any little interest he had in me or my play. Therefore all the more he wreaked on me his 'advice' about the Divine Voice, especially since he had not an idea to offer as to why Lazarus could arise without a miraculous mandate.

I suggested that he should come behind the scenes and call out reverently from his chair, 'Lazarus come forth!' I knew that his voice would sound so soft and soothing that the danger was it might deepen the sleep of Lazarus; but I wanted his co-operation to protect me from spiteful little mandrakes who would concentrate on irreverence in the play and nothing else.

Everything was ready to bear him to dinner. He was the only man who took a motor-car to cover fifty yards.

I saw the trousers striped grey and black and the short black coat disappear gradually into the motor. To-morrow he will read an account of my play in the papers. He will wonder why I should have waited to seek his advice after the thing was staged. What will he think of me then? I cannot say, but I know what he is thinking of now that the gong has gone, and that is about as far as I shall ever see into his mind. His branch of the Martyns cannot be descended from Nimble Dick!

I sat in the Abbey thinking of the gang who occupied the front rows. How many of them had been offered the alternative of service in Ireland to a long term in gaol? English magistrates, it was said, were giving criminals that choice. They had killed priests, shot a pregnant woman and tortured prisoners; yet they called the half-armed, totally untrained men who opposed their machine-guns and whippet tanks, cowards.

I remembered the account of one ambush – the only one, I think, that happened in County Galway. The local sergeant was acting unwillingly as guide to a lorry-load of Black-and-Tans. Very probably he was forced to act, for the Royal Irish Constabulary refused to co-operate with such ruffians. Along a lonely road in the bare West country, in sight of the mountain called the 'Devil's Mother,' the lorry came. The sergeant sat in the front seat beside the driver, who pulled up whenever he approached a spinney or rough ground to let his crew jump down and investigate, on guard against ambushes. The boys knew this, and they lay a hundred yards in front of a wood in a moor where there was hardly enough cover for a wild goose. They hoped it would be the spot where the lorry would come to a halt and a few of the Black-and-Tans would go ahead to search the spinney.

Lying flat on his chest, the captain would feel through it the rumble of the approaching lorry as it shook the light bog road. How many were there? He dare not raise his head to look. It was anxious work holding down, not knowing whether his party had been observed or not, uncertain whether he would be shot in the back without having fired a shot.

'Just look at that there wood, Jerry!'

He could hear the foreign accent ten feet away. It was harder on the half-a-dozen lads under his command: but his responsibility gave him courage. And they had their rosary beads. He counted thirty, forty, fifty paces as the advance guard separated. He gave them another fifty until he could hear them no more. A hissing whisper 'Soldiers, let them have it!' There were four men on each side of the lorry sitting back to back. Two were shot point blank. The driver got a bullet through his forehead. The two who had gone forward to the wood opened fire from the road. The sergeant jumped down and ran off unarmed.

'I did not like to quench him,' said the Captain.

Something like that was coming surely to some of my audience in the Abbey Theatre. And the devil mend them!

I had no programme. I was only interested in my own play. It was not necessary to have a programme for that. And as for foretelling what would follow, you could tell that without any programme. It would surely be something by Lady Gregory. I must get out before her namby-pamby humour deadens my spirits.

How much of her plays did she write? Yeats had spent many months annually in collaboration with her in Coole Park, and I knew how generously Yeats presented me, for one, with golden lines or ideas. I was wrestling catch-as-catch-can with a sonnet. I wished to get a simile for joy reigning in the dark places of a hospital. I had failed to grasp 'The happy hand of Chance.' Yeats murmured for a minute sonorously to himself and said, with a sudden emphasis of the 'leap':

'The blackbird *leap* from his dark hedge and sing.'

The Divine Voice! It made whatever was worth making in the sonnet. How much more would he not do for Lady Gregory? I almost got him to acknowledge his authorship of 'The Rising of the Moon.' I think he said that it was understood between himself and Lady Gregory that a play might be attributed to the one who had the idea!

Possibly Lady Gregory thought of the title, which was that of a well-known ballad. But the perpetual presentation of Lady Gregory's plays nearly ruined the Abbey. They were put on as curtain-raisers, comic reliefs, or they took the whole stage.

One who had contributed many hundreds of pounds to the Abbey, only to have a play of his cast unworthily, used to chaunt:

> 'I heard the pit and circle say:
> "Gregory bores us,
> And one by one we slip away." '

How different was the first play written and in part acted by an Irishman in Dublin! It was put on in some hired hall near Clarendon Street; George Russell's (Æ's) 'Deirdre.' The poetic mind had been awakened and inspired by Standish O'Grady's heroic fragment of Irish history. Æ was profoundly roused. He read theosophy into the tales of ancient gods and heroes, and compared them with the trilogy of deities he saw in every religion.

In his 'Deirdre' the lovers are being drowned by the uprising of invisible waves. They are supposed to be friendly and, in some mysterious way, beneficent waves, for Æ could not sustain the thought of anyone being injured. At the moment they were overwhelmed, the dark purple curtain which backed the stage opened in the middle. The golden-brown beard and full, fresh-cheeked face appeared. A sonorous voice chanted one long name:

'Mananann Mac Lir.'

It was the author, Æ! Shakespeare is said to have played the ghost in 'Hamlet' because he had a fine voice. Æ's only appearance on the stage was a partial appearance, the head of the God of the Waves of Erin, Mananann, the Son of Lir.

Then, farther up the town in Camden Street, Synge would be sitting watching rehearsals. He sat silent, holding his stick between his knees, his chin resting on his hands. He spoke seldom. When he did, the voice came in a short rush, as if he wished to get the talk over as soon as possible. A dour, but not a forbidding man. Had he been less competent it might have been said of him on account of his self-absorption that he 'stood aloof from other minds. In impotence of fancied power.' He never relaxed his mind from its burden.

I asked him if he did not intend his 'Playboy' for a satire to show up, for one thing, how lifeless and inert was the country where a man could be hailed as a hero for doing something kinetic even though it were a murder, and how ineffectual, for, as the event showed, even that had not been committed. He gave me a short glance and looked straight in front of himself, weighing me up and thinking how hard it would be to get the public to appreciate his play as a work of art, when one who should know better was reading analogies and satire into it already. He shook my question off with a shake of his head.

We were nearer to poetic drama than we shall ever be again. Intellectual life was astir. Joyce and I used to go to see how the actors were getting on with John Elwood, a medical student, who enjoyed the licence allowed to medical students by the tolerant goodwill of a people to whom Medicine with its traffic in Life and Death had something of the mysterious and magical about it. To be a medical student's pal by virtue of the glamour that surrounded a student of medicine was almost a profession in itself. Joyce was the best example of a medical student's pal Dublin produced, or rather the best example of the type, extinct since the Middle Ages, of a Goliard, a wandering scholar. The theatre off Camden Street was approached through a narrow passage. John Elwood got so drunk one night that he lamented that he could not even see the ladies stepping over him as they came out.

'Synge looks like a fellow who would sip a pint.'

'John,' I said, 'if you had done more sipping and less swallowing you would not have got us all kicked out.'

Joyce knew far better than I what was in the air, and what was likely to be the future of the theatre in Ireland.

Who can measure how great was its loss when Lady Gregory gave him the cold shoulder? Maybe her much-announced search for talent did not contemplate the talent latent in medical students' pals or wandering minstrels. After an unsuccessful interview he met us in a 'snug,' where, very solemnly, with his high, well-stocked forehead bulging over his nose, he recited solemnly, waving his finger slowly:

'There was a kind Lady called Gregory,
Said, "Come to me poets in beggary."
But found her imprudence
When thousands of students
Cried, "All we are in that catégory"!'

The elision of 'who' before the 'Said' in the second line is a
parody on the synthetic folk speech in Synge's 'Playboy.' And
the strained 'catégory' the beginning of his experiment with
words. She had no room for playboys except on the stage . . .
So Ulysses had to strike out for himself. Dublin's Dante had to
find a way out of his own Inferno. But he had lost the key.
James Augustine Joyce slipped politely from the snug with an
'Excuse me!'

'Whist! He's gone to put it all down!'

'Put what down?'

'Put *us* down. A chiel's among us takin' notes. And, faith,
he'll print it.'

Now, that was a new aspect of James Augustine. I was too
unsophisticated to know that even outside Lady Gregory's
presence, notes made of those contemporary with the growing
'Movement' would have a sale later on, and even an historical
interest.

'He's discovered a wonderful poem in 4 Faithful Place,
which he sent to Father Delaney.'

'Surely it is not

'There was a kind priest called Delaney
Who said to the girls, Nota bene?

Because I have heard that "not once or twice in our rough
island's story." '

Twitching and elusive, John did not reply. He was one of
those countrymen to whom a direct question suggests that the
answer should be withheld.

He kept his eye glued against a point in the window from
which the muffling of the glass had been worn.

Excitedly, 'There's three auld ones,' he said.

I was trying to recall what spark had been struck or what
'folk phrase' Joyce had culled from Elwood or me that sent
him out to make his secret record.

Secrecy of any kind corrupts sincere relations. I don't mind being reported, but to be an unwilling contributor to one of his 'Epiphanies' is irritating.

Probably Father Darlington had taught him, as an aside in his Latin class – for Joyce knew no Greek – that 'Epiphany' meant 'a showing forth'. So he recorded under 'Epiphany' any showing forth of the mind by which he considered one gave oneself away.

Which of us had endowed him with an 'Epiphany' and sent him to the lavatory to take it down?

'John,' I said, seeking an ally, 'he's codding the pair of us.'

But John could not be enlisted to resent.

'A great artist!' he exclaimed, using 'artist' in the sense it has in Dublin of a quaint fellow or a great cod: a pleasant and unhypocritical poseur, one who sacrifices his own dignity for his friends' diversion.

'A great artist! He may be codding the two of us, but he's codding himself!'

'Codding apart, John, why is he taking notes?'

'We're all on the stage – Jayshus, we're all on the stage since the old lady threw him out, Yeats, Roberts, Vincent, me and you – you're in for it worst, for you stood him a pint – Colum, Magee – we're all in a poem – "Hat unfix." ' John jerked a word or two out, trying with his intermittent mind to recall Joyce's poem probably confided to him but once. Hopeless!

'Gargle that and have another. I want that poem from Faithful Place.'

'Ask him for it when he comes back.'

He'll hardly give it me, I surmised, but long afterwards he did ... The door of the snug was pushed in; the three 'auld ones' appeared. 'Excuse us.' We made room. One of them wore her bonnet, toque or hat on the ridge of her left eye. Her friend's face was obscured. James Augustine reappeared. He evinced no surprise. Beside Elwood, the 'auld ones' intervening, he took his seat. As if nothing unusual had happened, he adjured them dictatorially with lines from his favourite Ben Jonson:

'Still to be neat, still to be dressed,
As you were going to a feast.'

'Well, now isn't your friend the queer body – and we're only recovering from a wake this morning!'

'Still to be powdered, still perfumed.'

295

James Augustine continued uninterruptedly:

'Ladies, it is to be presumed . . .'

John looked at me with dancing eyes the lids of which were as defined as a warrior's of the fifth century B.C. and something of an archaic smile hovered always on his well-cut mouth.

'Isn't he a real artist?'

Well-charged with diary of an evening's dissipation in Dublin, Ulysses could relax from listening to his companions' talk. But he sat on any resentment he bore by assuring himself that he would crucify us all in due course. Meanwhile, over-politely, he invited the old women to 'join him in a drink'.

'I know that yer laughin' at me,' she said recklessly, 'but, coddin' apart, I've reared five children and ye wouldn't believe that me father was a boat-builder beyond at Ringsend.'

'He must have been an artist,' yelled John.

Joyce rebuked John Elwood. John was as unaccountable as a faun.

'Madam, my friend is using artist in the Augustinian sense. St Augustine, you may remember, uses "art" to express the third manifestation of the power of the soul – practical life or "art" which comprehends all our activities from boat-building to poetry.'

She flung herself into a spate of words which held Joyce by their sound – sense yielding to sincerity.

'Eight children and the girls married and himself dead and me sons' father, and here am I in The Bleeding Horse and only one gentleman among the lot of yez! Not that I'm saying a word against the other two.'

Solemnly James recorded,

'Love still has something of the sea.'

Then, as if relenting from that detachment: 'Madam, another pint will do us good, though over there with the actors it only makes them talk unnaturally.'

'May God bless your lovely blue eyes, and hold His hand from your queer friends. Here's luck!'

'A boat-builder?' I inquired.

'Yes. In Ringsend, the town that thrun back Strongbow and sent him on to Dublin!'

Elwood nudged me.

296

'Every old one loves him and leaves us on our . . .'
'John!'
'You're as bad as them.'
'That poem. If you misquote it, maybe he'll give it to us.'
But James kept quoting Jonson still adjuring the three old
trots:

> 'Lady, it is to be presumed.'

So James Augustine mesmerized the old women. How much
the name equalled him in experience with the Saint will never
be recorded. It was far pleasanter and simpler than the ritual
of Yeats or Æ. I attended a lecture by Æ in Camden Street
and when, in answer to Yeats's invitation to comment, a man
in the audience asked: 'How many gods does your friend disbelieve in?' majestically Yeats remarked: 'My interrupter has
asked an interesting question. Æ will reply.'

'He's solemn enough now to be linked home! Have I time
to sing?' Elwood asked.

'Don't! John! Take a pull at yourself!'

'I'll recite then!' Who can resist an audience?

'This is what Joyce unearthed from No. 4. And he won't give
anyone a copy. It's paved by the cobblestones of the eighteenth
century, and in it a braver Dublin rings than we'll ever see
again! Where can we find men now who are not too cowardly
to speak of "bloody fine whores"? No bloody where! You're
all a pack of hypocritical funks!' And he broke into:

> 'As I was going down Sackville Street'

'Steady, John!' I adjured.

> 'Hey, Ho! me Randy O,
> Three bloody fine –'

'Who were they?' I asked.

'They're symbolical of course. Everything with him is. They
may be Patriotism, Politics and the Great Pox for all I know.'

'Present company always excepted and double exceptions for
Jimmy Joyce. The "auld ones" took up the chorus and were
singing now. Whisht!'

Released from cark and care, James had the old charwomen
singing, and at the same time reverencing him as if he were an
evangelist. America would have been his happy remunerative

297

exploiting ground if only he had been dishonest! He was gifted with a seriousness that was unremitting and could resist even his own jokes.

'How does it go, Anna?'

'I chose the one with the curly locks!
Hey Ho! –'

'That would be the Muse of Politics, John,' I remarked.

'Time – Gentlemen, Time! Now then – Please!'

'Good-night to you now, Master! You've a lovely pair of blue eyes; but I don't like the company yer keeping.'

'You,' said John.

'You!' said I.

'What about going to a shebeen in the kips to cleanse ourselves from Synge?'

'Apart from your quest for natural speech, I have my own reasons for going,' said I. 'For everyone has business and desires!'

'Yer a great pair of artists!' John shouted as we went into the night. And then as if thinking of the romantic bullies of Dublin's golden age he sang a stave:

'Whom did I meet but Tiger Roche?'

'Great, John!' I shouted. 'How does it go on?'

But the swift eyes eluded me, and he ceased to sing.

One of the first meetings of the Irish theatre, or rather of those who were about to produce Irish drama, took place in the Nassau Hotel. Maud Gonne sat on the opposite sides of the table. Synge was at one end by Lady Gregory. Patrick Colum sat next to me. Suddenly Yeats exclaimed in admiration of a scene he was reading:

'Who does he mean?' Colum whispered, amazed.

'Aeschylus!'

'Synge, who is like Aeschylus.'

'But who is Aeschylus?'

'The man who is like Synge!'

We talked while Yeats was reading. I was surprised at Maud Gonne's small voice. For one so tall and striking you would have expected a voice full and contralto: but no, here was a small voice. And like the man in Douglas Hyde's song, she had a large heart –

> I'd rather have if I got my choice,
> A large heart and a small voice.

A tall and tawny woman, the daughter of a Colonel in the English Army, greatly she inspired Yeats.

'It is hardly possible for anybody in Ireland to write anything at all without becoming a genius. I am off' – to Colum.

But Colum, who was fast becoming one, refused to discuss it disrespectfully.

The Abbey Players have now a theatre all their own. And the plays of the least inspired of that old group of nascent geniuses are played the most frequently.

Happy and wholesome days with genius in the bud and the status of a medical student's pal recognized as a profession!

'Medicals' were immune from molestation even in the most lawless purlieus of the town.

'Mebbe they're on midwifery duty, helping a poor woman. Ye never know.'

They were safe in every shebeen from the Gloucester Diamond to Hell's Gates when the 'kips' were in full blast. This side of the Yoshiwara there was never such a street as Tyrone Street for squalor with wildest orgies mixed. Here reigned the Shakespearean London of Jack Greene. Here nothing but the English language was undefiled.

The names of its brothel-keepers, bullies, and frequenters were typical of a city which, like Vienna, had forged for itself a distinct identity. There were certainly not Irish nor wholly English names. Dublin names, euphonious and romantic!

Now that the Abbey Players are world-renowned, I begin to realize that with such an audience and such actors an author is hardly needed. Good acting covers a multitude of defects. It explains the success of Lady Gregory's plays. It explains the favouritism enjoyed by the Fays. This is no place for me! I am off. But if I could father 'A Serious Thing' on the old Lady, it would never stop running.

CHAPTER TWENTY-THREE

Ely Place, Dublin. Like its namesake in London, it is a *cul-de-sac*. From St Stephen's Green, Hume Street runs into it at right angles, and Ely House, the residence of the long-dead Marquis, looks down Hume Street to the west. The prevailing wind, which is western, blows the dust of Hume Street against the great house, seven windows wide, and makes it unsafe to keep them open. Ely House is one of the few remaining palaces of the spacious eighteenth century which exist in Dublin without having fallen long ago into decay: old houses which were dedicated to mythological persons. Belvedere House to Venus, Ely House to Hercules. The Farnese Hercules stands like a pillar at the foot of the great stairs, which are balustraded by representations in gilt bronze of the wild beasts such as the Nemean Lion, which fell to his club and whose hide he holds for ever on his left arm.

Sir Thornley Stoker, the famous surgeon, lives in Ely Place, and in the eighteenth century, which he never really leaves; hence the house is filled with period furniture, of which he is a collector and a connoisseur. Chippendale, Adam, and old silver candelabra, match the silver jambs of the doors, and are contemporary with the silver linings of the great fireplaces, under their mantels of Siena and statuary marble.

A figure with hair silver as a dandelion in summer, pink porcelain face, sloping shoulders and peg-topped trousers in a suit of navy blue, came strolling down Ely Place from its garden end. He carried a malacca cane with an ivory top shaped like an egg; he strolled leisurely, as became a novelist, a perssonage, and a man of independent means. When he reached the long railings of Ely House he drew his stick across them as he went, causing a noise which he calculated would reach and irritate the somewhat strange and irascible owner. He passed on.

'Be sure you come punctually,' said Sir Thornley to me, 'it's a sign of bad manners to be late for dinner. Augustine Birrell is dining with us; but it's not for that reason that I ask you to be punctual, but for the general principle.'

The great dining-room was lit with candles, which of course were waxen.

'Nobody ever heard of paraffin candles at the time that this house was built; you see how much better the stucco designs appear on the blank walls in this mellow light. This is Mr Birrell; now I think we can all be seated. There is no use waiting any longer, and one has to consider the soup more than a tardy guest. Take your places, gentlemen.'

We had just finished the soup when the door of Domingo mahogany swung silently, reflecting the light. The butler said, 'Mr George Moore.'

Sir Thornley Stoker only half rose and turned sideways, holding his napkin like an apron in his lap.

'Sit down, Moore,' he said testily, 'sit down. We couldn't wait for you any longer.'

Moore went over to his empty chair, balanced it on its hind legs, admired what Sir Thornley would call 'the excellent skin' of its glossy Chippendale wood, and turning from his scrutiny, with a look of inquiry towards his host, asked: 'A cancer, Sir Thornley, or a gallstone?' referring to Sir Thornley's habit of buying after a big operation 'a museum piece'.

Moore resented the presence of Birrell. He had decided for the evening not to have read *Obiter Dicta* or, at the worst, if anyone mentioned it, to be unaware of its relation to Mr Birrell, or of Mr Birrell's relation to it.

Sir Thornley asked: 'The shoulder or the belly of this salmon, Moore? I'm chining the salmon. I killed this fish in the Slaney – King Harman's water – and I think we'll find it a palatable fish. Shall I help you to the shoulder?'

'No, I think the fin, Sir Thornley.'

'Now, Moore, don't be peevish. You are the last that should pretend to be careless about your food. I've just been reading your long letter in the *Irish Times* on the grey mullet. Nobody ever heard of a fin.'

'On the contrary, the Chineses – as my friend here insists on calling them – find sharks' fins delicious.'

These antics fail to draw Birrell, so Moore addresses his remarks to me. Then Birrell says, 'How is your brother Bram, Sir Thornley?'

'Haven't seen him for some time.'

'Is he living in Herbert Street, or is he in London at all these days?'

'He is engaged on scientific research somewhere,' said Sir Thornley.

'Not on the habits of Dracula?' said Birrell, with a laugh.

At this stage the mahogany door burst open, and a nude and elderly lady came in with a cry, 'I like a little intelligent conversation!' She ran round the table. We all stood up. She was followed by two female attendants, who seized whatever napery was available, and sheltering her with this and their own bodies, led her forth, screaming, from the room.

Our consternation held us in the positions we had suddenly taken. Birrell looked like a popular figure in Madame Tussaud's, Sir Thornley, with his knuckles on the table, inclined his head as if saying a silent grace. At last he broke silence with: 'Gentlemen, pray sit down.'

Nobody liked to begin a conversation, because the farther it was off the subject, the more purposely self-conscious it would seem. Sir Thornley recovered himself and spoke:

'Gentlemen, under my mahogany, I hope you will keep this incident, mortifying as it is to me, from any rumour of scandal in this most gossipy town. And now, Moore, I conjure you most particularly, as you are the only one who causes me grave misgivings.'

'But it was charming, Sir Thornley. I demand an encore.'

Sir Thornley rose, went over to Moore's chair, and pointing his beard into Moore's ear, hissed something. Then, taking the novelist by the shoulder, he pushed him to the door and into the hall, and out into the street. We heard the door banging and the yapping of her Ladyship's pomeranian dog.

Sir Thornley insisted on his guests drinking more wine. The dinner dragged on, Sir Thornley asking questions without waiting for answers, from each of us in turn. I was counting the minutes towards the end of this melancholy feast. After some minutes the butler leant over and said something to Sir Thornley.

'Did you admit that scoundrel?' said Sir Thornley harshly.

'He says, sir, it's a matter of life and death.'

'Will you, pray, excuse me, gentlemen? I have to leave the room for a moment.'

We could hear the inarticulate sounds of voices, and suddenly two loud screams. It transpired that George, on his way home, had been bitten by a mad dog and was in danger of hydrophobia. Sir Thornley had enlarged the two slight scratches on Moore's right calf and was screwing caustic into the wound. The yells increased, and through the door, which Sir Thornley had forgotten to close, we could hear him saying, 'I don't care whether you're in a dinner-jacket or not. You'll have to send to your house for my honorarium, which is five guineas, before you leave this hall.' Moore produced a wallet of flexible green leather and handed Sir Thornley a five-pound note, with 'I'll send the silver in the morning by my cook.' The butler opened the door, to let out George Moore, and to let in a little pomeranian dog . . .

George Moore returned up Ely Place, still straying his stick against the railings of No 8. Sir Thornley Stoker, far back in his dining-room, placed the *Graphic* on the *original* red leather of one of his chairs, stood up on it, so as not to be observed, and satisfied himself that the source of the corrugated irritations was the novelist whom some weeks ago he had saved from Pasteur.

I bought my house because of its Florentine knocker. This rattled loudly at a quarter to ten.

'I know where he is,' said Thornley, entering, 'I'll find my way up.'

I met him on the stairs.

'Where can we talk?' said he.

I took him into a little room that looked out on George Moore's garden – which was a glory of apple-blossoms and the deep hue of lilac beginning to unfold.

'As a Fellow of the Royal College of Surgeons, you've taken the oath of Hippocrates,' said Sir Thornley.

'I have,' said I.

'Well, I bind you by that oath,' he said, 'not to lift a finger in aid of that ruffian who lives opposite you up the street. He'll come over here, cadging for free medical advice. Remember, you are not a physician. I loathe the word "specialist", but your activities are on the surgical side . . .'

'What's wrong with him now?' said I, wondering how the oath of Hippocrates, who had forbidden men to accept any emoluments for medical services, could prevent them extending a helping hand to an invalid who sought it. Then suddenly I

303

had it – Artaxerxes! Moore was to be refused aid as Hippocrates had refused to help the Persian enemy of his country.

'I've noticed this morning,' said Sir Thornley, 'that that fellow who lives opposite to you up the street is about to have an attack of weeping eczema where it will hurt his vanity most. Already there are three little vesicles on that shiny forehead of his, and in a day or two they will be confluent or generally distributed. It will lay him up for two or three weeks, but remember, you are forbidden to interfere. He will come over to you, because I have refused to let him in, and he will try to pick your brains. Let him seek for aid anywhere but in Ely Place.'

I affected to be greatly concerned, hoping that Moore would not appear while Sir Thornley was shutting off aid, no matter how inadequate, from the nearest member of the profession. We spoke on other subjects. He corrected me in matters of good taste in furnishing; he said, as he got off the chair: 'Hepplewhite, not Chippendale. I hope you haven't been taken in.'

I was about to admit how little I cared, when I suddenly realized what an admission of vulgarity this could not but appear to Sir Thornley, who had made myself and most of the doctors in Dublin gentlemen by persuading us to buy a Chippendale table, with a lion's mask or shell, for our halls or waiting-rooms. I said I found them at home, and that I got them 'restored'.

'Good God!' said Sir Thorney; '"restored"! You are incorrigible. I suppose you had that mirror re-gilt.'

'I don't know,' I murmured, 'I'm not sure whether it's old or new.'

'Well, you should know,' he said, 'for these things make all the difference between ignorance and culture.' Then, going down the stairs, out of that great human heart of his – 'But, by the way, if that poor devil gets too bad, you may give him this . . . where can I write it?'

I provided pen and paper; and in the kindness of that troubled heart of his he wrote out a prescription. In the evening I saw George Moore ambling from the second last house on the left where he lived, but he still remained on the brown granite slabs of the walk on his own side. He passed Sir Thornley's but made no attempt to transform the railings into a harp of low tone. He was endeavouring to placate Hippocrates.

After dinner I was beckoned from the room.

'A gentleman wants to see you, but he won't come upstairs. I think it's that gentleman from the other side of the street.'

'Ah, my dear friend,' said George Moore, 'I want a word with you. Where can we go? Bring me to a private room with a good light.'

I switched on a lamp. He pointed solemnly to his forehead, leaning his finger, like the rod of Moses, and asked in an awe-struck whisper, slowly elongating the adjective, 'What are these loathsome things?'

I scrutinized his brow with a steady stare for as long a space as the solemnity of the occasion demanded, then, breathing a sigh, I diagnosed, 'Memoirs of your Dead Life.'

'Good Lord!' said he. 'Can it be possible? It must be thirty years ago.'

'Even unto the third and fourth generation . . .' I said.

To my astonishment he recovered quickly. In fact, he assumed an arch air and waved his stick, saying, 'Oh, well, that kind of thing can be cured.'

'But not by me,' said I. 'Very sorry! But with all these oaths of fellowship going about, and Sir Thornley watching, I can't touch you, until it gets into one of my departments. Your ear, or up your nose . . .'

'You don't mean to say I'm to be vivisected and tortured alive, till the disease gets into my ear? Do you think it will spread so far?'

'You may have absolute confidence in me. It will be in your ear in a few days.'

He went out expostulating, but I did not hear him threaten to consult anyone else. Perhaps he thought he could buy Sir Thornley, by the silence of his railings.

But I was wrong. Next day I saw the brougham of a well-known dermatologist in the street; two days later another physician was called in. They had accepted Moore's version of his Dead Life, and greatly increased the outbreak by applying an actual remedy to an imaginary disease because the second physician doubled the dose of the first. Moore came over to see me.

'I want to see you as a friend,' said he, 'even though your conduct is most unfriendly and inhuman. Perhaps you are satisfied now. The beastly thing is in my ear.'

305

I searched for the remedy of Sir Thornley. Luckily, I found it, committed it to memory.

'Have you dismissed your physicians, by the way?'

'Don't speak of them,' he answered, with a sigh.

'Well, if this cures your ear, you may apply it to the rest of your face, on condition that you do it at your own risk.'

'My face fell off this morning, in the bed,' said George.

'But there's a much more important condition,' said I.

'What is that?' he demanded. 'I'd do anything under the sun.'

'Well, you will do this out of the sun; for you must promise to remain for fully a week in your house. You must not go for one moment out-of-doors till this day week, which is Monday.'

'But, my dear friend, how can I go out-of-doors with this leprosy? I would want a leper's rattle . . .'

'You could rattle the railings, but don't do it in my part of the street . . .'

'Well, my good friend, I will remain indoors. I promise you that.'

'The promise will probably hold out until Sunday, for that's your cook's day out, and you used to dine with Sir Thornley, Lord O'Brien, or with me. You can't even come over to me; nor can I go over to see you. I don't visit patients in their homes.'

George Moore had refused my mother's request to exclude my name from *The Lake*.

'But, Madam, if you can supply a name with two such joyous dactyls, I will change it.'

It caused her much pain. And I came in for a lecture on the company I was keeping. 'Show me your company, and I'll tell you who you are!'

'But I am not George Moore!'

However, I was his keeper for a week. And now for revenge.

The one regret he often expressed was for his thoughtless attack on Mahaffy, made when he was full of enthusiasm for the Gaelic language. Socially, intellectually – in many ways, it recoiled on him. Now, if an invitation to meet Mahaffy and to make up the quarrel at dinner in the College Hall were to reach Moore on the first day of his isolation, it would exasperate him. And he could not break prison owing the state of his face. Yes. And another for Tuesday from Bailey. Bailey he knows so well and has dined with him so often that it will appear quite natural that he should invite his old friend. The bathos of this familiar dinner compared to the exaltation of a dinner with Mahaffy in Dublin's seat of learning will test his temper. It was not hard to get Bailey to comply. Let me see – for Wednesday Lord O'Brien. But Lord O'Brien said,

'Why should I ask that fellow to dinner?'

'Because he can't come,' I said.

Now I had put my foot in it!

'Can't come? What do you mean?' said the old Chief Justice, sitting up.

He had been called Peter the Packer because in order to get a conviction in the Land League days he packed the juries with twelve complacent men. He and I were not on very friendly terms since I had offered in answer to his advertisement for a shooting brake to hold twelve, a seven-seater limousine.

'But –' said the agent.

'If Peter the Packer can't get twelve into it, who can?'

I tried to explain the predicament. But this made it worse, for it only elicited sympathy for George Moore. I had to do a little gerrymandering. And Moore received what looked an invitation. That would be three. Now for a fourth. What a pity Sir Thornley's present mood admitted of no reconciliation! Also he knew the condition of the patient, and even if he did not, he took his dinner-parties so seriously that he would never have made a meal the subject of a joke.

Would Rolleston invite George? The difficulty, I could see, would arise from the proximity in which they dwelt. Rolleston might take it into his head to call with an invitation. Invitations had to be written. They had to come from acquaintances close enough to excuse their short notice. A difficult problem. Rolleston might not be inclined to see George Moore so soon again. I remembered, before the 'leprosy' broke out in 4 Upper Ely Place, a long argumentative wrangle over the date and the excellence of Angus O'Gillan. Rolleston had produced a superb poem 'From the Irish of Angus O'Gillan'. Its metre alone would distinguish it from any elegy. The theme was Clonmacnoise, an ecclesiastical town on the left bank of the Shannon below Athlone, which in the early centuries of Christianity became a Westminster Abbey of sorts wherein all the famous in the land were interred.

What a glorification of death! Rolleston's poem is well known, but it cannot be known enough. In any case, it is well for me to recite it to myself, for it is one of those poems which I always wish to have at call in my memory.

CLONMACNOISE

In a quiet watered land, a land of roses,
   Stands St Kieran's City fair;
And the warriors of Erin in their famous generations
   Slumber there.

There beneath the dewy hillside sleep the noblest
   Of the Clan of Conn
Each beneath his Stone with his name in branching Ogham,
   And the Sacred Knot thereon.

*   *   *

Many and many a son of Conn, The Hundred-Fighter,
   In the red earth lies at rest:
Many a blue eye of Clan Colman the turf covers,
   Many a swan-white breast.

'In the red earth! And the lovely women too!
Was it any wonder that Rolleston dressed like Alfred Lord Tennyson? His height justified it, his poem, and his trim beard; but he was a better-looking man than Lord Tennyson, and Lord Tennyson, though laureate of England, had done nothing better than 'The Dead at Clonmacnoise', whose heroism and beauty endow Death and make it partake of their glory.

But I am forgetting my hospitality to George Moore. There is no dinner for him on Friday. Let me see.

Ah! Sir Horace, of course! I thought of Kilteragh, with its perpetual house-parties, which invariably contained some American reporter of outstanding ability and a British Cabinet Minister.

'Don't you think, Sir Horace, that Mr McPherson should meet George Moore?'

'Hah, my dear fellow! Can you bring him to dine on Friday?'

'If you give me a note, Sir Horace.'

George will be summoned forth on Friday. Meanwhile I will

take a look at his windows across the garden from my back room.

Beauty for Saturday. There must be a beautiful woman pining in the Shelbourne to meet the famous novelist. Now who shall it be? If I choose Isadora Duncan, he may read in the papers that she is in the South of France. An actress of course, of course! Better still, a ballerina; and Anna Pavlova is appearing in the Gaiety and Count Markiewicz knows her well. Not so long ago, my friend, another 'George' was telling Joe and myself about the Count's cocker spaniel and Anna Pavlova, and of his own chivalrous exploit.

About eleven o'clock the other evening the Count invited this other George to go to the Gaiety to see Anna Pavlova when she should come off the stage. They found her in her dressing-room The Count spoke Russian, and George was introduced. He did not know what they were saying, but she looked at him and then questioned the Count. She was about to take off her costume.

'Do you mind if I change?'

'Oh, not at all.'

'But your friend?'

'George won't mind! Oh, my God, no!' the Count assured her.

'She stripped herself stark naked. She had a lovely body,' George said. 'The lines rippled down to the beautiful hips. Her breasts were firm and out-pointing.'

'Was she dark?'

'No, her hair was a sort of brown. But when the Count was having a whisky – she kept a bottle on her dressing-table – I noticed his dog mouching about. Presently he went off through the partly open door. Pavlova went on dressing. Suddenly she came to a halt and made an exclamation in Russian, pointing to a deficiency in her clothes. She missed her knickers. At once I realized what had happened.'

'Splendid fellow!'

'I went after the dog, which had escaped into the street with Pavlova's undies in his mouth.'

'Did you get them?' I asked breathlessly.

'I did,' said George solidly. 'And I brought them back.'

'I have not eyes like those enchanted eyes,' I quoted to myself, looking enviously at George, who had gazed on Nature's naked loveliness.

'Was she a Jewess?' Joe inquired.

'No, she was the loveliest figure I ever saw,' George admitted. 'She was a Slav.'

'A Slav to your passions,' Joe remarked.

Count Markiewicz would be charmed to pull Moore's leg, or anyone's leg. His six-feet-five made him kinsman of the gods. An invitation to George Moore to her suite for a light supper after the show. Exactly!

'And, by the way, Count,' when I had explained the limitations of the novelist, 'what about Sunday?'

'Oh, ho, ho, ho!' He roared at his idea before expounding it. His wife was dressing to go to the Vice-regal Lodge that night. He had to be there too. Leave it to him! 'The notepaper, and a soldier! It will be all right, Ho! ho!'

The scheme was to obtain the notepaper, write an invitation to George to dine with their Excellencies on Sunday night, and despatch it by a lancer.

'The lancer with pennon will look very well and the chain reins will jingle outside his windows. Very pleasant indeed! A martial memory!'

Now, it costs twenty shillings to detach a private of the Lancers from duty for even ten minutes. All he had to do was to ride up Ely Place and attract attention. If necessary a little boy would be sent on to knock at the door.

'Leave it to me,' said the Count.

Later we watched the horse curvetting in front of No. 4. We could see the red dressing-gown flashing and the white hair appearing and reappearing behind now one window and then the other. The Count deserved his bottle of whisky.

'It's very pleasant to sit here dispensing Vice-regal hospitality!'

'Very pleasant ... Not too much soda! ... Very pleasant indeed!'

But a maid was leaving Moore's house. Presently I heard a knock. A message from Mr Moore.

'Say I am not at home!'

'None of us is at home,' the Count added.

Before evening a letter was handed in. After assuring me of his complete recovery and his total lack of appreciation of what a few hours' extra detention could be expected to do, it continued:

'. . . I would have you to know that this is not an invitation. It is a command!'

'A relapse is utterly incurable,' I wrote. 'You promised to give the cure a chance by remaining indoors until to-morrow.'

As for commands, I said to myself, I hope I shall persuade the postman that three or four letters addressed to the addresses I have listed must be referred to me.

George Moore never knew the cause of his transient hebdomadal popularity. On recovering, he explained its sudden cessation to himself by his having had such a loathsome disease.

The lady friend of his to whom I told it in London, hoping that it would reach his ears, misunderstood the whole thing. She thought that the idea was to give him a lift into Vice-regal society which he never needed. 'And had he not every right to go?'

CHAPTER TWENTY-FOUR

'Hah! My Dear Fellow. Will you come with me to the Front? Just you and I? I am thinking of going out next week.'

Sir Horace gnarled on, over the hard vowel sounds of the next sentence he intended to utter. I guessed that it was to explain some reason for going out other than mere curiosity, something really of constraining and national importance.

Not wishing to appear hesitant, I replied before he could say more, 'Of course! Delighted. Splendid!'

But he hastened to assure me of the enormity of the undertaking.

'It's not a holiday. It is far more important than you seem to realize. I have written to Haig to expect us both at Headquarters. I mentioned your name. I have no doubt that I can work you in. I wrote to Haig about a fortnight ago that I should be ready to go to France by the 24th. The reason I am postponing your inclusion until the last minute is that I may any day get an excellent excuse for bringing you with me.'

I wonder for what great cause I shall be travelling. It is a first principle with Sir Horace that whatever he does must have a transcendental purpose. Sir Horace has so many national and international reasons for doing exactly what he pleases that I wonder how I shall fare when enlisted under 'an excellent excuse'.

I imagined us at the railway station amid the sadness of farewells – reassuring brave 'co-workers' with a handshake firm enough to be too expressive for words – everything packed, and at the last moment having to leave the train because we had forgotten to put in 'a national purpose'! Then Sir Horace remembers it, and we steam off determined come what may to co-operate with Haig.

We are not bringing Æ, was the first misgiving which flashed across my brain. Why are we going? It cannot be to fight, for I am not much of a fighter. I am given more to prolonging life than cutting it off in its bloom.

'Haig on the 24th!' he emphasized challengingly.

Does he think I am funking it? I am somewhat, but my nerve is within reason's control; and I can soon bring myself to the sticking place. Fearing that he might think what he had every right to opine, I hurriedly said – realizing with the assurance it lent that it was to G.H.Q. we were bound:

'You have only to ring me up. I am at your service.'

But all the time the question kept asking for an answer, What is Sir Horace up to? Lay the foundations of a gun emplacement? Declare a barrage open? Start a co-operative movement among the Allies? Their buying power is enormous! But their explanation was beyond me. Meanwhile I interposed:

'I am at present attached to three military hospitals. I suppose I shall have to give them some notice.'

'Hah, you know nurses!' He pondered. At last: 'You must not mention this, but there is on foot a project for getting Irishwomen to work in the American hospitals – a service, I am inclined to think, which might be willingly rendered if the matter were properly put after ecclesiastical sanction had been obtained. . . . Let me know your movements.'

'Forwards!' I cried.

Isn't Sir Horace wonderful! Here was our international purpose, our excellent excuse – Irish women, American wounded! But when, on his departure, the double mesmerism of Sir Horace's effect on me and my effect on myself by wishing to appear nonchalant in mid battle had worn off, things began to take a less assured form.

There were first of all submarines in the water which had to be sailed. True, Sir Horace said something about a destroyer which I did not clearly hear, nor did I, had I heard it, wish to make it seem that I counted on it. The word 'destroyer' is disturbing anyway. Then those aeroplanes which kept over Boulogne trying to drop things on the T.N.T. freighters, even a brick or a spanner, or one of the planes itself if shot down and the wreckage were to fall on the ammunition ship . . . shells too, even though we were only off to G.H.Q. No use assuring oneself that the one casualty that never occurs is that of a Commander-in-Chief. Killing a Commander-in-Chief simply is not done. Otherwise the war might stop, and what would those who are engaged in waging it do? It is not professional etiquette to bomb, shell, shoot or bury a Commander-in-Chief.

Sir Horace knew everybody. I narrowly escaped the Dardanelles, after saying glibly one night that even Homer knew that they were only to be commanded from the Asiatic side. Sir Horace had been at school with Admiral de Robeck. 'Hah! That's a good idea. One worthy of reviving, I mean. Longworth, make a note of that. I may send it to de Robeck by our friend here. Or I may go with him myself.'

But a watery grave was preferable to a land one only in that it would have been over by this. *Nunc habet pro tumulo toto* – what would Dardanelles be? – *ponto*. But France *The kind strange land, Whereon we stand* is not our country's clay. No, it would be somewhat *outré* to be buried in France. To rise for ever in an endless officers' mess. And there would be little use adding a proviso to my will that my remains were to be brought home, if all that were left of me were the heels of a boot. Boots? If the soles of my boots were to be painted white they would act as flags of truce and signals of peace in case I fell back on my second line. But these are thoughts unworthy of me.

How does one dress going perhaps officiously, but certainly unofficially, to the Front with Sir Horace Plunkett on a visit to his friend Haig? If I wear a tall hat it may attract the notice of the enemy, if any. A dentist whose hand had acquired such a tremor when at the Front that he could no longer draw teeth, still could draw, as he complained, the enemy's fire. He had not joined up for that! A tall hat would attract snipers. Plus-fours would be out of the question except in the base hospitals. If I ask too many questions before we are actually *en route* it may imperil my invitation. Meanwhile, I must make myself warminded. G.H.Q. is safe enough to cover a great deal of military diffidence. Discipline's the thing!

I took a turn down Merrion Street.

'In the name of God, what's wrong wid ye?' Jimmy speaking. A sturdy, short, reddish man in a bowler hat. 'I thought you were spavined or doing the goose-step.'

Coldly I replied: 'I am merely walking down the street.'

'I thought I'd seen a drill sergeant. What's come over you lately? I'll go a bit out of the way with you if I can keep in step.' And he suited his action to his words and walked along.

But any ambitions I may have had to fall like a soldier were dashed. I got a letter from Sir Horace complaining that because

I did not keep his intention secret he could not go. It seemed that Lord Granard asked him in the Club, 'Where are your tabs?' suggesting that he was already a General. He hated anyone who tried to pull his leg. Instead of going to the Front, he fell back on Kilteragh, and I never met Haig.

CHAPTER TWENTY-FIVE

Dr Tyrrell!

'Is it the benign doctor?' He came in a little breathless.

'Oh, oh! Yes, ah, my delightful friend, I nearly missed the train. We are staying out at Greystones. I am not familiar with the lanes. I was directed to a short-cut, but I had not time for a short-cut this morning. Ah!'

He relapsed mellowly into an armchair, concealing a smile at his satire on directions for short-cuts. He looked like one of the clean-shaved Caesars. His beautiful profile and *embonpoint* adding to the resemblance. I filled a tumbler one-third full of whisky, adding soda. He took it and remarked after a lengthy pull, as he sighed contently:

'There is nothing more disconcerting than an illness one has *not* brought on oneself.'

'Happy is he who discerns first causes; he can disregard the clamours of hungering Hell.'

'Oh, yes. How quick you are! *Felix qui potuit*, of course. Now I can set about curing myself with a tranquil mind. What happened was this. I was walking to the club with Willie Atkinson, when that little bandy-legged solicitor with the chattering teeth met us and invited us in. I thought it was into the University Club – the steps are about the same – but the surroundings were unfamiliar. The ceiling of the dining-room was blue and prankt with stars – Orpen, they say, painted the ceiling and added the stars. What superb genius he has! A lesser man might have painted them on the floor. "Welcome to the Friendly Brothers' Club," the little fellow said. "Here's luck, Perfessor." He called me "per" instead of "pro" possibly with the idea of choosing a stronger prefix.

'Well, of all the places I have drifted into! It was a discovery in a way, for I often wondered where the descendants of those who of old escaped death by duelling as the natural result of their bad manners had managed to conceal themselves.

'Friendly Brothers!

'Now had they called it "The Sick and Indigent Roomkeepers' Society," it would at least have had the advantage of

316

a magnificent if somewhat pretentious title. After a while we managed to escape, only to find that in the University Club drinks are no longer served in the Hall. And after we had scaled those steps!'

He took a sip and continued:

'No. They are to be served upstairs on the topmost flight – Bernard, of course, that old curmudgeon, instigated the Committee to make the rule. He thought we would be deterred by the climb. Would you believe it, as I sat resting in a window-seat, I saw him coming up the stairs? As cheerfully as I could, in answer to his very curt nod, I said:

' "They shall be afraid of that which is high."

'Parsons hate laymen to take their words out of their mouths. He frowned and went up to the Library. Had he been present at the wedding feast of Cana he would have soured the wine. Thereby weakening our faith. And this morning, owing to the vigilance of the village, I had no opportunity to undergo a cure.'

He paused and leant his face into his tumbler which I had replenished because I had to break what might be unpleasant news.

'Hearing that you had been to the Friendly Brothers with the little chatterer, I invited him to the picnic this afternoon. And now I am afraid he'll turn up. "The worst thing about him," as Yeats said of a colleague, "is that when he is not drunk, he is sober." However the absence of Mahaffy may compensate you for the inclusion of the moron.'

He asked with a show of interest why Provost Mahaffy was not coming. I said that I feared he blamed me for including Æ in a lunch.

'The Provost had a bottle and more of claret, and was just seeking a windless corner of the garden to smoke a satisfactory cigar, when Æ rushed after him and said: "Why won't you use your great influence, Provost, to have these scandals in Russia stopped? It makes my blood boil to think of the way they are being knouted and sent to Siberia!"

'Sir John Pentland Mahaffy, the only cleric who obtained a title in recent years, turned, displeased by the disturbance, and asked icily: "Let us get this right, my good man. Who is knouting whom?"

317

' "Oh, the Tsar is knouting the Russians and sending them to Siberia in thousands and thousands. It makes . . ."

' "Well, all I can say is," Mahaffy said genially, "that if the Tsar does not knout them, they'll knout themselves."

'But his afternoon siesta was spoiled; and now *nec mihi Apollo respicit.*'

Dr Tyrrell raised his glass as if toasting the relief he felt at the absence of the critical supervision which might be his lot if Mahaffy were to accompany us. There was little love lost between them. He murmured:

'I never quite forgave Mahaffy for getting himself suspended from preaching in the College Chapel. Ever since his sermons were discontinued, I suffer from insomnia in church.'

'Why was he forbidden to preach?'

'It's a long time ago now, but when he had overstayed his leave in Greece with Oscar Wilde by about a month, he made matters worse by preaching about the Unknown God. He told the congregation that the Athenian altar was erected to the unknown gods for the sake of foreign visitors who might use that altar for the worship of outlandish gods. And when St Paul claimed it for his particular God it was quite improper – "Think of the impertinence of this impudent little Hebrew talking to the Sages of the Ancient World in that manner." He added, "I can never quite forgive St Paul. There was an excellent University at Antioch, but he seems never to have availed himself of it. Never!" '

'So he was in Greece with Oscar Wilde?'

'Oh, yes. Are you not aware of that? Wilde got most of his superciliousness from trying to imitate Mahaffy. Mahaffy of course would call his attitude εὐτραπελία, well-bred arrogance; but the evidence for good breeding in great measure is absent.'

The doctor's snuff-box was beginning to behave eccentrically. He murmured to himself on a high-pitched note. He captured it just as it had disguised itself as a butterfly pulverized with brown.

'Wilde was the grandson of a Yorkshire land agent. But the Provost's well-bred arrogance is susceptible to good breeding. When an undergraduate called Birde caught him by the gown at a dinner in College and said, "Sit down, Mahouf!" he was

318

yclept Mahouf by those of heavenly birth, but plain Mahaffy by the race of Earth.

'When his friends awakened him next day, he realized the enormity of his rudeness. Birde, sober, realized that nothing could save him from rustication. So he resolved to play the man and gentleman by calling to make his apology to the Provost before being sent down.

' "Come in!"

' "I came, sir, to ..."

' "Now, who are you?"

' "Birde, sir."

' "What bird?"

' "I am an undergraduate, sir."

' "Of what College?"

' "This College."

' "And what do you want?"

' "I want to apologize, sir, for my inexcusable conduct at dinner last night."

' "What dinner?"

' "Dinner with you, sir."

'Realizing astutely that he was dealing with a gentleman because he had the good grace to apologize, Mahouf said: "Sit down, Birde. And mark this: a gentleman never takes the least notice of what another gentleman says when he is in his cups." '

The doctor commented after a pause, and sourly: 'He was only "in his cups" because he was dining with Mahaffy. Had it been me or you we would have been "disgwacefully dwunk".'

Later, after a dream with himself, he remarked:

'If you take the trouble to inquire, you are certain to find that Birde's father owned an excellent shoot.'

'The picnic party will be coming in on us,' I suggested, 'If we go ahead now, they can follow. Otherwise we shall be in the procession of motor-cars.'

The party had been arranged. The meeting-place by a lake in the Wicklow Highlands had been named.

The doctor found it hard to interrupt the progress of his cure.

At last we got into the motor. We had not gone three miles when, in passing Stillorgan, he remarked: 'It's amazing how motoring blows the alcohol out of one.'

I ignored the innuendo.

Nodding, he said: ' "οὐκ" forbids and "μή" denies, but seemingly Dublin has a more negative asseveration. It is at its best in an example. "Picnic" reminds me:

"Are you coming to the picnic, Mrs Murphy?"
"Picnic, me neck! Look at Mary's belly since the last picnic." '

'An excellent example,' I acknowledged. 'It reminds me of the invitation to a whist drive presumably held by that same lady, whereat the favours of the hostess were assessed only as second to the first prize, which was a bottle of stout!'

The presence of this third enclitic 'me neck!' proves that Dublin still uses the English language as emphatically as the Elizabethans could. And they could say more in it than we in spite of our increased vocabulary, rendered, as it is, anaemic by the abuse of words.

A greenish sea lay to our left. Howth shone incredibly, save to our greatest painter, Nathaniel Hone's retina, amethystine across the Bay. No whitecaps marked the footsteps of the wind overnight.

The three tips of Bray Head, purple like the Paps of Jura, appeared. The doctor opened his eyes, and putting the onus on me, said:

'If you are quite sure that this is the tower and town of Bray, I am reminded that I am still a member of its Country Club.'

Resigning myself to the imposition as I thought of an unwanted drink, I stopped, and we entered the Club.

'Two whisky drinks for my friend and me.'

He drank one, and, leaving the empty glass on the table, disappeared with the one that was full. Later, when he returned with the second glass empty in his hand, he looked at the first and asked, 'Been entertaining a friend?'

The plateau, rimmed far off by clear hills, is high. It is called the Calary Bog. The air was thin and fine and the far-flung light increased distances to the eye.

'Surely God in His infinite justice, and that rather contradictory quality of His mercy, never intended to lead us into a wilderness such as this without punctuating it pleasantly with a public-house?'

I looked at the buff-coloured waste. A deserted church with a clump of sycamores over-topped by its grey pinnacled tower.

One of those churches built to plan in the eighteenth century when the abbeys were left to fall into ruin was all that was to be seen. On the right, the watershed of the Roundwood lakes rose gradually.

'We have come to the utmost end of the earth,' he quoted, moaning to rebuke me, his guide.

'But, Sir, I see a mile or so off, on a gable, that blessed word "Hotel".'

At once he became vivacious and vociferous like Friar John of the Funnels in that marvellous psychological study the *Discourse of the Drinkers.*

'Do you know Father Claude of the High Kilderkins?' – How I wish I did! We have but few of them here. One or two, but by no means enough. And they that remain and those who admire are now subjects of suspicion of our obsessing Jansenists.

'Hotel!' he said. 'Now you know that, though an absurd word – a French word, and not to be compared to "Inn" – is very promising at this moment. I found an excellent hotel in Durham. When I entered, mine host appeared with a pint of port on a round salver.

' "An old custom, sir," he said.

'And only when I had imbibed it by the fire, did he ask me: "How long are you going to stay?"

'That was in Durham, a University town . . .'

Nearer we drew to the gable on the left. 'Hotel', it read certainly. But, to my horror, when we drew alongside – 'Powerscourt Temperance Hotel'!

The doctor, even without his eyeglass, which I think he used for reading only, could not have failed to see the sign. He hardly glanced at it before his disapprobation found words:

'That's this country all over! Not content with a contradiction in terms, it must go on to an antithesis in ideas. "Temperance Hotel"! You might as well speak of a celibate kip!'

I laughed so cheerfully and so long that the doctor's disappointment was appeased. He even smiled to himself. To distract him I said, 'That reminds me, the kips need either to be rebuilt, "moulded nearer to the heart's desire," or abolished. Their condition is awful – as awful, almost, as that of the banks. In the world of good taste the architecture of the Dublin banks is just as deserving of censure as the brothels

321

are in the sphere of morals. The banks have disfigured with their immodesty the quiet features of what was once a stately and dignified town. Guinness and Mahon's is the only exception. Pretentious display and meretricious design, medley of style and periods, vulgar mass supported by exotic pillars, all tend to confuse and to debauch the taste of the beholder, while dishonestly suggesting that solidarity in architecture is equivalent to financial security. This exhibitionism in architecture is to my mind more indecent and less excusable than a display of lingerie. Lingerie is at least necessary: Aberdeen granite in Dublin is both far-fetched and dear-bought. And it is libellous for the banks to go for their substance to Aberdeen. I have found Aberdeen a most hospitable, humorous and generous town; but defamatory legend makes all Scotland, especially Aberdeen, close-fisted and canny; that is why, even if we accept this calumny, it is so unnecessary for the banks to import their symbols of thrift from Aberdeen. I have a plan to reduce the enormity of both these outrages on good taste and good living: banks and brothels.'

'It will be interesting to hear it. They seem beyond redemption,' the doctor said. 'I cannot imagine how they can be remedied. What is your plan?'

'To turn the banks into brothels and the brothels into banks.'

'You don't mean to remove them all to the kips?'

'No. Just exchange the staffs of brothels and banks for the present. All future banks I would place in that street which is straight – but who dare call it so? – (from Lower Gardiner Street to Buckingham Street), each next door to a kip in the following order: Bank of Ireland, Mrs Mack's; Teasey Ward's, Belfast Bank; Munster and Leinster, Liverpool Kate's; Piano Mary's, Provincial Bank; Mrs Hayes's next to the Royal and May Oblong's next to the Northern Bank.

'Most improvisators in policy must be prepared to accept a medley and to countenance compromise ... forgive me if I am already using somewhat artificial language – a compromise might be reached wherein the over-rigid and formal lives of bankers would be gently offset by the more flexible manners of their next-door neighbours. Thus that "certain neighbourliness" would be achieved. The braced and the relaxed, the formal and informal would meet and merge into the mellow mediocrity which is Dublin life. The de-humanized prose of the

322

genial bank manager would lose the power which it has, when directed to women who are beyond reproach – that is, any reproach but his, "on behalf of my Authorities" – of creating suffering and insomnia once it arrived "By hand" in emancipated Mrs Mack's. Just think of Mrs Mack receiving the following composition and her reactions thereto: "Madam, While I do not want to press you unduly . . ." "Jaysus, girls! Excuse me, ladies, I meant to say 'oh, dearie me'!" '

The doctor, who rarely laughed, laughed now. He raised his head and the sunlight made for a moment translucent his wholesome teeth.

'Already I notice an improvement in manners, doubtless due to the compensatory recoil from the outrageous architecture of the banks, but, go on! What does the bank manager say?'

' "I must request you to put me in a position to report to my authorities that, as far as in you lies, you have done your best to discharge your liability . . ." '

'Liability,' the doctor warbled, smiling. 'And have you considered how the lady would reply?'

'I see her waving the letter before her love-learned sisters with: "Here! Will none of yez tell this fellow where he gets off?" '

The doctor agreed, opining that those who had intelligence in Love would know how to soften the harshness of the mechanical money machine and to humanize him.

'Later, then, in default of an answer by return, "Madam, a writ is now issued. Will you accept service at the law offices of this bank or at your present address?" Fresh Nellie might volunteer,' I said, ' "Tell him none of us would be seen dead in his kip." Thus would he be "told off".'

The doctor, who seldom punned, but he said, as if to himself, 'Telling a teller off?' Then he considered the subject as a whole.

'Yes; it is time something were done for the poor bankers. As it is they are condemned to lives as austere as the clergy's, but reaching, not as theirs does, to sanctity, but Sadism. Your idea of this neighbourliness is a good one, because we must in turn consider the effect the spacious and pretentious housing would have on the amorous inmates. Confronted by stucco pilasters, mosaic pavements and plaster ceilings, a projection into architecture as it were of their cosmetic paint and powder, they would gradually recoil from the meretricious gaudiness of their surroundings and come to yearn for something genuine and honest in their lives. Thus the vulgarity of the banks would be a salutary lesson to the late inhabitants of the brothels. Meanwhile the bankers, huddled and confined in the kips next door, would learn at first hand how the poor unfortunates had to live. They would have time to ask themselves how many families had their inhumanity reduced to status of bankruptcy: how many daughters of good families had their compound interest condemned to live in such "compounds". Piano Mary may once have shown, among her loving family, skill as a pianist. To help an embarrassed father she may have "gone as a governess" and slowly reached the level at which she is, or rather was until lately, to be found. How can a banker be expected to measure the iniquity of his usury without going to the kips? The kips would Christianize the bankers – that is, a certain proportion of them – just as the indecent display and exhibitionism of the banks would make all women who dwell in them revolt from any thought of flamboyant living.

'And when tired of keeping their money under a pillow or palliasse or in a vase on the mantelpiece, the bankers began building extensions, strong rooms and managers' offices in their respective kip, think how the rateable value of the whole city would be improved! Instead of having the most squalid, foetid, and miserable stews in Europe, Dublin would find itself without a kip of any kind except those "in process of alteration" by the bankers. Baths would be introduced; and with the sentiment of the Georgian period preserved, as in Guinness and Mahon's, the kips would be exemplary specimens of good and careful enterprise, while the banks would be efficient houses of correction for pretentiousness and display.'

'I saw you coming out of Mrs Hayes's!'

The doctor thought it over, smiling to himself; then facing me on a higher note, 'Or was it Mrs Mack's?' he asked, testing humorously my scheme.

'No!' I said indignantly. 'That was the Royal Bank!'

I will admit that until each had proved itself there might be bad times in store for bawdy houses and borrowing houses, but once merged, the morals of the bankers would be improved.

After all, it was not the Magdalen that the Lord scourged from the Temple.

Clanging the gears we jerked forwards. 'It is only ten minutes to Roundwood.' There was no time to be lost.

'This is worse than the lunch we had with Boss Croker when he produced the gold medals won by his bulldog and showed us the record elephant's ivory with "Them's the biggest tusks outside Africa . . ." '

'Ah, had they only been drinking-horns!' the doctor moaned. 'Neither ivory nor gold amazed me more than his use of "them" as an adjectival pronoun.'

Soon we found sanctuary.

'What a wonderful escape we had from dying of inanition on the desert crossing!'

'Yes,' I agreed.

'The monks of St Bernard would be well occupied if they built a monastery on the site of that "Temperance Hotel". The desolation reminds me of a Sunday I spent with Sergeant Dodd. Every minute I expected a neat-handed Phyllis to appear, but no! At lunch I would have died, only for the Christian negligence of the butler, who forgot to remove a heavy Waterford glass decanter of sherry from my side. As it was I nearly sprained my wrist. Days later my "host" had the audacity to ask me what I thought of a young subaltern who, incredible as it seems to me, got drunk in his house. "It shows marvellous industry," I said.'

We turned to the right to begin the long ascent. The great car moaned high into the hills.

'This mountain is Kippure, a celebate kip in its way, for there is not a licensed house among all its water-springs. The other picnickers are to meet us at two o'clock by Lough Bray.'

'But which of them has a car equal to this? And what time is it now, my dear friend?'

It was only one-thirty.

'Orpen will attend to you, sir, while I round up the guests. For losing us you would be left astray. The well-stocked hampers will be unloaded before long. And we will have an appetizer together.'

> *La concreata e perpetua sete*
> *Del deiforme regno cen portava*
> *Veloci, quasi come il ciel vedete.*

Light cumuli floated smoothly, sun-smitten, like nautili on the edge of the blue.

'Is the picnic on the top of yonder peak?'

'It is by the highest lake in the sunny highlands.'

'Don't forget, dear boy, that this altitude evaporates one's drinks.' He looked anxiously at the empty steeps.

'I have provided for that. There never were such hampers on these mountain-tops before. Even Æ's blood would boil at a lower temperature up here, and Mahaffy could afford to be sympathetic so high above the world.'

'Who are coming?' he asked, as if anxious for the supplies.

We entered a cloud of midges where the hills were thronged with streams. The wind-screen reflected the light behind my back directly into my eyes. The doctor took out his red silk handkerchief.

'When we are out of this!'

Again we turned to the right at the topmost crossroads.

Four-and-a-half miles now.

'They have approached by another road,' I said. 'We took a round course so as not to travel with them all the way.'

'How long will you take to do four miles?'

'Six or seven minutes on this track.'

'I can hold out that long,' he said.

The little solicitor had not come. He was sitting in his office twittering and shuffling pens and pencils in the inkstand before him. He could hear his head clerk, whose high blood-pressure and well-held alcohol gave him not a moment's rest, brow-beating with profuse expatiation a confused and intimidated client. His syringe had broken. He was left diddering alone until his messenger should return, in his lunatic asylum of an office, disapproving all the while of Dr Tyrrell, who unexpectedly had accepted a drink from him in the Friendly Brothers' Club, at one quarter-of-an-hour before lunch.

He would not, could not be a party to further frivolity. He mixed the tabloids with a little water. The injection reassured him. He was glad that he had the moral strength to resist the temptation of a unedifying picnic on the summit of Kippure!

'Orpen will be there, and Vera Hone and McGurk, the Master of Those Who Know, with Endymion, whom he found wading in St Patrick's Well. My friend, the rare Alabaster, has been invited: and Major McLoren who fought with love

326

even to the end in the person of Sylvia Langrishe, who is back from India now; my wife and her sister, without whom there would be no entertainment; a young American girl who has found peace through divorce, and our old friend McCabe.'

'The good McCabe!'

'Yes. He follows you for the language movement. He loves good style.'

'That is the upper lake. The larger one is just down there. I can see the cars assembled.'

He lifted an eyelid, but continued with his reflexion:

'That egregious ass, George Moore, used to snigger and annoy Douglas Hyde by suggesting that Joseph of Arimathea followed the Disciples for the sake of the language movement.'

'He held the Grail,' I said.

A hundred yards from the road by a path that borders a rivulet the edge of the lake is reached. An ancient crater makes three-quarters of an amphitheatre which opens to the south and east. The lake lies deep within. Beyond, the semi-circular cup is dark green like the colour that invests Eternity. Pinewoods lie in a level to the right and hem a crescent of white sand.

By the granite outcrops the feast was spread. One of the rocks made a natural table with its flat top. Hampers were unpacked. Hard by, a cottage provided hot water for those who cared for tea. The sun shone on the lead-bright water.

'Who will bathe before food?'

Luckily, before undressing I thought of the doctor. Where had he gone? I gave him to Orpen so that he might be looked after while I collected the guests, but, like little Musgrave in the ballad, Orpen 'had more thought of the fine women,' so he left the doctor stranded by a rill. I ran across the heather. The six minutes for which he could hold out had been exceeded long ago. I led him to the feast. He rebuked me gently with: 'It's amazing how many qualities of a drink water has!' I protested my regret for his being deserted beside the little rill when he should have been seated by a syphon. Soon his spirits revived.

'I see we have with us the Master of Those Who Know, our most excellent colleague, the Professor of Moral Philosophy, the divine McGurk. But who are the other men?'

327

'One is Alabaster, a friend of Orpen, the other is Endymion, whom McGurk brought, because though a little odd he is such a fine musician. McLoren is a Major retired from India, and the ladies are his friends – and mine ...'

'Friend,' he said, subsiding, 'it is good for us to be here. Alabaster? A strange name.'

'Yes. It is a derivative of Arquebuster – Herrick mentions it.'

'Come along,' they were calling to each other when we signalled that the feast was spread.

McGurk sat beside a Primus stove. Dr Tyrrell sat with his back to a large stone on the top of which fruit salads were displayed. The ladies fussed about with the dishes; all but Sylvia, who sat in front of McGurk, her dainty shoes almost touching his soles. We were on a high and pleasant shelf. To see the valley it would be necessary to walk a hundred yards to the road: whence to the south-east stood the peaks of the Golden Spears, the Head of Bray, and beyond, a floor of shining sea. Some miles behind, a point might be reached from which Dublin could be seen smoke-veiled in its plain: St Patrick's Cathedral seemingly still its highest and greyest mass beneath a pall of smoke, though Christ Church is higher. The dear and fog-crowned Athens of my youth!

Not far from where we sat the Liffey sprang to birth from the streamy mosses of Kippure – gathering water from that many-fountained hill before it could risk a long journey without being foiled by the flatness of its moors. For sixty miles it would wind through the loveliest valleys in the world to Brittas by Kilbride, where the Shankill river rushes to meet it through a gorge of rhododendrons and oaks, then, meandering, it will fall at Poulaphouca down to the level plain of Kildare, and to shine black and bright by Newbridge, and so on with many a winding to the Strawberry Beds for the first taste, at Island Bridge, of its salt and spacious home, Howth-guarded to the north beyond the Bull of sand and the old Green Plain, held southward by green Killiney and the shore that curves to Bray, to find rest at length beyond the Bay in the recreating sea.

The lake by which we lolled was a crater once. Our very table, tricked out with mica, was of igneous rock that told of old incredible cataclysms before man narrowed Time to be a measure of his years and superimposed his squabbles on the silver-shining granite that had reached eternal rest.

'If I merely say "tricked" in the doctor's hearing, later on,' I said to the Master of Those Who Know, 'we shall have a dissertation on "Lycida", together with a recital of its last half-dozen lines.'

He jerked his incoordinated six-foot-four. 'You filthy brute!' he exclaimed lovingly. 'And why should you fool the dear old man? Cannot you leave the beloved doctor alone?'

'Oh, well, I want to add to the enjoyment of the company.'

'By "clanging" the poor old man with "tricks his beams and with new spangled ore flames," etc. It's poor and cheap and reflects more on your intellectual limitations than on his.'

'I'll "clang" you on "you dirty brute!" and the other terms of endearment you have for me, before very long.'

'What exactly is your vocation, Mr Alabaster?' the lady with the beautiful name, Vera Hone, inquired.

Orpen interposed: 'We brought Ally along so that he might try out his patents for filling in lulls in conversations. Ally has a lot of patents.

'His job was in the Oriental department of the National Museum; but when he took to jumping out from a replica of an Assyrian tomb in the Egyptian section on little girls, the authorities superannuated him. Is not that so, Ally?'

'By a lake like this, as he tied a fly, Mahaffy said to me: "I have had sixty-five love affairs in my life. And I have never regretted one of them! Not one! But, of course, they were all before I was ordained." '

The doctor's high-pitched voice could be heard as he quoted aloud for our edification:

' "The King of Assyria was drinking himself drunk in his tent with the six and twenty kings who were with him and helping him." ' Then, as a commentary, 'You know Mahaffy would not have refused a little light refreshment in that society.'

'That was a marvellous dinner you gave us at Jammet's.' Orpen said.

Alabaster whinnied at the recollection.

He referred to Alabaster's answer to what he considered was an insulting 'bonus' when he resigned from the Museum. He gave a dinner in Jammet's to five people at £8 a head.

'Wall-paper like this, Jammet, with lobster sauce, unthinkable!'

Bill-posters appeared during the meal and plastered up new wall-paper. A carpet of a different colour was provided with the game.

'Let Ally answer for himself.'

But Ally preferred to tell how the landscape might be altered in the valley, if the farmers would pay more attention to the colour than to the character of their crops.

How self-effacing women can be! They can sacrifice themselves for the pleasure of others, reckless of the worth of their work or fame.

'This is cold punch, Professor!' my wife said.

'Oh, indeed?'

'Now, it is not a thing to be despised! The proportion of boiling water to fifteen-years-old Jameson was, before it cooled, in exact ratio to the amount of Falstaff's expenditure on bread as compared with sack.'

'I cannot refuse!'

'And a little more chicken?'

'The point is,' Professor McGurk interjected, 'whether we have improved on it since then.'

'Improved on what?' Sylvia asked.

'Life!' McGurk answered.

'I was talking about Homer – beautiful, beautiful that banquet of the gods where they stretched forth their hands upon the sacred fare! How delightful! But the point is, have we improved on it since then? Three thousand years have gone! The question I ask is, "Have we anything better to do than the gods did?" – "They stretched forth their hands upon the sacred fare!"'

He reached to his glass and threw back his head.

'Did they do nothing but eat and drink? Surely you have forgotten Love, Professor?' Sylvia asked.

'Love! My goodness!' He raised his face and quoted ecstatically: ' "But for us twain, come, let us take our joy couched together in love; for never yet did desire for goddess or mortal woman so shed itself about me and overmaster the heart within my breast." ' He struck himself dramatically.

Sylvia looked embarrassed, wondering whether it was a

genuine quotation, or a proposal, or both. But her doubt was solved when the Professor continued declaiming:

' "Nay! not when I was seized with love of the wife of Ixion who bore Pirithous, nor of Danae of the trim ankles who bore –"

Sylvia withdrew her foot.

' "If thou art fain to be couched on the peaks of Ida where all is clear to view." '

'In this world of appearance,' I said, interrupting, 'it is well that things should look their best when all is clear to view, else let us wrap ourselves in a cloud of gold.'

'Sylvia, what about a stroll in the wood?' McLoren asked, by way of relief.

' "It is as easy for a thing to be as not to be," ' I quoted, to draw the Professor.

Indignantly he turned: 'How dare you, you dirty brute! You have an impish mind with no respect for anything in this world of phenomena, not even for the great Hegel himself! For you, Reality simply waxes and wanes!'

By this time the word 'tricks' had germinated in the benign doctor's mind. With a little moaning overture pitching his voice high, he began:

> 'So sinks the day star in the ocean bed,
> And yet anon repairs his drooping head.'

He nodded.

> 'And tricks his beams, and with new spangled ore
> Flames in the forehead of the morning sky!'

His voice rose to a high treble so that he almost crowed when he repeated 'Flames'.

But the moral philosopher was annoyed with me.

'Scandalous! You dirty brute!' he grunted. 'Could you not leave even our dear old friend alone?'

A fiddle sounded from above us on a rock.

'Your friend Endymion, whom you found wading the other night in St Patrick's Well when you neglected to close the gate in the wall at the foot of Dawson Street.'

'And why shouldn't he wade if he wishes? He played Chopin's Sonata, the scherzo of it in B minor on my piano; and that's a thing you could never do!'

They had spent the night in the Professor's room improvising until dawn.

'I observe that he has laid down the sword for the violin. What is he playing?' the doctor asked.

'Our national anthem.'

'It's not the national anthem,' McGurk thundered. 'It's "Johnny, I hardly knew you"!'

'I have always held that that ballad should be Ireland's national anthem. It is full of a kind of steadfast courage that can revel in disaster. It is as if the very spirit of Ireland mocked and revelled in vicissitude, deriding death. The wife, Kathleen Na Houlihan, of course, of the war-broken veteran who hardly recognizes her husband repeats:

> "Ye haven't an arm and ye haven't a leg,
>   Huroo! Huroo!
> Ye haven't an arm and ye haven't a leg,
>   Huroo!
> Ye haven't an arm and ye haven't a leg
> Ye eyeless, noseless, chickenless egg;
> Ye'll have to be put in a bowl to beg,
>   Johnny, I hardly knew ye." '

But the doctor was recalling it, greatly amused.

'True,' I said sententiously to tease the Professor, 'recognition is hard to come by, particularly for minds which are not devout.'

But the benign doctor took up the theme:

'You spoke of steadfast courage, but that was all that was steadfast in Johnny. It goes on:

> "Where are the legs with which you run?
>   Huroo! Huroo!
> Where are the legs with which you run?
>   Huroo!
> Where are the legs with which you run
> When you went to shoulder the gun?
> Begob, yer dancing days are done.
>   Johnny, I hardly knew ye.
>
> Where are the eyes which were so mild?
>   Huroo! Huroo!

332

Where are the eyes which were so mild?
    Huroo!
Where are the eyes which were so mild
When of my love you were beguiled?
Why did you skedaddle from me and the child?
    Johnny, I hardly knew ye!" '

'Excellent! sir,' said Professor McGurk.

Encouraged, the doctor continued:

'If one were to treat that ballad with the reverence which it deserves, Dean Bernard's attention should be directed towards it, perhaps by you, McGurk, after I had translated it into Greek. You might describe it as a writing seen in vision on a wall in Patmos by a member of the Hermetic Society. Something like this might emerge.' He applied himself to his tumbler for a moment, then gathering his mind, composed *ex tempore*:

'Alas, for the going of Swiftness, for the feet of the running of thee,
When thous wentest among the swords and the shoutings of captains made shrill,
Woe is me for the pleasant places! Yea, one shall say of thy glee
"It is not!" And as for delight, the feet of they dancing are still.
Also thine eyes were mild as a lowlit flame of fire
When thou wovest the web whereof wiles were the woof, and the warp was my heart!
Why left'st thou the fertile field whence thou reaped'st the fruit of desire?
For the change of the face of thy colour, I know thee not who thou art!

'That is an excellent example, and an object lesson of what Dean Bernard and men of his ilk mean to the irrepressible spirit of our land. Dulling first, then deadening it and covering its grave with a formal foreign urn.'

'Huroo!' Endymion echoed. And his music mingled with the trees.

The lake was smoothening and beginning to reflect the few light clouds which had climbed the sky. The ladies had tripped

333

away and the fiddlenotes receded farther and farther until they were indistinguishable from the fitful sounds of *the wide world dreaming of things to come*.'

I removed a fruit salad that threatened to slide down and to enfillet, with crescent of orange and green, the dear old doctor's supernal brow.

The Master of Those Who Know said, with his back against a rock:

'Isn't it a nice bloody thing that when the women go off we are left here with nothing to do but go to sleep?'

> 'Sleep that softlier on the spirit lies,
> Than tired eyelids upon tired eyes,'

the doctor murmured.

For Heaven's sake don't go to sleep and leave me to keep watch here alone on behalf of intelligence which I am unable to sustain by myself.

Sleep in the sunlight, what could be better? It will leave the night free, bring what it may. And by the warm rock I nodded, until there came to me the image of a little child with velvet suit and lace collar in a public-house tempted by a coachman and wondering at the drink proffered to him in secrecy, sweet and bitter, sanguine as Life.

'Would you care for another raspberry cordial, Master Oliver?'

By 'Gis and by St Charity if it lead to a great calm like this above the world, with friends like these, in spite of the danger of its becoming a habit, I would say 'The Same Again'! and chance again my lucky stars.

Rolling Down the Lea

'There was the Liffey rolling down the lea'
SPENSER: Faerie Queen

Under the Plough and
the Lucky (unlucky)
Stars.

To

T. A. COSTELLO

μηκέτι ὑδροπότει, ἀλλ᾽ οἴνω
ὀλίγω χρῶ, διὰ τὸν στόμαχόν σον
καὶ τὰς πυκνάς σου ἀσθενείας

Paul to Timothy

CONTENTS

1 — 'No Mean City'

Ireland, like its fabulous islands in the Western Ocean, is visible only once in seven years. So now is the time to catch a glimpse of it. If you believe airline advertisements, you will imagine that all you have to do is to take your grip and step on board a silver-shining cleaver of the skies to reach Europe from America in the morning. The advertisements do not specify how long it may be between your grip and your step. That is why, to a leisurely soul like mine, air travel appeals more than a trip in an ocean liner or even in a windjammer. It is not necessarily so speedy or so regular.

I have flown the Atlantic off and on since the days when seaplanes took off at Foynes and landed at Port Washington. That was before air-ways became important enough to engage the attention of the 'Authorities'; and, as a result, to be endowed with pomp and spancelled with red tape. That is why some years ago it took two months and eight days before I could get a reservation. And when one came, it was at midnight with a quarter of an hour's notice, and no taxi to the airport five or six miles from Limerick at Rineanna.

I had used all the influence I could bring to bear to obtain a 'priority' by which I was enabled to get a seat in front of the many who were waiting. I got before them, and boarded a twenty-six seater with twenty-three empty seats. Do not think that I am complaining. That is one of the advantages of red tape: it disheartens the unsophisticated and leaves the old stager plenty of room. It also reduces possible casualties: in my case from a possible twenty-six to three. I will admit that the bird-like flutter at the last minute adds a thrill that suggests flying, a thrill that would be absent if you went by sea. Then there is the additional diversion that you never know where you may land. The last time I flew intending New York, I landed in Labrador. The long wait for the priority had conditioned me, so I had plenty of time on hand. I could pity the poor sea-passengers who would be put ashore at the irrevocable hour on schedule without a hope – except an iceberg – of seeing more than they had paid for: out of bounds for them was the silence and spaciousness of Labrador.

Red Tape, and not the serpent, is the cause of the Fall of Man. Eve, even without a mother to prompt her, took a coil of it; and had Adam where she wanted him for the rest of his days. His descendants have never ceased filling out forms.

In the days of the flying-boat you were provided with a bed; but in these modern times all you get is a chair that slopes backwards and suggests a shave or a haircut more than a sleep. Nevertheless, you can land at Shannon safely if the magnetic mountain in the vicinity has not queered the altimeter and brought you down in defiance of all the lines' red tape. But why dribble any farther? Let me shoot at the goal. There will be plenty of time, I can vouch for that, to describe my pleasant journey from the airport to the town. But here we are in the capital of Tín na nóg, the Land of the Ever Young.

Dublin. Dublin of the vistas! What names come to mind, names filling more than two centuries from the days of the gloomy Dean Swift, who left his money to found a lunatic asylum 'to show by one sarcastic touch no nation needed it so much', to Mrs Bernard Shaw, who left her money to teach manners to Irishmen; and some say (they would in Dublin) that, in spite of all his acumen, the man for whom it was principally intended failed to see the sarcastic touch; Oliver Goldsmith; Bishop Berkeley, who wrote 'Westward the course of Empire takes its way' and went his way to Rhode Island and gave his name to Berkeley, California; Hamilton, who discovered proleptically the Quaternion Theory by the banks of the Royal Canal; Burke, who thundered in defence of American liberation; Molyneux, whose nationalism caused his books to be burned by the common hangman; Fitzgerald, who anticipated Marconi in the discovery of ætherial waves; Mahaffy, who was the greatest Humanist of his time as well as the expeller from Trinity College of Oscar Wilde to Oxford; down to Yeats, Æ, and lastly James Joyce, in whose *Anna Livia*

2

Plurabelle the whole history of Dublin may be discerned by thought, this time cataleptic. All these men lived in Dublin, but most of them died elsewhere. Dublin, that stick of a rocket which remains on the ground while its stars shoot off to light the darkness and die enskied.

I could see that, over the way in the Green, the chestnuts were pinnacled with countless blossoms. Such a year for flowering Spring! The severest winter in memory must have done good in its secret way, for, though the Spring was cold, the blossoms were profuse and lasting. What a glorious morning! I took a turn to the left along Merrion Row. The One-Eyed Man had changed hands – most taverns do. It is Durkin's now; now it is Sweeney's; now it is Kennedy's. What is it that the old gloss, written a thousand years ago by a monk on the edge of his parchment, said about the fort of Rathangan? It had many captains.

> 'It was Aed's, it was Ailill's,
> It was Conaing's, it was Cuiline's;
> The fort remains after each man in his turn –
> And the kings asleep in the ground.'

'And the kings asleep in the ground.' The fort remains after each man in his turn. So it is with the Dublin taverns; but the change is quicker.

A café stood next to a locked gate, over which was an inscription cut in stone 'Huguenot Cemetery 1693'. I looked through the railings which protected it from the street. Within were a few oblong stones raised on four square pillars. The inscriptions were faded; but not so the lilacs which were holding their funeral torches over the dead. The gold of the laburnums was still to spend. It was 'in reserve', as became men who founded banks in the city that gave them sanctuary.

The best of Dublin was built between 1750 and 1800. After that the blight of Union, that Union which acted like a vacuum-cleaner and sucked everything into itself; but, unlike that machine, left vacuum behind. For more than a century Dublin was sucked dry to the tune of 'good form'; but the stately houses remain to show the grandeur that has departed. They are tenements, some of them, some of them are Government offices which lack the glamour of tenement life; but the rose-red shadows they cast in the twilight bring back the purple splendour of the prime.

The city of about half a million people is divided by the River Liffey, which is only fifty yards wide at its largest bridge. It should have been called the City of the Seven Bridges; but in the days such places were given names it had but a ford of hurdles and no bridge.

It is one of the most beautiful cities in Europe, with its five squares, its domes and the Palladian architecture of its public edifices.

The names of the squares and the streets record its history, which is the history of the English Lords Lieutenants or of the soldiers who held the country for their kings and queens. Rutland Square, where the Duke of Ormonde had his town house; Mountjoy Square, commemorating the good soldier who drove Don Juan d'Aquila back to Spain and to a court martial on the conduct of his invasion of Kinsale; Fitzwilliam Square – the descendant of that good Earl is still alive – Merrion Square, where the famous doctors lived from whose presence it got its nickname, 'The Valley of the Shadow of Death'. Here in No. 1 dwelt Sir William Wilde, the father of Oscar, a man of inordinate appetites famous in his own right: no mastoid operation can begin without the incision called after Wilde. In this first of the houses on the north side of the square also lived 'Speranza', the mother of Oscar who had her drawing-rooms darkened and joss-sticks burned at three o'clock in the afternoon. On the south side, within a door of one another, lived the poets, Yeats and Æ, who went to call on each other at the same time; Yeats passed with his head in the air, Æ passed with his head sunk in his beard, resolving many mysteries. On calling, each was told that the other was out.

About one third of the way along the vista of rose-red confronting the greenery of the square, the customary granite steps are replaced by ostentatious steps of white marble. This was the house of the famous sporting surgeon, Johnny

4

MacCardle, who may have missed a patient or two, but never missed a race-meeting. At one of these a jockey fell and broke his neck. Instinctively the crowd turned to the grand stand. They were right. The surgeon was there, but not exposed to the cold of the seats so much as to that of the ice surrounding the Heidseick. His acolytes took him by the Persian-lamb lapels and led him out protesting that there was no such thing as an urgent accident. He knelt down and found that the jockey's neck was a grating universal joint. He arose. Silence for the pronunciamento – 'Boys, he's dead; but I'll do all I can.' Doctors say that 'where there's life there's hope'; but here we are trespassing on the mysteries.

Aside, to the right before the long vista begins, is the great mansion where the Duke of Wellington, Blücher's protégé, was nursed. He was born in a coach on the way to Dublin. Hence, perhaps, his remark that 'to be born in a stable does not make you a horse'. He should have said '"Coach" does not make you a postilion'.

The long vista is closed to the east by a strange church. It stands in Mount Street Crescent; and its steeple consists of copies of two well-known architectural features super-imposed: one called the Lanthorn of Diogenes, the other the Temple of the Winds. The latter may have questionable appropriateness to a church; but so intent was the XVIIIth century on steeples that it was thought that no church could be complete without one, and this even though the main edifice was modelled on a Greek temple of the classical or pagan period. It took Dean Swift much of his caustic denunciation to prevent a brick spire from being stuck on the tower of Comyn's fine cathedral. Alas, the outrage was canonised and committed. Needless to say, this after the death of the pungent Dean.

Every man in Ireland is a 'character', that is to say that he has a soul of his own and expresses it individually; if words fail him, by actions. In Dublin some of these characters preserve their own self-respect or vanity, by veiling their malevolence in an assumption of friendliness. Malevolence is their nearest approach to superiority. Dublin, as Yeats called it, is a 'bitter' town. However, I was born there, and I am – who knows? – maybe somewhat astringent, so, when my sharp-nosed acquaintance hailed me with, 'Your book is banned. The Censors have banned it,' he could not suppress his glee.

'Naturally,' I said. And he was taken aback. 'Which one?' I then asked casually.

'*Mr Petunia.*' He had it pat.

'That's rather exasperating,' I said, as if I cared.

His interest rose.

'That's a nuisance,' I continued. 'I wish the Censors had timed it better, waited a month or so.'

He was all agog. So I *was* put out by his news.

'Why did you want them to wait a month?'

'It's a long recital,' I began. I hoped that he would carry away even half of what I was about to say; but I knew that he couldn't hold anything that had the least trace of subtlety in it; but I let him have it for whomever would get the garbled version.

'Try to remember this. When I voted for the Censor Bill, I did so eagerly because I realised that, during the periods that censorship was most astringent, literature was most remarkable. The Inquisition produced some of the greatest geniuses of Europe. And in England, in Oxford, the Martyrs' Memorial commemorates the golden years of English prose. And it is on the style of English prose that an Englishman relies for his salvation. If the Bible came to him through French, he would be damned beyond redemption; but it came to him literally illuminated by its translators.

'There was some heat in controversy in those days. Only for the king and the clemency of Pope Clement VII, Rabelais would have been burned at the stake for the matter of a comma; but he talked over the heads of the censors who would make anyone think that they were chosen as a rule for their ignorance of literature and their sensitiveness to the stimuli of lascivious suggestions. That is why the censors are always either old or celibate, or both, which make a vigilant censor. While they are nosing out smut, the author, if he is worth his salt, is getting by them with literature. It would seem, from a survey of the history of censorship, that censors were appointed as "interference" (a phrase from American football) to hold off the empty man while the player in possession gets by.

'With this in mind, I voted for as many censors as the Church and State thought fit to appoint. I knew that they would not interfere with good literature or deprive the nation of any writing that was thoughtful, spermatic and edifying.

'What was the result? I myself was one of the first to be banned. Little did I imagine that sex obsession would be more alluring than style.'

'Your books could not have been that way,' he interjected, only half understanding the argument. A thought made him vague.

'A moment,' I said. 'Don't interrupt your Stream of Consciousness. Now, as I could not consider that my lucubrations were in the tradition of great literature, literature that would be above the capacity of paltry people as the poems of the ollaves of old were above the heads of the uninitiated, I refused to submit my books to capricious censorship. Note: "capricious" means being like a he-goat.'

He began to wriggle. Reasoning made him restless.

'Hold it for a minute,' I entreated. Then, to arouse his curiosity, 'Don't you see what this means?'

He examined the question as a hen examines a speck of meal. 'It means,' I said with all the emphasis I could summon, 'that censors will have to send outside for their smut as a fish-wife with a hang-over sends out for a pint of porter in the morning.'

Inarticulate sounds of inattention told me that I was talking to an intermittent mind.

'Must I go on talking to myself, as the modern writers do? I said that to have my book banned at this juncture was exasperating. Do you know why? Because I was employing all the influences I could direct to have it banned in Boston. Now, that would be worth while, for any book that is banned in

7

Boston is boomed in the rest of the United States. But, just as some friends of mine were trying to make the Boston booksellers believe that my book, which is a study in psychiatry – I am referring to *Mr Petunia* – was at root pornographical, over comes word that it has been banned in Dublin. In Dublin, where they banned *Old Moore's Almanac!* with its harmless prognostications. That was enough for the Bostonians. They thought – don't you see? – that my book was about things that cast their shadows before: brassières and the like. How could the Boston censors stoop to that? It was most disconcerting. I, who had expected thunder, heard only a fiske. Instead of protecting works of genius, Irish censors are only protecting (commercially) religious pamphlets. I don't want to be banned in Dublin again. No one asks a eunuch for an opinion on divorce.

'Prudery and stupidity have been problems in every civilisation. All poets have been confronted by both. Censors.' I endorsed myself by a quotation from that blameless man, Gerald Griffin:

> 'Had bounteous Nature's counsel hung
>   Upon your will severe,
> Tom Moore had ne'er green Erin sung;
>   Nor Burns the Banks of Ayr.'

With what pity do we regard the old-maidish men who called Shakespeare 'Smutster and punster'.

'Brakki kekkax koax koax! If Aristophanes tried to get his "Clouds" played in Dublin! Holy smoke!'

He was gone like a cloud from the Moetic Lake.

The sun was shining. People were smiling. They were all well dressed. The faces of the girls were as gay as their costumes. Visitors were everywhere. Prices were higher than ever before, but there was money to pay them. There was not a shop or a store to be rented. Houses cost six or seven, aye up to ten, times more than they cost a few years ago. And this in spite of the fact that the city's taxes were 125 per cent. Englishmen were as plentiful as rabbits. After all, there must be some magic in Sean T.'s hat, I remarked to myself as I leaned on the parapet of Dublin Bridge, looking west. 'There was the Liffey rolling down the lea', changed from the days when the poet Spenser saw it, because it is now contained by walls on each side. But it is still rolling down the lea.

Geologists tell us that there was time when the Liffey did not roll down the lea at all, but rushed for Dublin Bay as directly as the River Dodder does. That was before the Liffey burst its banks at Poulaphoca to go meandering for sixty miles or so through the rich plains of Kildare, mirroring horses and trees in its black, still reaches, and tempting salmon fresh from the sea with little cascades, until, after its last fall at Leixlip, which is the name the Viking pirates who founded Dublin gave to the Salmon Leap, it took the tide where Iseult's chapel once stood, and rolled down the lea.

Today on both sides of the river the lea is covered with the most perfect examples of Georgian architecture that remain, now that a great part of London is demolished or replaced. Dublin stands about its river very much as when the City Fathers planned it at the end of the XVIIIth century. True, its principal street is vulgar and bizarre, with plaster palaces and neon lights that make the day tawdry and the night hideous; but in its guarded squares, uncrowded streets and quiet culs-de-sac and along the canals, a loveliness still lingers from a century that is gone. Among rose-red houses, public buildings of white stone rise, crowned with various domes of copper, green with age.

The pillared Custom House is reflected in the water when the river is brimful at high tide. They say that the architect of the Four Courts died of a broken heart because his plans for such another water-reflected pile were rejected.

It is well for him that he did not live to see stucco in the broadest street of the city or turf in the great park.

But I have promised to reiterate my trip to Dublin from Shannon port.

It is not my fault that the tale begins tangentially, and so is somewhat abrupt. But it was abrupter to me because I was

9

watching the large gold pieces that the sun was squandering under the trees that met over the road, and I was thinking that the woodbine would be already open on another planet, provided of course that it grew there.

2 — *'What durst you, Sir?'*

'Have you ever heard tell of What's That, the quean of Cootehill?'

Spring comes to Ireland gradually and lingers through all May and well into June. No petal falls from the chestnut pinnacles while lilac and laburnum bloom. The lilac waits for the laburnum to blossom, and they are still blossoming when the hawthorn whitens fragrantly and fills the tranquil air about it with heady balm.

They tell me that Winter here was colder than any Winter within living memory: man and beast died of cold; floods carried off the hayricks and laid waste the fields. There was great scarcity of fuel, and what turf there was, was damp. Even the long and lovely Spring could not make people forget the hardship they had endured. I wondered if the severe Winter was the cause of the unusually bounteous Spring, for, like many another, I find myself casting about for cause and effect. In this instance the old, deep-seated idea of compensation was at work. And I might have gone on following this dialectic had not the question stated above begun to intrude into what reviewers nowadays are pleased to call 'the Stream of Consciousness', which would appear to be a stream with no banks, in which modern novelists flounder in default of a current or an estuary. Incoherence is explained by 'Subjectivity'. In other words, the author is himself the subject.

Far be it from me to present myself as my own subject. I take very little credit for being conscious.

Where hedges rose, they were bright and black. I was in no mood to particularise. I wished to become a part of the genial scene.

Be this as it may, let me state here that I resented being asked if I had ever heard tell of What's That, not because it might have interrupted and disturbed my contemplation of the season's golden pomp (though of course it might have fitted nicely into my Stream of Consciousness), but because, though meant in all friendliness, it was over familiar, and therefore impertinent in its way. Of that I have no doubt, for unless such a question is asked by an old friend, it obtrudes on a man's dignity, implying as it did that he is interested in the *demimonde*. And a friend would have to be a very old friend indeed to ask me such a question. Only my besetting sin, which is, strangely enough, curiosity, could have made me tolerate such an intrusion and a taking-for-granted that I could possibly be interested. He is making me pay by his familiarity for giving me this lift to town. This is why, instead of saying 'I have not the slightest interest in What's That,' all I said was 'No.'

This led to an explanation which, in turn, led me unaware into a defence of the hoyting girl of Cootehill.

I can well understand why she was wont to ask the question from which she got her nickname among the lewder merchants and the surreptitious bank clerks of Cootehill. Being alone, it became incumbent on her to assume a maidenly unsophistication, and this, as the citizens should have seen, redounded as much to Cootehill's credit as to hers. In fact, had she for a moment permitted herself to become *blasé*, it would have reflected upon the township and brought it into disrepute, because it would have revealed the fact that Cootehill could support but one facile Venus, and that, as a result of the town's illiberality, she had become sophisticated, shameless and over- worked. But by exclaiming 'What's that?' she gave an impression of perennial innocence even though she had it not.

I could have quoted Herrick about a girl who 'is not for one but every night a bride', recurrently fresh; but I felt that it would have been lost on my interrogator. Instead, I defended Modesty in the abstract:

'There's a lot to be said for What's That,' I continued, 'for, by pretending to be innocent, she not only flattered each bank clerk, auctioneer and cattledealer by leaving him under the impression that he was the first to gain her favour; but she engendered in him a certain gentleness in love, for who would be so gross as to take advantage of a poor innocent without some "sweet, reluctant, amorous delay", as the Puritan poet has it? Think of the opposite. Would you have her shameless? There is nothing so revolting and demoralising as an immodest woman. Even the pagans of old felt this when they elevated Modestia to a divinity. Would you have her as devil-may-care as good old Mary Anne?'

'Good old Mary Anne?'

'Now, Stephen, don't pretend that you never heard of Mary Anne. She was or is a "roaring girle" of Dublin who, as the song made in her honour – well, not exactly in her honour, but about her – says, "She doesn't care a damn". Picture to yourself the effect of anyone not caring a damn in ethical Cootehill. Why, not only her name, but the names of all her paramours would be all over the town. The whole economic system of Cootehill would be dislocated. For instance, who would deal with a bank in that hamlet of righteousness if one or more of its officials were known to be given to chambering and wantonness? It could be overlooked but not forgotten in, shall we say? the case of an auctioneer who might be "going, going, gone", for all Cootehill would care; but a bank depends on stability, and stability in the last analysis depends on character, and character . . .'

'Wait till you hear what happened.'

'What?' I asked, weakly allowing myself to be diverted from the moral of my homily.

'She struck.'

'Whom?'

'Nobody. But she struck work because they called her What's That. And it served them damn well right. Talk of dislocation! You should have seen Cootehill. It was desperate: those who could not get to Dublin for week-ends applied for a transfer. One banker who was a bachelor resigned.'

Well might she exclaim, I thought:

'How many of our sex by such as these
Have their good thoughts paid with a blasted name
That never deserved loosely.'

And into my Stream of Consciousness came an old Greek play on how the women of Athens flouted all the men until they should give up their squabbles with another Greek State, and the stringency that ensued. The very thing that What's That did to Cootehill. What a play could be made of that for the Gate Theatre! It's too good for the Abbey. Anyway, in the Abbey it would have to be in Irish, and if you have a smattering of the language and an ignorance of history you may believe that there never was a gay woman in Ireland – that is, if you read history under proper direction. This pious hallucination will hold as long as the Irish are ignorant of their own history. If they had only an inkling of it, Grania would be black-balled for the Cumann na Mbyhan, which more or less corresponds loosely with the Daughters of the Revolution in America.

'One fellow made a kind of sneaking apology; and, dammit, what do you think happened? You could never guess.'

'I could. She accepted it,' I said.

'Accepted! She married him!'

Fresh and fair were the gems she wore.

'Now you see the virtue of modesty.'

'Are you codding?' was all my thanks.

'No, I'm not,' I said; 'for this is no subject for *blague*.'

Not only did her innocence implied in the question from which she got her name bring What's That a husband; but it kept sweet the good name of Cootehill.

Now, there are many Protestants in Cootehill. Protestantism is primarily a regulator of conduct more than a religion. It lays stress on the outer life. There are many Orangemen, too, in Cootehill; and you know how those rugged and illiberal men refused to yield an inch of their artificial Ulster and their slogan, 'Not an inch'. Therefore, What's That may be considered, with her abnegation, an embodiment of the Orange North. 'Not an inch.'

While good old Mary Anne, with all her liberality and large

14

discourse and 'There's a belly that never bore a bastard', becomes a worthy symbol of the South. Our problem, or rather, the politicians' problem, resolves itself into a merger of What's That with Mary Anne, North with South. Intangibility on the one part; illimitable invitation on the other. 'Not an inch' with 'Let them all come!'

'Wouldn't it settle things quicker if all the women were to take example by What's That and go on a local strike? Then the Orangemen could get a woman only in the South; and *vice versa*, which is Reciprocity, this would bring in the North.'

For a fellow of Stephen's type – that is, a fellow who is a bad listener – his suggestion was admirable. Why had I not thought of it? It showed at least that he had not missed the good intention and the trend of my remarks.

With my mind's eye already I could see troops of sex-starved Orangemen crossing the Border with drums beating and fifes askirl, migrating south to where the only complaisant women were.

Soon my mind outsoared any thought of carnality, and dwelt only on the great cultural influence our Mary Annes would have on the Men of Ulster, and of the sweet reasonableness they would engender in those dour and resolute breasts. The Ulster dames and damoiselles might co-operate in the great Union. I know that it is an opinion heretical in the South; but I cannot help but hold it – The women of the North are better looking than their Southern sisters. I began to think that the plan was not so preposterous as it sounded. One factor, a compelling one, was overlooked: the thought of the return of their terse and take-it-for-granted spouses and lovers would be enough to make the Northern ladies lenient and disposed to try any novelty; and what greater novelty could they find than the woman-shy swains of the South, the sootherers, the blarneyers, the palaverers, the playboys, the jongleurs? There was always the chance that they would take so long in their adulations that the ladies might be driven in desperation to ask them to be more practical and less poetic; and to do something pat. Unless the thought of the fast-working men of Ulster, with their technique of summary coercion let loose among their Southern sweethearts, might act as a spur to the men of the South philandering in Ulster. Who can say that to the Southern ladies it might not come as a great relief?

Meanwhile, the Dovetails and other liberal societies advancing in open order with banners flying gallantly – whereon is displayed a dove with wings addorsed and rising tail – to the Border with bagpipes playing many a ditty of loneliness and love-longing such as

'Saw ye my wee thing? Saw ye my ain thing?'

in dialect as a compliment to the North, would lead the Army in open order to dally with the disdainful maids and matrons of the North in an endeavour to convince them that Popery is no insurmountable obstacle to Union. What good is woman's franchise if she does not use it to unite opposites?

'Why open order?' Stephen asked.

'To facilitate infiltration,' I answered shortly, for I dislike being interrupted in a rhapsody. 'You would not have them serenading in mass formation?' I asked.

He thought that it would be unseemly to send an army against women, however obdurate.

'Not if they sang the National Anthem, "Neutrals are we".'

'Or "The Cock o' the North",' said Stephen.

If it fails in real life, it can be played in the Abbey Theatre.

A castle covered with Virginia creeper rose on our right. Woods spread not far away. They reminded me of a remark the Earl of Mayo made when we drove one morning to see the hydro-electric works that were being built on the Shannon. Every time we passed a grove of trees he would exclaim, 'Ha! They have not got rid of all the gentlemen yet!'

By which he meant to convey, not snobbishness, but the fact that only the owners of mansions had the sense to know that if you destroyed a country's woods, you exposed the soil to winds, floods and erosion. An ignorant farmer is not his country's pride, but its suicide.

I well remember that trip to inspect the Shannon works. We started off so early in the morning that we arrived in Limerick too early for lunch. We kicked our heels till noon. In Cruise's hotel we lunched at a table covered with smilax. The Earl had been recognised. After lunch we drove to the office of the Shannon Scheme. It was a large yard entered by an arched gateway. No one was about. After much blowing of the horn, followed by shrieks of the siren, a lame man wandered out.

'I have come from Mr McGilligan to see the Shannon Works,' the Earl announced.

'Mr McGilligan is out,' the man replied, standing to attention as he did so. He sensed the aristocrat in my companion.

'Of course he is. I left him in Dublin.'

'But this is his brother, Sir, and he's out at lunch.'

The Earl thought a moment, then he turned to me laughing.

'Well, as Lord French says, "What's the use of being Commander-in-Chief if you can't appoint your own staff?"'

His voice changed as we drove off with our permit.

'That lame chap is a good fellow. He served in the last war. That's where he got his wound.'

I didn't know where Lord Mayo got his information; but it and subsequent observations redounded to the credit of McGilligan's Shannon Scheme.

'Whose place is that? I used to know,' I asked Stephen as I pointed to the well-kept castle on the right covered with creepers and crowned by crenellated parapets. But Stephen did not know.

'Where are we?' I asked.

'We're in Roscrea. There's a Trappist monastery here. If you knew more about it you would be less interested in that castle.'

True enough! I might not be interested in anything of this world; but just to show him how far my knowledge of things religious went, I inquired if he were ever a guest of the monks of Roscrea.

'Were you?' he countered.

'Indeed I was.'

'And what did you bring out of it?' he asked, as surprised as he was satirical.

'I got this from a window-pane in the old house. It was cut with a diamond by the original owner of the place.' I recited,

> 'Mutton is mutton;
>   Pork is pork,
> And both are good to eat.
>   Ham is ham
>   And lamb is lamb;
> But only beef is MEAT.'

The writer must have felt this so intensely that the power of his spiritual mood, as Æ would say, attracted its opposite in a community of vegetarians. In fact it took many Carthusians to deliver his spirit from the flesh.

Strange! The moment I mentioned 'Carthusians' the name of the owner of the pleasantly seated castle occurred to me.

'Colonel Charteris!' I exclaimed. 'We must be in Cahir.' Another contrast. 'He gives shooting parties. At one of them the Marquess of Headfort dropped dead. He was a Senator with the Earl of Mayo in my time.'

My companion winced, but his car did not swerve.

'Dropped dead?' he asked.

I could see that he could not appreciate tragedy. To induce the calm which it should bring, I said, 'It's merely a matter of propinquity. Now, on the planet Neptune, where a day is as long as five of our months, and all our banks would go out of business, the Marquess would not have dropped dead, but subsided gradually, fortified (if we had inter-planetary communication) leisurely by the rites of whatever church claimed him. It's what they call Relativity now; but when I was at school we called it the third law of Kepler. Nobody then thought of broadcasting as a new discovery, something enunciated three hundred and thirty years ago. Indeed, it would have been impracticable then, for there was no semi-sophisticated public nor channels of publicity. So doth Slow Motion take the sting from death . . .'

He tried to think it out. He was hoping for a place where no one could drop dead, but he was of the earth, earthy.

'I ought to be driving you back to the Abbey of Roscrea,'

he said at length. His mind was still associated with death.

An empty cart approached, swaying on the rutted road. The driver tipped his cap. Then he leapt from his newly painted cart, which cheered the eye with its brightly painted reds and blues.

'Could I be lendin' you a hand?' he asked. It was his way of hiding his curiosity. 'Ye haven't run out of gasoline?'

Now, if Stephen would only gas himself and pass out for ten minutes, I might have an interesting talk with this native of the district. But what to me would be an interesting talk might not have seemed so to Stephen; and he would have interrupted. His manners lack reserve. Of this the reader has become painfully aware from the very first sentence with which this chapter opens. For this reason, and not for any lack of humanity in me, did I wish that he would pass out painlessly while I chatted with the carter. But such a stage of subterfuge was unnecessary.

The man turned to me after eyeing my grey felt hat.

'I would take you for a stranger in these parts?'

The thought shot through my mind: If he finds out that I am a native, I'll learn nothing. So I said, 'I hear that somewhere round here is the most horribly haunted house in the world.'

He eyed me suspiciously. After an anxious pause during which his eye never faltered, 'That would be Leap Castle,' he said, and pronounced it 'Lep'.

Now, Leap Castle is probably first on the books of the society that deals with haunted houses in the British Isles. I had heard much about Leap Castle from many friends. Some had been visitors to it, guests of the family called Derby, to whom it had passed. And Yeats, who loved such things, had more than once discussed with me the elemental that haunted it. This materialised in the form of a large black ram with a thick fleece. It had the face of a decomposing human head. When it appeared, the stench was overpowering. In spite of this Yeats affirmed that it was not an evil spirit. He may have said that it was not an 'elemental'! I am unfamiliar with the terms spiritualists apply to the different unearthly visitants. I remember that when he talked about it, his voice was grave and authoritative. I need not go into the various adventures of those who saw the ghost, nor associate the hauntings with the skeletons in armour that were found immured in the castle walls because in those days when a member of the garrison was killed during a siege his body was walled up. The besiegers were not to be counted on to give him decent burial.

There was a silence, during which his scrutiny continued. At length, 'It was burned down during the Troubles.'

I took care not to jump to the conclusion that it was burned down by the Black and Tans, irresponsible guerillas or gorillas loosed upon Ireland by Lloyd George. The places they burned were not as a rule homes of the gentry. Mansions were burned by the IRA because they might be occupied by the Black and Tans – so the explanation – but really because they belonged to men of English stock. But the underlying cause, I do not fear to affirm it, was the spirit of destruction inherent in the masses which is loosed whenever law and order are in abeyance. It would appear to arise from an inborn hatred in the unworthy for all that leisure and graceful living can produce. One need not go to Russia for examples. It is universal once the reins drop.

'So that is the end of it?'

He became secretive, almost furtive. But he did not wish so old and famous a castle to be summarily dismissed.

'There's nights when it goes on fire.'

I saw the empty windows filled with a red glow. I knew enough. That which haunted it was still there. Few spots on earth are favourable to ghostly presences, and they are reluctant to abandon those.

'I came to drive you from the airport, and not to have you talking about the ghost of Roscrea,' Stephen interposed.

'What else is there to talk about in Ireland except ghosts, from Finn mac Cool to Michael Collins? All ghosts. There is never a good word to be said for the living in this country. It is not until they become ghosts that calumny ceases. That is why I prefer ghost stories to speeches'; but I held my whist.

'Come on! Jump in!'

Misassociation has so often been my lot in life that I have become almost used to it. I jumped in.

I waved to the man with the red cart as we steered for Dublin. Had I said 'Cheerio', it would have been incongruous, as incongruous as J. J. Walsh when, in the middle of the epidemic of Gaelic revival, walking silk-hatted down the quays of Cork, he answered a fishwife's greeting, 'Laun braw' with 'Law braw, by Jove!'

We drove down the straight of the Phoenix Park. It is over two miles long, and it formed the finish for motor races years ago. Now it is like passing between dark walls. On either side, shutting out one of the pleasantest views on earth, long-drawn-out pyramids of melting turf were stacked mile after mile by de Valera's administrators.

'Gracious!' I exclaimed. 'Look what has happened to the finest Park in Europe. Was there no place else to disfigure than the Park?' I remembered what I was thinking about paltry people. 'It all goes back to housing,' I said.

'Housing?' Stephen inquired, puzzled.

'Maybe I was too quick. Let me explain. Those born in slums have a slum outlook. They have been deprived of beauty. They have become tolerant of dirt. And this is the result. They cannot comprehend what they are destroying. But if they thought for a moment about other people, they would not ruin what does not belong to them. This Park is a national possession; it is not owned by a gang that governs or misgoverns the country for a while. The Park is not a wood-pile or a turf-stack.'

I said no more because I was downcast with the thought that the people cannot or (what is worse) do not protest. They permit the slum-minded when in office to spread slumdom over everything that is fine and fair, mental and physical. How long, O Lord, how long, until we have an election to rid us of 'Dev.'?

I thanked him again for his great kindness in coming so far out of his way to drive me across country. He was one of the few good fellows who are unaccountably kind. I dwelt upon his kindness with gratitude, but his opening question still rankled a little in my mind because of its idiom, 'Have you ever heard tell?' Why couldn't he have said, 'Have you heard?' By using a tense which was a kind of past imperfect he suggested existence over a period of time, making What's That, as it were, a thing of the past, whereas she was alive, espoused and flourishing. It made me see, too, that his was the idiom I should have to adopt while living in a country of which I have ever heard tell.

3 — 'This Mortal Coil'

'Because he's a huer and a bastard!'

I had just left the haunt of ancient peace only to walk into MacGlornan. It is amazing what you may find once you come out through the wicket in the Front Gate. Trinity College was behind me, with its smooth lawns, its sleeping Dons and its golden memories. Talking of things golden, I had just left Richard Best in the College Park. He was walking from the Library, probably. He was in a hurry, so he asked me to come to his house any evening to continue our talk. Richard Best, the scholar. I remembered how, years ago, he confided to me that there was only one alternative: religion or scholarship. And I remembered, too, how George Moore had described his golden hair and his unageing, pink complexion, described him as one envious, for Moore's own hair that had been red once was yowden now.

'But I asked you a simple question. I did not mean to offend you,' I continued soothingly to Mac.

Over his tightly buttoned, thin raincoat, the broad, honest, yet fox-like face, with its high, hectic cheek-bones, stared at me with gleaming eyes.

'I had a job all right till he found out that I was a Stater.'

'Well, well,' I said sympathetically, while I tried to get the connection.

MacGlornan was an honest, earnest fellow in spite of the fact that he was a professional politician of the lighter sort. A 'ward-heeler' he would be called in the USA. I realised that he had just lost some appointment that had been promised to him because, on looking into his dossier, somebody had dug up the fact that he had worked at election time for the Government previously in power. As if such a thing mattered; but in the precarious profession of politics such conduct was unforgivable. So here he was, hungry, out of a job, a family to

23

provide for and no prospect where every 'Organiser' had been already appointed. No wonder he became excited when I witlessly asked him, 'What are you doing now?'

'Let me tell you that bastard goes into everything before he'll let a blind man get a job breaking stones.'

His mood changed suddenly. He felt that I was too remote from his affairs to be enlisted.

'Ah, to hell with it!' he exclaimed, impatient of unpleasantness, as all Irishmen are. 'Let's go somewhere and have a quick one.'

I regretted persuasively that I could not go. Even with the whole morning before me, I had no time for 'a quick one'. Politics had not as yet sunk sufficiently deep into my subconscious stream.

'Jaysus!' he exclaimed. 'Trinity College must have ruined you. They lock themselves up like the Friendly Brothers when they are drinking there.'

'Friendly Brothers,' I repeated. 'I have just met two of them, law-abiding citizens on their way to 42 St Stephen's Green.'

'Law-abiding! I should think they are. Those fellows came over here after, oh, bloody well after the Battle of the Boyne, to see what they could pick up; and they have formed themselves into a club to dodge danger. Friendly, me neck! They were raised on celery.'

Behind me, the Dons dreamed on. The politics of Cleon, innocuous now, and the decline of Athens were their concern. They could study as in a microcosm what had happened, and from that still life deduce what is bound to happen again. Humanity is human at every phase of its history; and Athens provides a pattern and presents us with a formula for all time. World politics is only Athens to the nth. Meanness, chicanery and self-interest, all were there. So clearly cut is the statue that we have ceased to analyse the substance. With this in mind, I grew tolerant, for what confronted me in the person of MacGlornan was but politics in action and very much alive. It would be an easy thing to scorn had it not been a part of life, or of whatever vitality Dublin can lend life. Athens was all life.

The minds of its citizens had less restricted curiosity and were suppler. The climate helped them with its most pellucid air. The difference between us is only one of degree of dampness. You must not blame Irish politics for not being as corrupt as Athenian politics: vanity, envy, deception, self-justification, endless expatiation, nepotism, honesty, courage, altruism, patriotism – all are here. The pace is slower; and they lack the magical mist of Time and an able panegyrist to make them classical and even edifying. I have never been afraid of Life such as it is. Why should I be now? The fact is I want a man of greater calibre than MacGlornan and more independent, to praise, denounce and project the situation so that I may get it into some perspective. I will wait until I come across one who is above the petty and immediate concerns of politics, an observer unmoved and serene.

I walked across what had once been College Green, upstream against the flood of oratory that was pouring out of Grattan's bronze mouth, too full for sound. Atkinson's poplin shop was to the left, and near it the National Bank, which hides in one of its vestibules Andrew O'Connor's magnificent statue of another orator whose words were, like Henry Grattan's, cast in bronze. The pillared Parliament House was on the right; its 'ironic' columns, as Joyce would say, held the Bank of Ireland now. Shelley commented on this when he came to Dublin at the beginning of the last century, so it would be presumptuous of me to comment on it now. I will only remark that the sounds therein of the adding-machines are dispassionate; and, if inarticulate, exact.

How pink and white are the complexions of the people! MacGlornan was like an apple. The girls looking into Atkinson's window are like Dresden shepherdesses – pinker than ever now by contrast, since the town is becoming more and more brunetted by hordes of dark, hard-eyed little men and fat, blowzy women, self-displaced from England for the flesh-pots of the capital of a food-producing country.

I am very careful to refrain from saying that Ireland is a strange country, just as I have come to deny myself comment on the shapes seen in a restaurant, for I never forget that I am part of the show. This Bernard Shaw overlooked when, after reading Joyce, he exclaimed, 'If such characters really exist, there should be a commission to enquire, Why?' He should have been prepared for them. He was born in Dublin. He spent his youth in it. He was part of the show himself. But he left it as soon as possible, you will object. That matters not. Dean Swift was born in Dublin. As Shaw himself says, 'That was enough.' He, too, was part of the show.

Here is a lady pink and white. Before me stands Dulcie. Her eyes are of that blue that is neither light blue nor violet, and yet not one blue, but two blues that are often melted into one, around large pupils. Now these pupils were all but level with my own.

She stood before me smiling, and never said a word. She watched my eyes, waiting for recognition to dawn. Thank God she did not say 'You don't know me.' She was anything but banal. I waited, too, as I gazed at her neck with its poreless Irish skin. Then up came the memory of Robin. I remembered his explanation, 'It's more matey', for sleeping in such a narrow bed. And this is Dulcie. How sweetly she smiled! Nothing inscrutable about it: the smile of a companionable woman.

I said, 'It's you that is looking well.'

She made a joke and smiled. I caught the glimpse of even teeth.

· I said, 'You have not altered. What are you doing? Where are you living now? Are you real or some personification of Ireland?'

She shook her head.

'And you have not forgotten Robin?'

'Could I ever forget him? Those were the days.'

She smiled regretfully, for the days when there was nothing bounded by any ring.

I marvelled at the power Robin had over women. He was 'rantin', rovin'', if ever a lad was. Bald and by no means good-looking, yet he was prepossessing. Maybe his dark eyes and his deep voice mesmerised them, and the way he had of taking the harm out of things by taking everything for granted. How Dulcie regretted him! Her eyes deepened. She was near to tears. I rallied her to cheer up:

'What a fine figure! Your regular features and your silken skin. You can pick and choose, though, as a rule; the lovelier the woman the more worthless the man she marries.'

'That won't be the way with me,' she said.

'Will you ever forget the trailer?' I asked.

She forgot to look embarrassed, but smiled gaily.

'You are asking *me*,' she answered and pointed to herself.

I went on, trying to give an imitation of Robin as he joined his friends at the bibbery asking in his deep voice:

'Will none of you blighters ever laugh?'

'He never gave himself a chance,' she said.

On this we agreed, nodding knowingly. She shook hands and went her way, leaving me with memories that were sad and glad. Sad, because Robin was gone, though it was just in time before infirmity caught up with him; and glad that Dulcie was happy and still fancy free.

What is about to be said now used to be said only of the Saints. Dulcie, when I knew her, had not been classified in that category. And yet she has one characteristic of the Saints, that is, of some of them: she has fragrance. Now, I hate perfumes as much as Flaccus did. Dulcie has no need for them. She has a fragrance all her own. I recalled what poets have said about a fragrant breath, hoping that it were true, but not convinced. I took it for something super-physical until I met Dulcie: breath or body, there it was: fragrance! Dulcie diffused fragrance. She is the only one I ever met who did.

They tell me that Ida of Louvain, St Colette and St Humiliana were as fragrant as sweet flowers. St Herman Joseph could be traced through the corridors by the sweet perfume he scattered. St Thomas Aquinas smelt of male frankincense. And I myself knew a lay brother who smelt of snuff. None of these explains Dulcie, who is not exclusively a saint.

There goes one serene mind in this passionate maelstrom, I

thought. Such a one I was seeking when I longed for serenity, for someone who could, calm and judicious, stand outside the lists. 'How is poor old Ireland and how does she stand?' That is what I would like to find out. Not 'how is poor old Ireland and *who* is going to stand?' as MacGlornan offered; and as O'Sullivan has it that O'Leary Curtis used to enquire.

4 — 'Lilli-bullero'

Yes; like another Napper Tandy, but not so devoted to the
bottle which produces the effect of political questionings, I
wished to know, 'How is poor old Ireland and how does she
stand?' I hoped to meet someone detached and serene who
would give me a dispassionate account of affairs of State.
Instead of that, what do you think happened? This is what I
got.

There is a little passage between shops before you come
quite up to Hely's. It leads to the Stag's Head. I was about to
turn into it when who should be coming out but my old friend,
the Senator. 'Old' he might be called, for he is past the Biblical
limit, but in Ireland 'old' is more a matter of date than of
decline. He was as upright and as sprightly as ever. He walked
on the ball of his foot. His bright complexion had not a trace of
the sallowness of age. As he extended a hand, one half of the
dark, double-breasted coat he wore came with it, as if to add
cordiality to the greeting.

His smiling, quizzical eye settled at last.

'Well, well, well! How's yourself?' he said.

'I can't complain.'

'You'll find a mighty lot to complain about before you are
here much longer.'

Now, I like to tell myself that I am not afraid of Life, though
I don't know exactly what it means. I felt something ominous
in the air. I knew the Senator and I have a great *gradh* for him.
He is a man of courage and of sound if somewhat vehement
opinions. A man exemplary in his private life. All of a sudden
he became as roused and as cryptic as MacGlornan, whom I
had just left. I may be unafraid of Life, but I prefer it not to
come at me like an avalanche of bricks until I have some little
preparation. The morning was smiling, but not so the Senator.
I had become apathetic towards contemporary politics,

whereas his indignation was growing every moment. At its peak point it became superhuman and impersonal, for he never mentioned a name.

He stood for a second on his toes, reminding me of the statue of the Liberator on his toes while the earth-breath came up through him in his recess in the National Bank. Here was another orator in another recess, only this recess was not between the National Bank and Dame Street, but between Dame Street and the Stag's Head.

'Get this,' he said, 'and don't you forget it. I am an old man now, but I will live to see the day when a British destroyer in the dead of night [I shivered, for I don't like the dead of night since they buried Sir John Moore] will put into Dun Laoghaire and slip that fellow away before the Irish People wake up and in their righteous wrath tear him in pieces for the way he has deceived them and for all the harm he has done to them.'

I could hear Demosthenes inveighing against the specious son of Macedon.

His nostrils ceased to dilate. He fixed me with his eye to see the effect on me of his prophetic phrensy. I had to remind myself that I was supposed not to be afraid of life. I tried to ease matters by pointing out that politics or diplomacy follow a certain pattern in given circumstances.

'The British always leave an amenable rebel with whom they can treat after an uprising. Take the case of Smuts. We have the same thing here, with this difference . . .'

I could see the pressure oscillating in the countenance of my friend. New trains of thought were opening up for him as he dallied with the parallel.

I tried to change the subject, but I succeeded only in increasing the tension. I must have been thinking of the systolic strain, for I found myself quoting the Minister of Health.

'I see where the Minister of Health in a speech at Clonakilty talked of a band of men and women with a curious sense of loyalty who were headed by a military gentleman, a major named Quisling; and his followers are known by the newly-coined word in the international language of contempt as the Quislings.'

His eyes began to quiver like the column of mercury in the apparatus they use for taking blood-pressure. They bulged from the pressure of associations behind them. These made him for the moment speechless. There were for him so many Quislings that he could not arrange them rank by rank. He had to shake somebody, so he seized my shoulder and began to asseverate incoherently. I tried to continue with the quotation; but he thought that it was a part of my speech. I made a mighty effort to distract him from the subject that I had unwittingly brought up. I talked of a less opprobrious theme – something pleasant, for a change. When I thought that he could hear, I said genially:

'I see the President has received the ex-Prime Minister.'

'Aye. You would think it was the stigmata he received.'

'The country has received them and no mistake,' I suggested, providing a wider field.

But a flash of his old wit dispelled the thunder.

'The Mikado receiving Houdini,' he suggested.

'The Mikado receiving Don Quixote would be more like it,' I replied.

'No, no,' he said. 'It's the other way about. The Mikado receiving a windmill.'

But I felt that other thoughts were fermenting. He would not remain long in his genial mood.

'Do you remember the morning that you brought Griffith and his party out to the mail-boat to meet Smuts? Griffith wanted to get a word with him before he reached Dublin Castle?'

'I do well. And I can tell you how Larry O'Neill made a fool of us all by announcing himself as the Lord Mayor of Dublin come to meet General Smuts. That was enough. The General avoided us by getting the Welsh sailors to hide him on the lifeboat deck until we went to the saloon. Then he escaped; and left us looking at Larry for a full hour. Afterwards, in the Mansion House, where there was a meeting, official this time, he advised us to have nothing to do with a Republic.

He said that he had tried one and it did not work.'

'Yet he worked himself up on the ruins of one,' exclaimed the Senator, with rising colour.

'Now, now,' I said quietly. 'That's all past and done with. We must take things and persons as we find them.'

'Let me tell you, there's nothing past in this country, however it may be with South Africa . . .'

'To proceed,' I said. 'We returned to the secret hide-out, in Dr Farnan's house, number 5, Merrion Square. It was about half-past seven in the morning when we arrived. We were rebuked for failing to get in touch with Smuts, and we were supposed to take our failure very much to heart, when suddenly the telephone rang. His Majesty's representative in Dublin Castle was on the line. I felt like a fool, after all my preparations: meeting the Lord Mayor – who, by the way, had us nearly late – at one place; Barton at another; putting Griffith up for the night and keeping ether handy to prime the cylinders lest there should be a hitch in starting the Rolls; and then hiding my car for fear it might give away our very secret hiding-place. You should have seen Griffith's face when he found that it was little more than an annexe of Dublin Castle all the time.'

He listened eagerly, as if he had not heard it over and over again.

'It served Griffith right for expecting that he could get anything out of Smuts.'

'I can understand him for not wanting to meet disgruntled disloyalists when he was over here on a mission for His Majesty's Government. But, as I told you, the British always leave someone on the outside left to play their game subsequently.'

'They're prime boys, both of them; and Prime Ministers as a result.'

I can't bear the onus of hatred, so, in a harlequinade as it were, I asked, 'Don't you think that the pair who were receiving one another at the Vice-regal Lodge yesterday saw the humour of the situation?'

'Where's the humour in it?'

'Surely there's humour in a fellow appointing one of his pals to "receive" him; and then his pal receiving him without a wink? They must know what a pair of play-actors they are.'

'What sort of cods are the Irish People?' he asked indignantly. 'It is they who have to pay for this sort of cod.'

He is taking things rather seriously, I had to admit. Imagine taking such a bright spot as the Vice-regal Lodge seriously. He poured question after question upon me. Most of them were rhetorical, seemingly, for he did not wait for an answer.

It is hard to survey politics without being mixed in it or contaminated by it. What right have I to set myself up in the gallery and look down upon the matadors? It may be somewhat cowardly, too. For instance, I should have expostulated with him when he was talking about Smuts. After all, Smuts saw that the Republic in which he was born was an inferior type of civilisation and as cruel to the natives as the Empire which, with its marvellous powers of compromise, made him a Field Marshal. It would have started another argument – this time directed at myself – and shrunk the Senator's stream. Suppose I had asked, 'What is the Republic of Ireland doing but trying to subjugate the North? From time immemorial to the beginnings of our history Ulster was always opposed to the rest of Ireland. Queen Maeve led an army against the *Men of Ulster*, and the Hound of Ulster held it up at the ford of Ardee. It is true that the present-day men of Ulster sent out for their allies to England and to Dublin, for F. E. Smith, and the briefless Carson, saw their opportunity and used bigotry of Ulster as a spring-board to wealth and honours. Ulster has been exploited over and over again because of its gullibility once you join in the Big Walk of the Twalft.

'And, to look at it another way, is this question of Ulster, coming up as it does at the very time that the last Prime Minister was kicked out of office, anything more than a red herring drawn across the path of the present Government just to distract and fool it by crying for the moon – a well-known trick of the last leader?

'Why not leave Ulster where it has always been, separate from the rest of Ireland and, to be fair in a muddy atmosphere, a model in many respects to the rest of the country? If Ulster depends on England, so did its champion seventeen hundred years ago depend on the men of the Mersai tribe beside the present-day Liverpool (he may have been one of them) and on a suffragette named Scota?'

Had I asked such questions I might have put an end to one spate only to open another. I would not have mitigated the indignities that ate into his flesh. He did not pause for want of breath, for he seemed to breathe continuously, like the air-pump of an organ; but his words had telescoped themselves. While he was disentangling them, I thought with some misgiving, 'If politics be Life, I am taking Life too seriously.' And I recalled the remark of a famous American general who observed, while the beauty of the Veldt was being pointed out to him, from an aeroplane, 'True; but is it necessary?'

Is any government necessary? The American Colonies managed in the early stages of the war without any regular form of government – that is, if Tom Paine be right; and he was there.

As the tapping of a chisel on the skull of a patient is said to augment the anæsthesia, I could feel faintly the hammered arguments of the Senator before I was enveloped in a dream state. They were the most extraordinary dreams, too – dreams that were apparently totally unrelated to the question, to the many questions that I could no longer hear. What did I dream of? It is hard to remember. Dreams are fleeting, and few of them reach memory, few remain.

I was kissing a Bible when the court usher or crier said, 'That is not necessary.' I pushed it aside. 'Take it up.' I grew confused. If the Bible had an universal influence it would be unnecessary to kiss it; but its influence could not travel far from it if you had to hold it in your hand. How far, then, can a Bible influence one who is taking an oath? How far from the Bible is an oath binding? Obviously a Bible cannot throw its influence all over the globe as can an etherial wave; and this must be in a way a dispensation of Providence, for if the influence of a Bible were global there would be need of only one Bible. Think of all the printers that would be out of work, not to mention the missioners and the Gideon bibles in every hotel in Belfast. Philosophical systems take the place of frustrating dreams for me: philosophical systems that luckily remain incomplete and irrational as a dream itself. There must be something of the Middle Ages still in my make-up, for most of the problems by which I am confronted in dreams begin with a question – 'Utrum?' as did the old theses. Whether there is more virtue in a salute from a man with a silk hat and a big head than from a man in equal social circumstances with a soft hat and a small head? Even in dream I was wary of the answer, for I could see the pitfall ahead of me, yet I could not avoid it, as is the way in dreams. Once I conceded that head and hat, I would be attributing merit to the intrinsic substance of the instrument; I would be admitting that your chances of recovery – in the case of illness – were better if your pulse were to be taken by a doctor with a gold watch than by one who had only a watch of gun-metal like that of Mr Bernard Shaw.

And then another 'Utrum?' in the case of greeting, in the case of shaking hands – a handshake that cost the country so much a shake was obviously, if not 'better' ethically, better at any rate than that of a one-armed man, shall we say? Just as the handshakes of the late Lord Mayor, Alfie Byrne, impressed New York more than the shakes of the skipper who had navigated him over the main sea deep. They say that even the hands of the clocks were shaken in New York; and, as for the prominent members of the more arcane – and more prominent on that account – clubs, their hands were in slings long after he had left. Therefore you are not going to tell me that there is not some innate virtue in a hat, or a hand, or a head? Thus the tempter; but I awoke to the sound of music. Incredible as it sounds, the Senator was singing a song. It was nothing less than the old ballad that had emptied two thrones in its time when sung to a well-beaten sheepskin:

'There was an auld prophecy found in a bog,
  Lilli-bullero bullen-an ah!
That we should be ruled by an ass and a dog,
  Lilli-bullero bullen-an ah!

'The prophecy's true, and has now come to pass,
  Lilli-bullero bullen-an ah!
For Talbot's the dog, and James is the ass,
  Lilli-bullero bullen-an ah!
  Lero, lero, lilli bullero,
  Lilli-bullero bullen-an ah!'

When I looked up there was nobody there. But the refrain
hung in the weather long after the singer had gone.
  Do I still dream?

5 — *Bridges on the Liffey!*

A great tranquillity is born of a slow-flowing stream. Gradually the distemper of politics left me. After a while I cared not who manned Rathangan Fort. Even the humourless pomp and pretensions of the fantastic fellows who aped English Royalty ceased to irritate or amuse.

The greater the foolery, the greater the pomp. I thought of the Irish People to whom the Senator attributed 'righteous wrath'. I wish I could attribute to them a sense of the ridiculous, which is a precious and a salutary gift.

'Will none of you blighters ever laugh?'

Farther to the West than the spire of the Augustinians, the great brewery veiled itself in smoke. A story told by Brinsley Macnamara, that bright intellect who not only can laugh but make others laugh too, came into my mind. The story of 'The Nine Naked Arabs' he called it; and he told how nine Arabian seamen from the Persian Gulf came to the docks of Dublin on a tanker, and, hearing the word *Guinness* so often repeated, took Guinness for the king of the country, and resolved, of their great courtesy, to pay their respects to such an august personage. The more they passed westward on their journey along the docks, the more the royal name was mentioned. The King's popularity was evident in that his name could be named by high and humble, lewd and learned, rich and poor. From a well-lit corner house an elderly woman emerged and, after gathering herself as for a dance, pirouetted round and round, testifying to the goodness of His Majesty. There were female dervishes, then, in this liberal country. They saw much symbolism in the greater illumination of corner houses than of others that stood in rows. His Majesty's influence extended to every corner of the earth. His name was named in every corner house.

From the bridge they could see the minarets of the great

palace. When they pointed to it they were answered by many reassurances of the name. And their response was accompanied by smiles and noddings of the head.

A tall, gaunt stranger with shovel hat and hair on the upper lip tapped the ground before him as he moved towards them slowly. 'Guinness?' he asked. When they made obeisance in affirmation, he pointed with his stick to the south bank of the river. They thanked him and crossed the bridge.

They passed four bridges. The first was metalwork which spanned the river in one low arch. At length they reached a long wall of brown, baked clay topped with stone. But here there was nothing to guide them. The wall was blank. They were about to retrace their steps to the last corner house when an urchin shouted 'Is it Guinness's yez are lookin' for?' He directed them southward by the side of the wall. Gradually the ground began to rise in gentle eminence.

'Guinness?' they inquired again.

By this time many citizens escorted them, and left them at the hall door of a private house. The house of a muezzin, in all likelihood. But the house was dark and the door was shut. It was after sundown. There was nothing to do but to prostrate themselves in evening prayer and await the dawn. In a row they lay with foreheads touching the ground until the last of the curious and sympathetic citizens had gone to rest. They prayed on. After midnight, and towards that darkness that is said to come before dawn, a gentle wind arose from the south. It stirred their burnouses' many folds. An officer of the law and guardian of the great walled palace of the King patrolled the raised path, which was somewhat above the level of the street for the convenience of sentries. He regarded them with some astonishment. Then, realising that to a bi-lingual member of the city's watch nothing should be unintelligible or inexplicable, he addressed them first in the official language of the country, and met with no response. Yet he respected them as men in an attitude of prayer. After a quarter of an hour, in which the wind was rising, he grew somewhat impatient. Worship he understood. He had never for a dozen years missed a 'short twelve'; but silence he could not understand.

However, thinking that they might be members of the stupid race of Sassanach, he condescended, as indeed he was often constrained to do in discharge of his duty, to speak to them with greater fluency in a Middle-Eastern dialect of English which was none other than that used throughout an Empire that includes every race under the sun except the witless who cannot comprehend the benefits of its sway.

'What d'ye think yez are doin'?' he said.

Still there was no answer. Their silence, then, was the silence of malice. 'Mute of malice.' And with that he was prepared to deal. As his truncheon descended, the wind, like a train-bearer, lifted the burnous of each kneeling figure. (Here I cover the mind's eye with a mental hand.) It was the south wind that justified the title of Brinsley's tale.

Yes; Brinsley is the last left of the men of genius whom I used to know in the old town. There was Joyce, who loved the Liffey and wrote about its rolling as no other man could. *Anna Livia Plurabelle* impressed Pat Colum because (I think he said) 133 rivers mingle with its wave. He said this in America, where Joyce is greatly esteemed for the scope of this sort of thing which his books afford: America, the home of the smoke-signal.

I know only two rivers that run into the Liffey in its course between Guinness's and the Custom House. One, I forget the name of it – Bradoge, I think – comes down from under Grangegorman Lunatic Asylum and enters Anna Liffey at the end of East Arran Street. They say that the trout in it think a lot of themselves. This megalomania may be due to their river passing under Grangegorman. The other, and this is the one that matters just now, has 'The Dolphin' disporting by its wave. You cannot see the Poddle because they have put it in a pipe. But it flows under 'The Dolphin' – you can hear it in the cellars – but it never gets into the wrong pipe.

The Corporation of Dublin did a great job in the days of George I when it built the granite walls that confine the Liffey's stream. There must have been a lot of mud and slob land before it was decided to fill in the marshes and to keep the river within bounds. And, centuries back, while it was unconfined, young men from the Dun on the south bank must have used its dark pool for a bathing-place. I remember how laboriously I tried to dig out from the Irish of *The Youthful Exploits of Finn* the story of how that son of Cumhall drowned the youths of Dublin while they were bathing in the Plain of Life! That was the way 'Liffey' was spelt then. It was wider and shallower then than the fifty yards width of it that flows unheeded now. It is discouraging to look at its course to the east, for that brings the Loop Line Bridge, with its grey steel cantilevers, into view. It is a perfect pediment for the warning 'Abandon hope'. This hideous structure shows, as plainly as if their souls could be seen, the total depravity of its promoters. It proves them to be 'utterly indisposed, disabled and made opposed to all that is spiritually good'. It reveals their abysmal ignorance, for they sinned against the Holy Ghost when they denied Beauty, which is one of the chief witnesses to the existence of God. But final impenitence was theirs, too. At the time it was proposed to build the grille across the mouth of the river which becomes nobler as it flows east, there were many citizens alive who could feel the enormity of the proposal and who spent time and money in an endeavour to prevent this outrage on the amenities of their town. But the promoters were stubborn and had their way. They knew what vulgarians were, and they knew how deep and subtle was the damage that could be done for generations to the citizens if they were to be deprived of the beauty of their expanding river, the romance of its masts and hulls lying still in the flat light.

They say that if an infant, in a foundling hospital, for instance, be left for months with a cover daily over its cot, it can never be brought up to the mental standards of the child that has been permitted to gaze about it, even though there be little comprehension in its gaze. The harm that William Martin Murphy and his gang of money-changers did to the Dubliners in depriving them forever of the view to the east can never be assessed because it has been done, and with it the power of appreciation and wonder has become atrophied. The atheists of beauty have declared themselves. This would be an old story and out of date, did it not point a moral, and point it strongly now. What happened to the Liffey then is happening to the principal street of the city now; and there are none to know the enormity of the crime, or even to recognise it for a crime at all, because have not other cities had their movie-theatres and their palaces of cement to brighten the night life of their citizens? New York has the abuse of light in the phosphorescent putrescence of Broadway and the greatest problem of juvenile delinquency of any city in the world. This may not be an example of cause and effect, but it is an example of coincidence which should not escape the notice of those who have the welfare of great cities in their keeping. Vulgarity is a form of crime because it overwhelms beauty, the harbinger of a Heaven which is always open. The fallacy of the cement palace is a message from the Father of Lies. Nothing that is born of ugliness can avail the spirit of man; nothing that can make him magnanimous or noble can come from an ugly town, any more than the infant can recover from the blotting out of its senses or the slum child forget the slum.

Those in authority would seem to have joined this conspiracy against the light. We see them dressed in black hats and in dark broadcloth, as if they would put out the light of day. Their pomp is as fallacious as the marble in the movie-halls of O'Connell Street and, worse than all, they know not what they do. They have blighted life for the people. Will these blighters never laugh? Never as long as we take them as seriously as they take themselves.

And yet there is the making of a great laugh in these playboys, a laugh that would puncture pomposity and expose humbug; for where will you see a greater farce than is enacted in these plays? Take an example:

Not long ago a miracle play was staged, not in the Rotunda, but in the Vice-regal Lodge. It was called 'The Reception'. It was a miracle play like 'Everyman'; but it had in addition another aspect of a miracle, the chief character, 'Bad Conscience' (black soft hat and black double-breasted coat), was received by one of his own creatures in a black, tall hat. It was as if a medium were to shake hands with his own ectoplasm. This seance was staged in broad daylight, for, as

41

most of the audience were 'paper', too close a scrutiny was not expected, nor indeed was any criticism at all anticipated. There was none. There was not even a comment. Nobody asked into what Bad Conscience was received. Nobody asked how came it that, by shaking hands with himself, so to speak, an honour was bestowed on Bad Conscience. Above all, nobody asked of what was the president President. The impression presumed to exist already in the minds of the audience, and which was the condition of their being invited free to witness the performance, and which the play was designed to perpetuate, was that the two chief characters of a sovereign (*sic*) republic were affirming their sovereignty. Nobody was inclined to point out the contradiction in the terms 'sovereign' and 'republic'. The marionettes were Lord Rugby's Players of the Vice-regal Lodge, who are producing more contemporary plays than Lord Longford's players at the Rotunda.

These farces are staged not always by Lord Rugby. At any rate, the actors are selected once by the Irish People, and then they can arrange to keep up the caste. But they are staged with the design to fool their audience into dreaming of a false freedom which few have the courage to question or to define. Don't take this from me, for I am so prejudiced against anything that is built on humbug and deception that I am biased; but take it from this clipping from an evening paper of the city of Dublin. And from a high-court judge.

'NO TURNING BACK

'What is freedom, that freedom that is supposed to be ours in this blessed Republic? If one were to ask a keen student of the higher politics he would probably say that it was the exercise of the God-given right of man to work out his own destiny in his own country without interference from outside sources . . . Parnell said something about no man having the right to set bounds to the onward march of a nation; but the question of where the onward march happens to be leading is surely just as important as the right to march at all. We in this country have been marching onward for a quarter of a century and it is very doubtful if anybody has any clear idea of where we are making for. Practice is so different from theory. We have a Constitution setting forth a lot of lofty principles; but who will say that the ordinary citizen, the man without "pull" or friends in high places, is one whit better off or enjoys any greater measure of fair play from the Government or his financial superiors and masters than he did before Mr de Valera presented his admiring subjects with the statement of their rights? We are all free, but at the same time we are in chains. We are taxed, directly and indirectly, to an extent that would have appeared unthinkable in the days of the Cosgrave regime. In a free country, it might be thought, there would be equal opportunities for all persons of equal merit; but in fact ability, personality and integrity of character count for nothing when a "big job" is "going" and the political jobbers take a hand in the game. The individual is hampered and restricted almost at every turn by arbitrary orders and regulations. No man, said Goldsmith, is so fond of liberty himself as not to be desirous of subjecting the will of individuals in society to his own. We are moved to these reflections by a remark of Judge Sealy at Nenagh Court when he said that the people were curtailed in every direction and that our freedom was freedom in name and not in substance. Our position amounts to this – that we have freedom to elect to power people who will deprive us of our freedom. We are free to make slaves of ourselves as we continue our interminable onward march, angrily sweeping out of the way any man who dares attempt to hold us up.'

And yet it could all be cleared away if the People would give a good guffaw in the right place. 'Will none of you blighters ever laugh?'

In the middle of the river between the bridges a cormorant appeared with a flat white fish in its bill. The fish was about six inches across, and could not be swallowed at once. The cormorant was unable to cut it in two. After shaking it violently for a while, the fish escaped, only to be caught again and brought to the surface. This went on for five minutes between the bridges in the middle of the town, and it did me good to see wild life so near the city.

The cormorant remained under the surface for a considerable time. It came up; but this time there was no fish.

I began to wonder how long it will take the Prime Minister to receive the President.

6 — *The Destruction Still Goes On*

Ignorance and apathy are unpleasant subjects which you cannot denounce without putting yourself deliberately or unconsciously into the position of an arbiter. To ignore them makes you an accessory; nor may an Irishman by removing himself from the scene escape injury when ignorance becomes criminal, as it does when it becomes iconoclastic.

Since childhood we have heard laments for the losses of our manuscripts, our goldsmiths' work, our ancient monuments. These losses we attribute to 'the Danes'. But we abstain from any inquiry that might uncover culprits nearer home. Yet 'the Danes' did not burn Cormac's chapel; nor were they the only raiders of Clonmacnoise; nor were their hearts warmed by 'the memory of the lime-white mansions' their right hands had laid in ashes.

Every country has its upsurgings of the savage who is innate in humanity. Seldom have savages tried, as they did here, to justify their ruinous acts, much less attempt to vindicate the destruction of a nation's monuments by the pretence that they were objects that had to be removed from the path of Liberty; as if the liberty that arose from such licence could contribute to the culture of society. But when the 'liberty' purchased by the destruction of what was comely and cultured in this country becomes a retrograde movement and rewards barbarity and slavery, it is time that the pretenders were exposed and pilloried.

This is no easy task when a nation has been faced about and blinded to all that makes it worthy of a place on earth, when its standards have been thrown down and trampled, and pretence set up in the seat of principle – when, in a word, national life is founded on a lie.

It may be that in the breast of the savage there smoulders fear of everything that is beyond his understanding, and that when what was unapprehendable becomes familiar, fear turns into hate and envy of everything that is beyond his capacity. Culture, the cousin of wisdom, points an accusing finger at him. Therefore he obliterates its every trace. When the contempt of civilised nations makes him realise what a barbarian he is held to be, he will endeavour by vulgar shows to make the people he has outraged forget the destruction of their heritage. Beholding these puppet plays, we cannot refrain from asking how many 'Receptions' at the Vice-regal Lodge will compensate for the destruction of the records in the Record Office, 'that even the Danes spared'; or how many town houses must yet be turned into Government offices to compensate for the destruction of irreplaceable mansions of the country's greatest century. This inherent vandalism the poet Yeats foresaw when he advised his countrymen to:

> 'Scorn the sort now growing up
> All out of shape from toe to top,
> Their unremembering hearts and heads,
> Base-born products of base beds.'

A gang of ignoramuses, headed by a man who is cultureless, cheerless, songless and alien in every way to the kindly Irish, undertook to compensate the people for their ruined heritage by a series of imitation English Punch-and-Judy shows. It is as if a spoilt lay brother dressed in black were to present himself as the equivalent of an insulted hierarchy and a despoiled cathedral.

'Romantic Ireland's dead and gone.'

A cuckoo has usurped the songbird's nest. The songsters are cast out to perish. The tradition is broken. The song that Finn loved to hear in Letter Lee must be heard in Ireland no more.

This is the explanation of the deliberate indifference to the nation's history and the attempted substitution of trumpery pomp for national tradition.

The destruction still goes on.

In the United States the value of monuments and ancient landmarks in the march of the nation is recognised. They are

46

cherished. Homes of great men are known and preserved. Records of the nation's great are collected. Their statues stand. The *genius loci* is honoured so that its spirit may inform the people and act as their growing inspiration through the centuries. The creative stress of those rare spirits whose lives were devoted to their fellow men is felt by all Americans in a deep and earnest mood. Britain, too, knows the worth of the example of its great sons and daughters. Whole districts are named after them. We read of the 'country' of those whose lives were spent in certain well-known parts of their native land. The houses where they dwelt are marked by entablatures. What a contrast in Ireland, where, with but very few exceptions, the birthplaces of its famous sons are unknown. How many citizens of Dublin can point out the birthplace of Swift, of Burke, or Griffith – men whose names are synonyms of human liberty? If such names cannot be associated with the spot of Irish earth their birth made sacred, what hope is there for the artists, the creators whose work made Irish culture known the world over? What hope is there for a generation whose unremembering hearts and heads are unaware of such men?

The tradition is broken.

It would seem as if the very existence of the fame of the great engendered envy and malice in the drab schemers of today. Not only is no effort made to preserve the names of the great, but the places that housed them or were made famous by them are razed to the ground. And the destruction still goes on apace: we read:

'One of the last links that bound Dean Swift with Glasnevin has been broken. The Temple in the grounds of Delville has been demolished because it stood in the way of a roadway to a new hospital. This temple, designed and built more than two hundred years ago, had, until decay set in, a medallion of Stella painted on its walls. The Latin inscription on the façade, *Fastigia despicit urbis* (it looks down on the pinnacles of the city), is said to have been suggested by Swift himself, and likely,

47

too, for the two senses of "looks down" are in character.'

And there is another reason for regret. The Temple, as everybody called it, was built over an arched vault in which the world-famous Drapier Letters were printed. That vault, where the remains of an old printing-press were found some years ago, has been cut in two by the new road. Near the Temple stood 'Stella's bower'. That has been partially torn down. A portion of the brick, arched roof has been cut away, probably for road-filling.

'But the citizens will probably be compensated fully for such a trifling loss by the historical appearance of the President in his silk hat to open the new road to an old woman's Home and by the significance of this for the nation.'

The path to the future. What is it? A pathological institute.

Delville! A name composed of parts of the names of Dr Delaney and his wife, Mary Granville. Delville, the house where the famous men of the period met – men who were not only forerunners of the Irish Literary Renaissance but helpers in the renaissance of the soul of Ireland, men who nursed it back to life and self-respect; the house where the Delaneys entertained Addison, Thomas Parnell, Stella, Dean Swift and Thomas Sheridan. An old woman's home has taken its place. It may prove to be an appropriate refuge for whatever may be left of the spirit of the nation.

And the destruction still goes on.

. In his castle of Tilira near Gort in the County of Galway some years ago, that great Irishman, Edward Martyn, was entertaining his literary friends, George Bernard Shaw, Arthur Symons, his cousin, George Moore, and, among others, the young Yeats. From a house a few miles away the widow of Sir William Gregory, an eminent Civil Servant, drove over to join the throng. Thus it came about that Lady Gregory was intoduced to Yeats. That was the beginning of a partnership in letters which was to last for fifty years.

Lady Gregory's house, Coole Park, was one of the many houses to be found in County Galway. It was a three-storey house built of native limestone and dashed a light grey. Like Rafort, near Athenry, it was one of the smaller mansions of the country. But its woods were its principal attraction – the Seven Woods of Coole with their beautiful Gaelic names. They are worthy of a better word than mine. Let us hear Yeats recite his wonderful blank verse that names them all:

'I walked among the Seven Woods of Coole,
Shan-walla, where a willow-bordered pond
Gathers the wild duck from the wintry dawn;
Shady Kyle-dortha; sunnier Kyle-na-no,
Where many hundred squirrels are as happy
As though they had been hidden by green boughs
Where old age cannot find them; Pare-na-lee,
Where hazel and ash and privet blind the paths;
Dim Parc-na carraig, where the wild bees fling
Their sudden fragrances on the green air;
Dim Parc-na-tarav, where enchanted eyes
Have seen immortal, mild, proud shadows walk;
Dim Inchy wood, that hides badger and fox;
Wise Biddy Early called the wicket wood:
Seven odours, seven murmurs, seven woods.'

In these woods walked the men who have raised the country out of that spiritual oblivion that engulfs all parochial appendages of a great Empire. On a tree in the woods their names were cut. Here Bernard Shaw went for his constitutionals; and, happily, the years have testified their advantage to his health. Here Moore was at his most mischievous on the very few occasions he was invited to Coole Park. Strange to say, it was not George Moore but Arthur Symons who deprecated the abduction of the young Yeats by the widow Gregory. When she joined the party at Tilira, Arthur Symons warned, 'Be careful of her, Willie. She has a possessive eye.' The warning availed not. Yeats went to reside at Coole: but luckily the prognostications of Symons as to the fate of Yeats's lyricism, 'She will put an end to his poetry', proved to be unfounded. Some of the best poetry he was to write was written by Yeats during his years at Coole Park. The house was magnified by his imagination into an ideal Irish mansion full of the courtliness of a century it may not have seen at all. His imagination endowed it with the traditions of the period he most admired, that century in which the Anglo-Irish mind flowered and 'the salt of the earth', as he called them, enunciated opinions, liberal for their period and since unexcelled.

What has been done to preserve these memories? A saw-mill marks the site of Coole and its Seven Woods. The very stones and slates of the house that welcomed the greatest geniuses of their generation have been removed by a contractor (building materials are scarce) to build an ecclesiastical structure within the walls of the disused Galway gaol. How truly Yeats's friend, George Russell (Æ), said: 'One of the very first symptoms of the loss of the soul of a nation is the loss of the sense of beauty.'

Someone, not unmindful of the fame of Coole, bought its hall-door for five pounds ($12). From it he cut a heart-shaped piece of wood which held the knocker. This he offered to the Dublin Municipal Gallery. It was refused because, no doubt, those who conducted a gallery of Ireland's great did not want such a stultifying reminder of the many acts of vandalism against 'the noblest of the things that are gone'.

'The President has received the ex-Prime Minister at the Vice-regal Lodge.' – Daily paper.

When I consider the drabness – drab as the sodden peat in the Park – and the soullessness of the present State, the paradox that puzzled me is resolved. The paradox was this: why did that efflorescence which is called the Irish Literary Renaissance manifest itself while the country was directly under British rule? The answer is that those engaged in the Irish Literary Movement drew their inspiration directly from an unbroken tradition, from the sagas, the legends and the speech of the country. There was no pretence about it. The undiluted language of the Gael was theirs. The old tongue had not been pidginised into a political shibboleth. Then, too, there was adventure in the air. Without adventure there is stagnation. The sagas had a vitalising effect on those who listened to them. They renewed the national spirit with a love that was genuine, strong and impassioned; poets became patriots and, in turn, poets made patriots. The soul of the nation, so long silenced and alienated by the denationalising system of education known as the Intermediate System, burst into song. The issues were clear-cut. The enemy was British domination with its universality or Imperialism, which, like a ten-cent store, was to contain everything reduced to one level (and nothing worth much) under one management or administration, an Emporium of Empire. The defence against this levelling was a return to nationalism, a recoil from Imperialism. There can be neither art nor poetry in a regime that is founded on politics which has debauched the very language of the country into ersatz Gaelic that is a confessed failure:

> 'Mr T. Derrig, Minister for Education, told General Mulcahy that eight essays had been received for a $500 competition in Irish on the life and works of Thomas Davis. The adjudicators did not consider that any of the essays was of sufficiently high standard to justify the award of the prizes.'

And this after twenty years of compulsory Irish! There is as much spent on this attempt to spell English in Irish characters – Bus, Incoim Tax, Telephon and Phuist – as would clear the disgraceful slums of our towns and raise the standards of living to include cleanliness, health and self-respect; or to perpetuate, by the preservation of their homes, the glory of our great men.

There are certain things that may not be justly compared with one another. For instance, it is not just to compare the cost of women's imitation jewellery with the cost of demolishing slums. They are not in the same category. But the cost of a tinsel court may be compared with the cost of slum-clearing because they are under the same dispensation, and that public; and the same men have the allocation of the money. Lately, some years ago, they were endeavouring to increase their own salaries, although not one of them, according to the then Prime Minister (and he magnanimously included himself), is worth more than £1000 ($5000) a year.

From the ends of the earth men come, are 'received' and find a home in an Irish 'republic', where a great number of its citizens have not a home of their own.

'Will none of you blighters ever laugh?'

7 — *Opposites*

Please forgive me for breaking off so abruptly in the last chapter. The fact is I could not help it. I got the hell of a shock. Suddenly out of my Stream (the Conscious or Unconscious, it is much the same to me) arose, came into mind, awful thoughts, like a litter of half-drowned pups coming up to accuse their owner. The thoughts had to do with people who go on denouncing others or hating them and what they stood for, and so forth. I began to recall things I had heard and read on the subject of self-righteous reformers just as I was becoming one myself.

This is the first quotation I remembered:

'The perfect men of the present day, however, are not constituted thus. They love to be sharp upon the faults of others and lenient towards their own, the result being that no advantage accrues to either. In their own conduct they are satisfied with a minimum of virtue and ability, cajoling others as well as themselves into believing this more than it is. But when it comes to estimating anyone else's virtue and ability, nothing seems good enough for them. The past is raked up and the present ignored . . .'

Now, that's the very thing I have been doing, being sharp upon the faults of others and easy on my own, with the implication that I could do things much better, and that I am a better man. And this, mark you, after denouncing the whole tribe of ward heelers. As for raking up the past, I even went farther back than the ex-Premier himself, who usually begins at Brian Boru. I must say that I felt a bit guilty, and was trying to acknowledge it to myself, when up came another, and this time a worse and more alarming memory. It came from George Russell (Æ), the Sage of Rathgar:

'There is a law in human Nature which draws us to be like that which we passionately condemn.'

And there is a bar-tender in New York who told me that in the Speakeasy days he was up so often before the beak that he began to look like him.

When these two revelations hit me together, I passed into shock. I wonder if I shall ever pass out of it – that business of being drawn to be like and, worse still, of looking like one whom I 'passionately condemn'. What would the Senator say if he met me metamorphosed walking down Dame Street? I don't know if this transposition includes having a body-guard; but I know that if it happened to me, I wouldn't care who took a pot shot at me. The sooner I got it over the better. But, holy smoke! what an escape! I wouldn't so much mind being turned into Sean T. about dinner-time, provided that I could snap out of it when the guests were going home. But!

The only thing to exorcise me and to prevent the other ghastly possibility is to go and get a large whiskey and a little water. That's a stream my opposite or ghoul will never cross. From this time on I will stop passionately condemning anybody. I am quite satisfied, perhaps too much so, with being myself.

I never before realised the wisdom of 'Love your neighbours'.

As I went my way towards the Dolphin on the Poddle, I took a surreptitious look at my hat. It was still grey, not black. Thank God! And I was still compact and middle-sized. But I felt strangely depressed. I took another look at myself in a copper bed-warmer in McBirney, the haberdasher's window. I made due allowance for the colour and the distortion, yet I resembled the Knight of the Rueful Countenance just a little bit. But when I meet Jack Nugent I will be all right. To be 'received' by him means something.

Outwardly, the Dolphin consists of brick walls, Victorian bricks and terra-cotta ornaments. There are nine weathercocks on the roof which can account for any wind. The Later Alcoholic style, appropriate enough for a tavern. Otherwise it has nothing to recommend it architecturally but a beautiful metal knocker. However, brick walls do not the Dolphin make. It is Jack Nugent and the boys within. What was it Dr Johnson said about there being more joy found in a well-run tavern than in anything else Man's ingenuity invented? Jack Nugent can tell you more about that than the learned doctor.

Jack Nugent is a pleasant, portly, welcoming man with a kind of chortle. When he laughs, he turns sideways, with his hand over his mouth, for his laughter ends in a fit of coughing. He often coughs without a cold. He has a retreating chin; but he wears an open collar for emergencies so that his necks may come to its aid. Sean T. has an open collar, too; but I don't think that either of them has been denouncing the other. It must have something to do with greeting and goodwill. Jack's mind is full of weights and dates and considerations of form. He is a hierophant in Ireland's oldest religion, which is the Cult of the Horse. Anyone who knows anything about reverence, not to mention good manners, knows that when an owner of all people is in conference with an expert on form it is no time to butt in with an interruption or a shout, as it happened once. The Earl of Fitzwilliam was in deep consultation with Jack Nugent at the foot of the stairs when who should come out but Jerry Cattermole shouting:

'There's no soap in your toilet, Nugent!'

The owner of the Dolphin turned on him with righteous indignation. His necks rushed reinforcements to his chin, which stood firm and did not retreat.

'Get out of here! How dare you come into any man's house with dirty hands? Go home and wash yourself!'

After giving this advice conversation was resumed quietly with the Earl.

Anyone who does not go to the Dolphin in Dublin is hardly worth seeking. To put it another way, anyone whom Jack Nugent does not know is not worth knowing. You may be sure of one thing: he is not a sportsman. This statement should be qualified a little. There are judges who, probably in order to preserve the adage, 'Sober as a judge', do their drinking privately at their clubs, at the King's Inns or in one another's houses; but not in the Dolphin. Then there are doctors who regard it as unseemly to be seen drinking in a public place. In the case of judges there is one exception. Judge Meredith was well known to Jack Nugent, not because he was a judge, but because he won the quarter-mile championship in his day and Jack's day, for Jack held the billiard championship for years.

To go back to Judge Meredith. I can still see his white calves twinkling as they carried his slight, flat body swiftly round the green of College Park. Even on grass he could always break two minutes for the quarter. Jack could tell you his times. The Judge was a scholar, a philosopher, a great student of Hegel. Maybe it was owing to the Hegelian dialectic that he could not make up his mind. If he began by being lenient to a prisoner at the beginning of a trial, he compensated for it by downing him at the end. So notorious was his vacillation that his architect disobeyed instructions and put only one toilet instead of two at the stairhead of his new house. The Judge had to acknowledge the wisdom of the omission and to accept the architect's explanation, 'In the case of an emergency, Judge, you might fall between two stools.'

With those whom Jack Nugent does not like there must be something very wrong. Their names are on a lot of dusty telegrams in a glass case in the hall to the left as you come in. They have been addressed to men who died in Jack's opinion, men who failed to live up to the easy standards required of sportsmen, so their telegrams are their obituary notices.

Still talking of decent fellows, I remember late one evening, when I was having supper in the Dolphin, I felt an arm about my shoulders and heard a throaty voice in my ear. It was mine host acknowledging me and welcoming me home. We talked of old times and of old friends: what Irishman does not love to muster them in his talk? When I came to Jimmy Montgomery, the Master of the Dolphin was silent. Slowly he shook his head. That was enough. I knew that my old friend Jimmy Montgomery, the Film Censor, had passed away. In a moment Jack Nugent changed from his solemnity and smiled.

'Did you hear this one?' he asked. 'The boys went to see Jimmy as he lay dying. "How are you, Jimmy?" they said.

"Just hovering between wife and death," said Jimmy with a smile.'

What better epitaph could a man have than a moment's solemnity, and then a laugh? I often heard Jimmy telling us how he had reversed the usual procedure and had drunken up the two public-houses his father left him.

I remember his reply when he was asked what he wanted on a certain anniversary.

'Two minutes silence.'

Jack Nugent sighed as he parted from me:

'Jimmy Montgomery was a grand fellow!'

A fine testimonial from a man who knows form so well.

But there are other decent fellows who are dead and gone. Happy Harry, whose speech was a series of propagating adjectives with an unvaried noun to give the adjectives an hold, is no longer at his table near the door.

Tall, striking Fred Weston, with a large, aquiline, embossed nose that perversely recalled Mr Gladstone, surveys the scene no more: dead as Jack Lister, who used to lean across a sidecar with the sun on his patent-leather shoes. All with the 'also rans'. They will have an anxious time in Heaven balancing weights against the jockeys' wings.

Amid the talkative throng you can find the habitués of the day. If you cannot, your foreground is not right. You will be more sib to them if you are going to Punchestown, Leopardstown, The Curragh or Baldoyle. There's the gallon Baron, with his race-glasses slung slantwise. He is too careful to trust them to the hat-rack, for there is no knowing if a tout or two may not have escaped the waiters' watchful eye, because on a day like this, when there is a rush of people coming and going in and out, it might be quite easy to slip a pair of race-glasses off just as you were taking down your raincoat. So the Baron explains with modern instances. 'Excuse me,' you plead, 'there's Hugh Harpur and Dudley Walsh,' which only makes it worse, for the Baron knows them all, and they know the Baron. They are not going to the races. No. They will keep on lunching instead, anchored by the conviction that they are too busy to go anywhere.

While I was looking in at the door, Willie slid as if he were on skis.

'You'll have a seat in a minute, sir. Jack's in York; but expected back tonight.'

His whisper was audible, though it came from a corner of his mouth.

I had to tell Willie that I didn't want a seat. I turned instead back to the left-hand bar off the entrance, where they serve lunch and drinks off the Aberdeen granite that is curved like a horse-shoe.

I am still a bit shaky after my narrow escape. The surest way to be different from anything I passionately condemned is to order myself a large Jameson and Thwaites for luck, since soda-water was invented in Sackville Street and Jameson is distilled in Bow Lane. Tom is sympathetic. You would think it was only yesterday I left the Dolphin.

'You may fill it up. Ha! That's the stuff. Tom, give us another just to make sure.'

I stopped.

Tom looked at me. He must be wondering what it was I wanted to make sure.

Pondering on such things, I was roused by an intense whisper from Tom: 'Dan Chaucer is good at four to one.' So Tom confided, having looked sharply from left to right. 'The third or fourth race; but you'll see it on your card.'

'Dan Chaucer me arse,' an unconsulted little citizen beside me remarks contemptuously.

His speech was in idiom, so I need not set his words down literally. I would have ignored the remark had I not known that, long before Freud, the Irish attributed negative properties to the lower portion of the alimentary tract. I took his comment as a negation of the barman's faith. It meant that, in the citizen's opinion, it was not only improbable but impossible that Dan Chaucer would win the third or fourth race. A copper-faced client on my right, who looked like something from the Levant, announced that not only did he own but that he trained Dusty Miller.

'Don't mind them,' the bar-tender said. 'Don't mind either

of them. They only come in here to try to pick up a few tips. Did ye see how quick the little fellow was to pick up what I whispered to you?'

What would the poet Chaucer have thought had it been revealed to him that part of his fame would be to have a race-horse named after him in Irlonde? And what would he have thought of the manners and customs of the modern Irish had he heard his name qualifying a word which, though he did not hesitate to employ it in his verse, lacked both dignity and respect even in his day?

As I sipped my antidote the problem of the names of race-horses bubbled up. How is it that their names in the aggregate come to denote race-horses and not running dogs, the names of which are as odd and fanciful, yet in some subtile way associated only with canine, and not equine owners. This problem kept me brooding until another question arose, and one that was not easily solved. It was this. How do they who name horses prevent them from being associated – by mistake, of course – with the products of Shanks in Barrhead, Scotland, or Murray Crane in the USA, manufacturers of toilet utensils both? How, in a word, is one to know that Adamant by Hanley out of Twyford, Ailsa, or Deluge, or Ladore or, more ambitiously, Niagara, are not to be looked for in hotel toilets rather than in paddocks? I confess that the problem baffled me. If it baffles me, it will baffle these touts, I thought. If I could have a word with Tom that would not be listened to by Copper Face or the commentator on Chaucer, something might be done. While one of the barmaids was cutting ham and trying to obey directions from Chaucer, I got Tom to the end of the bar.

'You know Shanks' patent urinals in the lavatory?' I asked.

Tom looked blank; a puzzled smile: then he nodded.

'How about giving me a tip to back "Shanks' Pat"? It's only a urinal; but it sounds like a winner!'

I left it to Tom and went back to my stool.

I was tracing the change of the times in the changes in the names of horses. In the days of unsung Victoria only classical or famous names, like the names of battles, were used in designating horses. You would almost trace their date from their names. Omdurman, Sevastopol, Khartoum. Then came the double names, and with them the decline; names such as Pay Parade, Goodwin Sands, Fleet Street, White Lodge . . . Tom whispered audibly:

'Here's something for your ear only. You can get a hundred to one now on Shanks' Pat for next year's Derby. Orby was not much of a sire, but Shanks' Pat has his dam's and Tetrarch's blood, and not a bloody word about it. He's not even listed yet.'

'Where can he be seen?' I asked.

Tom said mysteriously, 'That would be telling ye!'

Though the little fellow used no note-book, I could see that the tip had registered.

It registered on my other side, too, for Addis Ababa gave himself away by asking, 'Wot's this about Orby being a bad sire?'

'This is doing me good,' I said: and I went on thinking of the romance that is mixed up in the names of race-horses. I know how Bahram got his name from that great hunter. The Aga Khan could not have given his winner a better name. It fetched even me, who rarely mix gold with the Olympic dust. But I bet on Bahram, for I knew that he was as swift as the wild ass and that he could not lose. And wasn't I right?

Then there are fanciful names by which the fancy women of the less austere owners endowed their lovers' steeds, names which reveal the trend, and sometimes the limitations, of the ladies' imagination. Sometimes the owner names his horse after his lady, Lovely Anne. Sometimes the lady returns the compliment, as in the case of the French horse, Monsieur L'Amiral. Charming! I wonder what the old seadog said when she insisted on her whim. Sometimes ladies call horses after the pet name of their lovers. This is the only explanation of how No Nightie got its name.

Brands of champagne are used and names of cigars; both associated with racing women and men. Château Yquem, which those for it who go to the races will pronounce in their own way; just as Elysium can come to betray to the bookies who have their personal pronunciation the name of its owner's sweetheart, Alice. So, too, Euphegenia tells to all in the know that Fred Weston went round with Jenny Hughes . . .

'Excuse me, Mister,' the fellow on my left said deferentially. 'Don't think that I want to butt in. There'll be no getting it out of Tom, and the Derby's off almost a year. So there'll be very little harm in letting a fellow know who owns Shanks' Pat.'

I assumed the look of one whose confidence is more or less outraged. Then I softened somewhat and, with adjurations to the profoundest secrecy, not to mention mystery, I revealed the fact that Shanks' Pat was owned by a very high official of the Dail who, for conscientious reasons, could not enter it in his own name. The last part of my confidence convinced him. He had swallowed Tom's tip, toilet and all. Lest I might think that I had conveyed anything of an important nature, he said indignantly:

'Why the hell can't he run it in his own name? Doesn't he and his bunch get seven and a half per cent out of every bet? And why the hell can't he go to a race meeting, like every honest bloke in the country?'

'There I leave you!' was all I said.

Brave men are these gamblers. They blame themselves for their errors of judgement. They never blame the horse. They lose or win the making of a life of luxury and ease, yet they never pause to seize the prize. It all goes back into 'the field'. True votaries, their devotion never relaxes. Their courage never faints. For them is no fascination equal to the fascination of life and death when all is put to the touch. Their deity gives and takes away. Blessed be the name of the Horse!

Thinking thus, I was reminded of a tale told by Jake Brennan, of a gambler who for the nonce had lost his all. He was rolling down Park Avenue in New York some hours before the dawn. He was homeless. His eye caught a notice on one of the fashionable churches, 'Enter by the north court'. He entered, and fell asleep in one of the pews. When he awoke a funeral service was in full swing: flowers and candles. Turning to a lady of quality on his left, he asked, using Happy Harry's only adjective, which implies a certain disapprobation of the less fortuitous aspects of Life, 'Did you ever see so many . . . candles?' Her look knocked him unconscious again. On recovering, he inquired this time concerning the multitude of flowers. Again he passed out, to be wakened by a stentorian voice intoning loudly:

'The Lord gave and the Lord hath taken away.'

He brightened and, turning again to the lady, said:

'Well, if that isn't a fair shake, I'll . . .'

And he reverted to that Chaucerian usage of which we have already adumbrated.

So to the gambler the giving and the taking away are both parts of the game. It's a fair shake. That is all they ask, though the dice may favour them but once in twenty shakes.

Is it any wonder that the Dolphin should observe secrecy of a cult so important? Or that the principal shrine in Ireland of the horse should have its mysteries: mysteries concerning form, weights, tips, ownership, and mystery surrounding the movements of its priest whom Willie whispered was 'expected back' from York?

If the Dolphin be the shrine of mystery, do not forget that it is also the temple of Hope. Jack may be back from York 'any minute now'.

8 — *Lewd and Learned*

A woman was scourged in the House of Industry for some infringement of the rules. The Board met, and found that the porter whose duty it was to inflict such punishment as the Board awarded had been remiss in his duty. He was ordered to scourge the woman again, more 'conscientiously' this time, which meant more heartlessly; and he was fined a week's pay. His pay was six shillings and sixpence a week. A clergyman was a member of the Board. The porter was not as conscientious as the clergyman. This was in Dublin in the XVIIIth century, a century of magnificence and squalor, of 'Mud and Purple', as the poet O'Sullivan has it, a century of the most dehumanising existence for the paupers of Dublin and of every other town in the kingdom.

This was one of the most inhuman centuries of which there is indubitable record. It was the century of floggings unto death in the King's Navy. It was the century in which women were stripped and scourged in the lazar-houses and the pestilential prisons. The century in which the insane were chained and bedded on straw and exhibited to make an holiday. A century in which the death penalty was inflicted for an hundred offences. Much of this inhumanity is a thing of the past. The gaols of Ireland and England are the only places that still retain a remnant of the tradition. And the slums of the city still bear witness to the festering lives of the XVIIIth century poor. Yet during that period Dublin arose in stately buildings and gracious private houses unapproached for the beauty and the symmetry of their design. So out of the misery and suffering came the Pyramids of Egypt and the victories of the Nile and Trafalgar. Architecture outran hygiene in Dublin as well as at Versailles.

To one of the best examples of XVIIIth-century architecture in Dublin, the Provost's House, I was bidden to meet the

Provost and, with the American Minister, go with him to dine at what used to be the Chief Secretary's Lodge in the Phoenix Park.

The Provost is Dr Alton, a robust, restless man of middle height, which makes him all the more burly, oak-complexioned, robust, but not stalwart, a stout fellow who looks before and after. He looks *after* in his study of Ovid, on whom he is an authority; and *before* in that he has foreseen the future of Anglo-American culture. For this he plans to make provision by extending the present great library of Dublin University to accommodate American as well as British literature. But, like most of those who plan for the future, he lacks present funds. And yet years hence there will be a great discovery. Someone else will adopt – and plagiarise – the Provost's ideas, and not only be hailed as a foreseeing statesman, but be given ample funds to cement America and Great Britain and bridge the Atlantic by an intellectual bridge. This would bridge the estranging sea more lastingly and advantageously than any bridge of boats or aeroplanes. For Ireland it would be a peculiar advantage because to the fluency and grace of the English language as it is spoken in Dublin, it would add the vigour and imagination of the language as it is used in the United States. That language will expand in power and poetry with the growing power and expansion of the United States. Is it too much to prophesy, looking back at the old landmarks, that this will lead to unimaginable evolutions of art and literature?

This is what the far-seeing Provost has in mind. May success crown his plans for an Anglo-American library on Irish soil where one of the world's greatest libraries already stands. Thus he looks before.

In his looking after I am interested, too. Concerning his predilection for that sprightly fellow, Ovid, psychiatrists, who see far more than I would care to, might tell us that if the Provost had his way, and could control time and space and public opinion, he would choose to be Ovid. For this, of course, he would require to be born in imperial Rome about the time that the Emperor Augustus was becoming grandfatherly, respectable, and so censorious, and beginning to dodder. That was about the time that Ovid was rumoured to have spied on that other Julia, the Emperor's grand-daughter, as she was reclining in her bath. Yes, he would have to go back, for I cannot imagine anyone spying on a relative of anyone in power in Dublin who may be said, when allowances are made and mean things compared with great, to be in a position tantamount to that of Augustus – doddering apart. No, Siree! This ejaculation must have arisen from my subconscious. The Emperor, as is well known, banished the poet to barbarous and half-illiterate Tomi. Our censorious gaffer has gone one better: he has banished Tomi into Dublin.

But to return to Alton and Ovid. We left him spying on Julia, an action that is in direct contradiction to the advice the poet gives us in his *Ars amatoria*, 'Never spy on a woman'. I cannot see the Provost doing any such thing. He must have been inspecting the bath to assure himself that it was properly steam-heated, for I noticed his concern lest he catch cold. He has this in common with the poet: an interest in temperature.

He showed me parts of the Provost's House in which I had never been. He pointed out portraits which I had never seen. It was years since I was entertained by any Provost: admonishment cannot be called entertainment.

He demonstrated the white paint which had been applied to a Chippendale bookcase during a preceding consulate. The moral adduced was that paint could be taken as an index to taste. I remarked, 'It was *not* Mahaffy!'; and for once I was uncorrected in the Provost's house.

From the drawing-room, with its cylindrical ceiling and its columns topped with cornutes of gold, we descended to rooms below from which terraced lawns could be seen smooth-shaven and rolled, as they had been for decade upon decade. It was getting late. Soon the car would come to take us to dinner in the Phoenix Park.

From the finest example of an XVIIIth-century mansion left in the city, we drove along the slums which marked the nadir of that time. We were still in that century, in spite of electric cars, taxis and telephones. It is the mentality of a town that marks its date. I have been in prehistoric settlements which nobody has discovered in spite of their electric light. I am in the XVIIIth century still.

The Minister lives in the lesser of the two magnificent houses which were built when the English satraps ruled the land. They were built with true British soundness, and were comfortable and well proportioned, built with all the liberality which is associated with England, and which is undiminished by subject nations having to foot the bill.

The Chief Secretary's Lodge lies less than half a mile west of the Vice-regal Lodge. Though neither as large nor as well endowed with garden, lawns and ornamental water, the Chief Secretary's Lodge is commodious and comfortable. It is separated to the south by a sunk fence from a large field which is called the Fifteen Acres, though actually it is nearer 150 acres in extent. It enjoys the same view across the Liffey Valley of the Dublin mountains as the larger mansion. The Chief Secretary was any official whom the British Government of the time saw fit to rule Ireland. His appointment was political.

The Provost and I met some very pleasant people at dinner in the Lodge. How pleasant and charming or who they were, I do not think it advisable to write, because, just at this moment, while the cult is in favour of 'the Common People', pleasant and cultivated people are called 'the Ascendancy'. I have never met anyone who confessed that he was a common person, though I cannot avoid meeting many who are champions of the Common People. So it is hard to say whether or not I would like common people whom I have never met. I have met one or two who prefaced their remarks by 'speaking as a plain man; and I will admit that the role was appropriate. I don't know why they choose plainness or what prevents them from admiring the Ascendancy, who comprise the best people I have met. I know that they are called 'the Best People', but it is said derisively. Derision does not affect me (I sometimes deal in it myself). Being called a snob does not affect me; so I am quite eligible to admire the Best People.

We had a very pleasant evening. The best of Dublin in the

person of the Provost; and the best of Ireland in the person of the Minister's guests; and the best of the United States in the person of his wife and the wife of one of his guests. In the middle of the entertainment I reflected sadly how few of our citizens had the moral courage to like 'the Best People'. These are rarely dull. They never look cadaverous and offer it up to Ireland. They are always cheerful, even in adversity, because their courage is high. Like the best people in England, they cannot understand defeat. That is why I suspect they look upon the present regime as just a bore; pitiable and passing. I don't want to give them away to the head-hunters, for from them has come anything that, for the last two centuries, has redounded to Ireland's culture amid the civilisation of Europe. The head-hunters have still the same idea as the Common People had in the days when Quarles wrote:

> 'We'll drive the doctors out of doors,
>   And arts, whate'er they be,
> We'll cry both arts and learning down,
>   So, hey, then up go we!'

I don't want anyone to join this kind of ascendancy at the Best People's expense.

I left the house of the liberal and genial man who represented a great Republic.

The relation of a country's politics to the potential power of its best citizens is a theme which historians have not presented as a natural phenomenon. Yet for the greater part of the life of a constitutionally governed country and the whole life of a country suffering under a dictator the best brains have not been available to conduct the fortunes of their country. This would seem to be in the nature of things generally. It is in the nature of politics particularly. 'The inevitable tendency of the higher intelligence in all countries has been to separate itself from the practical concerns of men,' so W. K. Magee says.

Maybe this is all for the better, if not for the best. Think of what happened to Plato, one of the world's greatest intellects – sold in Ægina as a slave because he bored Dionysius the tyrant with his plan for an impossible Republic; and to come to our own day, think, if you can, what would happen to a city run by Bernard Shaw: it would be all a Convent Garden. It is not fair to expect that the best brains should represent a nation. This would leave all but kindred intelligences unrepresented. No; there must be a mediocre mind to represent what is the bulk of any nation: mediocrity. The higher the mediocrity, the better. Avoid the best, therefore, as you would eschew the worst.

Yet there were times when devotion to the common weal was the noblest aim and occupation of a nobleman's life. With the Cult of the Common People an awful fate looms over the Common People. It is that they may attempt to govern themselves. What have they to offer themselves but commonness? This they avow. The results of it in practice are as bad as the worst outrages against human liberty tyrants have perpetrated, because they may be disciplined only by 'liquidation'. But this is a lesson that may not be learned, because when the Common People become Communists they are herded and driven by their worst elements until they find themselves under a dictatorship as avaricious and as cruel as the ideals that distracted them were deceptive and destructive. It would seem as if politics have become the perquisite of certain banded vagrants who hate every evidence of civilisation and the humanities which proceed from civilisation. To politicians such as these, educated and self-disciplined persons do not appeal. These are 'the Enemies of the People'. And, in turn, the best and most liberal minds in the nation loathe and are repelled by the exhibition of narrowness and chicanery of those in power. Thus a nation is doomed to be divided and doomed to be led by its least competent and most unworthy citizens. Proof of this lies round us. Can the problem be solved? Very recent history gives a solution of the disparity between the competence of politicians and the specialised activities of devoted men. The common danger of the last war drew every American citizen into an united defence organisation in which the brains of the whole nation were pooled, regardless of personal avocations or opinions. For this, a threat to the existence of the nation is required. There was no such menace to Ireland, because England held over her subjects a protecting shield. Ireland, despite the mouthings of its politicians, has to be protected by British arms for military and economic considerations.

Another thought, probably a reaction to the pleasant evening, came to make me sad. Why is Ireland so susceptible to catchwords and demagogues? Why does she suffer aliens sometimes to take over her Government and to dictate to her, and make her resent the existence of the best citizens in the land? Yet there was a time – a time within my recollection – when the services of the most representative men of Ireland were availed of when the Senate was founded by William Cosgrave. True, it was under an agreement with Great Britain that one-quarter of the Senate was to consist of such men. This to President Cosgrave was no duress. That statesman saw clearly that no country could give an account of itself with its right hand tied behind its back. So he appointed such men as Jameson, Guinness, Lords Glenavy, Mayo, Granard, Headfort, etc., and the poet Yeats, who represented the spirit of the nation as no other man of his time could or did.

The reactionaries and the Little Irelander from foreign parts came into power, and the Senate was abolished. Then, when the Prime Minister at the time had contradicted himself sufficiently, it was established again. The nation waits until its rulers are over-ripe or rotten enough to drop off the bough. Ireland outruns its Government every ten years.

Instead of twenty-five per cent of men who had a stake in their country, there were fifty per cent of persons with outlandish names in the last Government, none of whom had any stake in the country; all of whom owe their position to fomenting hate and class hatred, farmers of grievances; all wavers of a red flag to the Brown Bull.

To find an answer to this and similar problems I had, first, to define what is meant by 'Ireland'; and then to suspend myself fairly (if I could) between the Best People and the Common Man. The result of this investigation was not comfortable. I saw the same force at work as that which turned Russia into a movable camp of slaves: the same undiscriminating pursuit of impractical ideas: the menace there and danger thereof; the imminence of that danger and its inevitability.

Absit omen.

9 — *A House in a Garden*

To restore my benignity I will go to Connemara. But I remembered Best's invitation. This will do just as well. I can postpone my departure to the Many-Coloured Land. I will go to visit Best this evening.

Best lives in 57, Upper Leeson Street, in one of those houses set far back from the highway with a garden in front and a garden at the rear. It belongs to a period when men insisted on space and privacy and life was unconfined.

He saw me as I walked up the garden path, and he opened the door before I had ascended the seven steps to the hall. The rooms on the right had the folding doors between them removed so that the rooms formed one long chamber with a view of flowering-trees and shrubs fore and aft. Laburnum and lilac leant over the path in the front garden. You could see fruit-trees flowering in the garden at the back. And the house was silent, as becomes a scholar's dwelling.

On a mantelpiece of black marble stood a Renaissance copy of the IVth century B.C. statuette of the Listening Dionysius, from the collection of the late Sir Thornley Stoker, who never tolerated anything but 'a genuine piece'.

Best's memory was better than mine; but we failed to recall an intimate name. Mrs Best in her quiet voice recalled it for us; and so the memory of old acquaintances flowed on.

'First, let me thank you for the notes you sent me of George Moore's funeral, and particularly of the funeral oration composed by Æ and delivered by you while workmen were laying Moore's ashes in the cyst. You got my version of the proceedings from Lennox Robinson? I gave him my article for you when I met him in the Waldorf Astoria in New York.'

Best hesitated a moment.

'I never got it,' he said.

I was taken aback. I had counted so much on Best getting the first copy of *Town and Country*, in which the article appeared. I was irritated. I assured Best that the last thing I did in the Waldorf was to put the magazine in Lennox's suitcase. This was early in the morning, before he set out for Europe. I apologised, and promised to write to London to ask him what he had done with it.

We talked of the eccentric funeral, and of Colonel Moore's difficulty in conducting a pagan ceremony in the middle of Catholic Mayo; and of the post-mortem pleasure George Moore must have felt (if ashes could be sentient) in putting his friends, and especially his religious brother, into such a predicament.

Lennox irritated me in another way. When I asked him when Yeats's remains were to be brought back from Cap Martin to Sligo, as he had willed, Lennox waived the question with, 'I don't see why anything should be "brought back".' Yet the French Government offered a battle-ship to carry the remains. That was an honour; and an acknowledgment of what the French thought of Yeats. More than his own countrymen, it seemed. Are we to make an exhibition of our boorishness and betray our inability to appreciate great art by not accepting this fine and generous offer of the French Government?

'Which French Government?' Lennox asked; and he went on handing out the sandwiches.

Best pondered. He had been unaware that the French had offered a battle-ship. He did not reply. He did not comment. Possibly he was wondering who would undertake the removal of the remains. I am sure that he expected nothing of the last Government. He would be right in that, for Yeats had denounced those in office and all their works shortly before he died: 'And great Art beaten down'. Anyway, I said:

'It is very hard to be angry with Lennox. He told me an amusing and characteristic story of Yeats when their friends had arranged a reconciliation between Yeats and the poet Seamus O'Sullivan. For some reason or other they had never cottoned to one another, as you know. You know, too, how Æ, in the kindness of his heart, had tried to persuade Yeats to

72

encourage the younger poet, and the answer: "Where is the wild dog which ever praised his fleas?"'

'O'Sullivan's repartee has not had such a wide publicity.'

'What was it?'

'"Where is the wild dog which ever knew its father?"'

'Probably it was tartness such as this that kept the men apart. Be that as it may, years later the day came when all was arranged. Yeats and O'Sullivan were to meet at some party in the Abbey Theatre and to be reconciled. Horace Reynolds, the author from Boston who knows more about Yeats and his writings than any Irishman, was a guest. Lennox told how that day Yeats had gone to the dentist to have a tooth extracted. But I cannot pretend to tell the story as Lennox tells it with his persuasive and unemphatic voice.'

'Do your best.'

'Lennox described how Yeats, who was to some extent an hæmophiliac, frightened the dentist by bleeding continuously after the extraction; and how the dentist put him in a bedroom upstairs, and then went out to dine and forgot about him. After dinner he suddenly remembered Yeats, who had a strange faculty for resigning himself to such circumstances, abandoned in the bedroom. He rushed back and released his patient. That explained why Yeats was very late in coming to the meeting. At last he arrived. He blinked in the light. Then he remembered the purpose of the party and, going over to *Horace Reynolds*, shook his hand and from the highest rung of his personality said, "O'Sullivan, I am glad to meet you after all these years."'

'I asked Lennox if it was put on as a pose.'

'Was it?' Best asked.

'Lennox does not think so. He attributed it to the dope or whatever it was the dentist injected.'

Best smiled quietly.

I said, 'I would like to think that it was an act. It would fit into the picture I have in mind of Yeats. But the injection gives him the benefit of the doubt.'

'Yes,' Best agreed. 'I can see Yeats resigned to being locked up in a bedroom as if it were all a part of some mystical ceremony connected with the operation: docile in the hands of the dentist.'

Before Mrs Best I could not discuss the Steinbach operation to which later Yeats 'resigned' himself without consulting anyone. The talk took a turn again to George Moore.

'By the way,' I said, 'I have a little bit of history which may serve to dispel the legend of George Moore which Susan Mitchell circulated. You know?'

'Some men kiss and tell. Some men kiss and do not tell. But Moore tells and does not kiss.'

'Yes,' I said. 'But in the light of what I have heard, all that stuff about Moore's impotence is nonsense and Susan. A lady who knew him intimately told how Moore talked with a friend a few days before her marriage. Moore said:

'"You are to be married on Wednesday? This is Friday."

'"Yes."

'"Once married, you cannot be unfaithful to your husband."

'"Of course not. What makes you think of such a thing?"

'"Because your only chance of being unfaithful is *now*."

'So that was the beginning of *The Lovers of Orelay*. And you know the rest. Her name was . . . but she is married now; and as for Orelay, there is no such place. Where the lovers met was at Avignon. I was there, and the hotel proprietor offered to show us the bedroom of the Lovers of Orelay. He was quite intrigued.

'When Moore published the story, his friend called on him. She was indignant; and she swore that she would never speak to him again.

'"When you need me," Moore said, characteristically ignoring her statement, "hum a bar of Schubert's *Tannenbaum*."

'Years after, when Moore was ill in Lady Carnarvon's Nursing Home, a stately figure dressed in black came out of his room and disappeared. George lay on his bed, which was covered with roses, and his face wore an ecstatic look. I spoke to him, and he said as one in a daze, "I have been in Paradise. I just heard a bar of *Tannenbaum*".'

Still on the subject of Moore, I remarked that Moore was

more revolted by the thought of old age than by death. He had resigned his somewhat unresignable nature to the inevitability of the latter. He refused to let the thought of it enter his mind, whereas the decay of a tooth, the greying of the hair – signs of age – repelled him. I tried to tell him how Epicurus, in his endeavour to rid men of the fear of death, said, 'While I am, death is not. When death is, I am not.' In other words, the two never meet. But Moore dismissed the subject impatiently. He hated contemplation. As for me, there is but little consolation in the Epicurean subtlety, for it's the dying that hurts.

'*Malheureusement, pour être mort, il faut mourir,*' Best added. 'Ah, there's the rub! Obviously, the best fate is to get out before you know what hit you. That is what Julius Cæsar is said to have preferred, if you believe the story that, when asked what kind of death he would choose, he answered, "A sudden one." And didn't he get it? He surely did. He lived by the sword and died by many daggers. There's something in a man's death that becomes his life, some connection between a man's greatness and the manner of his death. Who wants to die "a straw death", as the Irish called death in bed? Cæsar spent a great soul as became him: unperturbed by pain, he rebuked his faithless friend. Who could live up to him? In Shakespeare's case there was still another "rub". He was afraid that, bad as Life is, there may be something worse behind it. Awful thought! And one rendered all the more ominous because it was entertained by, so far as we know, one of the greatest intellects of all time. It is an uncomfortable thought with which to fascinate the mind, if we forget that the mind comes after birth and has as little to do with Life as the perfume, imperishable as it is, has to do with the fate of the rose-bush. The thought that if we became "abject from the spheres", as my friend the poet, Watson, phrased it, "there may be nothing to stop our fall". There is something to be said for the theory that if we have left our Golden Age behind us, we are unlikely to be steering for another Age of Gold. We may be on the downward grade *en masse*, for all we know. So let us not take a look at history, lest we think that there may be something worse coming to us and nothing to stop our decline and fall.

> 'Ay! but to die, and go we know not where;
> To lie in cold obstruction and to rot . . .
> To bathe in fiery floods, or to reside
> In thrilling region of thick-ribbed ice;
> To be imprisoned in the viewless winds,
> And blown with restless violence round about
> The pendant world: or to be worse than worst
> Of those that lawless and uncertain thoughts
> Imagine howling: 'tis too horrible!
> The weariest and most loathed worldly life
> That age, ache, penury and imprisonment
> Can lay on Nature is a paradise
> To what we fear of death.'

'Lawless and uncertain!' The Master of the Adjective!

'Shakespeare must have had a greater fear of death than anyone who is known to us, greater than Oliver Cromwell's, who feared it rightly, since he believed in eternal punishment; worse than Dr Johnson's, for Shakespeare had a mightier and intenser imagination than either. Goethe did not take it quite so badly. In one of his exuberant moments he assured himself that, "Death cannot be an evil because it is universal." But so is disease, and disease manages to be quite an evil universally. The best we can say for ourselves is that, for better or for worse (like marriage), we are all in the same boat. Perhaps that's what Goethe meant. I'm a poor philosopher. You need to be celibate to philosophise.

'Seeing that this is so, there is a lot to be said for the Friendly Brothers who remain friendly in the boat. That is why they limit and select the passengers: bores can put up with each other better than geniuses.

'My consolation is that all my forebears died; and I cannot be worse off than they are – provided we do not meet. After all, death is nothing unusual.

'Isolation and perpetual loneliness, the loneliness of an elemental, I admit would be hard to bear; but, then, one would have to be immortal to put up with it; but, seeing that gregariousness is a part of the make-up of human nature, such a fate would be outside the terms of reference, so to speak.

'Death has not got us yet, so what about using it meantime to enhance life? To me death is the turpentine in the athletes' liniment: it keeps the muscles tense. And though you can imagine life without it, it would be an unsustainable bore. In the present scheme of things, Life is quite impracticable without its scavenger.'

I was homilising too much, so I asked suddenly, 'Have you ever kept a list of the seventy-six corrections you sent George Moore?'

Best was George Moore's proof-reader, grammarian and literary adviser.

Best smiled. He thought little of his appointment as corrector of George Moore's grammar and syntax. Moore employed Atkinson and W. K. Magee as well as Best. You might think that he was one of these modern authors who are hardly more than editors of other people's brains. But Moore was more than that: he had words at his command. He could extenuate a story and, above all, he had a sense of style. Smoothness was its characteristic.

Now both smoothness and sequence are gone from the novel. The Subjective or Stream of Consciousness has been substituted. And the Subjective covers a multitude of sins. The so-called 'modern' novel appears to me to be a garbage-pail or ash-can which contains any or every cast-off remnant of living: old clothes, broken crockery, back numbers, stale food and decaying fish. I might have guessed that there was Chaos coming, for Joyce had his aerilon out and caught rumblings from Rimbaud, rumours of a revolt that cast its shadow before the revolution, and was destined to turn things topsy-turvy until hideousness took the place of beauty, and slavery the place of liberty, and discord the place of harmony, disruption the place of unity – unless the cohesion that the galvanised garbage-pail gives to its contents be considered an unity: the bucket in this instance being the Subconscious. Naturally, these 'moderns' in their obscurity were left to talk to themselves for the want of an audience. Joyce went one farther, and talked to himself in his sleep: hence *Finnegans Wake*.

The time is more or less ripe: it is the age of crossword puzzles, anthologies, detective stories and relative education; America hailed this Babel from the Berlitz schools of Europe . . .

'Americans are all detectives,' Best asserted. 'They love something that provides scope for detective work. The stupendous associations in *Finnegans Wake* must be a godsend to detectives. Particularly those who knew neither Dublin nor Joyce.'

I concurred.

'You and I would be anathema to the authorities on Joyce, because we knew him. Somebody sent me a book on Joyce and Dublin lately, written by some professor at an American college – don't forget that Æ said that you must be always on the look out for the specialist in America – with a photograph of the author. This showed a full-faced, compact-headed, alert young man. The painstaking thoroughness of his investigation was astonishing. He had consulted every street directory of Dublin of the period. He took as real, characters which were composite or mere figments of Joyce's imagination. He actually gave their addresses. Detective work, as you say; but it remined me of the Hollywood mortician who came over to measure Annie Laurie's chapel. The pity of it is that so much research and intelligence should be devoted to European will-o'-the-wisps and turned away from America, which is an inexhaustible source of inspiration.'

'Forms more real than living man,' Best quoted.

'Exactly,' I said. 'And therefore all the less vacuous.'

An investigator would be shocked to realise from our talk how little of a prophet Joyce appears to his own country-men.

Then I remembered the denunciatory poem printed on what resembled a galley-sheet that Joyce shot back at us from Flushing when he arrived in Holland. Printed abroad it was, as the quotation marks beneath and not above words showed.

'Surely you were not exempted from his indignation? You must have been included in *The Holy Office*, rhymed pentameters on a galley sheet?' I asked.

'It was *Gas from a Burner* that was on a galley sheet. *The Holy Office* was in two columns instead of the one column of *Gas from a Burner.*'

'That's the one I got. It was burned with my house. What did you do with yours?' I asked eagerly.

'I tore it up,' said Best.

'I was a recipient of *Gas from a Burner*, his invective against "Maunsell's publisher", who would not print *Dubliners* for fear of giving offence to the King.'

'Was it offensive?'

'Not at all. Joyce wrote to the King. His secretary wrote back saying that His Majesty took no interest in such matters. Both letters are published in the Preface to *Dubliners*. The publisher was pilloried in *Gas from a Burner*, and the rest of us in the first epistle, the one I am looking for. Magee was derided as one who would not

> "His hat unfix
> Either to pint or crucifix."

I was

> "One whose conduct seems to own
> A preference for a man of tone."

The man of tone was Trench, whom he called "Haines" in *Ulysses*. I wish I could find my copy now, but it was destroyed by the bandits who burned my house.'

'I tore up my copy,' repeated Best.

And then our interest turned to Best's pictures, of which he had a nice collection of the best-known Irish artists, from Nathaniel Home to Jack Yeats.

We went upstairs to inspect the pictures. I can recognise a Home anywhere; and a Jack Yeats. I am not so sure of the others, for my knowledge of painting is almost as wanting as my knowledge of music. I much prefer to see an armchair in a room than a piano.

'This is my Abigail Mosser,' Best said, 'and it is one of the finest of my pictures.'

That I could see. The drawing was exquisite, particularly the drawing of the eyelids of the girl, some French sitter she found in Paris.

'She painted a lot of portraits: everybody of her time, and that was pretty long. She must have been ninety-six when she died. She used to say, "Let me sit with my back to the light so that I may pass for ninety-three." She might be still living, but that she foresaw an increase in succession duty. She offered to paint me. I refused.'

'Why?' asked Best.

'One thing deterred me. Some of her sitters came to a bad end – hanging and that sort of thing. Take the case of Sir Roger Casement. She painted him, and what happened . . .?'

But my remarks were out of keeping with the tone of that peaceful house.

It was nearly eleven o'clock when we parted. The evening was still an evening. Darkness had not come on to bring with it night. I turned to the left by the canal and passed the lock gate off which Professor Reynolds fell and saved himself by anticipating the superfluous summons to 'Hauld on!' from the jarvies on the bridge.

The lock gates were not more worn than they were thirty years ago. There were no more rope rings cut into the wooden bollards, and the long handles of the gates were still sound enough to take your weight when you sat on them. Through one of the sluices the water rushed in a white cascade. How blessed is Dublin in its waterways and its silences, through which you can hear the noise of rural water! And how happy it is in that interesting people live within easy reach of one another to the traveller on foot!

Thinking thus, I returned home and to bed.

10 — *The Dublin–Galway Train*

It's a great thing to catch a train!

There are few running in Ireland now compared to what there were before we won our freedom, in which freedom, freedom from easy transport was apparently included. But enough of that! Here I am in the ten-fifteen bound for Galway, the capital of one of the Four Provinces, Connaught. I take care to choose a seat by the window on the right facing the engine, because that will give me a view of the now-disused Royal Canal. The railway company bought it up to avail itself of its levels, so now it lies free from the slow barges that used to be drawn by a mule with trailing rope, a long avenue of water lined by old elms.

For the first few miles I will be like one of those Chinese travellers who never write of the incidents or the inconveniences of their journeys; and they must have been much more irksome there than here.

I will not look out of the window at the dome of the Custom House when we are crossing the Liffey, because I will be travelling on the Loop Line bridge; and I do not want the old anger I felt at the men who permitted the city to be defaced by that eyesore to arise again. There won't be a word out of me until we reach Clonsilla, where the canal comes into view. We will pass by many a village with a lovely Gaelic name just like the one I have just mentioned, Clonsilla, The Meadow of the Willow Trees. Whoever lived in it is forgotten. Only the memory of his cell remains.

'Where are you going, sir?'

'Cootehill,' I replied unthinkingly.

The ticket collector stood in the doorway with something shining metallically half hidden in his right hand. He looked at me quizzically, then laughed.

'First stop, Liffey Junction,' as I extended my ticket. 'His nibs the stationmaster told me to take care of you.' He jerked his head over his shoulder. Much to my relief, he smiled. A breezy, good-natured fellow.

'Tell him you did take care of me. Do you expect a full train?'

'There's days they come and days they go. What moves them there's no tellin'; an excursion, maybe. But then again I've seen her half empty during an excursion. There's one thing certain: there's more going than coming.'

'Emigration to England?' I suggested.

'And why wouldn't they go? Good wages; and they don't have to be in before dark.'

'But if this emigration goes on, what will become of the Irish Nation?' I asked anxiously.

'I wouldn't mind that. There's plenty of English coming in; we are just exchanging populations.'

And a good thing, too, I reflected.

He turned my ticket upside down. After a careful scrutiny he punched it, then continued lightheartedly with a sigh:

'Never fear! They'll come back here to die. Ireland's a great burial-ground.'

Two young men with shining faces and Roman collars made of rubber came into the carriage, not emigrants they, but immigrants to the great theological college called Maynooth, by the side of the Royal Canal. They took seats beside each other, and one of them handed the collector tickets for two. He punched them reverently. Another pair of clergymen arrived; with them a broad-faced lieutenant of the US Navy. He had brown eyes widely separated over full, sunburnt cheeks that told of sun on the Pacific. It took the three some time to settle. At last they were seated with the lieutenant between them. They gazed at the two students, and their smiles died away.

The shouts outside ceased. We started. Silence settled on the compartment. Behind my magazines I tried to discover what was the 'deep determinant' that made me mention 'Cootehill'. One of the priests produced a little book, changed over and sat beside me, and began to move his lips.

I retreated into the Subconscious as the train crossed the

Liffey. Soon steep walls confined us: we were passing along the deep cut by Whitworth Road. Above our heads on the left was Mountjoy Gaol and the Royal Canal. Soon I saw a large round tower built of cut stone. It was much larger than any other round tower in the land, a copy, revealing, in spite of its size, the poverty of imagination in those who planned it to mark the tomb of Daniel O'Connell, the Emancipator and founder of the cemetery. Innovations were the cut stones and the surmounting cross: Glasnevin Cemetery, a great burial-ground!

If extension in size alone were to be taken as a sign of originality, surely that mild looney, Endymion, must be handed the palm for his invention of an ocean liner three thousand miles long; but they have not yet built one to cross the Atlantic instantaneously. The tallest round tower in the country takes its place to shorten Dan O'Connell's passage to Heaven.

At last the long water began.

Mile after mile the train went on. A lock appeared, a very deep lock, 'The Deep Sinking', the last, perhaps, before the long level across the centre of the country. Beside it stood the cottage of the lock-deeper, to whom life must be leisurely now, as by day he waits for barges that never come, and by night lies listening to the sound of water pouring over the gates or flowing through one of the open sluices. I wondered what lore is his: what tells him to open a sluice in the gate or when to let the water overflow; and what tales he tells to magnify the canal and increase his own importance. It would take a good shanachie to give significance to it now.

His wife came to the door with a cloth in her hand. Three bare-legged children with morning faces dodged past her skirts and lined up to salute the train, the train that had deprived the canal of any business and had given their parents long leisure to dally and produce. Strange, is it not, that out of idleness comes the greatest feat of creation in the world? So the children stood and saluted the compensating train, that, though it took many adults away, yet enabled those who were left to make up for their loss.

What a pleasant sight is a white-washed cottage with its roof of warm thatch; with its half door, little windows and deep eaves! How restful is the spell of it! How he who is borne past it longs to stop and remain! The outside has such allure that the pilgrim never thinks of the darkness within and the cramped space. So, too, it is with a yacht. The *Shamrock* showed her emerald hull and her gleaming copper keep as she cut the azure water, heeling over on a tack. White as the wing of a turning gull, her lofty wing of canvas spread: lovelier without than on deck, where all is bustling and alert; and where the canvas is more a concern than a joy forever. What constitutes the spell of a cottage nestling in the folds of the hills or standing by the long and lonely canal? Nothing but the promise of something stable in the flux, some straw to catch at as we hurtle on.

The more you regard the things outside, the less you become conscious of your journey. The moving panorama occupies your mind: so much so that you do not notice your passage until the terminus is reached. On the other hand, if you do not look out of the window, but fix your attention only on that which is in the carriage, you are not conscious of movement at all.

There are places on this earth where time seems to be speeded up and to pass more quickly than in others. One of these places is the city of New York, where the moon appears to take a week only to slide through all its phases. Other places there are; one of them is Ireland, where from crescent to full and to crescent again it takes a lunar month. Therefore life seems longer in Ireland than in America, though the proportion of centenarians is almost the same in either country. In America even a toothache would be welcome to arrest you and to make you think of your own individuality, to hold you for a moment in the swirl. There are more stabilisers than toothaches in Ireland: two of them were with me in the train. They teach that man should turn his thoughts inwardly and contemplate eternity, which is the cessation of motion, and so save himself from the transience of time. I get somewhat the same results by gazing at the long canal that is always the same:

one unchanging length of lilied water, no matter where you are.

This must be the reason why my Subconscious always chooses a seat on the right in my journey to the West.

But what will explain the recurring vision that comes to me more than once or twice within a season of a pool of water crystal clear, at the bottom of which a little fish lies over the sand with his fins moving transparently, while beyond the pool a tiny waterfall trickles? I know, of course, that this, in the view of the psychologists or psychiatrists, is very significant and very ominous. To them water is a symbol of the most discreditable significance . . . . Water is more than the symbol of Time made manifest. Oh, no. It is something far more compromising – something *endo-psychic*, in fact.

Whatever it stands for, the long canal of pellucid water takes its place now.

Over the Plain of Nooth white clouds spread wide and high. The two young men in the rubber collars rose and, awkward with embarrassment, begged leave to be excused while they reached over the other passengers' heads for their modest luggage. With an inarticulate murmur they withdrew.

Immediately the priest nearest to me became voluble and said to the naval lieutenant, opposite to him, 'I heard a good one at Father Caffrey's last night.'

The priest beside him nudged the abstracted lieutenant to listen.

The lieutenant came to life and asked, 'When do we come to Mullingar?'

His companion, pointing to the priest beside me, said, 'Father Paddy has a good one for you.'

This brought the lieutenant to attention.

'Spill it,' he said.

The narrator drew a silken ribbon down his book to mark the page and said, 'Father Caffrey – but it would be a bit before your time – told us of two old women having an argument during the Eucharistic Congress which was held in Dublin. It seems that the poor people – and they're full of devotion, God be praised – were vying with each other as to who would have the best decorations in their windows to celebrate the Congress. One woman, we'll call her Mrs Durkin, was showing no decorations at all. She was beginning to be the talk of the neighbours – she lived in Upper Dominick Street: you wouldn't know it. It's one of the poorer parts of Dublin. You might call it one of the slums. It's falling into decay, anyhow. Well, at long last, late one evening, what do two of her old cronies see but a picture – they were all hanging out holy pictures – a picture leaning out of Mrs Durkin's top front. The two old ones on the street below looked at one another and then took another look at Mrs Durkin's picture. After a good gaze, Mrs Kennedy, we'll call her, says to her companion, Mrs Cassidy:

'"It's St Joseph, be Jingo." Only it wasn't "be Jingo"; but, now mind you, they mean no harm by it – but the Holy Name. "It's St Joseph! be all that's holy," says she.

'Mrs Cassidy has a good squint.

'"That's no St Joseph," says she. "St Joseph has a trim beard – but St Patrick. I know him as well as Cassidy himself."

'"Ye must be losing yer sight, Mrs Cassidy. It can't be St Patrick, for St Patrick's beard goes down to his belt," says Mrs Kennedy.

'So they argued and argued, and were beginning to fight, when who comes out but Durkin from one of the licensed premises, that's what we call a saloon – and they turned to him and one says, "Mr Durkin," she says, "Mrs Cassidy and me were wondering who the saint is in your wife's holy picture up there in the top front. I says it's St Joseph. She says it's St Patrick."

'"It's neither," shouts Durkin, waving his fists. "But a better man than either. That's Charles Stewart Parnell!"'

It was perhaps too topical for the naval man. He smiled vaguely, but that was undoubtedly due to the fact that Fr Paddy had raised his voice to a pitch of indignation when imitating Mr Durkin's challenging assertion.

'I didn't get to bed until after four this morning,' he remarked. 'You would think that if it takes six hours for a hundred miles, it would pay the Company to put a restaurant car on the train.'

'We'll be at Mullingar in no time,' Fr Paddy assured him.

The lieutenant turned his wrist and looked at his watch. He closed his eyes.

'Hold it now and listen to this.'

His companion beside him said, 'There was a fellow from a parish not a thousand miles from here who met a girl in London and married her in a registry office. His sister got to hear of it, and she was indignant at an unreligious marriage like that: and why shouldn't she? He came over here with the young lady, and they stopped in a hotel in Galway: wait till you come to Galway, and you'll never want to go anywhere else. His brother started to call on them, and he said as much to the sister. The idea didn't appeal to her at all; but seeing that her brother had made up his mind, at last she says, "If you must go, on no account let on you know that the woman he's living with is his wife."'

The lieutenant went blank.

Fr Paddy explained, 'That's the way they look on it here.'

At last the train stopped. The 'Square Mill' – in another word, 'Mullingar' – had at last been reached. Many doors flew open, and a crowd rushed back towards the railway refreshment-room. In a moment there was a crowd four deep in front of the bar. Tea was handed out in containers. Bottles of Guinness reached those on the platform who could not fit themselves into the huddle in front of the bar.

There would be fourteen minutes for no apparent reason unless to give the passengers time to refresh themselves at a counter far too short to accommodate the occupants of one coach. The lieutenant emerged from the refreshment-room and was directed to a door marked 'Fir'. The translation underneath read, 'Gentlemen'. 'Ladies' was in English. Could it be that there was no equivalent for 'Ladies' in Gaelic?

I was still protected by my Subconscious when he returned. He smiled all around him. As the train started he took his seat with increasing smiles.

The cement wall enclosing the disused track for horse- and

dog-racing was slowly receding. It caught the lieutenant's undimmed eyes. It reminded him of something he was trying to recall. The clergyman beside me opened his breviary. Silence settled only to be broken by the lieutenant saying:

'I got something in the Dolphin last night. But it wouldn't be in your line, as you don't play horses; besides it's not until the Derby the year after this; and who knows where I'll be then? It's a tip about a yearling owned by – I don't know Irish, so I can't remember the name; but the owner appears to be the leader of the local Brains Trust. I wish I had written both names down. The horse is Pat, Pat something; but what's the use?'

Evidently there was none.

Fields in need of drainage spread on both sides. Here and there a substantial house of stone appeared. The reverend gentleman beside me closed his breviary and borrowed one of my magazines. At Moate the train stopped, but no doors were opened.

'Moate?' the lieutenant inquired.

The man beside him said:

'There's a great tumulus here – one of the biggest in the country. From it the town takes its name. In Ireland they call all the tumuli "moats".'

'Is there a moat around them?'

'Oh, no.'

'Then why are they called moats?'

No answer.

The second clergyman said:

'They get their name probably from the Norman word "motte", meaning a mound. There are many words of Norman French derivation that have passed into the language. The Normans were there longer than is realised. There are some of them here still; that is, their names – family names – are here. They are "more Irish than the Irish themselves", as the saying is. Your own name is an example. "Burke" was once "de Burgho".'

The lieutenant was all alert.

So his name is 'Burke'.

The expanse of the River Shannon shone as we crossed it hard by Athlone, the Ford of Luan. The hydro-electric installation on the river was compared unfavourably with the harnessing of Niagara. The politics that made it a failure on the Canadian side and a success on the American were expounded. The lieutenant saw that the magnitude of the work was too much for his audience, who did not like the Shannon to take a second place to any river, seeing that it was bigger than any river in England. After relapsing into silence for some minutes, he inquired:

'Is there a refreshment-room at Athenry?'

Neither of the reverend gentlemen could say. But one congratulated the naval man on the way he could remember a map. Another pause, and one of them said (the 'refreshment-room' must have reminded him):

'You were telling of that fellow with a hang-over in Boston. Well, here's one of a fellow who goes into an Irish pub. He was in a shocking condition.

'"For God's sake give me a cure," he calls to the barman.

'"D'ye think this is Lourdes?" the barman asks, after one look at him.'

The lieutenant's smile was puzzled.

'Nothing short of a miracle would have been any use to him,' Fr Paddy explained.

But at Athenry, the Ford of the Kings, the refreshment-room – if you could believe the guard – was over the bridge at the other side of the station; and there was only a minute's wait.

My seat was getting so hot and irksome that it ousted my Subconscious, which was motivated by the pressure of my body on the seat. Just in time!

'More and more,' I found myself repeating as I looked at the great square castle of Oranmore.

I left Dublin to recover my peace of mind only to find that the relaxation or suppression of the influences of the will which had inhibited my stream result in this suspicious word-association. Can't I even relax in a railway carriage but I must be pursued by endo-psychic existence?

There is not the least doubt about it, I am fast becoming a

case for Al Robitesk, Mayer, Wundt or Ferenczi. And to think of it: there is not yet a doctor in Galway with a name alien enough to be alienist enough for me! When they hear what an opening there is for them they will all slip into a country where any of them may wind up by becoming Prime Minister. Sean Robitesk, Seumas Mayer or Eamonn Wundt. All they require is an Irish-given name. No prophet in Ireland is a countryman.

Was it because I had sat on my Subconscious so long that I was compelled to say 'More and more' for Oranmore? If so, what are the complicated psychic influences that compelled me to say it? 'Oranmore: more and more!' I see it all now. I have found myself out: I have been liberated from the Subconscious by the Conscious. I may be going a bit bats. But where's Stekel? Where's Hitschman? Where's Bleuler? There's only Dr Bob MacLaverty in Galway who can explain and sublimate my mistake about Oranmore; and he's Professor of Obstetrics to the University, and that makes me feel all the more shy. Anyway, there's nothing for it but to confess to him that a young lady of my acquaintance has bought Oranmore Castle and is doing it up with power, light, hot and cold water and all modern conveniences; more and more! If the doctor will permit me, I will call on the lady to see how she is getting on in Oranmore.

I heard someone saying to the lieutenant: 'Yes, this is Galway. And why would you want to go farther? Why should anyone want to go farther? There is no farther to go.'

Why should anyone want to go farther than Galway? Why indeed?

Galway is the gossip capital of Ireland. It is not without significance that the statue in its principal Square should be that of a shanachie or story-teller. The citizens know (sometimes beforehand) what is happening in every county, and lack of information neither limits nor diminishes the tale. Therefore it came as no surprise to me to learn that I was expected. It used to surprise me to hear that I was welcome until I realised that that was but a figure of speech, an exordium indispensable to conversation.

You do not altogether leave Dublin by crossing the island to its western side, but you leave a great deal of bitterness and acrimony behind. Personalities take the place of politics in Galway. The first citizen of Galway was Morty Mor – Big Martin – who died a little while ago. Never did the Gaelic language record a death more majestically in three fateful words,

MORTY MOR MORB.

It had the language of Rome behind it, in which each word can fall like a stroke of fate. It is not as unbecoming as it would seem to talk of a dead man in a town where there are so many living persons about, because in Galway, as in China, the dead are more important than the living, so that a friendly reminiscence is enough to recall them from oblivion.

Morty Mor McDonough was big-headed and very tall. He dressed in black, for, since clergymen wear it, black commands respect; and as the greatest employer in the town, respect was his due. His character was as great as his power: he could talk up to the other men in black, and there was no cowing him. His rheumy eyes gazed slowly at you as he made up his mind. He was loyal to Galway town, the City of the Tribes, so loyal that he resented the visit of two missioners from Meath who came to collect for what they called the Maynooth Mission to China. They were astonished to find themselves refused. Conscious of power, they became insistent and brusque. Morty Mor spoke.

'I will not subscribe to a Maynooth Mission to China; but *I will subscribe* to a Chinese Mission to Maynooth to teach you manners.'

It was a new conception: a Chinese Mission to the great theological college of Maynooth or to anywhere at all! The Chinese do not send missions to proselytise 'foreign devils'. That is why it came as an original suggestion from Morty Mor. Suppose that the suggestion were to be adopted. How wonderful it would be if a sampan from China were to berth in the Liffey and its cargo of bonzes to come ashore and to proceed in a barge up the quiet waters of the Royal Canal to Maynooth! If they were not first subjected to a reception by the President and an urine analysis, their progress would be one serene procession in their reconditioned barge or houseboat. With what dignity would they acknowledge the salutations of the aborigines who would wave them on with cheers of encouragement on their unprecedented journey. With what gravity would they await, with hands hidden in their robes, the inrush of water that would raise them up to higher levels in the locks until, at last, the mule, garlanded and with harness decorated, would draw them westward through the long reach to the wall of Maynooth. How they would admire that wall, impassively comparing it with the wall of the Forbidden City that held the Old Buddha before the rising of the Boxers undid her. And then the reception in the *aula maxima* in Maynooth: yellow and purple; bonze, bishop and acolytes in one glory of double imperial dyes; the Imperial yellow of the Middle Empire and the purple of Imperial Rome!

Those introductions:

'T'as Yuan Ming from the Temple of the Haunted Dragon by the Peak of the Celestial Pool meet Dr Cod, Bishop of Ferns.' 'Ma Tu Fang from the Pavilion of Shining Truth by the

River of White Jade – Dr Scanlan.' (Afar off, voices singing, 'Hurry to bless the hands that play.')

It was so convincing, albeit a vision, that I began to detect a Chinese influence in the deportment of the Galway divines: a sedateness and weight, an *embonpoint* and amplitude, that endowed them with a ceremonious courtesy that had something in it of the Middle Kingdom.

I did not come to Galway to dream of China; and far be it from me to teach manners or anything else. I will turn my face to the South when the time comes, comforted by the thought that I never had a pupil.

What a town Galway is, beside its rippling, abundant river, swan-laden, salmon-full! The Corrib must be one of the largest rivers in the world for its length, which cannot be more than a mile or two. It used to turn many a mill. Its canalised waterways are there today, green-haired with weeds and overgrown; but as crystal clear as when they first rushed to the sea from Lough Corrib and Lough Mask.

If the mayor had any taste he would cut the weeds from the river-banks and let even wild roses, that ask for no gardener, take their place; and he would strictly forbid plastering with cement the faces of houses that owe their proportions to the influence of Spain, houses of cut stone that had large, oblong windows centuries before England emerged from half-timbered, casement-lit cottages. The few remains of historical houses owe their preservation to a priest who cherished history in stone. Now the stones are painted over and any travelling circus can hire Eyre Square.

All my wishes are fulfilled; but if I had one more wish it would be that I might be mayor of Galway even for one year – Galway, a cleaner Venice, with living water in place of the brackish, stagnant canals! The men who built those Galway houses with gardens giving on the mill-races felt the beauty that water has and its power to inspire. The sides of the mill-races now are filled with whatever rubbish lies out of reach of the stream. You need not be a landscape-gardener to see what a town of enchantment Galway could be made were its many water-courses to be lined with lilac, laburnum, woodbine and hawthorn; especially hawthorn, which is exempt from vandalism because it is unlucky to bring it into a house. These bushes would cost nothing or next to nothing to plant; and they would have a double bloom in the long Spring, a bloom above and a bloom reflected. The streets are clean; why should the banks of the clear streams be left as witnesses to the tolerance for ruin which seems to lie in the character of the Irish nowadays?

What has obsessed the Irishman with thanatophilia – this love of death, decadence and decay? The toleration of eyesores is its outward sign. Even the farmer, when he has prospered and moves to a larger house, leaves the old sheiling to rot and deface the landscape with its gable angles rising against the sky.

Spanish Arch must have been the sea-gate of Galway town. It abuts the river. Beyond it lies nothing but a few nondescript cottages and the empty dock. Its watch-tower is half gone, but the arch and one closed-up beside it are still strong.

So Clare Sheridan, the sculptor, has bought both the arch and the houses next to it. She plans to have a hanging garden on the top of the arch overlooking the rushing water. Her niece, Shane Leslie's only daughter, Anita, is restoring, not far away, the strong castle of Oranmore, the fortress that guarded the approach by 'the Great Shore' to Galway from the south.

This is not the first of the old XIVth-century castles to be rescued from utter dilapidation in Galway. Yeats restored the castle at Ballylee close to Coole Park. He called his keep Thor Ballylee, because he thought that 'castle' was somewhat ostentatious, although every large dwelling of stone built in Ireland before Cromwell came with his bible and his Black and Tans was called a castle.

Yeats was well aware of this toleration of ruin in the heart of the native. He knew that they would preserve nothing if left to themselves. He knew that out of their perpetual preoccupation with the past came a desire to make all grandeur portion and parcel of that Past. Therefore he composed the lines to be engraved on a stone of the door of his tower, praying,

'May these characters remain
When all is ruin once again.'

So why all this pother about ornamenting a town? The answer is obvious. In it lies the difference between beauty and ugliness, between grandeur and meanness, between cleanliness and dirt. A beautiful place engenders sentiments of pride and affection in the hearts of those who inhabit it. This gives rise to stability and to patriotism. Conversely, they who dwell in squalor, deprived of beauty, have nothing in their souls but a reflex of that squalor, discontent and hatred for all things lovely and pleasant. In this tragedy lies, and the road to rebellion until Squalor sits enthroned: all this in Ireland, the wealthiest country in the world.

Into Oranmore Castle builders are bringing baths and basins and hot and cold water. Electric power and light are already laid on. Great cisterns collect water from the slightly domed roof. Walls are being plastered and panelled. Even the dungeon or prison on the third floor which took a small boy weeks to clear of rubbish, in which a baby's skeleton was found, is being repaired.

Maybe this and other restorations are the result of the scarcity of houses. Whatever be the cause, it is something to be grateful for that people of taste are giving an example of what can be done in a town that has the enviable endowment of ancient walls and waters running beneath them – everything for its inhabitants but the eye to see.

I took tea with some friends. I soon discovered that there was much that I had missed in Galway. Apparently I had been thinking only of its natural advantages that could make it one of the loveliest towns on earth. Little did I realise that already it was a Cytherea, a shrine where Venus was worshipped. I thought that I knew the history of Galway. I had read Hardiman and studied the report of the Commissioners who were appointed to preserve its archives. But the enactments touching Venus only referred to fines for those citizens who permitted their houses to become houses of assignation for friars. It was all so long ago that I discounted it as accurate history. But though the friars who dealt in such real estate were long dead, from what I was now told I judged that the reign of an obscure Venus was flourishing still. At last I exclaimed:

'But if such things go on, how does society hold together in the daytime?'

I did not intend to expostulate or to appear incredulous. I merely wondered how such things could be kept clandestine in such a small town. I had often wondered how Anne Boleyn, Shakespeare, Mistress Fitton, Kit Marlowe, Ben and the rest of the boys 'got away with it', so to speak, where the houses were half-timbered and everyone knew the neighbour's business. The answer was now apparent: they didn't get away with anything. There were always intelligent observers about. So the beauty that I longed to see by the canals and river is hidden in the boudoirs of the town. It was a consolation in a way, but a way that was questionable.

While I was occupied with such thoughts as these, my hostess asked:

'Did you hear about the retreat for women?'

And I had been thinking that, by her account, their bedrooms were their retreats. But I was wrong! 'Retreat', in the sense in which the word was used, meant a religious meeting to hear sermons, to examine conscience, and to pray.

'I heard nothing about the Retreat.'

How could I? I was only just arrived.

'Oh, you must hear it. It was advertised for weeks: "*Women only*. On the 4th there will be a retreat for women; and sermons on the Sacrament of Matrimony".'

'Weren't all the men aching with curiosity to find out what the sermons would be like?'

She smiled complacently; then she went on:

'Well, the great day, or rather evening, came round at last. Every woman, including Mrs Dunne, that could get out, was there to hear a Franciscan Father preaching. Now, Mrs Dunne came from the Claddagh, and she had eight children, including ones that she was nursing, so it was no easy matter for her to leave the house. Anyway, she took the baby under her shawl and off with her to the Retreat. She was a bit late when she arrived and the sermon was in full blast. God help me! I shouldn't say that. But you know what I mean. The preacher had got himself worked up.'

The lady laughed so much at this point that my curiosity, inert for the most part about Retreats, was aroused. At last she was able to continue.

'Well, Mrs Dunne got in and found a place by the door. She listened for a minute to the sermon on Holy Matrimony and then said fervently as she turned to go: "I wish to God I knew as little about it as that fellow".'

I thought of the white swans stemming the Corrib and waiting for a word from the Franciscans of comfort to the birds.

With such things to concern them indoors, is it any wonder that there is apathy among the citizens regarding the appearance of their town?

12 — 'Going West on my Journey'

The jolting of the crowded bus brought up fond memories of
the Broadstone Railway Station in Dublin with its colonnade
of Ionic pillars built high above the level town. If there had
been no preceding architecture of the kind, the Broadstone
Station would have been the loveliest building in the world,
provided, of course, that no other contemporary building of
similar design existed. The Broadstone is altered now, like
many other good and stately things. It is a bus station. The
excuse, of course, was economy and, of course, that
inseparable carrot, efficiency. Look at the result: a sea-sick bus-
full of disgruntled passengers, and the broken bridges and the
ripped-up metals of the railway – uncertainty of travel and
certainty of delay. You pay for first-class tickets abroad to end
in the commune of a bus.

When the Athenians juggled the cash that the trusting Allies
deposited in the island of Delos, Athens was beautified. The
Parthenon was the result. Relatively a thousand times more
money has poured into Dublin lately since the ruination of the
railways than ever ancient Athens knew. The Hospital Sweep
has brought in hundreds of millions, some of which are spent
on hospitals, sanatoria, lunatic asylums and convalescent
homes – buildings that have a hint of medical philanthropy –
but not a red cent is spent on that which is as justifiably medical
as the hospitals: prophylaxis against disease by means of slum-
clearing and clean houses. It might be thought by some
archæologist or historian, if such be found, to take sufficient
interest in this trough between waves of culture, that the
hospital was the thing, and not the cure.

Millions will not beautify Dublin, any more than the
thousands subscribed did honour to O'Connell, simply
because culture, good taste, has been scorned 'and great art
beaten down'. So better build a few dozen more sanatoria and

coughing-stations to receive the casualties of the slums; but hands off the slums that produce such a prosperous harvest of hospitals without one colonnaded masterpiece among them all.

The bus jolted along. A woman beside me congratulated me on getting a seat. There were many people left behind. Would there be an auxiliary bus for them, or would they be left to stay the night in Galway town? She could not say; but I could, for I was forced, for the lack of bus accommodation not very long ago, to spend a night in the Railway Hotel. I was about to send a telegram to the President to put his Rolls-Royce or whatever car he favours at the disposal of myself and half a dozen benighted travellers, until I cooled and consoled myself by the thought that a night in Galway, in spite of its early-to-bed proclivities, was not such a hardship. The Manager of the buses explained the shortage by the sale of one hundred buses to Northern Ireland. Another effort to 'bring in the North'? He thought that I was wrong when I suggested that it was the late Government's way of encouraging tourist traffic: 'Not an inch.' And years ago you could reach Dublin in five hours. Now it may take two days.

The names of the places to which the buses go are printed in Gaelic. Native speakers cannot read Gaelic, but they interpret it by interrogating the conductor or the driver.

A landscape drenched after rain spread to the right and left. I remarked to the man beside me, 'It's rather unseasonable weather for this time of year.'

'Sure, it isn't this time of year at all,' he announced.

Where else but in Connemara can you meet a man living in the Fourth Dimension and yet riding in a bus? He is travelling: so Space denies Time.

On the left one far-off conical hill broke the long monotony. We passed a ruined castle or keep that stood solitary by the side of the road. It told of a lake or marshes that were drained, for it could not have defended any road now, so open was the ground. Stone walls demarking fields and drainage ditches were passed, proof of generations of toiling men who worked to reclaim land, the yield of which their landlords enjoyed –

sometimes. There were no landlords now; their places are taken by the Land Commission and the nameless legion of attorneys who own Ireland instead.

The ruins of Ross Abbey appeared on the left. Lough Corrib could not be far away, for the friars who built such abbeys loved the lakes or river which provided them with fish. Ross Abbey, with its square tower in the middle like that of Kilconnell near Aughrim, stood roofless. We were nearing Headfort, where the bus would stop and some of its occupants alight and relieve the congestion. The charm of Headfort consists in its being only seven miles from Cong. Bright-roofed, pleasant cottages cheered the scenery. There is little misery in the country; misery resides in the slums.

If there were no towns larger than Galway, there would be no slums. Galway has a population of nineteen thousand; and that is about the maximum a town should have. When the towns of the future are broken up and replaced by satellite villages to limit the devastating power of the weapons of modern war, there will be many Galways in the world. What a pleasant world that will be, although it will lack Galway's limpid streams.

I thought of the difficulty of moving crowded populations. The present system of emigration leaves too much nostalgia in the hearts of those removed. The solution is to remove self-contained portions of cities, for every city has villages within it such as the Chelseas of London and New York. People become homesick because their social life is uprooted: they miss the gossips of home. In other words, they miss the scandals of their home towns. Therefore, when founding a colony overseas, it is necessary to move the chatterboxes, the barbers and the dentists; for no man worth his salt will take his scandals vicariously on the movies and such-like substitutes.

Limpid streams! Was there ever a village more endowed with running water than the village of Cong? The name comes from the Gaelic 'Cunga', meaning a neck, for it is situated on the neck of land between the lakes of Mask and Corrib which a subterranean river joins. The Local Government Board, in the days when the British ran the country, cut a canal to enable boats to ply between the two large lakes.

The time came when the canal was finished and it was ready to be 'opened' by the leading members of the Local Government and other philanthropists. The waters of Lough Mask rushed in – and disappeared! The region was limestone, and the waters went to join the subterranean river which had been formed æons ago by the action of the acidulated waters on the limestone. Even the water went underground as a protest against British domination in those days; and yet the British yoke was mild compared with the acid infiltration of some of those in office since. In the old days anyone with a friend in court could, by assiduous drinking, drink himself into the Local Government Board. Now everything is dry: canal and all. And Sir Henry Robinson, who preferred good manners to go-getting, is dead.

Grey mill walls diagonalled by ivy rise from placid waters overgrown by lilies and flowering waterplants. Broken weirs and sluices show where the mill-wheels were. Under leaning woods, the escaping streams run free. Woods! 'They haven't got rid of all the gentlemen yet.' Lord Ardilaun planted the woods when he built Ashford Castle at the head of Lough Corrib. He must have employed the same architect as did Michael Nugent.

Cong, with its caves and subterranean river and many fountains, is the site of the Abbey where the remains of Roderick O'Connor, the last King of Ireland, rested for seven years until they were reinterred in Clonmacnoise. In Cong was the famous cross of Cong, a processional cross curiously wrought and marvellously designed. As an example of goldsmiths' craft it is one of the wonders of the world.

Into the bus an angler in the uniform of an angler came with his net and rod. Evidently he was an Englishman, because he was looking for someone with whom to talk. This is directly opposite to the accepted picture of the self-contained, tacit Englishman; but you should meet one on fishing bent in a foreign country such as Ireland where he is revered. Then he loosens himself in – sometimes, but not always – condescending speech. If we have accepted the exception he represents to the stage Englishman of the Dr Livingstone legend, more's the pity that he cannot see that all Irishmen are not stage Irishmen derived from Cruikshank in the pages of *Punch*. And he should be the last to talk of dirt, seeing that the bath was introduced into England only after the return of the Anglo-Indians who took one as a refuge from the heat, whereas the so-called Turkish bath was well patronised in Dublin long before Warren Hastings was impeached. However!

Is there anything more annoying than the famous question, 'Do you believe in fairies?' – a question usually asked with a hint of condescension? What makes such a question obnoxious is the logic of the questioner and the imputation in the word 'belief' with all its undistributed meanings. Added to this, there is the deep conviction within you that all such matter-of-fact people are utterly incapable of understanding what the instinct is, or the gift whereby the water diviner, for instance, is enabled to find water, or the unsophisticated poet to reach the general heart, or the man or woman who is 'fey' to see fairies. This conviction causes you to resent such factual people; you feel a resistance and you sense a lack of sympathy. You know that they would catch a butterfly in a rat-trap or use a gauger's rod to sound the procreant omnipotence of the unconscious mind.

Such inquisitorial people are frequently found. They have only a limited time to hear an answer to their question and neither time nor attention to hear you out, if you are foolish enough to answer. Their minds are already made up, and they cannot get out of them.

My way of dealing with such a question is to retort with another question. When they repeat, 'Do you believe in fairies?' I ask, 'What, here?' I will admit that this is too disconcerting to be polite, for it is obvious that no fairy would appear in the bus that goes from Galway to Clifden the wrong way round.

From this it will be obvious that there is a time and a place for everything. Far from the mechanisms of this atomic age are the gay, mischievous and appeasable fairies, denizens of rath and hill.

Though they partake not of human food, they suffered from the potato famine when millions of those who had eyes to see and spells to placate them closed their famished eyes forever or turned them away from the mystic circles around the twisted thorn. The emigrant ship carried away many of those with whom they were in sympathy; mass schooling and regimented education shut the minds of the rest.

Darby Doolin could tell you that much better than I. It was he who told the father of Oscar Wilde, Sir William, what caused this defection.

'Troth, Sir, what betune them National Boards and Godless colleges, and other sorts of larnin', and the loss of the 'pratey, and the sickness, and all the people that's goin' to America, and the craturs that's forced to go to the workhouse, or is dyin' off in the ditches, and the clergy settin' their faces ágin them, and tellin' the people not to *give in* to them, sarra wan of the Gintry will be found in the country, nor a word about them and their doin's in no time.'

Thus in beautiful musical speech was delivered an elegy on the fairies almost one hundred years ago.

But the fairies are immortal; they may withdraw, but they cannot be destroyed. They avoided commissioners, inspectors, school boards and examinations; survived the famine and the plague that followed it to carry off millions of their devotees, and withdrew into the Many Coloured Land amid the purple mountains and the reedy valleys of the West:

'The fairies, the whole pantheon of Irish demigods, are retiring one by one from the habitations of man to the distant islands where the wild waves of the Atlantic raise their foaming crests; or they have fled to the mountain passes and have taken up their abodes in those wild, romantic glens, lurking in the gorgeous yellow furze and purple heath amidst the savage, disrupted rocks or creeping beneath the warrior's grave.'

Well do I know where they are, for I have lived longer in Iol Daithe, Many Coloured Connemara, than Sir William Wilde. The wonder of this many coloured land lies in the change of colours, which are never for an hour the same shade. To name them in a language that has hardly a dozen names for colour would be impossible. Plum-blue, hyacinth, cyclamen and every flower that grows in the country would have to be enlisted, and then they would never give the impression of living and glowing hues. The mountain lakes are more than black; the mountains are lapis lazuli mixed with velvet brown; sea inlets take on shades that no words can name . . .

'Have you ever caught a leprechaun (is that how you pronounce it?) behind a bush?'

I followed his gaze up a slope blazing with gorse in bloom.

'Which bush?' I asked, hoping to please him by showing that in Ireland there was at least one factual mind.

Instead of being grateful, he got out of the bus. He had intended to, anyway; but could there be a more alluring place to get out at than Cornamona, 'the turn of the Turf', Cornamona of the lovely name?

Casleen na Kirka – the Hen's Castle – was out to the left, standing on its solitary rock in an arm of Lough Corrib. The great lake was no longer to be seen. The castle's ruins are kept from falling by the late Lord Ardilaun's provision, for the castle has a history of its own. Some say that it got its name from an enchanted hen that laid an egg for every member of a garrison during a siege. Others – more factual, like me – say that Grace O'Malley, the sea queen of the West in the days when Queen Elizabeth reigned in England, came to her husband's rescue when he was locked up by his enemies in the castle. Her husband was called the Cock; and the castle was called after her who had raised its siege.

The bus was entering the Joyce Country. There was a rumour of old that every Joyce had six fingers on each hand and six toes on each foot, a tale that must have arisen as a corollary to the gigantic stature of that famous tribe.

The rumbling mountains that, when far away, were diamonded by flashes of rainy sunlight, are now close by, fit haunts of those 'immortal, mild, proud shadows' seen by men with enchanted eyes and by the aritst, Jack Yeats, whose picture of 'The Others' is in my mind. His painting shows a countryman doubled with toil and hardship, leading a wretched donkey and cart along an exposed and endless road with one windswept tree beside it. Coming half from heaven and earth, 'The Others' may be seen clothed in dim gold, majestic, a vision which is the dream of the bowed man, his treasure and his sustenance: a splendour the very opposite of his lot. Here, where reedy pools and windy bogs have islanded a fair green knoll, 'The Others' have come down from their courts in the mountains which are richer than all earthly palaces. Only to those whose thoughts and feelings are intense enough to endow hill and glen with fitting splendour 'The Others' will appear. In this there is nothing that has not been known time out of mind.

> 'Democritus, the philosopher, writeth that we should pray we might ever see happy images and sights in the ayer, and that the good which is meet and proper to our nature may rather come to us, than that which is evil and unfortunate ... that there are good and bad images flying in the ayer which give a good or ill impression unto men, and incline men to vice or to virtue.'

The old biographer should have added that there are only certain places on earth proper to such images, for in certain places only may they be seen 'flying in the ayer'. If I am not already in such a place I soon shall be, for I am bound for a mountain-sheltered island in a lake not a mile from the Atlantic. Trees cover it, and it is ringed with the red-berried mystic rowan tree. There I will dwell actually as the poet Yeats dwelt in vision in Inisfree. Inisfree means Isle of Heather. The isle to which I am going is Freilaun, Heather Island. 'Midnight's all a glimmer and noon a purple glow' in both.

There I will abide with 'flying images' for a month or two and seek their good impression before returning to the river rolling forever down the lea.

13 — *Freilaun*

In Tully Lake there is an island eleven acres in extent called 'Freilaun', which means Heather Island. It lies midway between the nearest shores under the great rock of Letter Hill, which shelters it from the prevailing western winds. The lake is shaped like a long oval which has been contracted near the middle where the island lies. On the eastern shore there is a garage which is also a boathouse. A boat is kept beside it by a little pier. A few minutes' rowing brings you to the island where the boat can run into a harbour the size of the boat. When you step ashore you are at the beginning of a path that winds crimson-walled by fuchsia, and roofed by laurel, rhododendrons and flowering shrubs. After thirty yards the air grows warmer because of a copse of linden and sycamore trees. Before you suddenly a long, two-storeyed, limewhite house comes into view with a veranda of brown timber running along over the first storey. Between the house and the lindens is a little court paved with irregular slats, russet and brown and sea-green. The silence that reigns in the island may be broken only by a startled blackbird or a belted bee barging back, by and large, from a foray on the spreading flowers; or, in the long Spring, by a cuckoo that sounds as if it were close by. At evening, a pair of wild pigeons make love-lorn moanings as they settle in the trees.

A bank behind the house rises as high and shelters it with trees and shrubs from any breezes from the North. To the south the view is open over the lake to the Twelve Bens of Connemara, which seem quite near, though glistening Diamond Mountain, the nearest of them, is five miles away.

On the ground floor every window gives on the green and purple of the rhododendrons or the pink of rambler roses crowding the garden wall. Over the lawn on the west side glimpses of the lake may be caught between the larger trees;

but, though the house is in the middle of a lake, the lake-water is never heard lapping on the shore. It may be that the rowans, sallies and ivied trees that rim the lake keep away even the gentle sound of little waves.

Where the lake itself preserves the silence, it is needless to say that the ambrosial night is not made hideous by the brayings of a radio.

This is no place for the listless nor for the restlessness of youth; but a man well stepped on in years it suits well.

When I think that the poet Yeats spent a night on a rock beside Lough Gill gazing through the midnight glimmer at Inisfree, which he was never to reach to build his cabin, and of the years through which he longed in vain for his love, it is disturbing to know that the best poetry comes from a longing that must be forever unfulfilled. Yet here I am where I longed to be. All that I can do with my ease is to weave some light rhymes together about the passing away of comely things, and so sublimate my resentment against those who put buses in the place of the uncrowded trains.

There is plenty of tranquillity here in which to remember those nincompoops. I will see what will emerge. A few admonitory words, no more.

The comforting thing about poetry is that it requires no effort. It is one of the few things that will come if you leave it alone. So while the lines are murmuring in my ears, I will try to follow the path that goes round under the sheltering trees. Years ago, when the island was houseless but for the remains of a cottage, so undisturbed was it then that I came across a wild duck's nest with seventeen brown eggs. The wild duck nest no longer on the island; but on a smaller island to the south, called Half-Moon Island, from its shape, there is an heronry. You can see the birds nesting on the tree-tops with their legs hanging down through their nests. I rowed past it yesterday and startled at least a dozen herons flapping out from the undergrowth. Though they are said to eat eight pounds of fish daily, I do not disturb them, for nothing good comes from upsetting the balance of Nature. Huntsmen are learning this far away in the Everglades, where they now spare the alligators, for these feed on snakes, not fish; and they not only keep the serpentine breed down, but they keep the ground moist in the arid summer.

The water of Tully Lake is agate brown because of the bogs which feed it with their overflow. Bog water is acid; and it is this that accounts for the small size of the numerous trout.

The path comes into the open after I have struggled for ten minutes through the dense shrubs. It comes into the open if you call a miniature forest of bracken open ground. I wade through the bracken, and emerge on the stony tip of the island where the grass is tufted, showing that otters pass this way. Now, though the view of Half-Moon Island is unobstructed, not a heron is to be seen. They are away standing in the flags of some marsh or by the side of some tiny stream. Tully Lake is too deep for them to fish; and there is nowhere to stand in its reeds. One of them has gone to a station of his own by Roisinduff Lake two miles away. Roisinduff means 'the Little Dark Wood', and the lake is called after it. Some of that ancient wood still remains to justify the name that the old Irish, who were susceptible to the features of the landscape that surrounded them, gave to the Lake of the Little Dark Wood.

I know that heron's post well. It is where the water-lilies are huddled at the western side of the lake. One bird rose when I was going round the lake some days ago and flew away over the rising ground on solemn wings. He did not fly home to Tully Lake, for I watched him that was watching me; but he went out of sight where the land falls to the beach. There is a trickle of water there where a frog may swim.

If I lie down I might as well close my eyes because – I may as well acknowledge it – I cannot stand the sight of beauty for more than ten minutes, if so long. The view of the Benna Beola – the Twelve Bens – with the gold dust in the air that fills their valleys, because for me it is inexpressible, fills me with unrest. It is the same when I gaze upon a sunset over the Atlantic by Roisinduff. The sun sets behind the island of Inisturk and turns its purple into black with a luminosity in it. It would be hopeless to attempt to describe this – just as hopeless as it is to turn the Twelve Bens into words, because it is not the description but the spirit of the sunset that should glow in a single happy word. It would hurt too much to search it out. It would mean walk after walk through the wild wood; so be content to stare a while at the mountains, then close your eyes and hope that the everlasting mountains will take their place.

Why the devil I should want to stuff a sunset into one word I do not know. In the first place, no word could contain it; in the second place, there is no one word for it; and in the third place, if there were, I would not be competent to find it. So I may as well feel beauty while I last and cease to torture myself by trying to express it.

The aborigines who lived on the third island in this lake must have felt the beauty of their surroundings deeper far than I, for it was innate. When the last late Government tried to set their descendants down in the fallow lands of Meath, these mountainy men developed a homesickness that amounted to a disease.

Yes; south of Half-Moon Island is a round island not much larger than a tennis-court. It was once surrounded by large stones which were removed when old Blake, the Sunday man, built a cottage on Freilaun. A Sunday man is not necessarily a devotee, but one who could move freely only on Sundays, for on that day the King's Writ did not run; and debtors were safe. Blake removed the encircling stones and with them traces of one of the oldest of habitations – a dwelling on a crannoge or island (usually artificial) in lake or marsh. These may be compared to the pile-dwellings in the lakes of Switzerland. Why men wished to crowd on an island little larger than a large room is hard to say. It may have been to keep their children safe from the wolves that were a pest that could not be exterminated. Whatever compelled them who can tell? But that they lived on the crannoge in Tully Lake is indisputable: their bone needles were found there, and what else who knows?

So I am not the only one who saw the sun on the Twelve Bens and could only point to it. If you want to feel more than sensation can take, come and see it for yourself.

Why should I linger beyond the scent of the woodbine? I

will go back to the shelter of the lawn. There, beside a bush of broom and under a bank of wild roses, I will gaze at the screened water and cut off Eternity at both ends with the garden shears. Only by a garden shears may this be done.

There is light enough in June to go to bed without a candle; but a candle should be lit to bring back a forgotten light that is softer than electric light under the mellowest of shades. Bernard Shaw may have reason in keeping electric light out of his cottage. His reason cannot be that candlelight is more beautiful: he is thinking probably that the unknown rays of electricity are bad for his health; whereas candlelight is comforting. It is more soothing than electric light and easier on the eyes. It is astonishing how much light a candle can give. It is not enough for modern eyes to read by, though the greatest works in the world were written by it; but it fills a bedroom with a soporific glow.

It is important to quench a candle properly. If you do not, the smell of burnt candle-grease can keep you awake too long. It is bad enough to have the cuckoo's incessant song breaking the silence and bringing thoughts of the murder of birds of a better song, without a nasty smell in the room. Maybe, if I listen well, I can hear the water lapping; but all I can hear now is the occasional barking of a distant dog.

This is better than looking at a brick house on the other side of the street, I said when at breakfast I gazed through the window and saw walls of rhododendron mixed with mauve. The morning light was coming through the trees which veiled the upshot glitter from the water. All was very still. An ousel cock took courage and picked up the bread I threw upon the grass. But he must have seen me move in the room, for soon he took alarm and flew up into a tree.

I wandered down the path that leads to the little pier. What a sight was there! Two swans, stately on the water for all their wildness, moved slowly, dipping their necks for the red weed. This, it seems, grows only near the pier; and that is what brought the two swans so close to the shore. Between them six little grey cygnets, looking like floating balls covered with aigrette feathers, tried to imitate the parent birds, but their necks were far too short. The big birds kept the little ones between them to shelter them from the ripples and the breeze. I went back to the house for some bread; but the moment I raised my arm to throw it, they moved slowly but deliberately away. Leave them wild as they are. Why should lovely things be made dependable on crumbs from a man's table?

This is the first time that swans have hatched out on Tully Lake. On the upper lake there have been two swans for twenty years. They hatch out their eggs every two years, and drive their offspring away as soon as the white feathers take the place of the light brown. They are sent to fend for themselves by being driven out to sea, for Roisinduff is separated from the sea by only a ridge of beach fifty yards wide. Maybe the two on Tully Lake were swans cast out of Roisinduff. It is pleasant to think of these beautiful wild things neighbouring me so near. I am glad that there are no pike in the lake to drag their little ones down. There are no pike west of Lough Corrib, for Lough Corrib is a Rome to them from which no one runs away. They grow to such a size in that lake that they could attack and kill a swan. That must be why there are no wild swans on Lough Corrib. It makes my two wild swans all the dearer to me.

I have found a perfect way to observe the sportsman's ritual, which is to fish wherever there are trout. No lake in Connemara has more trout than Tully Lake or trout that are easier to catch. So, to prevent endless questions, 'What luck today?' 'What fly did you put up?' 'What's your heaviest fish?' I take the boat by myself and fish with neither fly nor hook upon the cast. After a little, good-natured people do not like to ask questions that would show me up as a far-from-Compleat Angler. I know that they pity me in their piscatorial hearts. I pity the fish. So the two pities balance one another. Meanwhile I can take a boat and drift on the lake without rumours getting about regarding my eccentricity.

This is not an original idea. I got it from the Chinese poet, Ching Chi Ho. He was banished from Court, so he spent his time in fishing; but, determined not to be disturbed, he used no bait. He probably did not use a hook, for you never can be sure that a fish may not take a hook just as well as a fly. At last, he was recalled from exile; but he refused to leave his fishing and his peace. I remember being so struck by the wisdom of the man that I tried to celebrate him in verse. I never can remember my own verses. To this I owe the remnant of my friends; but, if I can put my hand on the book, I will, by your leave, reprint the verses I made in honour of the fisherman to whom I owe my peace.

Another reason makes me loath to fish: I have a pet fish, an angel fish, round as a silver coin, and ruffled with two little fins swift as the wings of a bee. He has two long whiskers like a Chinaman's, which droop down from each side of his mouth as he swims to the side of his aquarium to look out for me. I feel that I could hardly face him again if I were the slayer of dozens of his kin who are all too easy to catch. So don't shout at me, 'Hi! You have forgotten your landing net!'

ANGLERS

That pleasant Chinese poet, Ching Chi Ho,
Who spent his time in fishing with no bait,
Recalled at last from exile, would not go
And leave the stream where he could meditate
And foil all interrupters with his ruse,
Sitting beside the water with his line.
Was it a wonder that he should refuse
When he could catch his rhythms half asleep,
Watching below the lilies fishes shine
Or move not – it was all the same to him –
And river mosses when he gazed more deep,
And deeper, clouds across the azure swim?

There's not a roof now on the courts whose schemes
Kept men awake and anxious all night long
Distracted by their working out; but dreams
He dreamt in idleness and turned to song
Can still delight his people. As for me,
I, who must daily at enactments look
To make men happy by legality,
Envy the poet of the baitless hook.

For the last week I have not seen the swans and their cygnets. They may be sheltering behind one of the islands, for the Summers here are not as assured as those of Maine or Vermont — Vermont, the county of America that most resembles Ireland. Even with the shelter of Letter Hill the wind from the Atlantic cannot be kept out. It does not whistle round the house, for that is embowered; but it blows white crests on the lake. If there is red weed only by the pier, it must go hard with the swans to find food in Tully Lake. Their young cannot be more than three weeks old. They are too young to fly, so they must be here.

The bell on the farther pier is ringing. That is the way the postman shows that he has come with the mail. He is an impatient fellow. The extra half-mile to the lake is an unwelcome stretching of his daily round. He waits for only two minutes. If no boat puts out within that time you have to wait until next day for your letters and newspapers. Not that I miss newspapers, for I make my own news here. But now I take the oars and put my back into it as I row to the shore.

I had to go to the hotel beside the upper lake. I met the chauffeur on my way, and he gave me a lift. He was coming for me in any case. He had a tale to tell that had him all mixed up. He was incoherent.

'It's a tragedy and no mistake!'

But to question him only made him worse. He hung his head.

'The swans?' I asked, fearing the worst. He nodded.

'A tragedy and . . .?'

At first I got it all wrong; but after a while I had it all straightened out. The parent swans had taken their young ones to Roisinduff Lake, and were driven off by the old couple who had held that lake for twenty years.

'And every time the male bird drove the other off, he killed a young one.'

'And you did nothing?'

'I went for my gun to shoot him, but by the time I got back it was too late.'

It was a tragedy 'and no mistake'. It saddened and silenced me. I knew now why I had missed my little birds. Then,

113

realising that they could not fly, I asked the chauffeur how they got to the upper lake.

'There's a story in that. They walked them all the way.'

I asked, 'Do you mean to tell me that the swans trekked the two miles by road? Why, the cygnets were too small to reach it through the bog. They would have been lost.'

'It took all day from three o'clock in the afternoon until sunset. The Civic Guard held up a truck that was going up the lane while they were moving; and you should have seen the old birds keeping the small boys away.'

Two miles by crooked lanes and road! The parent birds must have observed the way they would have to go from the air, and they had learned the route well, because from the ground they could see nothing but the hedges and the stone walls that hemmed them in.

'Did they go across country at all?'

'No. They went all the way by boreen and road until they came to the lake. And then the fight took place. I was on the other side of the lake, so I could do nothing until it was all over.'

For days I was depressed. I cannot look at the pair of swans on the upper lake as they float about, keeping a few yards apart, or shine by the side of the little flat green islet where they nest. That is what caused the fight. The older couple were nesting. I found that out when I questioned the man again. He told me that they had three eggs, one of which was light. He threw that one away. After what must have been more than the usual five or six weeks, when nothing appeared, he threw the other two away. I did not thank him for his interference or for his lack of it. I pondered on the design of Nature that two swans that may have been too old to produce living progeny should have killed six healthy little ones.

Why, I have often asked myself since, did the parents who were clever enough to follow paths mapped from the air, hatch out their six eggs by a lake that was deficient in food to feed them? Obviously, it was the dearth of food that made them take to the land and lead their young to a lake that, because of its muddy bottom, is rich in all kinds of water-plants.

Roisinduff is rich indeed. In it a water-fern has been found the like of which has been found in only one other lake, and that is in Cumberland.

'A tragedy, and no mistake!'

There has been no sign of the bereaved couple since. I wonder where they are gone. They may have gone to Kinvarra, where there are a games of swans, fifty or sixty in number dipping for whatever the subterranean river from Coole which emerges beside the old castle of Dungory, brings down from the Seven Woods.

I hope that, wherever they are, they do not associate the murder of their little ones with a man who may have frightened them off when he tried to throw them bread.

When an island becomes too small it is time for a ramble on the mainland.

I often dream of a pool of water crystal clear; now, with water all about me, I think of a pleasant lane that leads to wherever I will.

It is no farther than the swans went on that fateful journey; but I must not burden my memory 'with a heaviness that is gone'.

There is a grass border all along the boreen: wider on the left just as you enter it. Here tinkers come camping once a year. There must be a well somewhere in the reeds; but that is off the path, and I am not going to be diverted by water just now. The lane is hedged by dark-green furze without a yellow flower. This is strange. They say that 'Love is out of season when the gorse is out of bloom'. I do not wish to be an augur. Love is still able, even in Ireland, to take care of itself, blossom or no blossom on the gorse. I will leave it at that and walk along. One thing that delights me is that no gardener ever came here. Whatever grows planted itself; and did it well. There is just enough rough gorse to make the wild rose all the rarer and to keep the loops of the blackberries down. I notice one wild rose mixed so well with woodbine that it seems to have a double flower and two scents. It was 'quite canopied o'er with luscious woodbine' as it leant across the path. One good thing about woodbine is that it never strangles the shrub or tree that sustains it, whereas ivy kills whatever it embraces. No; I will not bore you by drawing a moral from that! Like most morals, it is all too obvious and trite. This is a lane in which it is better to linger than to go on. I will hasten slowly on my way to the sea behind Letter Hill. There, on the edge of the Atlantic, amid the many coloured mountains on the outermost shelf of Europe, dwell men who speak the immemorial tongue that sweetened the air long before the English language came out of the German lowlands. Centuries before Langland struggled with his stark monosyllables the Gael was speaking and singing in a flexible speech full of innumerable nuances of soft sounds. I am still in this winding lane with its ample grassy margins and inextricable tangle of wild flowers, bounded by walls seen here and there of mottled grey: a lane after my heart, unspoilt by man's regulations, free from all pruning, weeding or manuring, decent to last in its own order when all gardens are overgrown; a lane to go back and forth in; a lane I am loath to leave until somebody tells me that to *Lecanora parella* is due the mottling of the stones.

While I am enjoying this freedom from all formality, this garden in a waste, the thought is borne in on me with its questioning, 'What hope is there for anyone like me whose mind is fed on wildness, who resents all hints of the law behind order and is, nevertheless, elated and content?' This is more than the problem of the effect of environment on the creature, instead of what you might think should be the other way about. It is the problem of all Ireland except, perhaps, that constricted corner of Ulster where all is orderly and therefore ordinary. There the 'subjects' pay with all the Arts for their model farms; but I was born free. Cajoled by bigotry and distracted by a Saturnalia (in the middle of Summer!) in honour of a King who was a pervert, it never dawns on them that they are being exploited and enslaved. Their docility is dangerous. Like the slavery of Russia, it is a menace to the world. The graces of civilisation are withheld from them. For poetry they are given "resolutions"; for painting, Orange banners; and for music, fifes and drums. And in spite of all this they are not blind. Never forget that it was the Belfast University that was the first to honour Yeats, while the University of his natal town was dumb – the Silent Sister. There are no sex-starved censors in the North. And it was a Belfast bookseller who said, on reading *As I was Going Down Sackville Street*, 'If this isn't the best yet, may I die in a temperance hotel!'

Behind me rise the purple mountains diamonded by a flash

of sunlight or merging into the majesty of purple and gold. Before me lies the illimitable Atlantic, whereon float spectral islands seen once in seven years. Thus, once upon a time floated the Isle of Inis Bofin – the Isle of the White Cow – until it was accidentally disenchanted by some fishermen who touched it with fire. It could no longer float hidden from mortal eyes, for fire had the power to fix it forever on its base. This is the way that came about. From Omey Island, which can be reached from the mainland at low tide, went a fisherman and his son with a seed of fire laid on clay to broil the fish they might catch. They were not many hours out at sea until they heard about them the song of birds and the sounds of sheep and lambs. They thought that they had reached Hy Brazil; so they landed, bringing with them their catch of fish and their fire. They looked about. They beheld a lady full beautiful driving a cow that was no mortal cow to a lake. She touched the cow, and it turned into a stone. One of the fishermen went to remonstrate with her, and she instantly became a rock. Before any disaster the White Cow can be seen on the island which is inhabited by mortals now. This is a part of a legend, a part, much garbled, of mythology older than Ireland of the Moon Goddess in her three aspects. She is the lady 'full beautiful'; she is the White Cow and, lastly, she is the rock. But let us leave such exactness to mythographers.

Though the cow and its lovely herdess are petrified, nothing has happened to the fairies who can be heard carousing in the hills. They tempt men to eat their fairy food by throwing down showers of fish. A man who was going by the side of a rath or fairy fort was struck by an iris leaf thrown by one of its inhabitants; he drew his black-hafted knife and stabbed the elf. Terrified by what he had done, the fairy-killer ran for help and, on returning with some men, found only a heap of slime, 'like what a dead frog turns into', on the spot. An Englishman who lived there until recently declared, one day, he went out shooting, that he was surrounded by a troupe of fairy girls dressed in brown.

The long mountain at last falls into the sea with many a gully and indentation. Some of these were caves and roofed over within memory; but the ocean sent its sappers under them and blew their roofs off.

Cave na Mbhan is one of these. This is called in English the Cave of the Women; and legend has it that the bodies of two naked women were found floating there. As for the date, you will get no information, for exactness in dates is unknown; but if you refer it to 'the days of the Spanish Armada' you will be met by no denial, for that date embraces a lot of the romantic past. The Spanish Armada should be nothing to make dates by, for the way the survivors were treated on the west coast of Ireland is one of the disgraces of history.

The Cave na Mbhan had an interest for me because between the two world wars a merman was seen in it by two fishermen who told me about it by the aid of a 'witness' who had wished himself in on them.

Here in Connemara a 'witness' is a specious fellow who helps out unsophisticated people up before a magistrate for any misdemeanour or who happen to be the heroes of any event. He is the self-appointed counsel who, during the lunch hour, can weld the evidence and strengthen his clients' oaths. At other times such as this he is a 'producer'.

The story of the merman who haunts the coast of Connemara is too well known to be retold. It got full publicity in the English Press. Scientists explained him. 'It is possible that he may be a straggling dugong,' Dr Lepper, a member of the Royal Zoological Society, said. 'This very warm weather might bring a straggler; but it is a long way from the Amazon to the west coast of Ireland. The description given by the fishermen seems to me impossible. More probably the fishermen saw a great grey seal.'

Yes; it is a long way from the Amazon, but not from Hy Brazil. And I have yet to meet a Connemara fisherman who would not recognise a 'great grey seal'. They are all over the littoral waters. I shot half a dozen of them in less than half an hour not so many years ago. Regan and Hearne, men who have spent all their lives – except the years they were in the first world war – on the sea, are not unlikely to recognise a seal however 'great' when they see one. The great grey Atlantic seal is the enemy of all who go down to the sea to fish.

Now that the witness who came with them when they first told me of the merman is not about, I can renew acquaintance with them and talk about something else.

I passed the old castle that had had stone cannonballs stuck in its masonry. It is known as Renvyle Castle, and is said to have been cannonaded by that masculine sea-queen, Grace O'Malley, or in Gaelic, Granu Maille.

Round the western shoulder of Letter Hill I went until I came across one of the two men, the one who had a limp from a severe knee-wound he got in the war.

'It's a long time since we met,' he said.

I said that it was. There was a pause. I broke the silence. 'I often wanted to ask you why is "Fir na Mara" not used in Gaelic for the murruman or man of the Sea?'

He smiled tolerantly, as well he might, for he had heard the old language in his cradle; and he spoke it mellifluously.

'That's schoolmasters' Irish,' he said.

'Schoolmasters' Irish,' I repeated, and smiled, for now I realised with what feelings the real Irish speakers regard compulsory Irish. The stuff that is forced down the necks of their children in the schools.

He repeated 'merriman' for me. This is about the nearest I can get to the sound in English letters, the nearest I could get to it in any alphabet, for my ear is incapable of following the fine inflexions he put into the word.

'They will never teach Irish by compulsion. Nothing can be achieved by compulsion in this country,' I assured him. 'It's significant that there's more Gaelic in the Highlands of Scotland than there is here in its home.'

'And wouldn't you think that they ought to know?'

'What makes it more foolish,' I said, 'is that the principal enthusiasts are outsiders who never heard a word of Irish until they came into this country. Now they're all for it, although they cannot pronounce a syllable of it correctly. Under their tutelage it bids well to disappear as unpopular as any political shibboleth can be. They cannot speak a sentence that you would understand.'

'But a schoolmaster might,' he said with a smile, 'if they paid him well.'

'I read the other day that one of those fellows whose name is full of English letters staggered, lamented the fact that Gaelic is disappearing. Is it any wonder? The kind of stuff they're teaching now is not only killing Gaelic but making the girls disappear. The "language", instead of preserving the national spirit, is emptying the nation; over to England they go. When they come back,' the speaker said, 'they despise all things Irish. Pseudo-Irish, I would say. But do you know what's driving them out?'

'What would that be?'

'Boredom, boredom and more boredom. They are bored stiff by all this artificiality. If a Government bores people, it will empty the country of all its girls and boys. Either to Hell or to Connaught; but even Connaught is emptying now.'

He cast an eye over the water to the West.

'It's not to America they're going, but to England,' I said, for I thought that, looking West, his mind was on the United States.

After a pause he sat on the wall on which he had been leaning when I spoke to him. I knew that he did not disagree with me; but, like all natives, he took not the slightest interest in the politics of the day.

'You have been about the world a bit,' I said. 'Do you know how Brazil came by its name?'

He shook his head.

'It got its name from Hy Brazil, the island of the Blest to which St Brendan voyaged so far out there over the ocean. He thought that he sighted it in the setting sun.' And I pointed out to sea. By the depth of his silence I felt that he was gathering speech. But I went on: 'The Voyage of Brendan should interest all Irishmen. He may have been the first to discover what is now the American continent. He describes a floating island of glass. Which was scoffed at because no one recognised an iceberg from the description of one who saw an iceberg for the first time. On it were strange beasts with enormous teeth and speckled bellies: walruses evidently. When he reached the mainland he found no traces of the monks who went there before him. This looks like a forerunner of what happened to Columbus when he searched in vain for the settlement he had established on his first voyage. Neglect of our legends, which are primitive history, is to blame for our ignorance. Anyway, he called his island Hy Brazil, which is now Brazil.'

Pensively he said:

'There's a lot of strange sights after sunset on the sea. Sometimes all the sea lights up; and you see what might be islands far out where you know that there is nothing – at least by day.'

Words in Gaelic from his cottage interrupted him. He asked to be excused and went in. In a minute he appeared again.

'That was griddle cake. The wife would like you to come in.'

I demurred.

'It's no trouble at all,' he said.

So I went in with him. The table was being laid for three.

The cottage, in spite of the smallness of its windows, was bright enough inside. The door was open, and that helped to light the room. There were flowers in a pot on one of the sills. A tall dresser held the family crockery: blue and shining. The woman of the house dusted a chair for me and we sat down. There was yellow butter *go leor* and griddle cake. I had to ask for hot water to dilute the tea. If I drunk it as strong as it was, I would have had palpitation of the heart for the rest of the day. I felt that they pitied me.

Tea is the principal stimulant of the fisher folk; Indian, not China tea.

'Tim was telling me that he went to see you about the Merriman.'

'Yes,' I said casually. 'Years ago.' For I did not wish the woman to think that the sole object of my visit was to make more inquiries. It was a friendly visit, and to be treated as such. So I waived the Merriman off with, 'There's been too much talk about such things. Not that the newspapers believe them anyway.'

This had the effect of putting our hostess on her mettle.

'If they lived here they'd be wiser. But maybe they're better where they are.'

'Much better,' I heartily agreed.

'The butter's at your elbow. You're eating nothing.'

'I was thinking all the more,' I said.

Innate courtesy forbade her to inquire concerning the subject of my thoughts.

She stood up and filled my teacup. Then she passed me a jug of milk. That was a sign that her interest had not relaxed, so I went on:

'We were talking about St Brendan when he sailed to Hy Brazil, having sighted it at sunset out to the West; and about the islands that appear as if they were enchanted.'

She remained silent when I ceased. After the pause she said, '"Enchanted" is right. And why wouldn't they be?'

I pleaded ignorance, hoping to be informed.

'The old people do be telling of a queer island. It's an old story that it was reached by fishermen years and years ago. Hy Brazil you were talking about. It was Hy Brazil they landed on, and there was people to report it, too. Thousands of people seen it from the North. But this captain – he was more than a fisherman – if I remember rightly, he was a sea captain who used to sail to France. One time he was sailing out from Donegal or wherever he was. He found himself in a thick fog, so thick that he couldn't see the sides of his ship from the middle. He couldn't tell where he was, so he took soundings and let the vessel drift. It got shallower and shallower, and at last it got so shallow that he knew he must be near land, so he let the anchor drop. When he looked up, what did he see but an island with horses, cattle, sheep and black rabbits. That ought to have been enough to scare him out of his life. He took no notice; but went ashore with eight of his company; and after walking for a while they came to a castle and knocked on the door. Nobody answered no matter how loud they knocked. They walked all round it; but they couldn't get in. So they gave up and started to light a fire to cook a bite to eat. All of a sudden they heard a terrible noise. They took to their heels and made for their boat and rowed out to the ship. In the morning they saw a gentleman and his attendants on the shore and he waving to them. After a while they made up their minds to send the boat for him, and they brought him off. It was a queer story he had to tell them, I wouldn't go so far as to say that I believe it or not.'

She paused, and asked if we wanted more tea.

'That'll do you now. Go on with your story,' her husband said. He probably resented an artist's subterfuge to add suspense and relish to the tale.

'He said that he and his servants had been imprisoned in the castle by an enchanter; but that lighting a Christian fire wrecked the tower and broke the spell.'

'Only for that it might be fair enough,' her husband acknowledged. To him the enchanted island was apparently acceptable.

'I'm only telling you what I heard myself. I'm not making it up like a shanachie as I go along.'

'We know that. We didn't mean to interrupt you.'

But, like the castle, the spell was broken.

'Well, that's all there is to it,' she said, and began to clear the table.

'Regions which are fairyland,' I said to myself, but I could not help thinking that we might have heard more but for the man's taking exception to the enchanted castle. An enchanted island, yes; he had seen them off and on, but he had not landed on any of them.

Many of such tales have root in fact. Time, and that sibness to the supernatural which is the heritage of the Gael, exaggerate and magnify them until the historian loses patience. But when I remember the accounts of how savagely the Armada crews were treated by the Irish natives who despoiled them, stripped and clubbed them to death, having robbed them of their silks and jewels, I thought the story highly plausible. Suppose some island chieftain had imprisoned some suppliant grandee who, with the surviving members of a broken ship, had sought sanctuary with him who presumably was no friend of England and not afraid to defy her orders to kill all sailors of the Armada who tried to land, and who was holding him to ransom while awaiting the news from Spain; and that during the period of his incarceration some men landed on his island who looked like guardians of the coast, would he not have released the Spaniard for fear lest he should get into trouble with the authorities? If you substitute one kind of fire for another and read 'cannon' instead of 'Christian fire', the account of the cracked tower is not incredible. Grace O'Malley herself might have been the enchantress of the tale. It's a thing that you couldn't put past her, anyway.

By low stone walls white with lichen like flakes of flat foam, I walked back to the island, encouraged by the story I had heard for the evidence it gave of insistence on the supernatural. Nothing less will satisfy the Gael.

In this day of ours, when the seat of the spiritual impulses of man is placed in the lower bowel by a quack like Freud, one of the most prominent of the *'hostes humani generis'* of our time, it is refreshing to listen to a tale of something beyond the reach of psychoanalytic frauds. It saddens me to think of the seriousness with which such pseudo-scientists are accepted by an all-too-gullible public. I had leifer live in Belfast, that bright suburb of Glasgow where there are psychic cases only on one day in the year, than among those who believe in the constraining influence of the bowel on the soul. And no one sees the cynicism.

Compared with the treatises you read on anal fixations and other indecencies, the story of the enchanted islands of the West is sweet as morning dew and as fragrant as a lane lined with honeysuckle.

Were it not for the clouds off the Atlantic that break in rain, I would never leave Renvyle with its glimmering islands and its assured faith in wonders of the deep.

15 — *The Spirit of the Place*

By this time it should be pretty obvious who is the hero of this narrative. It is certainly not the writer. Who then? The country is the hero, the landscape if you like to call it that, or the *genius loci*, the spirit of the place, the pull of the earth, that nucleus smasher which can transmute anything. And, this being so, the history of the hero's vicissitudes is not out of place, even if we have to go back some time to find his lean years. I remember before an election – there were plenty of elections then if the Government found itself shaky – a gardener came to me to get my signature on his application for a blind pension.

'But you are not blind,' I objected, for I knew him well.

'I know that, sir; but I'll only have to go blind for a month or so, at the worst six weeks, till the election.'

'But why do you want to go blind?'

'Well, it's like this: them rabbits is a pest. They're eatin' all the grass. If I get the pension, I can buy a gun.'

In a Democracy it is very hard to prevent the country's money from being spent to return the gang to power or to keep it in power. But this being Ireland, it is not always the vote that is cast for efficiency.

There was a commercial traveller who visited a small village in which were two gombeen men – that is, two principal merchants who between them had the whole village on their books from which there was no escape, short of a windfall.

He solicited one of the merchants, 'I have not had an order from you for over a year.'

'And you'll get none. My business is ruined. The country's business is ruined, too. I'm burst. I'm bankrupt!'

'Well, you know who you voted for at the last election.'

'And I'll vote for him again; for that old blackguard up the street is not bankrupt yet.'

Those were the days when the bus drivers and conductors

looked forward to an election to improve the roads. It seemed that there was some connection between the state of the roads and votes. So money was lavished upon the roads until they became literally paved with gold, like the fabled streets of New York.

A vibration which caused me to bite my tongue shook the bus. The conductor was all sympathy.

'If it were not so full I could put you in the middle seat. There you'd find it easier.'

We were speeding along the road that Morton, who goes 'in search' of countries, declared to be the loveliest in the world, the road to Clifden; but we were travelling in a direction the reverse of his, for Clifden we had just left.

Ballinahinch would soon be reached, with its glimpses of the salmon-pools into which the Indian Maharajah, Ranji Singh, had piers built wherever a salmon had risen. Now, if it had been the Ganges, it might have been a considerable gesture in honour of the crocodiles; but a Connemara salmon could only regard the unusual obstacles as a few more boulders fallen from the hills, and changed his accustomed ways. It was hard to understand and impossible to explain. It would be worth while to have a few words with the gillie.

The bus was bounding along beside the ruined bridges and the grass-grown permanent way of the old Galway–Clifden train which it had superseded. Bounding, bounding along mile after mile *et nos mutamur in illos*. However, it was not my stomach that changed; but the stomachs of two children to whom the motion was a novelty. Send us an election soon, O Lord!

We passed a lake with one island on which there was a solitary pine. I remembered how once, early, before the morning mist had risen, that pine appeared out of a wall of luminous grey as if it were the work of some artist of China, one of those who knew how to paint mists so well. It appeared to be in the middle air, for the lake was as yet invisible, and so the level of the pine could not be judged. The lake itself was hidden, but the stream that ran into it was coloured like claret in the level light. The Many-Coloured Land!

The country opened as the Twelve Bens receded. The wet, yellow-green fields spread fenceless, for 'drains' took the place of fences or stone walls. A bridge with three arches of dark stone told of a road over a stream. Somewhere to the left a farm would soon come into view, a farm that was a most attractive arrangement of stone walls terraced in irregular lines on the side of a hill. A well-kept stone cottage unwhitewashed with lichened walls above and beside it made a symphony in grey. It was as if the stony heart of the land had been conjured and compelled to turn into a house with garden and garth walls all of living stone.

Soon came Ross House, or rather the grounds of what had been Ross House, for on the left we passed torn trees and broken walls, a broken gate that closed the entrance to what was once the avenue had been knocked down.

A cottage with garden walls had been built with stones from the fields, some of which had been carved with all the taste of the XVIIIth century. A prosperous tavern stood on the sweep which fronted the gate in the days gone by. Here the Earl of Mayo's remark would be out of place. The Land Commission are landlords now, and have but little feeling for 'demesnes'. The long-dead owner, Martin of Ross, wrote a comic Irish song. Probably, like Percy French, he soothed his broken heart with comic songs. It will be some time before a song sounds in Ireland again: anyway, not until after the election. When it does it may not be whimsical. Even our humbugs are melancholy now. Why? Some people cannot take affluence. It saddens them. Maybe, they pretend to be sorrowful like Tim Healy when he became Governor General lest people might think that he was too well off.

Somewhere between Moycullen and the town of Galway two lofty piers rose gateless. There is no sign of them now.

'Could those be the gate-posts of the long avenue of Ballinahinch Castle?' I asked and, as I feared, the question implied a history too old for a man of the conductor's age.

The story went that Martin of Ballinahinch – 'Humanity Dick' as they called him for his Prevention of Cruelty to Animals Bill – was walking with George IV in Windsor Great

Park (a little holding of seven hundred acres) when the King asked if he had anything as extensive in Ireland.

Martin replied:

'My avenue is fifty miles long.'

He might have added that his property in which His Majesty's Writ did not run was well over a hundred thousand acres.

We had travelled about fifty miles from Ballinahinch. Very likely the pillars we passed were the entrance gates to Martin's avenue.

Menlo Castle stood black and bare over the Corrib to the left. Menlo, a name carried by the Olivers of Galway as far west as San Francisco, is another ruin not caused this time by the civil war, but by a demented sister of Sir Valentine Blake who, wandering with a lamp one night, set the oak panelling on fire; and the ancient pile went up like matchwood.

Sir Valentine Blake was a famous character. He drank a British Admiral off a gang-plank. That is, the Admiral, who had pitted himself against the strong-headed knight, fell off his gang-plank as he was returning to his ship. A story made apocryphal, however, by the fact that Galway harbour could not accommodate a battleship and there are no gang-planks between a launch and a vessel's side.

Nevertheless, Sir Valentine was a good man at bingling. He was of so hospitable a frame of mind that Lady Blake kept the keys of the tantalus, so Sir Valentine had to plead the laws of hospitality when he saw the District Inspector of Police driving briskly to the castle with his small son beside him. Sir Valentine demanded the key. It would never be said that Menlo could not offer a guest refreshment. There would be two.

Later, he set the minds of his visitors at rest, for the fire in the haystack which he had come to investigate was not a case of malicious damage, but had been set by Sir Valentine so that he might have the pleasure of the Inspector's company.

A man of great originality was Sir Valentine, who could use fire to quench a thirst!

The conductor's shout, 'You've made it!' aroused me from

my reverie. He meant that the bus had arrived in time for me to catch the train to Dublin.

I looked in vain for a railway porter. Apparently the feud between the services was not over. No railway porter would deign to handle luggage degraded by a bus. A cheerful, toothless little fellow who answers to the Chaldean name of 'Seorsam' came from nowhere and refused to unload any luggage but mine. Some minutes elapsed before I could point out to him my baggage on the top of the bus. I feared that the engine-driver might share the porter's resentment and drive off without me.

'He belted her along well. You're in plenty of time. The guard has not come along yet.'

'Nevertheless,' I said, 'put those bags in a carriage for me.'

'I'll leave them where you can't miss them.'

He took them away and laid them by one of the doors that gave on the platform. Further entry evidently was denied him. I took the lightest bag and placed it in a carriage. I hoped to reserve a seat by doing so. I directed a listless youth who was the solitary porter to add the rest. I went back to look for my uniformed assistance. He found me. He ignored the late occupants of the bus. Evidently I had found favour.

'It's brightening up a bit,' he remarked. 'We've had a sprinkle and no mistake.'

'Will it keep off?' I asked.

'They say in Galway that if you can see the Aran Islands, it's going to rain. If you can't see them, it's raining anyway.'

In the comfort of a railway carriage I put together the lines I had composed on the coming fate of the Dublin–Galway train. If you can take the ballad, here it is in the making, for once it is completed I shall cease to remember it. I leave it to you to say, 'That's just as well.' Don't forget that it was made in the lean year when you didn't know where you were going in Ireland.

16 — *Hanta Pei*

> Everything changes:
> Time deranges
> Men and women and mountain ranges

Why the Devil can't Time let Wellenough alone?
He no longer stoops to set his '*Nil obstat*' on
Trusted, tried and comely things than he sekes to change,
Wither, age and alter them and the best derange.
This has happened just of late to the Galway train
That with passengers and freight crossed the central plain,
Pulling out from Dublin town that Liffey's stream divides
West to old grey Galway town, where Corrib meets the tides.
It strains at first, then settles down and smoothly rolls along
Past villages with Gaelic names that sweeten on the tongue:
Clonsilla, Lucan and Maynooth beside the long canal,
Where yellow-centred lilies float and no one comes at all,·
The long canal that idle lies from Dublin to Athlone,
To Luan's Ford: but no one knows who may have been Luan,
The Royal Canal that joins two towns and makes of him a dunce
Who holds that nothing can be found in two places at once;
A long clear lane of water clean by flags and rushes rimmed,
Where, crimson-striped, the roaches steer, and, by the lilies dimmed,
The greenish pikes suspended lurk with fins that hardly stir
Until the Galway train comes on and shakes each ambusher.
The lovely hills are left behind; but soon the rising sun
Will overtop the mountain range and make the shadows run.

> The light that flushes the hills was low;
> But now it gathers to overflow
> And shadow each bush on the central plain
> And gather the dews and catch the train.
> And light the steam
> In its morning beam,
> Making a fugitive rainbow gleam.
> Past walled Maynooth,
> Where they teach the Truth
> In the meadow called after Druidical Nooth.

Puff, puff!
That's the stuff
As if there weren't white clouds enough!

Like a charging knight with his plumes astream
The train comes on with its sunlit steam,
Past fields where cows are chewing the cud
To Mullingar, where the Square Mill stood,
Where the cattle-dealers, with rough red skins
And gaiters buttoned across their shins,
Wait for another train; they wait
For cattle-drovers to load the freight
Of blunt-nosed cattle with towsled coats
Bound for the East and the English boats:
Cattle-dealers replete with knowledge
That is not taught in an English college.

It blows
And goes,
A whale that feels
The pistons stabbing its driving wheels.

It reaches Moate, where a king lies still
Under the weight of a man-made hill.
On and on, until, quite soon,
It will come to the ford that was held by Luan,
Where, as in Spenser's pageantry,
The Shannon, 'spreading like a sea',
Flows brightly on like a chain of lakes
Or linkèd shields that the morning takes:
The lordly stream that protected well
When jar-nosed Cromwell sent 'to hell'
The Irish nobles who stood to fight
That Bible-bellowing hypocrite.

From the bridge you can see the white boats moored,
And the strong, round castle that holds the ford.
Over the bridge it slowly comes,
The bridge held up on its strong white drums,
To enter Connaught. And now, good-bye
To matters of fact and Reality.
Ballinasloe, where the hostings were,
Ballinasloe, of the great horse-fair
That gathers in horses from Galway and Clare,

Wherever the fields of limestone are:
Mayo and Boyle and Coolavin
Between the miles of rushes and whin
And mountains high in a purple haze,
Streams and lakes and countless bays
Of Connemara, where still live on
The seaside heirs of the Sons of Conn.
To Athenry, where the kings passed by
From whom was named the Ath-na-Righ.
It rests for a minute at Oranmore,
A square grey castle protects the shore.
The Great Shore, limit of Galway Bay;
And Galway is only six miles away!

The engine-driver can wipe the oil
From his forehead and hands,
For his well-done toil
Is over now; and the engine stands
Only a foot from the buffer-stop
(He eased her down till he pulled her up).
Oh, see the children jump about
As doors are opened and friends come out
With paper parcels. What endless joys
Are hidden within those parcels of toys!
The county ladies in English tweeds,
With leathern faces fox-hunting breeds,
And shoes that give them a look of men,
Have come to the station 'just to look in'.
But never an officer home on leave
Is seen; instead, they only perceive
The rakel, card-playing boys debouch
And pay up their losses with search and grouch.
Oh, what a wonderful Noah's ark!
Lady Philippa Merlin Park,
Holding her parasol half up the handle,
Is back from Daly's of Dunsandle.
Where gold-headed Daly delights the gazers
As he leads the field of his Galway Blazers.
The Stationmaster opens a door
And clears a passage for Morty Mor,
For Morty Mor is known to own
The principal works of Galway town.

He is not one of the county set
(Though he helps them out when they lose a bet);
His saw-mills hum and he sells cement,
Potash and lime to his heart's content.
The workers he sacks on Saturday night
Are back on Monday morn contrite;
In spite of his temper, deep at the core
The heart's all right in Morty Mor.
That little boy lost is found again;
He ran away to the end of the train,
For all he can taste in his youthful hour
Of splendour and terror and speed and power:
The harnessed hates of water and flame,
The engine brings with its seething steam.

The platform now is empty again;
And empty stands the Galway train.
(Strange that nobody came to call
On the lonely men in the urinal.)
Land that is loved in ballad and song,
Land where the twilight lingers long,
May you be crossed and crossed again,
Forgetting the bus and the aeroplane,
By nothing worse than the Galway train,
Who shall tell how, when I'm dead and gone,
Gaily the Galway train came on?
How it puffed with pride on a road of its own;
How it whistled, *Waeshael!* to each nearing town;
How brightly its brass and its copper shone?
It seemed to be painted to match the scene
Of boglands brown and the trees between
With its coaches brown and its engine green.
It brought the towns where it stopped good luck,
Goods, the result of a bargain struck;
And it never ran over a cow or a duck.

Now all is changed for an overplus
Of passengers packed in a reasty bus,
A crowd that stinks and the air befouls,
And children pewk as the full bus rolls.
(A popular government plays to the masses
And that's what they get who abolish the classes.)

Lady Philippa, whose share of charity
Fails when it comes to familiarity,
Lady Philippa, her feelings hurt
Because Democracy means such dirt,
Is sitting, a most disdainful rider,
With the man from her gate-lodge sitting beside her.
The Law of Change would be just a jest
Were we sure that all change were a change for the best.

17 — *Palmam Qui Meruit Ferat*

I could see the young poplars over the end wall of Ely Place as I was about to turn into it. I was not permitted to turn into it. One of those fellows whose names you never know, however well you may be familiar with the owner of the name, stopped me with a slow smile.

I was grateful to him for not asking, in that superior, half-aggrieved and wholly exasperating way, the question, 'You don't know my name?' Instead, he continued a conversation where he had left off ten years ago.

'As I was saying, that's a real anecdote, one that you could write.'

There are those who think that if something is recorded in writing, it becomes sacrosanct, immortal and no longer subject to the chances and changes of this mortal life.

'The story you told me?'

'Of course, what else?'

'Candidly, I have forgotten it. Let me have it again.'

In a swift, whispering voice he went on without pausing. The voice was not unpleasant. In fact, it was so soft and soothing that I was in danger of listening to the sound and not to what it conveyed, as the girls of Bryn Mawr listened to Æ. Swift as his utterance was, I could catch every word with little difficulty. I too was a citizen. The little Dublin man went on smoothly without inflexion.

'Surely you remember the story I told you about the Limerick Corporation and the aldermen who could not decide who was to be Mayor. If they voted among themselves, there would be a deadlock. That would never do. So, after much argument (I needn't tell you), they decided to repair to Thomond Bridge and to elect the first man who came across it. And who came across it but an upstanding young farmer leading a cart with creels of turf.

'"Would you like to be Mayor of Limerick?" they asked.

'"It would suit me nicely," says he.

'So they took him back and elected him Mayor; and Mayor he was, with the red velvet cushion in front of him and the mace on it. There's no telling the social reforms he made.

'One day while they were in session, his mother came to see him. There he was, Mayor of Limerick right enough. But he didn't seem to notice her. After looking at him awhile, she could stand it no longer.

'"Arrah, Pat!" she called out. "Don't you know yer own mother?"

'"I don't know meself," he said.

'You could make a good story out of that, particularly of the social reforms he put through.'

'What kind of social reforms?' I asked, suspicious as I am of all reforms.

'Wasn't he a farmer and didn't he know what the poor wanted. He was a socialist unbeknownst to himself.'

I thought for a moment. 'There's a story in that,' I acknowledged. 'And you have told it well.'

'Sure there is. And it's full of satire too.'

I turned as if to leave him, but he followed me to the end of Hume Street where it opens on Stephen's Green. Then he walked beside me. As if the thought impelled him, he took me by the arm.

'Do you know anything about palmistry? All the doctors are taking it up in Harley Street and lots of places.' Before I knew it, he had my right hand in his. He bent it back until the colour of the creases appeared. He bowed his head over it.

'Red!' he exclaimed. 'You're all right. Now, if those lines were yellow, it would mean anæmia. No; liver. If they were blue, it would mean that the auld ticker was out of order. I'm not coddin'. It's dead sure.'

He was so much in earnest that I could not bring myself to interrupt him.

'What a line of life you have! You'll live to be eighty.'

As much for his own information as for mine, he muttered

in the same swift way, 'The Heart line; the Hill of Mars; the Line of the Head.'

I could not permit so much earnestness to go to waste. He 'intrigued' me, as the antique dealers say when they are pretending to be men of taste.

'You can't tell me what that line means,' I challenged, pointing to a transverse indented deeply into the ball of the thumb.

He was silent for half a minute by the watch; and that's longer than you would think.

'I'll tell you what that line means.'

'What does it mean?' I asked, for I had never heard it explained.

'It means energy. Anything on the ball of the thumb has to do with vitality. That line's for energy.'

I have had less pleasant readings by far. He left me thinking as much of myself as if he were a copy of the *Reader's Digest* which aims at making you content. He had to go into his office, which was, oddly enough, you would think by the name of it, in the Board of Works. But not if you knew Dublin.

I went on my way rejoicing that I belonged to a city in which you can get a good story and have your hand read by a Civil Servant during the busiest hours under the chestnuts of Stephen's Green.

Ouspensky in one of his lectures in New York divided men into five classes or categories. The lowest two are more or less thoughtless automata who can speak only in clichés. The third are the 'self-conscious' class. Here 'self-conscious' is not used in the vulgar sense of shy or awkward, but in the sense of awareness of one's self as a rational being, one capable of reflection, of 'looking before and after' – in fact, individuals. The fourth class, geniuses, Plato, Shakespeare, Pasteur, Edison; the fifth, Avatars, Buddha, Confucius and the rest.

How does this apply to my subject which is of that city on the Liffey's banks and all that emerges therefrom or has to do with it? It explains why there are so many individuals in Dublin and why the first and second class – that of the robots – hardly is to be found in the old town. Everyone is of the self-conscious class, even if he rises only to a resigned self-pity, or, as is more frequently the case, to a self-righteous indignation against the slings and arrows, or against his fellow citizens.

Ouspensky would be as puzzled as Bernard Shaw if he came to Dublin.

There is something that has been puzzling me – worrying me, as they say in our town. It has no connection with Ouspensky's classifications, but it has to do with classifications of the literary figures in Ireland. The obstinate question is, Why is Dunsany not admitted into the hierarchy of the Irish Literary Renaissance? Before I could find an answer – an unsatisfactory answer at that – I had to determine who they were who decided who should be famous and who not. I found, alas, that the fame-makers were a little narrow and exclusive coterie the members of which excluded non-members from the pedestals they had assumed for themselves. This coterie consisted of the Directors of the Abbey Theatre which evaporated down to Lady Gregory. Her maternal and material instincts moved her to shoo off any possible rivals of herself and Yeats. Dunsany was the first to be ousted. There would be no pedestals for his Gods of the Mountain in the Abbey any more. Edward Martyn, one of the founders of not only the Literary Movement but of Sinn Fein, which was to free Ireland eventually, had been excluded from the very first. And yet he was one of Ireland's greatest sons, an aristocrat unashamed of his country.

In a less degree, for he never sought notoriety, Stephen Gwynn, one of the best poets Ireland has had for generations, soldier, sportsman, scholar, is hardly heard of in a Dublin that has run out of geniuses as the Abbey Theatre ran out of them when it sent out its SOS in 1903.

Being as curious as an old Athenian, I asked one of the geniuses who remains why Stephen Gwynn was not acclaimed as he deserves. The answer was Delphic, 'He has written too many books.'

'But his poetry? His *Ossian and St Patrick*; his poem of *Mary Queen of Scots* and, just lately and just as wonderfully as the eighty-year-old Robert Bridges, Poet Laureate's, *Testament of Beauty*, he has given us his *Salute to Valour*,' I asserted.

But it was the last oracle: Phoebus would speak no more. The water-springs were dead. But while she is being canonised, the *Advocatus diaboli* may submit that Lady Gregory was a fool not to welcome Dunsany. I, pleading for her beatification, will answer, 'No.' Dunsany was not unmonied. When it came to helping poets, he was not ungenerous, as, later, his support of Ledwidge was to prove. He might have been a greater patron of the Abbey Theatre than Miss Horniman. Why had he to go? For the same reason that Gregory of the Golden Mouth, as James Joyce irreverently called her, elbowed out Miss Horniman. Dunsany might prove troublesome. He might not be dominated. He might not kowtow. He could not be closit in Coole.

And so the classifier, the fame-bestower, left him out. No chivalrous explanation, I admit; so, when a baron cannot wear a lady's favour, he espouses his own cause and tilts for himself.

This and other examples, Sean O'Casey to wit, may explain why the principal hero and heroine of the Irish Literary Renaissance are comprised in the Abbey Theatre coterie.

It must be admitted that Dunsany is difficult and indomitable – traits that were enough to disqualify him where compliance was indispensable. Dunsany is self-centred and a Conservative.

Then, too, there was not jealousy, but a certain hidden envy of the man. Yeats, who was feudal at heart, could not trace his ancestry back in Ireland to 1181, even though his family possessed a cup that had belonged to the Butlers of Ormonde: William *Butler* Yeats.

Stephen Gwynn is a scholar and a member of the great Trinity College family of scholars and sportsmen. If Trinity College was anathema, it was all the more unlikely that, in Dunsany's case, Eton and Sandhurst would be welcome. So Gwynn 'dwelt apart' as far as the Literary Coterie was concerned. The coterie is gone, but the impression remains that every gleam of Irish genius went with it. No critics, or reviewers or authorities can take genius to the grave with them.

Time holds a tribunal whose decrees are far more reaching than those of Lady Gregory. Before it, when Martyn, Dunsany and Gwynn come to be summoned, they will find themselves exonerated from contempt of the earlier court.

Lady Gregory would have excluded Tommy Moore for the reason that she excluded James Joyce: he was not quite a gentleman. Contrari-wise, I can imagine his indignation if, forty years hence, an historiographer were to discover Dunsany in the Fields of Dis with, 'One of the Abbey Theatre, I presume?' What a welcome he would get from the shade who had rhymed so lightly when on earth,

> 'I heard the pit and circle say,
> "Gregory bores us."
> As, one by one, they slip away.'

Disconcerting as it is to realise that everyone is fenced and bounded by the conventions of the time in which he lives, it is more irritating to know that by some accident you may be more accurately pigeon-holed in a particular compartment of time. Yeats and his contemporaries, for all their awareness of the narrowing effects of politics on poetry – an effect of which Thomas Davis was held to be the chief exemplar – owed their fame to being the mouthpiece of the popular myth of the time, and not, primarily, to their poetry. Yeats happened to be the greatest poet of the period because he had the gift of creating rhythm from the inner relation between words and metre. Had he to rely on this to recommend him to the populace, he would be as out of it as Dunsany is or as Milton was in Charles the Second's day.

What is the remedy? Obviously, the populace cannot be taught poetry in time to recognise it before an exponent dies. This would not be in the nature of things, seeing that every poet, if he is worthy of the name, must be prophetically ahead of his time and untrammelled as far as possible by its conventions. The remedy for the poet is not to seek public approbation but to flee from it as stigmatising him and dating him – *Odi profanum vulgus*. Let him look to his accomplishment for 'its own exceeding great reward'. This has been done before. If it bring no peace of mind it is because the poet has no confidence in his work. Flaubert cared little for applause. And I have yet to learn that Shakespeare signed anything but his will.

Follow the road along with me,
Mulhuddart first, and then Clonee,
Meath of the pleasant watercourses,
And Rogers rude who deals in horses.

I have an invitation to dine at Dunsany Castle whenever I can. I remember one invitation that was sent to me because it was in rhyme. I will quote only one stanza: the others are in Dunsany's *My Ireland*, one of the best books on that country.

'Here in this fertile land
The port you may not touch
Waits you, and by my hand
The wild duck slain and such.'

That was one of many hospitalities. But here it is due to myself to explain why I might not touch port, lest it be thought that I had achieved the last infirmity of idle limbs, gout. I had not even poor man's gout.

What had happened was that, influenced by the luxury and the feudal lordliness of his house, I had asked Dunsany where he bought his port.

'From Sir George Brooke.'

Now, the family of Dublin wine merchants known as Brooke were so well esteemed by those who could appreciate good wine (and consequently were in power) that they obtained a knighthood for the head of the firm. He became 'Sir George' just as Kay, in the court of King Arthur, was awarded the accolade.

To Brooke's in Gardiner Place I went and ordered some dozens of 'the kind of port you supply to Dunsany Castle'. Sir George himself had it looked up; and I got the wine in due course. The associations of the port turned me for a day or so into a two-bottle man. But 'oh, the difference to me!

All the cuckoo-clock factories of Switzerland moved into my skull. Every time my heel touched the ground four and twenty cuckoos began to sing.

I went rolling down the lea.

On my next visit to Dunsany I accosted my host. I told him what his dark brand of port had done, and of my martyrdom to his house. Such an imputation had never been heard before. He caused an inquiry to be made. The butler reported with becoming concern. It transpired that his predecessor had for years devoted himself to the castle's cellar, and after a life of assiduity, succeeded in drinking a pipe of port that had been laid down when His Lordship was born. The port with which the empty pipe was replenished was from one laid down on the birth of Dunsany's heir, who was in his cradle at the time. Dunsany's dark brand was also in its infancy.

Even though a general election was 'due any minute now' I could not wait for the work on the roads it promised. I went in a private car.

You do not enter Dunsany Castle by the great gate over which two white jennets support the baronial arms with the motto, *Festina lente*. The family name is Plunkett, which is a corruption of the Norman French for 'white jennet'. To enter by the great gate entails the opening of gates here and there in the park. So you go past it to Dunsany Cross, on the right-hand side of the road, and turn slant-wise through a narrow Gothic arch, hence a short drive which passes the old church on the left and one of the mottes, mounds or duns from which the place may have derived its name, brings you to the wide gravel sweep in front of the castle which rises sheer from the 'fertile land'.

The trees appeared to be thicker and heavier than they were ten years ago; but this must have been imagined by me, for few eyes can detect the growth of an old tree. Ivy there was in abundance. The old church to the left where the barons lie is clothed in the bright-green, shiny leaf. Little of the grey stone was visible. This was one sign of Time's passage. The walls of the castle, too, were green, not grey. One tree stood shattered, but its cleft wood was almost hidden in foliage, for leaves in Meath are profuse.

The castle door is in the west tower, on the top of which Dunsany dreams and composes. He immures himself from noise, and any noise that reaches him from the broad meadows must be more muffled now, for the ivy vine has reached to the battlement. No one is permitted to see that skiey room which even the lowing of kine or the crowing of a cock can hardly enter. If no one may enter it but the poet, I felt that it was also forbidden to talk about it. I did not bring the subject up, for to do so might be construed as an attempt to get an invitation. He might not say it, but that is what he would think. But I wished ever so much to know if from its height – the Height of Constructive Contemplation, the Chinese would call it – the Boyne that became the Yann or the hills of Elfland to the south were visible as he looked over the desolate flatness that stretched to the rim of the sky and saw 'never a sign of Elfland, never a slope of the mountains', when the day threw off the blanketing clouds that comfort the herds of Meath.

Maunder, the stately butler who asked the Black and Tans as they were leaving the castle after raiding it, 'Who shall I say called?', did not come into the hall. Instead, an older man appeared, and said that his Lordship was in the billiard-room. I went straight back, for it is on the ground floor, and found him seated at a tea-table with light from the stained-glass windows throwing a nimbus around him and tricking my sight. He arose. In spite of his beard, he was no 'grey borderer on the March of death', but incongruously sprightly. We discussed his work. I tried to get from him the origin of his wonderful names. Where did he get Narl and Zend and Lirazel; Pendondaris and Babbulkund? They flowed into his brain. They were not derived as Coleridge's Alph, the sacred river, was from Alpha, nor from the names of Indian villages where the tiger prowls. I should have guessed as much. For that which is breathed into us is 'inspiration', and these names, each of which can translate the reader to translunary places, are certainly inspired.

A man grows older in proportion to the distance he passes

beyond Keats. I find myself attracted by Matthew Arnold, the passionless school inspector, and by George Meredith, with Shakespeare as a standby before the end. Dunsany has translated Horace, the most complacent poet of them all.

We discussed Yeats's rudeness in turning his back on people. Dunsany derived it from Yeats's study of those who had turned their backs on him. Yeats, according to this theory, is presumed to have taken this as the 'normal gesture of a "gentleman" who wished to impress others with his superiority'; so therefore Yeats adopted it whenever he played the gentleman according to his interpretation of one.

I wondered where Yeats had met gentlemen with such conformity of conduct, for the few I have come across are more or less eccentric, and none of them has mannerisms in common. Besides, turning the back is more in keeping with a constable on point duty than with a gentleman. But that Yeats had an exalted and romantic view of those whom he elevated to the rank of 'gentlemen' cannot be denied.

My standards of sympathy and sentiment never alter. Yeats's memory and Dunsany's mind are equally inspiring to me. My only excuse for enjoying another's foibles is that I am not sufficiently aware of my own. Conscious of this, and not wishing to be discouraged, I never pray to any power for the giftie to see myself as others see me.

We were talking about the refusal of a knighthood by Yeats when Lady Dunsany came into the room. She pointed out that Kipling had done the same thing. This was an act on a par with Yeats's and just as inexplicable. She quoted from Kipling's *True Thomas*:

'And ye would make a knight of me!'

Obviously Kipling was disgruntled. He spent his leisure in making himself disliked equally when he lived in Vermont and Sussex. His ambition may have been a peerage such as Alfred Lord Tennyson achieved, or an Order of Merit. His case I could understand; but not the case of Yeats. Influences I could name (and did name) were at work to remind him that a *volte face* from a member of the Irish Republican Brotherhood to a Knight of the British Empire would be worse than Rolleston's coat-turning from an Irish Republican Brother to a censor of the books for Republican Brothers imprisoned in an English gaol.

All three are with the unaccoladed dead.

As I passed through the hall on my way out, I remembered more of my host's achievements.

The hall is half-filled, if not adorned, by the head of a rhinoceros which thrusts its black snout three feet across the way. The white walls show up well the armour which covers them. There is a mace which was used for the laying on of hands by one of the Dunsany ancestors who was a bishop. He preferred a mace to a spear or sword, for the Church was averse to the shedding of blood; and he was a scrupulous Churchman.

Off the hall, and past the Magistrate's Room, is another deep in the tower. This room is decorated by the originals of Sidney H. Sime's drawings to illustrate Dunsany's earlier books, by some grotesque masks marvellously imaginative, made by the author, and a snake-skin the long tenant of which succumbed probably to a rifle-shot, for Dunsany is one of the best shots living. He shot a swallow in the wing with a rifle; but his modesty in sporting feats makes him attribute the fall of the swallow as much to the rifle blast as to good marksmanship.

The grotesque masks show another side of the artist which is concealed in his writings. They were the faces of denizens from some hollow or reversed Elfland. Yet there was no damnation or abomination of desolation about them, as there is in the great gulf where cackling laughter sounds in Joyce's last work. In some glass-topped case were engraved seals cut in silver.

Beside the fire a hidden door gives on what is now called a secret passage, but is in reality the winding stairs in the wall of the old tower, stairs such as all castles of the period have. This, then, is the way Dunsany climbed to the bedrooms of the visiting cricketers he haunted in lieu of a castle ghost.

I once suggested to the wise Mahaffy that the name Dunsany in its original form may have been 'Dunskeney', from the river Skene, which flows through the grounds, only to be met with the mild rebuke.

'My dear fellow, you will soon find out that in derivations the most plausible explanations are usually the least correct.'

I was not thinking about the Skene as a derivation of Dunsany now; but of it as the scene of an accident to his Lordship years ago when he had miscalculated the additional force the partial subsidence of the raft on which he was balanced would lend to the gunpowder in the torpedo with which he was experimenting when torpedoing himself. Gunpowder was in the blood. His father had a cannon charged with some sort of delayed or dud 'crack', so delayed that it blew the arm off the butler who was ordered to investigate it. It may have been an act on the part of Providence to get even with that unjust steward for his behaviour with regard to the pipe of port. I forgot to inquire if the butler died from the explosion or from his attempt to rival Perkaio, the dwarf who pitted his life against the contents of the great Tun of Nuremberg.

It is an open question whether or no Providence is concerned with port.

'Splinter me neck!' said McGlornan. 'It's a damn fine Government. It represents the people better than the old gang. And it's not because anything would be better than what we've just had. It's the men in it. Decent men and an honour to the country. Only for the war we'd have got rid of the old gang years ago. What do you fancy for the first?'

We were at the races. McGlornan, restored to affluence and to some extent power as a backer of the new Government, was more interested in horses. This was as it should be. It was the first race-meeting since the general elections that had changed the face of things.

I am not much of an astronomer; but the sun seemed to have added a few more billions to its candle-power: the gloom that had depressed the day was lifted now. Even the weather was better.

'Hi!'

A well-known 'bookie' was opening the rumble seat of his large sedan. In it was a bar fully equipped with liquid refreshments which could be used long before fatigue set in.

'I'll have to be going soon, but James will take care of you. See to them, James.'

It was not yet half-past twelve. As a rule I do not go to horse races; but if I have to go, it were well to go while there was yet a chance of getting a good place to park a car. But, early as it was, the enclosure was crowded without by the careless, happy-go-lucky tinkers, pedlars and fortune-tellers who come into being only at stated intervals which coincide with the different meetings which are held all over the island. You had to drive slowly while you ran the gauntlet of compliments (if there were women-folk with you) or abuse if you were travelling with male friends. Having shaken off a hundred offers of miscellaneous wares and dispensed a minimum of largesse it was possible to drive the car across the rest of the field that circled the enclosure.

Do not become impatient with this noisy rabble. Theirs is a tradition older than history, a tradition that is contemporary with the first Fair or any assembly where men are gathered for sport. Bear, then, with the mockery, the cries, the ructions which will come later, and the cheers when any recognised personage arrives. They were at the Games of Taillteann, and they will be in Ireland as long as there is a horse left to run. They are the congregation of the Cult of the Horse.

That cult, in contradistinction to the Cult of the Cave, is observed in the open air, and its votaries are orgiastic and unrestrained. They are given neither to sorrow nor repentance. They feel dimly injured when subjected to the law.

These people, who would be called 'vagabonds' by the uninitiated, interested me more than the horses in whose honour the assembly was called. True it is, you could not have a race-meeting without horses. But neither would it be a meeting without the rabble without and the race-goers within.

'You must be having an anxious time now that Blethers is dead,' I shouted after the hospitable bookmaker.

Ted Blethers was a trainer who originally had come from England and, with an Englishman's sense of business, had become the leading trainer in the Curragh, which is the Irish Newmarket. He dominated the 'field'. Now that he was dead, the law of probability reigned again, and with it a certain amount of uncertainty which was enough to make any bookmaker anxious.

New faces were everywhere within the enclosure: pink Englishmen and brown foreigners; fat women who were not homebred, and the usual lanky hunting-women whom we all knew, and the hurried, busy, long-nosed men. For years I puzzled over the problem, how comes it that race-goers have long, pointed noses? You never see a snub-nosed jockey; but that is not a solution of the greater question. It is, of course, a well-known fact that devotees of any kind become to resemble the object of the devotion. Thus husbands grow to look like their wives, and sometimes *vice versa*. This is in direct contradiction to the more alarming theory held by Æ. Everyone knows that. But why are long-nosed men found in all the enclosures where the Cult of the Horse is being celebrated?

You meet them at the Spring Show, the Horse Show, Punchestown, Leopardstown, The Park, the Curragh, Fairyhouse and Baldoyle. Owners do not have it. That I will admit; but, then, owners as a rule take up owning horses late in life, when they have made their pile and, wishing to become fashionable and to rub shoulders with the best people, are converted to the Cult, just as anyone wishing to avoid poverty becomes a Christian Scientist. It is among the lifelong devotees the long nose is found. You might think that this comes from poking into race-cards; but you would be wrong. These men need no race-cards. They carry them only for the same reason that a priest carries his breviary, although he knows the words by heart. Among the 'stewards' are to be found the longest noses. They are of the inner sanctuary, as it were. Do not go away with the impression that I may give thought to a problem and find myself unable to solve it. I have the backing of science behind me in my solution. According to Darwin, the tapir was the prototype of the horse. Immemorial ancestry! The Cult goes back beyond recorded time.

With the women it is different. Their noses are not necessarily sharp. Leather pigskin has affected them. They have been so much in the saddle that the leather has entered into their soul. They wear country-looking tweeds, made far away from the country by London tailors, and low-heeled shoes. They walk as much like a horse walks round the paddock as they can; and when they can indulge their whim, they have stables in which they breed horses.

One of them, a Marchioness, caught sight of me. She was a very successful race-goer. She never had any losses. Hence the interest she was taking in my hospitable friend. He had warned me weeks earlier that if I met her to keep off a certain subject which was her besetting theme.

She stood with legs akimbo in front of me, a bulk of

womanhood. Her voice was gentle. She really was a gentle lady when not crossed.

'What have you been doing with yourself?' she said.

'Lying fallow more or less.'

'See you again,' she smiled and moved on.

Her nose was blunt like the nose of a horse; and, like a horse, the sides of her face were flat. Why, then, when a horse has a blunt nose, should the noses of its votaries be long? Having strictly meditated this, I recognised the fact that those who had the longest noses spent all the Winter hunting the fox, and therefore there was a time element in the development of a nose. Owners, as I said, who, as a rule, are later postulants, have not had time to develop this 'proscenium of the face'.

Boss Croker, the owner of Orby, a Derby winner, had a stout nose like a pugilist. He was the only man with whom the King did not shake hands when he led in his winning horse. He had bid against His Majesty's representative at a sale of yearlings. He raised on his Glencairn estate the only Derby winner to be trained in Ireland.

Joe Magrath, the strong-armed man who saved his country when its fate was touch and go, is a great owner – he has a winner at nearly every meeting, yet he has a round nose.

The bookies were on their stands, shouting like muezzins. Refreshments were shut off until the end of the race. Ted's rumble seat was down. Bookies from the North were in evidence: Hughie McAlinden with the euphonious name was calling from his pinnacle. A fat English bookie laid the odds in guttural tones.

It may be very democratic to rub shoulders with every other worshipper; but I hate to be jostled. I hate to be butted in on when talking to a friend. I had this unpleasant experience at the rails in front of the Grand Stand. I had come across the Marchioness again, and she was asking me, 'not as a medical man but as an observant, intelligent human being', how I accounted for the fine fettle of the horse. I was wary at first, for this might be the very question of which I had been warned. Surely she is not going to give me Gulliver's Travels with its houyhnhnms with their neighing names? I was thinking of some non-committal answer, though the commitment in any case was not much, when up rushes a fellow with a small head and a jockey's ingrown chest and seized her programme. With a pencil he marked a paper.

'Thanks, Violet.'

He was about to rush away when I asked, 'Are you by any chance a stockbroker?'

He tried to look through me. I smiled blandly as I looked him up and down.

'Are you a stockbroker by any chance?' I repeated.

'What's that got to do with you?' he asked.

'I noticed that you have the manners of one. One glance at the market and off you go.'

Off he did go.

'You shouldn't have said that,' the Marchioness said. 'He fell off a horse and got concussion of the brain. Then he became a stockbroker; and a very successful one.'

'He owes his fortune to that concussion. His trade does not encourage imagination,' I concurred.

From the throats of tens of thousands of people came the dull cry, 'They're off!'

The shining horses passed us once. I watched the impassive faces of the monkey men who crouched on the horses' withers: watchful, alert, although their faces, with a deep line on either cheek, registered nothing.

Again they passed. This time they were in the straight, a cloud of colour with flashing limbs beneath. The turf became so sonorous as a drum. At last cheers broke the tension.

The board that announced the winners spelt out – Good Lord, it cannot be – SHANKS. If it spells out PAT I will consult an astrologer. But the final notice gave SHANKS MARE as the winner.

'So I thought,' the Marchioness remarked. 'What about some plovers' eggs?'

She led the way to the marquee of a Dublin club that found that exclusiveness was as bad an investment as the Exclusive, so it opened its doors to ladies in the last ten years. The air within was dank and hot and the grass underfoot greasy.

'I think we'll go to Ted's car.'

We left the enclosure and went to where the cars were parked. We found Ted's man dispensing lunch. When the Marchioness appeared the guests faded away.

James gave us seats in the sedan. He spread napkins on our knees.

As she sipped her champagne the Marchioness said, 'I asked you a question when poor Ned came to consult my card – for it is against his principles to buy one of his own – it is this: how do you account for the fitness, strength and speed of the horse?'

From the unnecessary look of rapture on her face I said to myself, 'It's coming now,' but I answered, 'Selective breeding.'

'Ah no,' she said. 'It's more than that.'

I remained silent but attentive.

'Can't you guess?'

Sadly I confessed, 'No.'

'Breast-feeding! Breast-feeding and nothing else.'

I saw four teats and only one foal.

'There's a lot in that,' I agreed.

'I should think there is. Take the case of yourself. I don't want to be personal – take the case of myself too. I can tell by you that you were a breast-fed baby. I – well, I will say this, I am not exactly a runt.'

She stretched her shoulders. 'The only child of mine that was not suckled because I got malaria is a disgrace to the family. He chases every woman he sees. He can't help it. He was deprived as an infant . . . Now . . .'

A man in pink, with a white face and white moustache under a tall hat, put his head through the window.

'So that's where you are. Violet, come out of it. You must watch the second race. People expect it.'

'Very well, Terence, I'll get going.' She lifted her bulk out of the car. 'You can stay here until Ted comes in or bore yourself stiff watching my mare lose.'

One of the aspects of Demeter was that of a mare. Under

the appearance of the Mare-Headed she was worshipped in Arcadia, and may she not have appeared in this Western Arcadia to us?

Back in the enclosure people were lifting their hats. The new Prime Minister was driving in. No one pretended to be pre-occupied. They all looked at the Prime Minister's car with respect. Already he had done more in three months than his predecessor did in fifteen years. He didn't stall and wrap himself in a cloud of words. He did what his predecessor, for all self-exhortation, had failed to do – establish a Republic. Costello did more: he persuaded the Prime Ministers of the Dominions to accept his decision to sever political ties with England. This was done without ostentation or hesitation. The quiet dignity of the man made him popular when he went to Canada and convinced everyone of the justice of his determination. Not that politics is of such importance now that economics has supplanted it.

He finds time to visit the races.

Was there ever an Irishman who had not a sentiment for a horse? I remember convincing the late Pat Hogan, Minister for Agriculture, that not only had Disraeli done more for Great Britain than the ex-Prime Minister had done for Ireland; but he had attended the Derby; and that made him more English than his counterpart here was Irish. Pat agreed.

Loud cheers came from the fields outside. Who was coming now? Rumour that is never wrong at an open-air assembly said that Joe was coming. He had been detained on business at the Curragh, but he was in time for the third race.

The sea of heads bobbed before me. Sadly I thought: A few years, and they all shall have disappeared like clouds that cross a hill. Other generations shall take their place. How few of those present shall be missed? How few even remembered? Three or four; and one of these shall be Joe Magrath, who has as many aspects as the Mare-headed One herself. Another will be William Cosgrove, who, in spite of his retiring disposition, will stand out for inflexible justice and honesty. And the present Prime Minister, Costello: he shall be remembered, not because he is in a series that is historical, but for the quality of his statesmanship; and for the fact that he is the first Republican Prime Minister.

Yet, in spite of this, and in spite of all his patriotism, his Government shall grow less and less popular because the Irish people outrun their Government every ten years (only the war saved the last Government). Like the Earth or the Marchioness, Ireland is a Mare-headed goddess. But, like Earth, she is also a goddess of death, and will enfold all her children in the end.

'It was Aed's, it was Ailill's,
It was Conaing's, it was Cuiline's;
The fort remains after each man in his turn –
And the kings asleep in the ground.'

This is a foregone conclusion; but how would it be if in the crowded fields out there another Zozimus should arise under the rim of gentle hills, or another Blind Raftery who should seize the sentiment of all race-courses, of all Ireland, and give it to us in everlasting rhyme?

There is room for every kind of character in Ireland and no one is likelier to become popular than the man who is poor. There is some sort of luxury in pity, and when a man is pitiably poor all the more eligible is he for Tir na nOge.

The fact is that no Irishman can endure being himself for long. This is not only an Irish trait; but one that is universal. It is common alike to fool and sage. George Santayana, the wisest man of our time, has expressed this sentiment in a poem where he wishes to escape from himself. You don't have to be a hero to be a receptacle into which the Irish people precipitate themselves. Anyone will do – almost. But think of what Ireland will do to you once you become the receptacle of its spirit. Think of what happened to Parnell. Knowing this, no Irishman wants to be himself. He wants to be represented by a hero who, like the victim kings of primitive times, perished after a little reign.

I may be given to apprehensions which are groundless for the most part; but it is beginning to dawn on me that if I don't withdraw from the scene, I may become a national hero. Don't think I am getting a swollen head, it's not much of a compliment and so not much of a boast. Just look at the heroes we have had! After all, very few people know me. That's what makes me so eligible. And once you become a trash can for the soul of Ireland, the Marchioness, the Mare-headed, will get you surely. I have no wish to become a national hero; I had rather they threw bricks at me than themselves; but strong misgivings obsess me that I may be, if I do not get away. It will not be so fateful if I become a figure of edification far away.

Maybe once a year, maybe not once in two or three years, the dream or vision comes to me of a small boy, who was myself, lying on the heather beside a mountain rivulet gazing down at a trout balanced about an inch or two above the sandy bottom of a little pool. Though the vision is pleasing, I do not linger on it because, though I am given to sentiment, I am not prone to being sentimental about myself.

Of late the vision has become more frequent, and so more insistent, for it recurs not only every week, but is before me night and day after every distraction or absorbing interest. The picture re-forms clearly and becomes clearer and clearer as the days return. This fact alone has made me decide to visit Roundwood and try to find again that mountain pool which cannot have been far from the house where I stayed; for a tiny boy may not wander far without being missed and chided on his return, and chided I was not.

To Roundwood, then, I resolved to go, prepared for the disappointment and the disillusion that is in store for all who seek to recapture the wonder and enthusiasm of their childhood. Beyond such a chasm as the years had deepened, what hope could I cherish to catch again the freshness and the magic that wood and rock and stream and hill held for a child who had been taken for the first time on a holiday from his native town?

I see that trout now as he lies safe below three feet of water, staying himself with an almost imperceptible movement of his transparent fins. I remember how I uncoiled a cast and tried to sink a fly that would not be submerged until I had tied a pebble to the gut and tried again. Down the fly went, and I held it in front of the little trout, but the trout took no notice of the lure. I returned to the house disappointed; but no one learned of my failure, for I was loath to acknowledge my inexperience, and I was far from certain that I had acted wisely in departing so drastically, through impatience, from the usual practice of anglers who wait for the fish to rise.

All I can remember that would mark the date is that it was a year of a great drought. The fish in the Vartry Lake were leaping two and three feet out of the water, and so close to the shore that I wondered why no one thought of putting a landing-net under them before they fell back. I see again distinctly (perhaps too distinctly, for memory is a magician) the crimson freckles above the band of gold which was their side, the brown of their backs that deepened into limpid black on the hard helmet of their heads; and I feel again the surprise and excitement of the suddenness with which they left the water, and the lovely curve of their leap into the air.

My trout lay so still near the bottom that I am beginning to wonder now if it were not a gudgeon, after all. Its back was greyish silver, and it was scarcely five inches long.

I remember the yellow-hammer that chirped incessantly, flashing black and yellow from its dipping tail as it swayed in the hedge between the road and the lake; but it will hardly be a landmark now.

Half a hundred years ago! Where will Beda Murphy be by this; and the maids who served that little inn?

From the railway station at Bray the drive was long, for there were no taxis, owing to the restrictions on motor fuel. A landau or a Victoria — one of those carriages that stretched between their pairs of wheels like an inverted Cupid's bow — was surely the kind of vehicle that took me to Roundwood in the days gone by. It seemed appropriate now. That's why I hired it. I liked the looks of the driver, a rubicund fellow in his early forties.

The drive was tedious, for the horse had to be walked up the many hills that led to the Rocky Valley. We stopped at Pluck's. Pluck may not own it now, for taverns change hands even as the Fort of Rathangan. The driver threw a rug across his horse and followed me into the bar parlour. There was nobody about. A round mahogany table, a horse-hair sofa and a few prints gave a non-committal greeting to all and sundry.

Outside a hen could be heard clucking. Sunlight slanted down into a narrow yard. After a long wait the driver obligingly went to search of an attendant. A girl appeared and disappeared. We were more or less intruders. It seemed that we had come in at the side instead of at the front door under the white porcelain letters of J. Pluck. We apologised for being there at all. This confused the barmaid or the skivvy, or whatever she was, into action.

'What d'yez want?' she inquired.

The hen made a commotion as the maid returned with the drinks.

'Don't go away,' I said. 'We'll want the same again.'

We left with the feeling that the management had conferred a favour by suffering our presence in the place at all. The barmaid took the relish out of the tardy drinks.

We emerged under the shadow of a 'decent' church that suggested with soaring spire heights yet to be won. The Rocky Valley was before us, the road escarped by granite boulders upthrust between broken acres of golden gorse. A few summer cottages hid among the rocks to the right under the shelter of a hill. After a slow climb the high ground on the right fell away and revealed a wide valley with a hint of a stream. The driver, who had failed to draw me into conversation, not for the want of a vocabulary but for fear that he might make the unforgivable mistake of taking a native for an American, began to thaw under the delayed action of the depth-charges we had put down at John Pluck's. He levelled his whip and, pointing to a large mansion of light brown stone crowned by a dome of green bronze, hardly visible in its trees, said:

'That's Powerscourt over there.'

'Powerscourt?'

'Yes, where the Battle of Agincourt was fought.'

On my answer depended his confidence.

'It seems to me that I heard something about movie men and a battle they staged here in Wicklow. So that is the place?'

'Begob, sir, you should have seen it. It took months. The longest battle I ever heard tell of. There was horses and spears and tents and knights in armour. You never seen the like.'

'Who ran it?' I asked and foolishly stopped the tide.

He had to consider what to him was a quite irrelevant detail. After much thought he said in a voice that had lost its enthusiasm: 'I think it was a man by the name of Rank was behind it.'

'Soldiers rank on rank,' I said, and was sorry for myself. It blows nobody good to gulp a drink. But the driver resumed the saga.

'They hired the Waterfall and pitched tents and bought up every old nag they could lay hands on and paid the boys well to dress up in armour and go charging at one another hell for leather with a long pole in their hand.'

'A pole?'

'Well, a spear. There's plenty of them about for keepsakes since. They have a round thing near one end and a point on the other. Regular spears they were, like the lancers used to have, only they had no flag on them. They spent a lot of money while they were at it. The "Powerscourt Arms" was full every night, and "The Royal" and every pub in Enniskerry. But they had to be up and mounted and ready to charge at cock-crow. And they kept the crowds out. That's why I'm thinking that they took Powerscourt because it has a wall about it to keep out the crowds.'

'But what had Lord Powerscourt to say to all this?'

'Sure wasn't it him that rented the demesne to them? It was Her Ladyship that did any objecting there was.'

'Why should she object when His Lordship didn't?'

'There I leave you. Women is queer. They say that when she came across an arm, a leg or a nose that had been lopped off the day before, she would pick it up on her spiked stick and say, "What shall I do with this beastly thing?"'

The picture of Lady Powerscourt going the rounds like a park ranger collecting paper amused me. It must have been a great battle:

> 'Arms were from shoulders sent;
> Scalps to the teeth were rent.'

But I had to comment aloud on the tale he was telling me.

'It must have been shocking right enough to find a leg or a nose in the demesne.'

'Shure, they were only artificial legs that was lost the day before and never missed.'

'The casualties must have been heavy?' I suggested.

'Faith, you're right; but they were mostly French. The English won every day and the people didn't like it. They began to blame the management.'

'What could they expect? Wasn't it an English company that was running Agincourt in Powerscourt?'

He thought that out, and reluctantly agreed that what they were staging had the backing of history.

'But that's the way it happened in the old days. The French got the hell of a beating. It must be true, for a nephew of mine who worked in the battle for a month on the French side – and didn't like it – got such a belting that he turned on the Englishman, a fellow be the name of Houlihan, and he sez to him, "Houlihan," sez he, "Houlihan, get this into your head and under your helmet, and don't forget it: if ye larrup me on the last night the way ye have been doing up to this, be Jabers, I'll reverse history." It's history all right. That's how I know.'

I felt the need of silence to think this out. The great Sugar-Loaf was behind us now. The old Gaelic inhabitants called that and the lesser Sugar-Loaf the Silver Spears. In that lies history, too, and more than history. The Anglo-Saxons, lovers of creature comforts, thought of food. The more unsettled warrior Gaels thought of forays. Wicklow was a battle ground long before they staged Agincourt beneath the Sugar-Loaf.

The road was more level now and the horse was relieved from strain. I had not spoken since I heard that threat of the driver's nephew to 'reverse history'. When I thought of it, I realised that it was not as absurd as it sounded. For what have the movies been doing but reversing history, aye, and distorting it? In after years scholars will try to delve behind the only history that they shall have – movie history. But who will believe them?

The driver was talking to his horse. I accepted the cue and inquired after the horse's welfare. This started the driver into more history; but this time it was personal and contemporary.

'You think that the country is prosperous, but God forgive you! Do you know that if it wasn't for the Old Age pension the mare and I wouldn't have a bite to eat.'

Evidently it was my destiny to be astonished.

I had never seen the country looking more prosperous. The people appeared to be cheerful and well-fed: misery was nowhere to be seen. But now I am told that it is all as deceptive as a movie. And what am I to think of an Old Age pension for a man who cannot be near fifty yet, not to mention sixty-five? I was dumbfounded. At last I said:

'Do you tell me that you are in receipt of an Old Age pension?'

'Aye; and only for it I might as well retire.'

'But I thought' . . . Where does thought lead me? I asked myself. The less I think the better. I began again:

'Surely there is an Inspector to interview you before the Government hands out an Old Age pension?'

'Av course there is; and two of them. But it was not me he seen at all; but an auld alibi out of the mountains.'

He jerked his whip over his left shoulder and indicated the O'Byrne County with its fastnesses and deep glens.

Again I was silenced. I pictured to myself that 'auld alibi', that old man of the mountains suddenly finding himself of growing importance as the value of the Old Age pension dawned on the tribesmen of hill and glen. Just as he had settled down, determined 'to husband out life's taper at the close', he is thrust forward to represent his constituency, the younger generation, who are helpless when it comes to being suddenly matured enough to be pensionable. I longed to cast eyes on that 'auld alibi'. Maybe, I shall meet him before my excursion ends. I have hopes, for I remembered Mahaffy's dictum, 'In Ireland the Inevitable never happens, the Unexpected always.'

After two hours the road passed by an artificial lake in fields to the left. Soon it afforded a glimpse of a natural lake, and then passed between three or four houses on either side. Two of the houses were longer and better kept than the others. They faced each other across the road. The house on the right was my destination..

The driver took my bag into the hall. He was enjoying such a welcome that I wondered if there would be any left for me.

But I was mistaken. Instead of being left standing in the hall, I was taken into the kitchen, which is the principal room of a country house; but nowadays not open to strangers. To be admitted to the penetralia was a compliment I appreciated, for I knew what it meant.

The driver was well known to the owners. He was a mountainy man, a clansman who never drove past the house with a fare who might be a good customer. But now it was the driver who had to listen to local histories. A grave and ancient man was the speaker. The daughter of the old man was the woman of the house. She appeared to be a widow, for to a husband she did not refer. This by itself would be a poor proof of widowhood in a court of law, but we were in a home now and it had more import. After talking to me for a quarter of an hour she turned to the old man and, to his surprise, announced that I knew as much about the place as herself. I had been here as a boy. This took the conversation far into the night. It was late when I went along the corridor to my room. In the morning after breakfast I would begin to explore.

Through a thin screen of pines the Vartry Lake gleamed grey. That was over the road; but, as far as I remembered, it was on the hither side the little stream flowed down. I went through the garden at the back. A few apple-trees stood with arms akimbo, covered with silver moss. Through the fence I passed and walked to the right through the fields. There was no sign of a brook. That was strange. Mortal things pass away, but a running brook flows on. If I go back and out on the road and then turn into the fields or, better still, go on until I come to a bridge, I may find it. There was no bridge. Perhaps the stream was too small to need a bridge that would cause a rise in the road. I left the road and made a wide semi-circle high up in the fields, but no brook was there. Then I thought of the heather. Maybe it was from a picnic I had stumbled upon the brook. The heather began far away, so far away I went. The ground rose brokenly into what in Scotland they call 'braes'. A high bank, too high to see what was above it without a climb, rose before me. What is that? Distinctly I heard the sound of water falling hidden from the eye. I should have known that in such broken ground the rivulet would be hidden. I reached the bank. I saw the little pool, with a wall of rock rising upright beyond it covered with brown wet moss. A broken trickle of water fell down to fill the pool. Eagerly I took in every detail: heather, ferns, moss, a leafy branch spreading half across to hide the pool from above. Would I look for the trout and risk a disappointment, or be satisfied with what I had found?

It was not any wonder that I had failed to find it at once. It lay low in the heather under a wall of wet rock, covered with dark brown moss, a few ferns and branches from a willow that took root out of sight. It was just a little basin in a mountain stream. But how clear it was! Had it not been for the ripple where the water fell into it, I could not have been sure where its surface ended and the air began. It was as crystal as the eyes of a wondering child.

I tried to see it as I had seen it for the first time. The branches I did not remember; but everything else was there: the trickle from the rock, the tinkle behind me where the overflow hid in the heather again, and the granite dust that formed its sandy floor. There was another difference: I could reach down an arm and touch the floor that had seemed so out of reach.

It was exhilarating, this sense of accomplishing something by my discovery. I realised now that it was not all a dream and that the persistent vision had its origin in reality. I stood up to follow with my eyes the course of the stream to where it went under the road. Just as I thought: it had not a bridge to itself. Instead, it passed through a square tunnel of cement, walled above the road like the side of a bridge. I marked the place. It was not more than a few furlongs from the inn. Hedges started again, gapped where the walls were. I could not miss it even in the dark.

How long I lay beside my pool I do not know. The morning

was still young. Half an hour would take me home when I wished to go.

I rose. I did not gaze down to see if there was a fish in that little pool. Instead, I leapt across it and caught hold of the boskage beside the tiny waterfall. I climbed up the rock and worked my way along the narrow channel of the stream. I have loved streams all my life, and I enjoyed wading up against the brook and splashing from half-hidden pool to pool. The climb grew steeper. I scaled many a replica of the pool I had left far below. I passed between two boulders on the level ground where the stream was absorbed amongst mosses and ferns. The ground grew firm and dry. I turned around the last bush of golden gorse that bloomed by the way, under a solitary boulder of granite, and a strange sight met my astonished eyes..

I had come upon a town not two hundred yards away. Houses and streets, carriages and horses, men and women and children, and the cheerful hum of life. A church beside its tall steeple that held a clock with gilt hands on a black dial. The church was the only building out of proportion. Another 'picture' in the process of being 'shot', I guessed. But there were no guards or fences to turn me back. I walked along the first street I came to, and looked about me. Shops and offices and private houses lined the way. Smoke rose from the chimneys, for the weather, though bright, can be cold in Ireland even in the summer. Motor-cars and motor-bicycles were absent. It was as if you were in Bermuda or some town in old Japan. A period picture, evidently. And yet there was no apparent sign that the buildings had been thrown up temporarily. They looked far more solid and substantial than anything I had seen in the studios of the West Coast. Whatever company is financing this must intend the set to be permanent for period plays.

Every detail has been carefully studied. The houses show signs of weathering. Even the cast-iron railings that guard the areas of houses that evidently are intended to represent town houses of the eighteenth century are eroded where they join the stonework below. Plate glass is absent from any of the windows, which are lit by many panes. Even the pavement shows signs of wear. An old town seems to have been transplanted completely; the trees that line the public squares are mature.

'Are you looking for anyone, mister?' a barefooted street urchin inquired.

I shook my head; he doffed his cap and went away. He is better-mannered than many I have met in the course of my many wanderings.

Down the street came a two-seated trap or carriage with the horses in tandem. That was a sight I had not seen for years. The man who drove it wore a tall silk hat. Though a young man, he sported side whiskers. Beside him sat a 'tiger' or little groom. He raised his whip in salute as he passed. I turned to see if there were anyone beside me for whom it was intended, for I could not take it that he meant the salute for me. There was no one passing. Strange!

Two ladies approached. On one side walked a little boy. He wore a large collar outside his coat and he walked demurely with his toes turned out. When he saw me he seized one of the ladies' hands. His mother and his governess, whoever they were, wore clothes that seemed strange to me. Their skirts swept the pathway and their sleeves were puffed out like legs of mutton and rose over the shoulders in two peaks. Their boots were buttoned higher than the ankle, the same as those worn by the small boy. They carried umbrellas with long handles. They walked leisurely, talking the while without hurry or even purpose. It seemed as if they were out merely to take the air. The singular absence of crowds was the only sign that there was a limit to the number of the supers. Look wherever I would, no policeman appeared on point duty. I failed to find a policeman anywhere, or any sign of traffic lights. There was not a telephone wire in the town.

Down a street a two-horse bus or tram came gaily, with a copper bell jingling between the horses. It ran on iron tramlines. These, too, were spread from wear and tear. I went down a street at right angles to the one by which I had entered. Crowds here were lining the way. A hum of excitement ran amongst them. A procession of some kind was about to pass. I took a place three steps up in front of one of the houses to get a better view. Presently a large coach came on, suspended by great leathern straps. Four horses drew it, driven by a fat and bewigged coachman with golden epaulets; beside him sat a footman similarly dressed. Within the coach, which had large windows of glass, sat an alderman with a lady beside him. On the seat in front of them lay a huge silver mace, on a dark velvet cushion.

The crowd cheered and waved handkerchiefs. The Lord Mayor. He bowed in acknowledgement of the cheers. Behind him, in gay red vests and helmets of shining brass, came the town's Fire Brigade. They drove by, riding in or clinging to fire engines, hose-carriers and a long ladder shining with fresh brown varnish. After these came what appeared to be the various guilds of the town, with large banners pictured with their emblems. Behind the banners walked men in civilian clothes, some of whom wore gold-fringed sashes across their breasts. They marked time like soldiers, when the procession slowed at a turn. They marched gravely without turning to look at the cheering crowd. Suddenly a bucket of water or of some fluid fell on my head and the heads of those who were standing shoulder to shoulder by me. We looked up. A small boy was held dangling by one leg from a top window of the house on the steps of which we were standing. A man who was holding him leant out of the window and waved his free hand. We took his gesture for a sign that he was punishing the boy for his mischievous act. After a while the procession moved past, and I was left standing on the house steps alone. I took out a handkerchief and began to dry my hat and coat, when the door opened behind me, and a lady, who looked like one of those whom I had met out walking, appeared and said gently, 'Won't you come in?' She spoke with quiet dignity, yet I knew that she was disturbed.

I removed my hat and entered a large hall with a brass rail just inside the door. A deer-horn receptacle for umbrellas and walking-sticks was just inside it. At the back rose a tall grandfather clock. Chairs stood against the walls, and over a fireplace was a large picture framed in cane of a paddle-steamer gay with bunting passing a crowded pier with a light-house at one end.

'We are extremely sorry for what has happened. My son, I am afraid, is very bold. Rest assured that he will be corrected.'

I made light of the incident, 'accident', I called it. I bowed and turned to go.

'You cannot go,' the lady said. 'You must have your wet clothes dried thoroughly, and you must stay to lunch. My husband will be in shortly, and will be glad to see you. He will not be pleased when he hears of Alec's escapade. He spoils the child.'

As she spoke a key turned in the latch and a small man in his early middle age entered the hall. He wore whiskers, like the rest of the cast. He looked at me in no unfriendly way, and then looked inquiringly at his wife.

'Alec threw a basin of water on the people who were standing on the steps of the hall door. This gentleman got the most of it. I have asked him to lunch while his coat is being dried.'

He extended his hand.

'If you have not noticed my name on the door – I don't suppose you did – it is Purefoy. I am a doctor. This is my wife.'

'It is extremely kind of you,' I said, 'but I cannot think of trespassing on your hospitality. After all, the accident was due to a boyish prank. I am wet already (I glanced at my shoes) through wading along a mountain stream.'

He followed my gaze, but apparently he saw nothing odd about my shoes. After a pause.

'Nevertheless,' he said, 'lunch is just ready.' He looked at his watch as if to confirm his statement. 'We will not let you go. Thackeray will attend to you . . . Oh, Thackeray,' as the butler appeared, 'while this gentleman's coat is being dried, I will give him one of mine.' He led me upstairs and, turning to his wife, said, 'We won't be very long. Better tell Miss Orr.'

We entered a large room made smaller by a double bed and mahogany wardrobes with three doors. He went to one and selected a dark coat for me. I handed my own coat to the butler, and I put the jacket on.

Dr Purefoy smiled and said:

'It's as near a fit as these things go.'

He took me by the arm, and in that friendly fashion we went down to lunch.

We entered another large room furnished with heavy mahogany chairs, sideboard and dumb waiters. Silver shone on the sideboard. On a dark grey marble mantelpiece in front of a mirror that went up to the ceiling stood a bronze clock between two bronze urns. From the direction of one of the windows Mrs Purefoy advanced, and with her another lady who was obviously the governess, Miss Orr. I recognised them both now. I had seen them in the street.

Dr Purefoy still guiding me by the arm led me forward and said, 'I think he should have a hot drink with his lunch.'

If these people are rehearsing, I thought, it must be the most thorough rehearsal to which any cast was ever subjected. Every word, every detail is Victorian. Was there ever such a scrupulous training for any play? I thought of the thoroughness and passion for detail that made Austin Strong have his eyes bandaged for three months in order to realise the problems that confront the blind. That was one man in a million; but here everybody was subjected to a discipline that must be exacting in the extreme. Even in their friendliness there was such a genteel reserve that I forbore – for I dared not be rude enough – to ask directly what they were playing at. I preferred to fall in with the play.

Miss Orr was gently bantered on the misconduct of her charge. She turned the rallery gracefully.

'All's well that ends well, we must admit.' Shyly she glanced at me.

'Yes, Alec has brought us pleasant company,' Mrs Purefoy conceded.

'Through no fault of his own,' the doctor said.

'I would have invited the baptism had I known its advantages,' I replied, trying to return the very polite compliment of Miss Orr.

To my surprise that young lady blushed.

After the fish, the butler placed a large cover dish on the table in front of the doctor, removed the lid with a little flourish and revealed a leg of lamb. This the doctor proceeded to carve. The butler handed round each plate as it was filled. 'Well, if this is not carrying the thing far, I'll be' . . . I said, but I said it to myself. I felt disinclined even to think otiosely in that company. I begged to be excused from drinking whisky punch so early.

Claret in coloured wine-glasses was served with the lunch. Neither of the ladies drank wine.

The talk was of the opera and of the fullness of the house. They were going to hear Madame Patti sing.

I asked Miss Orr if she liked grand opera. She said that she did, but that she preferred Chamber music. She seemed embarrassed to talk before the doctor and his wife.

The thought struck me – her employers were not including her in their party. A bread-pudding filled with raisins was next dispensed. Cream in a large silver ewer was passed round. I handed mine first to Miss Orr. She poured a little of the cream daintily on the pudding and passed the ewer to me.

The doctor rose and apologised for leaving before the end of lunch.

'But you will understand,' he said to me.

That was the only inkling, if it were so intended, that I got of his being wanted on the set. I supposed that they were glad to have me to test themselves out, as it were. I dismissed the thought, for it was uncomplimentary even to myself. Yet when we went upstairs to the drawing-room the idea recurred. They were rehearsing a Victorian 'at home'. I was the foil, the visitor.

The drawing-room was the largest room in the house. It went across the width of the building, and was lit by three large mirrors: two with the console tables and one over the mantel, as in the room below. One console table was very large. It covered half the side-wall of the room. In the centre stood a strange article of furniture. It was a piece that was comprised of four seats back to back. The middle of the sofa or divan was crowned with an urn carved from walnut. A grand piano took up one corner. Gilt clocks under glass domes with porcelain dials painted with Watteau-like scenes stood on the console tables. Here and there tables with glass tops showing bric-à-brac took up most of the space that remained. On the mantelpiece two lustre candelabra with long crystal pendants ornamented that marble shelf.

The ladies seated themselves on satin-covered chairs. I stood behind a chair the back of which was covered by a mother-of-pearl inlay, until I was invited to be seated. I felt very conscious of my rough costume and my wet shoes, which their politeness forbade them to notice.

'I am sorry that my husband had to go out. I never know when he may be called. You know the way it is.'

I nodded my head.

'Do you never accompany him?'

'Oh come, come.'

'You both are very photogenic,' I ventured.

They would not depart one iota from character. I knew that before they pretended not to know what I meant.

'You photograph well,' I said again.

They turned to one another.

'Evangeline, bring down the photographs.'

Miss Orr left the room.

'It is impossible to get Alexander to sit still. Mr Lawrence has to fix his head with an iron bracket before he takes his photograph. Miss Orr will show you what I mean.'

Miss Orr returned and gave a set of photographs in tissue paper directly into my hands. What is more, she stood behind me and leant over my shoulder as I unwrapped them.

I saw a small boy with a lace collar and large 'sailor' hat standing on a rustic bridge. In his left hand he held a fishing-net, the handle of which obviously served to steady him on the bridge. His full, broad face was turned to the beholder. Long golden ringlets fell down to his neck.

So that's the brat who inundated me, I thought, as I summoned a look of interest to my face. I turned to a second photograph. The subject was the same. I knew that if I turned my face it might touch the face of Miss Orr, who was leaning over my shoulder. I shuffled the pack of photographs.

'Does he like fishing?' I asked the governess.

It sounded very flat; but it was all I could say at the moment. To comment upon the likeness of a boy I had hardly seen would, I felt, be bad form. I pretended an interest I was far from feeling:

'Are there any more?'

'Oh, yes,' said Mrs Purefoy, rising and going to an escretoire, from which she took half a dozen cases bound in black morocco. One she opened by pressing a spring. A daguerreotype in a pinchbeck frame of an old lady in a silk dress which made her look like a house-keeper met my eye.

Miss Orr's face left my shoulder.

'My poor dear mother!' Mrs Purefoy said.

'Miss Lacey is here now, Madam,' Thackeray announced.

That, being interpreted, meant that Miss Lacey was not a visitor, but some sewing-maid. This proved to be the right interpretation.

Mrs Purefoy excused herself, explaining that she had to try on her opera dress. I was about to go when she added:

'I will leave you two alone for a little while. You cannot go until your coat is dry.'

Miss Orr stood behind me. I turned half around when Mrs Purefoy had gone through the door which Thackeray held open. I looked her in the eyes.

'When do you go on?' I asked, summoning my courage.

The result of my question was surprising. Miss Orr went over and sat on one of the four joined seats in the middle of the room. She bent her head into her hands. Her shoulders shook.

'Take me out of this,' she moaned. 'Oh, take me away.'

I wondered what book they were screening and what was her part. Something that had to do with an elopement, evidently. But why all this waste of energy? There was no one to see her.

Tears fell through her fingers; sobs shook her.

Good heavens! can she be in earnest? I asked myself.

'Why do you want to get away?' I asked. 'You know that I am old enough to be your father.'

She looked up with eyes like violets drenched and said:

'You are not half as old as that awful man.'

'The doctor?'

She nodded.

'But you have Mrs Purefoy to protect you?' I said.

'She's worse.'

I saw the position in a flash, a pandering wife.

'Take me away,' she said again.

'But . . . how? How could you leave this?' I asked. 'When do you mean to go?'

'Any time. Any time. Tonight when they are at the opera.'

She rose from her seat and fell on my neck. If there were ever an embarrassing position I was in one. Two heavy plaits contained her hair. I noticed that it curled in a golden ringlet behind her ear, and that it had seemed dark brown to me, which goes to show how much my mind must have been in abeyance that I should notice in a crisis such a trivial thing.

'Promise to take me away.'

'What is preventing you from going? Can't you ask for another character?'

'She will not give me one. Oh, promise, promise me.'

I was about to ask, 'What will I do with you?' when I remembered that only a fellow like George Moore would do a thing like that. The code they taught me lays it down that you do not argue with a woman who invites you to elope. She has given herself away. Do not make it harder for her. Go thou, etc.

'Where can we meet?' was all I said.

'By the church at eight. It will be dusk by then. There will be a service tonight. No one will notice me.'

I confess that, code, or no code, it did seem strange the way she recovered her wits. Mine were still dispersed. While I was trying to gather them:

'Promise,' she implored.

I could feel how round her arms were in their black silk sleeves of her governess's dress, her badge of servitude. All at once the pathos of her position overwhelmed me. I promised. She released me and walked slowly to a window. It was just in time, for Thackeray appeared with:

'Your coat is ready, sir.'

When I came back to the drawing-room, the ladies were preparing tea. Very politely I refused to join them. Where was it I had heard that on your first visit to lunch in a strange house it is not done to remain on to tea? The clock in the church steeple chimed five. I looked at my watch. It marked four o'clock. They had never heard of summer time, I realised.

'You must come again,' Mrs Purefoy said.

'I should love to.'

As I said it, I wondered if I would be welcomed again.

Outside I decided to have a look at the town. First of all I must locate the church I had seen when I first found the place. It stood past some flowering-trees at the top of a slight incline. It was not very far from the house I had just left. Round a corner, I retraced my steps and saw it. The black dial with the gilt hands pointed to a quarter past five. My watch was one hour slow. I had ample time to see the town. I was curious to find out for myself how far the thoroughness of the set-up went. The few shops I visited had shopkeepers who were familiar with their stock-in-trade. In one, a wine merchant's, I was invited into a back parlour by an old gentleman with charming manners. He would be what an old-fashioned lady would call 'a superior person'. Nowadays we would wonder how he escaped an OBE.

His lore was the outcome of the experience and study of a lifetime. He lit a gas-lamp and began to explain that wine was a living thing and that it had to be humoured as much as a wayward child (I thought of Alec and of all he had let me in for), port particularly, he said.

His ledgers were all kept in longhand. As he turned the pages over he spoke of many titled clients whom it was his privilege to supply. I felt that it was they who were privileged when he helped me to a second glass of port.

'You must forgive me from sampling a different pipe. As you grow older your palate will mature.'

Then the explanation of the whole thing came to me. The promoters, whoever they are, have decided to emulate by reconstruction a town that will provide all the ease and comfort of a departed age to people whom the helter-skelter 'the sick hurry and divided aims' of our time have distracted and driven half insane.

Rockefeller restored Williamstown; but here they have gone further: they have restored the period and the peace that enfolded its deliberate and sedate life of tangible joys. Old world it is; but, oh, the freshness of it all! A great idea, I thought, to go back fifty or a hundred years and build a model slumless town that would be a refuge from this runagate delirium of today.

As I left the house of the wine merchant, I looked back. I would call again. The brass plate on the door of his Georgian house read:

SIR GEORGE BRENT

A shining brass knocker. A brass-bound orifice marked 'Letters'. No more. That was an admirable touch! So they knighted good wine merchants instead of cirrhotic ex-Indian Civil Servants in those days.

It was getting on to six o'clock. Already boys were carrying one by one shutters, which they fitted to the windows from the outside. It would take time to make arrangements for the accommodation of Evangeline. It would not be necessary to explain the circumstances. I could send her to Dublin next day. I did not think that there would be a hue and cry before that. It would not be until she failed to appear at breakfast that her absence would be noticed.

Miss Murphy was delighted, she was sure. There were many empty rooms. All that she had to do was to 'air' one of them. Would the lady be coming to dinner? I thought not. They were dining early, so as to go to the opera. So that was the way it was. This I confirmed. Would they send the trap for her? I thought that it would not be required. I said, 'Leave that to me.'

It was six-thirty when I set out to keep my promise. I gave

myself ample time, because I intended to enter the town from the same approach rather than take the risk of failing to find it. I would walk, keeping the stream in sight; so that, if I approached by any other entrance, especially after dusk, I should know it.

I walked rapidly, so as to reach the stream while the light lasted. Once I had that for a guide, I could take my time till darkness gathered.

This time I took the road and, leaping over a cement wall, followed the course of the brook. I would skirt the rock and wait by the pool until it began to grow dusk. In the town they were an hour before us, for we were on summer time.

By half-past six I had reached the gorse-ringed rocks. I will shelter here for a quarter of an hour more. I will have time to reach the church and meet Evangeline. What was I letting myself in for? Was she quite sane? Maybe the doctor and his wife were sheltering her in their home and that she was subject to harmless hallucinations. For instance, what did she mean by saying that I was not half the doctor's age? If he were fifty, which I doubted, that would make me twenty-five. But hallucination or no, I had given my word to be at the church by eight. The light was fading now.

I turned round the rock and stared. There was no town! I walked forward to where I was sure a street had been, a street that started immediately out of gorse and heather as in a studio. There was neither street nor house. I looked back to get my bearings. There was no mistaking the rock. It was from that I went forward for a hundred yards, and here I am where the street with its comely houses on each side and, round the corner, the church with its clock tower, had been.

Maybe, maybe, in the of day it was farther than I thought. I rushed forward until the heather was up to my waist and I began to stumble between the tussocks. What can have happened? They could not remove even a village circus in an hour. They could remove nothing without leaving scars on the grass. The town was gone, the town where I had walked on firm pavement, where I had spoken to the citizens and eaten and drunk with them. That town was no subjective thing.

I thought of Evangeline under the tower waiting in vain for me. Once more I asked myself could I be in the right place. Had I not made a mistake by skirting the stream instead of wading up against the current? But still the unmistakable gate, the rock, was there. No town!

I did not know what to do or to think. I doubted my sanity. What magical trick was here, 'not a wrack behind!' I had a profound distrust of substantial things.

Overhead, in the middle air, I heard the chime of a bell.

21 — *Green Tape*

The branch office of the Munster and Leinster Bank was empty, not because of an economic war with England (that is another story) but because it was the lunch hour. I had come to see the manager; but he was at lunch. He would be back 'any minute now'. Delays were becoming a treat to me. Had I not already waited two months and seven days for a seat on a Transatlantic plane that was to take off 'any minute now'? That minute was approaching: it might be tomorrow. You never could tell. To judge by the advertisements, it was quicker to go to New York than to Cork, from actual experience of the train. So I lolled about the branch office, which was decorated by a calendar and a clock. The sound of an adding machine being tuned somewhere off carried the life of the bank over the lunch hour. Behind some vertical brass bars I thought I heard a sound of breathing. I crept close, taking the utmost precaution not to alarm whomever it might be. I stood still, hardly daring to respire. I glanced at the clock. Its hands were together. It was ten past two. I moved so that I could see diagonally through the bars. A blond young man was leaning over a black box of japanned metal. Fascinated, I stared transfixed. My gaze must have aroused him. Without lifting his eyes from the contents of the box, he murmured, 'Any minute now'.

A sound behind me broke the tension. A hand must have moved from outside, for one half of the swing door was thrust open and a man entered with rapid strides and two raincoats. He was spare, with square shoulders and a broad, red face. He took one look round the bank. The adding machine opened up; its staccato speech filled the air with sound. The newcomer turned and eyed me. I felt that the youth behind the bars had suddenly risen to his feet. He was coming closer as the man with the raincoats approached. I was between the two, with the adding machine on my right under the screened window. Abruptly the man with the overcoats removed his hat, changed it to his left hand and, holding his right hand out in greeting, stood and said with a slow smile:

'The poetry of motion!'

It was McWilliam Lynch, the sprinter. He referred to our days on the track when I used to compete in cycling events and he did the hundred yards dash.

A voice behind me whispered in awestruck tones:

'That's the manager!'

The manager and I shook hands. He seized me by the elbow and, rushing me across the floor, led the way to an inner room which a quick glance at the flying door marked 'Manager' told me was his office. The door swung to behind us. The manager hung up his hat. He pointed to a chair with polished arms.

'It must be fifty years ago,' he said.

I was about to assent when he held up his hand in a gesture that indicated silence and conveyed a warning at the same time. He tip-toed to a large safe or strong room embedded in the wall, swung the combination and produced two glasses and a bottle of Tullamore Dew. He spun the bottle in his hand, making a movie of the label.

'Twenty years old,' he said. 'I wish I was twenty years old again. I would be doing better than around twelve for the hundred.'

'Metres,' I inquired.

'Not likely. The hundred yards dash. I did that the other day in the Veterans' race.'

'By heavens, you're not a day older. What age are you, anyway?'

He said nothing, but raised his eyes to a clock over my head on the wall behind me. He filled himself another shot. I thought it an opportune moment to ask his help.

'What can I do for you?' he asked.

'I have run out of cash; but I have a cheque book . . .'

'Fill it in! Fill it in! Any amount. You see that clock? I shall be retired in ten minutes. Fifty years of service! Fill it in!'

'I have run out only of English money. This is a dollar cheque-book.'

'And what's wrong with that? Fill it in, and hurry up.'

'Well, of all the banks I have ever come across, this one beats Banagher.'

He pressed a bell. The blond young man appeared.

'How do you want it?' the manager asked me. 'Small denominations? Cash that.'

The blond youth went out gazing at the cheque.

While he was gone we resumed our conversation. It was the manager's last day, last hour, in the bank. He had bought a house on the river. He had all he wanted. He would make way for younger blood: give the boys a chance.

'When I came in and found the bank empty it put me in mind of the famous bank in the Midlands during the so-called economic war.'

'I know the bank. What did you hear?'

'I heard that there was no report from that branch for three weeks. None of the letters from Headquarters was answered, so they sent an Inspector down. He arrived and, right enough, the bank was empty. He had not expected to see any customers; but he did expect to see the staff. There was no sign of any of them anywhere. He rapped on a door. No answer. He tried a second door. It was locked. He went behind the rails and tried another door. Behind the third door he thought he heard voices. He listened. After a while he heard someone say:

'"Have a heart? I pass."

'Indignantly he tried the handle, but the door was locked. He hammered on the panel.

'"The Inspector."

'"Well, the gas meter's in the cellar."

'"But – but I'm the bank Inspector."

'Silence. Then a voice: "The books are on the shelf. Inspect away."

'He was speechless. At last his eye fell on the fire alarm. To teach the young pups a lesson, he pulled it. That would get them out. For a minute nothing happened. He looked out of the window, and in front of his eyes a pot-boy from the hotel across the street came hurrying with four pints of Guinness on a tray.'

McWilliam Lynch slapped his thigh. His eyes sparkled.

'That banks had liquid assets all right.'

The blond clerk came in with the change. When he had gone, McWilliam Lynch put the bottle and the glasses in the pockets of his raincoat.

'This bank has liquid assets *go leor* without this!' he remarked as we steered for the door.

It is a pity that I could not go that night to the dinner in honour of the retiring manager who had preserved his fitness for over fifty years. Seventy years young he was, and no mistake. Think of any man sprinting a hundred and beating men twenty years his junior at his time of life!

A man is all right in Ireland if he can keep time out of his joints.

Apart from its uncertainty, air travel restricts luggage, so I had to arrange to have my suitcases sent by sea. In order to do this an export licence must be obtained from the Government. But the Government office was in Dublin. To Dublin I had to go. Back to Limerick after, so as to be near the unaccountable plane. Forms had to be filled giving a list of socks, shirts, under- and over-wear, otherwise nothing may be exported from the country. To save weight my typewriter had to be sent by sea. Green tape was enveloping the tourist trade.

I had little difficulty in getting an export permit, because the Government is familiar with those whom smuggling interests, and I was not included among its familiars. There was far more trouble in getting my traps out of the control of the Customs.

The muddle of red tape is everywhere, and it thrives on its latest host, air travel. This curse of red tape is by no means confined to Ireland. It has grounded air lines and put thousands of travellers under what is tantamount to open arrest all over the world. I, as a sorry instance, could not risk taking an hour off from a vigil by the airport; and yet I had to come to Dublin to send my heavy stuff by sea. Two thousand years ago a man could travel from York to Byzantium with more dispatch and less annoyance than he can do now trammelled by passports, re-entry certificates, fingerprints, parents' marriage-lines and police releases.

I had to go to the quays for a shipping form. I was not permitted to fill it in without instructions. The shipping clerk had joined the great majority of those who would be back in a minute. After an hour, he returned or came in, for all I know it may have been his first visit to the office that morning. At last I gave from memory another list of what my suitcase contained. I had to take it to the customs shed – not Custom House any more. This was a mile off along the North Wall.

At the end of a shed a little fellow with an insignificant head was absorbed in another sheaf of 'forms'. He took no notice of me, although I was the only caller to the place. I knocked on the counter. At long last he came over reluctantly. When he read my name he became animated. He cried out in delighted surprise.

'Well, if this isn't a coincidence! My mother always said that I was the dead spit of you, and here you are!'

Though I am shy by nature and easily embarrassed, I accepted the compliment because my luggage was accepted with 'To hell with the list'.

Thank God, my fears of becoming a national hero are unfounded. We smiled our adieux.

Of one thing a traveller should be mindful when he revisits a country that seems to him to be changed: the change that is in himself must not be forgotten.

I must bear in mind that I am like a clerk in a clearing-house.

That which appears to be aged, torpid and outworn will to younger and more eager eyes be as fresh and bright as the Liffey in its high mountain cradle in Kippure. The old town has weathered many vicissitudes without my help; and I should be the last to attribute any more to her now. There will always be new and original characters in Dublin and, relying on that, I would not have the Liffey change its bed or cease from rolling down the lea.

THE END

ANNOUNCEMENT

The chapters of *Rolling Down the Lea* in which Dr Gogarty describes his journey to Galway and to Connemara (Chapters X–XVI) have a remarkable and delightful counterpart in a long and hitherto unpublished letter written over one hundred years ago by

MARIA EDGEWORTH

to her youngest brother Pakenham Edgeworth in India. This letter gives a detailed and spirited account of a

TOUR IN CONNEMARA IN 1833

undertaken by Maria Edgeworth in company with a rich philanthropist and his wife. It displays to admirable advantage the humour, keen observation and gay acceptance of discomfort characteristic of Maria Edgeworth, who was sixty-six years of age at the time of her journey. She visited and portrays several of the places mentioned by Dr Gogarty, and the contrast between the two so different travellers give piquancy to both their narratives.

TOUR IN CONNEMARA IN 1833
by MARIA EDGEWORTH

is edited by her great nephew, Harold Edgeworth Butler, and published in period-style as a foolscap octavo volume with a folding map. The edition is limited to five hundred copies.

It Isn't This Time Of Year At All!

An Unpremeditated Autobiography

Contents

Proscenium

Some years ago I was bowling along in a bus towards that Fairyland, Connemara, which is situated in the West of Ireland on the most westerly shelf of Europe far away from all the turmoil and grim realities of war. Outside there was rain, flooding and desolation. I turned away from the disheartening scene. Next to me I noticed a tall man seated. He wore a suit of navy-blue serge. I knew from the way his Adam's apple went up and down that he was tall. His moustache was golden and his blue eyes were looking straight ahead, fixed like all Irish eyes on futurity. In my best social accent I addressed him. I said, 'It is most extraordinary weather for this time of year.' He replied, 'Ah, it isn't this time of year at all.' He was evidently in the Fourth Dimension.

I have worked long at the enigma. I might have expected something like it so far away from all that is pedestrian and merely real. Suddenly, I thought what a magnificent title it would make for a book that dealt among other things largely with the past where it isn't this time of year at all.

Boys! O Boys!

O BOYS the times I've seen!
The things I've done and known!
If you knew where I have been
Or half the joys I've had
You never would leave me alone;
But pester me to tell,
Swearing to keep it dark,
What ... but I know quite well
Every solicitor's clerk
Would break out and go mad;
And all the dogs would bark!

There was a young fellow of old
Who talked of a wonderful town*
Built on a lake of gold,
With many a barge and raft
Afloat in the cooling sun;
And lutes upon the lake
Played by such courtesans,
The sight was enough to take
The reason out of a man's
Brain and to leave him daft,
Babbling of lutes and fans.

The tale was right enough:
Willows and orioles,
And ladies skilled in love;
But they listened only to scoff
For he spoke to incredulous fools,
And maybe was sorry he spoke,
For no one believes in joys
And Peace on Earth is a joke
Which, anyhow, telling destroys;
So better go on with your work:
But Boys! O Boys! O Boys!

* *Marco Polo.*

1 5 Rutland Square, East

It isn't this time of year at all. And why should it be? Why should a free spirit be subjected to a calendar? Why should there be workdays and holidays? Why should my winged ankles be thrust into a pair of jack boots? I did not come down from Olympus for that.

Gyroscope yourselves up into a region of calm and I'll tell you something. Days are the time it takes a planet to revolve on its axis and even that is not constant; our earth had once a four-hour day, twenty-eight days a week, enough to satisfy the most exacting labour leader; but there were no men upon earth then; the tides were over a hundred feet high and the moon was much closer. Perhaps before you are done you will think that it's close enough anyway. Between the stars it is all eternity. The universe had no beginning. It was always there. It will be there for all eternity.

All this stuff is as old as Kepler, who was a few hundred years before Einstein. If you have not heard of him, don't blame yourself but his lack of publicity.

I am not done yet. What about the years? There are none between the stars; but here they grow, cheer you, change you, age you and finally lead you to the slaughter, that is, into Eternity, where it isn't this time of year at all. That is the standpoint, it is said, from which Life should be surveyed, an interstellar standpoint; but while we are depending on the sun, let us, like a sundial, record only sunny hours. Who wants to read about misfortunes except when they are not his own? Misfortunes are part of character; so is Good luck; and when it comes to Good Luck I have a very good character indeed. But, in spite of my good character, do not think that I have not revolved upon my axis: 'Is it not fine to swim in wine and turn upon the toe?'

It may be a pity that this book is not in the modern mode of writing, that is, without a hero, without any serial sequence, without meaning and without unity except the unity of whatever comes into the writer's head. That is the modern or open-air lunatic asylum method. The 'thought chase' or the stream of consciousness. I will eschew that even at the risk of making myself the hero; using myself as the subject. This is no congenial task to me.

As 'I am a part of all that I have met' you can judge me on the principle of 'show me your company and I'll tell who you are'. Show you my company, that I will gladly do; and if I cannot keep myself altogether out of the picture the blame will be on you, for I am satisfied to sit in the proscenium, that is, the part of the theatre between the orchestra and the stage, while my company is acting: men and women some of them dead and gone but all ever present in the communion of memory; portions and parcels of the past who still guide us and carry us on. We are part of what has gone before. The past is more powerful than the present, for not only did it form us but nothing in it can be altered or destroyed. What we call the present is only a suburb of the past.

One of the most remarkable men I met used to say that to talk about evil spirits is to bring them about you, a variant of 'talk of the Devil and he will appear'. From this I concluded that it is an unhappy thing to talk of rogues, cowards, self-seekers, bullies, men obstinate in their vanity and other scoundrels. I have come across them all. If I name them, it is only because I want to anticipate history and to put what I knew of them in life on record. Some of them are heroes at the moment, heroes to the unreflecting masses, the 'common men', who are the heroes of the hour. Conversely, it is a wholesome thing to speak about the good if you wish to have them about you. That is what prayer is for; and though this history of sorts is far from

2

being a prayer, it will be filled more with the good and the brave than with evil men. And it will be all the pleasanter reading because of this. At least, I hope so. I have met more good than bad men. I have met men who had in them 'translunary things' and yet were not so extra-stellar as to lose human interest. After all, there is such a thing as being superior to mankind, like Holy Willie. There is no welcome, salvation or housing for such here.

No one can tell where he was born even though he was there. The mother of the Duke of Wellington gave birth to him in a coach on the way from Mornington to Dublin. A coach is not a place within the meaning of the act, so it can be argued that the Duke was born nowhere; and yet he won the Battle of Waterloo, with Blücher's indispensable help. The future Duke was nursed in Merrion Street on the wrong side of the river from Rutland Square.

Had I been born in those days, I would have looked down on the Duke's family, the Wellesleys, for where I was born is only a few doors from the Marquis of Ormonde's town house and the houses of many worthies. I am a bit of a snob and that's not on account of my Olympian origin either.

It is better to be born lucky than rich. My nurse used to say that good luck was poured on me at my birth. She did not make me lucky or happy-go-lucky, but she foretold it, and she was right; to be lucky means to have a cheerful temperament. You never see a melancholy or a tightfisted fellow lucky, and it isn't that that makes them melancholy. It's the other way about; it's because they are melancholy, they are unlucky. So a cheerful temperament means a lucky one. It means far more. It means a happy one, and 'To be happy is the chiefest prize'.

It is sad to think that there must be more melancholy people in the world than merry ones. More influential ones, else why should there be this dismal outlook on life, 'Vale of Tears' stuff, and so on? If you take life too seriously, it will make you serious about everything, trivialities included. Life is plastic: it will assume any shape you choose to put on it. It is in your power to take things cheerfully and be merry and bright even though you are surrounded by melancholics who cannot imagine anyone being good unless he is unhappy. They equate goodness with unhappiness, as some ladies in great cities equate culture with seriousness. To these snouts you will always be bad; and it's no use trying to appease them. They all are paranoids and there is no bottom to their private hell. Have nothing to do with them if you want to lead a good life that is a merry one: 'For only the good are merry.' I prefer to think of life's great optimist, Brian O'Lynn who, when he fell into a river, exclaimed hopefully, 'There's land at the bottom!' Tell that to the bluenoses.

But why anticipate the gloaming and the end? You cannot appease Death, not even by dressing up in black. Maybe, all gloom comes from such idea: placation by anticipation. Whether it does or not is not such a problem as how to live merrily surrounded by gloom.

Five Rutland Square, East, was a good place in which to be born. East is more promising than West. I was probably born in my mother's room which looked out east at the backs of the houses in North Great George's Street which, though not so good an address as Rutland Square, held many distinguished persons including the great Sir John Pentland Mahaffy, afterwards Provost of Dublin University or Trinity College, as it is also called; John Dillon, the patriot, had a house there and there dwelt Sir Samuel Ferguson, whose poems and influence are responsible for the so-called Irish Renaissance.

The Sun, I was told, dances on Easter Sunday. I watched and saw it dancing on the ceiling; and that early memory remains with me, for divine control was about and Heaven was signalling. The hard fact that there was a cistern near the bedroom window from which sunlight could have been reflected makes no difference; now is now and then was then.

In the garden behind our house were flowering wild

4

currants. I played there with my sister under the long pink blossoms. Dark evergreens stood in the black earth, walled up from the 'area' on which the servants' bedrooms looked. The house was built in a century when there was no provision for the health of servants, let alone for their comfort. The men for whom the houses were built were ignorant of the fact that the servants' health might affect the masters. Had that been common knowledge and had social consciousness moved along with it, servants would not have been buried underneath the street, and their bedrooms would have had at least one window by law.

An ornamental iron vase stood in a plot all to itself in the middle of the garden. And then the stables. Sometimes a horse would be led out and I would be mounted and held upon it. This is an early memory.

There is a hinder one of a green wave over my head. That must have been when my mother dipped me in the sea at Salthill by Galway town where her father lived. Could I have been more than a baby in arms then? I cannot compete with one of Dr Sarnac's patients who not alone remembers herself in her mother's womb but in her father's testicle! John Kiernan, even if he tried, could not compete with that.

I have gone back as far as I can and I am beginning to wonder how can my early memory interest anybody, seeing that it bores me. What does interest me is my forgetfulness of whole periods of time. But for sanity's sake don't let us become philosophical; that way smugness and madness lie. You all know what happened to Plato's Mr Dooley, who had to drink the hemlock because he bored people to death. And you all know what that dirty carbuncular character, Karl Marx, who hated mankind, did to mankind with his *Das Kapital.* These men lacked humour.

Had Plato had his way the country would have been filled with motherless morons, just as Russia is filled with people who cannot call their souls their own, for in them individuality is annihilated. Plato was sold at Aegina by the Spartan Ambassador to Syracuse; but Anniceris bought him and loosed him, before he had a chance to see life steadily.

Karl Marx's carbuncles are festering all over the face of the earth in a kind of chain reaction and debilitating masses of mankind. Philosophy? Cut, shuffle or deal have nothing to do with it. Philosophy is the result of a bitch of a wife or none at all. Socrates is an example of the former, Plato of the latter; but we must hand it to Plato for endeavouring to endear himself to us by his mistress, Archianassa, as George Moore credited St Augustine with doing through his mistress and his illegitimate child.

Philosophy appears in the decline of a nation; in Greece after Plato, in Germany after Karl Marx. I will not mention France after Bergson. It is expostulating yet.

Until they have philosophers, or too-smart alecks, there will always be an England. They should be warned to stop theorising now. In the United States there are no philosophers, so there is no decline. I trust that you will not mutter as an aside, 'There is no civilisation either.' Just you wait and see.

Philosophy, though you would never suspect it, is what makes superior people call poetry 'an escape'. The real escapers are not the poets but the punctual, the commuters, the philosophers and all who seek to impose a rule and a regimen on Life. Regimenting Life is precisely the role of the philosophers: they seek by 'rules' to shackle thought; and they call their rules 'logic'! They dare not emerge from the fane they have erected to save them from the outer darkness wherein may lurk monstrous and frightful forms such as are seen in the gargoyles of Notre Dame. Imagination and mysticism they fear to face; and yet some intrepid artist faced them and carved their images. What is worse, these normals have had the audacity to call the glory of their race mad. It is high time that the tables were turned and that the prosaic were looked upon as morons, and those races that held madmen sacred came into their own. Poetry can climb Heaven and harry Hell. Philosophy is an air raid shelter for old men.

It is with the unruly, the formless, the growing and the illogical I love to deal. Even my gargoyles are merry and bright; my outer darkness by terror is unthronged. My thoughts are subjected to no rules. Behold the wings upon my helmet and on my unfettered feet. I can fly backwards and forwards in time and space.

2 *Green Thoughts*

Michael answered the doorbell. 'Your father got Fairfield,' he said. There must have been a lot of talk between Father and Mother which Michael had overheard. About that I knew nothing; but, judging by Michael's excitement and the serious scraps of conversation to which I was not supposed to listen, I felt that there was achievement in the air.

'Fairfield, I know; but where is it?'

'An old house on seven acres, about. Just to the right of the road before you come to the Botanic Gardens.'

I knew the Botanic Gardens. They were never crowded; in fact, there were few visitors so it was a safe place for nurses to wheel a perambulator and to talk with the gardeners or the man in the Gate Lodge. Some years back I had escaped from my nurse, who was thinking less of children than of grown-ups, and I had made for a boat moored to the bank of the Tolka, the river that borders the Botanic Gardens and flows between it and the gentle slope on which the Convent stands. The boat slid away and but for an attendant who pulled me out I would be keeping silence now.

'Don't let on I told you anything,' Michael said.

I flung my satchel, the one made of pigskin of which I was so proud, on the back hall table and rushed upstairs. Mother said, 'Your father's bid for Fairfield has been accepted. You will have a better place to play in than the Square.' Mother did not like Rutland Square, for though it was reserved for householders who lived beside it, there were gangs in it, and statements scrawled on the Bandbox, 'Molly loves Gerry', and disparaging remarks about O'Duffy, the dentist, and ribaldries about old Corney Walsh. Mother may have resented the remarks about the dentist, for he was the first to assure the neighbours that her complexion, the talk of the town, was not artificial but perfectly natural. As a girl she was called 'The Flower of Galway', and it was not only because her father was John Oliver, the miller.

Fairfield lay in an unfashionable neighbourhood to the north of the city on the road that went past the Botanic Gardens and the Tolka Bridge where the two tram horses rested while a third was harnessed and the climb to the tram terminus begun.

If you went beyond the terminus you came to the Model Farm. There were no 'ribbon buildings' in those days, that is, buildings that followed the water, gas and sewerage pipes, and so lined the roads, without depth. Open fields surrounded the town. There was the Bull Field even before you came to Fairfield, and fields with walls built of mud before you reached that. Behind St. Joseph's Crescent there was a field which stretched behind Kincora Terrace and Oliver Mount, all of which my father built opposite Fairfield's boundary wall. Now, with Fairfield, he owned fields on each side of Botanic Road.

The old name of Fairfield was Daneswell because of a stone-roofed well that rose beside a mound at the farthest corner near the Bull Field. A little stream bordered by enormous willows trickled from the well into a little pool which was to be my heart's delight. There is something about water which allures me even though it nearly pulled me in. Let psychiatrists make the worst of that!

The Tolka is my earliest memory of a river. By its banks, on its island and in its water I spent many happy days. Its north bank was bordered by a hedge of hawthorn and a green field that sloped up to the Teachers' College. It began with the waterfall under Tolka Bridge. Its source, of course, was farther away, in Clonee or Ashbourne probably. I often wondered if I dived from the bridge would the water under its white roof be deep enough to save my neck?

From the island near the bridge small boys, including myself, could fish for gudgeon with bent pins. You could see the gudgeon turning on the bottom, under three feet of water, with their sides flashing as they rolled. Schools of minnow swam over them and in the stiller places 'pinkeens', with their back fins spread and their gills highly coloured, could be caught. But the gudgeon were the prize; they were four inches long, or four and a half; the minnows, more numerous, were hardly three inches and the pinkeens never so long.

In the long reach before you came to the ruined mill with its dangerously deep millpond, an odd trout would dart by in the clear, slow-moving water. Very rarely a kingfisher flashed, a blaze of bluish green, to disappear in the high bordering hedge. I can see that sudden turquoise flight quite vividly now.

Carey, the Gate Lodge keeper, groundsman and general helper, showed me the knoll where King Brian's tent had stood near the well during the Battle of Clontarf in 1014. One of the berserk Danes entered the tent where King Brian was on his knees giving thanks for victory. He attacked the King who, though over eighty years old, cut off the Dane's legs with one sweep of his mighty sword. But the wounds he had received were mortal. He is said to have died in his tent which was pitched on the mound beside the well. Yes, the place was rustic enough to have legends and the legends were probably as true as legends are. We found a pit with human bones at the edge of one of the fields, and the millpond in which King Brian's grandson was drowned with a Dane gripping his hair was less than half a mile away. Fairfield House was two stories high with a gable in the middle and a hall door in a rounded tower at one end.

Another tower half as high led into the garden. The hall was level with the ground. Behind the house was the most wonderful garden I ever saw. A huge yew hedge many hundreds of years old separated it from the kitchen garden. Fully grown yew trees sheltered it from the north. The yew hedge was mysterious: there were tunnels in it where you found hollow eggs. Blackbirds nested in it, and in the big yews at the end of the garden low down in the branches little birds slept 'all the night with open eye'.

In the middle of the garden was a circle of hazels, and in each of two smooth plots near the house stood an ancient mulberry tree patched with zinc where the branches had fallen. On the top of the garden wall to the east foxglove grew and wallflowers; they must have been used for simples in the days when foxglove was prized for its digitalis. Lily of the valley and mullein, for heart disease and rheumatism, were to be found scattered here and there. Diseases were cured from garden simples then, and these were not advertised.

Two rustic seats under the yews showed that the garden was planned for a restful place where you could sit and gaze on the smooth grass or let your eyes wander to the hazel circle of lighter green while at intervals a blackbird would dive cackling from the great hedge of yew.

The front of the house faced south. To the right its boundary wall was fenced with old elms. There were rows of elms in the fields and one, a magnificent specimen, stood solitary and symmetrical in the middle of a low hedge on which the maids spread clothes to bleach. Who would dream, as he walks the cement pavement that covers those fields now, that once a splendid tree stood there, with spreading roots that held fast when the Big Wind of 1902 laid low many a stately tree? This great elm had horizontal branches evenly spaced that sheltered many a country bird.

There had been large elms in Rutland Square too. The one that sailor McVeagh climbed, and won every small boy's heart, was tall; but it was black with city soot and it housed many sparrows and starlings but no country birds. No maids spread clothes to air beneath it.

My love of trees is a late trait, later than my love of water. Trees had a practical value for me then, particularly those that stood beside the gate. The upper part of one had been blown across the roof of the old coach house and had knocked off many of the little slates that roofed it, long before slates from Wales roofed more than half the town. The bole of this broken elm was hollow. That is what made me value the tree. Into this hollow I used to lower myself and shoot with a peashooter quite impartially all who rang the gate bell. The most dependable visitor was the rural postman; I must have learned punctuality from him. He called morning and evening. He would turn his florid face inquiringly at the welkin and the walls. He never suspected an innocuous elm five yards away. It was not until his spectacles were hit that he lodged a complaint. The son of the gatekeeper was blamed, but his alibi was waterproof so I had not to yield myself up.

To the fields and the stream and the trees of Fairfield I owe all that makes me feel at home in the country and restless in the town. To this little early touch of nature my love of solitude is due. I could lie for half an hour under the great elm and stare up into the green world of the branches and watch linnets and finches hop, or a single blackbird fly about in this unconfining cage. The pond was the scene of many an adventure with a heavy raft I made of pine logs that could hardly float. In a tin bath you could drift down the Tolka until you came, nearly came, to the millpond. I used to listen long to the stream from the well before I realised that streams have spoken through the ages to millions in unchanging tones, no matter what language the millions spoke. 'Water, first of singers, The sky-born brook'; and mine was only a trickle from a well.

True, I used to be taken to Kilbeg, the home of Farrell O'Reilly, my father's friend, for they both came from Royal Meath. But that country place was too large for a child. It had a river of dark water bordered with reeds but its invisible flow and its blackness were repellent; besides, it was forbidden. If I did not promise to keep away when the grown-up men were out shooting I would have to remain with the maids indoors. There was a wood but its trees were evergreen and all the same.

The liss, or fairy palace, was another matter. I would listen avidly to the men in the yard who talked about it, far too seldom for me. It was hard to get word of it except in a way that was meant to frighten but only made me all the more curious because I could see that they were frightened of it themselves. It stood in a field in front of the house, a raised square with a few twisted thorn trees on it which no man dare cut down. It seemed harmless; 'Ah, but just you wait till night.' But I was sent to bed long before that.

Kilbeg had a garden with many beehives. There was a well in the middle of the yard, but the door of it was always locked. The joys of Kilbeg were restricted. It had many fears; Fairfield had none. The Tolka, 'the stream that overflows', was not repellent. But both country places put a soul into me that is made of waters, fields and trees, with background of fairyland not too far away.

3 'And Then The Schoolboy'

Richmond Street School was about two miles away from Fairfield. Strange to relate, it was no pain to go to school. You could walk citywards up the slight incline until you came to the canal bridge with the long Whitworth Road to the left and the sunken railway parallel to it beside the canal. If you had time you could go by the canal bank and charge down the slopes as Robert the Bruce charged on De Bohun; or, loitering, wonder how long you would have to wait before you were big enough to jump from one side of the stone-edged lock to the other.

Over the bridge was a tavern, the Cross Guns, of which Mr McGuinness was the owner. In the little garden at the back you could see two young poplar trees yellow in the light of spring. It was disappointing that there was no signboard to show why it was called the Cross Guns. The right name may been the Crossed Guns. Who knows? But the Brian Boru to the right and behind you on the cemetery road before you come to the bridge had, and still has, the best signboard ever seen outside any public house. It shows King Brian of the Tributes advancing with his army to the Battle of Clontarf. He is surrounded by warriors but with little discipline, for they had not much discipline in 1014. Though he looks more like a crusader than an Irish king, the customers, who for the most part consist of mourners, mutes who drive the hearses and the more cheerful gravediggers, are not offended, for their thoughts are not on far-off kings and battles long ago. So Brian's banner flies uncriticised.

Only one of the boys came to school in any kind of a vehicle; that was Tom Kettle, who came in a governess cart, a little pony carriage with a door at the back. Two people including the driver, who sat sidewise, could sit on either side. The Kettles were originally a Danish family – all Norsemen are called Danes – and they had dwelt in the district around the village of St Margaret's long before the Battle of Clontarf.

'We came out of the sea along the Black Beach. We won all before us. We won it with our battle-axes. We hold it still. We have been in the neighbourhood ever since.' That is what Tom Kettle told me. The Black Beach is now Baldoyle, a name that conceals the Gaelic name, Baile dhu Gall, the settlement of the Dark Strangers.

Tom Kettle was dark. He had eyes like the eyes of Robbie Burns, the eyes of genius. He wore dark grey clothes with three buttons on the sides of his knee breeches such as all schoolboys wore. He would not hail any of the other boys when he came to the school, although his eyes looked here and there. It was as if he already had things in his mind that were beyond the school. He moved about in his governess cart, not to gather his books but because his energy made him restless. We were not in the same form, for he was my junior, and I don't remember seeing him in the playground at lunchtime; but I used to see him when he was called for to be driven home. His home was a gloomy house of dark stone two stories high with a northern aspect in the village of St Margaret's. It was the house of a strong farmer, Andy Kettle, who had crippled himself financially supporting Parnell.

My father never drove up in his mail phaeton with its two horses to call for me. He knew better than to differentiate his son from the sons of others who were, for the most part, working-men.

Richmond Street School was run by the Christian Brothers, the only native order Ireland has produced. 'Chisel your words', Dr Swan the president, used to say. They were the best educators in the country and that is why my father sent me there. They taught Irish long before it became a political shibboleth. My copy of *The Youthful Exploits of Finn*, interlarded as it was with pencilled translations, fascinated me with its opening sentence: 'Cumhal left pregnant his wife.' What did that mean? I knew that it referred to Finn mac Cumhal, the bald father of Oisin, grandfather of Oscar and great-grandfather of Diarmuid, the Irish Hector, the first gentleman in Europe, Diarmuid who never lied.

I knew none of the boys well; but I did know well the propositions of Euclid and to their clear unambiguous style I owe whatever smatterings of unequivocal English I may possess. 'The angles at the base of an isosceles triangle are equal.' Euclid called his fifth proposition 'The Bridge of Asses'. I am indebted to him for bridging for me the gap between geometry and English. To him, and to the fact that there were essays set once a week, I acknowledge my indebtedness, and to the men who taught so well.

There was an essay to be written about a country fair during the writing of which I had a vision of sorts: I could see a plain with banners and many-coloured pennons waving over white tents; some dim association perhaps with the sign of the Brian Boru. I saw, although I did not realise it then, that all writing depends on seeing and then projecting the scene graphically. It is not without significance that the Greek word for knowing is the same as the word for having seen: 'I saw, therefore I know.' Do you see?

4 *The Tipperary Hounds*

'To break the rainbow on the briar.'

The Master of the Tipperary Fox Hounds was in the study. It appeared that his underlip had become transfixed by his teeth as the result of some accident in the hunting field. My father was attending him. Mystery surrounded the Master as it did all my father's patients. This was a necessary precaution to prevent the children, by which I was meant, from telling about the patients to other children in the Square in the hearing of their nurses.

It must have happened about Christmastime because I remember many presents which were sent to us by the Master, Richard Burke. My sister and I got more presents that year than in all the years before put together. One present, a large board brightly painted, allured and disappointed me, a forerunner no doubt of disappointments to come later on from brightness and paint. The board, which was about the size of a small tombstone, oblong with rounded shoulders, was fitted with holes with nets behind. Into these you were to throw a ball. Whatever game it was escaped me, for I was able only to take in the bright colours without being able to appreciate the game. It was the beginning of my acquaintance with that very remarkable man, Richard Burke, Master of the Tipperary Hounds for forty years.

The Tipperary Hounds are unlike any other Irish hunts

in that they hunt in the season five times a week instead of the weekly runs of the Royal Meath, the Kildares and other hunts. And the Tipperary Hunt was exclusive; it had few members but all were devotees. Its headquarters were at a small hotel in Fethard which kept an excellent chef. Dr Stokes lived in the hotel and he was a fixture, an authority of some kind, probably a veterinary surgeon. Next to the Master, the chief member was Dan Maloney of the well-formed body and the ruddy face. When he blew his nose it took about sixty seconds to regain its deep purple hue. The Master lived at the Grove and there were hunters by the dozen in the stables as well as the pack in the kennels. All the members had to be endowed with independent means, for it costs money to hunt and to do nothing else. The Master had lots of money; so had his neighbour Lord Waterford, another leathery man and somewhat of a rival with his own pack.

I must have been about ten because I did not count when the Master was 'constrained by love' (it was the questing love of some rajah whom he had invited to the Grove) to make the rounds of his house after midnight. He stood with his riding crop in the doorway of my bedroom. He was gone in a moment.

Next day I was mounted on a horse called the Sweep. It belonged to his eldest daughter and was worth, so the groom said, eight hundred pounds – about fifteen hundred pounds in those days. They may have told me that by way of a caution. The value of the horse made me far more nervous than the intermittent gallops over the countryside. My ignorance saved me from timidity; I did not know, so I did not care, that my face might be broken by a horse baulking at a fence or by a fall over a low hedge with a quarry on the other side. Some such accident must have befallen the Master when he was delivered to my father by special train.

I learned some of the things that become a member of a fox hunt: not to overrun the Master of the hounds or to get in other members' way. I found out some of the mysteries that horsemen keep to themselves; for instance, all this about gripping with your knees. You can get a much better grip on the saddle by the calves of your legs with your toes turned out a little. That may be what all the mystery is about. You may leave it to the horse; he will know whether you know how to ride or not. And it is understood that the best seat on a horse belongs to the Master.

The morning was early. It must have been a cub hunt. There was no fear of my running over the Master; I could not see him, much less catch up with him. But there was a danger of my getting in some member's way. So I went off by myself and lost touch with the hunt. There were only eight or nine members out and no ladies.

What a lovely thing the country is! Underneath the springing turf and the softly breathing horse and the jump through the hedges that had not altogether lost their green. The dark, dull leaf of the bramble rose that looked so well with the dew on it and the red withering. Out from the hedge, the open country with the rounded outline of Slievenamon, the Hill of the Woman, far away in the brightening weather. They told me that Slievenamon was the scene of a competition among the women of Ireland and that some hero on the top of it was the judge. Slievenamon is in the heart of Tipperary, the Golden Vein. The country that Cromwell gazed on and exclaimed: 'A land well worth winning.' There is nothing to equal it in England, for the light there is different for one thing, and for another the land in England is not so fertile.

By riding over about twenty square miles of it I got to know the Golden Vein. Perhaps I had been riding over Fanning's farm (but it was years after, many years after) and the wretched land that, in spite of all geology, lay beside it. 'Is it in good heart?' I asked Fanning, the tall tavernkeeper who had in his veins Cromwellian blood, that is, the blood of the sour, jar-nosed humbug's troopers who settled in the Golden Vein. It was easy to draw him when it came to a question about his farm; or it may have been his brother's farm, and that of his brother's mother-in-law hard by. 'Fertile, is it? Many's the morning I had to get up early and give the sheep a kick in the rump to remind them to go on grazing.' 'And the land beside it?' I inquired innocently. 'Now I know nothing about it, nothing whatsoever.' When an Irish man wants to denounce you he knows nothing whatsoever about you. 'But I'll tell you one thing,' he continued. 'If it's as mean and meagre as the old wan that owns it, a blackbird would have to go down on his knees to get a pick out of it.' There was nothing mean or meagre under hoof in Tipperary of the blue limestone when I galloped over it.

I tugged my bowler hat hard down. Hats are worn, tall hats and bowlers, to act as crash helmets in case of a fall. No, I had better not go any farther. It will be hard to find my way back or to explain to the all-seeing Master at dinner before the guests, before the amorous rajah, if he is still there, why I deserted the hunt. Taking care of the Sweep will be no excuse. I wonder now if she knows the way home? 'Gone away!' The fox, or I?

Under a clump of trees I saw two stableboys with four horses. Remounts of course, one horse for the Master and one for Dan Maloney. At first they thought I was bringing them a message. Soon they realised that I was lost. 'They'll be here in half an hour if the run was west.' I was not interested. I was in a quandary; what hunting etiquette do you break if you are caught talking to the boys with the remounts instead of following the hunt? 'If you keep the hill to your left and walk the Sweep we will overtake you in about half an hour.' 'Thanks,' I said; and slowly turned, determining not to let them out of sight even at the risk of being sighted by the farseeing eyes of the Master or his friend. 'The hunt has left me,' I added; but you can't fool a groom any more than you can fool a horse. However, I imagined that it was much better than confessing that I had left the hunt. 'Walk the Sweep.' Have I been overtaxing her? It will all come out when I get back. This is certain: that a newcomer can do nothing right in a hunt. It would lessen the lore of the old stagers if such a thing were permitted.

The truth is that fox hunting bores me. If it bores me in informal Ireland, what must it be in formal England? The fact is, fox hunting, like horse racing, is a ritual, a religion in itself, the religion of the plain as opposed to that of the cave; and I have no vocation.

Why is it that people must have a purpose before they assemble? I cannot imagine Dan Maloney getting up and in the saddle at five in the morning in order to gallop over the fields while the dew is still in the hedgerows. Can you imagine people going for a first night to the opera if there were to be no interruptions from the stage? And yet everyone knows very well that people go to an opera chiefly to see how others are dressed. Then all this interesting assessing is interrupted by men in exotic costumes shouting in foreign tongues on the stage when the curtain rises.

Alas, there must be an ulterior motive for every activity. There must be hounds to ride to or leave. It may occur to you that it is somewhat roundabout and elaborate to go through all the ceremoney and ritualistic vestments prescribed for the killing or running to earth of a fox. Yet the 'best people' are right about one thing – they don't go in for abstract ideas. In fact they set their faces against anything of that sort. Have they not had warning enough in philosophers, politicians, idealists and so forth?

Businessmen! That brings up the thought of how a rich and retired merchant of London endeavoured to improve his social status; well, let us say status although there is no status in society if you mix with commerce in a direct way. He determined to join one of the exclusive hunts, to meet the 'best people' and be accepted by 'county' in the end. With this in mind he paid his subscription and sent down a dozen horses to one of the hunts. Somebody told him that a dozen horses was somewhat *outré*, even though times were hard and the fifty guineas a horse would not be an unwelcome addition to the hunt funds. He listened to advice and reduced his horses to five. He rode to hounds. He had not been long in the field when he realised that if he were to make an impression on the best people he had to make the county hospital first. That's where the flowers were and the sympathy. So he broke his collarbone. He was carried to the hospital; but no one called. Perhaps a collarbone was not enough? When he recovered he remembered that he had the other bone intact; if he were to break that and add concussion of the brain to his fall, he might become an object of concern. He developed concussion of the brain. No one took the least notice. He had overlooked one thing – the better classes are born concussed.

There is no doubt about it, some sort of limitation is necessary if you are to become an accepted, that is, a successful, member of a fox hunt.

5 'But O, The Heavy Change'

My father died in the same year as Parnell. I had seen crowds assembled to hear 'The Chief' speak from a house about eight doors above ours on the same side of the square. It belonged to a Dr Kenny who must have been a friend of the Chief because it was from a balcony of his house that Parnell addressed the crowd. All are gone now, crowds and all, 'without a fame in death' except the Chief. Dr Kenny is forgotten, for all his intimacy with Parnell. He must have felt important when he housed the Chief, though the crowds who make fame knew not, or little cared, from whose house the Chief spoke. So Dr Kenny got as little credit for housing the leader of the Irish People as is given to the manager of a hotel. Yet the entertainment of the aloof and cold man was apparently its own reward.

The death of a breadwinner is rarely a change for the better. In my case it was a change to misery and servitude. I was sent to a third-rate boarding school. The prospectus read: 'situated on a gentle eminence rising from the Shannon'. The name in Gaelic means 'the Sedgy Morass'. I will never forget that 'gentle eminence'. It was the only thing gentle in the situation, and even that was fallacious. However, the word 'gentle eminence' had a strong appeal to my mother, to whom words ever had a strong appeal, else why did she send me there? My brother never went to such a school, and now he is much taller than I. I was stunted; no wonder I am but five foot nine. I was starved; undernourished in body and soul at a most susceptible age. We were herded into chapel in response to some discipline of our disgruntled jailers at hours unsuited to a growing child. We were fed on what the boys called 'cow's udder', for there was no bone in that insipid flesh. I became so emaciated after a few months that I was not sent back but was bundled off to England where the routine was much the same, but the food was somewhat better and the school was cleaner. I never complained, for I imagined that no school could be otherwise and that all schools were miserably similar. It seemed I was right when I read about the Eton of fifty years ago. Yet Protestant schools as a rule were better. For one thing, they taught better; any 'public school' boy could outwrite us in Latin verses by fifty to one. We were taught to compose Latin verses like jigsaw puzzles, irrespective of ear. We used a 'gradus' to check the quantities of the vowels. The result of our labour was futility. Hexameters meant nothing to the teacher; there was no appeal to the ear, for he was deaf to 'The stateliest measure ever moulded by the lips of man'.

We read Xenophon in his Greek: the 'paradise', with game of every kind, and the words 'nobody caught an ostrich'. I could see the bird, with his short wings aiding his speed as he outdistanced the arrows. Yes, that was a relief!

But why was I not told that Xenophon was a man about town in Athens and that he added himself to the army to do a bit of reporting like another Winston Churchill? The invitation of the Persians to all the officers of the Ten Thousand mercenaries and the treacherous slaying at a banquet was withheld. And also how Xenophon refused to head the leaderless band unless he were (here the resemblance to Winston ends) chosen unanimously. That passage about his stripping off his clothes and marching ahead of the grumblers in freezing weather would have won my admiration, and my interest with it. Why was I not told what it was all about? 'It was all in the Introduction, so why did you not read it?' you will say. Perhaps it was; but it was no concern of small boys to add to their task, which was to pass their examination with as little addition to the 'terms of reference' as possible. Anyway, who ever read an introduction?

By the time I was ripe for 'the sweet and pleasant reading of old authors' the sparks of fervent desire for learning were extinct with the burden of grammar. Maybe I was 'hard to handle'. That I will concede. I will concede, too, that teaching such as me was no pleasant task. Nevertheless, traffic with the lads in black made life so uncertain that it seemed fruitless to learn. For instance, if you had the temerity to say to one of them, 'It's a fine day,' he would be sure to draw in his breath and answer with a sigh, 'Ah, well!' It put me in mind of the condemned Irishman who was standing on the trap door with a noose around his neck, when the padre asked him if he had any last request. 'Would you mind telling me if the floor is safe?'

They nearly took the mercury out of me. I will be fair; it may have been fifty-fifty, a 'fair shake'; but they should have known better than to expect anyone to learn that which the teacher hates. It gave me pleasure to underline in my translation of Plato: 'Knowledge which is acquired under compulsion obtains no hold on the mind.' I must have been docile. When I think of the uncomplaining and unquestioning way I suffered in two of my three boarding schools I know that I was docile, and a fool. I had done nothing to be treated as a criminal is treated, with dislike, suspicion and distrust. Walking in Indian file along the wall, which we had to do in each corridor! What was that for but to make you feel servile? Well, the sons of wealthier parents than my widowed mother had to submit to that treatment. When I got to understand it afterwards I realised that all this hardship was intended to wean boys from their homes. Homesickness was a part of the discipline. The school instead of the home.

I was experiencing a medieval discipline, the rule of some fourteenth-century monastery on the Continent. The Middle Ages were about us with their fears, discomforts, and their superstitions. Though it was in England it could not be called an English school. It was a religious jail. There must be something resilient or devil-may-care in me that saved me from becoming embittered and resentful for the rest of my life. The only result was a recoil from all they practised. I was thinking all the more of getting out from all that was going on within. In spite of three grave accidents I was saved by the gymnasium, the swimming pool and the playing fields. And, I must add, the pride I felt each time I saw my straight young brother walk down to the dais to take a prize.

When I returned to Ireland I had to mark time before I would be old enough to join a medical school. So I was sent to another boarding school. The best of the lot. There I met Tom Kettle again. He was about fifteen and as big as the biggest boy and his limbs were longer and better boned than most. Under a low broad forehead, which a lock of hair made lower, glowed those dark eyes of his which held always a playful smile. His restlessness revealed his courageous, liberal and unchained soul. His was the terse and graphic phrase. I remember his description of a racing cyclist entering the straight and preparing to go all out: 'he put down his head.' There comes under my eyelid a moving picture of his grey-clad figure scorching round and round the gravel cycling track of the school, his long legs pushing power into the pedals, his brown face bright with exercise, and a glow in his dark eyes that could light a room.

Though I was two years older I took to imitating him. I am easily influenced by those I admire. His honesty and enthusiasm could have influenced one less susceptible than I. The successes of his older brother Andy on the cycling track added to Tom's glory.

Very few had bicycles at our school. I got one for a present; and I got my heart's desire. Though it was a roadster I converted it, as much as such a heavy machine could be converted, into the semblance of a racing bicycle. The transformation was effected by lowering the handlebars, changing the saddle and removing the guard that covered the chain. I imagined myself equipped for racing, though the amount of road work that poor bicycle had to do would have worn out any racing model. I thought nothing of riding thirty miles a day to play football for the Bohemians in Dublin, and the same distance back after dark. I took no credit for this performance, for it caused no fatigue; but I regretted every mile that was not on the racing track because it detracted from the raciness of my machine.

The school authorities let me out so that I might decant my energy, lest it burst the staves. In summer I played cricket in the First Eleven. The only thing I remember is that I bowled out Captain Bonham-Carter of the garrison with the first ball. All in all I enjoyed this school, which was a great relief from my English education. They fed us well. They did not try to break your will and leave you spineless. There were fine trees about the place; and there was the Liffey, black and bright; and one of the prefects came from an old Galway family well known for their eccentricities, the mad Dalys. James Augustine Joyce was at the same school but, as he was four years younger, he was in a different grade, so I did not meet him there. It was not until later years, when we were at the Royal University, that we met. Then 'we two were nursed upon the selfsame hill', as Milton called the plain of Cambridge.

6 'Faire And Softly'

Doctoring was in our family, so off to see Dr Bermingham my mother took me. He was registrar of the Catholic University Medical School. His want of manners was so evident that, at the end of the inverview, when he pattered out: 'Here's a pamphlet in which you will find the answers to all your questions', holding out the pamphlet as he kept on writing, there was no one to take the extended brochure. I was driven out of Cecelia Street, up Dame Street, to be entered in Trinity College!

There, the registrar was Dr Traill, afterward Provost. Though he hailed from the North of Ireland his brusqueness did not make him rude. He was considerate of others, and therefore a gentleman. He won my mother's approval at once because he asked, 'Won't you be seated? And may I ask if you are related to my friend the late Dr Henry Gogarty?' After that it was Faire and Softly. As we drove away my mother said: 'Now that you are entered among gentlemen I hope that you will never forget to behave like one.' A large order among the wild medicos of those days! A hope that could not be fulfilled if I had to satisfy my aunt, who had not only the Almanac de Gotha by heart but Burke's Landed Gentry as well. Yet it must have gone hard with my mother to enter me in a Protestant university. The fact that it had been my father's intention to do so may have consoled her; and it was not then a matter of excommunication to enter Trinity.

Scholastically the time spent in the Royal University availed me nothing. I had to begin all over again in Trinity, but the rigours of examinations in the examination booths of the Royal stood me in good stead in a university which went in more for educating its students than in filter-passing them as if they were so many bacteria.

The time at the Royal was not altogether lost. I met a less disciplined class of student in the Aula Maxima: 'Citizen' Elwood, James Joyce, Cosgrove, and Joyce's friend Sheehy-Skeffington, an opinionated, bearded little theorist in knicker-bockers. We had great fun during my short time in the Aula Maxima. Dr Campbell, the Professor of Chemistry, was a lean old gentleman who wore an old-fashioned full-skirted frock coat and cuff links as large as a lady's watch. He would ask: 'What are the Halogens?' and answer the question himself, 'Chlorine, Fluorine, Bromine and Iodine, never found free in Nature, always combined.' When asked to repeat we would chant: 'Dolan, Hegarty, McCluskey, and Dwane, never found free in Nature, always combined' – the names of a quartette of students who would have nothing to do with us, being earnest and hard-working.

Surgeon Blaney lectured on surgery. We soon discovered that he was merely repeating the textbook on Surgery by Rose and Careless. He had a huge scrotum and a huge memory.

Our Professor of Zoology was Dr George Sigerson, the famous author and scholar. He practised psychology, and he was a friend of the famous Frenchman scientist, almost of the eighteenth century, Charcot. He had a mane of white hair and a snub nose which showed his Danish origin as much as did his name. Our textbook for the course was Thompson's *Zoology*, which contained every species of animal, fish and insect in the world. It was far too long to learn. None of us could expect to memorise all its contents except, of course, the Halogens, so we divided the book into boroughs or constituencies and elected representatives for each set of three of the animals or 'orders' in the book.

I was the member who represented snails, anodons – crayfish, lobsters, etc. – and the common earthworm. Simon Broderick a student from Youghal, stood for the crustacea, oysters that have their reproductive apparatus in their feet, spiders and jellyfish. Christian was the member for insects of all sorts. Cheers hailed the man who could get through the most patter before he was ordered out. If a man were asked about an animal not in his constituency the member for that animal hastily would rise to answer and rattle off sentences from Thompson by rote.

'I have noticed,' said Professor Sigerson, 'that those who are most noisy in class are most silent at examinations.' Then he would put on his tall silk hat out of which parts of the specimens that had been handed around class were sure to fall. Of more than thirty in the class, only five passed: the Halogens and Simon Broderick. Just think of his luck! He got every animal he represented and the result was honours, though he knew nothing about zoology but the three orders in his bailiwick.

The only specimen that came my way was Nautilus, the giant Norwegian lobster; and though I wrote word for word, 'The male seizes the female in his great claws, throws her on her back and deposits the seminal fluid on the ventral surface of the abdomen,' it availed me nothing. I failed dismally; and I also failed to get an *ad eundem*, which is credit for the exams which you had already passed, when I left the Royal and entered Dublin University. This goes to show in how little esteem the Royal was held by the older university. I lost a year or whatever time it took to matriculate in the Royal, pass its First Arts examination, and attend lectures on chemistry, surgery and zoology. I must have lost more than a year; yet what matter? I met many people whom, as I said, I would not have met had I been only in Dublin University.

Joyce lived in my direction; he lived at Cabra and got out at Dunphy's Corner while I stayed on in the tram until it reached Fairfield, about a mile from Joyce's home. He used to walk down to visit me and we would go back and forwards under the apple trees in the kitchen garden, for that garden had the longer paths. Perhaps it was when the blossoms were in the air that he got that first of his lovely lyrics in *Chamber Music:*

> My love is in a light attire
> Among the apple trees.

His lyrics were as spontaneous as those of the Elizabethans whom he admired so much.

One morning as we walked in the garden, shortly after I had entered Trinity, he asked me if I would lend him my .22 rifle. What he, who to my knowledge had never handled a gun, wanted my rifle for was a puzzle; but I obliged. I continued to puzzle until one day he said, 'You are eligible to compete for the Gold Medal for English verse in the Royal.'

'But I am a student of Trinity College!'

'You have passed First Arts in the Royal; I tell you that you can compete.'

'Why don't you go in for it yourself?' I asked.

'I am thinking of your rifle.'

When I had untangled the cryptogram I realised that he had pawned my rifle and was proposing that I should redeem it by winning the Gold Medal for English verse, then pawning that and regaining my rifle with the money. The credit for pointing out the way was to go to him. I won the gold medal, which duly went into the pawnshop for something like eighteen pounds, but my rifle never came out.

Another member of the Aula Maxima whom I would not have missed was John Elwood, called the Citizen to ridicule his advanced views. He was an ebullient fellow who always had a quizzical smile in his eyes and around his shapely mouth. In the semicircular portico of the National Library we would meet every morning when I was not at lectures in Trinity College. Opposite to the library, in which the bookless students used to forgather, was the National Museum; it also had a pillared colonnade. Its hall was circular and decorated by nude plaster casts, somewhat larger than life, of the famous statues of antiquity. One morning Joyce 'arraigned Elwood. He assumed an air of great gravity, as he was wont to do when about to perpetrate a joke.

'It has come to my notice, Citizen, that this morning, between the hours of ten and ten-thirty, you inscribed your name in lead pencil on the backside of the Venus of Cnidus. Are there any extenuating circumstances that may be cited in your defence?'

'He's terrific,' said Elwood when he recounted the tale. 'A great artist!' 'Artist' in Dublin stands for a practical joker or a playboy; someone who prefers diversion to discipline; a producer, an 'artifex'.

If I were to draw a Parallel Life between then and now there would be only the sad difference which a Frenchman has expressed better than I could ever do, no matter how hard I might try: 'When we grow old we think that we have taken leave of our vices, whereas the truth is that our vices have taken leave of us.'

7 'The Craft So Longe To Learn'

Dublin has more than a dozen hospitals. Vienna, a much larger city, has but one; but then disease in Dublin is a *modus vivendi* and it therefore assumes a religious aspect. There are Protestant, Catholic and Presbyterian diseases in Dublin. The Adelaide; Sir Patrick Dun's; the City of Dublin, commonly called Baggot Street Hospital; the Meath; and Stevens; these are all Protestant hospitals. Stevens deals largely with the police 'who also serve' but are liable to contract venereal disease while standing and waiting – on point duty! In the Adelaide only respectable diseases are treated. There are two 'hospices' which are not teaching hospitals though they are called by inviting names: the Hospital for Incurables, and the Hospice for the Dying. One would think that the latter might be a very good teaching hospital, for its students could make no mistakes unless, peradventure, somebody recovered.

The Richmond Hospital, which was chosen for me, is nearly neutral. It is in reality a chain of hospitals, the

Richmond, the Whitworth and the Hardwick; surgery is taught in the Richmond, medicine in the Whitworth, and fevers in the Hardwick, separated from the other two. The Richmond has more knights and Presbyterians than all the other hospitals in the town. There were Sir Thornley Stoker, his brother-in-law Sir William Thompson, and Sir Thomas Myles: Protestants all. The Catholic 'balance' consisted of Dr Coleman and Dr O'Carroll; Sir Conway Dwyer was afterwards introduced.

The Richmond Hospital stood at the head of Red Cow Lane and looked south over Smithfield market to the mountains beyond the Liffey. It was an old building reached by a transverse set of granite steps which an iron railing protected. Beatty, with his large beard, his hollow chest in its dark blue brass-buttoned uniform, was the hall porter. He interviewed the incoming patients and tipped off the medical students as to the proper manner to adopt with each. His recommendations were possibly influenced by monetary considerations – what profession is entirely free from such? – but this is mere conjecture. There were other porters about the place who recalled pre-anaesthetic days, days not far off from Beatty's powerful youth, days when porters held strong men down on the sinister table of dark oak and stifled their struggles until the surgeon's work was done. Dublin resisted anaesthetics, for disease in Dublin is religious, and has the Book not said that women must endure the pangs of childbirth, and so on ...?

In the external clinics or dispensaries, as they were called, varicose ulcers were dressed with red oxide of mercury, but never cured; running ears, eyes with trachoma and cases of tertiary syphilis were attended to day by day. This was a part of the medical student's training and could not be omitted. Another part, also indispensable, was to 'walk' the hospital and listen to the lectures delivered at the patient's bedside by the visiting physician or surgeon. We were taught to use our ears and eyes, that is, to be observant to an extreme degree. For instance, a certain physician would walk through the ward hurriedly at the head of his class and, when he had passed through, turn and snap, 'How many in there will be alive in the morning?' You were supposed to judge by the position of the patient in the bed (decubitus): a dying man makes no bulge of the bedclothes.

As we got hardened we used to count the faints when the newly come students saw a catheter passed through a stricture or an abscess opened for the first time. 'What and why is there such a knife as a bistoury?' the surgeon would ask. 'It is a curved knife, curved so that its converging edges will cut more rapidly.' That was the answer, and it brought back the days before there were anaesthetics, when speed was one of the prerequisites of a surgeon.

I was Sir Thomas Myles's clinical clerk, or intern. Sir Thomas was a powerful man with a flowing golden moustache, large blue eyes and regular features, a very handsome but childless man. My mentor in Trinity, Dr Yelverton Tyrrell, the wit and diseur, commented thus, 'Now if Lady Myles had selected some little croquet-playing curate instead of this Adonis, she might have had a dozen children.' Sir Thornley in his turn was supposed to be in love with the matron of the Hospital, Miss McDonald, who was very strong-minded, as indeed she had to be. Sir Thomas showed his magnanimity by quashing the rumour and adding, 'Every allowance should be made for Sir T. He has hell at home.' About Sir William, Sir Thornley's brother-in-law, there was no scandal. He was one of those whose grandeur depends on silence. If a grand manner could cure disease, Sir William would be the world's benefactor.

One of Sir Thomas's ward rounds led, most indirectly, to a night of scandalous outbreaks in the hospital. Sir Thomas was transilluminating a hydrocele, which is a tumour caused by serum collecting between the tunica vaginalis of the testicle and the testicle itself. This is usually the result of an injury. There were two lady students present, both Presbyterians, breastless, defeminised, with dry hair. They stood with their arms folded at the edge of the class, a class in themselves.

'Take a look through that and tell me what you see,' said

Sir Thomas to me as he handed me the transilluminating tube.

I gazed. 'The light that never was on sea or land,' I said.

'This is not exactly the consummation of the Poet's dream,' Sir Thomas said. 'The question is. What is the etiology of hydrocele? Dr Fulton is about to enlighten us.' Every medical student is called 'doctor' by his seniors, out of some kind of satire. The medicals don't object, for it carries immunity in the dangerous places in town. Fulton was tall, heavy and somewhat stooped, as if the weight of his face were too much for him. He had a large pale face, wide-eyed, small-nosed, with a long upper lip which a little fair moustache did nothing to diminish. We called him Clinoclaustes, which means Bed Breaker, for the story ran that his weight and vigour contributed, with his partner's aid, to the collapse of a bed in the Kips: 'The tailor fell through the bed thimble and a'.'

The Kips can wait for an explanation; the man with the hydrocele is getting cold in the bed. Fulton knew; his heavy utterance gave his answer weight. 'Good, Doctor. Now Lamb will give us the differential diagnosis between hydrocele and hernia. Dr Lamb?' While Lamb was gathering his wits, Tom Myles, as we called him familiarly, told the class how Gibbon, the author of *The Decline and Fall of the Roman Empire*, suffered from both hernia and hydrocele. From time to time his doctors used to draw off quarts of fluid from his hydrocele until one day his hernia also pierced and he died from peritonitis. Therefore the differential diagnosis cannot be over-emphasised. Lamb knew his work and when his answer came, Sir Thomas congratulated him in such a way that Lamb became, if possible, all the more studious.

Charlie, an outpatient, was a syphilophobe, and that is an almost incurable condition. You can contract it without getting syphilis, which Charlie probably did. Now we used to say that we could cure syphilis but not syphilophobia, that is, the fear of syphilis. It was a cheering statement because it implied that the patient was not to permit his misfortunes to depress him. That way suicide lies. Charlie told me that he had so much mercury in him that he couldn't stand with his back to the fire because the column of mercury in his spine would bump against the base of his skull and knock him out. I saw in the harmless Charlie a way of getting my own back on the inoffensively studious Dr Lamb.

First I must find out what were the doctor's hours of duty. 'He goes off every night at twelve,' Beatty said. Then he added, 'Thank you, sir.'

'Charlie, if I give you a prescription to clear out that mercury you must follow instructions to the letter. What time is it now? Let me see. It's half past twelve. Yes; you will want twelve hours. By the time you get home to take my medicine it will be, say, one o'clock. Very well. One o'clock. Say one-thirty to be safe. You will take these three tablets and in an hour or two your urine will turn green, a dark blue-green. Take plenty of fluids. You might even drink a few pints of Guinness; but the point to bear in mind is not to let any of the urine out of your sight. Preserve it in any vessel that can hold it and no matter how much there is – the more the merrier – bring it up here immediately for analysis before it gets stale. No matter what time of night it is: any time after twelve hours. Ring the night bell; ask for the house surgeon. If there is any delay say you are just up from the country with an urgent message for him. Understand? Got that?'

Charlie said, 'God bless you, sir.' There were tears of gratitude in his eyes.

That night, or rather in the small hours of the next morning, I was wakened by a cursing and damning and a crash of crockery. 'What the hell do you mean, Beatty?' It was Lamb's voice cursing. Someone had wakened him from his sleep – and he was a heavy sleeper – with an urgent message from the country and when he opened the package – he probably expected to find something like the package that came for me at Christmas – he was confronted by a large night jar or pot, full to the brim with a green fluid.

'Lamb, I am surprised at you. Using such language in the middle of the night; wakening the whole dormitory.' The voice of Richards, the student from Wales piped up. 'What has happened? Whatever ...' It sounded frightened. But the expected roar did not come from Clinoclaustes. Where was he? Experimenting somewhere?

Lamb's loud outrage continued: 'That damned scoundrel, Charlie, sends me up a pisspot full of urine stained with methylene blue.'

'I certainly would expostulate with him,' said Richards.

'Expostulate be damned! What's the use in talking to a madman? I'll report Beatty for wakening me when I'm off duty.' But Beatty was, according to Boss Croker's definition, an honest man, that is, 'A man who, when he's bought, stays bought.'

It was turning over in my mind, 'What's the use of talking to a madman?' and thinking that words are only the symptoms of certain diseases; and we are taught that you must not treat symptoms: you must not treat words with words. The disease causes the words. Words in this case were accessories after the fact. Treat the disease and the words will take care of themselves. What's the use of talking anyway?

Another noise. This time raucous laughter and cries came from the ward beneath mixed with snatches of bawdy song. The time for such singing was right but the place was not. What was that? Water? There may be a fire raging and that noise comes from the Fire Brigade. But firemen don't laugh while on duty. We pulled on a few clothes and went down to investigate. There was the clever Fulton, Clinoclaustes, drunk as a lord and wielding a fire hose. Some strange rowdies, apparently companions of his evening, were chasing a goat which leapt over the beds dangling a length of chain. One patient, a paralytic awaiting operation, jumped from his bed and fled to shelter.

For the amputation stumps cold water was not the proper treatment. 'There was a dozen of stout in my locker before I went off duty, where is it now?' Clinoclaustes asked angrily as he turned with the hose held like a rifle over his shoulder. Plaster from the ceiling was coming down in flakes. Some nurses, thoroughly alarmed, gathered at the door. Clinoclaustes stared drunkenly at them. A young nurse still in her teens, with her hair fallen in disarray, fled from the doorway.

Dr Lamb screamed, 'Call off your friends, Fulton. I won't be responsible for this.' After an interval the lights went on fully. Wet bedding and mattresses were removed.

As dawn was breaking quiet was restored. I thought that it was time to avail myself of my privilege of going home once a week.

Next day there was an atmosphere of foreboding: an extraordinary meeting of the Board. And we were all up before it. Lamb, as senior, and responsible for law and order, testified first. He said nothing about Charlie but he acknowledged that he was awakened by a noise. He said that he was a light sleeper (oh!), which made the noise lighter as it were. Some men whom he did not know were tampering with the fire hose. He, as responsible house surgeon, though off duty, put them out. Richards, the squeaky little Welshman, was only a spectator. 'Of what?' asked Sir William. This took a lot of floundering to explain. 'And you, Fulton, what have you to say for yourself?'

'I cured a case of paralysis. It was not a case of brain tumour but hysteria.'

'That will do.'

Fulton was, as they say in the 'varsity, 'sent down'. Dr Robert Woods, laryngologist and otologist, recently elected to the Board, had me to examine. I was at home. He did not ask what hour I went there. Maybe he forebore deliberately; but he had to administer a rebuke. I explained that, as one living within walking distance of the hospital, I was permitted to take my meals at home when off duty and to sleep at home once a week.

'And that was not too often,' said Dr Woods.

There was no mention of the goat. Beatty restored it, for a consideration, to its owner in Red Cow Lane.

Where were my wits when we were up before the Board? They were there all right but they were in abeyance, for I did not realise at the time that the reason for such outbreaks and such loose living among medical students arose from what would be called now 'occupational neurosis'. The young nurses, finding themselves confronted daily by dirt, disease and death, grew tough. Medical students went wild as a reaction. Youth betimes confronted with Death: The outcome of this unnatural juxtaposition was outbreaks of wild licence among the men, and callousness among the young nurses, most of whom were in their early twenties or younger.

And what about the demoralising effect of the way in which we were housed? At least I could have said that; but would they have been prepared for it? An old loft, with rafters showing above, in which we slept fitfully: dying men and corpses below, and groans arising to our sleeping place in the darkness. Is it any wonder that we had occasional outbreaks? Had you yourselves, our mentors, been always models of propriety? What about Tom Myles's brother, who used cops as castanets? What about Tom himself? Though they had endeared themselves to us by lawlessness in their student days, such arguments could not be proffered. Yet I must have sensed the connection between conduct – not to mention disease – and housing. Years after, I wrote that slums breed diseases and demoralisation. For example the incidence of tuberculosis falls fifty per cent when the family has two rooms instead of one.

How Tom Kettle abetted me in my campaign for better housing and the abolition of slums will be recorded further on. This is no place for a homily, nor am I given to homilies. If you catch me giving out a homily, shout 'Author!' as the unpaid 'ghost' is said to have done to the politician.

8 *Fugax Erythema*

Instead of being sacked, as Clinoclaustes was, we, that is, Lamb and I, were promoted from surgery to the medical part of the chain, the Whitworth Hospital. Medicine came before surgery, so it was a promotion to the older branch. There was a time when the barber-surgeon followed humbly at the heels of the black-garbed, triangular-hatted, cane-carrying physician, to let blood into his brass basin, curved like a new moon.

The Whitworth was an old building but clean. Its visiting physicians were Dr Travers Smith, Dr Coleman, and Dr Joseph O'Carroll, called 'Joc' on account of his initials. Travers Smith had married the daughter of Professor Dowden of Trinity College, author of *Shakespeare, His Mind and Art*. She was so homely and he so good-looking that, contradictorily, her homeliness broke up their home. Dr Travers Smith went to Cavendish Square, London, and married a widow after his divorce. Dr Coleman had also an unfortunate experience with matrimony; his wife, though a Roman Catholic, took divorce proceedings against him. He was always unobtrusive; we found him so. The scandal, because it was not of our making, but that of an unbalanced woman, did not stick.

Joc was such a martinet that he made his children send him letters written in French when they were on their so-called holidays. He took even the slightest thing seriously.

In the middle of the ward, on the floor, seated on many cushions and surrounded by mattresses, was a case of trichinosis. He jerked and fell off his cushions every few minutes because the worm acquired from measly bacon moved in a motor area of the brain. Had he been a clown in a circus, he would have been comical; but in the Whitworth under Joc he was indeed a tragic sight. The effect of the spasms on the other patients apparently never occurred to Joc, who exhibited his authority by upsetting the ward and making a central show. It was a characteristic projection of the little man.

Joc was lecturing. We all stood about the bed in respectful attention. In the bed was a young country girl with rosy cheeks. Joc ordered the nurse to pull down the bedclothes. There is a special way of pulling down the clothes so that a patient may not be exposed indecently. The nurses know it.

There are no gynaecological cases in the Whitworth. When the time comes for gynaecology you must go to the Rotunda Hospital, the Coombe or Holles Street.

Joc signalled impatiently. He wished to lecture on a red spot, or rather, on two red spots, that had been found by a nurse, a novice most likely, earlier the same morning. At last the knees were shown to Joc's liking.

'Gentlemen, you will notice two red spots on the inside of this girl's knees. Let us approach the problem scientifically and we shall thus be enabled to solve it. Now, first of all we must define the disease. We notice two red spots. What is the medical nomenclature for redness? No one answers. Must I send for Dr Lamb? No, I will not interrupt him. He, doubtless, is engaged on his duties. I will tell you: redness is known in medicine as "erythema". Now we will proceed to define the erythema. What gentleman will palpate it? Mr Kirby, take your hands out of your pockets and oblige me by palpating this erythema. No, no! You must palpate with two fingers of different hands or with the two hands, not one; and not with one finger! Is it smooth? You say that it is slightly rough. Have you asked the girl what is its history? No. Tell me, girl, how long have you had this trouble?"

She does not answer. She is overcome no doubt by being surrounded, with her legs half naked, by so many young men. 'Let us proceed. Nurse, did you notice this skin eruption yesterday? No. Now what do we have at our disposal? We have an erythema that appeared since yesterday: it is slightly rough, not smooth. Now, Mr

Kirby, press the erythema gently, and quickly remove your fingers. What do you observe? The redness disappears and returns quickly. Now with all these facts in our possession let us call some great foreign dermatologists into consultation. Suppose we are sending an account of this to Paris – we will take it that this girl is some lady's French maid ...'

A voice from the bed. 'I am only a dairymaid.' Tears, silent tears.

'Silence, young woman! We will write, not in French, but in Latin, with its vocabulary of words derived from the Greek. We will write thus, having saluted your colleague in Paris, "We have here a case of erythema, *recens, fugax, nodosa.*" That is: it wasn't here yesterday; that makes it *recens*; it disappears on pressure, *fugax*; it is slightly rough, *nodosa*. To a communication such as that we should expect an enlightened reply. Now, my good girl, you may speak. Tell us how long have you had this ailment and how can you account for it?'

'Oh, Doctor, is it any harm? I always waken up with it if my knees are crossed.'

9 *Pulver Olympicum*

It would not be fair if the impression were conveyed that a medical student's life was all work. There were many hours of leisure when off duty. Was not Isodore McWilliam Burke champion cyclist of England, while a resident in St George's Hospital, London? No wonder he was champion with such a dominating name: first in the field. My venture in the field was in the twenty-mile Junior Championship of Ireland.

The Amateur Athletic Association controlled, through its committees in the different countries that made up the

United Kingdom, all amateur athletics. It certified records, fixed the rules and suspended or outlawed all offenders. Larry O'Neill, a dark, serious, tubby little man all in black, black knickerbockers, and black-a-vised – but there was white cotton wool in his left ear – was its president in Ireland and he presided over the race to be held in the Pheonix Park, which, with its nineteen hundred acres, is the largest walled park in the world. It was walled to protect the residences of the satraps who represented the King in Ireland and were called Lords Lieutenant and Chief Secretaries. These, as a rule, were noblemen wealthy in their own right, sportsmen very often; but they knew nothing about the humble sport of cycle racing. Polo and fox hunting were more in their line.

The Phoenix Park was chosen for the twenty-mile Junior Championship not for its connection with the Lords Lieutenant but for its good roads: the better the roads the better the race. A four-mile lap was marked off to the south of the central highway past the Castlenock Gate, the Knockmaroon Gate, round the dangerous corner at the Furzy Glen, down the winding road, until the hill at the Hibernian School was reached. When the toiling cyclists climbed that steep they had the flat road east of the Fifteen Acres – about two hundred acres in fact – in front of them before they turned to the left and entered the central highway from which they had started. There were twin oaks on the left of the roadside about a hundred and fifty yards from where the finish would be.

Crowds already were assembled by the time I cycled up. Here and there the bright caps of the different cycling clubs could be seen in the crowd. There were competitors from the Al Fresco, as 'posh' as any club of its kind could be. Charlie Pease belonged to it; and not only was he the one-mile champion of Ireland but the winner of the Blue Riband Championship of England, which was also the mile. Charlie Pease was a gentleman and kept himself aloof, except in competitions, from the other members. Aloofness, for the most part, constituted a gentleman *in diebus illis.* Yes; by its members and its victories the Al Fresco was the outstanding club in Ireland. I was a member, though that would not placate my aunt!

The National was far larger; it had Tom Goss and Cockey Meade, the fifty-mile champion, among its members, and Alex Sweeney of the Carpenters too. There were competitors from various clubs in the North of Ireland; but as all the North was discounted and discountable by the men of Leinster, and that included Dublin, their competition was not taken seriously except for the hidden feeling of the gravity of a disgrace if any man of Dublin should be beaten by a fellow from the North. So, barring a wholesale accident such as that lamentable one that occurred during a ten-mile handicap which I won at Ballinafeigh near Belfast in Ulster, when all but four of a field of forty fell at a corner during the first lap, there was not a hope for the venturous sons of Ulster, whose hardihood merely made the championship more representative.

Old Blunden, a pompous member of a firm of attorneys – probably he was its head clerk – officiated fussily. He it was who would fire the starting pistol. Quite an official? Yes. The only serious rival, though I say it who shouldn't, to myself was Christy Dodd, the son of a wealthy 'potato factor' of Smithfield near the Richmond Hospital. His form was well known to the hospital porters as he scorched round and round Smithfield when it was empty in the evenings; and his form was relayed to mc. He was a bigger fellow than I but he had not half the experience nor the speed, on a smooth track anyway: and the finish in the Phoenix Park was smooth enough. I felt that I could take on Christy Dodd. Who was he anyway? He had never showed up at the fast-run races on the sand track at Ballsbridge.

'Bang!' The explosion so frightened old Blunden that he nearly shed his silk hat. We were off. We had twenty miles to go and the principal thing was to avoid being spilled or elbowed down the steep at the Furzy Glen. The men of

Ulster, full of suspicion, were leading in a knot. How could they know the terrain? All right. Let them lead and set a pace that would mean a record to the winner, who I intended to be. It might do no harm to warn them, for the simple reason that they would never believe me but rush all the faster because of the warning, to be careful at the corner or – crash!

This pace is terrific. And the worst of it is that you dare not use any of the competitors, except perhaps a club mate, for a pacer because you never could tell when he might wobble off and bring you down. It was therefore something like a consolation to think that at this pace there was sure to be a spill in the first lap, when the bunch rounded the corner at Furzy Glen.

We were going past the Castlenock Gate now at a hell of a lick. Another few hundred yards and we would be at the dangerous bend. It was now time to shout, 'Be careful, boys! Go slow!' I knew it! they started sprinting. I knew that they would, that they would take my warning for some Dublin jackeen's trick. What was that? I couldn't see, for I was riding last. I could hear the branches of the furze crunching. I could hear the shouting; and the groans of the spectators who had gathered at the spot. 'Geordie, are ye dead, mon?' Well, they would not take my advice. Was the race to stop for a dozen men from Ulster? Not by any means. Now let us begin in real earnest. Where is Christy Dodd? Right ahead. He was too good a rider to precipitate himself down at the Furzy Glen corner, which must have been known to him well.

Once the men who were strung out for the better part of a quarter of a mile were passed, they were passed once and for all. They never could catch up again. It's a very fast run downhill to the big climb at the Hibernian School corner. Very fast. There were no free wheels then, nor brakes either. There were places where it was necessary to backpedal. A pity? True; but it is better than a smash; and there would be the very reverse of backpedalling when it came to climbing the hill. I did not feel much distress. I must have gotten what is called your 'second wind'. Oxygenated thoroughly, as Sir Thomas Myles would say. We were cheered when we entered the straight for the first round. Possibly the cheers gave us credit for the absence of the North. For having survived them anyhow.

Charlie Pcase and the Maggot, Gibson, agent for the Osborne bicycle, stood ready with a tandem to act as pacemakers after the first four miles. What a pity that the Maggot fastened himself to such a cyclist as Charlie. I was hoping to shake off Dodd as the pace behind the tandem increased. How could Charlie go fast with the Maggot behind?

To get the pacemakers you had to take the lead, so in the second round I came into the straight first. 'How are you feeling, laddie?' 'Fine, Charlie,' I answered. The tandem got into its stride. 'Where's Dodd?' The Maggot said, 'You can forget him.' 'More pace,' I yelled to the Maggot. That shut him up.

On the grassy borders of the road were half-clad men, limping along. Some of their cycles were badly broken up. The ambulance from Stevens took care of the rest. 'Bit of a spill?' Charlie said, turning his small well-groomed head to look at me. Round and round, at what seemed too slow a pace for one sheltered as I was by the bodies of the two cyclists on the tandem, round and round we went. I did not like to offend Charlie, handicapped as he was by the Maggot, to ask for greater speed. He guessed what was passing in my mind. 'We're well within record.'

At last the pace was called off. 'It's up to you now,' the Maggot said as the tandem rolled away. At my side was that really dark horse, Christy Dodd! I resolved to start a murderous pace when I should reach the double oak tree. 'Not all the potatoes in Smithfield will help him when I really get going.' I said that to arouse my soul. I was really rather nervous when he showed up at my side after the punishing pace for twenty miles. 'Now!'

I must say that he did his best and it was very good but he was too big and somewhat lumbering when it came to really fast work. I hadn't time to look behind me. I won by fifty yards. Old Blunden tried dignity and taking it for granted. He attributed what I thought was a personal triumph to the club. He pushed officialdom too far. I dived into a pond beside the club's marquee. That night I couldn't sleep a wink.

At breakfast my mother saw it as she turned over the *Irish Times*. Inwardly she may have been proud but she certainly concealed it. 'Your professors in Dublin University will hardly find your exploit a matter for congratulation. If you must indulge in athletics, why not play cricket for the university, or join the Rowing Club?' If cycling appeared to her to be an ignoble pastime, the silence in which I received her rebuke was most noble. I was about to say, 'Don't I play football for them?' But I remembered how I played against them for my old club, the Bohemians, and the disparaging remarks in the weekly paper, *T.D.C.*: 'His game is that of a professional.'

Until I brought the conversation round to Charlie Pease I could not rest. I made it clear that he was a member of the Al Fresco Club and that he came from a distinguished Yorkshire family, one member of which, Sir Something Pease, was a member of Parliament. 'If your friend is a member of that family, he must be of a cadet branch, very cadet,' my aunt remarked. Then to soften it she said, 'God has blessed you with a robust body. Youth must find an outlet for its energy. If you can spare the time from your studies, you might join the Ward Union Hunt.' The stockbrokers, barristers, wheel-chair stag hunters – Saturdays only!

Morning was melting into noon as I walked down Sackville Street. The Dublin Corporation had not as yet changed the name into 'O'Connell Street'. The Doric column rose darkly, with Lord Nelson standing on its top, his sword touching the ground like a walking stick beside him; his right arm in an empty sleeve. In beautiful letters lined with gold were recorded his victories: Copenhagen – one would think that the less said about that the better; the

Nile; Trafalgar. They call his column 'Nelson's Pillar'; from it all the trams in Dublin start. I thought it the best of all the columns I had seen; and I think so yet.

When you crossed the head of Earl Street, you reached Clery's big shop. It was just as well that I looked into its windows, for in one of them I saw a poster advertising a coming cycle meeting to be held at Ballsbridge. 'Gogarty v Time' it announced. Before my mother sees that, I said to myself, it must be removed. I went in to speak to the manager of the shop. 'It will be in other places,' he explained. 'So why object to this?' I explained, and it was taken out.

I looked up and down the Liffey as I crossed its bridge. It is only fifty yards wide; but it bears no mean city on either bank: the Seventh City in Christendom. Guinness's great brewery stained the sky with its smoke to the west. To the east the red funnel of one of the brewery's cross-channel steamers brightened the Custom House by which it lay. The green dome of the Custom House shone on high. The light broadened as the Liffey neared the sea. Masts rose on the right. It is a merry morning. I wish that I had not had a restless night.

A few stragglers were standing outside the Ballast Office, which is what the Port and Docks Board Building is called. They were waiting for the ball to rise on its pole on the roof. That would mark twelve o'clock, and the time was exact because it was sent in from the Observatory at Dunsink: sidereal time by which people set their watches. Why I cannot say because no one in Dublin cares whether the time is exact or not and those who were watching the ball did not look as if they owned a watch. Perhaps it gave an air of earnestness to the day.

I met Alfred coming along Westmoreland Street. He was the only son of the Professor of Chemistry in Trinity College, Professor Emerson Reynolds, who had for factotum Clancy, the stepfather of Cockey Meade. Alfred wore a dark serge suit. On his shoulder he carried a light brown overcoat folded like a flattened tube. He was a fashionable and impressionable youth; that's probably what brought him to the café district where young ladies and waitresses would be about. He said that he was just strolling along. I said so I thought. He looked at me shrewdly, but my air of innocence must have reassured him, for, 'I have to congratulate you,' was his next remark. 'Yes. Thank you. I didn't sleep at all last night, I dived into the pond after the race. I blame that for my want of sleep.' He looked astonished. 'I was not talking of any race. Do you not know that you have won the Vice-Chancellor's Prize for English verse?'

That will balance things for me at home, I thought rapidly.

'The Vice-Chancellor's Prize is twenty pounds,' Alfred said. 'We should celebrate.'

'It'll have to wait until I am paid. I haven't got any money now.'

Alfred pointed with his thumb down Fleet Street. 'What about Weldon at the Back of the Bank?'

The Back of the Bank is the name of Kelley's pawnshop, which is managed by the over-astute Jimmy Weldon, a friend in need of medical students, and of most other students.

'One of your medals?' Alfred said encouragingly.

'No. No. I cannot celebrate now. I have to try for the mile record at Ballsbridge next week.'

I felt that my excuse was a little lame but I was glad to get Alfred away from Weldon's before he learned that my gold medal for English verse from the Royal University was reposing in Weldon's care. However, Alfred assured me that he would be the last man to urge me to break my training.

We walked on to the front of *T.D.C.*, that Palladian front which makes Dublin, with its other buildings, the most beautiful city in the country, though other towns have better sites. Cork for instance, on its island in the river Lee. I often wondered why there was not more talk about the beauty of Cork. I asked a Cork man. 'No buildings,' he said. That explained everything. The only building in Cork is the university and that looks like a convent or a reformatory.

In the case in the entrance hall of Trinity College was a notice giving the names of the winners of the Vice-Chancellor's prizes. I could see my name; but I could not very well stand gazing at it, not with the hall porters and students hanging about, so I assumed a blasé attitude and passed into the quad. From a door on the right a gowned figure with a beard like that of the poet Chaucer, carrying a bundle of papers, emerged. It was Professor Dowden. He was Professor of English in the university, and didn't he surround it with dignity? When he died they made a Plymouth Brother Professor of English. At least that is how the father of W. B. Yeats described Professor Trench.

A gloom hung over the place. I could sense it. What had happened? One of the students told me that my friend Bird was in trouble and up before Mahaffy, the vice-provost. He had shouted a well-known couplet at him the night before. Mahaffy was the best known of all the scholars whose industry had sent the fame of 'The Silent Sister', as Dublin University was called in Oxford and Cambridge, over all the world. Mahaffy's textbooks, *Lyric Poets of Greece; Dramatic Poets of Greece; Rambles and Studies in Greece*, taught Oxford and Cambridge Greek. So it was all the more heinous for poor Bird, drunk or sober, to shout,

'Yclept Mahouf by those of heavenly birth;
But plain Mahaffy by the race of earth,'

and to wave at him familiarly.

Bird at last came out through the narrow door in the wall that led to Mahaffy's rooms. He would tell nobody what had happened. To the anxious question, 'Are you sent down?' he shook his head. He looked moved, and no wonder. We left him alone to commune with himself; but it was not long before the whole incident and what had happened came out. Mahaffy listened to Bird's humble apology. Bird confessed that he was drunk. Mahaffy said,

47

'No one takes the least notice of what a gentleman says in his cups.' So Bird was a gentleman in Mahaffy's estimation; and that was the reason why Bird at first would tell nobody what had happened. Bird felt overcome by emotions of respect and gratitude. The apology had done it – if you ask me.

Mahaffy was the greatest don I ever met. The examination for fellowship, which leaves its successful candidates text-drunk and good for nothing but to draw the salary that goes with what is a lifelong appointment, and take a few pupils, had not the least effect on him. He had taken it in his stride as a matter of course. He had taken much more in his stride: long before Egyptology had become a subject for research workers, Mahaffy had written a book on the subject which after all these years has not been found wanting. He had a perfect musical ear, and that, they tell me, is a thing that appears only once in a century. He was a sportsman: he had with his single-barrel gun shot a snipe at Sir John Leslie's shoot in Glaslough, County Monaghan, at ninety yards. Sir Shane, who is now Sir John's heir, measured the distance and Sir Shane can be called as a witness if anyone doubts me, for happily he lives and rules Glaslough. I am usually accurate when it comes to sport. When Sir Shane's brother at the same shoot accidentally loosed his gun and blew the hat off Mahaffy's head, Mahaffy merely looked at the shattered garment and remarked, 'Two inches lower and you would have blown ninety per cent of the Gweek out of Ireland.' He could not, or would not, pronounce his *r*'s correctly. Maybe it was because neither the Earl of Fingall nor Lord Talbot of Malahide could pronounce their *r*'s except as *w*'s. From this you may have deduced that Mahaffy 'dearly loved a Lord'. But it would not be accurate to dub him a snob, for snob means *sine nobilitate:* Mahaffy had nobility and made it a point to associate with noble men. Also a snob is defined by Thackeray, who knew what he was talking about, being a snob himself, as one who worships mean things meanly. Too slick! And to such a great man as

Mahaffy quite inapplicable. He was as omniscient as the scholarship and science of his day permitted. Now people grow tired of omniscience.

It is related how one night the dons of the college conspired to get the great man on some subject on which he was not an authority and so could not talk. After a consultation they selected Chinese music as the subject that they would bring up, as it were, accidentally at dinner. They discoursed on Chinese music, traced its origin and its effect, and expounded the difference in the Chinese conception of music and the European attitude. Mahaffy said not a word. The dons, inwardly delighted, kicked each other under the table. When they had exhausted the subject, Mahaffy said, 'Gentlemen, you have fallen into two errors that I myself nearly fell into, and you know how I hate to do anything foolish, when I wrote the article which you have been discussing; for the Encyclopaedia Britannica twenty years ago.'

The man I loved most in Trinity was Dr Yelverton Tyrrell. He was a Senior Fellow, Professor of Greek, and on occasion an examiner for the B.A. degree. We called him 'the Divine Doctor'. He was a very liberal and genial wit. His close friend was Henry S. Macran, Professor of Moral Philosophy, for whom allowances had to be made; and Tyrrell made them. Tyrrell it was who awarded me the maximum ten marks in my examination for English in the B.A., but that was merely a preliminary reason for my love and admiration. He was the wittiest man of his day and what a day it was! Tennyson, George Meredith, Wilde, Browning, Swinburne, George Wyndham, Jebb and Jowett flourished then.

10 *We Ourselves*

Why could I not imitate Alfred Reynolds, who, even though he was aware of waitresses, conducted himself respectably? He was studying to be an engineer. But the life I led as a medical student, when you had to deliver fourteen babies before you could qualify, brought the slums about me and the Kips, as the redlight district of Dublin was called. It is true that there are few births in a red-light district, for grass does not grow on the beaten track; but the Kips adjoined the miserable dormitories of the city whose denizens were poor and prolific, and children crowded the gutters. Here on the mothers the medico could practise to fulfil the requirements of the curriculum.

To look at the different roles I played in what may be called different incarnations is like looking into an aquarium and watching the highly coloured fish swim by like bubbles flattened or made long.

One of my incarnations, which began long before I studied at the Royal and Trinity, was as a politician – it began innocently at the Stad, and inevitably ended at a tavern called the Bailey.

The Bailey is in Duke Street, off the fashionable shopping Street, Grafton Street. It is nicely situated; so is Davy Byrne's, which is a tavern opposite to it. Upstairs in the Bailey is the smoking room; in this room Parnell and his followers were wont to meet. That was the reason why Arthur Griffith chose the Bailey and had a few 'large ones' with his friends of an evening, twenty years or so before his unswerving purpose freed Ireland, and Ireland made him its first President. I knew him since the days when his first movement for freedom began in An Stad, Cahill McGarvey's little tobacco shop opposite Findlater's

Church at the corner of North Frederick Street. That was about 1899.

His friends were George Redding, the solid man from Guinness's Brewery; Jimmy Montgomery; Neil – all wits and rhymers in their way. Griffith never discussed politics with his friends or with anyone; but there was an awareness that if you were not true blue, that is, a Sinn Feiner, and Sinn Fein means 'We ourselves', you had no right to be in the smoke room with Arthur Griffith. Sinn Fein implied that you were in agreement with the principles laid down in Griffith's pamphlet, *The Resurrection of Hungary*, and the application of the policy outlined therein was to keep the Irish members of Parliament away from Westminster; make them stay at home and boycott Westminster. How successful was this plan, which was attributed to Hungary, history now can prove.

I remember one night at the Bailey, like hundreds of others ... Arthur was there, so was Jimmy Montgomery. Arthur had almost as high a complexion as Montgomery; he was shorter and stockier than his friend. He wore tight-fitting pince-nez which indented the sides of his nose in two red grooves. When he took off his glasses to polish them these grooves showed. His rolling gait gained for him the nickname 'Cugaun' or 'dove', from the Kaffirs over whom he was overseer when he worked in a mine in South Africa. This roll was caused by a shortage of both his *tendo Achillis*. Actually he rolled rather than waddled when he walked. He apparently did not dislike his nickname, for he used it as a nom de plume in the weekly paper, the *United Irishman*, which he edited, and which he wrote nearly all himself. He wore glasses, because his blue eyes were short-sighted.

Neil arrived and announced that it was Sunday and so he had to leave any minute now to relieve, at 6 p.m. prompt, his father who played the harmonium at a local chapel. I am always uncomfortable when people announce that they must leave at any hour. I like to think of such meetings as permanent. I dislike the transience implicit in such remarks. You never see a clock in a well-regulated tavern or if there is a clock it is an antique and in any case it never strikes the hour.

George Redding came in and hailed us with a kind of grunt as he hung up his hat. Lewey the waiter rushed in with a large one for George. 'Ah,' Griffith called Lewey, and he made an inclusive sign by circling with his finger. Then turning to George, he asked, 'Any news?' George is slow to answer. He felt in his waistcoat pockets and produced a cutting from a newspaper. 'I cut this out this morning. I think that it is an excellent piece of prose.' Then he read something about a prize fight on a windy heath, and waited for our remarks. Griffith said, 'Hum. The best prose writer and the one I take for my model is Dean Swift.'

That was news to me. It is only because I don't know much about prose that I missed the explicitness of the dean's style and that of Arthur Griffith. Both are unequivocal and clear. I take very little interest in prose. I can hardly remember the Lord's Prayer; but when it comes to poetry it is quite a different matter. That I can remember because of its rhythm, without which there is no poetry. If you cannot remember what is called poetry perhaps it is because it is not poetry; or you are not a poet.

The people I know have good memories. Neil can recite and write; so can George Redding, and as for George Russell, Æ, he is the man with the memory for both prose and poetry. How can you be a poet without a memory, seeing that Memory is the Mother of the Muses? This quotation cured Yeats when he was affecting forgetfulness.

It is a fact that in Scotland Calvinism produced poetry in the person of Burns, and many others, by recoil. Neil owes to pedestrianism his recoil into poetry, for poetry is a recoil from ugliness and decay. In Ireland the recoil from English injustice made poets of us all.

Recoil made Arthur Griffith the author of a ballad very hard to come by now, *The Thirteenth Lock*. As for George Redding, in spite of all the respectability of the brewery behind him, he can bend a verse with the best and shoot his arrow straight to the mark.

Oh, Marie Stopes, I never knew how far it
Was wise to mingle love and faith until
I saw the holy brother of Boyd Barrett
Lead his full quiver up Killiney Hill.

'The holy brother of Boyd Barrett' was one of three brothers whom an overpious mother ruined. The holy brother spent his days in church kneeling and his nights begetting children. His wife was redheaded, and his quiver full.

Lewey came rushing in with a round of whiskeys. Someone remarked that it was half past six. As the whiskey and soda slid under Neil's moustache, he put down his glass and, sighing, said, 'And therefore, ye soft pipes, play on.' Obviously his father would not be relieved at six to play heard melodies; but as those unheard are sweeter than the harmonium of any chapel, the defection of his son can be condoned.

When Arthur Griffith started to leave no one tried to dissuade him. He was inflexible even in little things, so off he went. When he was gone a certain restraint left with him. Jimmy Montgomery opened with a story about the down-and-out who rushed into a grocery store, slammed down two pennies and ordered 'Two pennyworth of soup powder!' then he turned with a knowing look and remarked, 'If you're living with them, you've got to feed them.' That he would not have told us had Arthur been present, not that Griffith was a prude; but there was about him something that made levity seem out of place.

I had been talking to Neil a day or two before about Friar John, one of the characters in Rabelais, who saw in one of those outlandish islands the Two-backed Beast, the merriest animal that exists. Neil, who has a fluency in rhyming unapproached by any living poet of my acquaintance and by few I have since read, started with a ballad about the too well known wife of a Professor of Romance Languages who in one of her exploits went off with a native Irish speaker, that is, one of the few who learned Gaelic in their cradle. He was a very near approach

to a tramp, hobo, or gaberlunzie man, and he affected that
role much to the discredit of the language:

> The song I heard and the song I sing
> Are one and the same and the self same thing:
> This is the story and thus it ran:
> She's away with the gaberlunzie man!
>
> That two-backed beast of which you speak,
> He wears no horns upon his beak,
> And the reason is not far to seek:
> It needs strong back where a back is weak.
> There's wisdom yet in the ancient rann:
> She's away with the gaberlunzie man!
>
> Then guard your foreheads whatever befall
> For the tallest forehead amongst you all
> And the wisest scholar that ever was born
> He yet may wear the cuckold's horn.
> 'Twas ever thus since Time began:
> She's away with the gaberlunzie man.

When Jimmy gallantly suggested that the lady in question
was 'more sinned against than sinning', Neil instantly
remarked, 'Like the trees on the canal.' There were wits in
the Bailey even though James Stephens seldom came in. He
has described his own impressions, so I will leave them to
him.

As I left the Bailey I met O'Leary Curtis, tall and thirsty,
with a skin so smooth that he seemed to have been carved
out of ivory. His voice was sweet and sad. We called him
the 'Japanese Jesus' even though he wore a black goatee.
He brought back another of Neil's quirks, a parody on 'The
Wearin' o' the Green'. Neil has it this way.

> I met O'Leary Curtis and He took me by the hand
> Said, 'How is poor old Ireland; and who is going to stand?'

He was persuadable if someone stood the drinks, no matter what time it was. He told me that he was selling electricity
for the Dublin Corporation and asked if I thought the

Church would help by having its altar bread prepared by an electric toaster. I could not hold out any prospect of comfort because I was not in the confidence of the executives. I told him where his friends could be found. His eyes brightened: hope of another kind would not be long deferred. I just saw Arthur Griffith in the street and the Bird Flanagan, so I came along. The problem of 'Who is going to stand?' would soon be solved.

Any mention of Bird Flanagan makes me uneasy. He is one of three brothers who would be better had they remained in Turgenev. Characters such as these are to be found both in the Russian author and in Dublin's fair city. Who is the Bird? Well, let me try to tell you. He went to a fancy dress ball at the Earlsfort Terrace skating rink dressed as the Holy Ghost and supported by two of the Holy Women. In the middle of the floor he laid an egg about the size of a football. The management interposed; he and his supporters were expelled. He went out clucking. But the name 'Bird' stuck to him since the incident of the egg. His father, an alderman of the city and a much respected man, sent the Bird to Australia twice but he flew back. Then he was sent to Canada, but he was a homing pigeon. The last we heard of him was from a friend who returned from Buenos Aires. He said that there was a large hole in its principal street. Looking down, he saw a man with a broad back and a red neck plying a pickaxe. He recognised the ensemble. 'In the name of God is that you, Bird?' he called. The Bird looked up. 'For God's sake get to hell out of here! It took a lot of influence to get me this job.' He spat on his hands and resumed his work. He was done with bad companions. A great 'artist'.

Dr. Johnson says – and I thoroughly agree with him – 'There is nothing contrived by man by which so much happiness is produced as a good inn or tavern.' I agree; but would my mother? Very doubtful. My aunt? Certainly not; and she would be very much upset if she knew of the 'low' company I was keeping.

11 'And That Sweet City Of The Dreaming Spires'

Why did I go to Oxford and when? If you must know – and I hate dates – it was in 1904. Much good may that do you. Now for the 'Why?' There were two reasons and many subreasons. Here's one of the principal reasons coming this way: wall-eyed in cap and gown over trousers of light grey stripes, my tutor, Smyly, came from his rooms on the north side of the Front Quad of Trinity. His trousers matched the colour of his eyes. I could see him on the opposite side of the big holm oak that stood in the centre of its square plot. Reason enough, you would say if you had met him. He never once tutored me, never once spoke to me: disapproved oozed out of him. That is why I rejoiced in the company of the Professor of Moral Philosophy, Henry Stewart Macran.

In Macran's rooms I met R.W. Lee, Fellow of Worcester College, Oxford. He was my second and sufficient reason. Good will and urbanity flowed out of him. You felt it, for all his reserve and self-possession. The personality of the man was an invitation. Time was no objection, I had plenty of time, so off I went for a few terms to Oxford. It is better to be educated beyond your means than to have means beyond your education.

One of the subreasons was that I could no longer compete in cycling races. Larry O'Neill, the little fellow in black knickerbockers and the lump of white wool in his left ear, who was president of the Irish branch of the Amateur Athletic Association and, afterwards, chronic Lord Mayor of Dublin, had suspended me for bad language at the Furzy Glen corner where all the cyclists from Ulster crashed. It is remarkable how gloomy fools impress the Irish public.

It was night by the time I reached Bletchley on my way to Oxford. A falling star streamed down the blue vault. I am superstitious, especially when I am feeling taut. Was the falling star an omen? If so, an omen of what?

Worcester College is the only one of the colleges of Oxford that had athletic fields in its own grounds. It is famous for its gardens and its lawn, where *Comus* is played in the summer under the trees. Worcester or Wuggins, as it is called in the slang of undergraduates, is at the end of Beaumont Street, a rococo façade dark and uninviting. But when you pass through the forbidding portal you come on a charming sight. In front is a sunk lawn. On the right, houses of sandstone three stories high stand in a row which ends at the house of the Provost. The flowery wall of a water garden closes the view straight ahead. To the left is a row of little two-storey fourteenth-century cottages. When I was admitted to Worcester I dwelt in the third one in the row from the Pump Quad. In the Pump Quad was the famous Daniel Press, called after the Provost. This was the private press that printed the poems of Robert Bridges, afterwards Poet Laureate. I owed much to H.S. Macran, and the friendship of R.W. Lee was not the least of the debt.

So to Worcester I went.

All the men at Oxford were between eighteen and twenty-two. I was a year or two older than the generality; but as I had come to Oxford to sample the place and to have a shot at the Newdigate, which is a prize for English verse, it mattered little. I was not reading for a degree. In fact I was not reading at all. I should have been studying medicine, but that is a subject which is inclined to pall, particularly on a bright summer day.

Instead of reading, I played a little soccer. I hired one of the earliest motor bicycles, an Indian, from an agent who is the present Lord Nuffield, the Henry Ford of England, and ran it to taverns in the many villages that adjoined the university. I met a Buck or Beau from New College who was as free as myself. He accompanied me and often drove the motor bicycle, which had a trailer that was really a trailer, for it trailed behind, attached to the bicycle by a metal tube. One a day when the driver turned too sharply I was thrown out and forgotten for miles on the road.

One morning there approached me, coming through the Turl against the light, a youth who could not help being comely – I judged by his walk, for his face was against the light; when he came level I found that my guess was right. He had auburn hair, hazel eyes and a pointed sensitive face. He was almost tall. It was Compton Mackenzie coming from Magdalen College probably to look into Blackwell's bookshop. He it was who wrote *Sinister Street*, a novel about the equivocal time of youth. It was a marvel how such a young man could have so much wisdom. His book was a 'best seller', and reader too. That was a long time ago; but long as it is, he has never fallen from the high distinction of his early book and this in spite of many books. He couldn't be looking for Christopher Stone, Scholar of Christ Church. I left Stone not ten minutes ago and he said that he had a lecture to attend. He said nothing about Compton Mackenzie. They were friends. Mackenzie became Stone's brother-in-law later, for he married his sister.

I might as well tell Mackenzie that Stone had gone to a lecture and tell him of the sonnet which Stone composed on the depravity of the age. Sir Somebody – I remember only his title – and the Hon. Mrs – that will do – had been the principals in a divorce at which all Oxford was laughing, for had not Slater, the venal detective, given intimate and amazing evidence? Slater would photograph your wife, or anybody else's who could pay, in the most compromising positions and give evidence that was most telling in any divorce proceeding. He would also do it vice versa. His magnifying glass and what it saw was the decisive factor in the famous divorce trial. Stone affected to be envious of the notoriety of Sir Something and to be blasé as befitted an undergraduate of the university, for it was the proper thing to be blasé before you began life. So he testified to his prowess before Jeune, who was Divorce Court judge. 'It needs not June for beauty's heightening.'

> My name is written on the mirrored brink
> Of Love by rosy-filleted finger tip
> Jewelled with perfidy. Mine amorous lip
> Sucks the dull stain of passion like the pink
> and blushing blotting paper starred with ink.
> This is mine heraldry: a trouser clip
> Found on the bed beside a bodice slip
> That dropped unseen while amorous draughts we drink.
> The slanderous cuckoo in the apple tree
> Fluted his horned unforgotten tune;
> Later, oh, Slater, on the ambrosial bed
> Spied a moon-glimmering spot misdirected;
> And all unmellowed plucked me, gloriously
> Before the summering up of pitiless Jeune.

It was stuck in my head because it is some of the cleverest, if not the very cleverest, writing I have ever come across. That cuckoo in the apple tree, for instance, and the epithet 'slanderous'; 'Cuckoo, cuckoo, a word of fear.' And 'apple tree'. Stay me with flagons; comfort me with apples. I am sick of love, as the character in Stone's sonnet was supposed to be 'sick and very sick'. And then, 'the summering up' of pitiless Jeune! Is it any wonder that I have never forgotten it? 'It needs not June!'

I made a few discoveries at Oxford. One was that it was not exclusively a home of learning; in fact, learning was bad form; for any exhibition of it at table you were liable to be 'sconced' – that is, dared to drain a five-and-a-half-pint tankard, and fined if you could not make it. I found that 'good form' was *de rigueur*. Conduct was the rule at Oxford, not scholarship, and this had been the vogue long before Matthew Arnold's father, who was an Oriel College man, invented 'the old school tie', which as everyone knows is the outward sign of devotion to a code. Good Form taught young men to hold their drink in silence; it prescribed the cane you took to church on Sundays; and it took for granted that any culprit should come forward and acknowledge his misdemeanour rather than have the whole college 'gated' and the innocent locked in with the culprit.

From what monstrous complacency came the cult of stupidity? It is fostered in the country's schools and universities where the country's leaders are educated. It is a dangerous thing and requires to be exposed. As I have pointed out, it began when the father of Matthew Arnold, an Oxford man and Headmaster of Rugby School, preferred character to brains. Rugby is not one of the leading public schools but it is one of the best known. From it the cult of the Old School Tie, that is, loyalty to the boys of the Old School (which means loyalty to the Empire) spread to every school in England, even to the jails. Character may be preferable to intellect; but this cult of character instead of brains presupposes a settled and unchanging civil service which in return presupposes an Empire. With the disappearance of Empire and the colonial appointments that went with it, the Old School automata of the civil service were out of a job. They were incapable of adjusting themselves to change. Their brains were atrophied when learning became bad form. The Empire has melted away and these men have become a clog on progress, so much so that witty Winston Churchill, who, as a wittier commentator remarked, spent the best years of his life preparing his impromptus, is said to have exclaimed, 'England is a Laocoön strangled by the Old School Tie.'

In Arnold's time the Empire seemed to be everlasting and unshakable. He is not to be blamed because he did not foresee the inherent suicide in the stupidity he so assiduously promoted.

I made another discovery, or rather I had my eyes opened to a fact that was unaccountable hitherto. There was a conceited, mulish, mediocre fellow who was the *most popular* man in our college. I often wondered why. It was not until F.C. Crawley told me that as nobody would take the trouble of putting him in his place he was made 'popular' instead. The principle was the same whereby mankind calls the Black Sea the Euxine; and country people call the fairies the 'good people' when in reality they are mischievous and vindictive. This was very valuable information. It explained why people accept certain politicians. To hold the skunk in them would raise such a 'stink' that it was long ago decided to let them alone.

But the Newdigate, which is an annual prize for English verse, was my aim. The verses, in that time, had to be in the heroic couplet, the metre of Alexander Pope and of all the bores of the eighteenth century, Oliver Goldsmith always excepted.

The verses which I sent in did not win the Newdigate. They obtained a *proxime accessit*, which, being translated, means runner-up. I was disappointed because, with every Vice-Chancellor's Prize (I got four of them at Trinity College, a record, they say, since the prize was instituted) and with the gold medal for English verse in the Royal, I had begun to think of myself as a professional as opposed to an amateur. I was disappointed, until I read the prize poem written by George Kennedy Allen Bell, now Bishop of Chichester, with its

> Only I
> Hear the lank eagles crying up the sky.

Then I knew that a better man had won: 'lank eagles.'

George Kennedy Allen Bell was a fine poet with a whimsey when the mood was on him. In Dublin he met Macran, and he learned that his ideas of philosophy – Moral, of course – were sometimes a cause of anxiety to his wife. This he recorded:

> You could be all things but a good
>   And wifely man;
> And that you would not if you could,
>   We know, Macran.

And the parody on Swinburne's *Félise* is not unbecoming

to one who wears a mitre. He shows the power that is in him with his straight

> Ilion, city of Troy
> And the tall grey towers thereof
> Fallen, and gone from joy
> And out of the hand of Love.

I am sorry that Chichester is so far away. I would like to hear its bishop preaching. Of one thing I am certain: I am sure that the reference in the last line of one of the best limericks in the language, which describes the effect of the attendance at matins of one of the citizenesses on the bishop, does not refer to the present incumbent.

> There was a young lady from Chichester
> Whose curves made the Saints in their nichesstir
> One morning at Matins
> The heave of her satins
> Made the Bishop of Chichester's breechesstir.

The next year the rule as to heroic couplets was changed. The Newdigate can now be won by any form of verse, even blank.

I had not won what I set out for, but quite accidentally I performed a feat at Worcester unprecedented in the history of the college. I drank the sconce. I have already told you what a sconce is. It is a silver tankard that holds more than five pints. It is called for as a punishment on those who transgress at meals by making a pun or quoting from the classics. As a rule I do not make bad puns, and I would hardly have tried a tag from the classics in such society. I sometimes resort to the classics to prevent my ignorance in other fields from being shown up, hoping that a change of language will change the subject. It was the resentment of the abominable Bamburger who sat next to me at table that was to blame for my being sconced. He knew that I was supposed to be reading medicine and because I forbore to answer his endless questions as to what was good for training in the way of food he hated me. He was to represent Oxford as a lightweight in the annual intervarsity boxing competition, hence his questions about what he should eat.

Bamburger called for the sconce.

'Now, Bamburger,' I said, 'you know the rules: if I drink the sconce without taking it from my lips, I am privileged to sconce every man at this table. I will sconce only you and that won't do you and your training much good.'

He called to the butler, 'Bring in the sconce.'

Again I protested: 'Look here, Bamburger, you don't know what you're up against. I am not referring to the Cambridge lightweight but to myself. I can drink as many pints as my pals put up. I was weaned on pints.'

It was unavailing.

There was silence in the hall when the butler with due ceremony bore in the sconce on a salver. It was full to the lid with cold ale. I felt 'mortified' as they say in Dublin. All eyes were on our table; and at the high table, where the dons were, conversation ceased. I received instructions: I was not to remove the tankard from my mouth until I had drunk it dry, otherwise I would acknowledge defeat.

I planted my elbows firmly on the table and raised the silver tankard to my mouth. I took a deep breath. I began to drink. The first two pints went down pleasantly enough. It would have been enjoyable if there had not been so much depending on the draught. You would never guess what affected me most. Not a feeling of repleteness. No. You could never guess. It was the awful cold that hurt me on both sides of the throat and went up into my ears. Don't believe them when you hear that the English don't know how to cool their ale. They keep it in the wood in a cellar and that does not conduce to conduction. (A pun! Enough to sconce any man.) I held on, conscious still. If this goes on I will pass out; but on it had to go. I suppose it took two or three full minutes, and two minutes are enough to die in. Look at the second hand of your watch to realize how long two minutes can be. To me, whatever time it was seemed ten times longer. At last I reached the bottom and I put my head back to drain the thing so that it would not drip when I held it upside down. Cheers broke out all over the hall; even the imperturbable butler permitted a gleam of admiration to enliven his countenance. The dons on the upper table looked down at our table. I tried to get the conversation going again and off myself.

'Bamburger, I warned you. Now you can take on.' There was little sign of approval for that because all the table was afraid of the pugilist. Next day he was knocked out in the first round by an accidental blow of the blond Cambridge man's head. No one pitied Bamburger and no one blamed me, for he was too ugly to win even a boxing match.

On the whole, I'd rather have drunk the sconce than won the Newdigate. Oscar Wilde won the Newdigate and landed in Reading Gaol. G. K. A. Bell won the Newdigate and became Bishop of Chichester. And, latterly, it was won by a woman who, I am sure, could never have achieved the sconce. The way I was treated from that day on, you might think that I had seen the Holy Grail.

To shed distinction on your college fills you with a lasting elation. I put up a record that puts Worcester ahead of all colleges when it came to the bibbery. Whether the dons appreciated my effort or not, I cannot tell. It would have been just like them to have preferred a winner of the Newdigate. I could not have won the Newdigate. Had not a star fallen over Oxford?

There is a gap in the sandstone ledge of the library roof. It gave way as I jumped from the library to the roof of the Georgian row of buildings, on the right as you enter the college. The gap is still there (if they haven't repaired it) to show that an Irishman can drain the sconce and still jump across a gap sixty feet up in the air, and leave his mark upon the college. The Provost had a leaden chimney about eight feet high which attracted attention one night. Next day it was found embedded in the sacred lawn of the quad. All were to be gated. I came forward.

At Oxford they practise the Greek adage, 'Nothing too

much.' Boasting and ebullience are bad form. Hence it becomes one to become blasé. I am ebullient on occasion, I admit. I hope that I am not boastful. The Provost forgave me. Like Bird of Dublin, I was 'in my cups'. The Provost blamed the sconce. Perhaps it is just as well they take thought of nothing but conduct in Oxford. It is the only form of education, and what more do you want? Is it not, after all, better than taking dejectedly a seat upon the intellectual throne? Some men never recover from education.

12 *Tancred*

Where did I first meet Dermot Freyer? I say it is a poor friendship that can trace its beginning. I must have met him during one of my frequent visits to London. After all, London was but sixty miles away and I could get an *exeat* easily.

When I met Dermot Freyer he was impatient to introduce me to his friend Tancred. 'But who is he?' So there were people who had not heard of Tancred? 'Well, Tancred is a poet who is very particular about *le mot juste*. He will stop lifts, if he happens to be alone in one, until he gets it. My father's house in Harley Street has an automatic lift and it has been so often out of use to the household, because it was so often in use to the poet, that I have been forbidden to invite him again. Let us meet him tomorrow in the Café Royal.' Now I don't like the Café Royal and never did. It is the meeting place of all self-conscious people, pseudo artists and real ones. Would he meet us in an ordinary pub, say in Tottenham Court Road?

Enter a knight just taken out of his armour. I have never seen an armoured knight except in museums, and Tancred looked jointed, as if he were accustomed to move only in armour. 'Ha! And how are *you*?' he said. 'Been roebucking lately?' It was Dermot Freyer who urged him on in spite of himself before one who would have been a stranger save for what Dermot had said in my favour. We had a few drinks before getting on to the subject of verse. It must have been winter because the piece Tancred read had just been composed and it was about a New Year's Resolution. There is no need to go into the delay, the forgetfulness of the subject, and the interruptions, common to a public house. I have not forgotten the lines. I guessed that 'reticule' and 'misrule' must have put many lifts out of commission. Here is the result:

New Year's Resolution:

> My assets shall not gild the reticule
> Of any rose-lipped daughter of misrule.

And there were many more but I cannot remember them now.

I do remember a poem of Dermot's; one about a little child. I remember it because when I went searching the corpus of English literature I could find only very few poems about children, and none of them as good as Dermot's. But it was long afterwards that I came across the lines in one of those privately printed brochures such as Blackwell publishes for enthusiasts.

> Little Dolly Dimplekin
> Has dimples on her cheeks and chin,
> And dimples on her knuckles too,
> Which show that Dolly's years are few.

Tancred knew every word that Herrick had written. He had some mysterious theory about one of Herrick's friends, Shadwell. According to Tancred, Herrick had locked up Shadwell in his *Hesperides*; and here and there you could hear Shadwell calling through the bars of Herrick's verse. He was probably calling for help; but it was all so mysterious that I did not inquire so I could not be sure. It would not have cleared the matter because Tancred was

66

incoherent about the dark mystery and Freyer laughed and laughed whenever I showed interest in Tancred's theory. I saw no symptoms of lunacy in this theory; no more than I saw signs of latent lunacy then in Joyce.

Freyer was a Cambridge man. Tancred, all I could find out about him was that he worked in the Stock Exchange. That is, he had to wear a bowler hat. A helmet would have suited him better. He was a close friend of Dermot Freyer, and that was enough for me. He knew literature and he wrote verse. So we three had something to talk about. Too much probably, because one night I nearly missed the 'Flying Fornicator' back to Oxford. It reached the city of the Dreaming Spires a few minutes before midnight. If you are not in college before midnight – an *exeat* is no help – you have to tell where you were and bring witnesses.

I don't know how the train got its name. It was used a lot by the dons and that, added to the irreverence of the undergrads, probably christened it.

13 *Chamber Music*

> I saw and hearkened many things and more
> Which might be fair to tell but now I hide.

James Joyce said, 'Do you know that we can rent the Martello Tower at Sandycove? I'll pay the rent if you will furnish it.'

Sandycove is about seven miles from Dublin on the south side of its famous bay. It lies a little to the east of the harbour which takes the mail boat from England early in the morning and late at night. The water between Dun Laoghaire and Sandycove is called Scotsman's Bay and is bounded by the east pier of the harbour and the two-storeyed, thick-wall Martello Tower, with the Battery close by the Forty Foot, a resort for strong swimmers.

The Martello Tower is one of the many towers which the English built along the southern coast of England and the south-eastern coast of Ireland *after* Napoleon's threat of invasion. Some say that these towers got their name from a sculptor's mallet, others from the name of the man who designed them. They all look like the muzzle of an old-fashioned cannon, ringed around the top. They have very thick walls with two little windows for each storey. The entrance is on the side away from the sea.

The rent for the Tower at Sandycove was only eight pounds all inclusive per year, payable at Dublin Castle. We took it; and Joyce kept his word and stumped up the rent from a prize of twenty pounds that he had won in some examination. I did the furnishing from unmissed things from 5 Rutland Square. 'It's a poor house where there are not many things superfluous.' I learned that at school from the poet Horace.

Well I remember how we went out to inspect and to take possession, for Joyce had an uncle who was a clerk in an attorney's office from whom we had probably heard that possession is nine-tenths of the law. He was careful to leave some article of his as a symbol of possession before we moved in. The only movable thing he possessed was a roll of manuscripts which contained a score or so of poems written in his clear handwriting. Later these were published in a little book he called *Chamber Music*. How they got their title remains to be told.

The Tower at Sandycove is built of clear granite. It is very clean. Its door, which is halfway up, is approached by a ladder fixed beneath the door, which is opened by a large copper key, for there was a powder magazine in the place and the copper was meant to guard against sparks which an iron key might strike out from the stone. There is a winding staircase in the thickness of the wall to the side that does not face the sea. On the roof, which is granite, is a gun emplacement, also of granite which can be used for a table if you use the circular sentry walk for a seat. Over the door is a projection from which boiling oil or molten lead can be poured down upon the enemy. Beside this is a furnace for making cannon balls red hot. There were no shells in the days when it was built, but the red-hot cannon balls could burn a wooden ship if they hit it. Happily these towers were never used, though they were occupied by coast guards until quite recently.

We lived there for two years, greatly to the anxious relief of our parents. Joyce had a job at an adjoining school. I had some reading to do for my medical degree. When the weather was warm we sun-bathed on the roof, moving around the raised sentry platform with the sun and out of the wind. In the evenings we would visit the Arch, kept by watery-eyed Murray, soon to become a widower, or go into the Ship in Abbey Street in the city to meet Vincent Cosgrove or 'Citizen' Elwood, our friends from the Aula Maxima.

To get into the city 'depended' sometimes; it depended on our being in funds. We could go either by tram or train provided that we possessed the fare. Early one day we wandered off in the direction of the city. We were certainly at a loss, a loss for fares or for the subsequent entertainment if and when we reached Dublin.

Joyce saw him first, a tall figure coming rapidly in our direction. I looked and recognised 'old Yeats', the father of the bard. He was out for his morning constitutional. As he came nearer he appeared an uninviting figure, old, lean, and very tall. His dark eyes burned brightly under shaggy eyebrows. 'It is your turn,' Joyce whispered, 'For what?' I asked. 'To touch.' Reluctantly, and with trepidation, I spoke to the old man, whom I hardly knew. 'Good morning, Mr Yeats, would you be so good as to lend us two shillings?' Savagely the old man eyed me and my companion. He looked from one to the other. At last he broke out: 'Certainly not,' he said. 'In the first place I have no money; and if I had it and lent it to you, you and your friends would spend it on drink.' He snorted. Joyce advanced and spoke gravely. 'We cannot speak about that which is not.' But old Yeats had gone off rapidly. 'You see,' said Joyce, still in a philosophical mood, 'the razor of Occam forbids the introduction of superfluous arguments. When he said that he had no money that was enough. He had no right to discuss the possible use of the non-existent.'

We quoted and parodied all the poets. Joyce could parody every prose style and get an equivalent sound for every word. It was chiefly the Collects or the New Testament he chose to parody, for that blind, bitter antagonism towards the teachings of his childhood – an antagonism which finally broke his mind – had already begun.

He could be very solemn about it.

Vincent Cosgrove was another mother's boy. He was cynical and amusing, pensive at times, and cynical with himself. He caused jealousy by walking out with Nora Barnacle, who was the girl with whom Joyce eloped to Flushing before he married her. She had beautiful auburn hair. Vincent came to an early end. He inherited a few hundred pounds on his mother's death and in a fit of remorse, after a few weeks in London, jumped off one of the bridges over the Thames.

To the Tower, on Sundays, Arthur Griffith would come, and sometimes he would come out for the weekend. He would not let himself be outdone by anyone. It was my custom to swim to Bullock Harbour from Sandycove before breakfast of a morning. You skirted along by the granite rocks, but about halfway to the harbour the rocks receded and you entered a round extent of water from which the shore was equidistant on two sides. There was no landing until you turned and swam again along by the shore.

One morning, as I swam back from Bullock Harbour, I missed Griffith. He had been beside me, between me and the rocks. Then I saw him under the water but even then I forebore to go to his assistance because of his anger if he found out. Things got too alarming so I pulled out that determined man. Though his body was scraped as I pulled him up the rock, no allusion was made to the incident when he recovered and walked back to the Tower. I desisted from going for an early morning dip after that.

Joyce very rarely bathed and never in the Forty Foot, which was below the Tower. Once, when we took a tram to Howth on the other side of Dublin Bay, he did get into the swimming bath at the north side of the Hill. I forget if I saw him in the water, but I remember seeing him naked on the side of the bath, carrying a sweeping brush over his shoulder and deliberately staggering along. I was about eight feet up the rock at the side of the tank trying to get a foothold for a dive.

'Jesus wept; and when he walked, he waddled,' Joyce announced.

I studied the naked figure. 'So that's what his uncle wants to make a half miler out of,' I said to myself. 'He'll never do it with that physique. Why, his knees are wider than his legs. He has lost his faith. Now what is to become of his form?'

One morning back in Sandycove I was shaving on the roof of the Tower, because of the better light – it is a good idea to shave before going into salt water – when up comes Joyce.

'Fine morning, Dante. Feeling trancendental this morning?' I asked.

'Would you be so merry and bright if you had to go out at this hour to teach a lot of scrawny-necked brats?'

Touché! He had me there: not a doubt about it. Why don't I think of other people's problems? I must develop a little sympathy: suffer with them; realise their difficulties. I am glad that he has a job, though it is only that of a teacher.

The golden down that would be a beard on a more robust man shone in the morning light. Joyce did not need a shave.

'Yes,' I said, 'that is enough to obscure the Divine Idea that underlies all life. But why be atrabilious about it?' He gave me a sour look. He turned and stooped under the low door.

'I suppose you will bear that in mind and attach it to me

when you come to write your *Inferno*?' I said.

He turned and made a grave announcement: 'I will treat you with fairness.'

'Put a pint or two in fairness and I won't complain.'

He was gone.

What would be the use of sympathy with a character like that? He would resent sympathy. He is planning some sort of novel that will show us all up and the country as well: all will be fatuous except James Joyce. He will be Judge Joyce, to whom Judge Jeffreys, the hanging judge, won't be able to hold a candle.

I knew that Joyce was incapable of writing a *Paradiso*, but little did I think that *Ulysses* would be a masterpiece of despair. And all the worse because it represented the *disjecti membra poetae*: the scattered limbs of a poet. Joyce was the most damned soul I ever met. He went to hell and he could not get out. He could not help it, and no one could help him; he was stubborn and contemptuous. He could not follow in his father's footsteps, for they were too zigzag. His father was an alcoholic, an old alcoholic wag. His mother was a naked nerve; and Joyce himself was torn between a miserable background and a sumptuous education. My cavalier treatment did nothing to help, nor did the attitude of his friend, the lighthearted 'Citizen', who insisted on seeing in Joyce 'a great artist': a droll.

Presently I heard him climbing down the ladder. I went into the overhanging balcony and called down, 'Don't stop at the Arch on your way back.' He never looked up but he raised his stick in a grave salute and loped off.

Added to the grievances of his upbringing, and they were many but unavoidable, was the outrageous conduct of 'Maunsell's Manager'; that is what he called an illiterate fellow from Belfast who, when he was not selling ladies' undies, managed – and ruined – Maunsell and Co., the publishers of nearly all the work of those in the Yeats circle. Maunsell's manager burned the whole edition of Joyce's *Dubliners* with the exception of one copy on the plea that the book contained an offensive reference to the King or

Queen. You may wonder why that should be any concern of a Dublin firm. Ah, but Maunsell's manager was a Belfast man who travelled in ladies' undies, wholesale, and some Belfast men are professional loyalists, combative only in times of peace!

I do not wish to pose as a blameless observer of my contrary friend Joyce. If in spite of myself I do, you will perhaps forgive me, though I confess that I aided and abetted him. I drank with him, lived with him, and talked of many things. I was called by one of his critics 'An accessory before the fact of *Ulysses*'. That, of course, is an extenuation of the truth. To know a man intimately does not make you an accessory to his subsequent action. I did my living best to cheer him and to make those thin lips of his cream in a smile. Very seldom I succeeded. I tried to show him by example how unnecessary and absurd was a seedy hauteur. Maybe I was wrong to try to make him genial. He must have regarded my efforts as the efforts of one who wanted to master him and shape him after the figure and likeness of the would-be mentor. He had the formal and diffident manners of a lay brother in one of the lower orders of the Church. But I was living with him and his constant air of reprobation and his reserve and silences annoyed me, for I took them to be a pose; and I detest humbug in any manifestation.

Joyce had 'a nose like a rhinoceros for literature'. From his appreciations and quotations I learned much. From Dowland's *Third and Last Book of Songs and Airs* he would quote, 'Weep no more, sad fountains,' and caress the end of the last stanza, 'Softly, now softly lies sleeping.' 'One lyric made Dowland immortal,' he would say. Another favourite and model of his was Ben Jonson's 'Queen and huntress chaste and fair.' Clarence Mangan's 'Veil not your mirror, sweet Aline' was often recited to show me what a poet Mangan was. Vergil's '*procumbit humi bos*' he would compare to Dante's '*Cade como corpo morte, cade*'. He tried not unsuccessfully to reform his style on the precision and tersity of Dante. That and his intensity, self-absorption and silence caused me to call him 'Dante' just to rally him from being 'sullen in the sweet air'.

I should have known better, for I was studying abnormal psychology under Connolly Norman, in Grangegorman Asylum who was one of the best teachers I ever met. But it is one thing to study lunacy in an asylum, another thing to recognise it in a friend. Had I succeeded in ministering to a mind diseased, Joyce would not be the greatest schizophrene who ever wrote this side of a mental hospital: he would never have been famous, and Dublin would have been less.

We are all more or less schizophrenic, divided as we are between good and evil, belief and disbelief, reason and emotion, and the conditioning of our childhood and the real experiences of maturity. That is the normal condition for which perhaps the word 'schizophrene' is inappropriate, for that word is associated with a pathological state of mind.

After all, who am I to talk about sanity? Out of four of my friends, two committed suicide, one contracted syphilis and the fourth was a schizophrene. Show me your company! I am showing them to you, for I would not have you think that I wasn't as good or as bad as any of them, but it was 'after my fashion'. In that lies a saving grace.

If I hate anything, I hate humbug or what appears to be humbug. That is why I preferred the Citizen to Joyce. The Citizen was as free as a bird. He was not inhibited. He laughed easily. Joyce had a grim sense of humour; he never laughed at all. He guffawed; but it was his way of being scornful.

Apparently it was payday at the school; for when Joyce returned he had evidently dropped into the Arch to see Mr Murray, who kept that tavern. He invited me to go to Dublin. He had a purpose in going to town but he would not tell me what it was and I knew it was useless to try to pry the secret from him. He liked to act mysteriously of set purpose. We hid the key of the Tower and walked to Sandycove station. We got out at Westland Row. Now the secret will be divulged, I thought.

Joyce said, 'They meet on Friday nights.'

'Who?'

He laughed at my want of understanding. 'The Hermetics.'

'Oh, Æ's crowd?'

'Precisely.'

He led the way to Kildare Street. We went up it to Molesworth Street and thence into Dawson. Joyce stopped before a large shabby office building and proceeded down the lane beside it for about thirty yards. He stopped at a side door and beckoned me. 'This is where Maunsell's Manager has an office. He lends it to the Hermetics on Friday nights.'

I knew that they met on Thursdays; but I said nothing. 'The Hermetics sound like nonsense to me.'

He bowed his head gravely. He was determined on some outrage, joke or insult and he assumed a pontifical air before it, as was his way. We ascended a stairway that was perfectly dark. He paused and listened at a closed door. No sound. Brazenly he opened it. The dark room was empty. After a long pause: 'Got a match?' he asked.

I lit the gas bracket. The room was empty but for a dozen folding chairs heaped against the wall. On the floor was a suitcase. The gas went out. We had no shilling to waste in the meter so we left.

In the street I noticed that Joyce was carrying Maunsell's Manager's suitcase. Larceny, I suggested. He said something about himself having been robbed by Maunsell's Manager. In the Ship we found that the suitcase contained a gross of samples. All were ladies' undies. We had a few pints. Joyce suggested a tour of the Kips – the red-light district – to distribute the undies to the various ladies. The proviso with each present was that the lady would write to thank the Hermetic Society. For all the ladies would know, the Hermetic Society might have been one of those rescue societies which were such a source of laughter in the Kips. Fearing that the bruit of an adventure in the Kips might reach home, I suggested that we visit the mistress of Sweeney the greengrocer, whose vocation kept her constantly indoors. This constancy was her only virtue.

We found her at home in Rutland Street, which runs down to Richmond Street from Mountjoy Square. Jenny produced some bottles of stout, then sent the one-legged girl who lived with her out for more. Joyce, with increasing dignity, suggested that she try on the undies. 'Belfast's best.' Jenny obliged with such zeal that Joyce gave her the dozens of underwear and threw the suitcase with them into the bed. As he did so, his toe struck the night jar or 'chamber' and it rang musically. I never saw the letter of thanks she promised to write.

Our sufferings, it seems, were caused by Mrs Murray, or rather by her wake, at the Arch. She was the wife of the big-headed, thin little publican who kept the nearest licensed house to the Tower. As old customers we were expected, if not invited, to attend. Entrance was by the back door because Murray evidently did not wish to bring any trouble on the house that would be disedifying at such a time. The local police, however, were aware of the bereavement and they sent the constable on duty to pay his respects *en passant* to the dead. Mr Murray himself served libations; such service for the living was a habit with him which he did not turn off, now that it had become almost a rite.

'Here's how!' said the local constable, then, remembering the gravity of the occasion, said innocently, 'Here's mud in your eye.' In the eyes of Mr Murray there were tears, their liquidity overflowed, for there was always a watery film on his dreary blue optics. It had been raining and the probability was that the earth of Dean's Grange cemetery would be muddy; but in the toast of the constable there could have been no allusion to that. His was a well-known expression, the meaning of which, if any, escapes me. Kirke and Lyons, the two fishermen who sold us lobsters, were among those present. The other mourners were habitués, that is, pensioners, and one ex-conductor of the Dalkey tram. There may have been others. I am sure there were but I cannot remember them. I do remember Joyce's gravity as he intoned a ritualistic parody which was his form of joking: he recited Milton:

> 'She must not float upon his watery beer
> Unwept.'

There was a hiatus after that and we wisely did not attempt the unguarded stairs of the Tower. The potato patch was much safer and drier than its occupants.

What a pattern leaves can make, or rather what a pattern can be made out of leaves. Wonderful, wonderful! The window by Burne-Jones in Mansfield College, Oxford, for instance – is it by Burne-Jones? These are potato leaves, leaves of the potato plant. By Jove, I am lying in a potato ridge! I lift my gaze. Above me is the Tower. Where is my companion? I found Joyce in the ridge next to me. He was wide awake and staring up through the potato leaves. 'I have the title for my book of poems – *Chamber Music*.'

14 *Imported: A Patriot*

During the Long Vacation from Oxford, the length of which is a reminder that in the days of old students were released from their studies to work at harvesting, I invited to the Tower Samuel Chenevix-Trench. His given name was Samuel but he had it changed to Dermot by deed poll. He was of Cromwellian stock and the son of a colonel in the British Army, but when he got infected by the Gaelic Revival he became 'more Irish than the Irish themselves'. When you come to think of it, the Irish themselves care little about patriotism; for them it has memories of despair, so all our patriots are imported and Dermot Trench was no exception. When he was at Balliol, and there are no fools at Balliol, he would round up men from Ireland or with Irish propensities – remember Oxford is the home of lost causes – and teach them Gaelic in his rooms in Holywell.

His forehead was wide, with that level space across it which Lavater considers an indispensable mark of genius. His eyes were grey and set wide apart. His legs and feet were as long as those of the men who govern England secretly. His long legs were slightly curved; not curved enough to be bandy but they deviated ever so little from the straight. He was not our guest at the Tower for long before he removed all the oil-lamp shades because they were not manufactured in Ireland but made of Belgian glass. As a result of his patriotism the place was filled with smoke. He refused to use boot blacking until it was produced at home. His shoes grew a mould of verdant hue; 'The Wearin' o' the Green' on his feet! He refused to smile at the jape. 'Not another grim character?' I asked myself. 'One is enough for me.'

Joyce was greatly impressed by what he took for Trench's Eton and Oxford accent. With formal courtesy he gave him his bed at the right-hand side of the entrance door and slept in a bed under the shelf which ran round the room. It was where the number two is on a watch dial. Immediately over his head was piled all the tinware of the Tower – pots, pans, plates and a fish kettle.

One night about one-thirty Trench awoke from a nightmare screaming, 'Ah, the black panther!' As he yelled, he drew a revolver from under his pillow and fired two shots at the hallucination before falling back exhausted. Quietly, I took the revolver away. Again he woke screaming. 'Leave the menagerie to me,' I said; and fired the remaining shots into the cans over Joyce's head. One by one they fell into his bed. He scrambled out, dressed, took his ash plant, and left the Tower never to return.

Trench is Haines, the Englishman, in *Ulysses* and there is an allusion, which may read obscurely, to a black panther, about the middle of the book. Joyce had a great respect for Haines the Englishman. I was blamed for all the shooting. Had Joyce practised instead of pawning my rifle, he would not have been so gun-shy.

Trench's pamphlet, *What Is the Use of Reviving Irish*, is written in the clear style of a Balliol man. 'Gaelic is a language of social genius; its use reveals the Irishman to himself and sets in motion the genial current of soul that has become frozen in an Anglicised atmosphere. It is the symbol of a native social culture which was dignified and attractive in lieu of being snobbish and imitative and for lack of which every man, woman and child in the country are denied their full expansion of personality.'

As an example of social culture, when Irish had become a 'political shibboleth' a high dignitary among the judges of the Supreme Court issued an invitation to a garden party, but instead of the script reading ' ... wishes the pleasure of your company at a garden party,' it read ' ... wishes the pleasure of your body in his potato patch.'

Trench, with an enthusiasm which is the mark of madness, or of genius, or of both, made himself into a fluent Gaelic speaker. When he went back to Oxford he fell into the hands of one of those poverty-stricken, designing fellows who farm Oxford, on the lookout for Trenches and for their sisters who may make rich wives. The fellow that got hold of Trench married a titled woman and lived on her happily, for him, ever afterwards. Trench himself blew his brains out for the hopeless love of Lady Mary Spring-Rice.

Just as Carlyle thought more of a bridge his father built at Ecclefechan than of any of his own books, Joyce thought more of the admirable tenor voice he had inherited from his father than of his literary works. When I was in England he wrote to me – the letter dated 1904 can be seen in the Public Library at Forty-second Street, in New York City – to tell me of a projected tour of English coastwise towns on which he would sing old English ballads and sea shanties. This was his idea forty years before such things were thought of, though they have since become the vogue. The tour fell through because for one thing Dolmetsch, the instrument maker, would not present the troubadour with a lute.

Another reason was a distracting SOS which Lady Gregory sent out from her Abbey Theatre. It had run out of geniuses. As everyone in Dublin was a genius, we all applied. I had little to offer so I did not seek the Presence; but Joyce called on Her Ladyship only to be instantly thrown out. He was not out of the top drawer: not out of any drawer for that matter. When he emerged, he addressed the Citizen, Vincent Cosgrove and me with the following impromptu limerick. He moved his fingers gravely as he recited:

> 'There was a kind Lady called "Gregory"
> Said, "Come to me poets in beggary";
> But found her imprudence
> When thousands of students
> Cried, "All we are in that category."'

Ignored and derided in Dublin, Joyce eloped with Nora Barnacle, who was a maid in Finn's Hotel, Lincoln Place. He sent me a postcard of himself dressed as Arthur Rimbaud, the French poet who tried to revolutionise the French language. Later, he sent two poems printed on galleys to his acquaintances – he would not admit a friend. These were *The Holy Office* and *Gas from a Burner*, a reference to the gas jet in the room where he found 'Maunsell's Manager's travelling bag', i.e., the suitcase with the twelve dozen undies which he removed and presented as has been recorded. He himself was the 'Burner'. That was in 1904.

Almost a year later I met the Citizen, who, with eyes dancing and his quizzical mouth smiling, asked, 'Did you hear the latest about the "artist"?'

'No.'

'He sent a telegram to his parents to announce the birth of his son.'

'Yes?'

'I always said he was an artist. This proves it. *Contra mundum* and no mistake!'

15 *Hospital Politics And Practice*

Flattery is all very well in its way; as the American said: if you don't inhale it. And to have a son can be flattering, if you don't subject the sentiment to analysis. I seldom analyse anything. I did not marry by analysis. And I was far from analysing myself or my son when he was born in Fairfield and placed in his perambulator in the garden daily under, but not directly under, the old mulberry tree. There was danger from a falling bough if the infant were to be put immediately under the tree.

A son can make you responsible. I became so responsible that I passed all the examinations which had begun to accumulate within a few weeks after marriage, and I became a qualified doctor. Examination passing is just the beginning. It is necessary to have practical knowledge of the craft; that meant a sojourn in Vienna.

Our infant son was left in Earlsfort Terrace, Dublin, with a competent nurse who had orders not to take the baby out of Earlsfort Terrace until our return. This was in order to prevent the child from being dumped in the dirty house of one of her cronies. A friendly doctor or two used to look in unexpectedly on nurse and child, so all was well except for the wrench it must have been for my wife to leave her infant son at home and follow a medico to Vienna.

It was no easy thing to get suitable rooms in that then great city. At last we rented the large chambers that had been the apartment of Krafft-Ebing, author of *Psychopathia Sexualis* and of course the instigator of that enemy of the human race, Freud.

What would you expect but sex in Vienna? It was protruding under my very nose. This was the way. After my wife had left, when I was settled, I gave up a large part of the apartment. One evening when my day at the hospital was done, I noticed the black and yellow uniform on a coachman and a footman who sat on the box seat of an ambling brougham but I paid little attention. On the stairs to my apartment stood a deeply veiled figure. I entered my room. I could hear the sounds of love-making intensely intimate coming from the other room! The lovers spoke English of all tongues – what a language to make love in! This obviously so as not to be understood if the landlady, who had rented the room as a rendezvous, overheard them.

> What they did, who may tell?
> But I do think 'twas nothing more
> Than you and I have done before
> With Bridget and with Nell.

Not wishing to be an eavesdropper, I went out, and slammed the other door as I went. Inadvertently I had locked the lovers in, for when I returned, darkling, from the Café Clinic at the end of the lane, I found a hole large enough to permit a person passing through cut in the great door. What would all the secrecy and precaution have availed a lady from the palace of K.K. Franz Joseph if a lady in waiting or whatever she was had stayed out all night? Obviously the officer had used his sabre.

What a city was Vienna in the last days of the Emperor! He was doddering. They used to tell the tale of how, when he opened the Donau Canal, all he had to do was to press an electric button to admit *Der Strom*. That is what they call the Danube there; but *Strom* is also the word used for the electric current. 'What?' asked the Emperor as he hesitated to admit *Der Strom*. 'Do you expect me to drown myself?'

The most civilised city in Europe; a city of music and the waltz, the city where even the girls in the kiosks are embalmed in love, city of the most ineffectual army in the world – not even excepting the Portuguese – and therefore all the more civilised. So civilisedly inefficient was its army that it was almost defeated by its only victory; for when it took Cordona's Italian army prisoner there were no regulations as to how to dispose of a captured force. The indiscretion has never been repeated.

In Vienna there were no trained nurses. Feudalism did not permit its daughters to do menial work unmarried, so nurses were recruited from retired streetwalkers. These administered the anaesthetics to a dozen women at a time in the gynaecological clinic; the doctor started when the patient snored. Surgery was savagery in the Vienna of 1907. There was a flag to be flown over that great hospital, the Krankenhaus, if one day passed without some inmate dying. I never saw it flown.

When I returned to Dublin I found it an easy town in which to obtain a livelihood. With my father and grandfather doctors before me, it was not hard to acquire a practice. I had had a thorough course in Vienna, where I studied under Bàràny and Alexander for ear work; under Chiari and Hajek for throat and nose. And I had something new in instruments – Bruning's bronchoscope. A bronchoscope is a tube with a bracketed handle in which there is a small electric bulb to illuminate the tube so that you can see directly into the lungs or gullet.

I was the first to bring the instrument to Ireland and, for that matter, England; but the code is strict in Dublin; medical etiquette there forbids advertisement. Since then I have noticed that certain surgeons in England and America have claimed the bronchoscope as their own so that a gullible public might think they had invented it.

The next thing was to acquire a house. Sir Thornley Stoker, whom I consulted, advised me to take the house in which Sir Thomas Dean, the architect of the National Library and Museum, lived. It was a Queen Anne house 'modernised' by Sir Thomas. It had a bronze Florentine knocker on the hall door and that decided me.

Sir Thornley himself lived in the great house in Ely Place which was built circa 1770 by the Marquis of Ely. It was nine windows wide; but three of them had been embodied in another house into which Sir Thomas placed Dr O'Dwyer Joyce. Sir Thornley wished to keep up the status of Ely Place and he did not hesitate to sacrifice his friends. Dr O'Dwyer Joyce made a large income by moving when he took a house in Merrion Square, the Harley Street of Dublin, which the wags called 'The Valley of the Shadow of Death'.

Sir Thomas Dean, according to Sir Thornley, was very hard up, so hard up that he would take eight hundred pounds, which in those days was worth far more than that, for 'A house built by an architect for an architect,' so Sir Thornley put it. Now it is not in me to take advantage of a man's property. I offered fifteen hundred for the place and so revived did Sir Thomas Dean become that it took my outraged man of business a week before he beat the unfortunate Dean down to twelve hundred and fifty. I never regretted taking Sir Thornley's advice. Though, of course, I would have made much more money had I followed O'Dwyer Joyce to the Valley of the Shadow of Death. I had enough to carry on; and what more does or should one want?

I stayed on in Ely Place. My house was at the end on the west side, for Ely Place ends in a cul-de-sac. The east side is longer, by five houses. In the fourth and second last of these dwelt George Moore. Moore used to say that Stoker lived in the eighteenth century because he had to live contemporaneously with the stucco of his home, called Ely House, which had the best stucco work of any of the Georgian houses in Dublin. All the good houses were Georgian because Dublin, the seventh city of Christendom, was built in the eighteenth century. It is the best thing that Orangemen ever built. Whether or not that be the cause, Sir Thornley – I was too young and too humble to call him Stoker, which was Moore's way of addressing the surgeon and of exalting himself and reminding Stoker that he was one of the landed gentry and owner of Moore Hall on lovely Lough Carra in County Mayo – did have stucco work of the best period. It was austere and graceful, not florid and over-flowery as the debased stucco of a later time.

Ely Place was closed by two gates which were the gates that protected the city at night before policemen took the place of the inadequate watchmen. These gates, if closed, would shut off the five houses in Upper Ely Place. These houses were built in 1800 and they were built of a different colour brick, which to me was a historical reminder of the ruin caused to Dublin by the Act of Union, passed by bribery and fraud in the very year those houses were built. The gates were rusty; they belonged to no one. I had them removed.

Life was very pleasant in 15 Ely Place. The teeming town was outside and unobtrusive. There was silence, and trees and a greensward in our cul-de-sac. George Moore kept the garden, and I gazed out on its greenery and composed verses while I waited for patients. Sir Thomas sent me the first. I was a 'specialist' on Nose, Throat and Ear; and if you specialise and are comparatively unknown, you have to wait until some colleague or other recommends patients to consult you. It was very kind of Sir T. and the faith he had in me was very touching. Then Sir Thornley Stoker, who had a rich and fashionable practice, saw to it that I remained solvent in Ely Place.

The next question was the matter of a hospital affiliation. Without a hospital after your name, practice in Dublin, and in any other city as far as I know, is greatly retarded. My luck came abruptly.

'The Board of the Richmond Hospital has the honour to invite Dr Oliver St. John Gogarty to meet Sir William Thompson in the Board Room on Wednesday morning, prox. at 9 a.m.' It was signed by all the members of the senior staff.

It should be understood that a student as a rule when he becomes a doctor does not hang around the hospital where he was trained. I did not. So what was the meaning of this epistle? We'll see.

Impatiently I waited until Wednesday dawned. I drove

over across the Liffey and up long and narrow Church Street, so called because of St. Michen's Church where they show visitors how the limy exudate preserves corpses, to the New Richmond with its bronze-capped towers. The members of the Board were formal and at the same time courteous. After some polite meaningless words, Sir William announced, 'You will perform for me a low tracheotomy on a patient whom you will find waiting in the auxiliary theatre. I will await your diagnosis.' So I was to operate in front of all the staff. What could that mean? It could mean that I was being tested, put through my paces; but for what?

A girl, about eighteen years of age, was waiting in the annexe to the large theatre. She was already anaesthetised, not too deeply. The anaesthetist told me that it required very little ether to put her asleep. I kept that in my mind. I took a stethoscope and examined heart and chest although there was a full report on her chart. I referred to the chart after I had made my own examination. I could see that the procedure registered favourably for me with the staff.

I did a low tracheotomy. 'When doing a tracheotomy never turn downwards the blade of the knife.' Well I remembered. Why low? Why was such an operation necessary? I could not go into that. I was obeying an invitation to operate. I had inserted the tube when by some awkwardness of a nurse it came out. When I tried to put it back, a dark object had moved up from the thorax and obstructed any approach to the trachea. It was the innominate vein, which had been pushed up from the thorax by multiple neoplasms, new growths. The poor girl suffered from lympho-sarcomata. That is why I found her chest semi-solid. That is why she went off at the first whiff of ether. I announced my finding to the staff. They had known all along this was a case of multiple sarcomata; but they liked to hear another opinion.

In a month I was invited to join the Richmond Hospital as Visiting Surgeon for cases of Nose, Throat and Ear in the place of Dr Robert Woods who had resigned. Why had he resigned? Sir Thornley and he were such close friends that Woods's eldest son was called Thornley. Woods, whose reputation was beginning to be international, was making too much money as a junior member of the staff. He had often, without knowing it, anticipated Sir Thornley in Naylor's Antique Shop and at many an auction of antiques. This, to a connoisseur, is an unforgivable fault.

It is all right to make money and flaunt it as you may; but to use it to thwart the man who considers that he has made you, no, oh, no! 'Sharper than a serpent's tooth,' etc. So life was made impossible for Dr Woods. He left the Richmond and I took his place. He was welcomed to Sir Patrick Dun's Hospital, which was quite close to his house, 39 Merrion Square. So I owed my election to hospital politics more than to any skill I possessed. I kept that in mind. I could not publicise the knowledge; but it prevented me from having a swelled head. I was the youngest surgeon on the staff. Shut up! You owe your job to a dispute and nothing else. Don't fool yourself. If you do, no one can lend you a hand. I remained a fast friend of Dr Woods until his death and that goes to show that he didn't resent my taking his job and that I did not fool myself into thinking that I had won it by any merit of my own.

I learned a great deal in the external department of the Richmond Hospital. But I was not out of hospital politics yet. One day an old friend of mine, the doctor who saved my little son's life when he had an undiagnosed appendicial abscess, called on my wife. They had had a long conversation before I appeared. Would I resign the Richmond and join the Meath Hospital, to which he belonged? There would be no entry fee in my case.

Let me explain. The doctors of the Meath, as in any other teaching hospital, except perhaps those religious hospitals where the money first goes to the Reverend Mother, cut up the students' fees among them. These fees, in prosperous times, came to many hundreds of pounds annually. Therefore, to get into the group of doctors, an entry fee of some fifteen hundred pounds or more is exacted. There would be no such fine in my case. I asked myself how much the Richmond Hospital means in private practice – nothing; but the Meath had the servants of all the rich people in the best parts of the city. It is also the County Dublin Infirmary and, as such, subject to some control or direction of the Dublin Corporation. Then he told me privately that the staff of the Meath were in a quandary because the Dublin Corporation wanted to nominate a certain Roman Catholic doctor to the staff. In my case the qualifications were higher; was I not an M.D. of Dublin University and a Fellow of the Royal College of Surgeons as well? My religion was right – not left – so, if I joined the staff of the Meath Hospital at once, the Dublin Corporation would be beaten to the draw; and they couldn't say a word against the election of a man with higher qualifications than their own nominee. The most important consideration was the selection of a staff member who would remain with the members of the staff, not with the Dublin Corporation.

I did as my friend advised. I sent in my resignation to the Richmond Hospital. It was not accepted, so for a long time I had two hospitals and double work. I was so busy that I often came home half anaesthetised myself by the ether fumes.

Now that you realise how hospital appointments are made and what is the deciding factor, you will forgive me if I do not take myself too seriously as a surgeon. Perhaps I was the exception that proves the rule. If so, I will grant you that I was exceptional.

There are some avocations which bring the representative in constant touch with the rich: architects, portrait painters, jewellers, antique dealers and picture dealers; but these people know only those who are rich whereas a doctor knows everyone, rich and poor; especially the poor because every morning he has to devote his hours to treating them. If he sticks to one part of the profession, that is, if he is a 'specialist' – a word hateful to Sir Thornley – his colleagues send him their patients and so he knows all the country. That explains how I, who was not born to the purple, got to know those who were.

16 *Dunsany*

The old road from Glendalough to Tara crossed the Liffey at the Hurdle Ford and thence, inclining to the northwest, passed between two strongholds, the castles of Killeen and Dunsany, about a mile apart, which straddled the road and took toll of travellers to and from Tara and Glendalough. I asked Mahaffy, who was an authority on everything, if the name 'Dunsany' was not derived from 'dun', a stronghold; and the river Skene which flows through the grounds? 'The most obvious derivations are usually incorrect.' So I gave up, having to satisfy myself with the derivation of Killeen, which means 'the little church'. Killeen Castle is held to the present day by the senior branch of the family of Plunkett, a name said to be derived from *blanche jenet*. There are two white jennets supporting the arms of Dunsany which are cut in stone over one of the gates. Both strongholds are in the territory of Fingall, or the Fair Strangers who occupied the eastern shelf of the fertile land which lies roughly between the rivers Boyne and Liffey and extends to Baldoyle, Baile dhu Gall, the land of the Dark Strangers of whom Tom Kettle was so proud.

The Fair Strangers were not only the Normans who subdued the Irish Pale which comprises the district but their ancestors too, who settled on the north coast of France three centuries earlier than the coming of the Plunketts to Fingall. The family of Plunkett traces its ancestry back to one Rollo, the Dane, who settled in Normandy in the year 800.

Killeen Castle, founded in 1181, was the larger of the two, as it is today. Castles of this kind were usually built on a *motte* or mound which was protected by a wooden stockade; but there is little reason to think that such was the origin of either Killeen or Dunsany. There is no trace of a mound on the actual site of either, though there are two large mounds in front of Dunsany.

Originally, such castles consisted of four square towers which formed a yard to hold horses, and cattle gathered from outlying herds in the event of a raid. These towers formed a definite pattern: the ground floors had the thickest walls and their roof consisted of an arch, not domed or groined but cylindrical. In the course of building, the cylinder was curved over bundles of brushwood which were set on fire to dry the mortar and fix the arch for the support of the floor above. In the east tower of Killeen the marks of the bundles of brushwood may still be seen on the mortar of the roof. At a much later period the connecting or curtain walls were raised almost to the height of the towers and pierced with windows to form the rooms of a patrician residence – all things being now at peace.

The entrance to Dunsany Castle is through a studded door under a four-centred, Gothicised arch in the western tower. On top of this tower, immune from noise, Dunsany dreams and composes. The only noise that could reach a resident less protected would be the not exotic sound of lowing herds or the crowing of a cock; but these might be mixed with the crunch of gravel under the tyres of unappreciative visitors. From such as these we find 'The Captain closit in his tower'.

Probably General Hammond, Dunsany's steward, when in Dublin at the sale of Sir Thornley Stoker's collection, was responsible for introducing me to Dunsany Castle. The general was sent to recover a prunus vase, one of a pair that used to be among the treasures in Dunsany. It was taken away by the curio-loving Sir Thornley when he went posthaste to attend the maimed butler whose arm had been blown off by a cannon. If I remember rightly it cost his present lordship eighty guineas to recover it.

The next incident was an invitation for my wife and me

to a ball at Dunsany. Now hunt balls are fashionable; and of these the Royal Meath Hunt, called 'royal' from Tara of the Kings, which lies in the heart of Meath, are the most fashionable even though they are subscription balls. A private ball is quite a higher thing.

This was a private ball. While it was in full swing I wandered through the castle searching for a place where I could sit in quiet and get the spirit of the ball without the action; for I am averse to group enjoyments of any kind. At last I found a settee in a corner of one end of which sat a tall young man biting a fingernail. His hair was fair, his forehead extraordinarily high, noble and unfurrowed. His mouth, which a slight moustache did not conceal, was imperious with a clear chin line under the cold beauty of eyes and brow. He looked as if he belonged to a race aloof from the pathos of the common concerns of mankind. It was my host, Lord Dunsany.

I took a seat beside him: there was none other to be had. I must have passed some remark about the ball. I am sure I did. I hope, that it matters little now, that it was not disparaging. Perhaps he would not have cared what I said, for he appeared to be avoiding the ball as much as I. He was tolerant for, before he left, I quoted all Herrick's *Hesperides* and I was about to start on his *Noble Numbers* when somebody drew my audience away.

That was the first of many times that I was his guest. He knew Herrick as well as I did. He knew Kipling. The first did not influence him as much as Herrick influenced me. Kipling, perhaps. But no poet likes to acknowledge that he is beholden to an older – or a contemporary one! You will look in vain for any of Kipling's jingoism in Dunsany's writings. Dunsany has travelled as much as Kipling, but he was not a commercial traveller by any means.

Dunsany's earlier poems tell of the wonders he saw when the hills of Africa looked like crumpled rose leaves in the setting sun. They tell of his thoughts by campfires and on the many journeys he made. They tell of the glamour of wild, unspoiled places in his *Mirage Water*. His is a

Vergilian regret that civilisation is the enemy of old simplicity:

> ... a glamour lost to woodlands
> Which were old when Caesar came.

'Old when Caesar came': with such things he is familiar.

Horseman, soldier, sportsman, poet and playwright, Dunsany is the most representative man I know. His is a full life, a life I would choose were I not content with my own. It does me good to visit him; and the effect of those visits I have tried to record in the sonnet's 'narrow room'. As I say, I am a highbrow and as such I make no excuse for this my traffic with the Muse:

DUNSANY CASTLE

The twin dunes rise before it and beneath
Their tree-dark summits the Skene River flows;
And old, divine, earth exaltation glows
About it though no longer battles breathe;
For Time puts all men's swords in his red sheath;
And softlier now the air from Tara blows:
Thus on the royalest ground that Ireland knows
Stands your sheer house in immemorial Meath:
It stands for actions done and days endured,
Old causes God, in guiding Time, espoused
Who never brooks the undeserving long.
I found there pleasant places filled with song,
(And never were the Muses better housed)
Repose and dignity and fame assured.

17 *Sir Horace Plunkett*

When first I knew Sir Horace Plunkett he was one of those figures who are not only accepted as great but can be used to show how backward you are if you cannot see in what their greatness consists. In these days if Sir Horace is mentioned it is because he was Lord Dunsany's uncle. Then Dunsany was Sir Horace's nephew.

Sir Horace had secretaries, and to give them something to do, he wrote letters to *The Times* both in London and in New York, and he even gave gratuitous advice to the governor of South Africa. He became a member of Parliament. You are not to read into this an example of cause and effect.

The British Government made him Minister for Agriculture. Then his secretaries were in a turmoil of turnips, mangolds and brussels sprouts. Cattle, corn, cheeses and poultry, hackneys, mules, jennets and jackasses had to be treated by statistics. There was an abundance, if not of poultry, of things to be done. Sir Horace had no time. He couldn't take a holiday. Those who did not know him feared for his health. Little did I imagine that I would be a recipient of one of his letters. Yet I was. Here it is:

Royal Irish Automobile Club
Dublin

Dear Sir,

A complaint has been lodged with the Club and submitted to the Committee who in due course passed it on to me as President of the R.I.A.C.

It would appear that on Tuesday evening last at dusk you drove at an alarming speed through the village of Cabinteeley and ran over a duck just outside that village in the direction of Dublin. You failed to stop, and, to all accounts and appearances took no notice whatsoever of the accident.

The complainant is John Nolan of Merrion Cottage, Cabinteeley.

I hesitate to act as judge in this matter until I shall have heard both sides; but, as we motorists are a small group who depend on the goodwill of the public, it is but common sense not to arouse any ill feelings either by speeding or ignoring any accidents which may ensue.

It is to all our interests that satisfactory reparation should be made to John Nolan for the loss of his duck and that you or your chauffeur should drive at a reasonable pace in the future.

It is not without reluctance that I write this letter; but our interests as motorists are seriously involved and those interests are prevailing.

Yours faithfully,
Horace Plunkett, President.

'Sidney's sister, Pembroke's mother!' I don't know why I made that exclamation. I knew that Sir Horace would be president of any club which he could form or which would invite him. He is an unsuppressible President, Chairman, Controller, Consultant Unveiler and Director of his own or others' creations. I bet that the Royal Irish Automobile Club is his idea. The contradiction of 'Royal' and 'Irish' is obviously Horatian. It lies behind the ineffectuality of all his efforts for 'Ireland'. I learned that from Griffith. I had to assure him that I had nothing to do with the club when I showed him Sir Horace's letter.

But the letter, worse luck, requires an answer. I must write something that will be final and put a stop to Sir Horace and his secretaries tilting at ducks. Sir Horace is in his element when writing letters, especially those addressed to an editor. However, the only publicity he can get out of me is to make a mountain – forgive the mixture of the metaphor – out of John Nolan's duck.

I began 'Dear Sir'. Then I realised that 'Dear Mr President' would be more agreeable. He is not my President so I hope that he won't think 'Dear Mr President' is placatory. Here goes:

Dear Mr President,

Thanks for your letter. I have killed John Nolan's duck twice. On the third occasion when the opportunity was presented to me I refused to be an accessory before or after its death.

The first time was about a week ago. The duck crossed the road and flew with the greatest reluctance under my wheels. It was pulled by a string which, when I got out of the car to discuss the 'accident', had disappeared. I gave the aggrieved owner, a surly fellow, one pound which is about five times the price of a duck.

The second accident took place the following evening. This time I found the string. The duck was dead when I killed it. I pointed this out to the owner who refused to give me his address. I am glad that you have it and his name. Pulling a dead duck across the public highway at dusk may not be an offence in the eyes of the law; but it is surely a matter for the Society for the Prevention of Cruelty to Animals.

May I point out that, as you drive frequently on the Bray Road, you yourself are in imminent danger of killing John Nolan's duck in spite of the fact that by this time *rigor mortis* must have set in.

Yours faithfully

That touch about the Society for the Prevention of Cruelty to Animals comes well from 'yours faithfully' as you will see; but it will give Sir Horace a vent, so to speak. He will not write to me any more but bring the case of Nolan's duck to the notice of the committee, probably the same set of ladies that called on me, and eventually become Chairman of the S.P.C.A. now that a new source of cruelty to animals in the shape of the automobile is found.

Revising my letter, I liked 'imminent danger'; it is one of those clichés that are inseperable from the noun, like 'aching' void. It will alarm Sir Horace. Think of the President of the Royal Irish Automobile Club running over a duck. That may be all very fine for a doctor to do – after all, there is an association between quacks and ducks – but for *the* President!

It is very easy to make jokes but very hard not to promulgate them. That is why I did not send the letter about the duck and *rigor mortis* to Sir Horace. There was another reason: Who was I to set myself up as an equal to men of the stamp of Sir Horace? That is one way of getting yourself considered to be an upstart, so the letter I will send will not be impertinent but one of thanks for drawing my attention to the incident; and it will state that Nolan is exploiting the new form of transport, motoring. That will be enough. No mention of the S.P.C.A. and no such address as 'Mr President' – just 'Dear Sir Horace Plunkett'. I remembered how I resented the familiarity with which a shirtmaker wrote to me. He had taken advantage of an introduction in the United Services Club. As a doctor I can meet anyone but that's no reason for taking advantage.

Sir Horace is the brother of that Lord Dunsany who charged a cannon full of double cracks; and, when it would not go off, ordered his butler to see what was staying the explosion. The butler thrust his arm full length down the cannon's bore. There was a sudden burst. The butler's arm was blown off. Sir Thornley Stoker was summoned from Ely Place. What he did I do not know; but I do know that he took a prunus vase with him back to Dublin. Maybe he settled for the vase. Who knows? Maybe, when Lord Dunsany's man of business wrote to ask Sir Thornley what his honorarium was (Sir Thornley, who was of the old school, always spoke of his fees as his 'honorarium', for who can pay a doctor all he owes?), it was another matter.

I hope that I know enough to take a hint from Sir Thornley's effort at ingratiating himself with Lord Dunsany and not make a pup of myself.

No, the furthest I will go will be to show Sir Horace's letter at Moore's dinner next Saturday. Moore does not like Sir Horace. He blames him for sooting up his garden by smoke from the chimney of the Board of Works which lies between his garden and Stephen's Green. But if it isn't the smoke it will be something else, for Moore has to find fault with everyone since he is not happy with himself. He held the great Mahaffy up to ridicule when he compared him, with his side whiskers, to a butler; and, though he is a friend more or less of Diana, Dr Tyrrell's intelligent daughter, he is trying to find fault with her father, who is not only one of the greatest scholars living but one of the greatest wits. What a fool Moore will be if he tries to contend with Tyrrell in a battle of wits. Can it be that he who is a cause of wit in others resents their wit?

I have not forgiven Moore for his attempt at wit when my mother called on him to object to the use of my name in his novel, *The Lake*.

'Madame, if you can find me a name which is composed

of two dactyls, like the name of your son Oliver, I will substitute it for Oliver Gogarty.'

Perhaps it was some dim memory of this that brought the quotation about 'Sidney's sister, Pembroke's mother' into my head. *Pembroke* is a sound equivalent for *Plunkett*, and *Sidney* for *Horace*. It was not easy to live a dactylic life if you are born a spondee. – Geōrge Mōōre!

I was so right as occasion proved. Sir Horace later on consulted me as a doctor. Years later. He telephoned, it was a matter of the greatest secrecy, a 'top secret' in fact. He was going to the front. Had he not been at Eton with Haig? The only thing that had deterred him from going there long ago was the want of a 'national purpose'. He had found one: Irish girls, nurses of course, were to nurse American wounded. Irishmen would follow of course. All Ireland would join in the war. The idea for the moment must be kept a dead secret. And he was bringing me! I was weak enough not to refuse. Who could refuse Sir Horace when he wanted something. Meanwhile, I had to carry the secret: I couldn't open my heart to anyone. And I was getting more and more nervous. The fact that generals were never killed did little to comfort me. I thought of getting the soles of my boots painted white just in case!

He would let me know in a week. Meanwhile, mum was the word.

I saw the two of us seated in a railway carriage in Westland Row on our way to the front. I had solved somehow the problem of what to wear. Sir Horace would see to that. We were seated just waiting for the soft steam to enter the cylinders and to bear us off to the Front. The train started. We were off! Suddenly, Sir Horace leapt up. He had left the national purpose on the platform. 'Stop the train!' The station master rushed up to ask what was the matter. 'That suitcase there!' The station master looked at a solitary suitcase but one that was all important. It contained the 'national purpose'. I woke from the nightmare. It was not until a week later that Sir Horace accused me of letting out his secret. It seemed that some members of the Kildare Street Club had asked him in a railing manner, 'Horrie, where are your tabs?'

But I had had a narrow escape. Of course, I never revealed the secret. Quite possibly Sir Horace himself did.

18 *The White Lady*

On an evening in December I was walking home with Newburn, who lived on the south side of Stephen's Green. It was about 6 p.m. and quite dark. He asked me into his house. I waited in the hall while he searched for the light switch. He did not find it. Instead I heard him fumbling in a closet under the stairs. At last he emerged and lighted the hall. He looked perturbed. 'Say nothing about it to my wife,' he said. 'I saw the White Lady coming down the stairs when I came in. I thought she had hidden herself under it. There was no sign of her. I searched with my foot to where the stairs meet the floor. That's what delayed me.' The house is old enough to have a ghost, I thought.

Then I asked, 'Who is the White Lady?'

'I'll show you her miniature as soon as we go up. Don't worry about it now.'

When we reached the drawing room there was no sign of Mrs Newburn. Her husband went to the mantelpiece and took down a miniature, framed in pinchbeck, of a young woman, half length, dressed in white. 'For God's sake keep this and take it out of the house. It may put an end to her walking.'

Mrs Newburn, a quiet woman, appeared. We had some desultory talk, she glanced at the vacant place where the miniature had been but she made no remark. Soon I took my leave. When I got home, I put the miniature in a drawer and forgot about it for many years. When I found it, seeing that nothing had happened, I put it in the back drawing room over the mantel. Years later when I took it down – I must have been telling someone about it – the blue paper at the back had come loose and showed some writing in faded ink. 'Mary Medlicott drowned at sea when crossing from Barbados 1771.' So that was the name of the White Lady. I wondered if she or her people had been the owners of Newburn's house. The painting on ivory was the work of the eighteenth-century artist, Nathaniel Hone. It was a valuable gift that Newburn had given me.

Newburn was the greatest athlete I had ever known. He could always break evens for the hundred-yard dash *except in competition*. One fine evening I went out to Ballsbridge, where I had permission to train by courtesy of the Royal Dublin Society. Newburn was practising the broad jump. After a few tries by way of warming up, he told us to stand by and be ready to measure his next jump. He took what I considered to be a very long run. He rose high in the air with his legs pulled up under him and his hands forward. Out came the long legs. He had landed. He swayed; thrust his head forward and threw out his arms. Old Stevens was there, who represented the Amateur Athletic Association; 'old' Stevens the boys called him, and it was not used in his case as a term of endearment. He had a tall silk hat and a frock coat. He was a small red-nosed man who took himself very seriously. Why is it that we permit unathletic old fogies to get into responsible places in athletics?

I took the chain with, I think, Tom Cronin, one of the trainers. Newburn had jumped twenty-seven feet eleven inches. 'Mr Stevens, come and look at this.' It was no use. A world's record, and far more than a world's record, had been made; but Stevens was mulish. 'Can he not jump back too? The wind may have been in his favour.' I lit a match. It burned without a flicker in the calm air. 'Do you want me to break my ankles?' was all that Newburn said. Of course, there was no turf mould for a jump in the opposite direction. A few of the boys who were training came to look at the astounding jump. They spoke to Stevens, who tried to put on dignity; was he not the representative of the

A.A.A.? 'God blast you, anyway.' Newburn was not the only man to be spanceled by stupidity.

Newburn must have been six feet six. He was, as I said a wonderful man. He could pitch the fifty-six pound weight higher over the bar than anyone in Ireland. The fifty-six pound weight competition was discontinued as a result. Why he did not run in the 220 I could never make out. An athlete, a runner, is said to be at his fastest at 135 yards. Newburn should have done under twenty-one seconds for the 220 in practice. In competition he was useless. He must have had a faint heart. Maybe it was not in athletics. He seemed not to set much value on his jump and he cared not when the fifty-six pound weight was abolished.

For a year or so he was in the habit of going to London. Eventually, he became 'elocutionist' to Eton College, which meant that he taught stutterers and those with inhibited speech. He showed me a few of his cases: deaf mutes whom he had taught to speak. Infinite patience was required for this. Infinite patience he had. Perhaps it was this patience that accounted for the light way he treated Stevens, who had deprived him of a record, unofficial as it might have been. I remember that Stevens, among other objections, had said, 'He has not jumped in competition.' As for his treating deaf mutes: I put down the fact that I was invited to meet Dr Moure of Marseilles to examine Don Jaime, one of the sons of the Kip of Spain, to my friend Newburn. Perhaps someone in Eton had heard him speak of me. I did not go because I knew that no treatment could give hearing to one who was born deaf. To teach such a one to speak was another thing; and that was Newburn's business.

19 *The House Of The White Garden*

Man is the measure of all things. Where did I hear that? At school, when the teacher told us that Protagoras held that not universal humanity was the touchstone, but man as an individual. 'Nothing can appear to you as it appears to me.' And Protagoras was the most famous of the Sophists. We are in the age of sophists again. Karl Marx is the greatest scoundrel of them all.

We need not go into that just here; but when I say that man is the measure of all things, I don't mean what the wily Sophist meant about two thousand five hundred years ago, but man as the whole of humanity. I do not mean that a blind man cannot be proved wrong if you accept Protagoras, but I mean that to universal man a limitation must exist.

He has to be his own norm: to him the whale and the elephant are large, the fly and the streptococcus small. He talks of a normal climate. What is his norm but his own temperature of 98.6 degrees Fahrenheit? He cannot think of anything without a beginning; he can hear only within eight or nine octaves; he can see only the colours of the spectrum; and yet he prides himself on his health, his pedigree, his colour, his inheritance and his nationality, all of which are outside his control; all matter of what we call good luck.

I was priding myself on my children as I walked with a son on either shoulder down a tunnel of hawthorn, willow, ash and alder to the sea. One son was brown, the other fair. All the forethought in the world could not have influenced Nature's lucky bag when they were born sound and lively! And what am I doing now but congratulating myself on something I could not help? Even Julius Ceasar believed in the goddess Fortune, who favoured him more than most men.

In Connemara, Garranban House stands on a rounded hill with trees on either side, a lake to the south, a landlocked bay to the north. It was a good place for the holidays; and my hospitable sister-in-law invited us all.

I was teaching the boys to swim. In Ballynakill Bay the water was brimming, tide-full and clear. The water made no ripple on the gravel. It shone with an opalescence that recalled the colours of spilled oil. The children had been taught to put their faces in a basin of water and to blow bubbles. They loved the game and it taught them how to control their breathing when it came to teaching them how to swim. The water won't get into their mouths and cause a panic.

Out I was, waist-high. I pay in a son until he is merged. I tell him that the lower he goes the more buoyant he will be. He floats along until he is stranded. The next step is to let him strike out; but not too fast. 'Turn your face sideways when you want a breath.' My dark son was conscientious: he put no leg on the bottom while he stroked with his arms; he did not keep time; that will come later. The fair son swam well. Then I noticed that he had one leg on the bottom. Well, well; don't let them get chilled. Home we go.

Looking back, I realise that those were the happiest days of my life. Did I realise it then? From what I know of myself I must have done so, but not as much as I do in retrospect.

This retrospectful look is what makes a Golden Age. That age was mine and it was contemporary. I had attained the greatest happiness that man can reach. I had dwelt in the Golden Age. Who can realise it fully until he leaves it, or it leaves him?

Who was I to be so blest? This is an enigma that I must refer to my Lord Mayor of Dublin, Larry O'Neill, who will, playing for safety as is his wont, answer with 'There I leave you.' As you cannot answer it yourself and as the chief citizen evades the subject, you can only fall back on the cliché, 'The ways of God are inscrutable.' They have little to do with desert.

As I let the boys run homewards a strange sight met my eyes. A man stood upside down in a field; at least so it appeared at a distance. On coming closer, I found Snodgrass, the artist from Birmingham to whom, with his wife, my generous sister-in-law had lent a house by the beach of the bay Rossdhu. His head was bent down between his legs; his backside towards me. A breech presentation! Odd! He was not studying astronomy with his hinder part, as the merry bard suggested that another 'artist' was doing long ago. No, he was getting a fresh view of the scenery with a different and unused part, so he said, of his retina! Odder still; but then you must be prepared for anything from an artist. They have different ways of looking at things from the more common folk.

Snodgrass had been recommended to me by my friend McElroy, one of the most generous and enthusiastic men I ever met; this is out of the character attributed to Scotsmen by those who seek to denigrate whole nations to distract attention from themselves. He sent Snodgrass to Ireland during the war. Snodgrass was rejected by the recruiting station to which he had to present himself because of chronic mastoiditis and a large polypus in his left ear. No subject for hardship and the trenches, but an eligible visitor from Birmingham. he was now with us in the Many Coloured Land.

So this morning I find him upside down studying Diamond Mountain, that glistens when the rain lights its quartz. The painting which he exhibited in Dublin proved that he had seen it with a fresh eye. I wish I had bought that landscape, seen by a foreign artist; but I was intent on having the children painted, and so they were. The painting, sadly mutilated by the louts whom an alien loosed on the country when he plunged it into civil war, still exists, patched up by some expert in Chelsea. So do three magnificent water colours of the children.

What a refreshing sight the Twelve Bens – or Benna Buela as the Gaelic has it – at whose head stands Diamond Mountain, must have been to a youth born in Birmingham and raised beside its underground canals. The Twelve Bens form a massif with twelve peaks which lies between Kylemore Lakes on the north and the lakes round Ballinahinch on the south. To the east it is bounded by the long stretch of Lough Inagh; to the west is the town of Clifden and the plateau which falls down to Garranban.

To the east beyond the Twelve Bens runs the only fjord in Ireland's coast. It is called Killary Harbour. It is said that a whole squadron of the British fleet could anchor in it; the only objection to that is the fact that one submarine at its mouth could hold the squadron.

It is not the long drive by the side of the Killary that enticed me out but the restlessness of a holiday on which you want to 'go places' regardless of whether they are interesting or not. But nobody can say that Leenane at the head of Killary Harbour is not interesting. It is full of interest, or of that feeling that you are missing something.

That is a delusion from which I suffer: I want to get the sentiment of a place whether it is there or not. To the denizens the village must be the hell of a bore when tourists are not about. They have nothing unusual to look for but the village idiot, and he has become a part of the local scene.

A word must be said about the village idiot and about village idiots in general. There is one, or there should be one, to every village in Ireland. In cases where villages have become overgrown and turned into towns, the village idiot is not so recognisable. He may have been elected to Parliament; anyway, he is not as easily found as in the more countrified hamlets where he is spoken of as 'a natural' and has been accepted as a part of the community, just as the odd thorn tree is accepted on the top of the fairy rath.

The Leenane 'natural' crossed the road as the car was coming to a stop. He had a sack, worn capelike across his shoulders though, for a wonder, it was not raining.

'Gar, come in outa that!' a voice called. He turned his head. So his name was Gar. Most of the naturals have no name or, if they have, a fellow such as I will go a long time before he finds it out.

The Leenane fool was spoiled by the tourists, who seized the chance of proving to themselves their own superiority by talking to him. But now after lunch there were few tourists about. I had a talk with the man who serviced cars in the garage across the road over from the hotel. After the usual exchange of compliments Jim told me that Gar had been abandoned by some tinkers, when he was about two or three years old, and widow Feeney insisted on taking care of him, which was better than letting him go to the workhouse. His name was Gar because it was the only sound he could make. The last census people wanted to know exactly how to register him. Naturally, they could get nowhere, so his surname was entered as blank on the files. He was called 'files' after that. His name was given to the recruiting sergeant as Gar Files and he would have been taken away to fight for 'freedom' – when is a fight not for freedom? – and to see the world, as the posters announced. He had a good chance of seeing the other world as well. But the widow Feeney tapped her forehead significantly and the sergeant nodded; and Gar Files was left to brood on ambition unfulfilled. So they thought; but the ways of a loony are wily. So were the sergeant's. They met in the adjoining village and Gar became a private in His Majesty's Expeditionary Force. Later, during the retreat from Mons, when the exhausted British soldiers fell asleep, cemented by their blood to the floor of some church, Gar woke up to find the beribboned uniform which had just been cut off a general beside him. Delighted, he put it on. The Germans came and took him prisoner. He was treated as a general while imprisoned and he received a general's pension from the British War Office. For all I know to the contrary, he has it still. Such is war.

I found Snodgrass admiring the weaver at his loom in a shed beside the tavern. He should have been admiring the scenery, I, in my ignorance, imagined.

It is hard to acknowledge that your ideas about art and artists are wrong. I was under the impression that a true artist would stand gaping at the wonderful colours among the mountains of the west. The only one who stood agape was Gar Files, and he was gaping not at the mountains, which he had seen to distraction, but at an automobile.

Don't think that idiots are amazed at anything new. Remember the story of the Congo natives who dismissed a hydroplane that landed on the river with 'White Man's juju'. As soon as Gar found out that it was not an army lorry to take him to the battlefield his gaping ceased.

Yes, Snodgrass would have a drink. That was understandable. What I could not understand was his meek-and-mildness. It took me some time to realise that the man was in a strange country and his only armour was distrust. He would not trust even the army doctor who certified him as unfit. Our idiot wanted to join up; the artist did not. It takes a 'private person', as the Greek calls the idiot, to make a private soldier.

The waterfall of the river was flowing white. There was plenty of water in its winding stream. Off to the south the road rose, and the long drive through the Joyce Country began. Paudraic O'Malley's house was in the valley. Paudraic was the first man 'on the run'. The Black and Tans, irregular troops whom Lloyd George loosed on Ireland, riddled his house from a Lancia lorry on the road. You could see the bullets gleaming in the mortar. But Paudraic was never taken.

Somehow I did not want to take the artist any farther. He was not interested in the scenery, in spite of his looking at it between his legs! No, in spite of his fresh eye his painting of the Diamond lacks true atmosphere, which goes to show that you can be an artist without atmosphere. Could it be that that upside-down view was put on to fool me? I used to favour an upright outlook until I met this subterranean Birmingham boy.

Why is it that I don't want to drive through the Joyce Country? I used to love to dawdle on through scenery that defies definition and possesses, as no other scenery in the world does, a magic that is almost tangible. Instead I feel as if I were visiting the reptile house in some zoo. I must cure this sensitivity. Who would be a slave to sensation?

Things were silent at Garranban. Something had happened. The children had to be put to bed. What is wrong? Are they ill?

The information came with the reluctance of indignation: the children had been invited to the artist's cottage on the beach. They had come back drunk – my children. And not for the first time or I would not have mentioned it. Again that feeling of malaise.

20 *The Society For The Prevention Of Cruelty To Animals*

One afternoon while I was waiting for patients four of them were announced. At first I thought that there was but one who needed advice or treatment and that the others had come just to look on and feel superior to their friend. I was wrong. None of them was in need of my services as a doctor but they asked if I would preside at a meeting for the prevention of cruelty to animals. It seemed that they were the committee. It took me a long time to satisfy them, if satisfy them I did, that my engagements prevented me from presiding at a meeting for a purpose that was so near to my heart. They left in silence. And left me guessing.

At that moment I looked out on the garden and there was a black cat stalking George Moore's blackbird. As keeper of the bird during the day, I have a bow with half a dozen arrows all ready: the bow has only to be strung, the arrow fitted and through the open window ... the cat was about fifty yards away or less. Often have I shot at that cat but never hit it. Sometimes my arrows deflect the cat from its quarry; sometimes I have to take the more undignified measure of shouting. This time, fortunately for the bird's sake and very unfortunately for mine, my arrow found its mark. The old ladies from the Committee of the Society for the Prevention, etc., must have guided the missile to punish me for refusing to preside at their meeting. In consternation I ran downstairs. As I did so I looked out through the little windows of the staircase. The cat had jumped the wall and was making off down the street after the committee with my accusing arrow, initials and all, stuck in his rump.

At that moment when despair was about to numb my faculties, a small boy knocked at the hall door. He was the boy with the evening papers. I opened the door and thrust a half crown into his palm. 'Drop the papers and get the arrow that is sticking into that cat.' For a wonder he comprehended. He turned and rushed after the animal, who was rapidly catching up with the committee. His bare foot pinned down the arrow just in time. He bore it back in triumph.

I restored the papers he had dropped and I was about to show my relief in another tip when I remembered that if I were too lavish it might arouse curiosity. He grinned with a conspirator's cunning. 'The cat got off,' he said. 'Next time shoot it in the head.'

Strange, this business about Cruelty to Animals and anti-vivisection societies. Old ladies all. In Latin countries there is unnecessary cruelty to horses. In England up to the time of Dickens there was cruelty to human beings. Even now the jails are sadistic, so is capital punishment although its theory is not an eye for an eye but that the criminal, having rendered himself anti-social, cannot justly be made a charge on the community, and must be killed. Was I to watch the blackbird being stalked and killed? Arrows a few inches off did not stop the cat, the only one that did was that attended by unfortunate circumstances. Had the old ladies rescued the cat and read my initials, which are unusual and unmistakable, on the arrow it would not have helped my career. I would have been branded as a monster. What is there for it but to offer to all such old ladies a compensatory poem?

God made the rat
And then above
The rat he placed
The playful cat
for GOD IS LOVE.

All of which touches the origin of Evil; and goes to show
that there are exigencies; that Nature has tears: '*sunt
lacrymae rerum*,' and so on.

21 *McGeehan*

One day as I was going out by the Front Gate, through
which I had entered Trinity College ten years ago, the
porters touched the peaks of their black velvet huntsman's
hats. I returned the salute. Had I driven out in my
automobile, then one of the half dozen in all Ireland, they
might not have had as much respect for me, though the
salutes would have shown little difference. College porters
are opinion makers; they also make reputations which,
once they are made, stick to a man for life. I am not 'a most
superior person', I wish to be unassuming and to remain so.

College Green was in front of me with Grattan on a
pedestal. His bronze figure addressed the college. His right
hand was upraised. There was no mistaking his statue for
that of an orator. I wondered if it were to be removed
secretly by night how many citizens would miss it by day. A
statue has come to be a subconscious landmark that no one
notices; but don't remove the pedestal.

The half-circle of a Palladian masterpiece, the Bank of
Ireland, which was Grattan's parliament house in the
eighteenth century, was on my right with a gap in the
middle of the curve, gaping for clients. Opposite, on the
other side of the street, were three or four more banks.
Traffic passed in a medley in front of the college. I felt like a
bather taken by surprise, for doctors do not walk in the
street.

That is a custom born of necessity, because a doctor is at the mercy of any of his acquaintances if he is caught in a public place; and, if he is caught, free advice can make hypochondriacs of us all. So the unwritten law is for doctors not to walk in the street; and I hope that I have explained the reason why. Take, for instance, the case of a gynaecologist ... now you see what I mean? It is not that doctors wish to pretend that they are busy; but they don't want to be consulted; accosted is the better word.

There is an exception I must admit. That exception is Dr Kegley, 'Surgeon' as he calls himself. At five o'clock every afternoon he may be seen – you can't miss him – walking up Grafton Street with his umbrella tightly reefed. He carries it with its muzzle pointing to the ground, its stock under his arm. He is coming from Jervis Street Hospital. Everyone knows that operations are all over in Dublin by noon. Kegley, who can operate only on hernias, wears a bowler hat; well, if that doesn't suggest a hernia; but you can't very well consult a man about a hernia in the open street, so Kegley is safe to stroll along the sidewalk with his umbrella tightened up. It may be a symbol of the tightened tendons of a corrected hernia; but 'there I leave you,' as Larry O'Neill said; Larry, the chronic Lord Mayor of Dublin. They tell me that I am too prone to look for symbols.

My misfortune was Hamish McGeehan. He stood with his shoulder pointed towards the college. He had seen me saluted by the porters; he was in wait. His greasy little eyes brightened as his podgy body turned. He, like Kegley, had an umbrella; but it was not tightly wrapped. His mouth was. Over his silver hair was a soft black hat which associated him with the Church, of which he was a blameless though insinuating son.

'I saw you coming out of Trinity College,' he said leaving me to defend myself for having belonged to such a black organisation. I looked at my watch.

'You'll have time to hear what your friend, George Moore's secretary, is supposed to have done.'

'Which one?' I asked, for I knew that George had two or three a year.

I knew that one of them had gone off to hide her pregnancy and to have her child in peace without the knowledge of the omniscient novelist. I also knew that pregnancy was not one of McGeehan's subjects nor was it one of his wife's for she led the fat and sexless life of a Chinese eunuch. He emphasised the 'friend' when he mentioned George Moore so that I would be sure to be in the wrong. If he were a man at all, I thought he would find something to laugh at in the supposedly omniscient – as far as women were concerned – Moore missing his secretary's condition, which was under his eyes. No; it must be something that is more discussable than sex and, if possible, worse.

'She has been stealing his manuscripts and selling them.'

I saw it all in a flash. I am afraid that my conscience is easy-going. The poor little woman wanted money badly to pay for her confinement, which had to be in the country to ensure privacy. Her morale was not helped by Moore's dictation. She took a bundle of his manuscript and 'went to see her mother', only to come back one.

'She hasn't stolen any of yours?' I asked.

The professor smiled as a man armed with a stiletto might smile.

'No,' he said. 'And I don't suppose that she'll bother to steal yours though you live in Ely Place.'

So it was a sin to live in Ely Place, contaminated as it was by the presence of George Moore!

'Miss Jago has been delivered of a fine boy: mother and child both doing well.'

'It has an official sound but for the "Miss". Who is Miss Jago?' I asked Hamish.

He smiled that smile of his which made you uneasy: it suggested that you either knew and were pretending you didn't, or that, if you didn't know, you were exposing your ignorance. The kind of smile that is called quizzical and it's not a bad name for it. I repeated the question snappily enough to stop that irritating smile.

'George Moore's secretary, of course. His present one. She told me that she had to go away to be with her mother.

Instead of that she went away to become a mother – all this, and he prides himself on his knowledge of women.'

I remembered Moore telling us that his secretary was away.

'What will he do when he finds out?'

'Why should he find out? Of course if fellows like you go about sneering he cannot help but find out,' I said.

'It's already all over the place.'

This is the kind of thing that would amuse Yeats, I thought. I shall have to wait until he hears it if it is 'all over the place'. I have secrets enough without adding an open secret to them. Yeats will take a different view from anyone. He will imagine Moore himself 'lying in', doing a kind of *couvade* as the primitive tribes do and receiving presents because his secretary has had a child. The more illegitimate the better for Moore. That will be Yeat's theory. But I cannot see Moore tolerating any scandals that affect himself; scandals are all very well for other people. They supply copy for Moore's books; but in his own household, NO!

You have to be careful how you part from Hamish. He is touchy. If you look at your watch and say that you must be off, he will be offended. If you linger he will become quarrelsome. I jumped into a tram. This Hamish is not the same as another Hamish, Joyce's friend. This man is some sort of professor in arts in the law. That's why he has that superior grin on his face. It was a long time before I could get the taste of him and his ilk out of my mouth.

There is in Ireland a kind of third person which, though married, is sexless. The male of the species is more a churchman than a layman; and the female of the species is more churchman than the male. These McGeehans like to 'keep in touch'. After a lengthy trial when there is not a kick left in them they get a job with more patronage than any bought slave has to endure.

Once in his job, he stays put for the rest of his life, which is filled with envy and hatred for all free and indifferent spirits. He strives to get them into his Holy Office and to exhibit them as a proof of his rectitude and his zeal. He has been so accustomed to prove his devotion that he can't stop.

The Church as a rule doesn't want to be bothered by its McGeehans. It considers that they are busybodies. If left to itself, the Church wouldn't care a damn. I hope you get the gist of what I am trying to show. Instead of selling smutty postcards at the doors of the great cathedrals, instead of carving the seats of the confessionals as did the monks of old, the McGeehans wear miraculous medals and burn your character at the stake.

It is pleasant at any time, except when it is raining, to cross from the Front to the Back Gate of Trinity. After you pass the great dark grey library and the New Square, the College Park opens on your right. It is smooth and green and, in the hottest summer, hardly ever burned. I was walking along under the young trees when I met Joe Ridgeway. He had a stutter but he was quite understandable. It was worth while to be patient with him because he always had a new subject, and one removed from the expected, to discuss.

'Did you hear that Lady Dudley got acute appendicitis and had to be carried into the nearest hospital, which was the Mater?' he broke out.

'You don't say?'

'I'm wondering who will operate on her. I don't know much about the doctors in the Mater; that's why I'm asking you.'

'Well,' I said, 'there's Blaney, Chance and Lentaigne. Chance is about the best of them; but as Blaney's leading by half a dozen masses and two benedictions, he'll be sure to get the job.'

'It means a knighthood for whomever gets it.'

'A knighthood! Then they'll remove her to a Protestant hospital, for they don't want to give knighthoods to Roman Catholics, except for politics, at least not until they've exhausted the privileged list.'

Ridgeway eyed me thoughtfully. He was pondering

something I had said. Ridgeway does not take a joke or a slight sarcasm readily.

'What do you mean "leading by half a dozen masses"? Leading what?' he asked.

'I meant it as a joke. Blaney is the most docile of the Mater staff, and the most devout. He kowtows to the nuns more regularly than Chance or Lentaigne. And, as the nuns have the apportioning of operations, Blaney has the best chance of operating on Lady Dudley's appendix.'

Ridgeway could not see it at all.

'What does a nun know about surgery? I'm afraid I don't understand.'

It was too late to hand him over to McGeehan at the Front Gate. I would have given a lot to see Mac's face as Ridgeway's difficulty, and my villainy, dawned.

I heard afterwards that they did remove Lady Dudley from the Mater Hospital. It would never do to have Catholic hands palpating a Protestant abdomen.

When I left Ridgeway he was beside the Pavilion. When I looked back he was gone. It was a way he had of disappearing. Maybe he went into the Pavilion. There was nothing mystical about Ridgeway. And yet I was not disappointed because what endeared Ridgeway to us was his faculty of disappearing. He was such a void, he had no room for an ache. That's why, if we didn't all like him. No one objected to him.

22 'Who Is Stella, What Is She?'

My wife ran the house in Ely Place so smoothly that everthing seemed to go by itself. We had the same cook for years until she became so blind that she sent up potatoes instead of apples for dessert one night.

On Friday evenings George Russell, a constant friend,

would come in from Rathgar; Yeats from nearby Merrion Square; Griffith very occasionally, for he was not a visiting man; Tom Kettle and George Moore and many others. Everyone could 'affirm his own philosophy' except George Moore, for he had only opinions, shocking ones, on gentle occasions; he could be Senior Wrangler for all his lack of philosophy. This I was presently to experience.

I had bought a picture from Jack Yeats without first consulting Moore, who considered his taste in artistic matters infallible. I had acted on the advice of Æ, who had said that there were only two artists whose paintings were worth buying in Dublin – Jack Yeats and Nathaniel Hone. In his own medium Jack Yeats expressed the spirit of Ireland as well as his better-known brother, William, did in his. The poems of William Butler Yeats are more famous than the paintings of his brother, for the living word when winged with music can travel farther than the still life of any pigment, oil, tempera or water colour.

When Moore saw the picture on the wall and remembered that he had not been consulted, he began, 'Oh, where did you get that? It's all a mess of green and brown.'

I mumbled.

'By whom did you say?' he continued.

'Jack Yeats.'

He shook his head. 'Well, if you are prepared to throw your money away without asking the advice which I am always prepared to give, it is your own doing. I cannot help you.'

'I bought it not because of the artist but because of its message to me. That green is the green of the eternal hills, the colour of Eternity ... '

'Now, my dear fellow, what colour is Eternity?'

I proceeded unperturbed. ' ... and the sea that makes immortal motion is filling up the bay. Soon the brown seaweed will be covered over and the long effulgence will brim Clifden Bay with water and with light.'

Moore listened to his own trick of turning one medium into another; painting into words. He went across to

115

inspect the picture at close range. 'Well, yes; but the next time you buy a picture ask me to come with you. You might have done worse. You have had a narrow escape. Good-bye!'

'Pernickety' was the name that described Moore.

He was walking in the garden one day with a lady as tall, if not taller, than himself. She stooped a little, but not from the neck. 'Back she had of bended yew.' Her complexion was as pink and white as Dresden china. She had high cheekbones and no chin: English, obviously. I recalled a love poem of my early period:

> The girl by whom I am beguiled
> Must have high cheek bones and a child.

There was no way of knowing whether or not she had had a child. But her cheekbones tallied with the invoice. She did not appear to be full-bosomed. Don't let that deceive you. You'd be surprised!

As Moore walked beside her he was gesticulating with both hands. At times his walking stick would rise heavenward as he raised his arms up in the air. The lady only murmured, her voice was soft and low. What can the argument be about? After his habit, Moore is carrying war into the enemy's camp: he is putting the poor lady in the wrong. But what is he doing in his garden at this hour? It is about three o'clock. He should be arguing with his secretary, 'composing,' as he calls the daily wrangle. Well, I wouldn't have to wait long to hear about it; not if I knew George Moore.

'Some men kiss and tell; Moore tells but does not kiss,' Susan Mitchell, Æ's secretary, said of him; quite untruly, I learned after. Lady Cunard was my informant and she ought to know. Yes, Moore would tell me, of that there was no doubt. And I would tell it, if it had a hint of scandal, to Yeats, who loved to hear a bit of scandal about Moore. It could wait. But could I? I was devoured with curiosity. His house is only sixty yards diagonally from my hall door. I could not well call before teatime.

116

When I rang and was admitted, I found Moore in the drawing room on the first floor. The folding doors were open, so the two rooms were thrown into one which went from window to window, the depth of the house. The mantelpiece was covered by little water colours of warm interiors with bright armchairs, and windows with curtains of bright chintz; obviously the work of a woman. Moore was putting on an air of fatigue.

'Those are by Stella,' he said languidly. 'I forgot – you do not know her. She followed me over from London. She has taken a house at Templeogue so as to be near me. Ah! Perhaps you saw us in the garden this afternoon. That was she.'

'Yes,' I said. 'I saw you in the garden. You did not seem exactly to be burning "with a hard gemlike flame".'

This reference to Walter Pater brought out one of his hissing laughs, which left you uncertain whether he was amused by your quotation or laughing at you for being so ostentatious with it.

'Stella is a charming ... or rather she can be a charming woman when she likes. But like all women she is unreasonable. She makes me angry at times.'

That must have been one of the times, I thought to myself. It accounts for his stick going up in the air in an ecstasy of expostulation.

'She has plenty of money and she ought to have more sense.'

I would soon hear what it was all about, provided I betrayed no curiosity.

'It is not your fault if people admire your writings, especially women,' I said, and realised at once that I had said the wrong thing. I should have said, in a grave voice, 'Oh?' or something as non-committal as that. But to imply that his writings were admired 'especially by women' was a *gaffe*. Conversation with Moore was always a *gaffe* and this was no exception. I would not now hear what the argument was about.

In a changed voice, as if the only thing I understood was

some sort of refreshment, he asked, 'Won't you have some tea?'

He was about to ring the bell when the maid came in with the tea tray. During tea I was cross-examined: 'I hope that you have not been indulging in art purchases without consulting me?'

I did not dare to say that I had fourteen Hones hanging in the room that looked out on his garden, the best room in the house with a southern aspect.

'Do you know Hone?' I asked, knowing that he did not, and was unlikely to be received by that very independent and particular old gentleman.

'I haven't time for that kind of thing.' He shrugged. Then, brightening, 'There's a picture for you.' He pointed to the large oil which hung over the mantelpiece, a picture of a flooded river, willow trees half submerged.

'The Seine?' I said.

'Of course; but the subject of a painting is the last thing you should think about. Look how the paint is put on. It is like cream. You see?'

I let my face fall into repose, because when it is in repose they tell me that I look quite idiotic.

'What are you staring at? *Claude* Monet was a friend of mine.' He put great emphasis on the 'Cluade'. 'We had many a long evening in the Nouvelle Athène. Those were my Parisian days.'

'It must be pleasant to have artistic friends?' I said.

'Oh, don't let me hear you use that word "artistic". It is a word that Stoker is always using. He knows nothing about art. Secondhand furniture, yes, but not Art. Oh no.'

The teapot was Sèvres. The spout had been broken and repaired. He caught me examining it. 'Oh, some foolish maid broke it. I had quite a row. The cook left because I held her responsible. If you can't hold someone responsible for the behaviour of those under them, you might despair of running a house, particularly in this country. Don't forget that you are to dine here on Saturday, Kuno Meyer is expected. Æ, of course, and Douglas Hyde.'

It was the first time that I had heard of it. I took the

118

invitation to dinner as a dismissal from tea. I left the author to renew his war with Stella, and found my way out.

At home I found a woman waiting, in a downstairs room, to be transilluminated; that is, examined for sinusitis by a lighted electric lamp placed in the patient's mouth in a dark room. (If there be a denture or upper plate, it must be first removed.) When it is being transilluminated, the face looks like 'a face carved out of a turnip', as Yeats described the face of Moore. Don't get the impression that Yeats was vindictive. He would never have made that remark had not Moore first described him as looking like an umbrella forgotten at a picnic. This is an aside.

While the eight-volt lamp was in the seated patient's mouth, I had the misfortune to touch a hand-basin full of water. Instantly I was flung down and spread-eagled upon the floor. I had grounded the electric wire and sent the town's interrupted current of more than two hundred volts into my chest. There was no sensation of pins and needles, but a tornado that went raging through my chest. I was all but electrocuted. I remember thinking of the agony of electrocuted persons. At last the flex broke: I was saved. Oh, the relief! A voice from the chair inquired anxiously, 'Oh, Doctor, am I as bad as that?'

Dinner at George Moore's would be an experience. You could trust George to provide entertainment for his guests, whimsical as well as culinary.

Kuno Meyer, the German scholar who was studying early Irish – that is, pre-Christian – literature, was the last to arrive. I came in the middle so as to avoid a tête-à-tête – had I arrived first – and to avoid expostulations and sarcasm – had I come last. It was Kuno Meyer who came last. Evidently he was forgiven. He was a very scholarly man on a subject of which none of us knew anything, except Douglas Hyde. And Meyer was crippled with rheumatism, so Moore had every excuse to make allowances for his last guest.

When we were all assembled, Moore said, with an air of

diffidence, 'Gentlemen, dinner tonight will be at best an experiment. I have engaged a new cook. She was well recommended. We shall soon see what her capabilities are.'

He sat at the head of an oval table with his back to the garden and the street. In the quiet cul-de-sac nothing stirred; neither vehicles nor foot passengers entered Ely Place after sundown. The soup passed scrutiny. Moore was acting as a gourmet of the most exquisite taste before his guests. He had been in France and we were paying for it.

'It is impossible to convince a cook that she should heat the tureen before pouring in the soup. In these old houses the stairs to the kitchen are enough to cool the soup. The real test of a cook, however, is the omelette. Now we shall see.'

If his attitudinising had not been so characteristic it would have been boring. But Moore managed to make affectation an effective part of himself.

He lifted the lid of the chafing dish. He replaced it with an exclamation. He went hurriedly into his hall, opened the hall door and blew a police whistle. He returned with a young constable whose helmet was held respectfully under his arm. Moore again raised the lid of the dish and, pointing to the omelette, said, 'Look at that!' While the lid was coming off, the constable's helmet was being put on. The constable gazed at the omelette, looked at us all, and then at the omelette. Moore said, 'I want you to arrest the perpetrator of that atrocity.' The young policeman stood bewildered.

Douglas Hyde said, 'Oh, serve us some before it gets chilled. How can you tell whether it is good or bad until you have tasted it?' Kuno Meyer looked as if he would have preferred to be back in Berlin with a stein of beer and sauerkraut. On Æ's bearded face there was an impatient expression. He wanted dinner to be dispatched with all possible speed so that the talk could begin, unimpaired by mastication.

I wondered if Moore had not gone too far by bringing in the police. It might be a *cause célèbre* for a week if it got into the newspaper. Stoker would hear of it and be duly impressed by the importance Moore attached to good cooking.

The constable at last spoke: 'On what charge, sir?'

For a moment Moore was nonplussed. Then he rallied and, lifting the lid, pointed with it. 'That is no omelette. Go down and arrest her for obtaining money under false pretences.'

I was about to say, 'We have had drama enough, now let us have dinner,' when I remembered that I was younger than any of the guests, and my host too.

Douglas Hyde said, 'If you give the constable a drink, we will forgive the omelette.' After expostulating and complaining that he was not supported in his fight for good food, Moore waved the constable and the maid out of the room. I could hear them whispering in the hall.

When the maid appeared with the next course, Moore, now an authority on wines, raised his decanter and announced: 'I get this from an old Frenchman who visits his clients in Dublin once a year. He sends it to me in a barrel directly from Marseilles. It is called St. Pierre de Mou. I have it bottled by an expert. Gogarty can tell you how excellent it is. I sent my dealer over to see him. Hyde, whiskey? The decanter is in front of you.'

Neither Hyde nor Meyer cared for wine. Æ was abstemious to the point of teetotalism. Hyde drank John Jameson, and as for Meyer, he drank whatever his German doctor ordered, or what the doctor in some spa in Hungary permitted. Hungary was the only place in which Meyer got relief from pain, and I am sure that it was not wine that was prescribed for him.

Suddenly Hyde spluttered, 'Moore, this isn't whiskey. What is it?'

'But I ordered it from Sedley especially for you.'

'It may be Sedley, but it certainly is not whiskey.' And in a quieter voice, 'Who ever heard of a man ordering his whiskey from a grocer?'

Trying to divert him from Hyde, I said, turning to

Moore: 'Anything will do for me.' I had released all his frustration: 'Never say, "Anything will do for me." You cannot go through life disregarding what you eat or drink. "Anything will do for me" is what a pig or some omnivorous animal might say to his keeper. For animals, food is merely nourishment, for men, it is a subject for art. Don't you agree with me, Æ?'

Æ hesitated a moment, until he had swallowed something, then, pushing his knife and fork past his plate, threw back his head and announced, 'Art means an imaginative control over your medium.'

'Precisely,' said Moore, interrupting the sage. 'Or changing the medium, as in a translation,' he added.

'No, no,' Meyer grunted. 'You do not change the medium, which is language, when you translate.'

Moore looked bewildered. It seemed that he was not on firm ground; that art, his favourite subject, was about to betray him. Hyde, who had become reconciled to his beverage, said: 'Take Meyer's translation of *The Tryst after Death*, where a warrior appears to his love with, "Hush, woman, do not speak to me. My bloody corpse lies by the side of the Slope of the two Brinks": that is more than slipping from one language into another. If you do not know the original, how can it be held that a translation is more or less than it?'

There was the danger into which Moore felt he might have slipped. He knew nothing about Irish, Old, Middle or Modern.

'I can give *The Tryst after Death* word by word from Meyer's translation,' Æ announced.

Moore said, 'Oh, if we are to have recitals, let us have them with the coffee upstairs.'

Upstairs in the drawing room, under the Monet and over the Aubusson carpet, coffee was served. Meyer was not allowed coffee, Hyde did not take it; Æ sat in a corner and accepted automatically anything that was handed to him. Whether he noticed it or not was another matter. He was longing for an opportunity to expound Plotinus or recite something.

'I wish that Hyde would tell us what he considers the best poem in his *Love Songs of Connaught?*'

'*The Red Man's Wife,*' Hyde answered without hesitation.

Moore pricked up his ears at the mention of that poem. 'What a title for a novel, *The Red Man's Wife.*' He threw up his hands.

'I have Hyde's book here.'

'We don't want it. I can recite it word for word. I don't want a book,' Æ announced. And he could, because he had the most prodigious memory for verse or prose of any man alive. Verily, Memory is Mother of the Muses, which saying was well borne out in Æ, who was a considerable poet himself in days when poets were rife.

'The singer of this is in prison. He is the rejected lover of the Red Man's Wife. Probably he committed some outrage. He is working himself up as he lies fast bound with "bolts on my smalls", that is, on every isthmus of the body, ankles, wrists, waist and neck.'

'Give us it without the surface anatomy, as Gogarty here might say.'

This was a reference to my being Honourable Anatomist to the Royal Hibernian Academy, an art school. Thus hurried by Moore, Æ began:

> "Tis what they say,
>> Your little heel fits in a shoe,
> 'Tis what they say,
>> Your little mouth kisses well too,
> 'Tis what they say,
>> Thousand loves that you made me to rue,
> That the tailor went the way
>> That the wife of the Red man knew.
>
> 'Nine months did I spend
>> In prison closed tightly and bound
> Bolts on my smalls
>> And a thousand locks frowning around;
> But o'er the tide
>> I would leap with the leap of a swan

Could I once set my side
    By the bride of the Red-haired man.

'I thought, O my life,
    That one house love, between us, would be;
And I thought I would find
    You coaxing my child on your knee;
But now the curse of the High One,
    On him let it be,
And on all the liars
    Who put silence between you and me.

'There grows a tree in the garden
    With blossoms that tremble and shake
I lay my hand on its bark
    And I feel that my heart must break:
On one wish alone
    My soul through the long months ran:
One little kiss
    From the wife of the Red-haired man.

'But the day of Doom shall come,
    And the hills and the harbours be rent;
A mist shall fall from the sun
    From the dark clouds heavily sent;
The sea shall be dry
    And earth under mourning and ban,
Then shall I cry
    For the wife of the Red-haired man.'

When he had concluded, the air seemed drained. Silence fell on the assembly. Moore got up from his chair to poke the fire, for though it was June the weather in Dublin calls for fires in the evening, even if the homeliness they bring would not be a justification in itself.

When Moore had finished attending to the fire, he stood up with his back to the mantelpiece and announced: 'I was walking in my garden on, was it Tuesday or Wednesday? Gogarty can tell you, for nothing that goes on in that garden escapes him. Stella – you all know her name – had followed me from London and had taken the moated grange in Templeogue. I had, it seems, neglected her for three weeks. That is what made her come in from the country and call on me in the middle of my work, and it was all the more annoying now that my usual secretary is gone to see her mother – oh, she is dying – and have to work by myself. Stella called. And I took her into the garden. Well, the upshot of it was that I had to go out to see her next day.

'As I pushed the gate open, she came to meet me halfway down the drive. I felt that soon there would be an explosion, so I said, "I don't care what your gardener has done to the herbaceous border, nor do I care what you have done to the house. There is a frightful tension in the atmosphere worse than thunder. Tell me, tell me, what is it all about?" At long last, after question upon question, she still sulked and would not speak. I turned to go when she said in a whisper, "George, you do not make love to me often enough." At that, I took her by the arm: "Let us go into the house." She shook herself free. "How dare you?" she said. Now what are you to do with a woman like that? She accuses you of balking and, when you show her your preparedness, she brushes you off. Next day, I left for Dublin, a little dazed, a little shaken. I assure you it is propinquity that breaks up more homes than divorce!'

The discussion in the garden was explained. I might have guessed it. And I had guessed aright when I thought that Moore could not fail to announce it sooner or later.

'That's all very fine, Moore,' Hyde said, 'but this business of bringing women over from London and giving them a house in the country will soon be all over the place. This is a talkative town and you are the last person it will spare.'

Moore raised his eyebrows in feigned surprise. He was as pleased as a child to be the centre of interest. I knew that it would be useless to call him a cad for giving a woman away. It would give him an opportunity to use his old answer: 'Of course I am. My brother, the colonel is the gentleman of our family.' Susan Mitchell is right – Moore tells and does not kiss, not enough anyway. Has he not divulged the fact by his account of his interview with Stella?

When I look back on my tolerance at the time and my lack, all our lack, of indignation, I can account for them only by the incredulity with which Moore's 'affairs' were regarded. They were so advertised that no one believed them. He was a novelist: his amours, and his characters, were fictitious.

Kuno Meyer, like Queen Victoria, was 'not amused'. Æ was about to philosophise when Moore went on in answer to Douglas Hyde. 'But, my dear Hyde, I brought no woman over from London. She brought herself. It was not I who took the house in Templeogue. Stella has money of her own. If an English lady cannot rent a house in Ireland to do a little landscape painting without being made the subject of gossip, Ireland is full of Calvinism still.'

Who has made her 'the subject of gossip'? I thought. The others, I felt sure, did too; but we all let it pass. Douglas Hyde had made his protest. It was Æ's turn.

'In India,' said the sage, 'there are temple prostitutes; women's virtue is subordinated to communion with the divine.' Æ had never been in India, but let that not prevent an Irishman from being an authority *in absentia*. This is probably one of the results of Irishmen being tenants of absentee landlords for so long.

Moore's face assumed a beatific look. 'I see a solution to the whole problem. Meyer, listen to this. Temple prostitutes; one for every priest and two for every bishop. Then there would not be all this rancour about sex: making salvation depend on atrophy of an organ.'

Æ said, 'You have been too hasty, Moore. You have misunderstood me. Good conduct is man's chiefest contribution to the deity. Temple prostitutes are used in India to remove any carnal distractions that may arise when a man is about to seek communion with the Divine. They come from the highest caste. I have not heard that they had any traffic with the priests. They give themselves only to members of the congregation. The idea is to dissolve sex, the entangler; to achieve *samadhi*.'

'They first decant the worshipper and then leave him to

his prayers, if he has any energy left with which to pray,' I added to help Æ out.

Æ, heartened, as I thought, began again, 'Now take Ramakrishna ... '

'I will not take Rama ... whatever you call him. I won't have you diverting me from my idea of having temple prostitutes for Ireland. It is in Ireland, not India, we have to live.' He hissed behind his moustache as was his habit when he laughed. He was ridden by his idea; he wanted us all to develop it for him.

Meyer announced that it was time for him to go. He got out of his chair stiffly, and changed his stick to his right hand. Moore went with him down the stairs. We could hear his stick tapping against the floor of the hall. The hall door closed.

Æ asked, 'How far is it justifiable for an artist to sacrifice the proprieties to his art?'

'Moore sacrifices himself,' said I.

'I don't quite follow you,' Hyde remarked.

'Take, for instance, the lady of the house in Templeogue. By hinting that he was more or less impotent, he gave himself away.'

'He gave both of them away,' said Æ.

'That is what I mean by sacrificing the proprieties. That is the only sacrifice to which he ever attains.'

'He lóves to shock people,' I interjected, for I hoped to be asked for an example: their silence invited me. 'He was on the same boat as Thomas Cook during his journey to the Holy Land when he was writing *Brook Kerith* which, only for me – I may be flattering myself; I am, of course, for he must have consulted others – would have been called *By Kidron's Stream*. For three weeks or whatever time it takes to make the journey from London to Palestine, he deliberately snubbed Thomas Cook, who he well knew was the great travel agent. But when they arrived at Joppa and Moore saw the horizon stippled with the humps of Cook's camels, he was impressed. Cook, noticing this, took his courage in his hands and addressed him, "You are the great novelist, George Moore?" "And are you *the* Thomas Cook? Why did you not reveal yourself to me?"

'Conveniently overlooking the snubbings through the voyage, Cook fell for Moore's expostulations: "I have heard that you are going to the Holy Land to gather local colour for your book. If I can be of the least assistance, I will gladly detail some of my men to show you the places of interest. For instance in the morning I will send round a guide to conduct you to the Holy Sepulchre ... "

'"Oh, for goodness' sake, nothing so hackneyed, Cook!" "Where would you like to go?" "Well, if you would ask your man to bring me to where the woman was taken in adultery ... " Cook was greatly shocked; so Moore had his joke.'

Hyde did not laugh. I began to fear that I was too shocking when I heard Moore on the stairs. When he came back to the room, it was evident that he was still full of his idea.

'What does Gogarty think of it?' he asked. 'I know that Æ thinks that my plan of introducing temple prostitutes in Ireland is an outrage on his favourite India. Hyde, you on principle cannot approve; but I have Gogarty to back me. He is not like Yeats, afraid to make up his mind.'

'It would narrow the basis of meditation,' I remarked, hoping that I would not be put to the question any further. Then I added, knowing that it would be provocative, 'I do not think that for Holy Ireland the word "prostitute" should be connected with the Church.'

'No; I agree,' said Moore, 'we must find some other word.' Then striking his forehead and leaning backwards, he asked as if inspired, 'What about calling them "Divine Decanters"?'

'Have it any way you like; but don't father it on me,' Æ said and he bade us good night.

I went with him, for I knew that Moore went early to bed. On the landing he exclaimed, to Æ's dismay, 'Divine Decanters! I am very grateful indeed. Divine Decanters!'

Leaving Moore to dream of ritual prostitutions, I

walked with Æ to where he could catch the tram to Rathgar. It was a mellow night, as so few in Dublin are. I remarked how pleasant it was; but Æ was still annoyed at the way Moore had treated his favourite philosophy or else he was wrapped in some meditation. He did not answer. I said that I was delighted with his remembering *The Red Man's Wife*. Still he said nothing. I went on to say that Kuno Meyer was almost morose: he had contributed very little to the conversation. He could have recited his wonderful translation of *The Tryst after Death*, where the ghost of the warrior speaks to his mistress: 'It is blindness for anyone making a tryst to set aside the tryst with death.' And then, ''Tis not I alone who in the fullness of desire have gone astray to meet a woman.'

'Moore didn't,' said Æ.

When his tram came he muttered something as he got into it. He seemed to raise his hand in a farewell gesture. He may only have been grasping the rail.

There was light in the third storey of Moore's house. He was going to bed still hugging his idea and wondering how he would fit it into his next book. So I thought. I hoped that it would save him from the dreadful nightmares of which he complained to me.

Why does he confide in me? And then why does he take it for granted that I am an atheist, that all doctors are atheists? Is it because we are supposed to regard all human beings as merely bundles of reflexes? Can he not give us credit for asking ourselves, 'Whence did the reflexes come?' It should be as simple as for the child who, when she was being instructed in evolution and taught that all life came from the sea, asked simply, 'Where did the sea come from?'

Yes; whence did life proceed? Even if we have to think of everything in terms of cause and effect, even if our intellect is that far limited, why are we aware of that limitation? What told us? Oh, quit philosophising, I said to myself, and come down to the consideration of George Moore. Well you know that for him you, Hyde, Meyer and Æ will be but puppets or marionettes in his next creation. I comforted myself with the thought that it is better to have God for a creator than to depend for existence on George Moore. Nightmares, eh?

23 *Walking Home*

On a day as I walked up Merrion Square, I saw on my left the beautiful fountain, called after Lord Rutland, which conceals the lodge of the attendant of the Square. On my right, in front of the National Portrait Gallery, stood the statue of Dargan, who led into Dublin the soft water from Wicklow's granite hills and made fountains for the town. A little farther, apropos of nothing but the White Man's Burden, the British Empire, was a statue to the man who discovered Mr Livingstone, the Bible reader from Scotland who got lost in Africa.

Imagine a statue to a man who discovered a Bible reader! Why, I could discover one or two every Sunday; and on Saturday the whole Salvation Army singing by Portobello Bridge! Had it been one of the pygmies who got lost in darkest London while trying to convert its citizens to the hunting of elephants and a simpler life, I could understand a statue to that misguided man. But to erect a statue to a fellow who dug out Dave Livingstone while he was trying to pervert the simple pygmies and dose them with an oriental anthology which contained forms of ideation alien to their thought would have made me laugh had I not seen the cynical message behind the statue.

We, the Irish, were being gradually proselytised into the British Empire, which contains trends of thought certainly alien to the Gael. This is subtler than the system of Intermediate Examinations. Will Arthur Griffith, who lives on 17/6 a week, be able to tackle it at all?

The red tiles of my roof were about a hundred yards

away when I crossed Merrion Row. On my right were three or four houses which in the afternoon never caught the sun. On the ground floor, and for all I knew the rest of the floors, were the offices of Mr McDonald, architect. He built the house for Mr Wilcox in Connemara and drove the salmon out of the adjoining lakes for years after dynamiting the rock for the foundations. Out he came and I ran into him.

What did I say about doctors avoiding the street? He weighed at least four hundred pounds, as became a cousin of Larkey Waldron. His collar was twenty inches around: his mouth was open, and his whole face turned upwards, for, even though your neck has taken over, you must breathe. He was gasping when I met him. To give him time to catch his breath, I stood and waited. Was he leaving his office or entering it? What did it matter? He was breathing easier now.

'How is Larkey?' I asked.

After a moment he gargled in his deep bass, 'Splendid. You should see him since his cure. A child can speak to him. I don't believe in this slimming. Tell me, do you?'

'Which side is he slimming?' I asked.

'I must hurry,' he said, as if to explain his breathlessness, and stepped into his office.

Hume Street enters Ely Place in its middle, like the shaft of a cross. At the near corner the rounded house of Mrs Foule, the Belgian wife of a colonel of remounts, opened its hospitable door on Hume Street. Ely House, once the town house of the Marquis of Ely (now Sir Thornley Stoker's), looks down Hume Street and takes the dust from it whenever the west wind blows.

The sun was setting beyond Stephen's Green, behind the College of Surgeons. If I were a novelist it should have reminded me of Goya, El Greco, Monet or Manet, Constable, Turner or Fantin-latour. It only gave me an increased respect for the man to whom 'a primrose by the river's brim' etc. I saw myself talking to him at evening in his village inn over a pint of the best. I would wait until the psychological moment. 'And did that primrose remind you of nothing?' I would ask casually. 'Sure it did. It reminded me of a trouser button which was missing from my fly.' 'Was that because of its association with water?' No, I couldn't ask that. If it were beyond him, he would think that I was frivolous and maybe fooling him. But how happy I would be in his company, while he drew on his pipe and sipped his pint and I sipped mine. He must have been as addicted to clear thinking as Larkey Waldron.

'Who is Larkey?' you will rightly ask. He is a brother of General Waldron but he lives in his own right. Don't mind George Moore when he writes of 'the obscene bulk of Larkey Waldron'. I admit that Larkey is a substantial man; he weighs four hundred pounds and over, but then he is a stockbroker to the Catholic Church; and St Thomas Aquinas was no lightweight and yet he wrote the *Summa* and fixed the school. Larkey has to do sums for the bishops and archbishops and invest money for the Little Sisters of the Poor. He lives sumptuously in a beautiful house on Killiney Hill.

Yes: Larkey is a great fellow in every sense. He sits in his office in Anglesea Street with two telephones and four mantelpieces by Bossi in the room. He wears a skullcap of black silk topped by a large pink rhododendron. He hasn't seen his feet for years.

He kept me on my own feet by refusing to invest £500 for me in the Dundalk Meat Packing Company when even Solomons, another stockbroker, lost money in that very promising speculation. 'Did you pick up this cash in the gutter?' Larkey asked. 'No,' I said. 'Then home you go with it.' Weeks later the whole thing burst. I remember leaving his office trying to console myself with the thought that I wouldn't like a layman to tell me my business so why should I try to tell Larkey Waldron his? Stocks and shares were his business; leave him to it. Luckily I did.

You won't be surprised now to hear that Larkey's hobby is clear thinking; and Dr Johnson. He lingers among the secondhand bookshops on the quays on his way from

Westland Row to Anglesea Street. He puts Murray the bookseller in his place, because he pays good prices.

Perhaps the sunset should have reminded me of a painter instead of Larkey Waldron. A good novelist should always be reminded of something artistic. George Moore, when he and I were crossing the railway viaduct at Donabate, was reminded by the sunset of Nathaniel Hone, the landscape painter who lived nearby. He said, 'I would give ten pounds to see how that sunset will imitate Hone.' I tried to save him five by pulling the communication cord, because the fine is only five pounds if you pull it wantonly. I knew that you could never explain to a railway guard that art is more important than an accident. He must have had artistic sympathies though, because he 'forgot' the incident for ten shillings! Instead of being grateful to me as I was to Larkey for moneysaving, Moore expostulated and told me that I was impossible. I bore that in silence. I could have retorted that he was a plagiarist, for years ago Oscar Wilde had said that Nature was always trying to imitate Art. Do not look for gratitude from novelists.

On the way home I took care not to pass close to Sir Thornley Stoker's house. If he came out I would be put to the question: what was I doing on the street? Sir Thornley is the arbiter of Ely Place, and of the behaviour of those members of the profession who are immediately associated with him. I crossed Hume Street hurriedly and, as I passed the letter box at the corner, I heard the staccato yelps of Lady Stoker's black Pom. Betty Webb, the secretary, was taking it for a walk. Had she met me, I might have met Sir Thornley.

Oh, what a relief to get behind my hall door! What etiquettical, nonsensical precautions is all this unwritten rule about doctors not being supposed to walk on the street; with the exception, of course, of Kegley, and Gibson the gynaecologist, both safe from open consultation.

Gibson has or had a bad stutter so he collects Waterford glass – explanation later, if I don't forget it. Now you cure a stutter by instructing the patient to imitate someone else, any character he may choose, always provided that it is an edifying character. You never hear an actor stutter; nor a singer. Gibson selected some person so highfalutin that unsympathetic students nicknamed him 'Bardelys'.

I went into my library to read before dinner. Now I have not got a library in my house; there are bookcases here and there in passages and in a few rooms; but there is no 'library' for the simple reason that I think that, wherever a book is, a reading man can make a library.

This reminds me – when Lord Kingston and I, after driving up from Castleforbes, which owes its restoration to Lady Forbes, an American, were having tea here, Kingston exclaimed, 'Now I know what was wrong with Castleforbes, there were no books around.' 'No,' I said. 'They were all in the library.'

Books are all over the house in Ely Place; that is why I maintain that books and not a room can make a library.

> And after him a finicking lass
> Did shine like the glistering gold.

That's what I was reading. To find such a picture you must read the *Gestes of Robin Hood* and, before that, you must be attuned to poetry. Otherwise, all is vain.

If you have no affinity for verse, better skip this, or you'll be bored stiff and to bore anybody is beyond me. I got such a boring in my schooldays that I have had enough for the rest of my life and I am resolved not to inflict boredom on even the most deserving.

As I read of Robin Hood, that hero of England, I began to think many things, because a well-known book becomes a kind of crystal for me into which I gaze and think of something else, as a crystal-gazer professes to do. I thought that I was quite wrong to blame or to poke fun at novelists because sunsets remind them of paintings. I could not expect sunsets to remind them of the back of Thesus, for instance, for that is sculpture; and has not to do with colour. Colour reminds some novelists of music. They used to be reminded of Beethoven, but latterly Villa-Lobos gives a more up-to-date touch to their memories.

I couldn't expect novelists, especially George Moore, who is almost illiterate, to be reminded of a chorus-ending of Euripides or something out of *Prometheus Bound*. Thinking of illiteracy reminds me of Dr Yelverton Tyrrell's reply when he was told that George Moore was about to pillory him in a trilogy which he was calling *Ave atque Vale*. 'Moore, of course, thinks that *atque* was a Roman centurion.' On this being repeated to George, he changed the title to the rather redundant *Ave, Salve, Vale*.

And yet illiterates can be stylists.

This bids well to be a great book because it is becoming boring. I cannot help it.

No; art must refer to art, for art represents the world of the imagination, and it is imagination that makes artists, not reason. Imagination is truer than reason is or ever can be. To those who think differently belong the Kinseys of this world. Yes; the artist must speak his own language.

I was thinking, probably at the same time, about the word 'finicking'. I know that it means 'fastidious' – so much the dictionary tells you – but it means, to me at least, far more. First of all it is like a present particle and suggests walking along with mincing steps; and there is the suggestion of 'fine' in it and of something fresh, inexperienced and young. 'Glistering,' too, is a better word for the lass's hair than 'glittering'. Dictionaries, which suffer from the rigor mortis of words, will tell you that 'glistering' and 'glittering' are the same.

Back of my mind was Robin Hood and the thought that the green wood is the backdrop of all the forests of England, in prose or rhyme. Merry Sherwood waves its branches in the Forest of Arden and in all the woodland scenes of the poets of England. And how England loves the greenwood and all that it contains:

> The wood wele sang and would not cease
> Sitting upon a spray.

That's what poets can do; they can summon up a vision of peace.

> And evening full of the linnets' wings.

They should never be rivals, or be jealous of the hierophants of another mystery. They have a religion of their own which is their own 'exceeding great reward', and it extends its salvation to them. Never should they feel 'The Necessity of Atheism'.

I laid down the ballads of Robin Hood and hunted out a copy of Yeats's letter to Moore. I am so bad at keeping, much less arranging, manuscripts that it is a wonder how I found it. Don't ask me how I got it. I came by it innocently. It was only a draft but it explained the bad feeling between Yeats and Moore.

Here it is – Moore tried to hide it in vain. It has to do with their collaboration for the two years it took to produce the rather trivial play, *Diarmuid and Grania*, two years of wrangling and, for Yeats at least, frustration after frustration:

My dear Moore,
You say both should make concessions. I think so too but I so far have made them all. I have acknowledged that you have a knowledge of the stage, a power of construction, a power of inventing a dramatic climax far beyond me, and I have given way again and again. I have continually given up motives and ideas that I preferred to yours because I admitted your authority to be greater than mine. On the question of style however I will make no concessions. Here you need give way to me ...

There is more of the letter, but I read no further because I saw the impossibility of any writer sacrificing his style to another.

What has any author got but his style? It is the man; and his manhood goes with his style. To sacrifice it is to obliterate himself, to ask to be devoured. So that was it.

That was the cause of the lifelong enmity between Yeats and Moore; and the abusive terms they threw at each other.

136

The fact that Moore revealed himself to be what modern psychiatrists would call a 'paranoid' was the cause of the quarrel and the subsequent abuse, and Yeats's mischievous delight at Moore's discomfitures. And was not Yeats right? His standing up to the older and the then more famous man, and his belief in himself, shows a grit that no one guessed was in him at the time; and the time was 1901.

Tonight is Friday night. I expect him after dinner and Æ and a few more. We have an embryo salon on Friday nights. My wife loves them. Now what will I talk about? Yeats likes men who ride upon horses. His poem on the Galway Races shows that. William the Conqueror died from a fall from his horse. William III of England also died as the result of a fall from his horse. George V fell from his horse in World War I. Yeats, the old Irish Republican Brotherhood man, will like that. Perhaps he won't like the 'William' part of it. Maybe I had better avoid the subject. I have it! I know what I will say, or rather bring out nonchalantly in the course of conversation. I will quote those lines by an unknown poet which I came across in the Bodleian. It will convey at the same time that I was at Oxford – even at the risk of Yeats's going to live at Oxford, I will say that I found them in the Bodleian. And what an effect they will have on Yeats! Why, they even affect me:

> Cupid abroad was lated in the night;
> His wings were wet from ranging in the rain.

After that I will keep my mouth shut.

Why talk on any subject when the best talkers of their time, Yeats and Æ, are coming? It will do me good to listen for a change.

If I had only listened, what a Boswell I would have been! Instead of listening, I keep on interrupting. I am as bad – well, almost as bad – as Stephens's wife, who prefers to chatter when her husband, the lightest lyrist of them all, should be talking or singing to us, swaying to the rhythm as he sings.

Lovely and airy the view from the hill
That looks down Ballylee;
But no good look is good until
By great good luck you see
The Blossom of the Branches coming towards you
Airily.

That is how Stephens recaptured the lines that Blind Raftery wrote in Gaelic, a hundred years ago, about Mary Hynes, 'The Blossom of the Branches,' who was one of those beauties who appear, in court or cottage, but one in a century, or less.

But no good look is good until
By great good luck you see.

The sooner I go to dinner the sooner I will get it over, and then for the feast!

24 *The Divine Doctor*

Jan was on the telephone. Jan was an engineering student in Trinity College. He was a close friend. He had worked hard on me on the morning of my wedding. He was my best man. We had been at that English school together; like the companions of Ulysses, we had suffered much. But we had also enjoyed much. One of Jan's enjoyments was the company of the Divine Doctor. Of him he was speaking now. Jan had an halt in his speech which grew worse when he was excited. He was excited and no mistake.

'The Divine Doctor is in a spot. He doesn't realise all its implications. I have him here at lunch. When can you come along?'

'What's happened?'

138

'I can't tell you on the telephone. I will meet you in his rooms in an hour's time.'

It is not easy for me to get out in the afternoon. I am in my office all the afternoon; but this was an emergency and had to be treated as such. What could have happened to the doctor? That he had a little diabetes, I knew. He couldn't have had an attack of coma? 'Doesn't realise all its implications.'

The Divine Doctor was Jan's name for Dr Yelverton Tyrrell, our preceptor, a perfect Greek. It was Dr Tyrrell who first 'hailed my light' (such as it was) in college. He was a Senior Fellow; and so could not be a tutor to college men; but his company tutored us. To him I owe all of the little acquaintance I have of the classics and all my love of the plangent word or unalterable line. Though he was thirty years or so older than us, he tolerated our company, sometimes he appeared to enjoy it; we were body servants promoted to boon companions. Now what could have happened to him? Jan's voice, allowing for lunch, was anxious. It did not suggest that anything sudden such as a stroke had happened to the doctor. I felt that it was something that had turned up while they talked at lunch.

It had nothing to do with pecuniary matters: the doctor's income was ample. It could not be a matter of health – I had dismissed that, though I knew that Old Tobin, a retired army surgeon who was the doctor's medical adviser, had said that the doctor had a little diabetes; a little diabetes does not put you suddenly 'in a spot'. It seemed more probable to me that the doctor had fallen asleep at some important public function or had made one of his bons mots about some self-important personage who had resented it and even had gone so far as reporting the doctor to the Board. There was little good to be got from conjectures: soon I would know what had happened to our benevolent friend. And yet as I drove along in a rickety cab I could not help wondering what has happened.

Maybe he has had a row with the Archbishop of Dublin, Dr Bernard, whose sharp nose he dislikes. It was bad enough when Bernard got the committee of the University Club to put all drinking out of bounds except on the top floor. Tyrrell's remark when he met his lordship on the stairs must have rankled; the irreverence of it! 'They shall be afraid of that which is high.' The first instance of acrophobia in literature. And when I thought of the doctor telling me how he had reacted to an invitation to dinner at the archbishop's palace. 'I wouldn't give it to that old curmudgeon to say that I got drunk in his house. I took the obvious precaution of coming drunk.'

In his rooms on the first floor at the northern corner of the West Front, the doctor was explaining to Jan, 'I was looking for a book when I came across thirteen bottles of Bass's ale. Now why were there thirteen and not twelve? I pondered on this – some messenger by mistake has left a baker's dozen or I have drunk eleven and forgot all about it? Anyway the thirteen bottles looked so forlorn that I did not wish them to think that they were ignored. Oh, here's Gogarty!' Then to me, after he had me seated, he said 'McCabe and I have just come from Jammet's where we had an excellent lunch. I think he will agree ...'

'What did you have, sir?' I inquired.

'Well, let me see. I think we had a few lobsters and of course we had a few whiskeys and sodas to wash them down.'

'Lobsters and whiskey!' I could not help exclaiming.

'Oh well,' said the doctor, smiling, 'I recognise your medical conscience; but I make it a rule to let my stomach fight it out.'

Then he said, 'What was I saying? Oh yes. After the thirteen bottles of Bass, I was beginning to grow depressed when, what did I find? Just behind the shutter I found two bottles of marsala. I had an hour to kill before the time came to yield myself up to the bosom of my family. Marsala as you know comes from the southwest corner of Sicily where the grape is so abundant that the natives never think of fortifying it with the cheap and trashy brandy that is put into so many light wines to help them in their journey overseas. It has a somewhat sulphurous aroma; but on the whole it is not unpalatable.'

There is not the slightest sign of trouble. Why did Jan call me?

As I was asking myself that, the doctor remarked, smiling: 'You know I would rather discuss two bottles of marsala than any other subject with Tom Thompson Gray.'

'Ah yes, ah, ah!' Jan stuttered. 'Tom Thompson Gray has been chivvying the doctor since the last meeting of the Board.'

'Let us be fair to Gray. I was appointed secretary and at the first meeting I must confess that I fell asleep. I was awakened by the roaring of the Provost, "What! No minutes? The whole meeting had gone to waste." Gray added, "Tyrrell, if you cannot keep awake at a Board meeting, you should resign. I do not intend to let this dereliction of duty pass. I will frame a motion to that effect for the next meeting of the Board." The next meeting is in ten days,' the doctor added.

Gloom was beginning to usurp mirth. No use going into it now. Gray is a bluenose. He hates the doctor and all that he stands for. How well the name gives the man: Tom Thompson Gray. How appropriate it is that Gray's portrait by Orpen hangs in the dining room of the only club in Dublin that drinks in secret, and in secret transports its members home. Gray's portrait is an excellent camouflage. Who would think, to see it in the dining room of the Friendly Brothers, that alcohol could possibly be about?

The internal fight was beginning to influence the field of battle. The doctor was growing despondent. Maybe it was at the thought of Gray. To cheer him I said briskly:

'We have ten days. A lot may happen in ten days. The Sultan himself may die.'

'If I have to resign,' the doctor said, 'you know what that would mean to my family and to me.'

'There will be no question of resigning. It will not come to that,' Jan said. 'Let's see, You have Mahaffy, and the

Professor of Moral Philosophy, and Smithers is a gentleman. How will Wilkins vote?' Jan muttered as he counted on his fingers.

'Oh, for God's sake, Jan, don't ford your rivers till you come to them.' Then to the doctor: 'What did you say when the Provost complained?'

'"I don't like listening to scandal," I remarked; but instead of placating him it only made him worse. "You call a plenary meeting, a disciplinary meeting of the Board, scandal?" he asked, infuriated. I should tell you that the Board was meeting to consider a letter of complaint and the case of a Greek student who was found with two women in his rooms in college. It seems that the parent of some lady student wrote a letter complaining angrily about the way the Professor of Romance Languages illustrated the performance in the Provençal Courts of Love.'

'Why did she take Romance Languages if she couldn't take the romance?' I simply couldn't resist.

But uninterrupted the doctor continued: 'The Greek student I hear, was astonished. He explained to the Provost that it was not unusual in his country to have one if not two girls in one's rooms for comfort before such an emotional experience as an examination.'

The doctor could not forbear to smile.

'If that was the same student who, when asked sardonically by Mahaffy during a Greek examination, "Where did you get that accent?" answered "In Athens sir," it will go hard with him.' I suggested.

Privately I took heart: there never has been a case of expulsion of a don during the centuries of Trinity College's life. I forgot at the time that this was not a case of expulsion but of resignation, and so of the curtailment of an income. Universities have to avoid scandal: it will be forgiveness for the doctor; a stiff reprimand for the student from Greece.

'I hear that they have put an organ in his rooms,' said Jan.

'To exorcise his rooms, no doubt,' I suggested.

'To me it seems a homoeopathic remedy invented to

drive out the effect of the smaller by the larger.'

The doctor groaned as he came out of a reverie.

'Talking of Mahaffy, let us be fair to him. Though there is no love lost between us, he stood up for me when he saw that Gray was determined on victimisation.

'"Gray would murder sleep," he said.

'"But he has left us without minutes," Gray insisted.

'"We have reached decisions without them before this. We do not want every peccadillo that occurs in college recorded in black and white. He who makes an occasional mistake does far more for truth than the pedant who spends all his life trying to appear infallible."

'If that wasn't a slap in Gray's face, I would like to know for whom "trying to appear infallible" was intended. Nevertheless, if Gray perseveres with his motion against me and the Board supports him, I shall have to resign.' So said the divine one with a sigh.

Again Jan counted on his fingers:

'But you have Mahaffy, and the Professor of Moral Philosophy, and Smithers is a gentleman. How will Wilkins vote?' he repeated.

'Oh, for goodness' sake, Jan, don't let us take it for granted that it will ever come to a vote,' I said.

I wanted to keep our friend's mind from revolving on things to come. We had a long way to go before the next Board; and there were many wires still to be pulled. Before you can pull a wire you must first locate it.

25 *The Opinion Of A Moralist*

In spite of the fact that I had corrected Jan for anticipating the voting of the Board, I resolved to ask my friend, the Professor of Moral Philosophy, what he thought of Dr Tyrrell's predicament. I went to see him early, before he should have gone out.

The Professor of Moral Philosophy received me blandly.

'Sauterne,' he said, 'is more suited to the morning than Guinness's stout.'

When the bottle was finished, I broached, not another bottle as you in your haste might think, but the subject. He knew more about it than I.

'I am afraid that the venerably dull members of the Board have agreed to support their fellow, Tom Thompson, in this matter. Very much afraid. I do not wish to dispirit you, my dear chap; but I can hold out no hope, no hope at all. It is the culmination of much resentment.'

Despondency fell upon me. I was more concerned about my friend than I could possibly be about myself and I am by no means an altruist. Strange that I could be sorrier for a friend than for myself. Was it because I could not believe that circumstances could possibly affect me? Perhaps it was that I felt a little elation at my friend's discomfort and at the chance it gave me of helping him. But why should I examine my motives when the question is, what can be done for the doctor, and it is urgent at that?

I remember gazing stupidly in front of me at the wall of the philosopher's room. A coloured print of a Norwegian marriage feast, and a newly presented plaque of him who philosophises without effeminacy, Mahaffy, of course. Mahaffy, who could be sarcastic in a genial way when the spirit moved him. I recalled his crushing question to a man who was claiming respect for Swift McNeill – 'You know, he is descended from Dean Swift.' 'By whom? Stella or Vanessa?' Mahaffy inquired with a smile.

Mahaffy was superior to the chances and changes of this mortal state; not so Dr Tyrrell.

'Who did that?' I asked, pointing to the plaque on the wall.

'Some little *émigré* sculptor called Brissac, who lives in Harcourt Place. We gave him the order because he was recommended to us as a promising artist. He is, as you can see for yourself, still in his promissory stage ... '

The professor smiled his sad and gentle smile. As I went

down the stairs I could hear him singing the rhythmic sentences of some old Moorish refrain:

> Allah, remember me;
> I have lived in Granada
> At the house of the falconer;
> And a woman taught me love
> In the evening before sunset.

Jan had a long face which shaded a smile when I met him again. He made me think of the Frenchman who said, 'There is something not altogether unpleasing in the misfortunes of our friends.' But Jan was, in spite of his intermittent way of speaking, sincerely concerned. We exchanged notes. It was evident that there was but little hope for our friend.

What goes on in the mind; and what has time got to say to it? Is it because it is immortal that it takes its time? Why should there be such a thing as a doorstep witticism: *esprit d'escalier?* That is, something that you think of when the opportunity has passed?

The opportunity for putting my plan for saving Dr Tyrrell into immediate execution was almost lost. Suddenly it came to me: not too late, thank goodness!

'The problem is as good as solved,' I said.

'Oh, is it?' Jan answered incredulously.

'Listen, will you. You know that plaque which his friends presented to Mahaffy on his birthday? Very well. If we can get one like it done of the doctor and get a splurge into the daily papers and build him up in such a way before the Board meets that it will think twice before putting a petty domestic, splenetic quarrel ahead of world-wide publicity, the thing is done. Any Board would be disgraced, and so would the college that persevered in calling for the resignation of such a distinguished scholar. Why, man, he is Honorary Doctor of Literature in Cambridge University; Doctor of Common Law in Oxford; LL.D. of Edinburgh; Doctor of Lit., Queen's University, and Fellow of the Royal Academy of Letters and something else in the University of Durham.'

Jan was not carried off his feet; but for an engineering student he was quite flexible. He said that he would be round later to see me. I told him to fix the commission up with Brissac while he was on his way. No time to spare. This was Wednesday, and the Board would meet on Tuesday. Yes; yes, I would take care of the publicity. But we would have to keep well out of it. Consent? Of course we would get the doctor's consent. It was tantamount to consenting to be saved.

Jan was quite right. I am thoughtless. He pointed out that we could not present the case to the doctor as I had presented it to him, Jan. We would not expect the doctor to enter into what was more or less a conspiracy, without loss of self-respect. No. We would have to proceed as if the idea had cropped up in the ordinary course of events. We would have to get a few names to preside over the unveiling, including the editors of the dailies and the London correspondents of the same. Sir Horace, of course, would do the unveiling and use the opportunity to discuss catch-cropping. I was to see the doctor as early as possible in the morning. Jan would drop in during our talk.

When an idea impinges on me, I am at first exalted, then the impact of the idea causes me to pass into shock. As a result of this I felt listless and despondent when I called on the doctor. I found him in a state, if not of despondency, of dejection, and in an irritable mood which with him took on a sarcastic tinge.

He was reading some comments that Mahaffy had sent to the daily paper about some poor old woman whom superstitious villagers had buried alive because they thought that she was a witch. Little did I know, though I might have guessed it, that the village in question was the vilage in which the doctor's father had had his parish.

'After all,' he said quietly as he laid down the paper, 'it is only a question of premature burial, which is not such an obnoxious thing as delayed burial, which Mahaffy so obtrusively represents.'

'Well, you cannot say with Shakespeare that she is one of those inhabitants of earth who "yet are on't". Perhaps it was she who "set the minister of hell at work". I am thinking of the obsession of Tom Thompson ... '

But the doctor was more interested in the source of the quotation than in its application. I told him that it was from Rowe's *Jane Shore*. I thought of Jowett's definition of a scholar as one who could point to his references. That is why the doctor had to get my quotation right.

'By the way,' I went on carelessly, 'there are certain friends of yours who want you to sit for a portrait bust. Later it can be cast in bronze.'

Then I added, and I thought that this was the height of diplomacy – it was as far as I have ever risen, almost to Talleyrand form: 'Sir, if I may make a suggestion, don't be too hard on Mahaffy. At any rate not until you have had a better plaque than his cast in bronze.'

The doctor took thought for a minute or two. At last he asked: 'You don't mean to tell me that Mahaffy approves of this?'

Now I was in a real quandary. What would Talleyrand have done, or rather Machiavelli?

Fortunately Jan appeared at the door.

'May I come in?'

'Come in, come in!' says the doctor.

I caught what sounded like a note of enthusiasm, not for Jan, of course, but for my suggestion. He wanted to tell it all to Jan. I rushed to anticipate him, for Jan could not yet know what we had been saying or how far the project had developed.

'Jan,' I said, 'you know the quotation at the base of Mahaffy's bust, *"Philosophoumen aneu malakias"*? What would you suggest for a bust of the doctor here?'

Jan hummed and hawed and spoke intermittently. But as it turned out eloquence would not have got him half as far as his halting suggestion, for it made the doctor take the bust for granted and jump to the consideration of the quotation that was to go on the plaque.

What Jan said was this:

'Isn't there? It seems to me that there is ... I can't recall it accurately though ... some remark of Dido when her city was being built ... It could be used to refer to the walls of the Classical School which the doctor has founded in college ... if you see what I mean. *"Meos muros vidi."* Those may not be the exact words. They don't scan. My Latin is rather rusty ... '

The doctor groaned. Then he softened, out of his affection for Jan.

'"*Muros*" means a partition wall like the wall of a water closet; the word you want is "*moenia*". And the quotation which you quite rightly attribute to Dido is "*Meo moenia vidi*": "I have seen my walls rising."'

'I cannot imagine a more suitable legend for a plaque of the doctor,' I added hastily.

So it was arranged!

Before the doctor had time to ask himself why this should be left to his most irresponsible friends we must rush the sittings through. I saw Brissac at once. He was delighted. He would do it for nothing. That was out of the question. What we wanted was a plaque the same as the one he did of Mahaffy; and we wanted it completed in two days so that it could be photographed for the daily papers. The deadline would be Friday. Saturday for the ceremony.

While Brissac was seeing himself elected as official sculptor to the university, Jan was entertaining the doctor to what was a 'holding lunch'. Jan was to engage the doctor while I instructed Brissac. When we got the doctor back to his rooms Brissac was to begin.

The floor had already been covered with tarpaulin, the dais in place and the clay prepared. Brissac was instructed not to insist on the dais but to start on the head whether the doctor posed deliberately or not.

Very few would be interested in a description of a sculptor in action and of a sitter in inaction. It is enough to say that all went well.

We had a scratch audience for the well-chosen words that we got Sir Horace to say at the unveiling. The photographers from the various dailies were enthusiastic; they imagined that they had made a scoop. 'Publicity' had been foreseen; and printed matter, explaining the occasion of the presentation to Dr Tyrrell, had been made available, for obviously neither Jan nor I could pose as the 'onlie begetter' of the plaque idea. So let us pass over the unveiling. Suffice it to say neither the plot nor its purpose was unveiled.

It was at the beginning of the week after the meeting of the Board that Jan got a word with the doctor. He did not allude to the Board meeting. He refused to dine with Jan and me. He was dining elsewhere.

Jan looked at me. I looked at Jan.

'It must have gone well,' we said together.

It deserved a celebration to itself. What a pity that the doctor could not be let in on this.

When I did see the doctor, in his rooms, I thought that his manner was somewhat distant or rather lofty, as if he had turned himself into an examiner again and I was 'up'. He sat at his table under the window, and he was writing. The table was crowded with letters. The wastepaper basket was full of envelopes.

'You must excuse me. I have a considerable amount of correspondence to deal with. I am trying to explain to the Master of Balliol why I did not give him timely notice about the presentation of my plaque.'

I felt superfluous. On tiptoe I withdrew. I regret to say that I was not missed.

Anyway, I knew where to find Jan. His hours were his own. He had drunk himself into the Local Government Board and was a treasured fixture, for he had not been found wanting during the prolonged initiation. Old history; ours was new. He gave the order, and I took my seat.

'I saw the doctor,' I began. 'He was answering letters of which there was a pile on his desk. He was so busy that he did not ask me to stay. He was rather short with me. Not a word about the Board. Not even a hint of a drink; not a "won't you be seated for a while until I get this letter off my chest." Not a thing. I slipped out.'

Jan hawed a little. 'When I saw him, he was rushing off to dine with the Provost.'

I could see that Jan was trying to read a real excuse into that, rather than admit to himself that he too had been brushed off.

We sat silent. How long I could not say, but it must have been for at least a few minutes; and that is a very long time if you follow it on your watch; but it was at least five minutes because, when I did speak, the outlook had changed completely. I am a slow thinker. That is why, when I say five minutes, I am not exaggerating.

'Do you know what has happened?' I asked.

Jan made one of his inarticulate sounds which was meant to show that he was surveying the situation in all its aspects.

'Nemesis has interposed. When we undertook to draw a red herring, no, a red gurnet, across the track of the Board, we little thought of the factors which were out of our control ... '

'Such as?' Jan asked in a hushed way.

'The stature of the man for one thing. How were we to know what an inundation would follow the publicity? Then how were we to know that we would have to keep out of the whole business for the obvious reason that, if our scheme were found out, it would stultify its object and render the doctor suspect as an accessory to a trick. I did not realise, but you did, that we could never tell the doctor that the only thing we could think of to save him was this publicity. When you remember the abject state he was in before the Board meeting and compare it with his present state, when the Provost asks him to dinner, you will realise how successful our scheme was. You will also recognise that the greater the success the greater the need for the preservation of our secret.'

'We have started an avalanche,' said Jan.

'If we could only get him out of the way. To take a holiday, for instance,' I suggested.

'We may have to get ourselves out of the way before very long.'

When I met Jan next day he had an air of reserve about him, something withheld, aloof. It was not until I told him that I had a letter by the morning's post asking me to call on the doctor that his good cheer returned.

'What hour did he happen to mention?' Jan asked.

'Four-thirty,' I said briskly, though I was far from feeling comfortable.

'Same here.'

'Rather formal this letter writing – disconcerting, what?'

'You know he never uses the telephone,' said Jan.

'Oh, so we're both up before the Board so to speak, only it is a one-man Board consisting of the doctor?'

I interpreted Jan's grunts to be equivalent to a more eloquent person's 'Well I'll be damned!'

'Well, young men,' said Dr Tyrrell, 'when I consented to sit for that plaque I was surprised by the haste and the suddenness of your arrangements. I have still to see the reasons for such a stampede: and many of my friends also have been taken by surprise; and they have written in no uncertain terms to complain to me about their treatment, as if I were responsible. Why was it so rushed?

'As for the artist: no one has ever heard of him, and, though far be it from me to suggest it, there are those who state that I was his most important subject.'

Jan looked at me. I know that he wanted to ask, 'What about Mahaffy?' I wanted to ask that question myself; but how could we?

'Nevertheless,' the doctor proceeded, 'he modelled me with my eyes half shut or altogether shut. One might think that was asleep. Then there was the publicity for which there was no discernible reason. It was little short of indecent; my picture, or rather reproductions, in Monday morning's paper of that fellow's (what do you call him?) bust that purports to be me. Then there is all the huggermugger about the donors. At first when they congratulated me I thought that the portrait was being presented to me by some members of the Board; but when I thanked Mahaffy he was astounded, genuinely so, I will admit. "My dear Tyrrell," he said, "is it not enough to immolate myself to a wretched artist to please Macran without adding you to the sacrifice? I am thanking my stars that the artist is not another Pygmalion and that my statue is not likely to come alive." His attitude left me feeling that I had become the victim of a practical joke ... '

'Sir!' we expostulated in unison.

'I won't go as far as to say that; but I cannot rid myself of the suspicion that the invitations to dinner that have been pouring in on me are not free from a touch of condolence; that they are intended to comfort me. Tonight I am dining with the Archbishop of Dublin, no very intimate friend of mine. It is the only way I can account for it. Who can tell how deserving an object of pity I may appear to such as he?

'On the other hand, you have always seemed to be good friends of mine. You have been indiscreet in this matter, though I have little doubt but that you both meant well.'

The doctor rose.

'Well I'll be damned,' said Jan when we got outside.

'You are already damned, so am I – in his opinion at any rate. Let me tell you this. It is the last time that I will try to save anybody. There are too many saviours in this world. Saviours always come to a bad end. The world is filled with people who are trying to do good and force others to do likewise. It is the cause of half the trouble on the planet.'

'I wish you would speak for yourself and leave me out of it.'

'You, Jan?'

'Yes. It was your idea, don't forget.'

'*Et tu, Brute!*' was all I said.

Jan looked at me. 'You need not take it so seriously. He is out of it this time but it won't be long before he is in the soup again.'

'Then it will be your turn,' I said; and led the way into Fanning's.

As if to comfort both of us Jan stuttered, 'After all we

were not as badly snubbed as was the fellow who broke in on the doctor's conversation with the rude inquiry, "Where's the urinal?"

'"Oh, go along that passage until you come to a door marked GENTLEMEN but don't let that deter you."'

26 *A Sea-Grey House*

I saw a model-T Ford trembling outside a shop in Nassau Street. I hastened home and asked for a compass and a map of Ireland. 'What new folly possesses you now?' my wife asked as I bent over the map. 'I am looking for the largest house farthest from the railhead in Ireland, something that may be even two days away, because this afternoon I saw an automobile that will bring that house within half a day's reach in – allowing for the lag in human thinking – a few years at most. I want to get it while it is almost unsaleable, while it is still cheap.' But she was not as enthusiastic as I; few people are.

I remember when I collected old mills, no one took any interest in my suggestions; and now what do you see? Temple Mills on the Liffey with its own power from the river. The owner has merely to pull a wire like a bellpull and he gets boiling water for his bath; his house is warmed and lighted and cleaned by electricity.

The mill at Swords could be adapted just as well. It had the advantage of a millpond on which water lilies lie, and a little brook to feed the pond. The rectory, 'a haunt of ancient peace,' stands beside the millpond, which is probably overgrown with weeds by now; but when I tried to collect it, the owner, a shopkeeper who dwelt beside it, became suspicious because I was too honest and I told him all the possibilities I saw. As far as I know, it is still a half-ruined store.

Then I tried to collect lakes, depending on the fact that sooner or later their beauty would be recognised by town-stifled citizens. Meanwhile, I could have them for a song and dwell by them in the summer. Before I had time to go into the title deeds, a sale came on in Connemara: Renvyle House with sixty or more rooms. It was less than nine miles from Garranban where the boys had learned to swim; Garranban; the open house! It was fifteen miles from the nearest town and the nearest town was seven or eight hours from Dublin; two days if the connection between trains was off. With automobiles running in my head and full of hope, I bought the place. An extra hundred pounds accelerated the sale. I had a house in the heart of Connemara on the edge of the sea on the last shelf of Europe in the next parish to New York!

Geologically it was a wonder: a storm beach enclosed a little lake which was fed by a brook that fell from a rocky rise on the south side. The lake was forty yards from the house, the house was less than a hundred yards from the sea. In the lake was a little peninsula, wooded still with the last specimens of the old Irish fir trees. It was called Roisindhu, the Little Dark Wood, and it gave its name to the lake. Above it rose Letter Hill, a mountain that, as the mists of morning lifted, could be seen, plum-blue, reflected in the lake.

It was Mahaffy who said 'plum-blue' when I found him early one morning seated outside the house watching the mist rise from the water and the mountain upside down in the lake. Letter Hill can turn to purple from blue-black as the light grows. On a fine evening the sun sinks double, a golden ball far out on the ocean, and a ball reflected in the lake, with only a thin green strip of land separating the real from its reflection. Far to the west and ending the view, the ruined castle of Renvyle stands. It was built, some said, by the O'Hurleys; and stone cannon balls were found embedded in its walls at the time of the auction of the house. Some said that these were thrown by the guns of Granuaile, Grace O'Malley, because she claimed the land on which the castle stood; but no galleys of those days could throw such cannon balls.

It was split in two on the orders from Cromwell to leave no fortress standing in Connaught. He had garrisoned the outlying island of Inisbofin, the Isle of the White Cow, with coast guards to prevent smuggling from friendly Spain. When he died these guards were abandoned and left to their own devices. They were not slaughtered, for the names of Heather, Hazel and King point to intermarriage with the people on the mainland.

There was an old library in the house. In it I found a first edition of More's *Utopia* printed at Basle; and what I should have appreciated, for it was unique, a first edition of Chaucer's lesson on the astrolabe to his son. It began, 'Little Lewis.' I should have presented it to the Library of Trinity College as I did the *Utopia*. But perhaps I only learned the value of the *Utopia* from Mahaffy when he came to visit me again some years after I had Renvyle House. The library went up in flames during the civil war; and with it the priceless book on the astrolabe, together with other irreplaceable things.

Touching the origin of Renvyle House, the story ran that a ship laden with a cargo of precious timber was wrecked on the beach hard by. Blake, the owner of the lands, was informed because all that went ashore between two points on the beach came under the 'manorial rights' which went with the property. Blake hastened from London – it must have taken him weeks, for model-Ts were far from being invented then. He saw the site on which stood a cottage owned by one O'Flaherty. He built between lake and sea. He pannelled the house with foreign wood and made his own glass, thick and uncouth but homemade. The roof he covered with great slabs from a slate quarry near by. In order to withstand the thrust of the Atlantic gales the roof was low, and the walls of the house were six feet thick in order to bear the pressure of the unmansarded roof. It was to report on the quarry of slates that I brought two Welshmen, of a Sunday, from a famous quarry of rustic slates in Wales and saw them back to the boat on the same day. About four hundred miles of a journey, nothing now, but quite an achievement then.

Some of the indoor walls were six feet thick, and where they were pierced, the doors were double. Sometimes the doors would open and shut by themselves. We took no notice of this, for we thought that it was the effect of draught in the corridors, or that the children were playing at hide-and-seek. It was otherwise when the Yeatses came to stay with us on their honeymoon; but thereby hangs a tale.

In the days when Renvyle House was built the inhabitants of the country dwelt either in castles or in cottages. Important people had to live behind battlements; it mattered little where the humble lived. It was strange, then, to find Renvyle unprotected by battlements or even window bars. The explanation was that its remoteness was its protection. There were no iron rails on the windows, which were less than breast-high from the ground; but a window of an upstairs room, the only room in the house with a northern aspect, was heavily guarded. Why was this?

I should tell you that the house was built like the letter H, with the crosspiece nearer one end. The house was built round three sides of a courtyard, the fourth side enclosed by a wrought iron gate. Galleries connected the two sides of the house, and off the upstairs gallery was the room with the barred windows. No servant maid would sleep in that room. There was a 'presence' there which could be felt, they said.

One day a heavy linen chest that stood immediately inside the door of this room somehow moved so as to prevent the door being opened. A man had to remove the window bars to get into the room to release the door. Was the house haunted? None of the country people would give a straight answer. Such a question caused silence, and sometimes made the person who was asked walk away.

One windy night I was sleeping alone in the west wing in a great four-poster bed, with old gilt on the posts which turned out to be made of tilting spears, rare enough, when I heard or thought I heard a person walking along the corridor. Whoever it was halted as if he had a wooden leg. Nearer and nearer the limping thing approached. The sound was plain in spite of the storm outside. I could endure the tension no longer. I jumped out of bed. Nothing was to be gained by cowering. I lit a candle. I pulled open the door suddenly.

The candle was blown out. I was alone in the dark with the thing in the passage. I tried to strike out. It was no use crying for help; any servants there were slept in the other wing where my shouts could not be heard or, if they were, would be put down to the howling wind or the waves on the beach.

I could not strike out; my arms felt weighted, as if I were exercising with rubber ropes. But there was no need to strike out or to shout for help because nothing happened. There was a silence of sorts, after a kind of sobbing. It took some time to find the matches.

So I have a haunted house. Splendid when I have company. I don't want to be there alone again. Wait till Yeats hears this. He will be interested. Interested, yes, provided that I do not attempt to rationalise it and to explain the affair away. No mention of the possibility of a nightmare. I am very much inclined to put it all down to a nightmare, with its muscle-bound sensation and the fact that nothing happened when I was sufficiently awake to open the door.

Why did nothing happen? You had better ask Yeats. Æ would be impatient and preoccupied with something he wished to say. He would waive the whole business aside as an infringement on what he saw in a vision: 'Immortal, mild, proud shadows.' Mine was anything but mild. Why? I never saw it. A nightmare could account for it all; but who can account for a nightmare?

Ash and sycamore trees sheltered the old place from the north and west, the points of the prevailing winds. Sycamore trees can thrive at the sea's edge; so can the ash. There was an ash grove to the northeast of the house. It looked lovely in the early morning when the level sun lit the clean boles and the bright grass growing up to the very roots. Later, in spite of a special stipulation and a promise to preserve the ash wood, some local oaf cut down all when Sir Something-or-other – Patrick, I think – Doran, head of the Land Commission deprived me compulsorily of half of the two hundred acres I had bought, when the estate was divided among the tenants. They were Blake's tenants, a scion of him who built the place. I have no tenants. And yet fellows like Larry Ginnell think that there should be more 'locals' than cattle in a land already over-populated.

To impress on farmers the value of a tree should be a matter for the schools. Instead of confusing their sons and daughters with *ersatz* Gaelic, it would be more practical, and better for the country, to impress on children the value of a tree. Shelter for cattle would appeal to them. For what cow could yield a proper quota of milk when exposed to the wind? If they could not recognise the importance of a tree as a drainer, that is, a dryer of land and a preserver of the country's soil, let it be hinted that it is just as unlucky to cut down a tree as a white thornbush. Thornbushes are exempt because they are preserved by superstition. It seems that the whole country was once run by superstition. If superstition works yet, let it save the trees. Except Iceland, Ireland has the lowest percentage of trees of any country in Europe, thanks to the ignorance of the farmer and the apathy of Anglicised commissioners.

A month earlier than the market, daffodils broke out under the trees; snowdrops came before them, closer to the earth and hidden in the grass for protection. Protection against the winds of February, not against frost; for winds, not frost, were the enemies on that western shelf of an arctic island made semi-tropical by the Gulf Stream from the United States. Flowers white and yellow beside the grey sea, and the aberrations of the Irish character alike are due to the beneficent current from America!

Dawns, sunsets, winds, trees and flowers can be found in any place that is cherished, and even in those places, if there be any, where no one has been.

There was something else, something indescribable but as real as dim colour or soft sound. It was the spirit of the place: the countryside was faintly magical even in the rain. Half tones told of it; and the soft atmosphere made you feel that you were in a region that was your proper home, a home where there was neither time, nor tide, nor any change at all, something friendly and akin and full of all that might be needed, if need were to arise; but it never did, for you felt that nothing was lacking. And you did not want to speak.

27 *The Coming Of Augustus*

If man were perfect, life, as we know it, would not be worth living. Think of it: there would be no need for religion with its sacraments; no need for Baptism, Confirmation, Communion; no need for Redemption even. More than this; if man were perfect there would be no movement in his world: everything would be static; there would be no poetry and no thought. The reasoning that leads to this conclusion should be less abrupt. Jumping to conclusions is not permissible even among philosophers. I am no philosopher, so I will stop here ... and introduce Francis Macnamara through whom I met Augustus John, a man of deep shadows and dazzling light.

Francis Macnamara was tall, golden-haired and blue-eyed. His nose was straight but it ended in a triangle that at times was red. He was a gangling young man. His father was squire of Doolin House, County Clare. It was said that he had taken advantage of the prerogative of all country gentlemen in the west of Ireland and married his cook. It was only a rumour of course, marriage and all, so let us leave it at that and concentrate on Francis. He went to Magdalen College, Oxford, where he learned to be introspective and to be aware of Art. How he met Augustus I do not know.

Francis had a pretty wife and a prettier sister-in-law. They were both French. The word went round – since everything in Ireland that is not in the newspapers, which are by no means general, goes by rumour – that Francis slept with his sister-in-law and his wife in the same bed to save hotel expenses. Correct enough, for his sister-in-law could not have had a better chaperone. In spite of these rumours, or because of them, I liked Francis, perhaps because of an additional rumour that he told his dentist, when asked his profession, 'I am a poet; and I teach poetry.' Now in an age when the common man reigns, that is refreshing. After all, why should a man be ashamed of his predilection? An artist is not; nor a musician and as for a tenor ... Must a poet subscribe to the lowbrows and hide his head? Francis did not. Though I never met one of his pupils, except his sister-in-law, I got a paper-covered booklet of his poems. I forget all – a bad sign – but a part of one; it was addressed to an aviator in the days when flying was a dangerous novelty:

The lofty mountains pointing at you stand.

That, I thought, is a fine image, giving as it does both altitude and speed. I can see the aeroplane speeding over the established mountains, high over their tops.

He was influenced by that fine forgotten poet, George Meredith. There were schools of poetry in ancient Ireland where the pupil had to study for fourteen years before he was considered proficient. Francis studied all his days. I cannot be sure that the adjective was 'lofty' in his line about the aviator and I cannot recover it now, for the little book is long ago out of print. It was probably one of those books of verse which Blackwell publishes for earnest youths and maidens at Oxford, and makes them pay for through their Muses. The last I saw of Francis was in a white-washed cottage in the Dublin mountains where he was reading Bunyan's *Pilgrim's Progress*. He tried to get me to read that book in vain. I much preferred to read of Lancelot and how love constrained him, than Bunyan mouthing morality from jail.

But long before Francis took to Bunyan and whitewash, he invited over from London Augustus John. And Augustus arrived in Dublin like a lion, or some sea king with golden moustache and beard. John is a Welshman; and a fair-haired Welshman is rare. So it is conjectured that the ancestors of Augustus were men who fought with Harold against the invader under William the Bastard from Normandy, and, after that disastrous day at Hastings, took refuge in the mountain fastnesses of Wales. It seems improbable, for the Welshmen so scorned the Saxons that they refused to extend to them the blessings of Christianity in the third century; so why shelter them in the eleventh? Augustus assuredly is descended from the Vikings who founded Haverford where he was born.

There must be more Welsh than Saxon in Augustus in spite of his colouring because imagination is the gift of the Gaels and Welshmen are Cymric Gaels, and you have only to look at his paintings to see what imagination Augustus has. Now he is the only man painting in England that matters at all. And that is why the English Government honoured him with the Order of Merit. The Order of Merit is the closest club in existence: it is limited to nine members. In the old days it suggested gout more than merit; but I give it credit for honouring the man whose imagination enabled him to see beauty in truth and who has more colour in his retina than any man I have met.

When I saw him for the first time I noticed that he had a magnificent body. He could have posed for the Nordic Man, whoever he is. He was tall, broad-shouldered and narrow-hipped. His limbs were not heavy, his hands and feet were long. When I told Æ of John's long hands, he at once began a theosophical dissertation on Lu, the Long-Handed god of all the arts, the Irish equivalent of Apollo. 'For, you see, there is a similarity and a relationship between all the gods of every religion.'

What to do with Augustus? No one talks art to an artist. Augustus was – and still is – a moody man. Francis had offered Augustus the freedom of the island, but such freedom is not free. You have to pay for it. Therefore, the first thing to do was to get suitable lodgings for Augustus. The Royal Hotel, Dalkey, would have answered, but it had no rooms vacant. But the house next door had.

Augustus was duly installed on the second floor; and his face looked out of the window when I called to show him what Dalkey had to offer. It had the Cosy Kitchen with a nice room behind the bar, which occupied the front room. The Cosy Kitchen was backed against a granite wall on the top of which tufts of pink valerian grew. It stood by itself and was full only on Sundays and other days of obligation. We sat for hours saying nothing in the little back room. Suddenly from his corner Augustus broke into song:

> 'In Jurytown where I was born;
> In Newgate jail I lie with scorn.'

It was a song about a highwayman and seemed appropriate when John put his vigour into it. But a strange thing: as he sang his body seemed to grow small. It was as if it all went into his voice. He dwindled.

> 'At seventeen I took a wife;
> I loved her as I loved my life.'

If he threw himself into a song it was a promise that he would throw himself into a portrait. Now there are artists whose selves I would not like to have painting me. One is Billy Orpen, high-shouldered, short-bodied, long-legged – he will be 'Sir' William later, wait and see! And there are others who are mean men. With Augustus it is different. His would be a personality to have in your portrait.

I know you will sense the fact that I look upon portraits as stamping grounds whereupon the painter may dance. The fact is that no one who is up in things artistic ever speaks of So-and-so's portrait but 'Did you see the John of Lady Ottoline?' I know that much about art and very little more. Augustus John has magnificent eyes so there the sitter is safe. I have already remarked on his perfect frame

162

so what more do you want? Shannon had not fine eyes, but he had a good mouth, so his portraits all show people whose mouths are comely. As for Leonardo da Vinci, that enigmatical smile of his looks out on life from every portrait he has painted. After this you will say that I have been impressed by someone's statement to the effect that artists, like children, paint themselves. And you will be right.

But what about the savage portraits he paints, such as those of Lady Ottoline Morrell and David Lloyd George? Exactly. He knew the rascality of Lloyd George, the schemer, the double-crosser and the rogue that he was. It is all there in that unscrupulous face. Lady Ottoline, in his opinion, stood for false values and they are in the humps on her breast and back.

Dalkey is a lovely place. It looks out over Shanagolden Bay that sweeps in a curve to the south, so like the Bay of Naples that the pretentious owners of the villas around, who have probably never been to Naples, have given their villas Italian names. The whole terrace, in the second last house of which Macran lives, is called Sorrento Terrace. There must have been a regular wave of Italianism, for you can see it beginning at Blackrock, where there is a house called *Qui si Sano* and so on. Energetic Browning's time.

The visit of Augustus was a great excuse to take a day off now and then. I called for him one morning and he was all set to go. We would pick up Joe Hone, who lived at Killiney, and go to Glendalough, the Glen of the Lakes, in Wicklow. Joe, for all his quiet ways and his delicate health, which assured old age, knew all the artists and he was acceptable to Augustus. On through the lovely country we went. Augustus, who was sitting in the back, could not be distracted by scenery, for beside him sat Vera Hone.

I decided against going into Pluck's at Kilmacanoge. It might be hours before I could get the artist out. The drive to Glendalough takes two hours. We could have drinks at the hotel that has a clear river at the back. We bowled along the Rocky Valley. Suddenly I heard the word 'Stop.' As it evidently was not meant for me, I didn't stop. Joe Hone did not turn his head, so why should I? High to the left rose the peak of the Golden Spear, called latterly the Sugarloaf. The past was more romantic than the present, though the present was romantic enough just now.

Glendalough is set in a deep valley, between mountains which are near on either side. It is famous for an early monkish town which was walled, and for its round tower and the Seven Churches. In the upper lake, about thirty feet up in the cliff, is an excavation, about eleven feet long and less than four feet high, for it is impossible to stand up in it. This is St Kevin's Bed. St Kevin was a pre-Patrician 'saint' whose chief act was to repulse the female in the person of Kathleen. He threw her into the lake below, and she sank. Was that why they called him an anchorite? Apparently he expected the human race to be propagated by fission. This and the graveyard prevent it from being a place of enjoyment for me. Yet we arrived; so it provided a destination, for the road could go no farther and the Austrian who ran the hotel was a friend of mine.

The Austrian stood a drink 'on the house' when he saw Augustus John. Austrians are sensitive and highly cultivated, and the proprietor immediately recognised an outstanding human being when he beheld the Master. I for my poor part stood on the wooden bridge behind the hotel and gazed so long at the water that I felt I had a thirst, and so in and ordered a drink. John was toying with his whisky. His pipe lay on the table, unlit. Would it be the right time to tell him about Gendalough? He might not like the story about St Kevin. He might be short with me. Well, it's a nice state of affairs not to dare to speak to an artist about scenery. I might tell him what Sir Edwin Lutyens told me about the churches when I took him to Glendalough. Why tell him anything? He is entertaining Vera Hone with his silences. I think that I'll take a stroll with Joe along by the lake where you can see the water through the pines. Joe will know all about Glendalough and early Christianity and St Kevin.

28 *Mr Short*

Donnycarney is on the way to Santry, famous for the Lord Santry who was 'reduced' to a baronetcy in the eighteenth century for running a footman through. I mention Donnycarney because Joyce loved the name and wove it into one of his exquisite lyrics. Donnycarney would be in the sequence of the alphabet if it were Carneydonny; but it would not sound so well. It would not be so magical, and the magic of words was dear to Joyce. What is the alphabet anyway? It was the first attempt to reduce language to its radicals: 'You have the letters Cadmus gave.'

There is another way out of Dublin, which has roads out of it as the Statue of Liberty has rays out of her head. This road goes out from the capital through Drumcondra. Somewhere about Drumcondra was a lunatic asylum, set in the fields far from the road. It was about to be condemned, because it was in private hands and the doctor who owned it was recently dead. I knew another private asylum owned by a friend of mine who lived round the corner from Ely Place in Hume Street. His name was Dr Swan. He had a beautiful eighteenth-century house out near Templeogue. The dining room had three windows in the end walls, which were curved. I dined there one evening with him and the matron of his mental home, which was built as an annexe to the old house with the curved walls.

Why am I writing about private asylums near Dublin? Because from one of them, the one deep in the fields out Drumcondra way, I got the idea of kidnapping the Chief Secretary for Ireland, who had the temerity to visit the country. His name was Mr Short. He looked like a horse coper. He was Mr Short at the time, 1918, though doubtless he was later lost in an alias of the peerage. He went round with an armed guard, a symbol of the love the Irish People bore to those who rule their country. To capture the Chief Secretary and to conscript him among the patients in the Drumcondra Asylum was an original idea and one that would evoke the laughter of the British masses who are ever fair-minded. They would laugh at anything awkward that befell a member of their government.

I passed on the idea to those who could work it out. It was accepted with enthusiasm. First the guard would have to be bought off. This was found to be impossible. That meant that he was a member of the Royal Irish Constabulary. If he were an Englishman, he would have seen the light; and few things are lighter than Bank of England notes. No: he would have to be bumped off. I have scruples about assassination, increased no doubt by an attempt on my own life.

England was ruling through the Chief Secretary. If he were to be driven up in a van to the lonely house near Drumcondra and registered as an Englishman whose relatives wanted his mental derangement to be kept as secret as possible, all would be plausible. Any assertions that he was the Chief Secretary and that it was an outrage to confine him would only confirm the wisdom of his family in having him confined in another country. He would be diagnosed by the hardy attendants as another case of delusions of grandeur.

Very sad: we all know what that means. Delusions of grandeur is the form of insanity that should be expected in an Englishman, Is not the British Empire based on delusions of grandeur? Grandeur for its officials: durbars and delusions for its subjects.

He would be well fed and well treated. The asylum, if he were discovered in it, would become famous and perhaps would not be closed after all. All his statements while he was a patient would be subsequently published. We would see to that. The reports would make good reading, even though they were made in the days before the mouthings of lunatics became literature.

166

All this was a good idea, an excellent idea; but there was the obstacle of the armed guard. He too might be accommodated, but first it would be necessary to disarm him, and, alas, alas, as I have said, he would have to be killed. That would more than counteract the farce of the whole thing, for the English masses would never tolerate murder. So it was that the hardheadedness of Northern policemen prevented the tables from being dissolved amid laughter, and saved the routine of Mr Short.

Now that we are on the subject, let us discuss the traits of a good lunatic. Augustine Birrell, another Chief Secretary whom later I met, would have been unsatisfactory for our purpose. His face would be against him for one thing. It was square and logical. And then he seemed to have been born with glasses. You could not imagine him decently with them off. He would have looked naked. Lunatics seldom wear spectacles. At any rate, they remove them from the dangerous ones. They are held to be superfluous in the padded cell.

Mr Birrell's forehead was not that of a lunatic. It was not made for a fine frenzy. It was flat on top – plenty of knowledge, no imagination. That must have been what George Moore sensed when he met Birrell – no imagination. Moore resented Birrell's using his position in the Cabinet to add authority to authorship. Moore had the instincts of a woman: he was always right. There was a time when Birrell was right too. That was when he was twitted about the insurrection which broke out during his term as Chief Secretary: 'I haven't the money to buy them all.' That was true so far as the officials of Dublin Castle were concerned, not one of whom resigned; but to the nation at large it had no application. Money could not have paid for centuries of British despoliation or have bought off a nation's desire to be free. All of which only points to that satrap's ignorance, and ignorance alone is not a qualification for lunacy.

Field Marshal Montgomery would make a typical lunatic because of his phobias and his beret. He hates smoking (aminophobia) and drinking (oinophobia) and coughing – 'There must be no coughing in my presence.' The warders could not clear their throats even on a Monday morning. He would issue orders (stratego-mania). His razor would be removed until he looked like a 'naval person'; and then he would grow worse. Now Winston is beyond a joke: – a subject for 'psychiatry'.

Once you are locked up in a bughouse, everything you say is used against you. The very natural wish to get out is used as a proof that you should be kept in. It is like a tea party with an old maid where every word you say is at cross-purposes and you cannot put yourself right in her eyes. Only it is much worse: you are licked before you start.

The only people who would get along quite nicely in a lunatic asylum are a king and queen, to whom boredom is first, not second, nature. They would never know that they were confined, but they'd be dazed if set at large. If by any mischance they grew restless, they could have shock treatment, that is, a series of electric shocks sent through the frontal lobe of the brain to ensure concussion. Everyone knows that concussion of the brain makes for conservatism and continuance and what more do you want in a monarch? If King George III had been confined all the time, America might not have been lost. From this you will see that there is much to be said for a lunatic asylum.

What about me? I would make an excellent lunatic. Already I know most of the ropes. Is it not a tradition that the heads of all lunatic asylums become affected in the end? Would it not be subtle flattery to persuade the doctors, warders, nurses and floor cleaners that they were qualifying for directorship? The more eccentric they got the less would they trouble about me. There may be something in it. Have I not lived in the rooms once occupied by Krafft-Ebing in Vienna? I am a harmless lunatic and I do not need to be locked up. Confine, rather, those Irishmen, the Royal Irish Constabulary, for instance, who would die before letting their disciplinarians down.

Here is the psychiatrists' imaginary report shorn of nine-tenths of its verbiage: 'Winston Churchill was born in the ladies' cloakroom in Blenheim on St Andrew's day. He was born prematurely – a seven months child. To the place of his birth may be traced his wish to pose as 'a naval person'; and the cloak and dagger acts that have characterised his life. His mental precocity is due to his premature birth.'

It was not called 'The Ladies' Cloak Room' in the days in which Winston was born; but psychiatrists cannot be expected to know everything.

29 *The City Of Dreadful Knights*

'Lunacy,' said Connolly Norman, 'is a condition where dreams overflow into life.' Bad enough, you will say; but what about dreams (and those of a pompous bully) overflowing into other people's lives?

'England's difficulty is Ireland's opportunity'; that is a wrong quotation. The correct one is, 'England's extremity is Ireland's opportunity,' etc. Now there is a play of words when you use 'extremity' that might suggest to some minds a kick in the rump.

Extremity, or difficulty, hardly accounts for Arthur Griffith shouldering a rifle. Yet I saw his sturdy figure clad in a dark green uniform marching in company with other men in uniform. No; this conduct does not agree with his constitutional methods. Bloodlessly by these he was to bring about separation from England in the very same way that Kossuth freed Hungary. Those who read Griffith's *Resurrection of Hungary* must have wondered, when they saw him marching in Dublin. What had happened? Did he at last come to realise what all who went before him to the gibbet or the pitch cap, in fruitless rebellion after rebellion, had realised and that is that England never opens anything but a trembling hand? The few hundred who marched with Griffith were unlikely to make 'England shake'. Rather she will dispense bland and lavish promises all redeemable, mark you, *after* the war.

Thus was John Redmond fooled and Tom Kettle, who went recruiting for his chief, John Redmond; but forbore to ask men to go to a battle he himself would refuse to join. He was not like Sir James Percy, owner of the *Irish Wheelman*, or Sir Simon Maddock, curator of Mount Jerome Cemetery. Both were knighted, one for keeping peace in the cemetery, no doubt, and Sir James for his enigmatical smile. Tom Kettle fell at Ginchy. Sir James, who stayed at home, was presented with a cutlass of Honour because of his efforts at recruiting for the Navy. Sir William Thompson was knighted for chaperoning Lady Aberdeen. Hugh Lane, the picture dealer, was knighted for admiring Manet, as Sickert, the artist, said.

The situation is becoming serious – what about my voluntary work in war hospitals and consultant to them all? That is sure to be awarded. The only thing to do is to write to Lloyd's and take out an insurance policy against knighthood. It is not as amusing or as farcical as might at first appear. It is quite serious. Apart altogether from the association with me of characters that have been knighted in Dublin, I will lose the bulk of my practice – such as is left of it – because the bulk of it is among Irishmen who are Nationalists. They are no longer filled with awe at knighthoods, not after the last accolades. And if I refuse a knighthood it will be said that I am one of the disgruntled Irish and I shall lose all the moneyed garrison and the Church of Ireland as well. A bit of a quandary; but there is one hope: Percy, Maddock and the rest *sought* knighthoods and only God knows what they paid for it. And what about the fellow who was made a peer for pretending to be a Prime Minister's bastard? Yes, but that's the peerage. We are talking about knighthood.

John Robert O'Connell was knighted for putting trust funds at the disposal of Lady Aberdeen. He was the smallest attorney in Dublin as far as stature went. It is told that when the accolade was over and Lord Aberdeen pronounced the words, 'Arise, Sir John,' the onlookers did not know whether he had risen or was still kneeling. Later he became a Benedictine monk. The abbot sent for him one day to explain that spats did not accord with the habit he wore. He was sent to the belfry where, if you can believe anyone, he went up with the rope and was never seen again. Thus the accolade was followed by an assumption. He had risen. Spats in the belfry!

I do not want honours either on the King's Birthday or the New Year. The insurance will compensate me and the premium cannot be great, seeing that the request is, if not unprecedented, unusual. Of course, no insurance will compensate me if Arthur uses his gun. That is a contingency that need not be considered; but coolness or the loss outright of his friendship must be. He whom Griffith thinks unworthy is unworthy indeed.

I could have hobnobbed with those in power, always excluding Lloyd George, who is a reflection on power and even on politics; but I did not take the trouble. I suppose a sense of what was befitting saved me. The cobbler should stick to his last, and the doctor to his patients and avoid the society of knights who could not sit on a horse. All this may be part of some divine event; but to me it is not yet revealed. Jimmy Percy, now Sir James, got a Napoleonic complex: the walls of the stairway of his house were furnished with pictures of Napoleon in many attitudes and after many glorious victories. He was depicted in the days of his glory, but there was no picture of him on the deck of the *Bellerophon*. Simon Maddock, not satisfied with his British knighthood, spent quite a lot of money trying to become a senator, after the Irish Free State was created. He died trying to save a parrot, whose only cry was 'God Save the King,' from a fire which broke out in his house in the cemetery. I am too prone to see symbols where there are none; so I desist.

Before I take credit to myself for having discovered that the less intelligent a general be, the more successful, I must

171

submit my discovery to the test of the converse; that is, whether the opposite holds good. Can I show that intelligence makes for bad soldiers? I have only two examples, but then my acquaintance with military men is limited. I was walking in Hyde Park one morning when I met Shane Leslie, now Sir Shane, with General Sir Ian Hamilton, who conducted the disembarkation after the gross and stupid insistence on the Gallipoli landing. It was said that he paid the most scrupulous attention to the prose of his dispatches, which never mentioned the two millions in gold which, according to rumour in London, was the price that Atatürk set for the escape of Irish and Australian troops from that deadly peninsula. Sir Ian talked about another general. He said, 'He could get a hundred thousand troops into Hyde Park; but he could never get them out.' This was for me an insight into military problems. I knew that London policemen could handle one hundred and thirty thousand spectators at a football final, and get them in as well as out!

30 *Stupidity Is The Only Wear*

When celebrating the Charge of the Light Brigade at Balaclava, the Poet Laureate, Tennyson, wrote, 'Someone had blundered.' Blundering or 'muddling through' would appear to be the *modus vivendi* of England. It is a great country that can make its empties pay for its full ones!

Tom Kettle, who saw the incident, told me that the appropriately named Kitchener, who could feed an army but not lead it, was carried out 'blind to the world' from 10, Downing Street by two flunkies and put into a taxicab. He was blind to the world physically when he had to be carried; and figuratively when he ignored and thereby discouraged the first – and last – outburst of Irish enthusiasm for a war ostensibly to free small nations. Ireland was ready to cross the seas and fight, when England was unwilling to submit to conscription, that, is to be drafted to fight for itself. Perhaps it was the belief, prevalent in Ireland, that 'a good fight justifies any cause'.

There were thin, half-hearted Kitchener Armies but no general enlistment at a time when England was up against a foe of its own weight and colour. It was no longer a battle against fuzzy-wuzzys but against a mighty enemy with modern equipment. English armies were on the run – 'delaying action' – from Mons and Le Cateau, and they delayed no one. The blundering became contagious. The French armies under Joffre attacked through Lorraine in the south and were bloodily repulsed when they should have stemmed the German onrush through Belgium. The result of the combined effort of France and England was to abandon all Belgium to Germany, a large part of France, and eighty per cent. of its coal. Then came Tannenberg, at which Hindenberg and Ludendorff slaughtered three hundred thousand wretchedly armed Russians or drove them into the marshes to drown. This was on August 30, 1914, when the war had been a little over three weeks begun.

To give Russia arms; that was the paramount need. The Baltic was closed. It would be necessary to force the Dardanelles. That portion of the Royal Navy to which this task had been assigned did its work so well that it left but one fort standing. This fort had but two long-range guns left and these had only thirty-five shells. Liman von Saunders had not yet arrived with his infantry to help the Turks. The road to Constantinople was wide open. Ah, but the Royal Navy had lost three battleships and at least five hundred men in opening it. Naval intelligence was unaware of the victory! There was a council of war on board the *Suffern*. The captains could not make out what had sunk their ships. They decided to break off action. It cost two extra years of fighting and the lives of millions of men, and it brought about the fall of the Asquith government.

Set a thief to catch a thief. Lloyd George, a Welshman, was made Prime Minister instead of Asquith. His job was to win the war. First he had to create two peerages and make one of his conspirators Viceroy of India, before his financial scandals could be hushed sufficiently. He began organising for victory by kicking the Commander in Chief, Lord French, upstairs to the viceroyalty of Ireland. Haig (of Haig and Haig), a Scotsman and a cavalry officer, was appointed in the place of Lord French. Lloyd George, with a rogue's nature, became suspicious of the most straightforward of men, Haig. He suspected that Haig's propensity to attack might cost so many lives that his own popularity as Prime Minister would be affected. Before he could blunder, America entered the war.

Here is a tale that will try your credulity. Haig's sister had married the great Irish whiskey distiller, John Jameson. Through the offices of Lady Fingall I was invited in the last year of the war to lunch at St. Marnock's, a delightful place where the Jamesons lived by the Portmarnock beach north-west of Howth Head and about seven miles from Dublin. After the lunch, I was taken into the study, or library, and asked with great seriousness if I could organise another rebellion so that the attention of Lloyd George might be diverted from her brother, the Commander in Chief, whom she had reasons to know Lloyd George intended to sack!

I explained as well as I could that it was not in my power to arrange rebellions. The implication did not dawn on me at the time. I was not sufficiently alive to what people like the Jamesons must think of me. Obviously, they must have thought that I was deep in the councils of the provisional government of Ireland. But this is a retrospective view of the situation. It goes to show, too, what the sister of the field marshal must have thought of Lloyd George. It is not the first time that a warrior has been fired for trying to win a war.

31 *Easter Week*

I took a few days off in Connemara before Easter, 1916. I was returning by train from Galway when the first rumours of the insurrection were heard. Rumour upon rumour as the train went along. It was delayed at Athlone, which is about the centre of Ireland, to allow artillery from the barracks there to go ahead to Dublin. Then I knew that there was something serious in the air. At Mullingar, fifty miles west of Dublin, the train came to a halt. It could go no further because the lines were cut. This evidently was to prevent the passage of guns to Dublin. It convinced me that the country must have risen, as it had; in spite of the efforts of Professor MacNeill to call the rebellion off at the last moment.

Dublin was 'up'. All the old ballads surged through my mind: 'The debt so long unpaid.' Every century had seen a rising against the oppressor and now we were in another rebellion. I felt that I was a lucky man.

There was but one car that could be hired at Mullingar. Needless to say, it was not a good one. Its owner charged enough to buy it; but what did I care? I had to get to Dublin, not to see patients on Tuesday morning but to see what was happening on Easter Monday, now. Just as I was about to start, a middle-sized, middle-aged man with a grey beard and a tall silk hat came hurrying. Would I be so kind as to let him share the car? He could not get one for love or money in Mullingar and he had to be in London to attend an emergency meeting on Tuesday morning. Love? Here was the well-known Larry Ginnell, member of Parliament for

Westmeath and instigator of the 'hazel-wand' treatment of the graziers.

Cattle-driving was then the vogue. Cattle instead of men were supposed to be the enemies of the country and those who owned cattle were to be punished by having their herds driven by the hazel wand. My own opinion was exactly the opposite. I regarded his membership in John Redmond's Parliamentary Party with disapproval, but it did not prevent me from giving him a lift.

I wondered what was the Emergency Session of the House of Commons which he had to attend? He did not tell me. It was one of those sessions so secret that a voter could not be confided in by an elected man. This is the habit of those on governments; once elected, they turn against those who elected them and form a commando of their own. Needless, to say I did not ask Larry what the secret session might be. I was hoping that the rebellion would put an end to all those who carried their complaints into the spider's parlour. Even though there might be more to complain of, let us have a parlour of our own.

We drove more or less in silence for an hour and a half. Then the member of Parliament woke out of his trance. We were going down Cabra Road – a detour of some sort was necessary – when a bullet struck the windscreen and a few others whined over our heads. This was most unparliamentary. I did not like it any more than the M.P.

At once the driver put out the headlights, Cautiously we came to the railway bridge at Cabra, which had been turned into a barricade. A boy with a rifle stood beside it. He said his name was John Fogarty. His name, of which mine is a corruption or a derivative, took some of the force out of my expostulations that a bullet had been fired through our windscreen. He explained that we were mistaken for 'military' because we drove with lights undimmed. And the Republic could not afford to take chances. Hence we were given the benefit of the doubt. Benefit? The shots over our heads were the beneficial ones. I told him of the artillery train on its way. He said that it did not mean anything because there were no shells. He seemed full of hope for the rising. I left him so. He could not have been more than sixteen.

If symbols were prophetic, I might have seen in the first shots of the Easter Week revolution, fired against friendly Irishmen, civil war. I did not forsee anything of the kind. I thought only of the generations of the brave who in every century had risen in dark and evil days to right their native land and had been met with the pitch cap, the rack and the gibbet. Lord Edward Fitzgerald, Robert Emmet, Wolfe Tone, all done to death, and a divided Ireland left.

Don't imagine that this has been accidental through the centuries. It is the result of a policy which is very old; secret and deliberate. Here is what Sir John Mason wrote to the Privy Council as long ago as 1550 concerning the government of Ireland: 'These wild beasts should be hunted aforce, and at the beginning should be so bearded, before the whole herd run together, as might know with whom they had to do; wherein *the old and necessary* policy hath been to keep them by all means possible at war betwen themselves.'

The leopard does not change his spots. The John Masons are in council in London; and they will find means to keep the Irish 'by all means possible' at war between themselves. Who planned and prophesied the civil war?

When I had dismissed the car and with it Larry Ginnell, M.P., I took a stroll about the city. Dublin seemed normal. The street lights were brilliant. But there were crowds about, and this was unusual, for the streets of Dublin are rarely crowded.

The air was full of rumours. Engagements had already taken place. Victory for the insurgents. Engagements with whom? I asked myself. Key points were 'occupied'. There was much military textbook talk going about. Enthusiasm too.

I grew melancholy. And this feeling of oppression was, if anything, aggravated by what I read on a poster that had just been pasted on a pillar of the General Post Office.

POBLACHT NA H-EIREANN

THE PROVISIONAL GOVERNMENT OF
THE IRISH REPUBLIC
TO THE PEOPLE OF IRELAND

Irishmen and Irish Women: In the name of God and of the dead generations from which she receives her old tradition of nationhood, Ireland through us summons her children to her flag and strikes for her freedom.

Having organised and trained her manhood through her secret revolutionary organisation, the Irish Republican Brotherhood, and through her open military organisations, the Irish Volunteers and the Irish Citizen Army; having patiently perfected her discipline, having resolutely waited for the right moment to reveal herself, she now seizes that moment, and, supported by her exiled children in America and by gallant allies in Europe, but relying first on her own strength, she strikes in full confidence of victory.

We declare the right of the people of Ireland to the ownership of Ireland and to the unfettered control of Irish destinies to be sovereign and indefeasible. The long usurpation of that right by a foreign people and government has not extinguished the right, nor can it ever be extinguished except by the destruction of the Irish people. In every generation the Irish people have asserted their right to national freedom and sovereignty: six times during the past three hundred years they have asserted it in arms. Standing on that fundamental right and again asserting it in arms in the face of the world, we hereby proclaim the Irish Republic as a sovereign Independent State, and we pledge our lives and the lives of our comrades in arms to the cause of its freedom, of its welfare and of its exaltation among the nations.

The Irish Republic is entitled to, and hereby claims, the allegiance of every Irishman and every woman. The Republic guarantees religious and civil liberty, equal rights and equal opportunities to all its citizens, and declares its resolve to pursue the happiness and prosperity of the whole nation and of all its parts, cherishing all the children of the nation, equally and oblivious of the difference carefully fostered by an alien government, which had divided a minority from a majority in the past.

Until our arms have brought the opportune moment for the

establishment of a permanent National Government, representative of the whole people of Ireland and elected by the suffrage of all her men and women, the Provisional Government hereby constituted will administer the civil and military affairs of the Republic in trust for the people.

We place the cause of the Irish Republic under the protection of the Most High God, whose blessing we invoke upon our arms, and we pray that no one who serve that cause will dishonour it by cowardice, inhumanity or rapine. In this supreme hour the Irish Nation must, by its valour and discipline and by the readiness of its children to sacrifice themselves for the common good, prove worthy of the august destiny to which it is called.

Signed on behalf of the Provisional Government
Thomas Clarke

Sean MacDiarmada Thomas MacDonagh
P. H. Pearse Eamon Ceannt
James Connolly Joseph Plunkett

Yes. She has 'seized the moment'. Ireland's opportunity! It is taken!

I got one of these proclamations and brought it home. It was printed on poor paper and there were at least two founts of type used. It was badly punctuated: things which witnessed the secrecy and haste of its printing.

I examined the names of the signatories first. Not one was known to me, except in one case and that was by reading of the exploits of James Connolly whose patriotism seemed to be the patriotism of a labour agitator. I had met not one of those who had proposed themselves as the Provisional Government.

The words were brave and true. However, I did not like that clause about cowardice, inhumanity or rapine. Did he who wrote that sentence know the potentialities of some of the 'Irish People'? Rapine we had and inhumanity. Absurdity, yes; but no cowardice. Not unless you count pretending that you are a citizen loyal to Great Britain when, on your way to join its army, your good intentions are frustrated by your arrest as a suspect!

As I said, I was studying the names of the signatories of the brave proclamation. I suspected that there was not a Protestant among the signatories. I would have liked it better if there had been. I must ask someone about the men who issued it.

I went round on the morrow to see Hicks, the furniture master-craftsman in Lower Pembroke Street. He snuffled and was bent on ignoring both the question and myself at first. It was a mannerism he had, instead of manners. I knew Hicks. After some desultory visitors had left the shop Hicks opened up. 'Tom Clarke is all right, an old Fenian. There's nothing wrong with Tom Clarke. Patrick Pearse? His father is a tombstone cutter over in England. Sean MacDiarmada has a bit of a limp. Eamon Ceannt is Edward Kent, born in England. Tom MacDonagh, I don't think he is a Dublin man. Jospeh Plunkett? Isn't he one of the sons of auld Count Plunkett by one of his marriages, the old fellow with the beard? He had one son anyway who was riddled with tuberculosis . . . But what the hell is all this about?' Don't alarm yourself. It was only Hicks's way of repudiating any information he conveyed.

His detached summing up of the leaders of the rebellion was typical. Hicks stood to lose everything; and yet, like many wealthier men, he kept dabbling in revolution. How can that be explained? You see it among the wealthy actors of Hollywood. Is it in their case a sense of guilt, of undeserving, that inclines them to placate the remorseless enemy of non-political wealth, Communism? I am afraid I shall have to act the Lord Mayor once more with, 'There I leave you.'

War is not altogether grim, at least not in Ireland. The cheap book on military tactics that the Command of the Irish Republican Army seemed to rely on must have directed that sentries be posted at key positions in 'occupied territory'. That probably accounted for the stationing of young Dan Crowley (sixteen years of age but soldier of the Republic) with his rifle at the top of Grafton Street where it runs into Stephen's Green. At the hour of tavern-closing which was about 11 p.m. he was on duty, He took himself and his duties seriously. It certainly was a serious matter to be caught with a rifle by the British Government; but that thought was not what was uppermost in his mind. He was thinking of the position he had to hold, to let no one pass. No one offered to pass because most of the citizens were indoors wondering what would become of them. Suddenly sentry Crowley heard singing round the corner in the direction of the Gaiety Theatre and of Mother Mason's and of many a 'pub'. The voice got closer and louder. You could hear the words now ...

> 'I robbed no man; I took no life,
>   Yet they sent me to jail
> Because I am O'Donovan Rosse,
>   A son of Grainn Ualie.'

An enormous coal porter swung into view, cap with button on the top; leather bands beneath each knee.

> 'I robbed no man ...'

'Halt!' the sentry challenged meekly. But the song was not interrupted. It roared more defiantly than ever. The son of Grainn Ualie was in fine voice.

'Halt!' the sentry repeated. This time the song it was that halted for a moment. The singer swung down the street. When he had passed the sentry by a yard or two, he looked back at his interrupter.

'Be careful now, young fellah, with the rifle, or you might get hurt.' And what was learned in sorrow he continued to teach in song.

I left Dublin after first notifying the public through the newspapers that I would be out of town. After all, if the country was to revolt, my place was with my family and not with the 'leaders' who had not consulted me. There were no Edward Fitzgeralds among them; no Wolfe Tone nor a Robert Emmet. I noticed that. No doubt there will be cases of cowardice and rapine. Give them time and all will follow the pattern of revolutionary history. Little did I guess that I myself would be the subject of rapine and arson and that an alien born in Lexington Avenue, New York, would plunge our country into civil war.

From none of those who signed 'On behalf of the Provisional Government' was I inclined to take orders. What did they know about government? Yet, to be fair, what could they know? In them, and only in such as they, did the national being reside, and the dream of freedom. Ireland was decapitated and deprived of its gentry so long ago, and even of its middle classes.

Look at myself. Here I am depending on the good will of a class that considers a fight for freedom mere obstreperousness. A doctor has to be all things to all men. These men have staked their lives on a throw. They have everything to lose; and they will lose all. England will send over just enough troops to arrest the insurgents and to execute the ringleaders. They have 'become obstreperous'; they have asked for it, and they will get it, for all their bravery. Meanwhile, when law is in abeyance what will happen to my family? Patriotism covers a multitude of sins. Kidnapping may be one of them. Before I am confined to the city, in the name of Liberty, let me get out.

I turned my face to the west.

Trains were still running. The Dublin-Galway train went nearly as far as Oranmore, about six miles east of Galway. It could go no farther because the line was cut. I got out, cursing the upset. I fear that my enthusiasm for freedom did not cover being marooned. I saw a railway truck, or sled, with wheels that fitted the line. With the help of some of the passengers we put the women, such as would go, and a child or two on it and ran it as far as Oranmore. Then I walked about half a mile looking for help.

Oranmore was deserted, at least the house at which I called was. I went back. There was no sign of the truck. Exasperated at having my journey interrupted, I cast about for a way to proceed. To remain on the deserted track was useless. But wait. It would be more direct than the road.

Against this was the advantage of the road, which might have an automobile on it going in the direction of Galway.

Perhaps the owner of the substantial house at which I had called might be back by this time. I went to see. I found him in. Yes; he would drive me to the Citie of the Tribes. He was the manager of the model farm at Athenry. He would not hear of remuneration. As he drove me I found out that he was a Britisher; that, is a Scotsman employed by the English Government to show the Irish natives how to farm. The fact that the natives took no notice was none of his business. Obviously he never thought that, upset as I was, my sympathies could be with the rebels. We did not discuss the rebellion. He was glad to drive me. A strange figure; but only strange because he was sitting between two stools: the secure stool of an established government and the provisional stool.

The nights were clear in the part of Connemara where we were. Sometimes, strange whistles sounded in the starlight. Snodgrass, the artist in the cottage by the beach, was full of nerves. Well, what does he expect? Artistic temperaments have to be full of nerves.

There was no sign of the rebellion down in Connemara. Evidently it had not spread to the small farmers, without whom no rebellion can be a success.

The newspapers came through. As I thought: the principals were held in prison in Dublin's infamous Kilmainham jail. There they awaited execution. General Maxwell was appointed to hold the city under military discipline. His idea of discipline was to shoot the rebels by twos, and extend the shootings over a number of weeks. This will go well in America where, in spite of all that is spent yearly in propaganda favourable to the British, the Irish have a voice. They can be 'obstreperous'. And this even though their patriotism has been made synonymous with Roman Catholicism, a religion that can never give a President to the United States any more than it can give a monarch to Great Britain. And the identification of the Irish cause with religion, called Transmontanism, is emphasised by British propaganda. Yet for all that, there are other critics of England, fair-minded folk, in America who may ask why a war to free small nations should begin by oppressing the one nearest to England. And General Maxwell is extending the killings in Dublin Town.

Over forty prisons in England were used to hold the rebels. Scotland and Wales were requisitioned. But ninety per cent of the prisoners were held in English jails – Portland, Dartmoor, Parkhurst, Lincoln, Wormwood Scrubs, Wandsworth, Pentonville, Reading, Winchester, Birmingham, Lewes, Stafford, Manchester, etc.

So the Ireland that seized the moment, supported by her exiled children in America and by gallant allies in Europe, and struck in full confidence of victory, ends in every available jail in the three kingdoms.

That fair-minded historian, H. G. Wells, commented on the farce provided by the spectacle of Galloper Smith on the woolsack as Lord Birkenhead, Lord Chancellor of England, sentencing Sir Roger Casement to death for doing the very same thing that he himself, a Liverpool man, had done in Ulster when with Edward Carson – a briefless barrister from Dublin – he threatened to bring in the Kaiser if Ulster were to be included in the Home Rule Bill.

What, you will ask, were two such characters doing in Ulster? Ulster is the principal springboard where bigotry can be played upon by outsiders who adopt the Great and Glorious cause. Thus it came about that a man from Dublin and a man from Liverpool got themselves preferment in England at the expense of Ulster. Carson became Lord Carson, and Galloper Smith because Chancellor of England, with the title of Lord Birkenhead. He sat on the woolsack; Casement stood on the trap door. Such is the hatred and fear of Roman Catholicism in Ulster and England.

The support of 'her exiled children in America' – that was quite another thing. It was not the time to notice it, when English propaganda was endeavouring to bring America to Europe's aid. Better leave the Irish alone. The figures will never be known, but English propaganda in the United States before America came to Europe's (and Britain's) aid must have far exceeded the $800,000 which is now spent annually by England on pro-British propaganda in America.

So Ireland's manhood, as represented by the secret revolutionary organisation, the Irish Republican Brotherhood and her 'open military organisations', the 'Irish Volunteers and the Irish Citizen Army' were distributed among the prisons of England, Scotland and Wales. Arthur Griffith was in prison; his policy became all the stronger because of that. The first by-election in April, 1917, was won on the principle laid down by Griffith: boycott Westminster.

It was decided to put Count Plunkett up as a candidate because his son had died before a firing squad the year before in Kilmainham jail. The count was a count of the Holy Roman Empire, a slow-going man above middle size with a fine forehead and a long forked beard. There must not have been much behind the fine forehead because, after he had won his seat, it took all his backers could do to explain that he won it only because he was pledged not to go over to the Parliament in London. It took a lot to keep the count out of the limelight. Joe McGuinness won the second election; and the abstention policy of Sinn Fein was growing stronger. Not all 'Ireland's manhood' was in prison. It is difficult to put a whole nation in jail.

Griffith, Collins and Barton with the amiable Duggan were over in Hans Place, in London, fighting for fiscal control of their country. Nothing mattered so much. Economics rule the roost. Freedom and Liberty could come afterwards; they were political shibboleths used to fool Indians and such. What was 'freedom' compared with economic control of the country's wealth? Griffith and Collins were plenipotentiaries. Mark that. De Valera stayed behind. He was too important to go into the breach. He left that to 'plenipotentiaries'. Erskine Childers, whose typewriter never ceased night and day, was watchdog; and his job was to report everything. It was the one mistake of his life when Griffith yielded the leadership to De Valera. In fact it cost him his life, and the life of Collins went with it.

On the opposite side of the table sat Galloper Smith (Lord Birkenhead now), Churchill and Lloyd George: 'Could Satan send for such an end worthier tools than they?' Lloyd George bluffed – his bluff had carried him on through life. He spoke in Welsh to his secretary, Jones; politeness itself when you think of it. Winston scowled, as far as his face was capable of scowling; and Birkenhead, an admirer of Collins, sat pale. No word spoken at the table could be altered; but in Lady Lavery's house, 5, Cromwell Place, the talks could go on and not be recorded.

At last the 'Treaty' was signed by Griffith, Collins and Barton. Barton afterwards repudiated his signature; but then he was a cousin of Erskine Childers – Irishmen both!

The Treaty was brought back and passed by the Dail, by a majority of six. De Valera stormed – it was easy to storm; but where was he when Lloyd George and his trickery were being faced? De Valera did not go to the country. Oh no! The country had first to be roused.

32 *You Carry Caesar*

It is all very well to talk of wearing a revolver. Instead of you wearing it, it wears you. If you carry it in a hip pocket, your trousers sag on that side; one leg becomes longer than the other and you are inclined to trip. If it will fit in a coat pocket, the sight is liable to stick, and, as for the holster, leave that to detective stories. Now you will wonder what this is all about. I will try to explain.

On some occasions when I had finished gossiping in the Staff Room of the Richmond Hospital, I used to stop my car outside Tommy Costello's oculist's shop and go in to pick up the gossip of that part of the town which was known to me only as the external department of the hospital. He assured me that it was good for trade to have a well-known car seen outside his shop.

It did me good to call on Tommy. He had been a racing cyclist and, if he was not in the first flight, he was useful in increasing the field for others to beat. He used to complain of shooting pains down his right leg and tell me that he was being slowly poisoned with arsenic. I sent him to an X-ray man who reported that he could find nothing the matter, so I put him down as a hypochondriac. Soon he would forget his ailment and tell me about his dogs, which he kept behind the shop.

But one morning – it must have been late in December – he was full of mysterious whisperings. He waited until a customer had departed and then drew me into a little dark room behind the shop. Mystery and more mystery. At last he began: 'Last Sunday I was taking a stroll along the central road in the park. There was a group of four men in front of me. I heard them say distinctly, "We'll get Gogarty first."'

'What does that mean?' I asked.

Tommy went on, 'Two of them had belted coats like trench coats. The other two were taller. They looked back and saw me, and shut up. I stooped down and patted one of the dogs.'

Tommy knew things I did not know. He knew that mystery was in the air and, though he did not tell me directly, his manner was meant to warn me. It was enough for me to get his message and the warning implied. 'Remember what I told you and don't forget that you are a senator,' he said.

I met Desmond Fitzgerald, the Minister for Foreign Affairs, a few days later. To my surprise he took the message seriously. I did not mention my informant's name, though I will say this for Tommy, he had not bound me to secrecy though he was exposed to reprisals if it leaked out that he had warned one of the government. Now I was really astonished when Desmond said, 'You must go armed.'

'Oh hell!' said I.

'You are not leaving this office until I hand you a revolver.' He gave me a Colt with a long handle that did not suit my grip. Just to please him I took it. 'You must promise me to wear it,' he said.

The captain of the government guard saw it as I was leaving. 'Let me tell you one thing: you should never put that under your pillow. Wear it between your knees and shoot through the bedclothes if you are surprised in bed.'

What had I let myself in for? First I had called on Tommy and he had told me what he overheard in the Phoenix Park. Then I report this to Desmond and he makes me promise to carry a revolver! In fact, he gives me one. And now the captain of the guard, obviously an expert, tells me how to wear it in bed!

For a few days I tried carrying it. I forgot it in the toilet of the Shelbourne Hotel and a nervous fellow came shrieking out, 'There's a revolver on the seat!' I had to get it back from the manager.

I could not sit down with any comfort in a chair. The boys in Kit Marlowe's day wore daggers in their belts and they had to push them behind them and out over the edge of the bench when they sat down. I tried to feel warlike; but it soon passed. The spectacle of an armed doctor was too much of a contradiction for me. At last I threw Desmond's revolver in the drawer of my dressing table among ties and odds and ends. For that I was very sorry as it later will appear.

All the members of the government had themselves locked up in what was known as the Government Building, a building which was intended for a college of science under the British regime. The regiment guarding it was drawn mostly from the North.

Civil war brought treachery with it. Evidently the government did not trust the troops immediately about them. From that alone I saw how serious the situation was. John MacNeill, the dreamer who nearly wrecked the rebellion of Easter Week, J. J. Walsh, Minister of Posts and Telegraphs, Desmont Fitzgerald, William Cosgrove, and some others were in residence, which was little more than protective arrest.

I was free and accessible because it was easy to get into my house: a doctor is always accessible, or should be. That's what added to my anger when the raiders raided mine, a doctor's house.

It also helped me to be contemptuous of the kind of riffraff that had taken advantage of the civil war under the guise of patriotism. Had not the selfish and vain – I mean some of them – done so? It was under a pretence of impersonal devotion to a country in which they were not born, and to which they belonged not with the closest bonds, that they raised the civil war. Really their concern for their own ends and their vanity egged them on. Of course the watchdog, Erskine Childers – 'that damned Englishman,' as Griffith called him – was not far off to 'advise'. It was remarkable that between them they did not bring back the English. Never could the English have found a better excuse: 'Look at the Irish now. They cannot govern themselves.'

How far the British were behind Childers will never be known. If he were a member of their secret service, the one thing is certain is that it would remain a secret. Suffice to say that Childers spent his youth and manhood in the English service. Gerald Balfour said of his book, *The Riddle of the Sands,* 'If it is a novel, it is one of the best ever written. If it is a true account, it is the creator of the Baltic Fleet.'

One evening about eight o'clock on January 12, 1923, if I remember rightly, I was lolling in my bath. The bathroom was next to my dressing room. I was alone in the house but for a few servants. My family had gone to the country for the Christmas holidays. I lay in the bath and steam filled the room. I was trying to turn off a tap with my toes when I

189

felt something cold on the back of my neck. I looked around. There was a gunman in a belted trench coat of dark blue material.

'Out! And be quick!' He waved the gun.

'If this is murder, may I scribble a few lines to my wife?' Pale and agitated, he again threatened me with the gun.

'For a housebreaker, you seem very nervous,' I said.

Through the door of the bathroom I could see two gunmen on the stairs. I put a towel about me and cursed myself for leaving the gun in the drawer of the mock Chippendale table in the dressing room. To open that drawer it was necessary to place a foot against either leg of the table; even then the drawer was jammed.

Oh, how I regretted that gun now! I could have blown the head off the unsuspecting gunman and then rushed at the two guarding the stairs. Who expects a naked man to be armed? Slowly I drew on the trousers of my dinner suit and put on the comfortable old shoes which were down at heel. The other two gunmen were now in the room with me, while I dressed.

I looked in the mirror. My face was almost white. That does not come from thought. Maybe it does: what about 'sicklied o'er'? But the pupils were dilated. However, my thinking was unimpaired.

I was thinking that even if I could get my gun out, and find the trigger guard unobstructed by a tie or two, I could never beat the gunman who had his gun in my kidney to the draw. Geometry was against it. He had to move his finger only half an inch and my spine would be shot through. Besides, if I opened the drawer, it would reveal the fact that I had a pistol and 'justify' the already worked-up gunman in putting an end to me. He could discharge my revolver after I was dead. No, I had better leave the drawer alone.

Over by the fireplace I saw a pair of riding boots with trees in them. If I could get the tree out, I would have a weapon. But the brain, which was beginning to get hysterical with fear and excitement, thought absurdly of Fergus McRoy and his wooden sword. Amusing if the situation were in accord.

'Put those bloody pumps in your pocket and put on these.' I was handed a pair of skiing boots and an old coat of buffalo leather with the furry side in. They must have found these on the back stairs. So there was probably a gunman there and I was counting on those back stairs to make a dash for it. Hopeless now.

Clad in a pair of trousers, a white shirt, a great coat and heavy shoes, I was led down. A hunchbacked woman was waiting in the hall. I noticed that the telephone wire had been dragged out. A large sedan stood at the door with a big fellow at the wheel. The little crippled woman got in beside him. Evidently she was used for the purpose of making it look like a social visit if they were interrupted by the guards.

A gunman sat on either side of me; I could feel the pressure of a gun on each kidney. Another sat in my lap and lay back. I was crushed into the cushions and completely out of sight. We started.

'If you shout when we are passing any of your bloody soldiers, you will be blown to smithereens.'

Well, Julius Caesar was in a like position when he was taken by pirates in the Adriatic, and he promised them that he would crucify them all. They took it laughingly; but they were all crucified later.

'Wouldn't you like to be — now?' He named the unhallowed name.

'Anything but that,' I mumbled, my mouth smothered by the gunman's back.

It dawned on me that maybe I was being taken for a hostage for the two men that were held prisoners in Dundalk jail. They had been executed that morning! It won't be a rest cure for me when the gunmen find that out.

To say the least of it, my position was precarious. One of the corner boys asked: 'Isn't it a fine thing to die to a flash?' 'Better,' I muttered, 'than to be that scoundrel.' But oh, what waste: my life for theirs! If and when I get out of their clutches, it will be my turn. This was little better than associating myself with Julius Caesar: but then there is no accounting for a mind distracted by fear.

We reached the last house by the Liffey bank – at the time vacant – where the river meets the first weir at Trinity College Boat House. Here at full tide the water can be nine feet deep.

I was bundled through the small gate in the wall.

'Can I tip the driver?' I asked. That made them all angry, the driver most of all.

I was taken into a dark cellar, evidently a coal cellar, and made to stand against the wall. Seven men in two ranks stood in front of the door. One of them began to strike matches. Those in the front row evidently did not trust him. He might claim that he had no hand in the shooting if they were caught. There was an altercation. 'How can I strike matches if I have to shoot?' he said.

Somebody struck another light. I could see the pistols wavering in the front row. I remember thinking that it was more for the sake of the firing squad than of their prisoner that they bind his eyes. Now I realised why a victim gave gold to the headsman to dispatch him quickly. The match went out. I took two steps to the side. When I tried to get back so as not to show the white feather to such little jackeens, my feet were stuck to the ground.

I have seen films where the crowd sticks to the ground and is unable to move. It must have been thought, and my contempt for the undisciplined rats, that made me able to stare them down.

The captain of the gunmen ordered, 'Soldiers, forward and seize prisoner. We are going for a lamp.' Five men came forward and led me out.

I noticed that the house was parallel to the river, which runs west to east. It was in the small cellar at the east end that I was stood against the wall. Now I was being taken to the west end of the house with the river not twenty yards away. The corner boys took me to what had evidently been a music room. Music books were scattered on the floor, which had been torn up along the wall. The torn-up planks and some of the music books were piled up to make a fire, for the night was very cold. The fire soon blazed; but the unheated chimney smoked.

'Is it a part of the Republican programme to gas a prisoner before shooting him?' I asked.

'What d'ye mean?'

'There's too much smoke in the room.'

'Ye won't notice it when they come back with the lamp.'

They were shivering from cold. I tried to lecture on small arms. 'Those automatics are dangerous. They have to have the lock drawn back before they will fire. Let me show you.' I reached for one of their guns; but there was nothing doing. With my ear on a stalk I listened for the return of the sedan with the lamp and the head gunman. Then I would be shot and my body thrown into the flooded river.

I bowed my head and groaned. 'You fellows have given me such a fright that I'll soon have diarrhoea.' I waited for the remark to soak in.

It is a vulgar notion that fright produces diarrhoea, whereas the fact is that all the secretions of the body are dried up.

Whether the remark had sunk in or not, I was terrified that the motor would return – 'Quick, a guard,' I said hurriedly. The fools seized me and stuck the gun into each side of my heavy coat. In the near darkness I slipped my arms out of the coat, while I remained inside it.

Up rushed the outside watchman, on whom I had not counted. 'What's all this?'

'He has to go out.'

It was dark outside but I feared that the eyes of the outside watchman would be accustomed to the dark. By the feel of gravel under my left foot and the smooth cement threshold about an inch above the gravel under my right, I knew that I was clear of the house. In a broken voice I said to the guards, 'Would you mind holding my coat?'

They were still holding the coat as I was going swiftly down the river with the current. The black water had swallowed me up.

Oh, how I rejoiced in spite of the shock. Now for the Caesar act! But I had some swimming to do and the river was icy cold. I tried to grasp overhanging willows but they passed through my numbed hands.

Cross to opposite bank? What a fool I would be! The gunmen would rush over there. It would take them only some minutes to cross the bridge at Liffey Bank and to break into the grounds that went beside the stream. I floated along and I vowed two swans to the river if it bore me safe to shore.

Our good Father Liffey received my gift duly.

The lights of the city began to appear, or were they the lights of the houses by the river? I was looking and wondering when all at once I felt that I could no longer breathe.

I am too young for a heart attack; and I can swim easily. What is the matter?

I pushed my face under and it came up clear. I could breathe freely now. What had happened? A cake of foam had choked my nose and mouth.

At last a submerged willow was directly in front of me. I put my arm round it and I was immediately swept under. For this I was ready. When I came up on the other side, I got my other arm along it and gradually moved ashore. After crawling slowly up the muddy bank I tried to stand up. At first I could feel only my knees; all was frozen from the knees down.

I made my way to a lighted house and looked through the window. Four women and a man were at supper. One of the women saw me and the table shook. Now all but the man were shaking and moaning. My mind was working like a dynamo. I must have looked a sorry sight, pale and with but one shirt sleeve, with blood trickling down my forehead.

'I am not dead,' I gasped.

The moaning ceased. I had been taken for a ghost. No one had ever come into that house from the river before.

They refused to give me help. Were they afraid of reprisals? Who knows or cares? The man said, 'Come along with me.' I did not tell him who I was. Maybe he guessed. Least said, soonest mended. He took me down the garden and opened a door in the wall. 'There is the depot across the Phoenix Park.'

I crossed the park and suddenly felt very weak. Suddenly I was caught in the glare of a searchlight. With my only sleeve raised, I walked along the beam. After a while I came to the depot railings. A sentry asked me who I was but I could not answer; I could only make hiccup-like noises.

Evidently the sentry feared a ruse; there must have been firing behind me. He would not let me in. Some officer came, and by this time I could speak: 'I am Senator Gogarty ... I have been kidnapped ... I have just escaped.' He caused the gate to be opened. The police surgeon, whom I knew, took me in charge and I was put to bed. Hot bottles and hot tea.

About two in the morning, after much telephoning and red tape, three armoured cars were sent for me. I rode in the middle one and passed in triumph through a city that saw me going to my death some hours ago.

Such are the vicissitudes of politics. I did not think of it in that way at the time. If I do so now, it is because I can regard the incident dispassionately.

I was taken to the Government Building and I was given Desmond Fitzgerald's bed, but I did not sleep for hours. I am afraid that planning retribution kept me awake. I remained in the Government Building for three weeks. Meanwhile, a telegram was sent to reassure my family. They returned to Dublin at once.

I used to slip out of my house, which was but a block and a half from the Government Building. When the ministers got to know of it, I was given a guard of eight men. The steed had been stolen but was found and guarded now!

My kidnapping would not have been believed had the government boys not found my coat. A few days later a man called with a bullet, evidently from a .38, its nose somewhat bent. It was dug out of the spine of the ringleader who had raided my house and carried me off. O'Leary was his name. He was a tram conductor on the Clonskea line. He had died 'to a flash', shrieking inappropriately under the wall of the Tranquilla Convent in Upper Rathmines. Later the others were caught.

I felt normal again. It was said of my father that his

enemies all came to a bad end, I had taken after him.

I did not know what the government thought of my arrest and escape. I did not like that proof which depended only on my coat. But when Senator Bagwell was taken from a house in Howth, there was no uncertainty. It was clear that an effort was being made to intimidate senators and so prevent any laws, punitive and otherwise, from being enacted. Promptly the government announced that twenty prisoners would be shot if Senator Bagwell was not released unharmed forthwith. He was 'allowed to escape'. That was the turning point: opposition was broken. Later, when I inquired why a similar proclamation had not been issued in my case, the Prime Minister said, smiling, 'You escaped?'

The newspapers did not share any scepticism that may have attended my escape. They were full of it. One of them published a photograph with an arrow pointing down the wall by which I fell into the water. To get it the photographer must have used a boat. One paper said that the gunmen might as well have expected to hold an electric eel as to hold me. That pleases me very much.

Credit must be given to men like Senator Bagwell, Jameson and Guinness, and Lord Mayo. Very easily they could have thrown in the sponge. They held on instead. Once they had resigned themselves to a change in the order of things, they set themselves to accept the Free State. They gritted their teeth. They did not turn tail even though they had been brought up with affinities for England, as indeed we all had, though with less to lose.

Renvyle House was burned, all but the rooms of the caretaker at the end of one wing. How the flames were controlled at all is a mystery; but it was no mystery to me to realise that the peasantry were hand-in-glove with those in the civil war for reasons far removed from 'patriotism' as far as the civil war was removed from it; the peasants wanted my land and they cared not how they came by it.

Lord Mayo's house was burned. Here there were pictures of historical import, all destroyed, together with evidences of a culture second to none in Europe. That is why I say that De Valera did more harm to Ireland than Cromwell; he had more to destroy. Compensate senators as the government later did, no compensation could restore these things.

Of all I lost in Renvyle House, I remember chiefly a self-portrait of my mother at sixteen with her auburn hair divided in the middle, her plain blue dress, and all-pervading air of sweetness and simplicity. No compensation can restore that.

As I have said, a guard of eight men and a sergeant was now assigned to me. The guard occupied a small room off the hall. One of them wounded himself and blew the leg off a Chippendale chair during his guardianship.

During odd evenings firing from the streets would break the drawing-room windows. The guard would reply after an interval, which I timed at nine minutes. Were they in collusion with the enemy? They might have been: everyone must live; or he thinks so, and does not always consider the means.

One man who disregarded the shots through the windows and the falling plaster was Æ, who came to see us every Friday night, rain or storm. So absorbed was he in affirming his own philosophy that he either did not hear, or ignored, such interruptions as shots through the windows and, nine minutes later, my guards' prompt reply. The ottoman on which the philosopher sat was removed out of the line of fire.

It is one thing to have a guard but another to have patients searched for arms. Neither makes for confidence, security or, in a doctor's case, practice. Luckily, I had enough patients in London and other parts of England to form the nucleus of a new practice.

With much reluctance I moved to London, where I was feted as a hero. I did not know that I was one. I thought that it was the hospitality that I might expect as one who had made a dramatic escape from De Valera's civil war. It took Seymour Leslie, a first cousin of Winston Churchill, to

197

disabuse my dream. 'You arrived at just the right moment, when London had nothing better to do,' he said.

Every Wednesday I made it a point to cross to Dublin in order to take my place in the Senate. I would not give it to De Valera to say that his tactics had kept one voter from voting. For a while I was met at the boat by a guard in mufti. Of course, I could not know whether they were the enemy or not. It would have been easy for the enemy to masquerade as my guard and meet me at the mail boat and carry me off again. I had a Colt which I displayed as I sat on the back seat. Had the automobile gone by an indirect route, I intended to blow out the driver's brains and take the consequences. Luckily, nothing diverted the car. This, I think, goes to show that I was somewhat nervous and shaken by the kidnapping though I did not feel it in the excitement of escape.

It was harder to bear the confinement on the boat – I was forbidden to go on deck until the vessel docked at Holyhead and a representative of Scotland Yard met me. After a while I handed in my Colt to one of the big five in New Scotland Yard, which is directly over the Thames and looks across the river on St. Thomas's Hospital, where the son of the man who received my revolver was an intern. For all I know, it is still in the drawer in his office, though he himself is long ago departed. His name was Kearney, if my memory holds.

33 'They Had Nothing Better To Do'

The dislocation of my practice was compensated to some extent by the pleasure I got from meeting old friends in England. Compton Mackenzie edited and owned *The Gramophone*, a thriving magazine. Christopher Stone owned Field Place, Horsham; that was where Percy Bysshe

Shelley was born. I went down to Sussex to stay with him.

Dermot Freyer came in and out of his famous father's house in Harley Street, where there was a lift which his friend Tancred used to stop between two floors until the right word was found for whatever poem he was composing. I think that Sir Peter Freyer's patience was at last worn out by his son's friend. His son, too, may have fretted it somewhat, especially when he put under 'Amusements' in *Who's Who*, 'Trying to pass Half M.B. Examinations.' Perhaps the editors of *Who's Who* thought that it was the great surgeon they were listing and that he meant that his hobby was presiding at examinations.

Lady Leslie, the witty and vivacious, was my great friend. To her I owed introductions to people that I, in my walk of life, would never have met. She knew everybody. She it was who told me of Count Keyserling, gross and unkempt, who came for a week and stayed for three weeks until his hostess had to leave her town house to get rid of him. There I met Benjamin Guinness, the banker, who was restricted to three divorces by his bank!

At Lady Lavery's, in 5, Cromwell Place, and at George Moore's house, in Ebury Street, I often called. I had the misfortune one day of telling Moore that I had lunched with Lady Ebury, the wife of his landlord.

'She has the best cuisine in London. What did you eat?'

'To tell you the truth, I never noticed. I talk so much.'

He threw up his hands. 'You are a barbarian. Tell her to ask me.' But I was on no footing to advise Lady Ebury as to her guests. I was hardly a guest myself. Three weeks elapsed and no invitation came to George. He wrote a letter to *The Times* headed 121, Ebury Street, and beginning, 'From the long slum in which I live.'

I met the Duke of Connaught, the best-mannered man I ever knew. When he, with his hand to his ear, heard who I was, he told me that that morning he played eighteen holes of golf and spent two hours in the saddle and 'What do you think of that?'

'You are theatened with immortality, sir.'

Later, at lunch in his place, he remembered that and repeated it to Sir John Leslie, who was harder of hearing than the duke.

'What was that? Did he say "threatened with immortality"?'

In Lady Leslie's house in Great Cumberland Place I met two crown princesses of Greece. They were young girls, pink and white. 'Make a deeper bow than usual; and do not speak until they speak to you,' I was instructed. It seems that there are few themes to discuss with royalty. They must be born to be bored. If they spoke of the weather, one might be tempted to refer to 'Moving forever onward through most pellucid air', through which the Greeks of old went. But the Greek princesses probably had never been to Greece!

Yes, certainly I was feted even if 'London had nothing better to do'. Strange how susceptible I was to titles: Lady Leslie, Lady Leconfield, the Duke of Connaught, Crown Princesses; the Earl of Granard, Senator. It was rather amusing to find his house in Halkin Street with gates locked and guarded. It must have impressed the King, who dined there every second Friday. It did not impress me. Lord Granard's castle, at Castleforbes, had the hall blown in; but there was method in the madness of the bombardiers. Though they had orders from headquarters in Dublin to burn Senator the Earl of Granard's house, they only made a gesture. They did not want to be unemployed.

Much the same thing happened to Sir Hector McCalmont in County Kilkenny. He warned the locals that if his place were injured he would remove his racing stable elsewhere. Economics limited De Valera's policy of ruin: he could not bring civilisation altogether down, though he gave the country a lot of rubble.

My office was in Grosvenor Street, in the same street as Bruce Bruce-Porter – were there two spiders on his coat of arms? – and one of the mistresses of Edward VII.

I met Galloper Smith, who was now Lord Birkenhead.

His house was in Grosvenor Gardens down by the Victoria Station. I lunched there once or twice. I remember what a good mimic his daughter was. I must have forgotten the part he had played, for I kept thinking how Griffith took to him. Ah, it was because of the Galloper's admiration for Collins and not because of Griffith. The Galloper was a great rake. There have been many great rakes in English history; Charlie Fox was one. Wilkes another; and now comes Lord Birkenhead. I am wondering what Lord Birkenhead saw in me. Could it have been an affinity? I hope not.

Mrs Benjamin Guinness was a lavish hostess. Had it not been bad form to look a gift horse in the mouth, you might have wondered how expensive was the Guinness establishment. Many a lunch had I in Great Cumberland Place or Street. The evenings, too, had their entertainment. Nelson Keyes and Tallulah Bankhead combined to keep the boredom away. I remember laughing so much at Nelson Keyes that I forgot who it was he was impersonating! Whatever it was, laughter dissolved it. I remember being so amused that I secretly commended the bank for forbidding Benjamin to get rid of the third Mrs Guinness! Tallulah, raging on with hoarse voice and distorted features, was giving a parody of some prominent actress. Everyone laughed and I felt so indebted to Tallulah and our hostess that I invited them both to lunch at the Berkeley, which is a well-known hotel restaurant at the corner of Berkeley Street and Piccadilly. They came; but the spell was gone: it was day for one thing; and it was another for another.

When I wonder that I have forgotten what made me laugh so much at Nelson Keyes, I forget that the things that amuse so much can rarely be remembered. How often do you hear someone trying to tell a good story he heard overnight and failing utterly?

One morning as I walked down King's Road, Chelsea, I ran again into Seymour Leslie. 'I suppose we will meet at dinner to-night?' Now our hostess was reputed to be the biggest lion hunter in London. In fact an American girl who did not know the idiom once said to her, 'I hear that you are a great shot.'

For a moment which was, alas, too transient, I was filled with hope that I might appear to be 'a big shot' in the lady's eyes. Seymour quickly disabused all such vain misgivings when I asked the question, 'Who is her guest of honour?' 'The Unknown Soldier's widow.'

Our hostess, who often gave a tea party to Freyer and myself, one evening accosted us: 'You two are always laughing, standing over there in a corner. What are you laughing about?' I waited for the onus to fall on Freyer.

'About Tancred,' he said.

'Who is Tancred?'

Then I chipped in, 'Oh, he is a friend of Freyer's.'

'Well then, see that he comes to dinner here – let me see – oh, on this day week.' It was an order issued by 'She who must be obeyed.'

Freyer and I took counsel together. 'It will be rather difficult now that Tancred lives in a mild mental home,' Freyer said. 'But, as you are a doctor, the doctor in charge may let him out if you ask him as a favour. Surely Tancred is harmless.'

Dr Travers was very obliging. He would let Tancred out provided that I guaranteed to return him by midnight. A cinderella part!

It was Wednesday when Fryer and I turned up. Dinner was at eight-thirty but so far there was no Tancred. Perhaps he has got over-excited seeing that he is to be enlarged for the dinner. Perhaps Travers thought better of it and determined not to let him out after all. Perhaps Tancred is depressed. It was getting on for nine and everyone was restless, also hungry, when the door burst open and in rushed our friend.

'Well, well, well,' he said. 'It is awfully kind of you to invite me to dinner on the recommendation of those two oddities over there. You know I would never have been discourteous enough to come late but a very remarkable thing happened to me as I sat in the subway. By the way, I must tell you of a perfectly infallible method I have of judging character. It is quite infallible. Yes, quite ...' He broke off into a wild laugh.

Our hostess was too puzzled to be amazed. 'What is it?' she asked faintly.

'What is it? Let me explain. It is, like all great inventions, simple in the extreme: I simply judge people by the advertisements under which they sit. Now then, how came I to be late? I'll tell you. There was a lovely girl in a corner of the coach. She had a golden costume and stockings of light bronze. We were all alone. Now one would think that the social amenities would be somewhat relaxed three hundred feet under the earth's surface. Not a bit of it! She was sitting under Green and Black's tea, 'Used by all the big pots.' I at once realised that she was a big pot herself. But she took absolutely no notice of me. Why? Amazing! Surreptitiously I stole a glance at the advertisement under which I was sitting. SPARKLING MOSELLE! No wonder the poor child was frightened out of her wits.'

Our hostess did not appear to see any out-of-wits stuff in her guest. However, when at twelve, precisely, two quietly uniformed men without epaulets tapped our friend lightly on the shoulder, it may have occurred to her then. Probably it did, for neither Freyer nor I ever saw the interior of her house again.

I met an old friend, Lady Islington. Years back before taxis were used at all, she insisted on riding on a jaunting car in Dublin. The horse bolted, which showed unusual energy in a hackney. Her ladyship persisted in attributing the stopping of the runaway and the saving of her life to me although the exact fact is that the horse ran into a member of the Dublin Metropolitan Police and was 'taken into custody' with the jarvey.

Lady Islington was delighted with Dublin, which is the largest Georgian city extant, and it was this Georgianism that attracted her. She instructed me to buy Henrietta Street for her. Henrietta Street is a slum which, it was rumoured, Alderman Meade purchased for £900, which was then about the equivalent of £1400. Some of the finest examples of Georgian architecture were in Henrietta Street before the houses were denuded of mantels, stairways and doors; all except the two houses on the right as you approach the Inns of Court, which are now some sort of convent. For once in my life I was sufficiently businesslike to put the matter in the hands of – not a lawyer, oh no! – but an architect.

I chose Charles – I think that was his first name – O'Connor and asked him to get in touch with the man of business who represented Lady Islington. I cannot take much credit for this precaution because it arose, not from a knowledge of business, but from my knowledge of the transience of enthusiasms, especially the enthusiasms of ladies. I did not wish to be left with a slum on my hands and no answers to my letters of expostulation. O'Connor reported that, as a result of the habitation of slum dwellers for so long, the woodwork was impregnated with acrid odours which could not be got rid of, so the houses were useless for anything but tenements. Visions of fashion being revived, and of the north side of the city coming again into prominence, faded before the architect's report. So Lady Islington contented herself with her Adam house in one of the London squares, and with her moated house in the country.

It was to that house I was invited and in that house I stayed. I remember the tapestry which hung on the wall of my bedroom, and the house with its towers of rosy brick at the corners. The house rose from the moat; and the towers at the corners were capped with green bronze. That is all I remember. I cannot tell in what shire the house was, but I remember the long drive through the park and the oaks that stood with their branches out at right angles and not slanting upwards like the branches of quicker-growing trees. I remember Lord Islington's cigar after breakfast; as for the rest, it is harder to recall than a dream.

So ended my pleasant interlude in London, if you can call it an interlude where the fun was all on one side.

And then I went to south Sussex, to Petworth House. Petworth House is one of the greatest houses in England. It belongs to one of the largest landowners left in that country, Lord Leconfield. He ran his own pack of hounds, the Petworth Hounds, and they say often ran a fox to earth without leaving his own demesne. He had a disability or two: one was that he could not whisper. That was due probably to his having to shout across fields and spinneys as the hunt progressed.

To that house I was invited. I arrived about dinnertime; and, as there are no cocktails or other refreshments before dinner in a well-conducted English house, I felt somewhat depressed. This was not lessened by my being ushered into a small room where his lordship was seated with a blub-faced fellow beside him. The blub-faced fellow was Winston Churchill, who had loosed the Black and Tans on Ireland. Before I could speak to mine host, I was attacked by Churchill, who spoke as if he had a cleft palate: 'Gogarty, now that you have got your liberty, what are you going to do with it?' I took a very long count. When at last I pulled myself up, I answered very distinctly, 'Oh, we are going to use it to discriminate between our friends, *Mister* Churchill.' He gave a grunt, rose, and, as I thought, left the room. I turned to Lord Leconfield, 'Why is your guest so unamiable?' His shouted reply alarmed me: 'Don't you know? Nobody can trust the fellow. He crossed the Floor twice.' This was an allusion to the ratting of Winston, who was born a Conservative, then became a Liberal. On that occasion he suffered the greatest insult ever offered to a man in the House of Commons: when he entered with the Liberal party, the Conservatives rose to a man and left the House. Another grunt and this time Winston left the room.

Afterwards I met Winston as he was crackling up the stairs (his right knee emitted the rhetoric). 'Are you playing polo these days?' He did not answer. I was snubbed, ignored, brushed off. Doubtless he was going up to study *The Decline and Fall*.

And then I remembered Mrs John Jameson's request

when her brother was about to be sacked by Lloyd George. Probably Churchill thought the same, and in his opinion I had no right to be in Petworth House. And, if you are to judge by his host's distrust, neither had he. My mind went back to F. C. Crowley's theory of 'a popular' man.

34 *Politics And Palls*

'You must accept the governor-generalship. I won't have Healy, a man who betrayed Parnell.'

So spoke Griffith to me. I remember the incident well. We were walking along Nassau Street, passing a house with a large 8-in. gilt wood.

So I am not 'Down among the Dead Men' after all. In fact, in Arthur's opinion I am a better man than George Russell, Æ; and like Larry O'Neill and Nelson's Pillar, I stand where I did twenty years ago.

Now don't tell me that the mind cannot think of more than one thing at the same time. Mine thought of half a dozen things at once. The first was that Tim Healy had been working for the job and that pressure was being put on Griffith to accept him. What chance had I against Tim Healy? He had been in Parliament for more than thirty years and he had influence with those who were forming the Free State; and he probably was over in London now wire-pulling. Another thought that sprang up simultaneously was that the very fact that Healy had betrayed Parnell was in his favour. Parnell betrayed himself; but if Healy got the credit for it, it would help him now with the Church whose tool he was; and the Church was the real ruler of Ireland.

'When I wanted a place to meet certain emissaries from England, you risked all and lent me your house. When I asked . . . he hummed and hawed.' Griffith was referring to his meetings with Asquith and the disguised Lord Derby.

Politics has rewards out of all proportion to the merits of the subject, I thought. Then I thought, I cannot accept the job. I don't want the limelight. I am not a leader any more than Griffith is. Little did I think at the time that the post required little leadership, or character for that matter. Then, at the back of my mind there was the distinction to accept money from the nation; but this I could not say very well because Griffith was in receipt of a salary which he had earned by twenty years of hard work in grinding poverty. The post of governor-general was a sinecure. The governor was a mere rubber stamp or figurehead. Why should anybody take money for his convictions?

We walked on in silence while I pondered how to get out of the difficulty without offending Griffith, who was so well disposed towards me. I felt that, try as he might, he could not appoint anyone who would not be a nominee also of the Church; and I certainly was not likely to be one. Perhaps it was this thought, that Griffith could not 'deliver the goods', that made me so unenthusiastic.

Yes: I should be enthusiastic. I should thank Griffith. I was about to do that when luckily we sighted Jim Montgomery, who hailed us and pointed down Molesworth Street in the direction of the Bailey. For a while the crisis had passed. Jimmy's smile was meant for us both. To Griffith he said, 'Well you've certainly done it. You have taken England's hand off Ireland's throat and out of her pocket as you said you would.'

Griffith was silent; but he was pleased for all that. We entered the Bailey and went upstairs to the smoking room. The usual desultory talk. Griffith did not talk politics when there were people about. 'How are you making out, Jim, as a film censor?' 'Oh, between the Devil and the Holy See!' And so we walked on.

There was a call from the Government Building: Could I come at once to see the President, Arthur Griffith? He is far from well. I stopped whatever work was in hand and rushed down about two short blocks to see the President. I found him lying on a pallet in a small room at the back of the offices of the Minister for Justice on one of the higher floors. Seorsam McNicholl was in the room.

One glance and I asked for the telephone. It was necessary to get permission to move anybody from the Government Building, and for this permission Generals O'Murleigh and O'Sullivan had to be consulted.

'Where do you propose to take him?' I was asked.

'To the nuns' private hospital in 96, Lower Leeson Street.' I could not think of a place less likely to be raided than the nuns' private home.

The President was removed in an ambulance and the best room in 96, Lower Leeson Street was prepared. His blood pressure was very high. It is not necessary to go into details of his illness. When he was more or less conscious, he complained bitterly at having been removed from his work, particularly at such a time. However, his complaints failed to alter the fact that he was a very sick man and required both rest and isolation, especially from such friends as McNicholl.

A few days passed. I was not happy that I had to choose the nuns' home because of the fact that a member of the visiting staff of St Vincent's Hospital, which was round the corner in St Stephen's Green and in connection with which 96 was run, had the rather unprofessional idea that he could call without ceremony on any doctor's patient. Besides, there was no protection from nurses' gossip as there would have been had I sent the President to Elpis in Lower Mount Street. But this was regarded as a Protestant nursing home and, of course, was out of bounds for such a man as the Catholic President of the Irish Free State.

He remained in the nursing home for over a week. The last time I saw Arthur Griffith alive he was sitting uncomfortably in a chair in the middle of the room. On his knees were the day's papers. He could read them upside down as well as straight for he had been at one time a compositor.

'When will you let me out of this?' was his only question.

'When you are fit to leave.'

'I am fit.'

One morning there was a call from one of his nurses. Could I come at once? Mr Griffith was far from well. I took my time, for I thought that he was again giving trouble about being in a nursing home. I arrived to find him dead. He had never recovered from seeing, as he thought, his life's work ruined by treachery. George Washington beholding the devastation caused by Benedict Arnold on the property of the people is a case in point.

The funeral of Arthur Griffith went through historic College Green. The West Front of Trinity College looked out on the Bank of Ireland. Behind us in Grafton Street many shops continued to do business. Why did I not realise it then? While those of the people of Ireland who had not been split by the Splitter were in a state of emotion, business was being 'carried on as usual'. Economics stood while politics shook to its foundations. The Founder of the Irish Free State was being carried to his grave: 'The blood of some of the members of the Government' (*Irish Independent*, March 18, 1922) was waded through. The first victim was dead. The next was to follow within ten days. The Splitter and the Morrigas had spoken. Michael Collins was ambushed and killed in County Cork on August twenty-second. But there was business 'as usual' in Dublin. The Irish people could be as divided as possible so long as England had control of its markets.

I thought of the little man who lay dead before us. I had known him since 1899 or perhaps earlier, in the days of An Stad. Poverty did not shake his devotion. He was a poor man all his life, poor to the verge of starvation. Unbribable, firm, courageous, lovable, and fast to his friends. I remembered carrying his rifle as he marched through College Street. He was in the green uniform of the Volunteers. He was surrounded now by the soldiers in the green uniform of a state that was his own creation. They marched with his funeral cortege. My eyes were filled with tears.

Michael Collins was dead. Misfortune upon misfortune!

Behind and above the right ear of Michael Collins there was a small irregular wound in the bone of the skull. There was no exit wound. A ricochet evidently. He had been ambushed in his Lancia; not very far off from where De Valera was hiding. He died in the arms of Emmet Dalton and his body was brought to Dublin by boat from Cork because the railway viaduct had been blown up. Of the arrival of the boat with the body in the rainy darkness, I have written elsewhere.

For days he lay in state in the Town Hall, and Doyle-Jones, the sculptor, did a magnificent head of him in white bronze. Collins, who alone held Ireland together in the two years of the Black and Tan, Lloyd George and Hamar Greenwood outrages. There is a curse upon Ireland politically: she betrays her own children.

35 'Trowle The Bonnie Bowl With Me'

Going down Molesworth Street, I met Monty, the Film Censor. He was leaving his office and turning west, which is in the direction of the Bailey.

'Stepping westward, eh? A wildish destiny?'

He smiled as we crossed Duke Street together and went upstairs to our Parnassus in the Bailey.

George had come from the Brewery. Neil was there and, for a marvel, James Stephens. Neil was 'in possession' so Lewis took the orders.

Stephens spoke up: 'You know Neil has just published his poem about the wasp that got into the Rathmines bus, which was filled with sour-faced men and fat women. The bus was going citywards. How does it go, Neil?'

Neil would not say. Stephens remembered the admirable last line: 'That sunlight joined the sun again.'

George Redding moved his chair to make room for me.

In a low voice he told how he was summoned by the Board of the Brewery and asked if he were prepared to go to London. He answered that the interests of the Brewery were his interests. I was saddened at the thought of losing George.

Stephens had to be off and he left unobtrusively. He was an unobtrusive man. The most lyrical poet of them all when it came to lyricism, Yeats not excepted. But Stephens' flights were short and few.

I once asked James Stephens if he were ever sacked. 'No,' he said, 'but I sacked once myself. Macready's, a firm of attorneys, were paying me the enormous sum of 12/6 a week and a partner of the firm announced, "Owing to our policy of retrenchments" – one of them had just run off with a woman to Canada – "it will be necessary to reduce your salary to 10/-".' Stephens' answer was to take his hat and walk out.

He was by far the best scrivener and stenographer any firm ever had. He could do, and he often had to do, the work of three men. And after his gruelling day, he could write a lyric with the best; or compose *The Crock of Gold*, a 'best seller' of world acclaim.

'That short story of Stephens', "Hunger," is largely his own experience,' I said. 'Poverty ground the little man all through youth, but Poverty never got him down nor suffering either. When Lord Gray sent his lady friend a copy of *The Crock of Gold*, he wrote something like this – and it shows what a judge of character was Lord Gray:

'James Stephens is quite young, about twenty-seven, married ... He was hungry for weeks as a boy, slept in the parks, fought with the swans for a piece of bread. He lived on the kindness of poor people who liked the queer little fellow, and yet he has grown up with the most independent spirit. Nobody can get a whimper out of him ... He is small in stature but quite big inside, large and roomy.'

As far as my quotation went, it only bored the company. Neil was the first to show resentment.

'Oh, for God's sake!' he implored. 'It used to be dogs: now it is swans.' Neil was getting to his acerb state.

'There's a magnificent portrait of Stephens by Tuohy,' I remarked.

'I understand that the painter committed suicide,' Neil shot out.

'What's this about the telegram, "All is forgiven provided you don't come back"?' Monty asked.

My eulogy of Stephens had gone awry. Moral: You should never praise one Irishman to another Irishman.

> If I were as wise as they
> I would stray apart and brood;
> I would beat a hidden way
> Through the quiet heather spray
> To a sunny solitude.

I said to myself part of a poem by Stephens to the goats; and I beat a hidden way. I got out; no one protested at my departure but Monty followed. 'Time to go. Neil was getting sarcastic,' he said.

As we walked along, we spoke of Neil; he begins a drinking session in silence. Once the guilt feeling, or whatever it is, is drowned, he grows humorous and witty and then later on he becomes everyone's enemy. He sees an enemy in a friend.

'Half the trouble with Neil,' Monty informed me, 'is that he realises now that Arthur Griffith did not like him, and so he takes it out on any of Griffith's friends who survive.'

'You are taking Neil's politics seriously. Surely Griffith never cared what Neil thought?'

'You are wrong there. Griffith never forgave disloyalty to the cause and with disloyalty he had reason to associate Neil.'

'Why had he reason?' I asked; but Monty ran for his bus. As I watched his running figure, I realised that Monty, like Æ, would not say anything disagreeable about anybody. There was no doubt about Monty's loyalty. Had he not hidden Mulcahy when Mulcahy was head of the resistance movement?

Was I right about Æ? He could get indignant at times; and his indignation knew no bounds when he was informed about Neil's attitude to Griffith and the Treaty.

> Praise in your maudlin verse the men who died.
> Look black and bitter when their judges pass
> Who not to see your country glorified
> Would stop the drinking of a single glass.

Why is it that I like something imperfect even in a bar? It may be that I am afraid that perfection is too transient. It may be – awful thought – that I want to feel superior. Well, knowing myself as I think I do, although I do not dwell on it, I will venture to say that is not the answer. The probable reason is that I am afraid of perfection. My Eden requires a serpent.

I should have seen that something was brewing when Neil refused to help Stephens out when Stephens was praising and trying to quote Neil's poem about the wasp. Neil, of course, thought that Stephens was being superior, for what poet is not secretly jealous of another? Dublin's a bitter town. The country is not.

There was a time in pre-Christian Ireland when the Bard was the arbiter before even the king. Perhaps instinctively Neil remembers this and is forever acerb and discontented because of the fallen glory of the poets.

36 *Sir Horace And The Bearded Diphthong*

Sir Horace was dissatisfied with his own death which occurred without his being aware of it in Ireland while he was absent in the United States. Absenteeism could not be carried any further. Bad enough you would think but what was much worse: his obituary notice occupied only one-third of a column and most of that was taken up with a history of his family rather than of himself: not a word about the national purpose to which he had devoted his life! He resolved that such a thing would not happen again. With this in view he collected funds in the USA to found a paper of his own which would have at least a page describing his work for the country and black leads between the columns when he came finally to die. It was to be called, 'The Irish Statesman' (meaning Sir Horace). All that was wanted now was an editor, a man who would see eye to eye with him and give credit where credit was due.

Yeats who was fast to his friend could not have suggested a better editor than Æ (the first letters of aeon, that is the vicar of Hermes Trismegistus on earth). Was Æ not editor of *The Farmer's Gazette* – as you are doubtless well aware farmers are the backbone, etc.

The Irish Statesman would have a wider appeal: what do they know of Ireland that only Ireland know? Its leading articles would deal with problems that were not parochial but world wide. American sanitariums, not sanatoriums, catch cropping and the economic status of the pigmies of the Congo, British tonnage in foreign harbours, with a little poetry here and there. No; Sir Horace could not have had a better – not only an editor but co-adjutor than Æ.

214

Yeats if he were influenced at all must have remembered that when the National Theatre which afterwards became the Abbey, ran out of geniuses, Æ answered the SOS and contributed his 'Deirdre'.

Yes; Yeats never forgot how Æ had rallied to the call with his Deirdre, which was played in the Temperance Hall in Clarendon Street. 'Deirdre' with a name so weary that it deterred me from taking the least interest in her and her legend, was Æ's first and only play. Deirdre was a beautiful princess who was shut up by King Connor in a tower until she should be nubile. She fell in love with Naisi and ran off with him and his brothers to Glen Etive in Scotland. King Connor sent his battle champion, Fergus McRoy, to promise them safe conduct if they returned. Relying on the word of a king they returned only to have the king slay the brothers. Deirdre committed suicide and fell on her lover's corpse.

Æ could not bear suicide and murder on or off stage. He caused Manaanan McLir, god of the sea, to send an anaesthetic vapour which put them to sleep. The audience was not put to sleep because the bearded head, framed as if decapitated in the middle of the curtains announced in a cavernous and alarming voice, 'Manaanan McLir.' The god appeared *ex machina* and all was well. It put me in mind of the legend which makes Shakespeare play the ghost in his own play.

An invitation to lunch at Kilteragh, Sir Horace's new house in Foxrock, the fashionable suburb off the road to Bray. He has had it built with a revolving room on the roof in which he sleeps. There is a quotation from Kipling about an ashlar over the fire place and dadoes by Æ on the top of the library walls. These are the best paintings that Æ has ever done.

I think as I turn over the invitation what an escape I had when I forebore to be smart and uppish when answering his letter from the Royal Irish Automobile Club. And the hardest thing for a man of middle culture (and no family to brag about) is to refrain from smartness. It is worse than

215

the fellow who begins his after dinner speech by being reminded of something. Such people never do anything: they are always 'reminded' of it. The only difference is that Sir Horace 'reminds' others. I shall have to put up with being a 'man of middling culture' as Marcel Arland, speaking of France said, 'Every man of middling culture has at some moment identified himself with Rimbaud.' I have never identified myself with Rimbaud. I left that for Joyce. Resent as I will being a man of middling culture what can I do? Go to lunch with Sir Horace. That's the first step. The second step is to listen to the people you will meet there. And don't butt in. Listen! There was a planted circle in front of Kilteragh with a rockery in its centre. Cars could drive round it when they entered and left.

The butler took my hat and gloves. I could hear voices and Sir Horace's voice that cackled with culture while it explained something in terms of something else. 'My dear fellow.' That must be Mahaffy; and so it was. Nobody stopped when I was announced. All the acolytes stood in a circle round Mahaffy while he stood head and shoulders over them all. He had a superior smirk or perhaps I should have said smile on his face. Mahaffy paused. The butler had a chance. 'Yes. Yes,' said Sir Horace. 'Won't you lead, Sir John?' So Sir John Pentland Mahaffy led us into the luncheon room. I was last man in; so I thought until someone came from somewhere and pushed me on. It was Anderson, one of Sir Horace's indispensable secretaries.

'I see your architect has scamped the cornice ornaments. No one can be expected to believe that they can support themselves on the corners without a hidden support. And hidden supports are quite contradictory to the principles of architecture.' Sir John smiled, inviting criticism. Sir Horace was talking to some English civil servant, probably the permanent under-secretary, an important person – there is always an important person at Sir Horace's. Anderson, who had pushed me into the room, sat opposite with his florid face. He increased his permanent and proprietary smile and answered officially for Sir Horace.

'You see, Sir John, we are newcomers. When Sir Horace found that his place was in Ireland he had to get a house and get it quickly.' That was the official answer and it contained the hidden flattery of 'found that his place was in Ireland'. Sir John, however, did not listen. In spite of the warning against monopolising the conversation contained in his 'Prolegomena to the Art of Conversation' he laid himself out to hold the table. At last he saw his chance. Sir Horace had paused in his explanation of the Irish question in its immediate application. 'Winchester I presume' Sir John said addressing the Englishman. The Englishman nodded without, however, withdrawing his attention from his host. Probably he made a mental note that if they were all as harmless as Sir Horace, the reports about the increasing realisation called Sein Fein could for the moment be discounted.

'I thought so,' Sir John said, and smiled his enigmatic smile. The Englishman was made to realise that Winchester was inferior to Eton.

Fr. Findlay was talking cheerfully about prospects. He was whole-heartedly in favour of them. Yes; indeed. Another harmless man for who would expect revolution from a Jesuit? Gill, whose beard had given George Moore such amusement, was tired. Overwork? Distinctly so. But remember it was all in an important cause, fresh, original, nascent, kinetic; and Sir Horace was at the helm.

'What's that you are eating?' Mahaffy asked.

'Yogurt,' Sir Horace said; and he too was overcome by weariness. Whether he got his weariness from Gill or Gill seeing that weariness in good cause was one of Sir Horace's attributes, reminded and reinfected Sir Horace somewhat in the way that a yawn spreads. The Englishman must have realised the enormity and importance of 'the national purpose'. I was in no position to tell: I was lunching for the first time with one of Ireland's regenerators with half a dozen secretaries. How could I decide which was wearier than the other?

'You are missing this excellent fish,' Mahaffy remarked.

217

(He was an authority on everything, cuisine included.) Now it was Æ's turn. Æ was busy forming agricultural banks all over the country. It was the most creditable of all Sir Horace's works. It failed to please Arthur Griffith however, He attacked Æ in a savage article entitled 'Down among the dead men,' evidence of Griffith's anger that a man of Æ's intelligence should be abstracted by Sir Horace from a direct attack upon England. Griffith failed to realise that, left to himself, Æ had little interest in politics, which he considered ephemeral compared to the eternity of philosophy and art.

The British Government possibly on the report of the important guest at lunch gave Sir Horace an ivory gavel, which he waved importantly at men of his own ilk as Chairman of the futile Convention. Griffith gave the country the Irish Free State which later became the Republic under the Prime Ministership of John Costello and not under de Valera, who had 15 years which included a civil war to declare it.

Arthur Griffith's miserably financed weekly, *The United Irishman* was, in spite of its poverty and the mockery of a more popular and vulgar periodical, waging a slowly eroding war with the greatest empire on earth. Griffith naturally could not bear to see genius wasted and misdirected, resented Æ's devotion to Sir Horace. When I expostulated with Griffith about his attack on Æ, he grunted and not speak as one who thought that I should not want an explanation. Anyhow the harm had been done. I felt that if I defended Æ more, I would be down among the dead men too. What Griffith wanted was Æ's loyalty to Ireland and not to an Anglo-Ireland which Sir Horace personified. Æ, who was not an extremist, was supposed to abandon his employer and to join the, to all appearances, down and out party. He was asked to choose between the dilettantism of the arts and the seriousness of politics. Had I but known it the aristocrat of the time was the enemy. It did not occur to me then. I sided with Griffith because hatred of injustice was engendered in me. And I hated humbug. I knew that Sir Horace was considered an ineffectual humbug or he would not have been chosen by that arch schemer and rogue, Lloyd George, Prime Minster of England, to act as Chairman (Sir Horace could not resist) of a Convention set up for no other purpose but to delay action. It sat appropriately enough behind the Trinity College clock. Of course, as was intended, the Convention could not agree even about its own terms of reference. It petered out. Sir Horace wrote to the papers regretting it.

Sir Horace got himself wrong with the extremists and was now through his Home Brighteners getting himself in wrong with the Hierarchy of the Catholic Church which dominates the country. The Catholic Church looks askance at any attempt to influence the mind of the peasant from without: 'This Summer intrusion of superior young men and women from English Universities coming over here in the guise of Home Brighteners weakens the National Idea and seeks to divert the minds of the people from the goal. They are all of them English Protestants. What can they know of Ireland who only England know? And what can they possibly know of our Holy Religion for which our forefathers bled and died?' This has the ring of the Emperor Chien Lung's answer to George III. Sir Horace failed to realise that there are times when religion identifies itself with patriotism and so becomes the only touchstone.

Mahaffy turned and strode across the lawn, with his left foot a little inwards, towards the summer house at the end of Sir Horace's very solid pergola. 'Who was that gumptionless fellow who talked about Siberia after an excellent lunch? That's the worst of lunching with Sir Horace, who seems bent on getting the most immiscible people together. It would be useless to talk to that limited fellow from Winchester whom Sir Horace invited over here to listen to his ideas. If he wished to hear facts about the country let him come to me. Meanwhile, this looks like an excellent cigar.' Mahaffy wandered on in search of Sir

Horace's summer house before lighting it because no one but a vulgarian smokes in the open air. Æ overtook him on the smooth lawn. 'Sir John' he panted. Mahaffy turned and asked with raised eyebrows, 'What is it, my good fellow?'

'Oh, Sir John we all want you to use your great influence. The Czar is knouting thousands and sending them to Siberia.'

'The Czar is knouting whom?' Æ was nonplussed for a moment but he came on again. 'Oh, the Russians. If you write to *The Times*.' Mahaffy looked at him, 'Get this into your head once for all: if the Czar does not knout them, they'll knout themselves.'

Oh, the wisdom of Mahaffy, 'if the Czar does not knout them, they'll knout themselves.' And that was many years before they knouted themselves and liquidated millions as well as sending whole nations to Siberia. Good Lord how right he was. When I say 'Good Lord' I am invoking the spirit of righteousness in man that has kept the idea of goodness before him and led him through the vicissitudes for thousands of years.

The butler came across the lawn and found me. 'Sir Horace would like to speak to you in the library.' I entered the house and was shown into the library. Sir Horace said, 'I want you to know that I laid the fellow who trailed the duck by the heels.' I knew it! Sir Horace himself ran over that duck!

37 *Confusion Compounded*

Let us prescind from the fantasy of Chief Secretary Short in the asylum near Drumcondra and proceed to consider Ireland as an open-air lunatic asylum.

I was the first to reject the sentimental symbolism of

Ireland under the sobriquets of Dark Rosaleen, Kathleen na Houlihan, or the silk of the Kine, females all, and substitute a man, one Endymion, a genial joker whom the Moon touched, seeing that she loved him – Endymion, a lunatic, maybe; but the typical Irishman, good-natured, humorous, cynical.

Who would I commit to my asylum which is in the open air for it includes the whole islands? I would commit Einstein because of his notoriety derived from an unthinking mob which pretends to understand him, and because of the fact that he does nothing to disillusion them. Once in, he would be constantly on the move and running round in circles, because, otherwise, as he himself might say, he might be measured. By the same token all measuring rods and rules would be kept out of sight because, if he found one, he would alter it.

And who would be the director of this open-air asylum? De Valera, of course. He would promise 'freedom' to all the loonies; and they would hail him as their deliverer. Of course he would not let them out! His job would be over if he did. How well he would get on with Bertie Einstein! They would have both politics and mathematics with which to confuse and confound themselves and each other if necessary; and those of the inmates who took themselves seriously.

Think of all the confusion implicit in Neo-Euclidean geometry. Why not? Remember that the whole country is more or less mad. There would be Relativity dished up as a discovery. Time would be mixed up with Space and called a time-space continuum. An equation would appear with t in it; that is 'time'. You might as well throw in colour; and noise. De Valera would be sure to add a spot of politics: 'the day is not far distant from the Republic continuum.' There would be the Fourth Dimension with Document Number II as its charter. Einstein would hide behind the Fifth Amendment. All this built upon the measurement of farms in Egypt after each inundation of the Nile!

Mystical mathematicians, who cannot express themselves clearly; though Truth is always clear. What do you call a fellow who tries to pull wool over your eyes and hides, if chased, like a cuttlefish in a roil of words? All right, call them that. Bertie doubts if there are twelve who understand him, and he is proud of the misunderstanding of the inmates. And yet it is not only in an asylum that one understands his jargon. That's why I have him in. He has learned the value of confusion; the other fellow was born confused.

Suppose that the loonies clamoured to be let out? That is unlikely, seeing that they do not know that they are in. If they shouted, De Valera would answer, 'Presently, as soon as you can appreciate the difference between liberty and true freedom.' Bertie would add, 'Don't disturb me. I am bringing the Cosmos into an equation.' Don't tell me that there is no positive value in a negotiation. Bertie and Eamon would get along famously.

'The swifter the river, the nearer the bridge.' Now what does that mean? I confess that it came to me in a dream. Bertie was expounding time-space while Eamon was spouting in an *ersatz* Limerick brogue about true freedom. He was very earnest about it. Politicians are always earnest, preoccupied and serious. Now where do they get that; and what do they take us for?

Why should not politicians be cheerful sometimes? Why should we be asked always to look ahead and always to be on our toes? Why should we not sit down and enjoy the blessings which we have? Oh no; that would never do! The tension between the goal and Man's inadequacy must be kept up. And Bertie and Eamon come from a race of experts at the game; the experts include Freud. The carrot must be held in front of the ass, or else stuck up his proctodaeum to give him an 'id'. In either case he would GO AHEAD. It would never do to have a contented public because there would be no place for politicians at all. So it begins to dawn on me why politicians must always be serious, solemn and even, like De Valera, lugubrious. He always looks lugubrious. It is his melancholy that makes him such a good politician.

It is somewhat the same with Bertie. That 'postulate' of mine about the river and the bridge will illustrate the nonsense Bertie spouts. And even though it is not political, it is stuff and nonsense all the same. If he were to be asked what connection there was between the swiftness of a river and a bridge, he would define both a river and a bridge; but leave the connection out; or, perhaps, put it in because it does not exist. It is something like De Valera's notion of a republic. That is why I have the two playboys, or rather melancholy humbugs, in the same house. Both are fiddlers with words and depend on the public's love of mystification. Einstein belabours the obvious; De Valera buries it under a tumulus of words.

Have you heard of the nitrous oxide or laughing gas experiment? 'No.' Let me tell it to you then. Some there are who under the influence of laughing gas are filled with a desire to solve the riddle of the universe and to tell it to all and sundry. When I was under gas, it seemed that I was beneath a sheet of ice and if I could only tell the skaters above me two words, all would be solved. Yeats had a similar experience, but he put it more poetically, 'Gogarty, I felt that the riddle of the universe could be written on a blade of grass.' And Einstein wants to reduce the indefinable cosmos to a formula, a laughing gas hallucination. That is why I have him in.

Absurd as the picture is, wouldn't it be more cheerful if De Valera were to dance – his black coat tails twirling – to the tune of Bertie's oral fiddle-faddle? It would be droller still if in his dancing he were to pettifog. Everyone would know that his *id* was speaking, and that it spoke the truth for he couldn't help himself.

Yes, it would be a wholesome and laughable thing if De Valera were to dance. How could he? you will ask. When did you see a great funny man? And De Valera is a great man if there is any truth in the remark attributed to Sir Joshua Reynolds, 'The greatest man is he who forms the taste of a nation, and the next greatest is he who corrupts it.' So how can you expect the next greatest man to play the Dancing Dervish?

Pettifogging would be too terse and too reflex to be effective. Especially as sight is more important than sound. This was borne in on me during some political campaign or other at which I spoke from the top of a limousine. I admit that the engine was kept running, for I never can be sure what the effect of my unvarnished oratory may be. There was another campaigner on the top of an adjoining car. He could not be heard for the cheering. He had worked himself up so effectively that his coat nearly fell off. His shirt sleeves were exposed by the emphasis of his harangue. The audience roared applause; and the applause was so loud that whatever I was saying was drowned in the shouting. Anyway, our man was returned, and not by the skin of his teeth, mark you.

It is passing strange that so few politicians, 'leaders' or dictators have been amusing. It would seem that wit has no place in politics. I am inclined to that opinion. There are exceptions: Lloyd George was a wit; so is Winston, if given time. Aneurin Bevan is a wit. So was J. H. Thomas, another Welshman who had to resign from the British Cabinet in disgrace. We all know how Lloyd George dealt in Marconis. 'Great wit and *dodging* sure are near allied.' Yet there have been honest men who were witty, Benjamin Franklin, for instance; in Ireland, Tim Healy, and his namesake, the priest. Wit and politics do not go together; therefore wits should not dabble in politics. And yet it is sinister to be devoid of humour. Savonarola, Stalin, Stafford Cripps and Hitler took themselves and everything else seriously. Look at the results!

224

38 *Renvyle Is Rebuilt*

The government were compensating those who had lost their houses in the civil war. In order to obtain compensation, an attorney had to be employed. I engaged the firm of Arthur Cox to obtain the monies to rebuild Renvyle. This was done expeditiously.

I did not like to interfere when it came to employing an architect. The one that Arthur Cox commissioned turned out to be an ecclesiastical architect, one accustomed to drawing plans for a church to seat six or eight hundred as the case might be. They were all barn-shaped with yellow pine seats and a window at the eastern end shaped like the gear wheel of a bicycle. That is why the new Renvyle House has Gothic fireplaces!

Apparently it had been a good fire; give them credit for that. China vases had been fused and had run down the walls. A great oaken beam had fallen into the well which was underneath the old house. So I was told. I had not the heart to visit the ruins. All I had by way of details was from the terse foreman of the Belfast builders.

There were certain restrictions on the compensation. For instance, pictures were left out. This prevented anyone from claiming that half a dozen Rembrandts had been burned. Antiques, too, and books.

The new house was intended for a hotel. As I could no longer afford to keep a country house I conceived the idea of making the country keep me. But it was not Ireland that rallied to the cause; most of the visitors came from England and the North. However, our friends could be franked.

Yeats and his bride spent part of their honeymoon in Renvyle. Yeats laid the Renvyle ghost which, in spite of the fire and in spite of the fact that the room it haunted had been turned into a ladies' toilet – a running stream they dare not cross – could be conjured still.

My wife built a four-roomed cottage in the grounds sixty yards from the hotel but hidden from it by a wood and hedges of dense fuchsia. There we could remain aloof from the visitors; but it was not as peaceful as the old house had been when it was private and Mahaffy came and sat outside it in the morning watching the mist rise from the lake and the mountain: 'I declare it is plum-blue.'

Meanwhile there was the house on the Island in Tully Lough, Freilaun. Freilaun means Heather Island. So does Innisfree, where Yeats lay for one whole night on the shore of Lough Gill, building through the midnight glow in his imagination his small cabin: 'I will arise and go now.' But it was never his luck as it was mine to live actually on a Heather Island.

There were eleven acres in the island and a house built by one of the Blakes who was a 'Sunday man', that is, a man who could only appear on Sundays when the King's writ could not be served. We added some rooms to the old house and lived there in blessed silence.

Outside, to the east, stood a five-branched plum tree. In a dell to the north was a plot where raspberries grew. The house was surrounded by great sycamore trees and plane trees. These made the island very warm, warmer than any of the houses on the mainland. In Tully Lough was another island called in English Half Moon Island. It is a heronry. I hope that my son-in-law, who owns Tully Lough now, will let the heronry alone. A third island was evidently a crannog, that is, a prehistorical island settlement. The ancients often built in lakes, doubtless to safeguard their children from the wolves and other wild animals that infested the land of old when it was nearly all one forest of great trees. I think that the Sunday man removed the surrounding stones that rimmed the crannog when he was building his four-room house on Freilaun.

There are otters in Tully Lough. I neither trapped nor shot them because nothing good comes of disturbing the balance of nature. It is a thing for which I was thankful: to be allowed to live in a lake and not to disturb the wild life around me.

How blessed is silence! In the raucous, shouting towns no one can hear the music of the spheres, which is silence. Noise is the loud laugh which bespeaks the empty mind, or, worse, the guilty mind that dare not be still. Here in the moonlight it is possible to decipher print if the moon is full. The only sound that breaks the silence of the night is lake water lapping and the bark of a distant dog. The noise of the bark is as necessary as the snake to Eden, so that the blessedness may be realised and felt.

The sea is only half a mile away. To get to it you must row over to the mainland and then go up and downhill. One of the British Government harbours is there; a rock at its entrance is covered at high tide. No place to bring in a fishing boat; but curraghs and sea gulls can make it and sometimes they do. The harbour has a purpose, at least I have found one for it; it makes a good place from which to dive and the shelter of its sea wall keeps the water more or less smooth.

At Renvyle the sea is closer, only a hundred yards from the house. There is a rock to which to swim. The rock stands up in the water and is more than forty yards off when the tide is in. When the tide is out some sand is exposed. So are the anemones and mussels, which cling to the rock. In front of Renvyle house is the lake of the Little Dark Wood and the little promontory that carries the wood. Ash trees bend back to touch the walls of the house and guard them from the Atlantic storms. When the sun is setting you can see its globe in the sky and in the lake at the same time. If you are lucky you may see the Green Glint. If you have not been lucky and see it you will be 'made up' for the rest of your born days.

What is the use of regretting one place when you are in another?

39 *The Again Coming Of Augustus*

A telegram from Wales. Augustus, on his way from Fryern Court in Hampshire, had run into a tar boiler. But he was on his way. When his car would be repaired he would be with us. He did not say when. (He never did say 'when'.) So I had to wait in daily expectation.

I hoped that Lord Howard de Walden, the peer who sponsored all Welsh geniuses, had not roped in Augustus again. You might think that once at Chirk Castle Augustus would never leave. But that would show that you did not know Augustus. He had not George Moore's satisfaction at being entertained by a peer of the realm. Augustus would not forget his suitcase deliberately at Chirk as George Moore told me he did, so that he might be invited again.

But suppose that a Welsh gloom, black as pitch – I am not thinking of the tar boiler – has enveloped Augustus, such a gloom as descended upon the table at that misassociated dinner party at Chirk. The tale I heard – I think Francis Macnamara was the narrator, was that in the middle of the silence the Bishop of Liverpool, who thought that a bishop should be 'all things to all men', tried a seemingly incontrovertible question of Augustus, who sat beside him dressed as a gypsy with an earring in one ear: 'Don't you think, sir, that every man should take unto himself a wife?'

'I have two!' Augustus boomed. The gloom deepened.

Days passed. Then came a rumour from Galway that Augustus had been seen. He had a commission to paint a beautiful American girl who had come to Galway with her husband all the way from Philadelphia to have her portrait painted. I hoped that there was truth in the rumour. It meant for one thing that the tar boiler had not daunted him. It also meant that he had not gone visiting, in spite of all temptation, in his native Wales.

I remembered his aversion to one castle. That was when he came as a Distinguished Guest of the Irish Nation, in 1928, to attend the Irish games. Many distinguished people helped the government to entertain. The Countess of Meath threw her house open. Dunsany put Augustus up at Dunsany Castle. In Dunsany Castle there is little self-indulgence, so somebody, perhaps it was I, must have spoken to his lordship about the idiosyncrasies of the artist. The result was that every room which he was likely to visit contained a siphon and its companionable decanter. There was a decanter everywhere except on the stairs. It was too much. Augustus blamed not the siphons but the castle, from which he fled unceremoniously.

At last he arrived. He had driven from Galway with one hand. And now he is at work on a portrait of the beautiful American and all is going well.

I believe that there are people who bring you luck. Just as I believe – only more so – that there are people whose very presence is a menace. This, you will say, is sheer superstition; but remember that I am Irish, and the Irish believed that their kings were half magical: one glance if it fell on you would make you lucky for life. Yeats in his unpublished poem *Crazy Jane and the King*, contrasting the Irish idea of kingship with the English store-dummy king, has a line, 'Saw the lucky eyeball shine.' And Augustus comes from wizard Wales. He is lucky.

Why do I take to the Welsh? It cannot be that they are amoral. It cannot be that they have the highest rate of illegitimacy in the Three Kingdoms. Nor can it be that they are free and easy and that they have 'no complaints'. I know: they do not have to be superior to everyone else. There are no cold, superior Welshmen. Yes, after much cogitation I have discovered why I am attracted by Welshmen. And their women are charming too. No one is afraid of them. No one is afraid to marry them.

There are few bachelors in Wales whereas in Ireland, with a population of less than four million, there are five hundred thousand bachelors. Why? Don't ask me. I am biassed; but this is certain: no one ever heard of a Welshman dying, as one of the ancient leaders of the Irish did, 'from an excess of women.'

Mrs Hope Scott is the sitter, a slender, sinuous, dark-haired beautiful woman and a great horsewoman. Her husband is a tall athletic man with a gift for turning a verse.

Talk of Penelope's web! I found Augustus early one morning undoing with turpentine the face he had painted the day before. And Scott had only two weeks' leave from the USA! It took six weeks, I think, before Augustus was satisfied. But is an artist ever satisfied?

I remembered how his long sinewy artist's hands had tugged at the ivy when we were both staying in the old house just after it had come to me. It was then I taught him to drive a car, or rather I was there when he drove off in a Ford, and could not stop until it had run out of gasoline, somewhere by the side of Lough Fee! I followed fearfully in another car and watched him take corner after corner full speed ahead. I have recorded the facts of that first drive of his and in that record I compared him to a Viking. 'Like a Viking who has steered, All blue eyes and yellow beard.' Now I find how right that was. In his book *Chiaroscuro*, he tells that Haverford, where he was born, had been a Norse settlement: Haverfjord. Sometimes you find the truth in a rhyme though you may be unaware of it.

One evening he came back late. He had been out in his car alone. He said that in the dark someone had sat behind him and had left him only when the lights of the house were seen. It was an eerie story that befitted an eerie time and place, midnight on the extreme shelf of Europe. He would sit for hours on a ridge overlooking Tully Lough painting on panels of sycamore wood where Croagh Patrick, far off, shot its cone into a niche of coloured sky. A Japanese battleship-builder bought the twelve panels that he painted while he was at Renvyle.

230

40 *The Hawk's Well*

Yeats and his wife came to stay with us and Augustus went to work on a portrait of Yeats. Where the original is now I do not know, but the portrait represents the poet in his old age. He is seated with a rug round his knees and his broad hat on his lap. His white hair is round his head like a nimbus and behind him the embroidered cloths of heaven are purple and silver. It is the last portrait of Yeats. It is reproduced in *As I Was Going Down Sackville Street*.

Poets require little entertainment. They can entertain themselves. If you want to entertain them therefore leave them alone. But something was in the wind. Yeats was in consultation with my wife and I was not invited to take part in their planning. At last the news broke: Players from the Abbey Theatre were coming to produce Yeats's *The Hawk's Well*.

An explanation of *The Hawk's Well* and similar plays is necessary. Yeats got his idea from the symbolic Noh plays of Japan. His imagination was excited; he saw a new mechanism, with the stage on the same level as the room. He could have a theatre wherever there was a large room that would hold forty or fifty persons. But the audience must be 'readers of poetry'. Did he mean to bring out at last his poetic plays, shelved for forty years? My wife said that he had, in his own words, 'attained a distance from life which can make credible strange events, elaborate words.' All this, mark you, was by way of explanation, or was it an apology for what was about to happen?

'He wants to show us the masks and costumes designed by his friend Edmund Dulac. He is tremendously excited. We have ample space in the large room.'

231

Indeed there was space enough, for the large room was larger than most drawing rooms. It was over forty feet long and it had a folding door that could be used for entrance and exit by the players.

I had not been consultd. Very well, this meant I was spared such obnoxious details as the reservation of the ground floor of the east wing for the Abbey Players.

It may not be all very well to be a poet – fifty per cent of them are distraught – but it must be very intense to be a dramatist. What I am coming to is this: there is Yeats in the loveliest spot on earth – it was Bob Flaherty who, having seen all the world, called Renvyle the loveliest spot on earth – and Yeats, instead of enjoying the place, is constrained to bring in help from without, to wit, his Abbey Players.

Lady Wellesley has remarked somewhere that Yeats never noticed natural scenery. That may be, but that he did at one time observe it narrowly is obvious from his poems, which never once bring in exotic or impossible scenes, but always things most apposite – the speckled eagle cock of Ballygauley Hill; the yew that has been green from time out of mind; the long grey pike that broods in Castle Dargan lake.

Well, he loves excitement; and there is this to be said in his favour: there is no way to give anyone an idea of a play you have written that compares to having it produced, acted and seen.

I had never seen *The Hawk's Well*, although it must have been on something during my frequent visits to the Abbey if there was any room for it between the plays that Yeats attributed to Lady Gregory and which were played *ad nauseam*. If I did see it, one thing is certain, I never saw it with Dulac's masks, head-dresses and costumes, nor did I hear his music.

It may be that all this shadow of an objection to having the peace of the place disturbed by players is an affectation of mine. I shall find myself pretending that I am so full of resources that I do not require any outside help to enjoy a holiday in a lovely place. Now I find myself looking forward to the play; so my attitude was all nonsense.

It is to be on after dinner, that is, about nine o'clock tonight. Yes, he is quite right, time hangs heavy after dinner, especially on those who do not indulge in the illiteracy of cards or, worse still, billiards.

Much more than forty people had come to see the play. Who told them? I had imagined, foolishly when you come to think of it, that a play and players can thrive privately. So that is what all the whispering was about: to get an audience. I thought that they must be 'readers of poetry'. Well, who would have thought that Mrs — and the ash-blonde daughter ever read poetry?

'Oliver!' It was the voice of Augustus. 'We have been looking for you everywhere. Come in! The play is beginning.'

Yeats was already speaking when I entered. I tried to sit in a back row. But the speaker paused until I went forward. His pause made my interruption more noticeable. He resumed at long last when I was seated. But where was Augustus John?

'As I was saying, I have found a form of drama that is at once aristocratic and distinguished . . . ' He is resuming the poetic drama that he reluctantly set aside when he found that a theatre, in order to support itself, had to stoop to the masses, I thought; but I was wrong. 'I have created an unpopular theatre, that is, a theatre which does not depend for existence on crowds and the box office. I have found a form that does its work by suggestion, by complexity of rhythm, colour, gesture, symbol, not by direct statement, I have not altered basically the Noh plays that were intended for nobles, but I have made them suitable to our conventions of aristocracy . . . '

How the audience must be flattered!

'I, as you will see shortly, have discovered the theatre's antiself.'

Should he explain? Perhaps not. Everybody will think that they require not intellect to appreciate his play but, what is rarer than intellect, understanding of symbolism;

and who can limit its wide suggestions? Every man for himself! Evidently the audience thinks that it is up to them to supply mystical emotions. They are all flattered. That's what the speaker wants; and ...

'Perhaps I had better adumbrate the suggestions – not their significance, for that would be to limit them. The well, then, is the well of immortality or of wisdom, if you will. The hero approaches and find an old man seated there waiting for its bubbling. He has been there for fifty years.'

When the play was first written Yeats was fifty years of age.

'The well is guarded by a woman who is possessed by a hawk; call this woman intellect. She dances a magic dance which draws the hero off in pursuit and sheds sleep upon the old man. The song I have written for this play would suggest that the hero is Cuchulainn. I know well that you would not have me be explicit. Let it rest at that.'

> I call to the eye of the mind
> A well long choked up and dry
> And boughs long stripped by the wind,
> And I call to the mind's eye
> Pallor of an ivory face
> Its lofty dissolute air,
> A man climbing up to a place
> The salt sea wind has left bare.

Whatever sort of face Cuchulainn had, it was not an ivory face; but Yeats's face is the colour of ivory, and so was the face of Dante, who was 'Mocked by Guido for his lecherous life'.

Don't think that my thoughts distracted me from the speech. I remember it well.

'The masks, costumes and the music are by my friend, Edmund Dulac. Let us begin.'

Applause. Loud applause, all the greater in volume because of the room.

Thanks be to Heaven, Yeats at last is enjoying himself! Even the presence of a few old dames, to whom poetry – no

234

matter how you use your imagination – can have no appeal, does nothing to diminish the poet's satisfaction. That I knew by the assured way in which he spoke. Often when he spoke he used his audiences for guinea-pigs as it were; using the audience to sound out the effects of his words. Now he had no need of such subterfuge. He was master of himself.

No, I had never seen *The Hawk's Well*. The Old Lady of the Abbey Theatre repelled me by continually inserting the few plays she was supposed to have written and attaching them to everyone else's work. Once I tackled Yeats about these so-called plays of Lady Gregory. 'You cannot tell me that she wrote *The Rising of the Moon*.' He, although he tried to be evasive, acknowledged this: 'We decided that whoever found a suitable title might have the words too.' As I suspected. Yeats, who had a fine sense of humour, did not want the comic to interfere with his fame as an outstanding poet who must, in conformity to the English idea, be totally lacking in humour, so he let Lady Gregory get away with the comics. That interchange actually took place. I do not remember the year, but I remember the conversation and how triumphant I felt when what I had long suspected from observation turned out to be correct. I have a sticky memory.

The Hawk's Well was played even as its author would have wished. It proved to be a supernatural presentation, the like of which has never been seen before on any stage. I know nothing of Japan, but they could not have produced anything as satisfying and as moving for Europeans as *The Hawk's Well*. The crisis faded into a magical dance. What a lovely thing Dulac made out of the human hawk woman!

I knew that Yeats was very well satisfied; but I also knew that to praise him would detract from the mystical impression he had produced. So I left him alone with his glory.

41 *Looking Back*

The sun was setting, a red ball over the vast sea. A thin strip of green divided the sea from the lake with its promontory, the Little Dark Wood, before me. Around the lawn on which I sat was a wall of fuchsia; and behind me the house.

The test of life, I thought, is, would you live it over again?

Assuredly I would, and with little change and no 'apologia'.

Doctoring is not all. I went into politics with my eyes open. I never forgot Dr Kenny. At the same time I went on doctoring, and kept it up for thirty years. But politics gave me the opportunity to put into effect that which was borne in on me as of the first importance by my experience as a doctor – the abolition of slums.

A one-room tenement breeds twice as much tuberculosis as two rooms. Housing was the key not only to health but to morale. And politics offered a chance, if not to get slums abolished immediately, to point out the remedy.

There were many difficulties in the way of slum clearance. Not the least of these was the slum snob. 'Many a good man was born in a slum'; that I heard in the Senate. But why should a good man have to be born in a slum?

I promised to tell how Tom Kettle helped in the movement for better housing. He was giving evidence before one of the numerous committees. He said that he wanted to obtain entry to a typical slum, one situated in one of the old Georgian houses that had become derelict. Upper Dominick Street was selected because each side of the street was lined with houses of the best period, that had fallen into decay. The time was late at night. Tom, careless of how it might be construed against him, told how he was accosted by a whore and taken to a front room that had been the drawing room in better days. 'There was a family in each of the three corners; but as we approached the prostitute's corner we approached civilisation: there was a screen around her bed.'

I remember backing the Censor Bill. I knew that, when censorship was most active, literature was most alive.

What was the result of the passage of the Censor Bill? A gang of peeping Toms was let loose on every writer in the country; the censors smelled sex in every realistic literary creation; in one year they banned more books than the papal Index Expurgatorius had banned in fourteen years. They held up tourists at the ports of entry while they were searched to see if they carried any 'objectionable' book. By the way, the books which were objected to were not indicated. The censors had gotten out of hand. They were interfering with human liberty, not to mention the Tourist Industry. I should have foreseen to what extent lascivious old men in a Jansenistic country could go. I must acknowledge that my attitude towards censorship was wrong.

You may say that my experience of politics was an experience *in parvo*. But let me tell you that Irishmen are the most expert politicians in the world. The size of the country has nothing to do with its politics – there were three or four towns in ancient Greece each at the other's throat; and the Peloponnesos would fit into Ireland many times. Tammany, with the great city of New York surrounding it, is but a suburb of Dublin.

There is always this consolation in making mistakes: they prevent you from becoming complacent, self-satisfied and smug. I have another regret, but the circumstances were not altogether within my control. I might have purchased the Tower at Sandycove, where Joyce and I lived, from the British Government when it was clearing out of Ireland. I would now be the owner of it in fee simple. Why did I not jump at the chance? I did, but I was put off by a fellow, some little jack-in-office of a clerk in Dublin Castle, who wanted by delaying to impress me with the importance of the job he was doing for me.

Now when I think of the buildings that are close to the Tower, I am almost consoled. But that Tower was an ideal house. It could be locked up for a year with the utmost assurance of security; and when opened again it would be found to be dustless. The only things necessary to secure it against were pigeons, and they could be kept out by strong bars within the windows a few feet from the outer surface of the wall.

There is another form of consolation in the remark made by a public figure in one of his more idiotically inspired moments: 'History is useless because we do not know what might have happened had it gone the other way.' Or some such words that without the saving effect of a thorough Irish bull reveal a muddled head. Had history 'gone the other way', would it not still be history? I quote it to show how confused the mind of a 'leader' can be. However, I wish history had gone the other way just once and that I owned the Tower at Sandycove. De Valera could not have burned that.

Another regret I have is that I was not suspicious. This was not due to any magnanimity but because my head was in the clouds and, when it was not, I was too much inclined to leave responsibility to others. Thus it was that we were robbed of the estate which I made over to my mother by a deed of gift when I reached the age of twenty-one.

One day she said to me, 'Your father died intestate. Instead of putting the estate in Chancery, as legally I was bound to do, I spent the income on your education and the educations of your sister and brothers. Now you can put me in jail.' I found that a deed of gift to my mother would cover the situation, and made one accordingly. Had I inquired into the credentials of my mother's attorney I would have found that he had been struck off the Rolls, which is a rare disgrace for an attorney. Instead, I permitted him to make away with the whole property before my mother's death, which occurred within a few years of the deed of gift. Her attorney, or solicitor as they call them in Ireland, was an insinuating, bony-headed little scoundrel who had robbed his way to seeming prosperity. His supply of widows was limited only by his obscurity. He had met my mother at the altar rails, for he haunted the Jesuits' Church in Gardiner Street. That was enough for her. She had the uttermost confidence in the rogue. The result I have described. An automobile ran over him and his large head was fractured.

Struck off the Rolls; Reinstated. Struck off a Rolls He broke his head; And now Dishonesty lies dead.

But the lines I wrote for his epitaph were little consolation.

Often I wonder, is the inherent tension between a raving moral maniac such as the biblical Jehovah and Man's inadequacy suitable for all nations? The Orientals have it not, yet they manage to live lives without dishonour. They cannot understand Original Sin. I can, not quite dogmatically perhaps, but the question is, Does the tension created by the attempts of poor humanity to appease a raving deity do any good? See what it has done to the Jews who started it.

Is it natural for Irishmen? What would they be without it? You may ask; but is that not like asking what is the use of history because we don't know what might have happened had it gone the other way? All I will say is that I am not the first Irishman to query the tension between Perfection and Inadequacy. Pelagius did it in the fifth century in the form in which it was presented to him – he said that there was no such thing as Original Sin. He had to be suppressed. It was either he or the sacraments. It comes to this: You cannot have a religion of suffering without Original Sin. In other words, man is not perfect. The Bishop of Hippo knew that; and it was he who fastened Original Sin on the innocent infant, who can only cry when being baptised.

The worship of Jehovah does not seem to have done the Jews much good. 'Suffering is the badge.' Take Cardinal Newman, for example. He was the son of Dutch bankers called Neumann, and wrote *Apologia pro Vita Sua*. That was in the '60s in Oxford.

What a place Oxford must have been then! Oxford Movement Number One. Tracts, sermons and dejections. Oxford must have been full of 'pi-jaws' then.

I must prefer to laugh at the tale of the absent-minded and undejected president of Trinity College, Oxford, who, when asked what the four statues on top of the church tower represented, said, 'The Holy Trinity.' 'But there are four,' the GI objected. 'Of course,' the president explained. 'Three Persons and one God.'

Think of it! I might have been saved! But, to reverse the problem, as Mahaffy said to the zealot who cornered him in a railway carriage and asked, 'Are you saved?': 'To tell you the truth, my good fellow, I am; but it was such a narrow squeak it does not bear talking about.'

From the Christian Brothers Primary School, where Brother Swan told me to chisel my words, to Dublin University there is an unpleasant lustrum. Dublin University, let us call it Trinity College, a name which is more often used, healed me and gave me of its best. The Divine Doctor, the Professor of Moral Philosophy, Henry Stewart Macran, whom I knew familiarly as Fafnir, one of the dragons of the ring; and the great John Pentland Mahaffy, one of the greatest intellects of a day that was full of outstanding men ... There the education was certainly classic and by no means scientific; and though we had a great scientist in the Engineering School, Professor Fitzgerald, one of the first men to experiment with a glider and the man who discovered wireless before Marconi, we kept him there. The Divine Doctor used to quote Plato whenever a mathematician was mentioned: 'I have hardly ever known a mathematician who was capable of reasoning.'

Often the thought strikes me, Have I ever left Dublin

University? Certainly I have never sought to improve on the universal outlook on life. With Lachesis I sang of the Past, with Clotho of the Present and, thus equipped, I can look, as I do now, at the Future with assurance.

The politician has to strike an average; he has to deal with a cross-section of humanity. He has to make allowances; this means that he has to treat men as inferiors. To succeed he has to be, as Tom Kettle said, somewhat of a mountebank. He has to cherish the Plain Man. He has to pretend that whatever he does is for the Plain Man's good, when in reality it is for his own aggrandisement. For me to pretend to be a Plain Man would be just a harlequinade. Someday I will get away from this humbug to where there is a genuine Republic.

Fairfield is gone that I thought was fixed forever. I like to imagine that it was there to fall back upon no matter how far I wandered. I would not like to be shut in it all the time because I could not tolerate eternity. But it was good to dream that some things did not change for all the flux.

> O grant me, Phoebus, calm content,
> Strength unimpaired, a mind entire,
> Old age without dishonour spent
> Nor unbefriended by the lyre.

My strength is unimpaired, my mind is entire, and as for being befriended by the lyre, Sir William Watson in his *Retrogressions* has these lines that notice me:

> Three Olivers before your time
> Were not unknown in prose and rhyme;
> One was the paladin or pal
> Of him who fought at Roncevalles;
> One gave Drogheda to pillage;
> And one wrote 'The Deserted Village';
> But sorra an Oliver ever was seen
> Compares with him of Stephen's Green.

I lived in Stephen's Green for three years beside the Shelbourne Hotel. My office that was is now a bar; appropriately, you may say. Now who is looking for symbols? But when all is said, and though the name of the book is *Retrogressions*, which means that he considered himself reverting to an inferior state, Ireland – remember that he suffered from melancholia – I feel greatly complimented, particularly since Sir William wrote some of his best lyrics while retrogressing in Ireland.

42 *Samain*

Lough Corrib, on the north, sends an arm due westward to meet a river that flows through the valley of the Joyce Country. In this water stands Caisleen na Circe, the Castle of the Hen. Legend has it that the husband of Grace O'Malley was besieged in that fortress and that she raised the siege. He was eke named, The Cock; and so to celebrate the story of how she came to his assistance, it is called the Castle of the Hen.

Another story goes that a magic hen laid an egg daily for each man of the garrison during a beleaguerment. The castle is in ruins now. The late Lord Ardilaun, one of the great family of Guinness, kept the ruin from falling down. To reach it, a boat is necessary.

The road from Cong skirts Lough Corrib until the Joyce Country is entered. The Joyces were a giant race. Each Joyce had six fingers and six toes. That is not unknown. In Ireland it is a mark of gigantism. The Hen's Castle and the giant Joyces and the unworldly atmosphere of the place make you feel that you are travelling through a legendary magic land.

One evening as dusk fell, I was driving along by the north of Lough Corrib to the west. It must have been in the autumn, for all the hillside to my right was covered by dull red fading fern, bracken and the dark green brambles of the withering blackberry. In that soft climate there is no winter, nor is there any loss of colour, though the colour be fuscous and subdued. The hillside was not bare. To the left the mountains hid the sun setting in vaporous light and here the gloaming lay without a gleam on water or on hill.

Suddenly, as if a backdrop came forward, the land seemed to open out, light shone on a fresh earth and bright grass; all figures moved in beauty, birds sang in blossoming apple trees.

I was gazing at the Delightful Plain, I was gazing at Mag Mell, and I gazed without astonishment, for what I saw seemed in the order of things.

Students of the ancient lore of Ireland know that Amairgin, the poet, gave to the Tuatha de Danaan the lower half of Ireland, that is, the territory under the earth and under the waters outside the garish light of day. The Sons of Mil received the upper part; and once a year on the last day of October and on the first day of November there is common territory between the upper and the lower parts. The Tuatha de Danaan are said to have come from the isles of northern Greece in time out of mind and to have brought their magic with them. They were well satisfied with their award, for were they not given Tir na nOc, the Land of Youth?

It was on the last day of October that I came to enter the Joyce Country on my way from Cong.

Magic! There is magic in the West; and it is everywhere. It is everywhere in the world only we do not recognise it. We call it Good Luck or Fortune, What does it do but show that there are outside powers that rule our lives?

In the West of Ireland it is understood, it is taken for granted. When I saw the Green Glint in the evening sky an old man told me that I was made up for life.

> Yesternight I saw in a vision
> Long-bodied Tuatha de Danaan;
> Iron men in a golden barge;
> Saw the eyes that never wink

Mirrored on the winking wave:
Eyes a righteous king should have ...

And again, in the same (unpublished) poem, Yeats testified:

Saw the sages meet the king,
Seven fingers cautioning;
Saw the common people surge
Round a wave-wet landing stair,
Banging drum and tambourine;
Saw the lucky eyeball shine
On the lewd and learned there.

'Lucky eyeball'! Good Luck; it is magic all the same. I cannot explain it. Why should I? You know what I mean and why I was not astonished when I beheld the Delightful Plain full of fruit and flowers? All my life was a longing for it. Fools may call this longing, Thanatophilia, a Longing for Death; no, I long for immortality in Tir na nOc. There the monotony which I cannot sustain on earth would not be with me, for in Tir na nOc you escape from human time. Three hundred years there are but as a day in the upper half. There the denizens know nothing of old age; they have escaped from human Time. So have the dead, you will say; but the dead are not wakeful and aware as are those who dwell in Tir na nOc.

This longing for youth, this dislike of old age is pre-eminently an Irish trait. Blind Raftery, the poet, who was born in Mayo but spent his days in Galway town, his face to the wall (i.e., blind), playing his music 'to empty pockets', says in the last line of his famous poem, *The Country of Mayo*:

'Old age would never find me and I'd be young again.'

And in the twentieth century, Yeats in his *Seven Woods* tells how the squirrels rejoiced: 'As if they had been hidden in green boughs Where old age cannot find them.'

244

The ancient Irish had no Valhalla in the heavens. They had their Land of Youth in their own country, under the earth and under the waves. No one made the earth. When it came to making such things, that was a blacksmith's business. Under the earth and under the water there was an idyllic life where even eternity could not bore you. This means very much to me because even beauty, if dwelt on too long, begins to pall. But in Mag Mell, the Delightful Plain, it is otherwise: Mag Mell . . . why not call it Fairfield? That was the delight of my youth and in Tir na nOc I will see it again. I'll be young again in Tir na nOc.

In the West of Ireland there is magic everywhere. It is behind religion, for what is religion but the supernatural regulated? Reason cannot affect it, for reason was given us for a safe-conduct through our daily life; but magic deals with eternal values.

Some day, on the first of November perhaps, the earth will be opened and I shall enter into no strange realm but the realm of youth renewed.

Boys! O Boys!